D0146034

*Behavior
Therapy*

Second Edition

Behavior Therapy

Concepts, Procedures, and Applications

GEOFFREY L. THORPE
The University of Maine

SHERYL L. OLSON
The University of Michigan

Allyn and Bacon
Boston • London • Toronto • Sydney • Tokyo • Singapore

To Carol, Beth, and Tim
To Jerry and Sian

Library of Congress Cataloging-in-Publication Data

Thorpe, Geoffrey L.
　　Behavior therapy : concepts, procedures, and applications /
　Geoffrey L. Thorpe, Sheryl L. Olson.—2nd ed.
　　　p.　　cm.
　　Includes bibliographical references and index.
　　ISBN 0-205-19338-2
　　1. Behavior therapy.　　I. Olson, Sheryl L.　　II. Title.
RC489.B4T58　　1996
616.89´142—dc20　　　　　　　　　　　　　　　　96-38718
　　　　　　　　　　　　　　　　　　　　　　　　　　CIP

Printed in the United States of America
10　9　8　7　6　5　4　3　　　　01　00　99

Contents

Preface

Behavior Therapy is intended to serve as a book for use in college and university settings. We believe it will be most appropriate for the following:

- An undergraduate course in behavior therapy
- A graduate course in behavior therapy, supplemented by further readings
- Undergraduate and graduate courses in psychotherapy, supplemented by additional texts or readings for the other major approaches (psychoanalysis/psychodynamic and humanistic/existential)
- Any interested reader—layperson, student, instructor, or psychotherapist—looking for a comprehensive but manageable survey of the field

We selected our topics to meet the needs of instructors teaching a general course in this area. As a result, this book includes major sections entitled Theories, Principles, and Techniques as well as Applications with Specific Problems and Disorders. The *theories* chapters cover traditional behavior modification (drawn from the principles and techniques of conditioning and learning) and contemporary cognitive-behavioral interventions (drawn from social learning principles and cognitive therapy techniques). The *applications* chapters cover a wide range of problems and disorders in residential and community settings, with greater emphasis on outpatient practice. We have focused entirely on mental health problems—the most popular and best-developed field of application for behavior therapy.

Our aim has been to provide an engaging, readable survey of theory and practice, broad enough to cover the field sufficiently without going to encyclopedic extremes. Some books on behavior therapy focus entirely on outpatient treatment and supply lengthy reviews of research studies. Others focus on behavior modification exclusively and provide extensive illustrations of the use of reinforcement in self-management and in residential settings. We have tried to cover both areas thoroughly, integrating theory and practice and drawing extensively from our own clinical experience.

Although we have provided essential background information, studying this book will not in itself qualify its readers as behavior therapists. Clinical practice normally requires graduate training in one of the mental health professions, such as clinical or counseling psychology, social work, psychiatry, and psychiatric nursing, together with supervised experience leading to independent professional licensure. We hope that some readers not currently enrolled in graduate programs will be inspired to seek professional training in one of these disciplines.

In preparing this Second Edition, we have had the benefit of constructive criticism from users of the original book and from the professional reviewers. Mylan Jaixen, our Series Editor at Allyn and Bacon, graciously allowed us more space in which to accommodate these suggestions and add our own improvements. Consequently, this expanded Second Edition enhances the original text by including the following features:

- Many more *case examples* are given. Each section or chapter begins with one or more clinical vignettes to add color to the presentation and to provide a context for the theoretical material.
- Two *new chapters* are included: Posttraumatic Syndromes and Personality Disorders. Another addition is the Epilogue: Conclusions and Prospects.
- *Expanded coverage* of Behavior Disorders of Childhood is presented in two chapters, to accommodate material on recent developments.
- *Fuller explanations* are given of theories, concepts, and methods in order to provide a clearer, more detailed exposition of essential points.
- Reference to the *DSM-IV* of 1994 supplements discussion of traditional diagnostic categories and outlines the major features of clinical disorders.
- A *general updating* of the text includes important new developments and references from the 1990s, such as Virtual Reality Graded Exposure for specific phobias, panic control therapy, the role of acceptance in behavioral couples therapy, attributional models of posttraumatic stress disorder, eye movement desensitization and reprocessing, constructive narrative as a metaphor for cognitive-behavior change, rule-governed behavior in operant learning, and more.

We would like to acknowledge the helpful contributions, direct and indirect, of several colleagues and students. These include Roger Frey, Joel Gold, Jeffrey Hecker, Peter Ippoliti, Peter LaFreniere, Cathy Loomis, Ron Miyatake, Doug Nangle, Tim Nay, Jeff Parker, Richard Ryckman, Sandra Sigmon, Laurence Smith, Linda Yelland, and Janice Zeman at the University of Maine, and Christopher Peterson at the University of Michigan. Kathy McAuliffe, Rhonda Ouellette, and Shelley Rollins provided essential technical assistance in the psychology department at the University of Maine, and their help is much appreciated. The students who have taken courses in Behavior Therapy and Psychotherapy at the University of Maine are thanked for their enthusiasm and for stimulating their instructor to keep up with the field.

Sincere thanks go to the editorial team at Allyn and Bacon for their consistent encouragement, tactful promptings, and dignified acceptance of a litany of authorial excuses (mostly for tardy delivery of copy). Sue Hutchinson and Mylan Jaixen were models of patience. We are indebted to Bob Swan for urging us to submit the original prospectus, and we look forward to working with Cory Blackman and his associates as they make our work known to the wider professional community.

The help of Lynda Griffiths and her colleagues at TKM Productions is gratefully acknowledged. Thank you, also, to the following reviewers for their helpful comments: Mahlon Dalley, University of Northern Colorado; William Lydecker, Gustavus Adolphus College; Dudley McGlynn, Auburn University; and W. Stephen Royce, University of Portland.

Our families have been an enduring resource throughout, and we dedicate this book to them.

Introduction

Mike knew that his days in college were numbered unless he could get his act together and start some serious studying. But, despite his good intentions and his repeated attempts to sit at his desk and begin reading in earnest, he always seemed to end up daydreaming, or picking up his guitar "just to practice a chord or two" by way of a little break, or talking to a friend on the phone. He was in real danger of failing all his courses. At the urging of his friends, he finally asked for help at the campus counseling center, where his therapist taught him a principle from learning theory known as *stimulus control.*

All Mike had to do to increase the efficiency of his learning efforts was to connect the appropriate situation, sitting at his desk, with the desired behavior, active studying. That meant that all the time he was at his desk, he had to be studying, and all the time he was studying, he had to be at his desk. If he was at his desk and he started doing anything other than studying (such as reading the comics or daydreaming), he had to get up immediately and go somewhere—anywhere—else, breaking the connection between the situation and the unwanted behavior. It did not matter at first how much time Mike spent at the desk. On the first day of this program, even five minutes was enough to please his therapist, provided that those five minutes were spent studying, not daydreaming.

After following this straightforward procedure for a couple of weeks, Mike found that simply the act of sitting down at the desk was sufficient to focus his attention on his school work. The stimuli provided by this limited environment had come to exert a form of positive control over Mike's behavior. He was able to extend his concentration and studying time enough to pass his exams at the end of the semester.

Mary Ann had spent over ten monotonous years as a patient in a state hospital. At the time of her admission, she had acted in ways that her neighbors considered bizarre (such as talking loudly to unseen government agents in the middle of the street outside her house) and she had completely neglected her personal hygiene. Her problems were professionally diagnosed as reflecting a psychotic disorder, but most of those dramatic symptoms had subsided long ago. Mary Ann now followed a weary routine of being awakened in the morning, shuffling into the dining room for a meal, lining up for medication, and pacing up and down the ward, alone with her thoughts. There were plenty of other people on the ward, but they also followed solitary routines with little social interaction.

Mary Ann occasionally attracted the attention of staff members when she started screaming loudly for minutes on end, for no apparent reason. Staff members tried to comfort her and made a point of spending more time with her than usual whenever she had a screaming episode, but she continued to scream every few days. A new program was introduced by the staff, designed to encourage socially appropriate behavior and to discourage the kind of activity that would appear out of place in the street or at the shopping mall. The new program called for the staff to ignore Mary Ann when she screamed but to show an attentive interest in her when she was not screaming (and any time she was behaving in a socially acceptable manner). This was very difficult for the staff at first, because in the first week Mary Ann's screaming bouts were louder, longer, more frequent, and more annoying than ever before. Eventually, however, she stopped screaming altogether, and she responded positively when staff members spent more time with her.

This program of behavior modification was based on principles of *positive reinforcement* (in this case, increasing "normal" behavior by providing social attention when Mary Ann was behaving appropriately) and *extinction* (removing social reinforcement by ignoring the screaming outbursts). It was successful in helping Mary Ann stop screaming, it allowed her more opportunities for positive social interaction, it required no additional hospital resources, and it brought the client and the ward staff together in a constructive fashion that could pave the way for further improvements in her social skills and behavior.

When Mindy's relationship with her boyfriend ended she became depressed and eventually consulted a psychotherapist. Mindy tearfully explained that she had tried very hard to save the relationship. She had stayed at home practically all the time so as not to miss a phone call from her boyfriend. He had once noted that she was a little overweight, so she had immediately embarked upon a severe dieting and exercise regimen. She had made sure that he could find nothing to object to in her, always agreeing with him and going along with his plans, even when these involved his not seeing her for days at a time. When her boyfriend finally ended the relationship, Mindy thought that there was only one possible conclusion she could make: She was utterly unlovable.

Carefully and supportively, and in the course of several weekly therapy sessions, Mindy's therapist asked her to take a critical look at some of the assumptions she had been making. Following the principles and procedures of *cognitive therapy*, the therapist argued that Mindy's depression was caused less by the ending of the relationship itself than by the discouraging and demoralizing thoughts about herself that she had adopted as a result of the break-up. Mindy learned to see that one person losing interest in her did not necessarily make her completely unlovable by anyone. She realized that even if some behavior of hers did turn someone off, she did not have to view this as a permanent personal defect. More generally, she came to see that disappointing events did not have to reflect badly on her at all.

In addition to this cognitive therapy approach, the therapist suggested that Mindy might wish to pay more attention to her own feelings and preferences, rather than becoming excessively amenable to someone else's wishes. Mindy acknowledged that she had always found it difficult to stand up for herself and that she had tended to assume that other people's ideas, wishes, and preferences were always more valid than her own. Mindy's therapist suggested that they use *role-playing* simulations to help her practice various forms of self-assertion. For example, the therapist would take the role of the boyfriend and Mindy would be herself as they re-enacted some of the upsetting conversations that had occurred during the relationship. In therapy, however, there was the difference that Mindy would rewrite the script of these conversations, recasting herself as an autonomous, independent woman who could freely assert her own opinions and feelings, agreeing or disagreeing with the other party as she chose. Practicing in the safe environment of the therapist's office allowed Mindy to experiment with self-assertion, putting it into practice in her everyday life only when she felt comfortable in doing so. Before she terminated therapy, Mindy had significantly improved her social skills, reduced her depressive mood, and enhanced her self-confidence.

Mike, Mary Ann, and Mindy had different lifestyles, different problems, and different levels of participation in their treatment, but the common factor is that their therapists used behavior therapy techniques to help them overcome their problems and enhance their functioning. Stimulus control, positive reinforcement, extinction, cognitive therapy, and role-playing are samples of the treatment interventions commonly used by behavior therapists, and all of them are described in greater detail later in this book. Less obvious than the treatment techniques, but at least as important, are the general concepts and theories, and the specific client assessments and problem formulations, that direct the appropriate use of behavior therapy in particular clinical situations.

The introductory chapter that follows explains how behavior therapy, based on concepts of empiricism and behaviorism and grounded in experimental psychology, developed in the 1950s as an alternative to psychoanalysis. We use Sigmund Freud's case of Little Hans, and the John Watson and Rosalie Rayner case of Little Albert, to illustrate the theoretical differences. We also supply a brief history of behavioral techniques, touching on treating fears of frogs in seventeenth-century England, curing alcoholism in Roman times, and helping a British ballerina to gain control of her urination. We also describe the more recent developments that expanded behavior therapy from its focus on conditioning to its inclusion of various cognitions, ranging from self-statements to attributional styles. We conclude the chapter with an outline of clinical practice issues in behavior therapy, illustrated by one of our own case studies.

Chapter *1*

Behavior Therapy and Its Origins

Behavior therapy is one of the leading psychological approaches to contemporary mental health work. It is aimed at helping people enhance their functioning and overcome difficulties in practically any aspect of human activity and experience. Its techniques have been applied to education, the workplace, consumer activities, and even sports, but behavior therapy as a clinical enterprise is mainly concerned with the assessment and treatment of mental health problems.

As a distinctive and coherent form of psychological treatment, behavior therapy began in the 1950s when a small group of psychologists and physicians, dissatisfied with the traditional theories and techniques of psychotherapy, developed new treatments from the methods and results of experimental psychology. The link with experimental psychology was the important feature that distinguished behavior therapy from the other approaches. Its earliest procedures were developed from principles of classical conditioning and operant learning.

Behavior Therapy Techniques

Behavior therapists use a wide variety of treatment techniques today, but a handful of original methods first described in the 1950s and 1960s still serve as the clearest examples (Erwin, 1978). Classic books such as *Behavior Therapy Techniques* (Wolpe & Lazarus, 1966) described systematic desensitization, the token economy, and aversion therapy as leading examples of the new procedures.

Systematic desensitization, derived from pioneering laboratory experiments by Joseph Wolpe (1958), is most commonly used to reduce a client's unwanted fears of particular objects or situations. The technique involves progressive training in muscle relaxation, construction of a graded list of feared situations (an anxiety hierarchy), and careful presentation of scenes from the hierarchy for the client to imagine while deeply relaxed. Progress is carefully monitored by the therapist, and the client controls the presentation of scenes from the hierarchy by signaling the therapist to pause when anxiety arises. As you will see in the following chapters, most behavior therapists today reject the theory that inspired Wolpe to develop systematic desensitization, but it remains true that the technique can be highly effective in allowing the client to confront undesired fear patterns in a way that facilitates therapeutic change.

The *token economy* is chiefly used in hospitals and other residential facilities as a system for rehabilitating long-term patients who have grown dependent on institutions. Based on operant learning principles, the token economy provides rewards to patients when they display helpful, adaptive behaviors such as caring for their appearance and personal hygiene or interacting appropriately with other people. Staff members provide tokens—poker chips or special tickets—immediately after the patient has performed a specific behavior that has been targeted for improvement. Patients trade the tokens for more tangible benefits, such as extra food items or off-ward passes, later in the day. Ayllon and Azrin (1968) developed the method from laboratory research on *positive reinforcement*—increasing the rate of specified behaviors by means of the contingent presentation of food or other reinforcing stimuli.

Aversion therapy is the label for several procedures involving the use of painful or unpleasant stimuli to help clients reduce unwanted, but persistent, behaviors. *Covert sensitization* is an aversion therapy technique in which clients imagine scenes that pair the undesired behavior with a highly unpleasant consequence. For example, a client who wishes to quit smoking might repeatedly imagine a scene such as lighting a cigarette, experiencing the sensations involved in inhaling the smoke, then suddenly feeling queasy, dizzy, and nauseated, vomiting messily and profusely and ending up with feelings of shame and disgust. The method is self-administered by the client under the guidance of the therapist, who typically supplies lavishly detailed, lurid descriptions of the aversive consequences to be imagined (Cautela & Kearney, 1986). Applying covert sensitization to problem behaviors such as cigarette smoking or overeating allows clients to gain control by providing a form of punishment for their own behavior.

Systematic desensitization, the token economy, and aversion therapy illustrate some of the key features of behavior therapy. The procedures were originally drawn from laboratory research on learning. They are guided by experimentally supported theories of behavior change. They focus directly on real or fantasized samples of the client's problem behavior. Treatment progresses systematically from easier to more difficult learning tasks. Using these techniques, the therapist presents stimuli, observes responses, and carefully monitors the client's progress during treatment sessions, making adjustments to the procedure as necessary.

Theoretical Background

The innovators who introduced behavior therapy developed it as a constructive, practical application, in the clinical arena, of learning principles drawn from laboratory experimentation. At the same time, they proposed behavior therapy as an alternative to traditional, psychoanalytic therapy.

Behavior Therapy versus Psychoanalysis

Apart from the biomedical approaches, psychoanalysis was the dominant theoretical orientation in the mental health field when behavior therapy first appeared. Psychoanalysis began in Europe in the 1880s, when Viennese physicians Sigmund Freud and Josef Breuer studied the causes and treatment of *hysteria*. Patients with this puzzling disorder showed few, if any, actual biological abnormalities on medical examination, yet they displayed what appeared to be symptoms of physical disease, especially impairments in sensation or movement. Most physicians of the day dismissed such problems as the result of deliberate faking by the patient.

In 1880, Breuer treated "Anna O.," a young woman whose problems have been cited as classic symptoms of hysteria. These included paralyses of her limbs, problems with vision, a nervous cough, eating problems, and memory disturbances. Anna also had sudden dissociative episodes in which she would seem distracted and mutter words incoherently. Breuer took the unusual step of listening closely to what Anna was saying during these episodes. She began to speak more and more about her recollections of events that had had an emotional impact on her, such as memories of herself at her father's sickbed (Malcolm, 1982). Anna's condition improved when she reported previously unrecognized motives and feelings relevant to her symptoms. This meant remembering the time, place, and what she had been feeling when the symptom first appeared.

For example, one of Anna's symptoms was a strong aversion to drinking water, so that she could hardly bring herself to drink even when extremely thirsty. She could not remember anything that might explain this. But during a treatment session, she was able to recall having once seen her lady companion letting a small dog drink water from a glass. Anna also realized that she had experienced strong feelings of disgust (at what she saw) and anger (at the companion), but she had not expressed these feelings at the time. She was able to drink water immediately after this treatment session, and she had no further difficulties with drinking. Her other symptoms were also treated successfully by what Anna herself called "the talking cure" (Breuer, 1895/1989, p. 68).

Freud's original idea had been to explain the origins of hysteria in terms of disturbing, emotionally significant memories that the client could not call to awareness without special help. But he went on to develop an extremely broad-ranging theory of human behavior with unconscious motivation as its central theme (Farrell, 1981). Freud came to believe that the mind had structure and was composed of different elements that could come into conflict with one another. For example, one element, the *id*, contains strong instinctual drives, continually welling up, that may lead the individual to act recklessly and destructively in pursuit of immediate pleasures. Another element, the *ego*, is the executive part of the mind that can suppress the destructive drives by mobilizing mental defenses against them.

The chief aim is to keep awareness of these unacceptable drives out of the individual's consciousness, because (the theory states) such awareness could overwhelm the ego and lead to mental breakdown (Lapsley, 1994). One form of defense, surprisingly enough, is the formation of a neurotic symptom. For example, Anna O.'s "hysterical" symptom of aversion to water was thought to protect her from her unconscious feelings of disgust and anger. It follows from this view that any attempt to remove the client's presented problem directly, such as by having Anna practice drinking water a little at a time with the therapist offering reassurance and support, would be doomed to fail because to the psychoanalyst, the problem is really a symptom of underlying distress. Even if direct treatment did work, the ego would have to develop another defense against the unconscious material, and this defense might involve a symptom even worse than the original one. This doctrine of *symptom substitution* was commonly raised by psychoanalysts as an objection to behavior therapy in its early years.

Freud also believed that one's personality is formed by significant early experiences. An individual progresses through a standard series of potential challenges in the first few years of life, each marked by the part of the body most closely associated with pleasure at that point in development, and by a particular unconscious threat or conflict. For example, at the age of 5 or 6, a child enters the *phallic* stage of development and has to deal with the *Oedipus Complex*, somehow coming to terms with unconscious impulses to become sexually involved with the opposite-sex parent and to rival the other. This raises unconscious fears of punishment from the same-sex parent. At any stage, *fixation* may occur if the child experiences too much, or even too little, frustration in resolving the unconscious conflict. A fixation (a form of mental blockage or hang-up) may lead to the development of neurotic symptoms later in life when circumstances remind the person of the original challenge. For example, consider the case of a young woman who, under stress from competing for a highly paid job, develops a *phobia* (a specific, unwarranted fear) of heights, so that she avoids elevators and air travel. A psychoanalyst might speculate that this client did not pass through her phallic stage smoothly in childhood, and therefore continues, even as an adult, to be perturbed by any thought of rivalry or competition with someone else. In other words, the client is unconsciously (and symbolically) troubled by the notion of rivaling her mother by going up in the world. By preventing her from taking a job in a high building or a job requiring frequent flying, the symptom partly resolves the unconscious conflict by putting a stop to the threatening rivalry.

Criticisms of Psychoanalysis

From the very beginnings of behavior therapy, its proponents have lambasted psychoanalysts for their unscientific approach to clinical data and for their extensive use of intuition and speculation. For example, it was not uncommon in the 1960s for psychoanalysts to view children's bed-wetting as a sign of depression, because it could represent "unconscious weeping." A psychoanalytic play therapist, noticing that a child looked under the slip cover of the sofa during a therapy session, interpreted this as a symbolic and unconscious attempt to look under the mother's skirt to see the feces. Behavior therapists do not deny that it is *possible* that those interpretations are correct, but the evidence offered by psychoanalysts to support such theories has not met even minimal scientific standards (Miles, 1966).

The most influential early critique of psychoanalytic thinking was published by Wolpe and Rachman in 1960. These authors examined Freud's famous case history of Little Hans, a 5-year-old who had developed a phobia of horses (Freud, 1909/1955). In explaining the development of Hans's phobia, Freud argued that Hans was really troubled not by horses, but by unconscious Oedipal conflicts. Hans's unconscious wishes, fears, and defenses included a desire to have sexual intercourse with his mother, a dread of castration by his father, and the displacement of his fear of his father onto horses, who then symbolized the father. The phobia also served the purpose of keeping Hans near his mother, because, since the streets of Vienna at that time were bustling with horse-drawn traffic, avoiding horses meant not going outside the house at all. Freud supported his formulation by commenting on a variety of incidents noted by Hans's father, including:

- Hans played at horses, bit his father, told him not to "trot" away from the table, and compared his father's mustache to a horse's muzzle.
- Hans liked to follow his mother into the bathroom. He said one day he would have children and she would be their mother.
- Hans described a fantasy in which the plumber came with a large drill and took away Hans's behind with a pair of pincers, then did the same to his penis (Conway, 1978; Freud, 1909/1955).

Not convinced by Freud's ingenious account, Wolpe and Rachman argued that (1) Freud had presented no scientific evidence that Hans's fear of horses bore any relationship to his sexual fantasies, (2) Freud's conclusions were based entirely upon assumption and speculation, and (3) the case report provided no factual support for psychoanalytic hypotheses about ego defenses and unconscious conflicts.

Wolpe and Rachman (1960) suggested that *conditioning* is a far more credible explanation of the development of fears than psychoanalytic theory. They pointed out that Freud's own account of Little Hans's history contained a description of an obvious learning experience: A horse pulling a bus fell over in the street, presumably eliciting fear. This is based on Hans's statement: "It gave me a fright *because it made a row with its feet*" (Freud, 1909/1955, p. 50, original emphasis). Hans himself believed that this was the origin of his fear of horses: "When the horse in [sic] the bus fell down, it gave me such a fright, really! That was when I got the nonsense [i.e., the fear]" (p. 50).

Criticisms of Psychoanalytic Therapy
Because treatment is linked closely to theory, it is not surprising that behavior therapists have also criticized psychoanalytic therapy. In the early 1950s, practically all psychological treatment was based on psychoanalytic assumptions. Writing at that time, Hans Eysenck[1] (1952) made a strong attack on psychotherapy in general, arguing that there was no scientific evidence to support its usefulness. His review of studies on the effectiveness of psychotherapy revealed widespread methodological flaws, such as imprecise and biased measures and an absence of control groups to assess patients' progress without treatment. Eysenck estimated the expected course of typical disorders *without* treatment, so as to provide a baseline from which to gauge the effects of psychotherapy. He concluded that about two-thirds of the time, a neurosis[2] could be expected to resolve itself, or show *spontaneous remission,* within two years, whether or not therapy was provided. When he reexamined the uncontrolled data on the effects of psychotherapy, Eysenck observed that treated clients also showed a two-thirds improvement rate over a two-year period. He concluded that patients might as well save themselves the time, trouble, and expense of seeking therapy.[3]

Prompted by Eysenck's arguments, scientifically oriented therapists began to conduct controlled experiments on the effectiveness of their interventions. In 1961, Eysenck made the further recommendation that therapists design more exacting studies of treatment effectiveness. Not only should treatment produce better results than no treatment but it should also surpass the effectiveness of "nonspecific treatment," or the elements that would be present in any therapy situation—talking to a concerned listener, having faith in the therapist, describing one's problems in detail, and so on. Traditional therapy failed to meet this standard (Wilkins, 1979). Understandably enough, Eysenck's views have been extremely controversial in the mental health field (Rachman & Wilson, 1980), but among behavior therapists, they have been well received as an important stimulus to active research efforts on the effectiveness of behavior therapy.

Empiricism and Behaviorism

Behavior therapy draws its philosophical support from the traditions of empiricism and behaviorism. The central belief of followers of *empiricism* is that words and concepts make sense only when linked to direct experience. An empiricist would have trouble with typical psychoanalytic concepts because so many of them—like the unconscious, the ego, and fixation—are abstractions far removed from observation. Empiricists also reject intuition, conjecture, and theoretical speculation as avenues to achieving reliable knowledge. This means practically rejecting the whole theory and method of psychoanalysis. Because behavior therapists prefer the experimental method and scientific hypothesis testing, they clearly accept empiricism as their guiding principle.

Originally, *behaviorism* was the label for the views of experimental psychologists who focused on studies of overt behavior and rejected observations that could not be verified by other scientists (Miles, 1966; Rachlin, 1976). John B. Watson (1878–1958) was the most famous advocate of behaviorism, if not its actual pioneer (Hergenhahn, 1992). Conducting experiments on maze learning in rats during his studies at the University of Chicago, Watson soon realized that it was much easier for observers to agree on whether a rat turned right or left than on whether it was happy or sad while doing so (Rachlin, 1976, p. 54). As a result, Watson abandoned speculations about the states of mind of his rats and focused entirely on observations of their overt behavior, eventually viewing this as the only feasible method upon which to base scientific psychology. (Consistent with this, Watson also rejected *introspection*, or examining one's own mental processes for information on psychological principles, because any results from this approach cannot be objectively verified by others.) Among the several versions of behaviorism that have been put forward over the years, *methodological behaviorism*—the view that only observations of behavior, not speculations about mental life, can form the practical basis of a psychological science—has proved most popular among experimental psychologists since Watson.

To illustrate the importance of behaviorism to behavior therapy, the study most commonly cited by behavior therapists as an alternative to psychoanalytic case studies was one of Watson's. This famous case of Little Albert demonstrated the potential of conditioning as an explanation of phobic behavior.

Little Albert

Watson and Rayner (1920) sought experimental evidence to support speculations that emotional responses could be conditioned. Albert B. was an infant whose mother was a wet nurse at a home for invalid children, and he was selected for study because he was healthy, well developed, and emotionally stable. At the age of 9 months, he was presented with various stimuli in a standard behavioral assessment of fear. His reactions were recorded on film. The stimuli included a white rat, a rabbit, other animals, masks with and without hair, and burning newspaper. He showed no fear in any situation. The first time Albert did show fear was when a sudden sound was made by striking a steel bar with a hammer.

Watson and Rayner sought to answer four questions:

1. Can fear of a white rat be conditioned by presenting it while a steel bar is struck?
2. If so, will there be any evidence of transfer or generalization to other stimuli?
3. What happens to such responses over time?
4. If the emotional responses do not disappear spontaneously, can suitable methods for removing them be found?

When Albert was 11 months old, the experimenters presented the white rat together with the sound on seven occasions in two experimental sessions one week apart. The result was "as convincing a case of a completely conditioned fear response as could have been theoretically pictured" (Watson & Rayner, 1920, p. 5). Five days later, Albert withdrew when confronted by the rat without the sound. He also responded negatively to a rabbit, when he had not done so previously. Throughout this session, Albert was given blocks to play with between the presentations of the other stimuli. He showed no reluctance to play with the blocks—in fact, he played with them more energetically than usual. Without further conditioning, he reacted somewhat negatively to other stimuli, including a dog and a seal fur coat.

Two weeks later, the dog, the rabbit, and the rat were presented in conditioning trials with the sound of the steel bar so as to "freshen" Albert's reactions. Afterwards, when he was tested with the animals in a different place, he showed less fear. One month later, having had no contact with the animals in the interim, Albert showed slight negative reactions to them. At that time, he was taken away from the hospital, so the experimenters could not undertake their planned experiments on removing his fears. Watson and Rayner had thought of several methods for doing this, including constant exposure to the stimuli to get Albert used to them, feeding Albert while presenting the stimuli, and developing constructive activities around the stimuli.

Watson and Rayner (1920) had not been able to remove Albert's conditioned fear because he left the hospital, but Mary Cover Jones (1924) tried one of their suggestions with another boy who already had a phobia. The boy, Peter, overcame his fear of a rabbit when the therapist exposed him gradually to the rabbit while Peter was being fed.

The demonstration of conditioning in Little Albert does not prove that all fears are learned, and as a case study is open to at least some of the criticisms that behavior therapists have leveled at Freud's report on Little Hans (Cheshire, 1975; Harris, 1979; Marks, 1981a, 1981b). But the Little Albert study was vitally important in providing a plausible alternative to psychoanalysis. The study called attention to classical conditioning as a possible theoretical mechanism for the development of abnormal fears, as well as to extinction as a potential treatment procedure for overcoming them. Nonetheless, Watson joked that Little Albert might, as an adult, consult a psychoanalyst for help with his phobia, and find his aversion to rats blamed on the poor resolution of his Oedipus Complex (Pierce & Epling, 1995).

The links between behavior therapy and behaviorism have been so strong that some writers in the mental health arena use the terms interchangeably (Thorpe, 1977). It is clear that most behavior therapists would have no trouble identifying themselves as behaviorists. But today, many behavior therapists, especially those who favor cognitive therapy interventions, would not describe themselves as behaviorists in the tradition of Watson. Instead, they would accept a modified version, *emergent behaviorism*, that allows them to retain their commitment to empiricism while making inferences from observed behavior and studying such challenging phenomena as imagery, thinking, and dreaming (Craighead, Craighead, Kazdin, & Mahoney, 1994). The difference between Watson's traditional behaviorism and emergent behaviorism will become clearer in the following chapters. Generally speaking, behavior therapists who apply operant learning techniques with the most severely disturbed clients in residential settings tend to favor traditional behaviorism, whereas behavior therapists who use cognitive therapy to treat outpatients with anxiety or depression tend to favor emergent behaviorism.

The Development of Behavior Therapy

Defining Behavior Therapy

Some definitions of behavior therapy describe its techniques and emphasize their links with learning theory (e.g., Eysenck, 1964; Wolpe, 1982c). However, there is more to behavior therapy than its techniques. Behavior therapy also involves a set of attitudes about mental health work in general, such as dissatisfaction with psychoanalysis and willingness to deal directly with specific target behaviors. (Another limitation of defining behavior therapy by its techniques is that other fields, such as education and advertising, also draw specific procedures from learning theory.) It is possible, as an alternative, to describe behavior therapy in terms of the general approach or clinical theory of its practitioners (e.g., Kazdin, 1978; Yates, 1970). However, this is hard to do without making the definition too broad (Marks, 1981b).

Although it is difficult to provide a formal definition of behavior therapy that satisfies everyone, the common characteristics of behavior therapy methods and principles can be described as follows:

> *Behavior therapy is a nonbiological form of therapy that developed largely out of learning theory research and that is normally applied directly, incrementally, and experimentally in the treatment of specific maladaptive behavior patterns. (Erwin, 1978, p. 44)*

Precursors of Behavior Therapy

Treatment techniques similar to those of behavior therapy have been described throughout recorded history. A form of systematic desensitization was described by the philosopher John Locke in seventeenth-century England. He wrote about practical techniques for removing a child's fear of frogs by means of graduated, nonthreatening encounters with them (Marks, 1981a). Classroom management techniques similar to the token economy were devised by Joseph Lancaster in the early nineteenth century. He used a system of rewards to maintain attention and academic progress in large classes of school children. Proctors dispensed tickets to the children consequent upon desired behavior, and the tickets could be exchanged for "prizes" (Kazdin, 1982). Aversion therapy was used in ancient Rome by Pliny the Elder, who described a method for discouraging alcoholism that involved pairing drinking with unpleasant stimuli (Franks, 1985). The technique involved placing putrid spiders in the bottom of the sufferer's drinking vessel. (It is not clear which was the more aversive, the taste imparted by the putrescence or the shock of suddenly seeing the dead arachnids.)

Various treatment techniques derived from experimental psychology were described and practiced occasionally in the first half of the twentieth century. These included methods for removing unwanted habits such as nail-biting (Dunlap, 1932), for deterring alcoholics from drinking (Lemere & Voegtlin, 1950), and for controlling nocturnal enuresis (bed-wetting) in children (Mowrer & Mowrer, 1938). The Mowrers had developed a "bell and pad" apparatus that responded to the presence of moisture by sounding an alarm. At the onset of urination, the bell would awaken the child and prompt him or her to inhibit further urination until visiting the bathroom. The technique was inspired by classical conditioning procedures.

These techniques are "behavioral" in the sense that they were derived from conditioning principles and applied to specific problems of clients. However, they were not implemented in the context of a holistic clinical approach to assessment and treatment, and for that reason, they do not truly represent behavior therapy. More than simply the use of certain techniques, behavior therapy involves a "systematic application of conditioning principles to clinical disorders" (Wilson, 1981, p. 157). This point has also been made by Wolpe (1982a), who argued that principles are more important than techniques in behavior therapy.

As a comprehensive treatment approach, behavior therapy began in the 1950s when influential books by the field's pioneers first appeared. Common to the work of these psychiatrists and psychologists was an interest in exploring learning-based alternatives to traditional psychotherapy. At first, this work proceeded more or less independently in South Africa, England, and the United States (Franks, 1985).

Joseph Wolpe's Contributions

As a newly qualified physician in South Africa in the early 1940s, Joseph Wolpe was working at a military hospital that served soldiers suffering from war neuroses.[4] These men had all seen service in the Second World War and were suffering from anxiety-related problems in the aftermath of their combat experiences. Wolpe initially employed treatment procedures drawn from psychoanalysis in his work with these patients, but he found the methods to be limited in effectiveness and generally disappointing (Wolpe, 1981). For alternative ideas on the treatment of anxiety, he read the literature on *experimental neurosis,* a generalized pattern of fearful behavior sometimes seen in laboratory animals following experimental conditioning procedures.

In a series of laboratory experiments, Wolpe discovered that experimental neuroses in cats could be overcome by eliciting feeding responses that compete with anxiety. Conclusions from these experiments led him to develop the concept of *reciprocal inhibition,* a general principle of behavior change that relied upon countering anxiety by a competing feeling-state (Wolpe, 1958, 1982c). (Wolpe identified several activities in addition to feeding that suppress anxiety in humans. One of these is relaxation training, which plays a prominent part in the systematic desensitization technique that he developed.) Although feeding (and relaxation) can inhibit anxiety, the reverse is also true in that anxiety can inhibit eating. (People sometimes find comfort in eating when anxious or under stress, but they can also go "off" their food and lose weight under prolonged distress.) Because the inhibitory process can work both ways, the principle was labeled as reciprocal inhibition. The publication of Wolpe's (1958) *Psychotherapy by Reciprocal Inhibition* was a significant event in the history of behavior therapy.

Wolpe's approach with clients and patients resembled routine clinical practice more than a formal research program (Yates, 1970). In common with several other behavior therapists who worked with neuroses in the early years, Wolpe viewed each client as equivalent to a participant in an individually tailored experiment (Shapiro, 1966), and this approach continues as a strong tradition in behavior therapy. Wolpe's work was distinctive because of its foundation in laboratory experiments, its basis in clearly stated theoretical principles, and its stimulation of practical, goal-oriented treatment techniques.

Contributions of the Maudsley Group

While Joseph Wolpe was beginning his investigations into behavior therapy in South Africa, Hans Eysenck was establishing the first British graduate program in clinical psychology at the University of London's Institute of Psychiatry, affiliated with the Bethlem/ Maudsley Hospital. Eysenck had visited the United States to learn about clinical training programs in psychology and had been disappointed to see the strong influence of psychoanalytic thinking on assessment and treatment practices. Always extremely critical of psychoanalytic approaches because of their lack of experimental support, Eysenck insisted that they would have no place in his program. Instead, he proposed "the development of a theory of neurosis and treatment based on modern learning theory, particularly Pavlovian conditioning and extinction" (Eysenck, 1984, p. 3). Eysenck was supported in this project by his colleague Monte Shapiro, who had been dismayed by the wide gulf that separated traditional clinical training programs from mainstream psychology (Yates, 1970).

Before behavior therapy was established in Britain, the typical student interested in a career in clinical psychology would progress through the usual undergraduate curriculum—scientifically oriented courses in learning, motivation, perception, social behavior, developmental psychology, research and statistics, and so forth—before going on to a graduate program in clinical psychology. But the usual graduate program, Shapiro argued, required the student to forget about mainstream psychology and, instead, to study the works of Freud and interpret projective tests, describe character defenses, and delve for unconscious meanings underlying clients' behavior. Why not make clinical psychology more like psychology? The efforts made by Shapiro, Eysenck, and their colleagues in London to devise a scientifically oriented clinical psychology were essential to the development of behavior therapy, not only in Britain but worldwide.

Eysenck viewed common clinical problems like anxiety and hysteria as resulting from the interplay of personality factors and learning events. This inspired his associates to begin to use learning-based treatment methods, such as the Mowrers'(1938) bell and pad treatment for enuresis. The Maudsley psychologists also devised new treatments. Shapiro, for example, emphasized clinical assessment by means of objective, standardized tests and later took a single-case experimental approach to assessment that led directly to practical treatment ideas (H. G. Jones, 1984; Shapiro, 1966). Like Wolpe, the Maudsley psychologists drew their treatment interventions from the theories of Pavlov (1927) and Hull (1952). However, in treating anxiety problems, Shapiro and his colleagues tended to use graduated real-life tasks rather than systematic desensitization (Franks, 1969).

The Case of the Enuretic Entertainer

The first report on a patient treated by behavior therapy in England described a 23-year-old woman who was troubled by an excessive frequency of urination (H. G. Jones, 1956). She was a dancer with several theatrical companies, so her need to visit a restroom at least every half hour had become detrimental to her work. She had also developed fears of performing in public, and her self-confidence had declined considerably. The appropriate medical tests had revealed no physical abnormality.

In collaboration with the attending physician, Jones treated the patient by means of a form of biofeedback. A "cystometric apparatus" was devised that allowed various volumes of fluid to be introduced into the bladder; measurements of fluid volume were displayed on a scale visible to the patient. The readings showed that her urge to urinate arose with relatively low volumes of fluid, and it was found that the muscles that normally inhibit urination were weak. By gradually learning to tolerate increases in fluid volume while trying to relax, the patient was able to gain control of her urinary dysfunction in just five treatment sessions. To complete the treatment, the therapist implemented a program of "graded re-education," based on learning principles described by Guthrie (1935). The patient gradually learned to perform in public again by practicing her dancing in front of progressively larger audiences.

Contributions of American Operant Learning Theorists

The United States may claim to be the birthplace of behavior therapy for several reasons. First, behavior therapy has clear origins in the work of U.S. psychologist John B. Watson on behaviorism and in his ideas about potential applications of learning principles (Erwin, 1978). Second, U.S. psychologists developed a variety of learning-based techniques to treat a broad range of problems from nail biting to alcoholism (Kazdin, 1982). Finally, the work of B. F. Skinner (1904–1990) and other operant learning theorists led directly to practical therapeutic techniques.

In a series of studies in standardized learning environments, Skinner showed that animal behavior is modifiable by controlling the consequences of specified responses. In a typical experiment, a pellet of food was delivered to a food-deprived pigeon if, and only if, it made a designated response, such as pecking at an illuminated disk on the wall of the experimental chamber. If the pigeon's response rate increased as a result of this procedure, the delivery of food was said to reinforce the pecking behavior. With suitable modifications, this work was extended to human volunteers, and the same general learning patterns were seen. In his important book, *Science and Human Behavior,* Skinner (1953) showed that operant learning principles provide a basis for understanding the whole spectrum of human behavior, normal and abnormal.

With his colleague O. R. Lindsley, Skinner extended his work on operant learning from the laboratory to the hospital ward (Skinner, 1961). The purpose of this research was to find out whether chronic psychiatric inpatients would also display typical learning patterns. The result was that the patients behaved just like the pigeons and students, except for an occasional interruption by "brief psychotic episodes"[5] (Skinner, 1961, p. 218). Skinner also noted that his standard learning procedure "provides a highly sensitive baseline for the observation of the effects of drugs and of various forms of therapy" (p. 218). In an unpublished progress report in 1954, Lindsley and Skinner were, in fact, the first to use the term *behavior therapy*[6] (Yates, 1970).

Although this research did not involve treatment, it paved the way for the development of therapy based on operant learning. Sidney Bijou, for example, applied reinforcement methods to the behavior of children and developed measurement techniques that could be used in clinical applications (Bijou & Baer, 1966). Teodoro Ayllon (1963) demonstrated that operant learning methods could be used to increase adaptive behavior in chronic psychiatric inpatients, and he developed the token economy from the same principles (Ayllon & Azrin, 1968).

Broadening Behavior Therapy

The pioneers of behavior therapy in the 1950s and 1960s were excited about replacing psychoanalysis with treatments based on experimental psychology and "modern learning theory." They viewed their project as a creative, humane, and ethical undertaking, providing clients with brief and straightforward treatments that actually work (by contrast with the vague, prescientific, long-term, and ultimately unproductive efforts of psychoanalysts). If Jones's "enuretic entertainer" had been treated by psychoanalysis, she might have spent years in daily sessions on the couch, trying to construe her problem as reflecting "unconscious weeping" or unresolved Oedipal fixations. Reducing her urination frequency would have been far less important to her psychoanalyst than achieving insight into her unconscious conflicts and personality dynamics. Instead, with behavior therapy, she regained control of her bladder functioning in five treatment sessions, and went on to overcome her public performance fears by a systematic program of graduated real-life practice.

But behavior therapists' enthusiasm for experimental psychology, for laboratory experiments, for practical treatments, and for technical terms such as *conditioning, reinforcement, punishment*, and *behavior modification* was not shared by others in the mental health field. Psychoanalysts and humanistic therapists chastised behavior therapists for dehumanizing people—for treating them like laboratory rats and pigeons, for using behavior control techniques like rewards and punishments, and for seeming to ignore people's unique humanity. Many behavior therapists agreed, not that behavior therapy *was* dehumanizing but that the language of conditioning gave that misleading impression.

Beginning in the 1970s, many behavior therapists, especially those working in outpatient settings, found themselves using conditioning terms less and less and, instead, were stressing the importance of people's perceptions and appraisals of events in influencing how we respond to them. This coincided with an emphasis on clients' cognitions and imagery processes, and on the complex interaction between the environment and one's own self-regulatory processes in determining human behavior. But before these theoretical adjustments became widely accepted, and before behavior therapy was able to join the mainstream as an accepted tradition in mental health work, its proponents had to confront several unfair challenges to its humaneness and its ethical stance—challenges that had given it a distinctly negative public image.

The Public Image of Behavior Therapy

Woolfolk, Woolfolk, and Wilson (1977) showed that the very term *behavior modification* tends to evoke negative associations. Undergraduate and graduate students viewed a videotape of a teacher using reinforcement methods with children. All students saw the same videotape, but it was given different introductions for different groups of viewers. One introduction portrayed the video as an example of behavior modification, and included references to B. F. Skinner, behavior shaping, and "controlling the behavior of laboratory animals." The other introduction presented the video as "humanistic education," and cited Carl Rogers and the importance of "feelings," "self-esteem," and a "growth-producing relationship" (Woolfolk et al., 1977, pp. 186–187). The students made ratings of the teacher's competence and the efficacy of the teaching method. As you may have guessed by now, the results were that the ratings were significantly more positive when the videotape was presented as "humanistic education" than when it was presented as "behavior modification."

O'Leary (1984) examined the index to *The New York Times* for references to behavior therapy and found 35 relevant articles between 1968 to 1983. In the earliest articles surveyed, behavior therapy was usually portrayed negatively, with several articles criticizing the use of behavior modification in prisons. However, the coverage of behavior therapy research advocating "controlled drinking" for some clients with alcohol problems was seen as balanced, and from 1978 onward, articles on behavior therapy for anxiety and depression were generally favorable. O'Leary noted that sometimes medical practices that had nothing to do with behavior therapy (such as brain surgery, medication, and electroconvulsive therapy [ECT][7]) were wrongly identified with it, adding to the "bad press."

Unfortunately, some negative public reactions have been entirely justified, although these reactions have been not to behavior therapy proper but to unprofessional work perpetrated by unqualified or unethical practitioners in the *name* of behavior therapy. For example, in the late 1960s, a psychiatrist with a limited knowledge of operant learning used ECT as *punishment* for psychiatric inpatients who would not work at assigned jobs (cited by Feldman & Peay, 1982). To say that this practice betrays the clinician's ignorance of behavioral principles is an understatement (as will be seen in Chapter 3). It also represents professional incompetence and blatantly unethical behavior on several grounds. The clients did not give their informed consent to treatment; they could not opt out whenever they chose; intrusive medical treatment was given without a clinical rationale; a mental health intervention was attempted by a clinician untrained in the appropriate methods; and the list goes on (see American Psychological Association, 1992; Keith-Spiegel & Koocher, 1985; Stromberg et al., 1988). Although it is true that behavior therapists may use painful stimuli in therapy under certain exceptional conditions, the proper use of aversion therapy of this kind is carefully monitored by the professions, and clinicians follow well-regulated protocols that ensure that the client's well-being is of paramount concern (e.g., see Favell, 1982).

Behavior Therapy Enters the Mainstream

In the 1970s and 1980s, behavior therapists continued to elaborate their theories, evaluate new procedures, and debate the nature and compass of their approach. That process has helped disarm much of the inappropriate criticism that was directed at behavior therapy in the early years. Several important figures have enriched behavior therapy by extending it beyond its early limits within learning theory.

Albert Bandura set the scene for behavior therapists' interest in cognition in his book *Principles of Behavior Modification* (1969). As a strong advocate of learning principles as the foundation of behavior change, he has reminded readers that conditioning is not an automatic process. People are not pushed around by a merciless environment, and they do not respond passively to their surroundings, becoming conditioned by random stimuli. People respond more to their views or perceptions of their surroundings than to the objective environmental contingencies. Skinner (1953) would have agreed with Bandura that behavior influences the environment as well as the other way around, but Bandura went further and deliberately included people's thoughts and expectations in his account of human behavior. In his *social learning theory* formulation (Bandura, 1977b, 1986), environment, behavior, and symbolic or cognitive processes in the individual are assumed to interact continuously. An important element of the theory is the concept of *self-efficacy,* the principle that clients' expectations of personal effectiveness play a vital role in successful coping behavior.

Arnold Lazarus, one of the originators of behavior therapy, co-authored the influential book *Behavior Therapy Techniques* with Wolpe in the 1960s (Wolpe & Lazarus, 1966). Since then, he has encouraged behavior therapists to expand the scope of their assessment and treatment interventions. To Lazarus, pioneering behavior therapists such as Wolpe and Eysenck seemed more interested in conditioning principles than in clients' thoughts, feelings, lifestyles, and social environment. Advocating the expanded versions of "broad spectrum behavior therapy" (Lazarus, 1971), "multimodal behavior therapy" (Lazarus, 1976), and "multimodal therapy" (Lazarus, 1989, 1995), he urged behavior therapists to assess all aspects of clients' lives and functioning and to use any promising treatment, behavioral or otherwise, when appropriate. In advocating *eclecticism*, in which practitioners do not commit themselves to a single approach, Lazarus is careful to make a distinction between two kinds. *Technical eclecticism,* which Lazarus recommends, refers to drawing *techniques* from different sources; *theoretical eclecticism*, which Lazarus rejects, refers to the use of varied *theories*. Trying to combine varied theories—for example, explaining a phobia in terms of both classical conditioning and Oedipal fixations—would only create confusion, but the carefully judged selection of different techniques—such as aversion therapy, systematic desensitization, hypnosis, marital counseling, and medical care for a client with alcoholism—can only bring benefit (Lazarus, 1995).

Lazarus's critics have pointed out that some of the treatments he has recommended lack empirical support (Franks & Wilson, 1975), and that, in any event, the idea that behavior therapists are unfeeling, naive, and mechanical is seriously mistaken (Wolpe, 1976). Yet, Lazarus has retained a broad commitment to social learning as a theoretical foundation for his work (Lazarus, 1987, 1995). Most of his treatments are drawn from behavior therapy, rational emotive behavior therapy (Ellis, 1995), and cognitive therapy (Beck, 1976; Beck, Rush, Shaw, & Emery, 1979; Beck & Weishaar, 1995). Lazarus's innovations have significantly improved the image of behavior therapy for those people, otherwise sympathetic, who were deterred by the exclusive focus on conditioning in the early writings.

Like Wolpe, *Isaac Marks* is a psychiatrist who has conducted extensive research into behavior therapy. Like Lazarus, Marks (1981a, 1981b) has taken issue with Wolpe's emphasis on conditioning theory, but for different reasons. Marks has argued that it is far from certain that neuroses have their origin in conditioning or learning events. Citing Little Albert to support a conditioning theory of neurosis is no more convincing than citing Little Hans to support psychoanalytic interpretations. Marks has agreed that learning-based treatments have been extremely successful in the treatment of neuroses, but has argued that this does not prove anything about the origin of clients' problems. Although some of his points have been countered by other theorists (Wilson, 1981a; Wolpe, 1982b), Marks has maintained his view that confining behavioral interpretations of neurosis to conditioning phenomena is unjustified and needlessly narrow. Instead, he advocates an "empirical clinical science" in which data take precedence over theory.

Donald Meichenbaum contributed to broadening the scope of behavior therapy by pioneering the cognitive-behavior modification (CBM) approach (Meichenbaum, 1977). His research in this area began when he observed that patients hospitalized with schizophrenia would sometimes talk to themselves in a constructive way. For example, when taking psychological tests requiring concentration these patients would speak aloud, reminding themselves of what they had to do, and actually improved their performance in the process. Impressed by the clinical potential of self-guiding speech, Meichenbaum launched a series of experiments on impulsivity in children, inattention in people with schizophrenia, and speech anxiety in students. Some studies led Meichenbaum to adapt procedures from an earlier version of rational emotive behavior therapy, rational-emotive therapy (Ellis, 1962). The success of experimental versions of such techniques led Meichenbaum to add a cognitive dimension to behavior therapy procedures (Meichenbaum, Gilmore, & Fedoravicius, 1971). He has recently focused on *construc-*

tive narrative (see Chapter 4) as a metaphor for cognitive and behavioral change (Meichenbaum, 1995).

Rosemery Nelson-Gray represents a group of clinical researchers who have developed behavioral assessment as a major focus within behavior therapy (Nelson, 1983). Behavioral assessment has always been essential to behavior therapy, but Nelson-Gray and her colleagues have broadened the field by carefully studying the utility and limitations of assessment and by delineating important directions for its future progress (Nelson & Barlow, 1981). This work has shown that the detailed attention to specifics required in behavioral assessment sets it apart from traditional assessment practices and has led to significant advances in the study of treatment effectiveness. At the same time, this specificity has also posed problems by limiting therapists' ability to make generalizations about clients' behavior in different settings. These points will be amplified later in the book.

Behavior Therapy in Clinical Practice

Professional and Ethical Issues

Behavior therapy is not a profession in itself. It is a specialty within mental health work, cutting across the academic disciplines and professions in which mental health practitioners are trained. This means that behavior therapists have a range of professional backgrounds, including clinical and counseling psychology, psychiatry, social work, and psychiatric nursing. Because of behavior therapy's original emphasis on conditioning, learning, and experimental psychology, it is not surprising that psychology predominates and that most behavior therapists are psychologists. Whatever profession they belong to, behavior therapists qualify as practitioners through the academic discipline in which they received their training, so that anyone wishing to practice as a behavior therapist must first qualify in a mental health profession.

In the United States and Canada the professions are regulated at the state and provincial level. For example, every U.S. state regulates the practice of psychology in order to protect the public. This means that psychologists who offer direct services must be either certified to use the title *psychologist* or licensed to perform certain professional functions. Candidates for licensure are usually required to show that they have the appropriate education, supervised experience, and moral character to function as professionals, and they normally have to pass written and oral examinations as part of the licensure process (Stromberg et al., 1988). In most states, licensure as a psychologist automatically involves being bound by the *Ethical Principles of Psychologists and Code of Conduct* ("Ethics Code"; American Psychological Association, 1992), whether or not the psychologist belongs to that association (Keith-Spiegel & Koocher, 1985). Especially relevant to the practice of behavior therapy (or any other form of psychotherapy) are the principles and standards in the Ethics Code dealing with the psychologist's competence to implement particular treatments, and the client's informed consent to participate in assessment, therapy, or research. Additional coverage of these topics will be provided in later chapters.

Comparison with Other Specialties

Given that behavior therapy is a specialty, not a profession, how does it compare with other specialties? Apart from behavior therapy, the other chief theoretical orientations in mental health work are biomedical, psychodynamic, and humanistic/existential. Behavior therapy differs from these in several ways. By contrast with biomedical therapists, behavior therapists do not prescribe medications or diagnose physical diseases.[8] By contrast with psychodynamic therapists, behavior therapists do not look for unconscious motivations or conflicts in clients, and they do not view greater self-understanding as the essential goal of therapy. By contrast with humanistic and existential therapists, behavior therapists are not necessarily concerned with a person's search for meaning in life, and do not view the relationship between therapist and client as the most important factor in treatment.

Behavior therapy does have some elements in common with the other approaches, however. Like biomedical therapists, behavior therapists are problem focused and goal oriented, deal with here-and-now issues, and take a scientific approach to developing new treatment methods and evaluating their effectiveness. Like psychodynamic clinicians, behavior therapists attempt to assess clients' problems thoroughly and recognize that people are not always fully aware of the reasons for their own behavior. Like humanistic/existential therapists, behavior therapists see the client as the important decision maker about goals and issues to be dealt with in treatment. Yet, despite these similarities, behavior therapy is unique as a comprehensive system of psychological treatment. It originated in the work of behaviorists and experimental psychologists. Its practitioners deliberately use specific behavior change techniques and are committed to scientific evaluation of their effectiveness. It is guided by empirically based psychological theories that are continually developing in response to new findings from the laboratory and the clinic.

General Approach to Treatment

It is easiest to describe the clinical practice of behavior therapy by contrasting it with psychoanalytic therapy. The authors of a classic experiment that compared these two approaches illustrated the chief practical differences between them by providing a list of definitions that were accepted by leading practitioners (Sloane, Staples, Cristol, Yorkston, & Whipple, 1975). These definitions, still accurate enough more than two decades later, are paraphrased from Sloane and associates (1975) here.

In *psychoanalytic therapy,* clinicians are likely to do the following:

• Interpret the client's feelings about the therapist.
• Examine the client's efforts to resist the success of therapy.
• Take an interest in the client's dreams and use the material in treatment.
• Maintain some anxiety in clients as long as it does not disrupt behavior.
• Explore childhood memories.
• Discourage reports of symptoms, interpreting them in symbolic terms if the client does mention them.

In *behavior therapy,* by contrast, therapists are more willing to do the following:

- Give advice.
- Take a keen interest in the report of "symptoms."
- Attempt to reduce clients' anxiety.
- Adopt a variety of active treatment strategies such as relaxation training, desensitization, practical retraining, training in appropriate assertiveness, role-playing, and habit modification (Sloane et al., 1975).

Assessment

Together with presenting a new treatment approach in mental health work, behavior therapists provided an alternative to traditional assessment (Kanfer & Saslow, 1969). Any form of assessment in the mental health arena is influenced strongly by the practitioner's theory of abnormal behavior. Consistent with psychoanalytic theory, *traditional* assessment is concerned with identifying a client's defensive styles and unconscious personality dynamics. Consistent with behavioral theory, behavioral assessment attends to conditioning and learning phenomena, such as the behavioral contingencies, reinforcers, and stimulus pairings operating in clients' natural environment, and their responsiveness to such events (Nelson, 1983).

Behavioral assessment usually begins with a detailed examination of specific environmental influences on the client's behavior. Guided by learning concepts such as conditioning and reinforcement, the therapist inquires about the situations in which the problem behavior occurs, about possible pairings of stimuli within those situations, and about the possible reinforcing or punishing consequences of the problem behavior. Questions such as How? When? Where? and What? are typical features of assessment interviews in behavior therapy, consistent with the focus on the specifics of behavior in situations; the question Why is rarely asked because it is less useful (Wilson, 1995).

Behavior therapists often make direct observations of behavior in the natural environment in order to gather data and test hypotheses about potential conditioning and learning events. Whether information is gathered via an interview or through direct observation, assessment often leads directly to treatment. To take a simple example, a behavior therapist observes that a parent appears to be reinforcing a child's temper tantrums by giving attention as a consequence. An appropriate treatment plan based on this assessment information would be to ask the parent to reschedule the attention giving, breaking the contingency between the problem behavior and the potentially reinforcing consequence.

Behavioral assessment of personality is based initially on the straightforward idea that people tend to repeat the behavior that was reinforced when they last encountered a situation. The behavior may or may not be produced in a different situation, depending on the learning contingencies that applied there (Mischel, 1968). Consequently, there is little interest in personality traits or dispositions assumed to reside within the individual. Instead, behavior therapists assess the client's actions, thoughts, and feelings in particular situations, avoiding assumptions about the cross-situational consistency of behavior. Current assessment practices in behavior therapy reflect recent cognitive and social learning formulations in which the interaction of environment, behavior, and symbolic processes within the individual is stressed (Wilson, 1995).

Treatment goals are discussed carefully with the client, who is the chief decision maker, with the therapist serving as a resource. (Exceptions may occur in the case of very young children or severely disturbed adults for whom other responsible people have to make decisions on treatment.) Issues presented by the client are taken seriously and assigned primary importance, although the therapist may become aware of issues that the client does not initially regard as important (Swan & MacDonald, 1978; Wilson, 1984).

The Therapist-Client Partnership

Behavior therapists' theoretical positions would seem to demand a different style of interaction with the client than that involved in traditional treatments. Behavior therapists may seem more accepting of the client, in that the problems presented are not viewed with suspicion as the product of irrational unconscious forces. The client can validate the truth or otherwise of a therapist's ideas about the problem, because no faith is placed in unconscious motivation. Because of its focus on self-control (teaching clients how to use behavioral principles), behavior therapy is educational rather than "healing," with the therapist taking a facilitative role. There is much emphasis on behavioral monitoring and homework by the client between treatment sessions and troubleshooting with the therapist within the sessions. Rather than trying to remove problems within the individual by modifying unconscious dynamics, the behavior therapist works with the client to plan experiences that encourage the development of new skills. All of these factors contribute to a collaborative working relationship in which the therapist is seriously concerned with becoming fully oriented to the client's goals and expectations, and with delivering interventions that bring clear, practical benefit. Such a relationship is central to the practice of effective behavior therapy (Newman, 1994; Wilson, 1995; Wright & Davis, 1994).

Unfortunately, some early writings mistakenly gave the impression that relationship factors are neglected in behavioral treatment interventions. It is true that behavior therapists do not assign a *central* role to the rapport between client and therapist, but that does not mean that it is ignored. In their report, Sloane and colleagues (1975) commented that successfully treated clients in both psychoanalytic *and* behavior therapy attributed their improvement to similar factors, including the therapist's personal qualities, being encouraged to face challenging issues, and being understood by the therapist. Behavior therapists are occasionally surprised when their clients perceive relationship factors to have been vitally important in their treatment. Evans and Robinson (1978) presented excerpts from a client's diary that she had kept privately during her behavioral treatment. It showed that she was impressed by the idea that she could learn to solve her problems constructively. But it also showed that she derived immense comfort from her therapist's supportive assurances that she was special and not necessarily a disturbed specimen of humanity!

The psychoanalytic and behavior therapists in the Sloane (1975) study showed unexpected similarities in the attention they paid to the therapeutic relationship. Marmor (1975), representing the psychoanalytic view, noted that "the behavior therapists made virtually the same number of interpretive statements as did the psychotherapists"[9] (p. xvi). Wolpe (1975), from a behavioral perspective, wrote: "This book is . . . sure to benefit the public image of behavior therapy by its dispassionate testimony to the fact that behavior therapists are no less human and humane than therapists of other orientations" (p. xx). Such comments illustrate how misleading it can be to rely entirely on the technical writings of behavior therapists for information about behavioral practice (Goldfried, 1980). There is more to behavior therapy than employing specific techniques, and the therapist's interpersonal skills and clinical judgment are essential factors in the choice of suitable interventions and in dealing professionally with the client's ups and downs during the course of treatment (Woolfolk & Richardson, 1984).

In a survey of clinical practice in members of a behavior therapy interest group, Swan and MacDonald (1978) found many discrepancies between what behavior therapists write about in research journals and what they actually do in the clinic; they generally spend more time focusing on the therapeutic relationship and less in implementing specific techniques than had been expected (Wilson, 1995). As an illustration of some of the elements of behavior therapy in practice, this chapter will conclude with the following case example.

THE CASE OF FRANK T.

Frank is a divorced white man in his late twenties. He has been in therapy for more than a year, meeting his outpatient therapist once a week for an hour each time. His therapist is one of the authors of this book. Frank has several problems. He is a recovering alcoholic, having abstained from alcohol and followed the principles of his anonymous fellowship for five years. From his earliest years he learned to feel anxious when around other people. He was teased and tormented mercilessly by the other kids at school because he was thin and scrawny. Frank has not avoided people completely despite his fears of them, but he certainly avoids becoming the center of attention if at all possible. If he ever does find himself the focus of people's attention, he acts foolishly and lets people make fun of him for that. Frank has tried to convince himself that they are not really criticizing him, but his clownish behavior. In this way, he deflects more serious and telling criticism.

In adult life Frank has kept largely to himself. He has found it extremely difficult to deal with people in a straightforward manner. Painfully anxious about expressing his opinions or feelings, Frank has often agreed to requests he would have rather refused. When he is angry about someone's behavior, he tries to "get revenge" by indirect means rather than confronting the person directly. For example, when his employers did not give him a raise, he secretly vandalized equipment at the work-place. In his drinking years, he socialized with people often, but he saw himself as using alcohol as self-medication to reduce his fears. He has almost always avoided close relationships. Frank was married once, but this lasted less than a year and was a difficult experience for him. His wife had initiated the marriage. One of the problems in the marriage was that Frank had a sexual dysfunction; he was unable to feel relaxed enough to enjoy sexual encounters, and this interfered with his ability to function normally.

When Frank asked to see a therapist, his most pressing concern was not his social anxiety or his difficulties with intimate relationships. It was his problem with *exhibitionism,* a sexual disorder that led Frank to derive sexual pleasure from exposing his genitals to unsuspecting strangers. Although Frank would drive miles away from his hometown to do this, and he usually chose the hours of darkness for this activity, he was very fearful of being recognized by a friend or acquaintance or, much worse, of being arrested. He was also disturbed by this behavior in other ways. After each episode of exposing himself, he would feel depressed and near-suicidal. He wanted to be rid of this compulsion to expose himself and to be able to have a normal sexual relationship with someone.

Frank and the therapist agreed to focus on three issues: his exhibitionism, his avoidance and fear of close relationships, and his general social anxiety. It was agreed that one central issue was that he handled his fears, resentments, and concerns in an indirect fashion. Instead of asserting himself self-confidently with friends and work-mates, he deliberately acted as if he did not wish to be taken seriously. Instead of responding forthrightly to criticism or disappointments, he performed surreptitious acts of vandalism. Instead of confronting his problems with intimacy directly by seeking a suitable sexual partner, he furtively prowled the streets of a distant town and displayed his genitals to a stranger.

The treatment plan included several procedural elements designed to help Frank handle social and sexual situations appropriately. The theory that guided Frank's treatment is that therapy will be successful when he has gained (1) new social skills, and (2) a realistic sense of confidence in his ability actually to use those skills successfully in real life. Specific treatments included training in social skills to help him act more assertively and reduce his social anxiety. Covert sensitization was also used to help redirect his sexual arousal from exhibitionism. Frank would imagine a situation in which he was about to expose himself, and then would immediately create a vivid image of a realistic, unpleasant consequence. With the encouragement of the therapist, Frank became adept at imagining a sequence like this:

> He was driving around in his car, looking for a suitable victim. A woman, walking alone, appeared. Frank stopped the car and got out. He began to loosen his clothing. He was feeling strongly aroused sexually. Suddenly a police car pulled up, its lights flashing and its siren wailing. The officers looked on Frank with contempt as they handcuffed him. At the same time, one of Frank's workmates arrived on the scene. This workmate was the biggest gossip at the factory. News of Frank's arrest would soon be all over town. He would obviously lose his job. His crime would be reported in the local newspaper. Frank felt physically sick with shame. He thought ahead to the prospect of a long jail sentence, in protective custody as a sex offender.

Frank imagined scenes like this several times during a series of therapy sessions. He was distinctly uncomfortable during these therapeutic fantasies, but he felt strongly that the procedure was helpful and insisted on continuing. Frank not only kept the therapist updated each week on his progress but he also completed rating scales each day to reflect the strength of his urge to expose himself. As reported by Frank, the urges declined gradually, and as the weeks went by, it became clear that he was no longer exposing himself.

Another technique used in Frank's treatment was role-playing or behavior rehearsal. Aimed at increasing his self-assurance, reducing social anxiety, and improving his judgment and skills in dealing with people, this technique calls for therapist and client to enact brief episodes from real-life situations involving assertive behavior. Here is part of a transcript of one of the sessions:

Therapist: What would be a good example to take?

Client: Well, let's say if I was at work and someone was annoying me. Like my job's picking up something off the floor, and someone threw something on the floor or something.

T: OK. Can you think of a particular person it might be? I guess some people might be easier than others?

C: Yes. Yes, it's about the same; well, there's a guy, Mike. Say Mike, yes. He's always throwing stuff on the floor.

T: Well, let's suppose you're cleaning up the floor. And there's old Mike standing around there, he just finishes a pack of cigarettes, then he just throws the pack on the floor, right near where you're sweeping, right there. How would you be feeling?

C: Very angry!

T: Right, so you're feeling angry. So imagine I'm Mike. I may not look like him, but imagine I am, OK! So, I'm Mike, I've just slung this thing on the floor, and I go on talking to someone. What do you do?

C: I don't know, I'd probably say: "Mike, could you pick that cigarette packet up? I'm trying to keep this area clean, and . . . "

T: "Oh, sorry, Frank, I didn't realize you were sweeping up in here. Hey, sure, I'll pick it up!"

C: "Yeah . . . "

T: Now, how would that be, if he reacted that way?

C: That would be good!

T: So that would be all right, OK? You'd get what you want, he'd pick up the trash; you'd feel—what—OK about being assertive?

C: Yes.

T: Maybe he won't do it again! Where was that on your scale? (*Note:* The therapist and client had agreed on a scale of difficulty that ranged from 0 [no problem, easy item)] to 10 [extremely difficult, maximum fear].)

C: That was probably a 2 or a 3.

T: How did you actually feel while we were just doing that?

C: Not too bad, a little nervous.

T: OK, well, let's do it again, see what happens. Are you willing?

C: Yes, sure!

(Later in the session . . .)

T: You're not used to it, it's new, but it's going very well.

C: Right, right. I don't come over very direct very often. Going over this, I realize it. I hardly ever come out directly. Sometimes I go round a different way, like I'll go over to the next guy that's working and I'll say, "Jeez, isn't Mike a frigging slob, look at all the stuff in his work area!" and all stuff like that, joking, like . . .

T: I could imagine that not being as satisfying in a lot of ways. It's indirect, you're not actually confronting Mike, and the other guy might tell Mike you've been criticizing him behind his back. . . . Let's have the same thing, I'll be Mike, and this time see if you can tell Mike—me as Mike—how you are feeling as well as what you want me to do, OK?

C: OK. You've just slung this old box down where I'm sweeping. "Mike, I'm . . ."

T: "Frank, yes sir! What can I do for you?"

C: "I'm upset, angry, because you threw that package on the floor, and I'm trying to keep the floor clean!"

T: "Oh, I didn't even realize you were sweeping up in here. OK, sorry, I'll pick it up. That was dumb of me. OK?"

C: "OK, thanks."

T: How was that?

C: That was all right. A little more anxiety there!

(Later in the session . . .)

C: There's another guy at work that I've almost said something to, and the guy's name is Joe. He's a guy that'll really get on my . . . he'll call me stupid or something, and sometimes he sounds like he's joking and stuff, and I've come so frigging close to coming out and saying something, and not quite; and it's getting so I hate the guy so much, I feel like even if I was assertive, I wouldn't lose anything anyway, even if I did lose a friendship. In a way, it feels easier.

T: Have you figured out what you'd like to say to him?

C: Well, he'd call me stupid or something, or something ridiculous would happen and he'd say, "That's an idea old Frank would have thought of." Sometimes I laugh, it almost seems funny, and other times I get real angry and I just feel like telling him, "Joe, I'm not stupid, I don't like being called stupid, I get angry when you call me stupid, and I don't feel you have any right to call me stupid."

T: That's excellent, right there! Right there!

Frank's treatment also included *cognitive restructuring.* This is a general term for several procedures aimed at helping the client abandon unhelpful thinking patterns, and begin to think more constructively about situations, behaviors, or personal characteristics that have been the source of past difficulties. At its simplest, cognitive restructuring can mean pointing out the client's tendency to defeat his or her own ends by engaging in demoralizing thinking patterns. At its most complex, it can take the form of an elaborate cognitive therapy that has been shown effective in treating severe mood disorders (Beck, 1967, 1972; Beck, Rush, Shaw, & Emery, 1979; Beck & Weishaar, 1995). It entails teaching the client precisely how to challenge unhelpful assumptions and attitudes and how to replace them with more appropriate cognitions or thoughts. This example from Frank's therapy is at the simpler end of the spectrum and illustrates how unhelpful it can be to dwell on negative thoughts:

T: We know you *can* act assertively, but you don't always do it. What's the difficulty, then? Is it that you don't know what to say, or because you're giving yourself all kinds of reasons for not saying it, or because you feel uncomfortable about it, or . . .

C: I don't know. . . . Before I get into a situation like that, I'll start thinking. Like, before asking for that raise, things started to go through my mind, like, "Do I really deserve a raise? Should I go in and ask them? Or should I work another week and try as hard as I can and then ask them for a raise? Am I doing good enough?" And then I, I do that, and then I start thinking what I'm going to say, and all that stuff goes through my mind and I get confused and . . . Jeez, and then I think it's easier if I went in when I first started thinking!

T: That's true, there can be a real advantage to being spontaneous. Because the more time you spend thinking about it, "Oh, gee, what if this happens or what if that happens?" and trying to convince yourself that you need a raise, you can give yourself all kinds of probably conflicting messages about whether to do it or not!

Theoretical Comments

From the perspective of a behavior therapist, Frank's problems can be understood by examining his learning experiences, and the behavioral procedures that are helpful in his treatment can also be interpreted in learning terms. Frank's social anxiety may have arisen because of a long series of unpleasant experiences when others tormented him at school. His exhibitionism may have become established as a habitual pattern because of its effects: It provided relief from uncomfortable sexual tension that he could not relieve in other ways. He may have learned to act foolishly because others encouraged him to do it (because it was entertaining for them) and because it allowed him to avoid really opening himself to criticism.

The treatment procedures may also be understood in terms of learning principles. Covert sensitization provides a new learning experience by pairing stimuli in a manner similar to conditioning studies, and it probably also encourages the client to adopt more constructive attitudes toward controlling his own behavior. Behavior rehearsal, primarily a method of skills training, may also be useful as a technique for unlearning anxiety. The various cognitive restructuring techniques encourage a form of learning that is effective in modifying important attitudes and other thinking patterns.

The learning principles that apply to understanding Frank's problems and their treatment have been studied by experimental psychologists as classical conditioning, operant learning, and observational and cognitive learning. The following chapters describe these principles and the behavior therapy techniques that were derived from them.

Chapter Summary

Behavioral techniques have been described throughout recorded history, but behavior therapy as a systematic approach to mental health work began in the 1950s. Established as an alternative to psychoanalysis, behavior therapy was influenced by empiricism and behaviorism and is chiefly characterized by its links with experimental psychology. Having rejected psychoanalysis on theoretical and empirical grounds, pioneers of behavior therapy in South Africa, the United Kingdom, and the United States developed new treatment procedures that were inspired by principles of conditioning and learning. Since the 1950s, behavior therapy has been broadened by the contributions of several creative people. The actual practice of behavior therapy has many elements in common with traditional therapy, including the development of a close therapist-client partnership. Yet behavior therapy is distinguished from other approaches by its use of specific techniques addressed to specific problems and by its grounding in psychological research.

Endnotes

1. Eysenck has been a leading advocate of behavior therapy who established the first professional journal in the field, *Behaviour Research and Therapy,* in 1963.
2. *Neurosis* was the term used to describe a variety of disorders involving some form of anxiety. Since 1980, it has been replaced by other terms (see, especially, Chapters 7 and 8).
3. The time, trouble, and expense involved in a course of classical psychoanalysis can be considerable. The time alone could run to several years of sessions at the rate of three to five per week (Arlow, 1995; Menninger, 1958). Psychoanalytic psychotherapy, more commonly practiced than psychoanalysis proper, has typically been much briefer, especially in recent years (Auld & Hyman, 1991).
4. Contemporary behavior therapy for disorders like these is reviewed in Chapter 8.

5. To a mental health professional, a *psychotic episode* refers to a bout of disturbed behavior that may last for days or even weeks. Skinner, who was not a clinician but an experimental psychologist, was referring to momentary periods during which patients appeared to be responding to hallucinations.

6. Perhaps this is ironic, because the alternative term *behavior modification* has become strongly identified with treatment based on operant learning principles, whereas *behavior therapy* tends to refer to the whole spectrum of behavioral and cognitive interventions.

7. ECT involves deliberately inducing seizures in the central nervous system in order to relieve severe, otherwise untreatable, depression. The method is used rarely—only when other methods have failed and under careful medical supervision (*Harvard Mental Health Letter,* 1995).

8. Behavior therapists whose professional backgrounds are in psychiatry or psychiatric nursing are qualified to provide medical care, of course, but behavior therapy itself does not involve medical interventions.

9. Most writers use *psychotherapy* broadly to include all approaches, including behavior therapy; some, especially in the United Kingdom, use the term to refer to psychoanalytic and other psychodynamic therapies, contrasting psychotherapy with behavior therapy, as in this quotation.

Theories, Principles, and Techniques

This section of the book, which consists of Chapters 2 through 6, covers theoretical principles, treatment procedures, and research and assessment methods. The material presented in this section provides a basis from which to approach the remaining chapters of the book, those that describe specific clinical applications of behavior therapy. In Chapters 2, 3, and 4, we will explain the theories behind behavior therapy, describe the principal techniques, and illustrate their use with examples from our own clinical work. Chapter 5 deals with the methodology for gaining new findings in behavior therapy, covering the chief techniques used to test hypotheses both in clinical practice and in programmatic research. Chapter 6 is concerned with the practicalities of behavioral assessment and treatment planning in clinical and research contexts.

It is helpful to make a few comments on terminology as a preface to Chapters 2 through 4. We shall take a broad view of *learning*, viewing it as a process of adaptive change in which people adjust appropriately as they interact with their environment. Instead of offering a formal definition, we describe learning as encompassing the principles of classical conditioning, operant learning, and social and cognitive learning. It is easier to see learning principles and processes at work if one views interactions with the environment as the interplay of stimuli and responses.

The term *stimulus* refers to any detectable change in the environment. The environment can be within or outside a person, so a stimulus can be anything from a hunger pang to a loud noise. The term *response* refers to any specific activity of an individual that can be detected. Although the technical language of learning may suggest an emphasis on the mechanics of human behavior, implying perhaps a sort of mindless adaptation to whatever the environment imposes, we do not view learning as a one-way process of passive adjustment. In altering, adjusting, changing, and modifying behavior according to the feedback one receives from the world, one is usually altering *it* in the process. Oon future occasions, then, one interacts with an environment that has already been shaped by our one's past behavior.

Furthermore, despite behavior therapists' commitments to some form of behaviorism, contemporary theories of social and cognitive learning clearly recognize the interplay of behavior, the environment, and the *person* in determining psychological processes such as learning: "In the social-cognitive approach, the influence of environmental events on behavior is largely determined by cognitive processes governing how environmental influences are perceived and how the individual interprets them" (Wilson, 1995, p. 198). Far from being a robotic automaton, the person in contemporary behavior theory is assigned a central role in selecting the stimuli to be attended to, appraising the situation in the light of personal meanings, and evaluating his or her coping resources in determining which behaviors to bring into play.

Chapter 2

Classical Conditioning Principles and Anxiety-Reduction Procedures

Susan[1] had been so terrified of spiders for so long that she never really believed that she could completely overcome her phobia. As she told her best friend after she terminated her course of therapy, she didn't know who was more surprised at the result—she or the psychiatrist who had recommended behavior therapy. Susan had had many misgivings when she first made the appointment with the psychiatrist. Her phobia was so severe at that time that she was too afraid even to say the word *spider;* the psychiatrist could only figure out what she was afraid of after they had played an elaborate guessing game. To give him an idea of the severity of her phobia, Susan explained that she once saw a tiny one (i.e., a spider) out of the corner of her eye while driving, and in her panic, she had nearly driven off the road. He suggested that a minor tranquilizer might give her some relief, but Susan was reluctant to take drugs and asked if there was an alternative. The psychiatrist recommended that she consult a psychologist specializing in behavior therapy.

Susan's friend wanted to know what actually happens in behavior therapy. Susan found it difficult to describe. She explained that she and her therapist had used at least two separate treatment techniques, and if she had had a different problem, such as depression or obsessional thoughts, different techniques would have been used. One form of treatment she had had was called *systematic desensitization* and it had involved a great deal of relaxation, which had been very pleasant and calming. Then she had imagined a variety of scenes involving spiders, taking the easy ones first. She and the therapist had carefully worked out a list of spider scenes and Susan had placed them in order of how much anxiety they evoked, using a scale from 0 (no anxiety) to 100 (total panic). The first scene, rated at 5, was: "Your neighbor tells you she saw one in her garage."

The therapist had spent several therapy sessions training Susan in relaxation techniques before they actually started the desensitization. The treatment itself began with half an hour of relaxation induction, then the therapist gently described the first scene from the list. Susan concentrated on imagining the scene while continuing to relax deeply. If she ever became anxious while imagining a scene, she simply told the therapist, who backed off immediately and concentrated purely on relaxation instructions for a few minutes before returning to the imagined scene. They followed this procedure for several weeks.

Eventually, Susan started confronting real spiders, following a procedure called *graduated real-life practice.* Before Susan arrived for a session, the therapist had found a tiny, dead spider, put it in a jar with the lid tightly closed, and placed it on a table in the clinic's conference room. Susan started at the opposite end of the corridor outside the conference room, and gradually moved closer, pausing when she felt too anxious to proceed. She tried to move beyond that point, taking her time and regrouping after every step. Over just three sessions, she progressed to the point at which she could touch the glass jar with the spider inside. Only a few more sessions were needed to remove her anxiety completely. When Susan returned to the psychiatrist for a routine follow-up four months after her first visit, he had asked how things were working out with the psychologist. Susan replied by taking a glass jar out of her pocketbook, opening the lid, tipping a large spider from the jar into her hand, and saying: "I think I'm cured, don't you?"

In this chapter we shall focus on a group of techniques that were developed chiefly for use in outpatient settings. Most of these techniques were designed to reduce *anxiety,*[2] a pervasive clinical problem that was regarded by traditional clinicians as fundamental to the "neuroses." Assertiveness training, systematic desensitization, aversion therapy, graduated real-life practice, and various forms of flooding were initially inspired by principles of classical conditioning and extinction, and were described in significant early books such as *Behavior Therapy Techniques* (Wolpe & Lazarus, 1966) and *The Causes and Cures of Neurosis* (Eysenck & Rachman, 1965). Our discussion of these techniques begins with an outline of the theories from which they were drawn.

Theoretical Principles

Basic Concepts

Classical Conditioning

To study *classical conditioning,* we begin by identifying a reflex response, one that is triggered routinely by a particular stimulus. In humans, these reflexes include the eye-blink response to dust or a puff of air in the eye, and the reflex of the patellar tendon (the knee-jerk reflex) in response to a tap in the right place by the doctor's hammer. Such reflexes appear routinely without any particular training, so they are assumed to be un-learned or unconditioned. Classical conditioning takes place when a *new* stimulus acquires the power to produce one of these reflex responses. The term *classical conditioning* refers both to the experimental procedure itself and to the results of that procedure.

In other words, suppose you have a reflex that makes you sneeze whenever you are within two feet of a flower. You have had this reflex all your life, and as far as you know, you did not have to go through any elaborate learning process to acquire it. Therefore, your sneezing in response to flowers is unlearned, or *unconditioned*. The stimulus is the flower, your response is the sneeze, and the reflex is the stimulus-response relationship (your tendency to sneeze in response to flowers). Because this is an unconditioned reflex, the flower is an *unconditioned stimulus* and the sneeze represents an *unconditioned response*. Classical conditioning is a process through which a new stimulus takes on the power to evoke the unconditioned response. For example, suppose that your friend Chris normally evokes no particular reflex in you as far as you are aware. But one day Chris approaches you with a large bunch of daffodils, and you break out into an uncontrollable fit of sneezing. By coincidence, the same thing happens again the next day, and the next. On the fourth day Chris comes up to you again, and you start sneezing—but Chris is not carrying any daffodils today. Classical conditioning, which we shall describe next, provides a description of the process through which Chris became a stimulus capable of eliciting your sneezing reflex.

Ivan Petrovich Pavlov (1849–1936) was a Russian physiologist interested in the workings of the salivary reflex in dogs. The usual experimental procedure was for the researcher to place meat powder (the stimulus) in a dog's mouth. Without special training of any kind, a healthy dog responded quickly by producing saliva (the response). As a result, the salivary reflex could be studied quite conveniently. The dogs used in the experiments were restrained in a special harness, and a hole had been made surgically in each dog's cheek to allow drops of saliva to be collected in a tube and measured.

Although his training was in physiology, not psychology, and his research was designed to throw light on digestive processes, not learning phenomena, Pavlov is best known for his studies of conditioning. He showed that stimuli that previously did not call forth a reflex response like salivation may come to do so following a particular experimental procedure. That is, he demonstrated that dogs could learn to salivate in response to a bell being rung, or a whistle being blown, or even the presentation of a diagram of a circle on a piece of white card. The experimental procedure that produced such unexpected results involved repeatedly presenting the new stimulus a fraction of a second before the reflex-eliciting stimulus. This *pairing* of the two stimuli was made repeatedly until the response normally produced in the reflex began to be produced by the new stimulus. Pavlov discovered this phenomenon entirely by accident.

When they were new to the situation, Pavlov's dogs did not react particularly when a white-coated laboratory assistant entered the room. However, the stimulus of meat powder in the mouth routinely elicited salivation, whether or not the dogs were used to the laboratory. (The meat powder stimulus and the salivation response together form the salivary reflex, an unlearned or unconditioned reflex.) The appearance of the assistant routinely preceded the delivery of food to the dogs. After a few days of exposure to this standard sequence of events, the dogs began to salivate as soon as the assistant appeared. This phenomenon, now well-known as *classical conditioning*, was Pavlov's accidental discovery.

In classical conditioning, the new stimulus (the entry of the assistant) takes on the power to trigger salivation because the presentation of food, the reflex-eliciting stimulus, always followed quickly. The pairing of these stimuli (the assistant and the meat powder) in just the right way results in an increase in the number of stimuli that can kick off the reflex. At first, only food elicited saliva, but after conditioning, both food and the appearance of the assistant could do so. When conditioning has occurred, the previously neutral stimulus (the assistant) has become a *conditioned stimulus.*

At first, this new phenomenon was a distinct annoyance that tended to disrupt Pavlov's experiments; his careful measurements of the timing of the salivary response were thrown off by the presence of these "psychic secretions." Yet, he began to make a systematic study of the phenomenon. Because the comings and goings of laboratory assistants were too haphazard to allow precise experimentation, Pavlov substituted the ringing of a bell, a stimulus that could be precisely controlled and timed. Pavlov (1927) reported a series of investigations to determine the ideal circumstances that produce conditioning: the time interval between stimulus presentations, the duration of each stimulus, and so on. The general procedure is depicted in Figure 2–1.

Notice that the meat powder is the unconditioned stimulus and the salivation the unconditioned response in Figure 2–1. Presenting meat is a stimulus to the animal because it represents a detectable change in the environment. The dog's salivation is a response, an activity that can measured by an experimenter. For meat to produce the response requires no conditioning (learning), so the response is unconditioned. But when the ringing of a bell produces salivation in a dog, conditioning must have occurred. What the salivation is called depends on which stimulus elicited it. If meat powder is the stimulus, the salivation is an *unconditioned response.* If the sound of a bell is the stimulus, the salivation is a *conditioned response.* If the bell produces salivation, the bell has become a *conditioned stimulus.*

One aspect of conditioning that Pavlov soon discovered was *stimulus generalization.* Suppose that meat powder usually elicits about 10 drops of saliva, and that, after conditioning, ringing the bell produces about 5 drops. Pavlov observed that a stimulus similar to

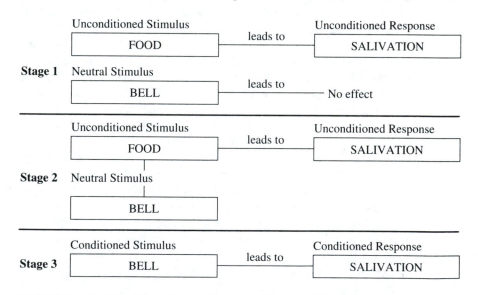

FIGURE 2–1   The Three Basic Stages of Classical Conditioning

Source: From L. A. Lefton, *Psychology,* 2nd ed. Copyright © 1982 by Allyn and Bacon. Reprinted by permission.

the ringing of the bell would also produce salivation, but not as much. For example, ringing a different bell with a lower or higher pitch might produce 3 drops of saliva. Interestingly enough, there was a systematic relationship between measures of the conditioned stimulus (the pitch of the bell, for instance) and measures of the conditioned response (number of drops of saliva). The more similar the stimulus was to the original conditioned stimulus, the greater the response.

The counterpart of conditioning is *extinction.* In the extinction process, the conditioned reflex gradually dwindles away (the conditioned stimulus loses its power to produce the conditioned response). The procedure involves presenting the conditioned stimulus repeatedly without the original stimulus, the unconditioned stimulus. For example, if the laboratory assistant appears repeatedly without the meat powder being presented immediately afterwards, the appearance of the assistant will eventually fail to evoke salivation. Notice that, like conditioning, extinction refers both to the procedure and to the effects of the procedure, or the process. The extinction *procedure* ("experimental extinction") involves repeatedly presenting the conditioned stimulus without the unconditioned stimulus, and the extinction *process* is the fading of the conditioned response to the conditioned stimulus.

Drooling in dogs is of no great practical significance to psychology in itself, but the principles of classical conditioning have been extremely important. Because it can occur whenever a new stimulus is repeatedly presented together with a reflex-eliciting stimulus, behavior therapists have taken classical conditioning seriously as a possible explanation for some mental health problems. Take the example of anxiety. As an emotion that involves various bodily responses like changes in heart rate and respiration, anxiety can be studied as a reflex response, conditioned or unconditioned. Certain stimuli—unexpected loud noises or sudden falling, for example—will automatically produce increased heart rate and respiration as unconditioned responses. If some other stimulus event, something that does not normally produce the response, occurs immediately before the unconditioned stimulus, then the new stimulus can come to provoke responses that might be labeled as anxiety.

Suppose someone is looking at an abstract painting in an art museum. Further suppose that the painting elicits no particular response in the viewer. Suppose, even further, that an earthquake strikes, and the museum visitor is in fear of imminent death as the walls and floor tremble violently. Assuming that the visitor survives the earth tremor, any further encounter with the piece of artwork could, by classical conditioning, immediately produce feelings of terror or alarm. Because it was paired with stimuli that elicited fear, the picture has become a conditioned stimulus. If the person had a similar reaction to other paintings by the same artist, that would be an example of stimulus generalization.

Clinical Implications

Behavior therapists have used classical conditioning principles to understand how clients' problems developed and to devise treatment procedures. Consider the example of Frank T., introduced at the end of Chapter 1. His social anxiety may have arisen because people were repeatedly paired with threatening and painful experiences, so that people became conditioned stimuli that evoked anxiety in Frank. Covert sensitization, a technique that was employed to treat Frank's exhibitionism, can also be understood in terms of classical conditioning. The unpleasant fantasy imagined by the client (being arrested) is seen as the unconditioned stimulus, which leads to uncomfortable reactions (fear, shame) that form the unconditioned response. The idea is to turn the stimulus that used to encourage the abnormal behavior into a conditioned stimulus for an unpleasant response. In Frank's case, the aim was to make the sight of a woman walking alone (in the context of his inappropriate desire to expose himself) elicit responses of concern, apprehension, and discomfort.

Classical Conditioning of Anxiety

The fear that signals genuine danger is helpful, of course, but the anxiety that the clients of mental health professionals experience can be highly distressing and potentially handicapping. As you will see in a later chapter, the negative behavioral effects of anxiety disorders can include avoiding objects or situations that are objectively harmless, engaging in compulsive rituals designed to ward off the threat of danger, and suffering impairment in routine behavior. For example, a client with a phobia of heights might avoid using elevators; a client with fears of contamination by unseen filth might engage in prolonged cleansing rituals; and a client with a social phobia who is giving an important speech before a large group might find his or her performance disrupted in one way or another by anxiety. In developing treatments for anxiety problems like these, the behavior therapy pioneers drew their theoretical principles from laboratory research on learning, especially classical conditioning, and were particularly impressed by the famous demonstration of fear conditioning in Little Albert by Watson and Rayner (1920), as described in Chapter 1.

Recall that Albert developed a new fear of a white rat when the researchers paired its appearance with the sound of a steel bar being struck. Because the boy's behavior showed typical classical conditioning phenomena such as stimulus generalization, Watson and Rayner speculated that naturally occurring phobias might also have developed through classical conditioning. Accordingly, behavior therapists tried to understand a client's anxiety reaction as a conditioned response (CR), resulting from the accidental pairing of stimuli in his or her environment. This view led to the study of extinction procedures as laboratory parallels to psychological treatment. For example, a phobic client who fears and avoids spiders may have developed the CR of anxiety after an unpleasant event of some kind coincided with the presence of a spider. Treatment would be based on the principle of extinction; the technique would be to encourage the client to confront the conditioned stimulus repeatedly in the absence of the unconditioned stimulus. That would mean confronting the spider without the unpleasant event that presumably was present when the phobia started. Since we assume that the unpleasant event is now history, the client is really operating under conditions of extinction anyway, and the therapist simply needs to hasten the extinction process.

THE CASE OF SUSAN B.

Susan, who was introduced at the start of the chapter, had developed her phobia of spiders after a single terrifying event. She was 10 years old when some of her cousins were visiting on a hot day in summer. As part of a game they were playing, her brothers and some of the cousins bodily forced her into a small shed in the backyard and locked her in. It was dark, hot, and stuffy in the shed, and she found it hard to breathe. Feeling panicky, she struggled to push the door open without success. At that moment her hair brushed against a large spider's web, and several large spiders crawled over her face and under her clothes. She screamed and struggled to get out, but the other children thought it was all part of the game and laughed at her. When she was eventually released after what seemed to her to be an eternity, Susan was trembling and crying and looked pale. She felt weak, and her parents noticed that she was tense and shivery for over an hour after the episode. The family doctor was called in and sedating medication was required. This single experience marked the beginning of her phobia.

Years later, Susan continued to be distressed and handicapped by her horror of spiders. Anything that even resembled a spider, such as the leafy stem of a tomato, startled her so that she would shy away. On one occasion she suddenly saw a large spider when she was ironing some clothes. She screamed, flung up her arms, and the iron crashed through a window. As she explained it, her reason for seeking therapy was that she and her husband were planning to start a family. "What would happen," she wondered, "if I were holding my baby when I suddenly saw a spider?"

Theoretically, the experience of being shoved into a cramped, hot, and airless shed while finding it hard to breathe and with escape impossible constitutes an aversive unconditioned stimulus (UCS) in Pavlovian terms. This stimulus situation would automatically elicit reflex responses that could include sensations of alarm and fear (the unconditioned response, or UCR). The spider, simply by its presence as an attention-getting stimulus, can become a conditioned stimulus (CS) by pairing with the UCS. As a result, responses similar to those initially provoked by the emotion-arousing event are elicited in the client by the sight of a spider, or, by stimulus generalization, by the sight of anything that looks like one (such as a green tomato top). Treatment following from this idea would involve some form of extinction procedure so that the feared stimulus loses its power to evoke anxiety. Susan's phobia was successfully removed after a course of treatment with systematic desensitization and graduated real-life practice, two of the treatment procedures described later in this chapter.

Classic Studies

Conditioned Suppression

Estes and Skinner (1941) described a laboratory study of anxiety that produced the phenomenon of *conditioned suppression*. Rats responded to a schedule of positive reinforcement, pressing levers to obtain food in the usual operant learning procedure. While the rats continued to respond, the experimenters suddenly presented an audible tone that was sounded for three minutes before terminating together with a brief electric shock. The tone-plus-shock stimulus combination was delivered at random intervals, unrelated to the rats' behavior. The results were that the rats began to slow their response rates at the onset of the tone and before the shock was delivered. The authors had therefore demonstrated "the conditioning of a state of anxiety to the tone, where the primary index was a reduction in strength of the hunger-motivated lever pressing behavior" (Estes & Skinner, 1941/1968, p. 245). Because the sound of the tone, after conditioning, suppressed the lever-pressing, the effect was labeled *conditioned suppression.* Extinction of this conditioned suppression was seen when the tone was presented for prolonged periods of a half hour or more without the shock ensuing.

Conditioned suppression has some parallels in clinical settings.

THE CASE OF LARRY

Larry, a mill worker with social phobia, was so apprehensive about attending safety meetings at work that he would make up any excuse not to go. But, since the meetings were mandatory and could be convened unpredictably and at very short notice, Larry was often unable to escape in time. To make matters worse, the foreman in charge of the meetings had been promoted to this position over Larry, who had competed for the job and lost despite having worked for the company longer than any other applicant. Larry avoided this man whenever possible, and always felt uneasy in his presence.

At the safety meetings, the foreman would randomly call on people to speak, and Larry's chief fear was of being thrust in front of the room and finding himself tongue-tied and embarrassed in front of the group. If he had been alone at home, he could have easily stood up and delivered a few sentences about safety procedures. He might even have managed fairly well in front of the group, if the foreman had not been there. But the knowledge that his rival was watching his every move while he spoke had the same effect on Larry as the tone had had on the rats of Estes and Skinner: In each case, the behavior was disrupted. Larry stuttered and forgot what he was going to say; the rats slowed down their lever pressing. The foreman, like the tone to the rats, was a reminder of aversive experiences (disappointment at not gaining the promotion), so that the mere presence of that conditioned stimulus was enough to suppress Larry's current behavior.

Wolpe's Experiments

In a series of laboratory experiments beginning in the 1940s, Joseph Wolpe (1958, 1981) deliberately induced conditioned fear[3] in cats in order to find efficient ways to remove it. His intent was to learn what he could about *removing* the cats' conditioned fears, apply these findings in the clinical arena, and then use them to develop treatments for his clients with anxiety disorders. The behavior therapy techniques of assertiveness training and systematic desensitization were derived directly from the results of these studies with cats.

The impetus for Wolpe's experiments with cats was the work of Jules Masserman (1943), an American psychiatrist who had produced lasting fear in cats by placing them in cages and delivering electric shocks as they approached food. After he had delivered a series of such shocks, Masserman disconnected the shock mechanism and observed the cats for signs of conditioned fear. How did Masserman know that the cats had become fearful? There were two indications: First, the cats would escape from or avoid the cages when given the opportunity (they had not done so before the shocks were introduced). Second, when the cats were forced into the cages, they would not eat there, even if they had not eaten for some time and were presumably hungry. Furthermore, the cats' experimentally induced fears *persisted* long after the shock was disconnected. Masserman had to provide "treatment" to remove the fear: He would place a cat in the cage and then force the cat toward the food by means of a movable partition. When the cat began to eat, the anxiety would fade away gradually.

Masserman's studies of fear conditioning in cats were partly inspired by psychoanalytic theory, which traces anxiety disorders ("neuroses") to conflict between opposing impulses. In the 1940s most theorists assumed that conflict was essential to the development of any neurosis (Yates, 1962). This notion was supported by Pavlov's (1927) findings on *experimental neurosis,* a phenomenon in which laboratory dogs developed strong fear of the experimental environment as a result of conflict between opposing responses after difficult training tasks. Because these original studies of Masserman and Pavlov suggested that approach-avoidance conflict was necessary in inducing conditioned fear, Wolpe included similar procedures in his studies.

It is important to note that Masserman's experimental procedures allowed more than one process to operate. Not only were his cats subjected to approach-avoidance conflict but they were also subjected to aversive *classical conditioning.* Initially, the cage was a neutral stimulus that elicited no particular reflex responses in the cats. Electric shock can clearly be seen as a UCS, one that automatically elicits UCRs of pain and fear. Pairing the cage with shock allows the cage to become a CS, eventually eliciting responses (CRs) similar to those elicited by shock. Thus, the cage can become an aversive CS, eliciting conditioned fear (or anxiety) as a CR, by classical conditioning. Furthermore, one would predict that, once the shock unit has been disconnected, the CR would undergo extinction (because the cage, the CS, is no longer paired with the shock, the UCS). Masserman's technique of forcing the cats toward the food by means of the movable partition could therefore work by extinction, because the cats were exposed to the CS of the cage environment without the UCS.

Fear Conditioning.   Wolpe (1958) induced conditioned fear in 12 cats. These were divided into two experimental groups of 6, each group following a different procedure. The first procedure was similar to that of Estes and Skinner (1941); the 6 cats in this condition were shocked individually in an experimental cage following the sounding of a tone, each cat receiving 5 to 10 shocks. The second procedure was similar to Masserman's (1943); these 6 cats were first trained to approach food in response to the tone, then they were shocked as they approached the food (the idea being to create conflict between approaching and avoiding the food). All 12 cats showed "neurotic symptoms" after the shocks were discontinued: (1) they resisted being placed in the cage, (2) they gave signs of anxiety when inside the cage, and (3) they refused to eat meat pellets anywhere in the cage even after three days of starvation. These responses were greater, and more generalized, when the tone was present.

There were few differences in the responses of the two experimental groups, so Wolpe had shown that inducing conflict was unnecessary in creating such experimental neuroses (Wolpe, 1982). The procedures and their effects can be seen as examples of classical conditioning, and there is a parallel with conditioned suppression because the cats would not eat in the presence of the cage or the tone.

Removal of Fear.   For 3 cats, Wolpe followed Masserman's (1943) technique of forcing them toward food during experimental extinction. The procedure was effective, as it had been for Masserman. The remaining 9 cats were treated differently because "the fact that the neurotic reactions of the cats were associated with inhibition of feeding suggested that under different conditions feeding might inhibit the neurotic reactions: in other words, that the two reactions might be reciprocally inhibitory" (Wolpe, 1958, p. 55). Wolpe fed the cats by hand in the cage under experimental extinction conditions; no tones or shocks were presented. Eventually, 4 of the 9 cats learned to eat from the food box in the cage. The remaining 5 cats, which had not responded to the hand-feeding procedure, were offered food outside the cage and were gradually brought nearer to the experimental cage. All cats eventually learned to eat from the original cage.

The Return of Fear.   No further shock was delivered, but the tone was reintroduced after the anxiety-reduction procedures just described. Anxiety returned in all of the cats. To remove the anxiety again, Wolpe fed 2 of the 9 cats at decreasing distances from the cage and the tone. The other 7 cats were fed in the cage without the tone; the tone was presented briefly, the cat was fed again, a brief tone followed, and so forth. Then the tone was switched on and sounded for a prolonged period as the cats remained in the cages and fed there. Eventually, the tone became a safety signal.

Comments on Wolpe's Experiments
The procedures Wolpe (1958) used to produce conditioned fear allowed classical conditioning to operate. However, he found that the normal extinction procedure—repeated exposure to the CS (the cage or the tone) without the UCS (the shock)—was completely ineffective; a cat would not eat in the cage after fear conditioning "though it might be left there with the food for days" (Wolpe, 1981, p. 45). The anxiety seemed to have produced a total suppression of feeding in the conditioning environment (Wolpe, 1982, 1990).

Although it seems surprising that the cats' anxiety did not extinguish after the shock was discontinued, there is a parallel in the experience of clients with phobias. After her own experience with fear conditioning, Susan B. continued to fear spiders for years, despite the fact that she had encountered them many times since the original incident without anything unpleasant happening to her (other than the anxiety itself, of course); she had certainly never again been locked in a shed. As you will see in Chapter 7, this notorious persistence of phobias led theorists to look for a second factor (in addition to classical conditioning) in explaining conditioned fear and avoidance behavior. But Wolpe, working with theories popular in the 1950s (Hull, 1952), concluded that anxiety is simply an unusual type of conditioned response that is extremely difficult to extinguish.

Reciprocal Inhibition
Because exposing the cats to the CS under conditions of extinction was not sufficient to eliminate conditioned fear, Wolpe proposed that anxiety has to be countered by a competing feeling state before it can be reduced. Accordingly, he fed the cats as part of the extinction procedure. Feeding competes with and inhibits anxiety, and anxiety competes with and inhibits feeding. He called the process *reciprocal inhibition* because the competing

process goes both ways. Wolpe stated the general principle as follows: "If a response antagonistic to anxiety can be made to occur in the presence of anxiety-evoking stimuli so that it is accompanied by a complete or partial suppression of the anxiety responses, the bond between these stimuli and the anxiety responses will be weakened" (Wolpe, 1958, p. 71).

In using reciprocal inhibition to eliminate the cats' conditioned fear, Wolpe found that it did not always work simply to start feeding them inside the feared cage. Some cats first had to be taken some distance away from the cage until a point was reached at which they could be induced to eat. Interestingly, Wolpe could always find a point for each cat at which eating overcame the anxiety, and he discovered in the process that there was a linear, inverse relationship between a cat's anxiety and its distance from the cage (the further away from the cage, the less anxiety). He could therefore bring the cats gradually closer to the site of the original fear conditioning, feeding them at each step, and allowing them time to tolerate each new situation before proceeding further.

Wolpe used this combination of techniques—reciprocal inhibition at each step in a graded progression of feared stimuli—in designing behavior therapy techniques for people with various anxiety disorders. He observed that a wide variety of responses can be used to inhibit anxiety, including feeding, sexual responses, muscular relaxation, and aggression.

Treatment Procedures

Assertiveness Training

Wolpe's (1958) research with cats quickly led him to the idea of reciprocal inhibition, but it did not immediately suggest the technique of systematic desensitization for which he is best known. In first applying reciprocal inhibition to clients, Wolpe (1982) tried to encourage them to enact behavior that ran counter to the anxiety that arose in their daily lives. The most common procedure here was to encourage clients to adopt a policy of assertiveness with people. He was influenced in this by the work of Andrew Salter, who had described a general approach to treatment of neuroses ("conditioned reflex therapy") based on Pavlov's (1927) theory of personality (Salter, 1949).

Salter had assumed that people naturally tend to be "excitatory"—that is, spontaneous, outgoing, expressive, and not inhibited by worry and fear. However, many people learn to inhibit their behavior excessively because of their upbringing by strict parents and other authorities, so that neurotic behaviors emerge. Acting on this theory, Salter tried various methods for encouraging clients to be excitatory rather than inhibitory. He urged clients to express feelings and opinions spontaneously and forthrightly, to look people straight in the eye, to use the word *I* unashamedly, and so forth. Impressed by Salter's work, Wolpe initially used assertiveness training extensively with his neurotic clients. However, he soon found that "assertion toward persons" was irrelevant to many neuroses and was effective only with certain kinds of social anxiety.

Wolpe's assertiveness training technique usually involves persuading the client of the disadvantages of being nonassertive and then urging him or her to begin acting more assertively in real life. The assertive responses Wolpe recommends contain references to anger in many cases, and he excludes expressing anxiety from his definition of assertiveness: "Assertive behavior is the socially appropriate verbal and motor expression of any emotion other than anxiety" (Wolpe, 1990, p. 135). The reciprocal inhibition process takes place in the natural environment. Because anger reciprocally inhibits anxiety, socially anxious clients are advised to start being more assertive in their everyday relationships. Expressing displeasure and annoyance would inhibit anxiety and allow its extinction to take place in real life. Hence, reciprocal inhibition takes place automatically when the client follows the therapist's directive to be more assertive.

Most of the time, instructions and coaxing to be assertive are sufficient to increase clients' assertive behavior and to reduce their social discomfort, but Wolpe also uses *behavior rehearsal* (originally called "behavioristic psychodrama") on occasion. In behavior rehearsal, the therapist and client role-play scenes from everyday life so as to help reduce the client's anxiety about forthright self-expression. When necessary, the therapist suggests more appropriate verbal responses and gives feedback on suitable gestures, eye contact, firmness of voice, and so forth (Wolpe, 1958, 1990).

Although assertiveness training was often helpful to clients with social anxiety, it was not always effective (Wolpe, 1982). Wolpe began to use Jacobson's (1938) relaxation training methods because they provided a means of reducing anxiety arising from any source. Typically beginning with 6 to 10 relaxation training sessions, Wolpe would expose clients to graduated fear stimuli in real life. When difficulties arose in arranging suitable real-life experiences, he began to deal with imagined stimuli, prompted by the work of hypnotists. This led to the development of Wolpe's best-known treatment method, systematic desensitization.

Systematic Desensitization

An informal description of *systematic desensitization*, as given by Susan, the spider-phobic client, to her friend, appears in the introduction to Section II. There are three key elements to the procedure as a behavior therapy technique: relaxation training, development of the anxiety hierarchy, and the presentation of hierarchy items for the client to imagine while deeply relaxed.

Relaxation Training
Wolpe (1958) adopted the relaxation training procedure of Edmund Jacobson (1938) as a means of inhibiting clients' anxiety during systematic desensitization. Jacobson had reported that relaxation exercises bring not only pleasant subjective feelings of calm but also many objective health benefits, especially in alleviating anxiety- and stress-related problems. One of Wolpe's most creative contributions was to incorporate relaxation methods into his experimentally derived treatment technique. Several versions of relaxation training have been described, but research has not clearly shown that any particular method is preferable (Hecker & Thorpe, 1992). One that involves teaching clients systematically to tense, then relax, various muscle groups is in common use today (Bernstein & Borkovec, 1973). The rationale for this approach is twofold: (1) it is easier to relax a muscle group from a state of tension than from a normal, resting state; and (2) alternately tensing and relaxing helps the client to learn to distinguish the sensations associated with each state.

The Anxiety Hierarchy

The anxiety hierarchy is a carefully prepared list of items, ordered along a dimension of gradually increasing anxiety-eliciting potential, representing a cross-section of the client's feared situations. A fictitious example that could apply to someone with a phobia of heights would literally consist of a series of steps. The first item, describing a situation eliciting minimal anxiety, might be "standing on the bottom rung of a step-ladder in your kitchen"; the second item might be "standing on the second rung"; and so forth. The last item, the most anxiety-evoking item in a list of 20 or so, might be "climbing to the top of a commercial radio antenna in a high wind."

In practice, few anxiety hierarchies follow such a logical, linear sequence. You might think, for example, that a test-anxious college student would experience slight fear one month before a major exam, moderate fear one week before, and extreme fear sitting in the classroom the minute before the test is handed out. The reality is often surprisingly different, so that on a genuine hierarchy, the item at the top, representing maximal anxiety, could be "studying in the dorm, the night before the test," whereas actually taking the test might be only halfway up the list.

Behavior therapists try to compile hierarchies that include the whole range of clients' fears related to a particular topic. For example, relevant dimensions of anxiety for a client with *agoraphobia*[4] could be how crowded the situation is, how far the client is from home, whether the client is alone or accompanied by a trusted companion, and whether the route away from home involves crossing bridges or passing through tunnels. To simplify hierarchy construction, clinicians usually ask the client to rate each potential item on a 0 to 100 scale of *subjective units of disturbance* (or *SUDs*). The lowest (easiest) item might receive a SUDs score of 5, and the highest 95 or 100. Typically, anxiety hierarchies have from 12 to 20 items. Susan B's anxiety hierarchy is presented as an example in Table 2–1; the hierarchy of a client with agoraphobia appears in Table 2–2.

TABLE 2–1   Sample Anxiety Hierarchy (Low to High): Phobia of Spiders

(Taken from the authors' files; the client was a 32-year-old woman. SUDs units are given in parentheses.)

1. Abbie (neighbor) tells you she saw one in her garage. (SUDs = 5)
2. Abbie sees you, crosses the street, says there's a tiny one across the street. (10)
3. Betty [at work] says there's one downstairs. (15)
4. Friends downstairs say they saw one outside their apartment and disposed of it. (20)
5. Carrie [daughter] returns from camp; says the rest-rooms were inhabited by spiders. (25)
6. You see a small, dark spot out of the corner of your eye; you have a closer look; it isn't a spider. (30)
7. You are with your husband. You see a tiny spider on a thread outside, but you can't see it very clearly. (35)
8. You are alone. You see a tiny spider on a thread outside, but you can't see it very clearly. (40)
9. You are reading the paper, and you see a cartoonist's caricature of a spider (with a human-like face and smile). (45)
10. You are reading an article about the Brown Recluse. (50)
11. You see a clear photograph of a spider's web in the newspaper. (60)
12. You see a spider's web on the stairs at work. (70)
13. You suddenly see a "loose tomato top" in your salad. (80)
14. You open a kitchen cabinet and suddenly see a large spider. (90)

TABLE 2–2   Sample Anxiety Hierarchy (Low to High): Agoraphobia

Taken from the authors' files. The client was a 51-year-old woman. SUDs units are given in parentheses.

1. Going to the local store, 50 yards away. (5)
2. Being in the butcher's shop when it's empty. (10)
3. At the beautician's. (15)
4. When walking, crossing a main road. (20)
5. In the QuickSave, pushing a shopping cart. (25)
6. At the butcher's, 1½ miles away. (35)
7. Taking a casual stroll along the main road for 15 minutes. (40)
8. Using an elevator. (45)
9. Talking to a neighbor in the street. (50)
10. Meeting a friend when walking in the street. (55)
11. In the Cooperative Store when there are about four other people there. (65)
12. In the doctor's waiting room when it's full. (75)
13. In the butcher's with five other customers. (80)
14. In a store, waiting in line. (85)
15. Walking in a large shopping mall. (90)
16. In the crowds at the town's largest shopping center on a Saturday morning. (95)

Presenting the Hierarchy Items during Treatment

After several sessions of preliminary relaxation training and construction of the anxiety hierarchy, systematic desensitization proceeds with the pairing of relaxation sensations with the items of the hierarchy. The first item, the one with the lowest SUDs rating, is described carefully by the therapist, and then the client is asked to continue to imagine it for 15 seconds or so. Two or three presentations of the item are given, separated by pauses for continued relaxation. Typically, clients use a prearranged signal, such as a slight wave of the hand, to indicate the appearance of anxiety or tension. At this signal, the therapist immediately asks the client to terminate the imagined scene, and proceeds to reinstate deep relaxation and calm before introducing the hierarchy item again. Each scene is presented several times without a signal of anxiety from the client before the next item is introduced.

Wolpe (1982) has explained that because the anxiety-countering effects of relaxation are relatively weak, only weak anxiety responses should be evoked during treatment. But repeatedly presenting a weak anxiety stimulus to a deeply relaxed client will eventually reduce its fear potential to zero, and then the next item on the hierarchy may be presented. When the anxiety associated with a hierarchy item has been weakened, the next stronger item will also have been weakened. Figure 2–2 shows Wolpe's depiction of this process. Reducing the anxiety associated with the first item, item A, from 5 to 0 simultaneously reduces the second item, B, from 10 to 5 (the shaded area disappears). It is as if the anxiety hierarchy represents a ladder, and reducing the anxiety connected with each step is like sawing the bottom rung off the ladder each time (see Figure 2–2).

Wolpe's systematic desensitization technique has clear parallels with his original research procedures. He used feeding to inhibit conditioned fear in the cats, but he uses progressive relaxation training to inhibit anxiety in his clients. With the experimental cats, he introduced them gradually to the cages in which they had been shocked, and he presented

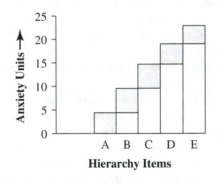

FIGURE 2–2   The Desensitization Process (When the anxiety-evoking potential of A is reduced from 5 to 0, B automatically is reduced from 10 to 5, and so forth.)

Source: From Wolpe, J., T*he practice of behavior therapy,* 4th ed. Copyright © 1990 by Allyn and Bacon. Reprinted by permission.

the tone for progressively longer intervals; with his clients, he exposes them to successive items from individually tailored, graded anxiety hierarchies. The cats were exposed to actual feared situations, but the clients confront imagined scenes. As in the animal work, the clinical application of systematic desensitization involves giving the client control over the rate at which feared items are presented.

Analogue Research on Systematic Desensitization

In describing the results of "treatment on reciprocal inhibition principles" in three sets of clients, Wolpe (1958) reported a "general average of about 90% of highly favorable outcomes" (p. 216). This claim of high success rates in 210 clients with various disorders (anxiety state, hysteria, reactive depression, obsessions and compulsions, neurasthenia, and others) is particularly notable in that treatment periods were generally short as compared with traditional psychotherapy. The treatment methods used, particularly SD, were described in enough detail to allow careful replication. As a result, scores of studies of SD and other Wolpean methods have been stimulated since the original work was reported.

Initial analogue studies of SD were reported by Peter Lang and his colleagues in the early 1960s. Lang and Lazovik (1963) were the first to show that SD could effectively be implemented in a laboratory setting with snake-fearful college volunteers. The study clearly demonstrated the superiority of SD to no treatment, and it is notable in the use of a fear-relevant behavioral-avoidance test as part of the battery of outcome assessment measures. The researchers asked the volunteers to approach a live snake in a glass case, and recorded how close to the snake they could get before being stopped in their tracks by mounting anxiety. The authors provided enough therapeutic contact to the treated subjects (14 individual sessions) to encourage confidence that the experimental procedures formed a suitable parallel to routine clinical work. A second study (Lang, Lazovik, & Reynolds, 1965) included a pseudotherapy comparison condition in addition to a no-treatment group, with the result that SD was shown to produce effects over and above those attributable to certain nonspecific therapy events.

Other studies were designed to assess not only the superiority of SD to no treatment or to treatment interviews in general but also the relative importance of procedural elements within SD. Studying snake-phobic volunteers, Davison (1968a) compared four experimental conditions: (1) SD proper, (2) SD but with hierarchy items that were irrelevant to subjects' fears, (3) SD with an appropriate hierarchy but without relaxation induction, and (4) no treatment. The results indicated that all the elements of the usual SD "package" are necessary to the procedure. However, this study may be criticized in that subjects in the no relaxation condition (3) were *yoked* to condition (1) subjects in their exposure to hierarchy items. That is, "no-relaxation" was confounded with "no control over progress through the hierarchy." Later work with snake-avoidant college students (McGlynn, 1973) and phobic clinic clients (Gillan & Rachman, 1974) produced contradictory results to those of Davison. Data showed that, while exposure to relevant stimuli is vital, the relaxation component is unnecessary. Furthermore, the data revealed that it is *not* essential to therapeutic progress for clients to control their exposure to hierarchy items by terminating scenes when anxiety arises (McGlynn, 1973).

In a landmark study, Paul (1966) provided convincing evidence of the effectiveness of SD by comparing it with traditional psychotherapy methods. The participants were drawn from a university community and had severe fears of public speaking. The therapists were experienced clinicians from the community whose orientation was psychodynamic. Paul had to teach the therapists how to implement SD, which they initially regarded as unlikely to prove helpful as treatment. Assessment measures used to assess anxiety before and after treatment consisted of an impressive battery of measures that included a behavioral test of fear (an actual speech before a group of raters), a series of self-report inventories, and physiological monitoring of pulse rate and skin conductance.

All participants received five sessions of therapy and were randomly distributed among four treatment conditions: (1) traditional insight-oriented therapy as usually practiced by the therapists; (2) SD; (3) an attention-placebo condition; and (4) no treatment. The people in the attention-placebo condition were given a pill to swallow. This was really an inert substance that they were told had impressive tranquilizing properties. Under the influence of this "drug," these participants performed a repetitive signal-detection task that was, in fact, quite dull but that they had been led to believe was highly stressful. The rationale given was that the beneficial effects of the drug during the experimental task would generalize to real-life public-speaking episodes. Post-treatment assessment revealed the short-term superiority of SD to all other methods. The results were consistent in the three behavioral domains that were assessed (self-report, overt behavioral, and psycho-physiological). A follow-up study two years later confirmed that the effects of SD were lasting and that there had been no emergence of new symptoms (Paul, 1967).

Further experimental work on SD has been devoted to assessing alternative explanations for its apparent success as a method. *Expectancy of benefit* is one such possibility, championed by Kazdin and Wilcoxon (1976). However, this is a complex issue because, despite genuine methodological problems in much desensitization research, it cannot be shown convincingly that positive expectancy of benefit actually brings about improvement in itself (McGlynn, Mealiea, & Landau, 1981). Another important matter concerns the type of participants in experimental studies of SD; findings obtained with student volunteers do not always hold in clinical samples. SD with clinic clients will be evaluated in a later chapter.

Wolpe (1982, 1990) has criticized the use of between-groups experimental designs in evaluating SD and other specific methods. Pointing out that behavioral assessment is essential to behavior therapy, he opposes arbitrarily assigning clients to one of several treatments in an experiment. In clinical work, SD or any other behavioral treatment technique is usually prescribed after a suitable assessment process with the client. Because they involve assigning participants to conditions randomly, group research designs cannot replicate the procedures of routine clinical practice; they "show statistically significant improvement in groups of patients, but leave the fate of the individual case obscure" (Wolpe, 1990, p. 345).

Aversion Therapy and Anxiety Relief

In some forms of *aversion therapy* that were popular early in the history of behavior therapy, classical conditioning procedures were used to help the client avoid situations or behavior that are closely connected with inappropriate behavior. Early examples of aversion therapy are the use of painful but harmless electric shock to discourage interest in a variety of stimuli ranging from inappropriate sexual partners (such as inanimate objects or animals) to undesired behavior, such as substance abuse or addictions. Electrical, chemical, and even imagined stimuli have been employed as unconditioned stimuli (Brownell, Hayes, & Barlow, 1978; Davison, 1968b).

In *anxiety relief*, the offset of an aversive stimulus can operate similarly to a positive stimulus. This means that if a neutral stimulus is paired with a shock being switched off, the previously neutral stimulus can become positive.

As originally described by Wolpe (1958), "anxiety-relief" was used as a treatment for anxiety in the client's day-to-day life. Some 10 to 20 times per session, the client receives an electric shock to the hand at a level that he or she has previously selected as "uncomfortable." The client is instructed to endure the shock "until the desire to have it stop becomes very strong" (Wolpe, 1958, p. 180) and then to say "Calm." At that point the therapist immediately turns off the shock. After two or three sessions, Wolpe reports, many clients can reduce spontaneous anxiety episodes by use of the word *calm,* although the results of this method apparently vary a great deal from client to client.

Thorpe, Schmidt, Brown, and Castell (1964) reported success with a variant of the method in a series of eight clients. The problems treated were phobic anxiety of clouds, elevators, and tunnels (one male client); obsessive-compulsive neurosis (one female client); compulsive overeating (one female client); and various paraphilias or unwanted sexual preferences (five male clients). These authors noted that in many published reports of behavior therapy, treatment addressed not the problem behavior itself but, rather, symbolic representations of it (such as color slides used in aversion therapy, or imagined scenes in SD).

Accordingly, they reported the development of a technique in which printed and spoken words served to represent the problem being treated. For each client, a series of words or phrases denoting the presented problem (e.g., *fear of clouds*) was prepared. The phrases were printed on a disk that could be revolved slowly so that they appeared successively in an aperture visible to the client. As each phrase appeared, the client read it aloud and immediately received a brief, painful shock. The last word on the disk was always a relief stimulus describing the stimulus to be approached rather than avoided (e.g., *clouds*), and its presentation guaranteed that no further shocks were forthcoming. The typical duration of treatment was two weeks with daily sessions. The authors described the procedure as "extremely effective," in that the use of words in place of overt behavior within treatment sessions was successful in producing improvement in real life. However, several short-lived but unpleasant side effects were observed in the clients (depression, general anxiety, gastric ailments, and nightmares), and treatment had to be discontinued in two clients because of their dissatisfactions with the procedure.

Thorpe and associates (1964) concluded their report by remarking that reciprocal inhibition may have been involved in the therapeutic process. However, in a later process study of the components of anxiety relief, Solyom, McClure, Heseltine, Ledwidge, and Solyom (1972) were unable to rule out other factors, including the noxious stimulation itself (which could remove some of the reinforcement of being in therapy) and habituation to the phobic stimuli presented.

Exposure Methods

Beginning in the late 1960s, systematic desensitization and anxiety relief were gradually replaced by methods that encouraged clients to confront anxiety-provoking stimuli directly. Joseph Wolpe had believed that simple extinction procedures were not sufficient to eliminate phobic anxiety, citing the results of his own experiments with cats and accepting the prevailing theoretical views. But the conclusions Wolpe drew from his own experiments can be questioned. Like Masserman, Wolpe had found that his cats *could* overcome their conditioned fear simply by being made to confront the full conditioned stimuli of the cage and the tone (without any more shocks, of course). Yet instead of focusing on that finding, Wolpe paid more attention to countering anxiety by feeding the cats, and to exposing them gradually to progressively more threatening stimuli, leading him to develop the complex systematic desensitization procedure. What if this elaborate desensitization procedure were unnecessary? Research both in the animal laboratory (Wilson, 1973) and in the clinic (Marks, 1981) showed that neither reciprocal inhibition nor graduated exposure to conditioned stimuli were essential elements in the elimination of conditioned fear.

These findings converge with recent advances in theory. Instead of emphasizing the automatic conditioning of responses to stimuli by the pairing process, contemporary learning theorists stress that one learns that different classes of stimulus event are correlated. Classical conditioning therefore involves the development of *expectancies* as one learns that the CS predicts a particular UCS (Rescorla, 1988; Thompson, 1994; Wilson, 1995). Eliminating the unnecessary anxiety evoked by a CS means altering the client's expectation that an aversive UCS will follow. As we shall show next, straightforward exposure to the relevant stimuli is the essential technique.

There are several possible procedures for exposing clients to phobic stimuli in a therapeutic way, but the essential dimensions that have been studied are (1) protective versus confrontive and (2) imaginal versus real-life (or *in vivo*) exposure. Figure 2–3 illustrates how those two dimensions of exposure can classify the anxiety-reduction techniques described in this chapter.

Graduated Real-life Practice

Behavioral treatment of many anxiety-related disorders includes some form of *exposure* to feared stimuli. In SD, the exposure is to imagined, not real-life, stimuli, and it is protective because the challenging stimuli are introduced gradually while anxiety is deliberately kept low by deep muscle relaxation (see the upper left corner of Figure 2–3). In *graduated real-life practice,* sometimes referred to as "graded practice" or "successive approximation," clients face actual feared stimuli without relaxation but following a graded hierarchy. Introducing the stimuli gradually constitutes a protective, rather than a confrontive, form of exposure (see the lower left corner of Figure 2–3). As in SD, the client may withdraw from a situation at any point if the anxiety exceeds a minimal level.

Susan, the spider-phobic client who was described in the introduction to Section II and earlier in this chapter, was treated partly by systematic desensitization and partly by graduated real-life practice. In her case, treatment proceeded fairly rapidly, and she needed only three real-life practice sessions. In the first of these, she was able to travel the length of a long corridor toward the tiny, dead spider in a glass jar, only balking at the last few feet. In the second session, she was able to touch the glass jar, and in the third, she could hold the spider in her hand. A few days later, she noticed a live spider in her car as she was driving, and she brushed it away without thinking. A few seconds later, with a sudden shock of realization, she was struck by the certain knowledge that she had finally overcome her phobia.

	Protective	**Confrontive**
Imaginal	Systematic Desensitization	Implosive Therapy Imaginal Flooding
In Vivo	Graduated Real-Life Practice	Exposure In Vivo

FIGURE 2–3   Dimensions of Exposure (The four combinations of protective versus confrontive and imaginal versus real-life exposure, and their corresponding treatment techniques.)

Graduated real-life practice was one of the earliest behavioral techniques to be used in Britain. In an early report of behavior therapy with two phobic clients, Meyer (1957) described the successful treatment of agoraphobic symptoms by applying the "experimental method and learning principles." Referring to the earlier case report of H. G. Jones (1956; see Chapter 1), Meyer argued that his demonstration was similar but paid more attention to individual differences in personality structure. The theoretical rationale was as follows. Clients with phobias display such intense anxiety in the feared situation that they are not amenable to therapy. According to the principle of stimulus generalization, however, if a stimulus is presented that resembles the phobic stimulus but evokes less anxiety, the therapist can attempt to substitute an "adaptive" reaction for the unadaptive one. Next, the client can learn to deal with a graded continuum of similar situations.

The clients were both in their forties, a man and a woman. Both had complained of blackouts and had been suspected of suffering from temporal lobe epilepsy. They avoided situations involving crowds, travel, and being confined. The female client had five sessions of graduated real-life practice. The therapist accompanied her on various outings in central London, taking bus rides, entering crowded stores, traveling on the subway, using elevators, and so forth. She responded well to the procedure and she had maintained her improvement four months later when reinterviewed. The male client had had more generalized fears than the woman. Systematic desensitization was not helpful to him because he could not produce anxiety in response to the hierarchy items. Meyer used anxiety relief instead, applying electric shock to the client's fingers and terminating the shock when it became unbearable and the client said "Calm yourself." Treatment sessions were divided between aversion relief in the office and graduated real-life practice. Initially the results were not impressive, so the therapist administered a stimulant drug to aid conditioning; after that, clear therapeutic gains were made.

Confrontive Exposure: Implosive Therapy, Imaginal Flooding, and Exposure In Vivo

SD and graduated real-life practice involve dealing with anxiety-evoking stimuli cautiously, one step at a time. Like entering a cold swimming pool by hesitantly going down the steps at the shallow end, these protective methods take time—and the caution may be unnecessary. The procedures to be described next are the behavior therapy equivalent of diving in at the deep end.

Confrontive exposure (sometimes called *flooding*, making the swimming pool analogy quite appropriate) may involve imagined or real situations (see the right-hand boxes in Figure 2–3). As Marks (1972) described it:

> *Flooding is not a fixed technique but comprises a wide range of overlapping allied procedures. Common to all the methods is the principle of confronting [clients] with the stimuli that distress [them] until [they] get used to them and/or the evoking of intense emotion during treatment. The term flooding is best restricted to those forms of confrontation that evoke intense emotion. (p. 129)*

The first confrontive exposure technique of this kind was the *implosive therapy* of Stampfl and Levis (1967), using imagined stimuli. These authors expressed regret that learning-oriented therapies had been developed entirely independently of the traditional psychodynamic approaches and argued that a suitable integration could be made. After a review of the laboratory evidence on fear conditioning, Stampfl and Levis speculated that not only external stimuli but also thoughts and imagery connected with painful experiences would be avoided. Any "defensive maneuvers" of the client that successfully avoid such thoughts or images could be strengthened by reinforcement principles. To Stampfl and Levis, this view admits psychoanalytic concepts of repression and the like into a learning account of psychopathology. Arguing that experimental extinction is the appropriate therapeutic principle in the treatment of neuroses, they predicted that extinction would be most effective when the subject is exposed to the original conditioning situation that elicits the greatest fear.

Boudewyns and Shipley (1983) noted that clinicians and theorists wrongly rejected confrontive exposure methods for years, uncritically accepting a series of false assumptions. These include Wolpe's (1958) concern that unprotected exposure to feared stimuli risks "resensitizing" the client. That concern arose partly from the results of studies of shock avoidance in dogs by Solomon and his colleagues (Solomon, Kamin, & Wynne, 1953; Solomon & Wynne, 1954). The dogs' behavior had failed to extinguish after many trials, leading the researchers to conclude that anxiety-motivated avoidance was extremely resistant to extinction if not entirely unmodifiable. The later work of Morrie Baum (1970) showed that the apparent irreversibility of conditioned avoidance is a myth. Abandoning the misleading assumptions of Wolpe and others led to the development of "direct therapeutic exposure," defined by Boudewyns and Shipley (1983) as "repeated or extended exposure, either in reality or in fantasy, to objectively harmless, but feared, stimuli for the purpose of reducing negative affect" (p. 3).

The implosive therapy technique of Stampfl and Levis (1967) involves prolonged confrontation by the client of relevant fantasy material. The therapist describes scenes that contain the appropriate fear cues in such an involved and dramatic way as to arouse great anxiety. When a sufficiently high level of anxiety has been provoked in the client, the therapist continues to describe the material until the anxiety decreases. The therapist repeats the procedure, introducing variations in the material described as necessary to continue to evoke anxiety. The session is not ended until there is a significant reduction of anxiety in response to the material. In presenting fantasy material the therapist is guided by an "avoidance serial cue hierarchy" derived from the client's current concerns and presented problems, together with issues prompted by a psychodynamic formulation of the client's case. Apart from including psychodynamic theme material, implosive therapy closely parallels the "forced solution" that Wolpe had used with his cats (the "blocking procedure"; Baum, 1970) in that

> *the therapist forces [clients] to be exposed to some of the anxiety-provoking cues that [they] partially avoid ... outside of the treatment session by means of [the] symptom. Therefore, with the avoidance response circumvented, greater exposure to the cues will occur, and subsequently greater extinction will be effected. (Stampfl & Levis, 1967, p. 501)*

The authors describe implosive therapy as having proven successful or at least shown promise in the treatment of neurotic, psychotic, and personality disorders. A typical course of treatment lasts from one to 15 sessions, and it is unusual for therapy to proceed beyond 30 hours of active treatment.

Since the Stampfl and Levis (1967) report appeared, a great deal of research on confrontive exposure methods has been reported (Marks, 1972, 1981a, 1981b, 1987). In methods using fantasy material, the psychodynamic themes have been abandoned by most researchers. The term *imaginal flooding* is commonly used to describe prolonged exposure to relevant fantasy material without psychodynamic content. Implosive therapy and imaginal flooding involve confrontive, imaginal exposure, as indicated in the upper right corner of Figure 2–3.

The remaining combination of procedures, confrontive exposure in vivo (in real life), has been labeled *exposure in vivo* (see the lower right corner of Figure 2–3). Isaac Marks (1981b) has conducted a long series of studies of confrontive real-life exposure in the treatment of phobias and obsessive-compulsive disorder. Not convinced that conditioning explanations of phobias have been scientifically proven, Marks has promoted exposure in vivo as an empirical clinical method that may rest on any of several theoretical processes: extinction, habituation, or other forms of acclimatization to originally feared stimuli. Because it is not proven that anxiety disorders are caused by conditioning, Marks prefers to avoid terms such as *conditioned stimuli* and *extinction.* Instead, he describes the feared situation as an *evoking stimulus (ES)* and the behavior that it calls forth, such as phobic avoidance or compulsive rituals, as the *evoked response (ER).* The task of the therapist is to identify the ES and present it until the ER is reduced. Experimental work addresses the important parameters of the procedure, such as imaginal versus in vivo stimulus confrontation, brief or prolonged exposure sessions, and so forth.

Not all forms of exposure to the ES will be therapeutic (or lead to response decrement). Research results to date suggest that stronger evoking stimuli require more prolonged exposure sessions before anxiety declines. Reiss (1980) has illustrated this by showing the relationship between stimulus intensity and stimulus duration in determining whether exposure will be desensitizing (helpful and therapeutic) or sensitizing (risking increasing the anxiety) (see Figure 2–4). For example, suppose that spider-phobic Susan had been treated by exposure in vivo instead of by SD and graduated real-life practice. She would have confronted large, live, threatening spiders in the very first session, and her therapist would have strongly urged her to stay in contact with them despite her high anxiety. If Susan could have held her ground for a prolonged period (say an hour or more), it is quite possible that she would have reduced her anxiety significantly and in a lasting way in that very first session. But, if she had fled in terror within the first two minutes, it is unlikely that this high level of exposure for such a brief period would have resulted in her anxiety being reduced—in fact, it could have increased.

Figure 2–4 shows the relationship of *CS duration* (how long Susan remains in contact with the spider) to *CS intensity* (how much anxiety the spiders evoke). Duration is on the upright axis, intensity on the horizontal. If the intensity is low (tiny, dead spider in a sealed jar 20 feet away; left side of the graph, at intensity 1), then even a fairly short exposure of a few minutes (low down on the graph, at duration 1) may be enough to reduce Susan's anxiety. But the same exposure time (duration 1) would *not* be sufficient to allow anxiety reduction if the stimulus intensity were high (large, live, active spiders, 2 inches away; right side of the graph, intensity 2). The graph shows this by indicating that any combina-

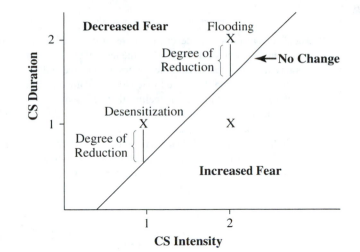

FIGURE 2–4 Theoretical Effect of Different Durations and Intensities of Conditioned Stimulus Exposure on Anxiety Expectancies

Source: From Reiss, S., Pavlovian conditioning and human fear: An expectancy model. *Behavior Therapy, 11,* 380–396. Copyright © 1980 by the Association for Advancement of Behavior Therapy. Reprinted by permission of the publisher and the author.

tion of duration and intensity that falls below the diagonal line will lead to *increased* anxiety, whereas any combination above that line will be therapeutic and lead to *decreased* anxiety. Intensely anxiety-provoking stimuli can be presented in a therapeutic way, provided that the duration of exposure exceeds a certain minimum time interval (intensity 2, duration 2, for example).

The protective exposure methods (SD, graduated real-life practice) lead to improvement even with brief stimulus presentations, because they evoke only weak anxiety. The confrontive exposure methods (imaginal flooding, exposure in vivo) are effective also, despite their use of stimuli that evoke intense anxiety, because exposure is prolonged.

Chapter Summary

Behavior therapy techniques used in the treatment of anxiety-related disorders were originally stimulated by principles of classical conditioning and by experimental neurosis phenomena. Research findings and theoretical developments have improved the practice of behavior therapy and modified its techniques. It was commonplace in the 1960s for behavior therapists to use systematic desensitization, aversion therapy, and anxiety relief with outpatient clients. Today, however, these methods are rarely reported and they have been supplanted by graduated real-life practice, imaginal flooding, and exposure in vivo.

Endnotes

1. "Susan," whose phobia is described more fully later in the chapter, is a composite of three clients treated by one of the authors in the last several years. Each incident described is true to life in having been drawn from the experiences of these three individuals.

2. The terms *anxiety* and *fear,* used extensively in this chapter, have been defined as follows: "*Fear* is the usually unpleasant feeling that arises as a normal response to realistic danger. *Anxiety* is an emotion similar to fear, but arising without any objective source of danger" (Marks, 1987, p. 5).

3. We consider the term *conditioned fear* to be equivalent to the term *anxiety.*

4. Agoraphobia—an anxiety disorder in which the client tends to experience panic attacks and to avoid crowds, public places, and traveling far from home—is considered in detail in Chapter 7.

Chapter *3*

Operant Learning Principles and Behavior Management Procedures

Harold was a single man in his forties who had spent over 20 years as a patient in a county psychiatric hospital. At the time of his admission for treatment, Harold's problems had been labeled as *manic-depressive psychosis,* but a sad combination of lack of social support in his community and less than progressive discharge policies at the hospital left him still on the ward long after his original problems had been resolved. In common with many other patients on his ward, Harold suffered mostly from apathy, having grown accustomed to the hospital's monotonous routines. He was not entirely withdrawn, however. He often conversed with the ward staff in quite an animated manner, usually dwelling on his favorite theme—his belief that he had an undiagnosed physical illness that gave him frequent seizure-like falling spells.

Although the hospital's efforts at discharging patients left much to be desired, the medical care was excellent, because the psychiatric hospital was allied with a general hospital located on the same grounds. Extensive medical evaluations had failed to identify any sign of physical illness for Harold, yet several times a week—always with several witnesses—he would suddenly collapse gracefully to the floor, remaining supine as the staff members and other patients came running to attend to him. Although the medical staff refused to call these episodes "fainting spells" (because they were not fainting spells), the label stuck, and Harold became known as "the fainter."

His habit of collapsing to the floor so often was the chief problem keeping him in the hospital. Previous attempts to discharge him to the community had always been defeated, because—usually on the same day of his discharge—Harold would take a spectacular fall in a shopping center or other crowded location, and would shortly afterward make a dramatic return trip to the hospital by ambulance. Because Harold's problem defied medical explanation, the treatment team decided to explore the possibility of using a psychological intervention based on operant learning principles.

The last chapter covered the various behavioral techniques that were inspired by laboratory studies of classical conditioning. In this chapter, we will discuss the principles and applications of *operant learning*, an approach that has had a strong influence on much of the behavior therapy practiced in the United States and around the world.

Theoretical Principles

The central figure in any discussion of operant learning is B. F. Skinner (1904–1990), whose prolific empirical and conceptual contributions to behaviorism brought exciting innovations not only to experimental psychology but also to education, business, and mental health work. One of Skinner's most important concepts is the distinction between respondent and operant behavior (Skinner, 1953). *Respondent* behavior usually involves reflex responses, involuntary activity in glands and smooth muscles, and is modifiable by classical conditioning procedures in which stimuli are paired independent of the subject's behavior. *Operant* behavior usually involves overt activity controlled by skeletal muscles, behavior that operates on the environment and that is modifiable by altering its consequences. Whereas respondent behavior and classical conditioning are relevant in understanding reflexes and emotions, operant behavior and operant learning apply to the whole range of active human behavior—speaking, doing, working, playing, avoiding, learning new skills, and so forth.

Classic Studies

According to Skinner (1953), early studies of operant learning were prompted by Darwin's theory of the continuity of species—the idea that humans are not fundamentally different from other animals. Original experiments by Thorndike (1898), for example, were designed to assess whether or not cats could think. His studies of learning and problem solving in cats launched a long series of investigations into animal behavior processes in the decades that followed. Thorndike would place a cat in a "puzzle-box"; the only way the cat could leave was by operating a door latch successfully. At first, the cat would make various highly inefficient attempts to get out of the box and would take a great deal of time in the process. Gradually, its efforts would improve. Eventually, after many experimental episodes (trials), the cat would discover the technique of unlatching the door and would escape efficiently each time it was placed in the box. If the experimenter kept a careful record of how long it took the cat to escape, it could be observed that the delay (the escape latency) would gradually decrease.

Thus, Thorndike had identified a gradual *learning curve* that looked similar to graphs produced by people's responses when learning a new skill. In this sense, Thorndike had shown that cats could "think." But in the process of conducting his experiments, Thorndike realized that he could study learning in cats without making any assumptions about their cognitive ability. Because the whole string of behaviors that led to the door opening was successful and produced "a satisfying state of affairs," then the cat's solution to the puzzle became "stamped in." The most efficient behaviors were stamped in most strongly. This stamping-in process as an explanation of learning was termed *the Law of Effect,* an early version of the operant learning principle that reinforcement strengthens behavior (Hergenhahn, 1992; Pierce & Epling, 1995).

Skinner (1953) pointed out that the learning curve produced in Thorndike's studies was not the most direct reflection of the learning process in general. It was really a combination of two things: (1) the cat's learning process and (2) the complexities of the specific learning task studied. Seeking to simplify the experimental procedure, Skinner developed a laboratory arrangement suitable for studying the behavior of rats and pigeons. The standard experimental chamber that he devised (popularly known as the *Skinner Box*) was deliberately made as featureless as possible, so as to avoid eliciting unwanted reflex responses.

The standard chamber Skinner used for pigeons consists of a temperature-controlled rectangular box. One of the internal walls has a tray in which food (grain) may be presented and a disk that the pigeon may peck. Lights of various colors and in different positions may be presented on a display panel. Typically, the pigeon is kept at a lower body weight than it would maintain if given free access to food. This makes it more likely that food will serve as a suitable motivating consequence in the experiments. The experimenter sets up the apparatus so that any behavior of the pigeon that results in the disk being pressed has a particular consequence. In the most familiar example, a response to the disk automatically causes food to be delivered to the tray. Under these circumstances, pigeons learn eventually to peck at the disk repeatedly. Disconnecting the food mechanism, so that pecking the disk has no particular effect, usually results in a rapid decline of the pecking response.

It is not known which stimuli, if any, elicit behavior of this kind. Unlike salivation, blinking, or knee-jerks, behaviors like pigeons pecking a disk or humans running a marathon cannot be readily sparked off by presenting a stimulus. Skinner has pointed out that the active behaviors just mentioned are distinctive in that they operate on the environment. He used the label *operant behavior* to describe this kind of activity. (Although operant behavior is not thought of as having been elicited by a stimulus, the term *response* is still used.) If operant behavior cannot be produced reliably by presenting a stimulus, then it presumably is not reflex behavior. What, then, does cause operant behavior? Skinner's answer is based on a newer version of the Law of Effect. As in Thorndike's studies, it is the consequence of the behavior that is important, not so much the stimuli preceding it.

In the standard experimental situation used by Skinner, pigeons usually learn to peck at the disk repeatedly when food is presented as a result. The experimenter does not cause the pigeon to make this response by presenting a particular stimulus. Instead, the experimenter establishes a *behavioral contingency.* A contingency is an if/then relationship. If the pigeon pecks at the disk, then food is delivered. Setting up a behavioral contingency may or may not lead to the pigeon producing the response. It depends on which stimuli are used as consequences, how long the delay is between response and stimulus, and other factors. Practically, the experimenter can simply find out by trying out different arrangements. The important point is that Skinner made monumental progress in understanding learning when he focused on the study of behavioral contingencies.

In everyday life, people are continuously operating under the potential control of behavioral contingencies. Just as gravity affects people all the time, whether or not there happens to be a physicist around to study it, so behavioral contingencies are always operating, whether or not an experimental psychologist or behavior therapist is on the scene. If you study effectively, then you will pass your exams. If you exceed the speed limit when driving, you may have to pay a fine. If you go to the dentist, then you may experience short-term discomfort but, in the long run, you will have trouble-free teeth. Behavioral contingencies range from the simple to the complex, and are seen everywhere. Studying, driving, and visiting health-care professionals are operants. People are not compelled to do these things, by contrast with reflex responses like sneezing when there is an irritant in the nose. People have choices. They choose whether to study or go to a party, whether to go to the dentist or to the beach. Despite this sense of choice and control concerning people's operant behaviors, learning theorists such as Thorndike and Skinner have shown how behavioral contingencies exert a powerful influence in encouraging certain responses and discouraging others.

Basic Concepts

Reinforcement

The process by which certain responses are encouraged is known as *reinforcement*. As in other contexts, it means "strengthening." An army calls up reinforcements to boost its strength. Reinforced concrete is strengthened by steel rods. Behavior is strengthened by the process of reinforcement. The procedure involves establishing a behavioral contingency in which the behavior to be encouraged is followed by the presentation of a certain stimulus. If the behavior does increase during this procedure, then reinforcement is operating. Researchers have to find out, empirically, which consequent stimuli actually work as reinforcers.

Consider the example of the food-deprived pigeon in the standard experimental chamber. The experimenter has arranged that food will be presented automatically whenever the pigeon makes the designated response, but not otherwise. If the pigeon makes the response (pecking at the disk in this case), the particular consequence engineered by the experimenter follows (food is delivered). If the pigeon makes any other response than pecking at the disk, no food is delivered. Under these circumstances, the pigeon's rate of pecking at the disk may increase. The experimenter can find out whether the food is responsible for the increase by disconnecting the food delivery mechanism to see what happens. If the pigeon's response rate eventually slows when food is no longer presented, the experimenter concludes that the food had been reinforcing the pecking.

At first, the experimenter may have to wait a long time before the pigeon even approaches the disk, let alone begins to peck at it. Because pecking at disks in psychology laboratories is not a reflex, the experimenter cannot elicit this response directly. How soon the pigeon begins to peck seems to be a matter of chance. Once the pigeon does make the response, it can come under the control of the reinforcement contingency. The experimenter can speed up this process by the method of *shaping*. This involves dividing the learning task into a series of smaller steps. The experimenter presents an easy task first, and when this has been learned, a more difficult task is presented. In this way, the pigeon's behavior progresses through a series of *successive approximations*[1] to the desired, final performance. For example, a first step in a shaping program could be to present food whenever the pigeon enters the half of the chamber nearer to the disk. In other words, movements that bring the pigeon nearer to the disk are reinforced. When the pigeon has responded to this contingency and spends most of the time in that half of the chamber, the experimenter can begin a new contingency, requiring now that the pigeon point its beak toward the disk before food is given. Eventually, the reinforcement is delivered only when the pigeon pecks at the disk.

Reinforcement, in operant learning terminology, is not the same thing as reward. Rewards are sometimes given to encourage people to repeat certain behaviors; in this sense rewards are similar to reinforcers. People are rewarded, though, not responses. Likewise, responses are reinforced, not people. Rewards and reinforcers are stimuli. A stimulus that has the effect of rewarding someone may not work well as a reinforcer. For example, a military decoration may be an ultimate reward for years of valued service. But it is unlikely that the medal actually served as reinforcer for all the specific behaviors that were produced during those years. Reinforcers are usually stimuli that may be delivered repeatedly during a learning process. Research has shown that small, immediate reinforcements are more effective in promoting learning than large, delayed ones (Logue, 1995).

Positive and Negative Reinforcement

The examples we have given so far involve *positive reinforcement,* so called because it involves *presenting* a stimulus that strengthens or increases the response it follows (see the upper left square in Figure 3–1). Normally, these stimuli—positive reinforcers—are seen as rewarding events, those that one might imagine are desirable from the subject's perspective.

However, behavior may be reinforced or encouraged in ways other than the presentation of a desirable stimulus, such as food or money. *Removing an undesirable stimulus may reinforce behavior.* For example, the behavior of taking aspirin to relieve a headache will be reinforced if the headache goes away. Similarly, imagine that the laboratory pigeon is subjected to a tremendously loud, bone-jarring noise. Pecking at the disk switches off the noise for several seconds. If the pigeon increases its disk pecking, then reinforcement is presumably taking place. In this case, the reinforcement is known as *negative reinforcement* because behavior increases when something (the noise) is *withdrawn* (see the lower left square in Figure 3–1).

The same situation applies when someone uses insect repellent at a picnic. If the insect repellent works and keeps the bugs away, and if the person keeps using it at picnics as a result, then negative reinforcement is operating. Positive and negative reinforcement both reinforce (i.e., strengthen or increase) behavior. Which is which depends on whether a stimulus is presented or withdrawn following the response. Figure 3–1 provides the definitions of the different response consequences.

Scheduled Consequence of the Response:	Effect on Behavior:	
	Behavior Increases	**Behavior Decreases**
Stimulus Is Presented	Positive Reinforcement	Punishment (Response-Contingent Aversive Stimulation)
Stimulus Is Withdrawn	Negative Reinforcement	Punishment (Response Cost)

FIGURE 3–1   Four Types of Response Consequence in Operant Learning (Each of the four has an extinction counterpart when the consequence is no longer contingent on the response.)

Negative reinforcement operates in *escape learning.* In the laboratory, the experimenter can produce unpleasant stimuli that the subject can escape by making a designated response. If response rates increase, then negative reinforcement is strengthening the behavior. *Avoidance learning* is similar to escape, but in this case the subject can prevent an aversive stimulus from occurring at all by making the response. A driver may take the car in for servicing at periodic intervals in an attempt to prevent mechanical breakdowns on the highway, for example.

Punishment: Response-Contingent Aversive Stimulation and Response Cost
When behavior decreases as a result of a behavioral contingency, it is possible that some form of *punishment* is operating. (Other possibilities are that the behavior is under extinction after positive reinforcement or that a contingency that positively reinforces low response rates is in effect.) The clearest example of punishment is found when response rates decrease after a stimulus has been presented contingent on the response. Another term for this is *response-contingent aversive stimulation (RCAS).* If the pigeon pecks at the disk and, as a result, the aversive loud noise is presented, the pigeon may slow its response rate. This would be an example of punishment. If a child touches a hot stove and burns a finger, and if the child stops touching the stove as a result, then the contingency operating is RCAS or punishment (see the upper right square in Figure 3–1).

To complete the 2 × 2 table (lower right square in Figure 3–1), *response cost* occurs when the subject's response has the effect of removing a stimulus, and this is followed by reduced response rates. If the pigeon's responses to the disk have the effect of taking food away, and if the pigeon pecks less often during this contingency, then response cost is operating. A familiar example in human behavior is the fine imposed by a court as a legal sanction. If drivers reduce their rate of committing minor traffic violations when they are fined for doing so, response cost is the contingency operating.

Extinction

In operant learning, *extinction* refers to the procedure of disconnecting a reinforcement contingency and to the effects of this on behavior. Imagine that the pigeon's disk pecking has been reinforced with food for some time, but the experimenter now switches off the mechanism that delivers the food. Pecking at the disk has no effect. The pigeon ultimately produces fewer and fewer pecks until, eventually, no further responses are made. Extinction of an operant response has some elements in common with extinction of a classically conditioned response.

The four types of behavioral contingency described here and shown in Figure 3–1 *all* have an extinction counterpart. In describing positive and negative reinforcement and the two forms of punishment, we focused on situations in which the person or animal is in the *acquisition* phase of the learning process, producing new behavior. Through reinforcement, subjects learn to increase their response rates. Through punishment, they learn to decrease them. Whichever way the response rate goes, new learning is taking place. Extinction is the procedure in which the learning situation changes and the previous contingency is removed.

In the example of positive reinforcement, extinction is in effect when the pigeon's peck is no longer followed by the presentation of food. A common result of extinction in this case is for the pigeon to slow its response rate, although this does not usually begin immediately. Typically, the subject will respond even more energetically for a while after the reinforcement mechanism has been switched off. Anyone who has lost money in a vending machine is familiar with this. Depositing the money and pushing the right button are the responses; the soft drink or candy bar is the reinforcing consequence. But if the machine takes the money without dispensing the goodies, one encounters an extinction trial. The tendency is to pull and push at the machine with increased vigor at first, before the more stable effects of extinction take over and the individual stops responding.

In the example of negative reinforcement, extinction is in effect when the insect repellent no longer works in keeping the mosquitoes away. A typical result is for the person to stop making the response of spraying the insect repellent (and probably throw away the can in disgust).

Extinction of a punished response involves the same principle but is likely to have the reverse effect on the behavior. When the stove is cold and no longer delivers RCAS when the child touches it, the child may be more likely to touch it again (if there is a reason for doing so). When the state police stop patrolling interstate highways and issuing tickets for speeding, drivers' compliance with the traffic regulations may decrease.

Discriminative Stimuli

Reinforcers are not the only important stimuli in operant learning theory. Behavior is not reinforced or strengthened overall, so that it occurs more often in general. Learning a new dance step may lead the person to display this behavior more often on the dance floor but not necessarily in the classroom or at a funeral. The *situation* is important. Learning takes place in particular situations, and reinforcement takes place in the context of specific environments. Therefore *discriminative stimuli*—the stimuli that provide the context for learning and reinforcement—may have an important influence on behavior.

This does not mean that the stimuli that set the context for reinforcement are like the conditioned or unconditioned stimuli that elicit reflexes. Instead of provoking the response, they set the occasion for it. Operant learning theorists call them *discriminative stimuli* because they help the learner discriminate, or distinguish, the occasions on which the response will produce the reinforcer. One familiar example is the traffic light, which exerts an influence on people's driving behavior. A green light indicates that a particular behavioral contingency is in effect: Driving ahead will probably work out satisfactorily. The green light does not force the driver to disengage the brake and push the accelerator. Similarly, a red light does not force people to stop; it has the influence it has because it indicates the behavioral contingency (in this case, driving ahead will probably be punished).

Schedules of Reinforcement

So far, we have described the typical operant learning procedure as if there is a high degree of consistency and predictability for the learner. That is, we have assumed that every time the pigeon pecks at the disk, food is delivered, and every time a driver double-parks or speeds, a fine is levied. In real life, the contingencies are not usually so predictable. Starting with the research of Ferster and Skinner (1957), operant learning researchers have made extensive studies of the effects on behavior of a number of *schedules of reinforcement.*

We will continue with the example of the pigeon whose pecks at a disk are positively reinforced by the presentation of food. When every response is reinforced, the term used is *continuous reinforcement.* After continuous reinforcement, the effects of extinction are usually quite rapid. This is a clear disadvantage of continuous reinforcement, if the goal is to make the learner relatively immune to the effects of extinction. Imagine encouraging a mute patient to speak by using continuous social reinforcement; that is, every time the patient speaks appropriately, the therapist smiles and nods in an encouraging fashion. Now imagine that, because this therapy was so successful, the patient leaves the institution and begins to deal with people in the community for the first time. What would happen if the patient's first attempts at conversation were not immediately followed by enthusiastic smiles and nods? Right away, there would be an extinction trial for which the patient had not been prepared. It is generally more realistic not to rely entirely on continuous reinforcement in therapy programs for this reason.

What are the alternatives to continuous reinforcement? Various schedules of partial or *intermittent reinforcement* have been studied by operant researchers (and can be seen in everyday life). Skinner (1961) originally discovered intermittent reinforcement by accident (or, as he poetically put it, serendipitously). He had been making food pellets for the laboratory rats one weekend. His intention had been to leave the rats in the experimental chambers for several hours, so that they could feed themselves by responding to the reinforcement contingency (that is, they could produce a food pellet by pressing a lever). On this occasion, there was not enough food to last the weekend, and the store that supplied this specialized product was closed. Skinner made the best of the situation by spreading the food out as much as possible. The food dispensing device consisted of a magazine with a series of slots, each of which took one pellet of food. Instead of filling every slot with food, he left many of them empty. As a result, the rats' lever pressing would not always produce a food pellet. When he returned to the laboratory some time later, Skinner was surprised to find that not only had the rats continued to press the levers in the usual way, but their learning curves were more consistent and stable than usual. He had discovered that intermittent reinforcement can be more effective than continuous reinforcement.

One aspect of this phenomenon makes a great deal of sense, intuitively: the effect of intermittent reinforcement on extinction. Skinner observed that if the rat had received food not after every lever press but after an average of three presses, for example, it would make many more responses under conditions of extinction. In the acquisition phase of the experiment, roughly every third response produced food, but which particular lever press would pay off was unpredictable. Under conditions of extinction, when no responses produce food, the arrangement has much in common with the acquisition phase, in which many responses did not produce food either. When conditions of extinction resemble conditions of acquisition, it is difficult to make the discrimination and determine which contingency is in effect (D'Amato, 1970). Whatever the explanation, one practical consequence of intermittent reinforcement is that the effects of extinction are delayed, and more responses are made under extinction (Angermeier, 1994).

An example familiar to many clinicians concerns appropriate child-raising practices. Parents often ask for help in dealing with uncooperative behavior in their children. A typical example is when the child makes a fuss at bedtime and repeatedly cries or asks for attention after the parents have put the child to bed. Parents familiar with operant learning know that it is unwise to keep going in to comfort the child in a situation like this, because that could reinforce the behavior and keep it going indefinitely. But sometimes the parents will report that, despite their efforts to be consistent in ignoring the persistent crying, they just had to give in last night because the child was making even more of a fuss than usual. From the therapist's point of view, this is very understandable but quite unfortunate in terms of what the child learns. By attending to the child one night after several nights of ignoring the fussing, the parents have now intermittently reinforced the behavior with the likely effect of making it even more immune to the effects of extinction. Greater patience on the parents' part would have been desirable, but of course *their* behavior was being influenced by a contingency. Comforting the child, thus removing the unpleasant crying and fussing, was reinforced![2]

Several standard reinforcement schedules have been studied by laboratory researchers. Some of the best known are briefly described next. Numerous studies have shown that rats, pigeons, and people responding to these schedules learn to make the most adaptive pattern of responses. That is, they behave so as to gain the maximum possible reinforcement. If the kind of response consequence is not specified, assume that you are dealing with schedules of positive reinforcement.

Fixed Ratio (FR).   In a fixed ratio (FR) schedule, a given number of responses is required before reinforcement is delivered. The easiest example is continuous reinforcement, in which every response produces reinforcement. One response is required per reinforcement, so the schedule is designated FR 1. If two responses are required, the schedule is FR 2, and so on.

Variable Ratio (VR).   In similar fashion to FR, a variable ratio (VR) schedule specifies the number of responses required to produce reinforcement. This time, the number of responses required varies randomly around a given average value. For example, in VR 3, roughly every third response produces reinforcement (sometimes the second response, sometimes the fourth, and so on). This arrangement is particularly likely to keep the learner responding, even for a considerable time, after extinction has been put into effect. A friend's cigarette lighter appeared to work on a schedule of VR 12. He would routinely wear the skin from his thumb as he persisted in his attempts to get it to work. It always did, eventually. Perhaps if his lighter had not operated so intermittently and unpredictably, he would have given up smoking some time ago. Variable ratio schedules are also at work to encourage gambling in all its aspects. The payoff for gambling is well known to be intermittent and unpredictable, thus reinforcing a stable rate of responding.

Fixed Interval (FI).   The interval schedules have a time component. Instead of requiring so many responses, interval schedules are set up to reinforce the first response that occurs after the particular interval has elapsed. Therefore, only one response is required per reinforcement, but the response is only reinforced if it occurs after the interval has expired. Earlier responses have no effect. For example, trying to use a computer before its initial programs have been loaded will go unreinforced, but going ahead after the system has been booted will produce the desired consequence. Some authors compare the FI schedule to working for a weekly wage (Angermeier, 1994) or studying for preliminary tests in college (Goldiamond, 1965), but this is misleading because in the FI schedule, the *first response* after an interval is reinforced, earlier responses having no effect. For most employees, refusing to work until Friday afternoons *will* have an effect, and bring about a consequence involving punishment or extinction! And possibly some students study for tests *as if* the schedule is FI, believing that the only studying that will be reinforced occurs on the night before the test; but, realistically, the likelihood is that a long chain of appropriate studying behaviors is required to produce the reinforcement of passing the test.

Variable Interval (VI).   In the variable interval schedule, the time interval that has to elapse before a reinforced response can be made varies around a given average value. A schedule of VI 30 seconds means that the first response that occurs after 30 seconds, on average, brings reinforcement. This schedule tends to produce stable, high rates of responding.

Differential Reinforcement of Low Rates (DRL).   This schedule is similar to fixed interval because the first response after a given time is reinforced. In the DRL schedule, though, any responses occurring before the interval has elapsed do have an effect. They reset the timer. That means the learner has to wait for the whole interval to elapse again before a response can be reinforced. Therefore, reinforcement is only delivered if the subject has separated the responses by at least a certain minimum interval. One professor reinforces the verbal behavior of graduate laboratory assistants on a DRL schedule, not wishing them to be entirely silent but refusing to tolerate constant chatter (Angermeier, 1994).

Because these different schedules call for widely varying patterns of responding, operant learning theorists have learned that observing behavior without knowing the reinforcement schedule operating can be deceptive. For example, an experimenter might see a laboratory pigeon pecking away vigorously at the disk in the standard chamber, receiving grain at intervals. Another pigeon, in a different chamber, is pecking at a very slow rate and also receiving food. Which pigeon is hungrier? The answer is that the experimenter cannot tell without knowing the schedule operating. The first pigeon might not be particularly hungry, but it might be responding to a variable interval schedule. The second pigeon might be extremely hungry, but it might be responding to a DRL schedule (Schaefer & Martin, 1969).

Sequences of Schedules

Much of everyday human behavior consists of elaborate sequences of responses. Making a pot of coffee, getting dressed to go out to a social event, and taking a college course all involve combining several different acts into an organized sequence. This is quite different from simply repeating a single response a given number of times. Not only is everyday behavior more varied than the typical laboratory examples but it also seems to go on for lengthy periods without any obvious reinforcement being provided. In the case of making the pot of coffee, drinking a cup of coffee at the end of the sequence could qualify as the positive reinforcer, of course. But how can the coffee reinforce the whole sequence of necessary responses—opening the coffee can, cleaning the coffee-maker, measuring out the right amount of water and coffee, and so on? Operant learning theorists find the explanation in studies of conditioned reinforcement and chaining.

Conditioned Reinforcement.   *Conditioned reinforcement* (also known as *secondary reinforcement*) refers to the use of stimuli that have acquired their power to reinforce behavior. Reinforcers such as food, water, and sexual activity are assumed to be primary reinforcers, because people do not have to go through special educational procedures in order for these stimuli to work as reinforcers. By contrast, other stimuli that can reinforce behavior seem to have taken on their power to do so through learning. Examples are a friend's smile, a large *A* written on a test, and money. These are all examples of conditioned reinforcers.

To return to the laboratory pigeon, imagine that it has been responding to an FR 1 schedule of positive reinforcement. That is, every response produces food (continuous reinforcement). Suppose that the experimental chamber is always brightly lit while this is going on. What would happen if, the next time the pigeon were placed in the chamber, the chamber was lit very dimly? The pigeon may or may not begin to peck enthusiastically at the disk. Suppose that the experimenter had arranged things so that, if the pigeon were to peck at the disk just once, the chamber would again be brightly lit and the pigeon would be back on the original FR 1 schedule. Pigeons *are* able to learn a sequence like this, and a typical result would be for the pigeon to learn to respond once in the presence of the dim light and again in the presence of the bright light. In this simple example, the sequence of events is that the chamber is dimly lit; the pigeon pecks at the disk; the light brightens; and after another peck at the disk, the pigeon receives food. But, despite the simplicity of this example, thoroughly understanding a behavior sequence of this kind means bringing in several concepts—conditioned reinforcement, discriminative stimuli, and chaining.

Really, the pigeon is responding to a series of two FR 1 schedules: one while the light is dim and the other while the light is bright. But the pigeon only gets the food at the end of the second part. What reinforces the behavior during the first part, when the light is dim? Researchers have established that in a situation like this, the bright light can work as a reinforcer for the first response. That is, the bright light becomes a conditioned reinforcer. It is, at the same time, a discriminative stimulus because it sets the occasion for the next response.

Chaining.   Operant learning theorists refer to the chain schedule when a subject has to meet the requirements of two schedules in sequence, with different stimuli present during the schedules, before reinforcement is delivered. In the preceding example, the schedule would be chain FR 1 FR 1, calling for a series of two responses under different conditions of lighting. In a chain, the transition from one stimulus to the next (e.g., from dim to bright light) is an interesting aspect, because the second stimulus works as a reinforcer and as a discriminative stimulus.

In one experiment, Ferster and Skinner (1957) presented pigeons with a chain FR DRL schedule. This meant that, first, the pigeons had to respond to a fixed ratio schedule, then a new stimulus was presented, and they had to respond to the DRL schedule before food was delivered. The pigeons learned the sequence well and responded quite rapidly in the first part and slowly in the second part, consistent with the schedules operating. What was interesting about this was that the stimulus that introduced the DRL component could reinforce a high rate of response (the FR component) and discriminate a low rate of response (the DRL component).

Chain schedules have much in common with the *token economy* programs used in clinical settings (described more fully in Chapter 14). In a token economy, conditioned reinforcement operates when specific behaviors are reinforced by tokens. The tokens have acquired their reinforcing properties through their association with the back-up reinforcers for which they can be exchanged. One consistent research finding has been that, in a token economy, it does not matter how soon after the response the back-up reinforcer is presented. It is essential, though, for the conditioned reinforcer—the token—to be presented immediately after the response. The same is true in the laboratory in studies of chain schedules. Studying the effects of delay of reinforcement in token economies, Osborne and Adams (1970) concluded, "The results suggest that delays in token presentation may reduce response rates, while delays in token exchange [for back-up reinforcers] may be less important to maintaining behavior. These findings would appear of some importance to the design of token economies" (p. 14).

After reviewing laboratory studies of chaining and conditioned reinforcement, Kelleher (1966) drew a similar conclusion: "The programming of the stimuli in second-order schedules [such as chain schedules] seems to exert far more control than variables such as the average frequency of primary reinforcement" (p. 207).

Both quotations show that immediate reinforcement is essential for optimal learning, but the reinforcers do not have to be "primary" ones. Most often, the important reinforcing stimuli are conditioned reinforcers. Commonly, these are stimuli that have been associated with completing steps toward a goal. Effective reinforcers for a psychiatric patient on the way to rehabilitation include smiles and praise from a therapist. Effective reinforcers for a college student on the way to graduation include good course grades and words of encouragement from professors.

Rule-Governed Behavior

Before completing this review of basic concepts, it is important to address an obvious question about operant learning in people: Why is it necessary to provide elaborate behavioral contingencies and reinforcement schedules to encourage certain response sequences, when all that has to be done is to ask the person to do it? Skinner (1953, 1966) objected to this circumvention of an operant analysis of behavior, arguing that human behavior is ultimately controlled by the actual contingencies operating, not by words. Part of the appeal of Skinner's approach is that it can deal not only with the behavior of verbal individuals but also that of animals, preverbal children, and people with communication difficulties. Yet behavior therapists always talk to their verbal clients and patients about the goals and methods of therapy and about the specifics of the treatment plans being proposed. Sometimes, verbal instructions are all that is necessary to solve a problem. Sherman (1990) cited an example from Martin and Pear (1978), who

> state the first rule of remediating a deficiency: "If you want someone to do something, first try telling him" (p. 229). This is illustrated by an amusing anecdote retold by one of the authors. While working on his master's thesis at an institution for the retarded, he tried to utilize positive reinforcement to teach a woman who worked in the kitchen to stack plates and dishes in one area and cups and utensils in another. After several sessions with little or no progress, one of the nurses finally told the woman to "put the plates and dishes here and the cups and utensils over there" (p. 229). That was that! (Sherman, 1990, p. 24)

Asking or telling clients to change their behavior is certainly not always effective, though, as you will see when we return to the case of Harold in a few paragraphs. Another issue here is that some studies have used behavioral contingencies *and* verbal instructions to modify behavior, making it difficult to tell which procedure was responsible for any observed change. For example, Ayllon and Azrin (1968) reinforced working on ward assignments in a group of hospitalized individuals, then altered the contingency so that the patients received the reinforcers whether they worked or not. The results, as depicted in a famous graph, were dramatic. Work behavior declined rapidly to zero when reinforcement was no longer contingent on the behavior; it immediately increased to full strength when work was again reinforced. But in addition to altering the contingency, the researchers told the patients they were getting a vacation with pay!

Contemporary operant learning theorists recognize the importance of *rule-governed behavior* when behavior is controlled by stimuli that specify the contingency operating (Pierce & Epling, 1995). Such contingency-specifying stimuli are rules, instructions, advice, and laws, and they can be seen as discriminative stimuli that set the occasion for adaptive behavior. Theorists contrast rule-governed behavior with *contingency-shaped behavior* (the type of behavior discussed so far in this chapter). One of the differences between the two types of behavior is that rules affect how the behavior is performed, whereas reinforcement contingencies influence response rates and the likelihood of the behavior being enacted (Pierce & Epling, 1995). Ultimately, rule-governed behavior increases or decreases depending on the actual reinforcement contingencies operating.

Clinical Implications

Behavior therapists assume that operant learning principles are at work not just in specialized laboratories but also in the natural environment in which people go about their daily activities. Similarly, the same learning processes are at work in normal and abnormal behavior. Understanding abnormal behavior in terms of operant learning principles can lead directly to treatments based on the same principles.

The general approach in applying operant learning to problem behavior is first to identify the behavioral contingency operating. Conceptually, this is as simple as ABC: Identifying the contingency means identifying A, the *antecedent events* or discriminative stimuli; B, the *behavior;* and C, the *consequences,* or the reinforcers at work (Kazdin, 1994). The contingency operating for Frank, the client with exhibitionism who was introduced in Chapter 1, was A (antecedent): the sight of a woman walking alone in the park; B (behavior): exposing his genitals; and C (consequence): the woman's reaction of surprise and Frank's experience of sexual arousal and excitement.

Specifying the contingency in this way immediately points to several possible treatment interventions, varying in subtlety and sophistication. For example, Frank could simply be encouraged to avoid A, the particular set of antecedents for his problem behavior (driving to another town at night; hanging around the park; looking out for unaccompanied females). His behavior at B could be the focus of treatment; he could practice talking to strangers in public in a socially appropriate way as an alternative to his paraphilic behavior. Or the consequences at C, a highly reinforcing set of stimuli (the victim's reaction; his own pleasurable sensations), could be altered so that they lose their reinforcing potential—for example, by means of the covert sensitization procedure that was actually adopted in Frank's treatment. Changing the consequences of the undesired behavior is usually the preferred technique and most consistent with operant learning principles (see, for example, Scotti, Schulman, & Hojnacki, 1994).

In clinical work, behavior therapists find many situations in which it is possible that an unwanted behavior is being maintained by *positive reinforcement.* A child may act disruptively in class when the teacher responds by giving attention, for example. Acting on the hypothesis that the teacher's attention may be reinforcing the problem behavior, the behavior therapist advises the teacher to ignore the child next time it happens. This strategy is aimed at placing the disruptive behavior under conditions of extinction. It may or may not work, ultimately; but if extinction does occur, the problem behavior is likely to become even worse for a time before it extinguishes. Accordingly, behavior therapists have to be patient and to persist with their extinction programs for long enough to give them a fair trial.

Take the example of Harold, introduced earlier as the "fainter" whose pattern of frequently falling gracefully to the floor before an audience of concerned onlookers was the chief problem keeping him hospitalized. The behavior therapists who were called in by the ward staff to advise on treatment immediately considered the possibility that positive reinforcement was at work. Perhaps Harold had few opportunities for rewarding social interaction on a ward with so many withdrawn patients, and perhaps the social attention he received whenever he "fainted" was highly reinforcing. Behavior therapists would not want Harold to be deprived of social attention, but they would want to help him find more appropriate ways of obtaining it.

The plan they adopted began with a careful conversation with Harold. They told him that his falling behavior was not the result of a medical problem, and they expressed their willingness to help him stop this behavior so that he might be able to leave the hospital and get on with his life. He said that he could not help it, and that he really did have a medical problem. The behavior therapists indicated that they would try to respect his view, but that they disagreed with it, and they told him they wanted to make quite sure they were not making his problem worse by paying too much attention to it. They explained that the medical staff had approved a plan in which the ward personnel would no longer rush him to the medical clinic whenever he fell to the floor; in fact, they would ignore him entirely. Instead, everyone on the unit would make a point of talking to Harold whenever they could, provided that he was not falling to the ground at the time.

Eventually, this plan was successful in reducing Harold's problem behavior on the ward, but there were several ups and downs before treatment was considered successful. Early on in the treatment program, one of the behavior therapists (the author of this chapter) had a very humbling experience. The therapist entered the ward one morning and saw Harold, relaxed and smiling, engaged in quiet conversation with another patient. Full of enthusiasm for behavior therapy, and mindful of the potential benefits of positive social reinforcement for appropriate behavior, the therapist approached Harold with a warm greeting and said something like, "Harold! It's great to see you looking so well! How are you doing today?" to which Harold replied, "Well, now that you mention it, not so well, doctor," and languidly collapsed to the floor with an elegance and grace that a prima donna ballerina might have envied. Luckily, although clearly disappointed by this early setback, the behavior therapist persisted with the program and, ultimately, Harold was able to obtain attention in more socially acceptable ways.

Behavior therapists have to remember that one does not always know in advance which stimuli will prove to be reinforcing. Sherman (1990) gave the example of a developmentally delayed child who would attend to school work for 30 minutes only when this behavior was reinforced by allowing her to spend 5 minutes alone in the coat closet. Normally, that procedure would be considered a *time out* from positive reinforcement, a procedure often used as a form of punishment (Kazdin, 1994).

Negative reinforcement has been an important (though until recently, neglected) principle in understanding and treating various behavior disorders (Iwata, 1987). A clinical example of negative reinforcement was described by Patterson (1982). Seeking to understand aggression in children, he examined the interactions between the children and their parents to see what might be reinforcing the problem behavior. He noticed that whenever the child did something unacceptable, the parents would attempt to punish him or her by nagging, yelling, and generally expressing disapproval. In response to this, the child would become more and more aggressive. Eventually, the parents would give up trying to control the child. In other words, the child had succeeded in stopping the parents' attempts at punishment! Making the parents stop complaining can reinforce a behavior (the aggression) by negative reinforcement.

Chaining is a helpful concept in assisting patients who have difficulty with appropriate behavior sequences. An example is helping someone to get dressed. It is best to start with the behavior closest to the completion of the chain, assuming that successfully completing the task of putting on the item of clothing is reinforcing. Suppose that the patient has a zippered coat to put on. Rather than handing the person the coat and helping him or her to go through each stage—putting one arm in a sleeve, then the other arm in the other sleeve, and so on—it is better to begin with the coat already on, then go back one step. For example, the person starts with the coat on, then the therapist unzips the jacket a little way, and the person zips it up. Next, the jacket is unzipped completely, and the patient learns to engage the zipper and do up the coat appropriately. Next, the jacket is unzipped, and the patient takes one arm halfway out of the jacket, then puts the arm back in and fastens the zipper. And so it continues. This procedure, sometimes called *backward chaining,* can be practical, effective, and efficient, and it follows appropriate learning principles in reinforcing the component behaviors step by step (Neisworth & Madle, 1982; Sherman, 1990).

Treatment Procedures

Applying operant learning concepts to mental health treatment has been a controversial idea. Recall from Chapter 1 that students observing a videotape of reinforcement procedures took a very negative view when they were told the methods were derived from operant learning (but not when they thought it was humanistic education!). There *are* grounds for concern. Operant learning methods are often used with nonverbal people and with institutionalized individuals, raising potential concerns about ethical and humane treatment. It is vital that mental health professionals use treatment to enhance their clients' functioning and relieve their distress, rather than to facilitate the smooth running of an institution or to control its inmates. Imposing a behavior therapy program on a client could undermine his or her self-determination (Yoman, 1996), but withholding behavior therapy could violate a client's right to effective treatment (Stokes, 1995).

Fortunately, clinicians helping people with chronic mental health problems are using the language of empowerment in addition to the technical language of clinical science (Fairweather & Fergus, 1993; Nelson & Walsh-Bowers, 1994). Behavior therapy, which is aimed at removing specific problems straightforwardly in the context of a collaborative working relationship with clients, is well suited to the newer set of role expectations in which consumers participate democratically in clinical decision making. This "consumer input" has led to advances in research design so that the "experiences, goals, and aspirations of consumers/survivors are being used to define and measure mental health service outcomes" (Scott, 1993, p. 3).

The same approach has been actively embraced by the government agency that funds research on mental health services (National Institute of Mental Health, 1991). Finally, recent complaints about the poor preparation of clinical psychology students for working with chronic mental disorders have led to proposals for new curricula and models of service delivery (Millet & Schwebel, 1994; Smith, Schwebel, Dunn, & McIver, 1993).

Some recipients of mental health services, such as those represented by the National Alliance for the Mentally Ill, acknowledge many of the assumptions of the professional establishment and accept the concept of mental illness (Preskorn, 1995). But other professionals (Szasz, 1990, 1995) and people who have received mental health services (Firestar, 1993) object strongly to concepts of mental illness and the entire language of the "mental health system," particularly the term *patient*. Yet others find the term *consumer* offensive in implying a devalued status (Stanek, 1993). Nonetheless, as a consensus on appropriate terminology continues to crystallize, advances in the egalitarian, respectful, and congenial delivery of mental health services to informed recipients are undeniably in progress.

Habit Modification

Before turning to examples of reinforcement and punishment, the therapeutic potential of straightforward habit modification is worth noting. Many of these ideas follow from Guthrie's (1935) contiguity theory of learning. This theory stresses the importance of pairings of events—not only the stimulus-stimulus pairings familiar in classical conditioning but also the stimulus-response pairings, even in the absence of obvious reinforcement. For example, many drivers who do not usually fasten their seat belts think it would be a good idea to do so, but somehow they keep forgetting. Anyone can readily develop the habit of fastening the seat belt simply by making a point of doing so repeatedly. In this case, it is a good idea to get into the car, fasten the seat belt, then put the key in the ignition—and to follow that sequence every time. It can be helpful to repeat this whole process several times before driving away: Get into the car, fasten the seat belt, then put the key in the ignition. Then get out of the car, shut the door, and open it again, repeating the procedure. People who routinely fasten their seat belts often do not even think about it when doing so; following this straightforward habit modification procedure—simply repeating the desired behavior—can rapidly establish the new habit.

As another example, consider the problem behavior of a child each afternoon on returning home after school. To the great frustration of the parents, the child invariably walks through several muddy puddles on the way in from the school bus. Next, the child opens the front door, walks in, passes straight through the hallway, and travels the length of the living room, leaving a trail of mud across the carpet. The ensuing conversation goes something like this:

Parent: How many times have I told you not to do this! Every day it's the same! You come all the way in here, tracking all kinds of mud in, when I've repeatedly told you to take your boots off in the hallway before coming into the living room!

Child: Sorry, I won't do it again.

To Guthrie (1935), there is no mystery about the child continuing to repeat this behavior pattern, despite the parent's reprimands. People tend to do what they last did in the same situation. Therefore, the most likely behavior from the child the next afternoon would be walking through the puddles, tracking mud all the way from the front door to the living room, being reprimanded, and then going back to take the boots off. To change this habit, the child would have to be led—perhaps quite literally—to perform the whole behavior sequence properly. That is, the parent tells the child to return to the school bus stop, to approach the house, to open the door, then to stop, take the boots off, and finally enter the living room. If the child can perform this sequence just once, it is now more likely that it will be repeated next time.

Reinforcement

From the viewpoint of an operant learning theorist, practically all human behavior is influenced by reinforcement. In trying to understand the causes of an undesired behavior, it is therefore a good bet to try to find the reinforcer that is maintaining it. A variety of problem behavior patterns may be explained in this way. For example, Bijou (1963) has argued that ineffective use of reinforcement by parents may delay behavioral development in children. Not reinforcing behavior often enough or soon enough produces too "thin" a schedule of intermittent reinforcement and leads to extinction. Theories like this have led to numerous applications of reinforcement in treatment programs. These have often been remarkably successful.

Azrin and Foxx (1971) devised a rapid method for toilet training institutionalized people who are profoundly retarded, for example. The method is a combination of several techniques, including shaping, positive reinforcement (both primary and social), and some punishment procedures. Nine patients were successfully trained in approximately four days. Findings like this indicate the tremendous potential for reinforcement methods in treating individuals who are severely disturbed.

Baltes and Lascomb (1975) consulted with nursing home staff who were concerned about the behavior of one of the residents. She was an elderly woman who had developed the habit of screaming loudly at intervals during the day. The therapists noticed that the resident's screams were always followed by the swift appearance of nurses and other residents, concerned to see what was wrong. Each time, the staff members would urge the resident to stop screaming, and would eventually go away, feeling frustrated at their difficulties in dealing with this annoying behavior. The therapists formed the idea that the attention of the staff might be reinforcing the resident's screaming. Accordingly, they sought to rearrange this unhelpful contingency. They began to spend time with the resident when she was *not* screaming, to make sure that she could gain attention appropriately without having to resort to this inappropriate behavior. This appeared to be helpful, but the resident would occasionally scream even when the therapists were already present.

The treatment plan the therapists adopted was as follows. When they were with the resident, they would pay attention to her, give her candy, and play her favorite music on a tape recorder. Whenever she screamed, they would switch off the music, remove the candy, become silent, and look away from her. When she stopped screaming, the therapists would pay attention again. This strategy proved quite successful. By systematically alternating periods of treatment and no treatment, the authors of the report were able to show that placing the screaming under conditions of extinction was indeed responsible for the improvement.

This example illustrates how positive reinforcement can unintentionally sustain unhelpful behavior in a client. It also shows how reversing the contingency—placing the unwanted behavior under conditions of extinction—can prove valuable as therapy.

Other examples of reinforcement can be found in cases of so-called hysteria, both old and new. Today, problems in physical functioning that cannot be understood medically are labeled as *somatoform disorders* (American Psychiatric Association, 1994). These include certain paralyses of the limbs, sensory problems, and pain symptoms that seem more related to behavioral than to biological processes. As we indicated in Chapter 1, the pioneers of psychoanalysis began their work with such patients. Consider the following case study:

THE CASE OF ELISABETH VON R.

Elisabeth von R., a patient of Sigmund Freud's, was a young woman who complained chiefly of pains in her legs and difficulties with walking. No medical basis for these problems had been found. Her father had died after a long illness not long before she began her treatment with Freud. Elisabeth had taken the role of nurse to her father in the last two years of his life, and as a result she had given up any social life she might otherwise have had outside the household. According to Freud's account, Elisabeth lost her symptoms as a result of recapturing the significant emotional memories that were associated with them.

One of the painful memories was of the onset of a symptom when she had felt guilty about her father's condition. The context was as follows. She had gone out to a social event for the first time in some months, and while there, she had spent much of the time with an eligible young man. They had walked together for a while after leaving the gathering, and Elisabeth had arrived home later than planned because of this. On returning home, she had found that her sick father had taken a turn for the worse while she had been away. She had felt guilty for having left him and felt unsteady on her feet as she heard the news, holding onto the door frame for support. Freud also discovered that Elisabeth's leg pains started with a sensation in one of her thighs. This happened to be the part of her leg on which her father had always rested his leg while she changed his bandage (Breuer & Freud, 1895/1974).

Although Elisabeth von R. was treated by the founder of psychoanalysis, her problems could also be understood from a learning perspective. First, she had spent a great deal of time looking after her father, an invalid whose problems included a leg ailment. Through her observations of his behavior, Elisabeth could have acquired a great deal of information about the symptoms of such disorders. She could have hardly failed to notice that her father gained support, sympathy, and attention during his illness. Second, after her father's death, Elisabeth found that she was still expected to work in the household rather than to attend social events. When her own walking difficulties emerged, she was relieved of those household responsibilities. In addition, she was able to receive sympathetic attention from other people. Psychoanalytic therapists recognize that a patient like Elisabeth may gain benefit from her symptoms. One form of benefit, *secondary gain*, results from the practical rewards brought by the problem, such as being attended to by others and not having to work around the house. What psychoanalytic therapists would call secondary gain, behavior therapists would call reinforcement.

This two-stage theory of problems like Elisabeth's was put forward by Ullman and Krasner (1975). First, the person observes somebody else gaining some reward from having a medical symptom. Second, the person's own complaint of symptoms is reinforced. In Elisabeth's case, being relieved of duties and chores would be negative reinforcement and gaining attention would be positive reinforcement, both having the potential to strengthen or maintain her problem behavior. This does not necessarily mean that Elisabeth was deliberately faking her symptoms. Operant learning mechanisms could strengthen behavior in just this way without the person understanding clearly what is happening.

Somatoform Disorders and Positive Reinforcement

A more recent example of similar processes was reported by Kallman, Hersen, and O'Toole (1975). The client was a man in his early forties. He had complained of back pain for 15 years, and he had had numerous hospital admissions for inability to work. Five years before the current hospitalization, he had retired from his job outside the home. He received an income because of his disability. Medical investigations could not adequately explain the symptoms. The therapists noticed that the client received a considerable amount of help from his family. Whenever his problems flared up again, family members would take over the chores and bring him breakfast in bed. Because of their suspicion that reinforcement may have been playing a part in the problem, the therapists tried social reinforcement as therapy.

Three times a day, a research assistant would spend 10 minutes talking to him. At the end of a visit, she would ask him to walk if he could. In some phases of the therapy, she praised him specifically for his success at standing; in other phases, she only praised him for walking. Whichever response was selected for reinforcement increased, indicating clearly that there was a specific reinforcement effect (not simply a general increase in his morale because of the visits). Things went well at home for a month before the client was brought back to the hospital with the original problems at full force. It turned out that the family had once again reinforced the problem behavior by attention. The therapists explained behavioral principles to the family members and used videotapes of the family's communication to make the point. After that, the client's improvement was maintained at home for at least three months.

Other illustrations of the use of reinforcement to treat somatoform disorders were provided by behavior therapists in the 1960s. Brady and Lind (1961) had shown that a patient who was apparently blind could respond to visual stimuli after this had been specifically reinforced. Zimmerman and Grosz (1966) made a similar demonstration. They treated a patient who was functionally blind but whose visual sensory apparatus showed no medical abnormality. He was asked to press one of three keys, each of which was located under a diagram of a triangle, for a long series of trials under different conditions. One of the triangles was always upright, oriented differently from the others. Pushing the key under that one switched off a buzzing sound, but responses to the other keys did not. The position of the upright triangle (right, left, or center in the display) was altered randomly from trial to trial. The therapists had told the patient that correct responses would switch off the buzzing sound. If the patient responded consistently so as to switch off the buzzer, this would be clear proof that he could respond to visual stimuli. The actual results were the exact opposite: He *rarely* responded so as to switch off the buzzer—so rarely, in fact, that his performance differed significantly from chance, indicating that he was using visual information to avoid making the correct response!

Reinforcement was also used in the treatment of two patients described by Meichenbaum (1966). One was a man who seemed unable to keep his eyes open. On examination, it was determined that this problem helped him avoid social conflict situations, so that it was being negatively reinforced. Treatment that involved helping him deal more effectively with social conflict was effective in resolving the eye problem. The other patient, a man with apparently paralyzed legs, received treatment in the form of positive reinforcement to encourage his walking. Staff members selectively praised him when he made specific improvements in his walking. It worked, and he was still doing well eight months later.

A detailed analysis of behavioral contingencies showed that the involuntary movements of an institutionalized man with a tic disorder were being reinforced by escape from situations that placed demands on him (Scotti et al., 1994). However, in this case, as in some other behavioral investigations of this disorder, the behavioral intervention suggested by the analysis of contingencies was unsuccessful.

Punishment and Aversion Therapy

Punishment has strong emotional connotations, and in everyday speech the term is commonly associated with abuse, ridicule, and revenge (Axelrod, 1983). In view of its unfavorable public image, how could a mental health professional possibly justify using punishment as therapy? Part of the answer has to do with what punishment means.

Take the example of the man who wishes to quit smoking cigarettes, so every time he thinks of lighting one he snaps a thick elastic band that is tightly stretched around his wrist. This is an example of punishment, but one that does not seem too unpleasant or controversial (at least, it does not involve abuse, ridicule, or revenge). Another example of punishment occurs when a telephone company begins to charge its customers a fee for using the directory assistance service. Contingent on making the response (calling for directory assistance), a cost is incurred (the fee charged), which has the effect of reducing the frequency of the behavior. This is a definition of *response cost,* a form of punishment. Consumers may object to the new charge, but they would probably not view the new policy as inhumane, abusive, or cruel.

Suppose that a client joins a group of people who are trying to help each other lose weight. Every participant deposits $10 at the outset. Each week that a client loses weight, $1 is refunded. On weeks when there is no weight loss, there is no refund. Is forfeiting the money a form of punishment? To behavior therapists, it is, and its use can be justified if (1) the client voluntarily accepts it and (2) it works.

Consider the example of Frank in Chapter 1. He imagined unpleasant but realistic scenes so as to help him control an unwanted habit (one that is also severely sanctioned by the community). That technique, *covert sensitization* (Brownell, Hayes, & Barlow, 1977), is recognized as a form of punishment.

To many of you, examples such as these do not conjure up the negative impression that the word *punishment* often evokes. Yet, these examples are instances of the punishment methods sometimes used in behavior therapy. In view of this, it is reasonable in evaluating punishment methods to avoid bracketing them all together and taking a general stand for or against. It is more constructive to appraise each kind of punishment procedure separately, deciding how effective it is and whether there should be limitations on its use.

The most controversial form of punishment used in therapy is, presumably, the use of painful electric shocks in an attempt to suppress certain behavior. Clearly, this is punishment, and of the most extreme kind. How could its use ever be justified? It is true that on rare occasions, in response to compelling clinical need, behavior therapists may actually deliver painful stimuli to clients in treatment programs. In hospitals or institutions such treatment may proceed only with careful safeguards and with oversight by an independent review panel. In this section we shall describe some punishment procedures and give examples of their use.

Why Use Punishment?

Some of the abnormal behavior treated by behavior therapists is dangerous in the extreme. "S" was a severely disturbed hyperactive 6-year-old who displayed many bizarre behaviors (Risley, 1968). The client had been diagnosed as brain damaged as a result of an infection before she was 1 year old. She did not speak intelligibly. Scars from many injuries were evident on her body. These injuries were all the result of her chief problem behavior—dangerous climbing activity. She persisted in climbing on houses, trees, furniture, ledges, and so on despite many falls and injuries. As Risley described it, "Her front teeth were missing, having been left imbedded in a 2- by 4-inch molding from which she had fallen while climbing outside the second story of her house" (p. 22). Her parents were thinking of having her institutionalized.

Lovaas and Simmons (1969) have described the self-destructive behavior of some children who are psychotic or severely retarded. Common behaviors in this group of patients include banging the head or arms against sharp or hard objects, biting themselves, and hitting themselves in the face with fists or knees. Those authors go on to say that, frequently, "such children have removed large quantities of flesh from their bodies, torn out their nails, opened wounds in their heads, broken their noses, etc." (p. 143). Some children try to gouge their eyes out, risking detached retinas and blindness; others have produced kidney damage by self-punching (Carr & Lovaas, 1983).

A severely retarded, nonverbal adult woman repeatedly bloodied her face by slamming her arm into her eye and temple. Unsupervised, she would hit herself over 400 times in 15 minutes or so. Every less intrusive form of treatment that had been attempted had failed, and a program of punishment for her self-injurious behavior was being contemplated. This would take the form of a quick slap to her thigh when she hit herself. Without successful treatment, this client would continue to be heavily medicated and kept in physical restraints for her protection (Sherman, 1990).

It is in cases such as these that behavior therapists have sometimes used painful, but physically harmless, electric shock to attempt to put a stop to dangerous, self-destructive behavior. However, these methods are not used unless others have failed. Carr and Lovaas

(1983) described the series of less unpleasant methods that should always be tried before the use of shock is contemplated. "One does not begin the treatment of severe behavior problems by using electric shock" (p. 222). The series of methods is as follows: reinforcing other behavior, placing the problem behavior under extinction, taking the patient out of the reinforcing environment temporarily, and having the patient practice behavior incompatible with the problem behavior. These methods will all be described here.

If all these methods fail, shock may be used, but there are some further requirements. First, an independent committee of concerned people should oversee the therapy (the committee would ideally include representatives of the patient's family, the clergy, physicians, patient advocates, and so on); second, therapists should always experience the shock themselves at the start of each therapy session. Behavior therapists give ethical concerns the highest priority whenever the use of punishment of this kind is contemplated (Favell, 1982; Kazdin, 1994; Sherman, 1990). In addition to the ethical requirements delineated by the mental health professions and by behavior therapy interest groups, the courts have sometimes imposed restrictions governing the use of electric shock in a therapeutic punishment program. For example, in one legal decision,

> *shock was restricted to extraordinary circumstances, such as when a client is engaging in self-destructive behavior that is likely to inflict physical damage. Moreover, shock should be applied only when another procedure has been used unsuccessfully, when a committee on human rights within the institution has approved of the treatment, and when the client or a close relative has consented to its use. (Kazdin, 1994, p. 414)*

Punishment has advantages and disadvantages (Axelrod, 1983). When it is used, it is because positive reinforcement is not always effective in treatment plans aimed at eliminating destructive behavior. Nevertheless, a dominant theme in the use of punishment as therapy is "when clinicians wish to eliminate one behavior through punishment, they should simultaneously reinforce the desired behavior" (Axelrod, 1983, p. 2). Advantages of punishment are that it can be effective, it can bring quick results, it may lead to complete removal of the problem behavior, and there may be desirable side effects. Disadvantages of punishment are that it can evoke negative emotional responses, it can produce aggression, and it can disturb the patient's relationship with the caregivers (Sherman, 1990).

Differential Reinforcement of Other Behavior

The *differential reinforcement of other behavior (DRO)* procedure involves delivering positive reinforcement when the patient has not made the undesired response for a specified period of time. The procedure demands a stimulating environment with adequate numbers of staff members. It is quite time consuming, and the staff members need a certain degree of skill to implement it. As a result, in many inpatient settings, the use of DRO is unrealistic (Carr & Lovaas, 1983). When DRO is used, it is often used together with *extinction*. In the example of the self-destructive psychotic child, extinction means identifying the reinforcer for the unwanted response (the head banging, for example) and then deliberately withholding that reinforcer when the head banging occurs. In many programs, staff members have begun with the hypothesis that social attention is reinforcing the behavior. Extinction therefore means ignoring the child whenever the head banging occurs.

Extinction was tried with three self-destructive children treated by Lovaas and Simmons (1969). Staff members ignored self-destructive behavior and left the room if a child began to do this while staff were present. Extinction was effective in the two boys to whom it was applied. However, several treatment sessions were needed before reliable effects were produced, and each boy hit himself several hundred times before the behavior declined to acceptable levels. Another problem is that the effects of extinction were limited to the situation in which it took place. That is, if a boy stopped hitting himself after 10 days of extinction in his room, he would not necessarily keep this up when he returned to the dayroom. Extinction would have to be arranged in every specific environment that the boy entered. For these reasons, Lovaas and Simmons concluded that extinction is impractical and its results are not rapid enough for the technique to be recommended.

Response Cost

The next technique, *response cost*, is "a punishment procedure in which a positive reinforcer is removed contingent upon the occurrence of a specific behavior, with the resulting decrease in the future probability of the occurrence of that behavior" (Pazulinec, Meyerrose, & Sajwaj, 1983, p. 71). Using response cost as a punishment technique requires that the patient already possess a number of positive reinforcers. Only in that way can a reinforcer be removed, of course. One way of doing this is to give the patient a number of items first and then subtract a fixed number of them contingent on the appearance of the behavior to be punished. In a token economy, in which all patients in a ward or other residential group have a certain number of tokens available, it is easy to have a system of "fines" in which tokens are subtracted when the undesired response is made. An advantage of response cost is that, as a form of punishment, it is relatively well accepted by all concerned. (Sherman [1990] has pointed out some disadvantages, however, and recommends that prominence be given to concurrent positive reinforcement of incompatible behavior.) In the example of telephone operator assistance, cited earlier, response cost was effective in reducing the number of requests. But it was also easy to put into effect, there were few objections by consumers, and there were hardly any reports of adverse "side effects."

Time Out (TO)

The notion of *time out* (TO) dates from the original laboratory work of Ferster and Skinner (1957), who referred to it as a time period in which the subject was prevented from making the particular response studied in the experiment. It became clear that time out from positive reinforcement was aversive, in that laboratory animals would learn to make responses so as to escape and avoid it. In its clinical applications, TO is intended as a fixed period of time in a less reinforcing environment, contingent on behavior (Brantner & Doherty, 1983). The actual procedure has several variations, ranging from having a single therapist withdraw attention for a brief interval, to removing the patient from the treatment environment to an isolation room for several minutes. An example of the use of TO is given here, described by Wolf, Risley, and Mees (1964).

A boy, Dicky, was occasionally self-destructive and often threw tantrums. During these episodes, he would throw down his eyeglasses, which were necessary for correcting a serious vision problem. The therapists established a TO contingency in which Dicky was placed in his room for 10 minutes every time he threw his glasses. The method was entirely successful, as shown by the use of a reversal design in which the contingency would occasionally be altered so as to gauge its effect. Unlike the example of extinction for self-destructive behavior, as cited earlier, the effects of TO with Dicky showed some strong generalization to other settings. When the problem behavior did reappear in a different environment, it was quite easy to remove the problem by the same method.

Overcorrection

As a treatment for disruptive behavior in a residential setting, *overcorrection* was described by Foxx and Azrin (1973) as a "positive practice procedure" to "require the disruptor to practice overly correct forms of relevant behaviors" (p. 2). There are two types of overcorrection: *restitution* and *positive practice*. The rationale for overcorrection is to "overcorrect" the environmental consequences of the disruptive act and, in the same situation, to practice "overly correct" relevant responses (Foxx & Bechtel, 1983). If a patient disturbs the physical environment in the disruptive act, the restitution type of overcorrection is appropriate. For example, if a child spits on the floor, then he or she might have to wipe clean the area of the floor that was spat on as well as the rest of the floor. When there is no physical disturbance to the environment, then positive practice is appropriate. A psychotic boy who hits himself in the head with his fist would practice making arm and hand movements incompatible with self-injury. In all cases, the activity used in overcorrection is performed contingent on the appearance of the disruptive behavior.

Advantages of overcorrection are that the consequence of the problem behavior is not an arbitrary fine or other punishment; rather, it is a relevant and realistic consequence—one that could make sense outside the institution. As Foxx and Bechtel have pointed out, overcorrection automatically contains an element of TO, because the time spent in the overcorrection task cannot be spent on other, potentially reinforcing, activities.

Harris and Romanczyk (1976) described the use of positive practice overcorrection with an 8-year-old retarded boy. His self-injurious behavior took the form of head banging, which had been severe enough to shatter automobile windshields. Contingent on head banging, a therapist would guide the boy's head in a fixed pattern of motions and then the same with his arms. This activity would last for five minutes. If any further head banging occurred during the overcorrection, the timer would reset to zero and a further five minutes of overcorrection would be required. After little more than two weeks of treatment, the frequency of the behavior had declined from a daily average of 6 to 76 episodes to 0. The procedures were practiced separately at the boy's home, with similar results.

A form of positive practice overcorrection has been used successfully with clients with tic disorders. The technique, *habit reversal,* chiefly involves identifying and practicing competing responses incompatible with the tic (Azrin, Nunn, & Frantz, 1980; Azrin & Peterson, 1990; Peterson & Azrin, 1992).

Comments

Further clinical applications of punishment and other operant learning procedures are discussed in later chapters. The methods based on reinforcement, as opposed to punishment, have consistently been preferred by practitioners of behavior therapy, and research evidence bears out the impression that the positive methods are more constructive and better received by clients or patients and the community. Nevertheless, in those extreme cases in which all other methods fail, it clearly seems appropriate to use aversive procedures when doing so can rapidly remove a life-threatening behavior. In such cases, it can be unethical to withhold effective treatment.

Chapter Summary

Operant learning phenomena are essential to behavior therapy. Discriminative stimuli take on the power to influence and direct behavior when responses come under the control of reinforcement contingencies. Because behavioral contingencies are always present, they exert their influence on both normal and abnormal behavior in any situation in which behavior occurs. Behavior therapists believe that abnormal behavior is understandable when the contingencies operating are known. Changing the contingencies can change the behavior.

Applying operant learning methods in the clinical arena requires sensitivity, competence, and professionalism in service providers. Even in institutional settings, it is usually possible to foster collaborative, egalitarian working relationships with clients. The potentially disturbing topic of using aversive stimuli in therapy programs is not as controversial when certain facts are recognized. Aversive methods only rarely involve actually painful stimuli. The procedures followed include a wide range of activities, from imagining unpleasant consequences to subtracting points in a token reinforcement program. Painful stimuli, such as harmless but unpleasant electric shock, are used only in cases of extremely dangerous self-mutilative behavior when other methods have failed and when approval has been given by the client and by a committee of responsible people. Aversive methods have provided effective therapy in some cases when all other techniques have failed.

Endnotes

1. Notice that this term was mentioned in Chapter 2 as another name for graduated real-life practice, showing that the development of that technique was influenced by operant learning principles.
2. This is a good example of negative reinforcement.

Chapter *4*

Social Learning Theory and Cognitive-Behavioral Therapy

Martin[1] was doing well in college but had begun to experience unpredictable, terrifying anxiety attacks that led him to seek psychological treatment. His chief worry was that if he had a major panic attack during a class (or, even worse, during an exam) he would have to flee from the room. This would not only be embarrassing and difficult to explain to his classmates but it could also impair his hard-won academic standing. There was also the lurking fear that, if he ever did have to leave a class abruptly because of intense anxiety, he might not be able to return for fear of having another attack. As he explained to his therapist, Martin was not at the point that he avoided any situations because of anxiety, but he was concerned that he might if his anxiety problem continued its present course. He felt this concern was well-founded, because he had had a mild history of anxiety and avoidance in childhood.

Growing up on a reservation separated from the nearest town by a river, Martin had, with most of his family and friends, led a life somewhat isolated from the community in which most of the jobs and educational opportunities were to be found. His early education was in an elementary school on the reservation taught by members of a religious order, most of whom were bilingual in English and French. Martin therefore grew up with a strong sense of identification with both Native American and Franco-American cultures. His first anxiety episode, recalled as vividly as if it had occurred yesterday, had struck in early adolescence when he was walking across the bridge from the reservation to the town—to begin his first day at a new school in the predominantly white, English-speaking community across the river.

Martin rapidly grasped the concepts of graduated real-life exposure that his therapist explained in one of their first meetings, but as it was clear that avoidance of situations was not a central problem, Martin preferred to focus treatment on managing, controlling, or coping with anxiety as and when it arose. Two treatment techniques were used. One was based upon the *rational emotive behavior therapy (REBT)* of Ellis (1995); the other was drawn from the *stress inoculation training (SIT)* of Meichenbaum (1977, 1995).

First, Martin learned to identify, and dispute, any unhelpful or needlessly demoralizing thoughts he was entertaining in the context of an anxiety attack (thoughts such as, "What if the anxiety gets totally out of control and I freak out? Suppose it gets worse and worse and I end up not being able even to leave my house because of anxiety?"). Second, he practiced imagining specific situations that tended to arouse anxiety, and at the same time rehearsed a series of self-statements designed to help him cope successfully (such as, "I can use the sensation of mounting anxiety as a signal to me to use my coping exercises" or "Even if I *did* encounter severe anxiety in class, I would not necessarily have to leave and I might find that I can cope with the situation reasonably well"). As the treatment had been conducted as part of an experimental study of these two forms of cognitive-behavioral therapy, Martin's therapist later had available a wide range of reliable data to confirm that substantial and lasting progress had been made (Hecker & Thorpe, 1989; Thorpe, Hecker, Cavallaro, & Kulberg, 1987).

In the decade following the introduction of behavior therapy in the late 1950s, a variety of effective, new treatment procedures appeared, each developed from the principles of classical conditioning and operant learning. Outpatients were treated for phobias, compulsions, addictions, and bed-wetting as if these disorders were the result of classical conditioning. Systematic desensitization, assertiveness training, aversion therapy, and flooding gained increasing acceptance after their initial clinical applications had proved successful. The problems of inpatients with schizophrenia and mental retardation were treated as learned behavior that could be reinforced or extinguished, and the results were often equally impressive.

But by the early 1970s it was clear that some clinical problems had received little attention from behavior therapists. The problems that *had* been dealt with successfully included situational anxiety problems in outpatients and specific behavioral excesses and deficits in inpatients—problems that can easily be construed in terms of learning principles. The problems that had *not* yet been dealt with effectively were the more diffuse disorders such as generalized anxiety, depression, and marital problems. Several developments within behavior therapy converged at about this time to inspire an interest in cognitive procedures and processes. This new perspective improved therapy effectiveness in many areas, including the more generalized problems that had not responded well to conditioning methods. In this chapter, we will describe the cognitive-behavioral orientation and its techniques, origins, and theoretical basis.

Theoretical Principles

The general notion that people are influenced more by their perceptions of, or thoughts about, events than by objective reality has a long history. Freeman and Reinecke (1995) quoted the Stoic philosopher Epictetus as follows: "What upsets people is not things themselves but their judgements about the things. . . . So when we are thwarted or upset or distressed, let us never blame someone else but rather ourselves, that is, our own judgements" (p. 183). If people are upset more by their thoughts than by actual events, it follows that treatment could be aimed at helping people think in more benign and less disturbing ways.

This approach was enthusiastically put forward by several European scholars in the 1500s. In 1558, English physician William Bullein recommended "for the passions of the mynde good counsel." In 1592, Jean de l'Espine advocated, as treatment for emotional distress, "words, reasons, arguments, discourses and demonstrations." And in 1600, John Downame, a puritan divine of London, described "spiritual physicke to cure the diseases of the soule," an early form of psychotherapy for anger involving "a soft and milde answere" and "wholesome counsayle and good admonitions" (Hunter & MacAlpine, 1963). In the early 1900s, French pharmacist Emil Coué, who had studied with the hypnotists Liébeault and Bernheim at Nancy, popularized the technique of *autosuggestion,* characterized by frequent repetition of the sentence "Every day, and in every way, I am becoming better and better" (Bromberg, 1975).

The imprecision and anecdotal quality of these early forms of counseling and psychotherapy seem far removed from the scientific credentials of behavior therapy as put forward by Joseph Wolpe, Teodoro Ayllon, and other experimentally minded therapists. But by the late 1960s, critics were questioning behavior therapists' claims to scientific rigor. Much of the criticism was aimed at the adequacy of conditioning explanations of abnormal behavior, and research was demonstrating that meaning and appraisal processes play a vital part in determining people's reactions to stress:

> *Too much research was emerging that highlighted that it was not the so-called stimulus consequences, or reinforcement, that influenced an individual's behavior, but rather how the individual perceived the relationship between his or her behavior and critical events. Moreover, the individual's awareness of the contingency of the consequences was a primary determinant of learning. (Meichenbaum, 1995, p. 143)*

Social learning theorists Albert Bandura, Walter Mischel, and Julian Rotter paved the way for the development of cognitive-behavioral therapy techniques by stressing the importance of those personal factors and self-regulatory processes that intervene between stimuli and responses. Learning is viewed as an *active* process, reflecting learners' continuing efforts to organize and reorganize their patterns of experience and behavior (Freeman & Reinecke, 1995; Meichenbaum, 1995; Persons, 1994). For example, in his important book, *Principles of Behavior Modification,* Bandura (1969) reviewed the relevant research and concluded that people respond less to the objective behavioral contingencies than to those contingencies as they are perceived. He identified the development of *expectancies* as an essential element in the processes underlying classical and operant conditioning. More recently, other learning theorists whose early work was behavioristic have emphasized the importance of expectancy modification in people and in animals (Reiss, 1980; Rescorla, 1988).

Bandura's theoretical work combined with other developments to inspire interest in cognitive factors in behavior change. Even the earliest behavioral techniques include subjective elements, often depending heavily on the client's ability to adopt certain attitudes, to entertain certain ideas, and to create certain kinds of imagery. Systematic desensitization involves asking the client to imagine scenes and to judge anxiety levels. Wolpe's (1958) approach to assertiveness training often meant giving the client a pep talk. And even aversion therapy, in which a client would agree to receive painful stimuli in a conditioning program designed to decrease interest in undesired behavior, included subjective elements that undermine any claim that the client was being passively conditioned.

Imagine the child molester who looked at color slides of young children and was given brief, aversive shocks. The client would be actively involved in rating the desirability of the slides during treatment, and in many such programs, those ratings would serve as the sole criterion for progress. A successfully treated client would thereafter avoid children as sexual partners, despite the clear realization that there would be no shock even if a child were approached. This observation could be consistent with a non-cognitive conditioning view of the therapeutic process, of course, but some writers interpret this same observation as an indication that cognitive processes within the individual play an important part. Their argument is that there is nothing automatic about the conditioning process, which is only successful if the client attends to key stimuli, mobilizes certain expectations, and uses the information acquired during treatment in an active self-control process that continues when the client has left the clinic (Rachman & Teasdale, 1969).

Systematic desensitization, assertiveness training, and aversion therapy can be viewed as following principles of classical conditioning and operant learning, but it makes more sense to many behavioral clinicians to invoke cognitive concepts such as images, thoughts, and expectations in describing the therapeutic process. Behavior therapists began to deal with such concepts at a time when these were not generally accepted by experimental psychologists, and, as a result, behavior therapy was criticized (see, for example, Locke, 1971).

Classic Studies

Studies of covert conditioning, placebo and expectancy effects, and behavioral self-control and self-management attracted the interest of behavior therapists who sought to move beyond strict conditioning interpretations of behavior change.

Covert Conditioning

Beginning in the mid-1960s, Joseph Cautela developed a series of behavior therapy techniques that depend entirely upon clients' active mobilization of certain covert processes. These *covert conditioning* methods require the client to fantasize performing specific behaviors (either undesired behaviors to be discouraged or adaptive behaviors to be encouraged), then to imagine encountering punishment, extinction, or reinforcement procedures as a result (Cautela & Kearney, 1986). The *covert sensitization* method used in the treatment of Frank T's exhibitionism (Chapter 1) was developed by Cautela. In the 1970s, covert sensitization began to replace aversive methods that had used electric shocks as punishing stimuli (Brownell, Hayes, & Barlow, 1977). Proponents of the cognitive-behavioral orientation within behavior therapy argued that if clients could resolve such difficult problems as exhibitionism by imagined, rather than actual, punishments, then cognitive processes and procedures deserved greater professional attention.

Placebo and Expectancy Effects

Another strong influence on behavior therapists' interest in cognitive processes was researchers' appreciation of the importance of expectancy effects in psychological therapy. After Eysenck's (1952) criticisms of psychotherapy, which he faulted for not having proved effective, behavior therapists took pains to assess their treatment interventions very carefully. After Eysenck (1961) added the criticism that psychotherapy had not proved any more effective than ordinary conversations between a client and an understanding listener, behavior therapists tested their procedures against generalized forms of therapy (having the client talk about personal issues to a counselor in an atmosphere of trust). This meant showing that a particular treatment was better than "treatment in general." The usual outcome of studies like these was that focused behavioral techniques such as systematic desensitization did fare better than generic counseling methods, yet it was also found that the less specific methods were often quite helpful in themselves (Kazdin & Wilcoxon, 1976). Such findings demonstrate the potential contribution of cognitive factors such as expectancy to treatment effectiveness.

Behavior therapists were also impressed by studies revealing the contribution of expectancy to emotional states. Schachter and Singer (1962) had illustrated the importance of subjects' expectations in determining how they described their feelings. Emotion was aroused in volunteers by injecting them with adrenaline. Participants' descriptions of their feelings depended on the context. People who were led to expect that they would feel angry tended to report feeling angry. Those who were told that they would just feel agitated tended to be vague about what they were feeling emotionally. These indications that the cognitive factor of expectancy influences emotion helped encourage the development of cognitive approaches within behavior therapy.

Self-Control and Self-Management

Behavioral *self-control* and *self-management* programs were found useful and began to be popular in the 1970s (Kanfer & Karoly, 1972; Watson & Tharp, 1985). The central feature of behavioral self-control programs is the individual's deliberate alteration of the contingencies influencing specific problem behaviors. Take the example of Janet, a college professor who was determined to quit smoking. At home, where no one else smoked, or in her office, where smoking was not permitted, she had little difficulty in abstaining (despite the occasional craving). But if she ever stopped at her friend Margaret's house, all was lost. Margaret was a chain-smoker who liked others to smoke with her. She would greet Janet with the offer of a cigarette and the confident assertion, "Go on, have one. One little cigarette can't hurt you!" Janet's best intentions were no match for this situation, and she would reluctantly (yet eagerly) accept the cigarette, then feel miserable afterwards for having given in and strayed from her program.

Using behavioral self-control procedures in a case like this involves changing the contingency that reinforces the unwanted behavior. This is an especially difficult example, because the problem behavior is smoking the cigarette, and the positive reinforcement derives from smoking the cigarette. The primary contingency is "If I smoke the cigarette, then those pleasant sensations will follow." Ideally, changing this contingency would mean somehow removing the reinforcement involved in smoking (having the tobacco manufacturers make cigarettes taste disgusting, for example). More realistically, because her problem (like most problems requiring self-control strategies) involves a *chain* of contingencies, Janet could move back one or two steps in the chain. The earlier the chain can be interrupted, the better (Watson & Tharp, 1985). For example, she could help herself avoid smoking by altering the secondary contingency "If I visit Margaret, then I get to smoke." This could mean persuading Margaret never to give Janet a cigarette under any circumstances. Another option would be to avoid the contingency itself by not visiting Margaret!

The idea of self-control is important in outpatient therapy. Operant learning techniques could be appropriate when the client wishes to overcome an unwanted habit, whether it is smoking tobacco, failing to study for tests, or exhibitionism. But operant conditioning somehow seems unsuitable for an outpatient setting. As an example of the limitations of a conditioning approach, consider an outpatient who consults a behavior therapist for advice on how to handle a habit problem. If the client were in a residential treatment setting, there would be few difficulties, provided that the client is able to give informed consent to therapy and is willing to be an active participant.

An existing token economy, or a new individualized program, could serve the client's needs well. Principles of reinforcement or extinction, used consistently by a well-coordinated ward staff, would be likely to bring rapid benefit. But would these techniques be used with an outpatient? Would the therapist spend the weekly one-hour therapy sessions handing the client tokens for appropriate behavior during the interview? Or encourage therapeutic progress by stuffing candy into the client's mouth? Absurd! This would be entirely unnecessary. A voluntary outpatient who is self-possessed enough to request therapy, to find the way to a therapist's office for outpatient appointments, and to identify specific problems for treatment would presumably not need to be passively "conditioned." Instead, he or she could be told about the essential principles of conditioning and learning, and then could employ the techniques in the natural environment between therapy sessions, with the therapist serving as a resource and general troubleshooter. This is where self-control comes in.

Goldiamond (1965) set out a rationale for using self-control procedures with outpatients and gave several examples to illustrate his points. Following the lead of Skinner (1953), he stated, "If you want a specified behavior from yourself, set up the conditions which you know will control it. For example, if you cannot get up in the morning by firmly resolving to do so and telling yourself that you must, buy and set an alarm clock" (Goldiamond, 1965, p. 853).

Stimulus Control.   One direct application of operant learning takes advantage of *stimulus control* procedures (Kazdin, 1994; Pierce & Epling, 1995). This is the approach that was used in the case of Mike, the student whose difficulties with studying were described in the first few pages of this book. Because reinforcement always takes place in a certain context, that context can set the scene for the reinforced behavior. In other words, stimuli connected with a behavioral contingency can become discriminative stimuli. Goldiamond took advantage of this principle in devising a program for a college woman who lacked motivation to study. The procedure was simple: She was to use her desk for nothing but studying. If she wanted to write letters or do some light reading, she had to go to another room. If she was studying at her desk but felt sleepy and started to daydream, she was to leave immediately and do something else, somewhere else. In this way, being at the desk was always associated with active studying. It did not matter, at first, how much time she spent there, as long as all the time that was spent there was spent in active studying. Eventually, simply going to the desk pulled powerfully for studying behavior.

Another client described by Goldiamond (1965) was a married man whose behavior toward his wife alternated between yelling at her and sulking. A treatment plan was developed in which appropriate behavior other than yelling was encouraged and reinforced. The client was advised to eat out frequently with his wife (so that the surroundings would discourage yelling) and to discuss interesting topics that did not involve the relationship directly (such as a mother-in-law's "crazy ideas about farming"). To deal with the sulking, the therapist advised the man to go ahead and sulk as much as he wished, provided that he always did this while seated on a particular stool out in the garage. When there, he could rehash all of life's various injustices and mutter grumpily about them to his heart's content. The point was to connect the sulking with just one particular environment, so that, eventually, all the other places would lose their discriminative function and would no longer set the occasion for sulking.

Self-Reinforcement.   It is difficult to imagine a behavior that could not be increased by *self-reinforcement*, an important component of most self- control programs (Goldiamond, 1976; Kazdin, 1994). The principles are straightforward enough. If you would like to learn to play the guitar, for example, yet you soon tire of regular practicing, you could set up a reinforcement contingency for yourself. If what you really like is reading a novel or watching television, you could make sure that you do one of these things immediately after a half-hour session of guitar practice, but not otherwise.

A common problem in self-control programs is that people do not use self-reinforcement often enough or soon enough after the behavior to be reinforced. If you decide to reinforce your novel-writing behavior by contingent dishes of ice cream, it probably will not work to eat the ice cream only after you have written 100 pages. Self-reinforcement should be "big, sassy, and fast" (B. T. Yates, 1985, p. 38).

Activity of various kinds can be a powerful reinforcer. Simply find an activity that, given the choice, you engage in very often. Next, use this activity as a reinforcer. Premack (1965) observed that, when rats deprived of water for 23 hours had the opportunity to run in a wheel or drink water, they spent more time drinking water. When a contingency was established so that water was available only after the rats ran on the wheel for a few seconds, the rats ran on the wheel; drinking reinforced running. Then the rats were given free access to water, and eventually they spent more time running than drinking. When a contingency was established so that the running wheel would only turn when the rats drank water for few seconds, the rats drank water; running reinforced drinking (Pierce & Epling, 1995). This is the *Premack principle:* "Of any pair of responses or activities in which an individual engages, the more frequent one will reinforce the less frequent one" (Kazdin,

1994, p. 34). This implies that if drinking coffee is a high-frequency behavior and studying for tests is a low-frequency behavior, a student could be advised to drink coffee only after beginning work on the studying (Homme, 1965).

The Premack principle also works for one of the authors of this book, for whom watching mystery movies is a high-frequency behavior and writing chapters for a textbook is sometimes a low-frequency behavior. When I finish this section, I'm watching a Sherlock Holmes episode, but not before!

A clear advantage of self-reinforcement programs is that they can be applied to covert events, such as thoughts and fantasies (Homme, 1965). Someone troubled by obsessional thoughts with a depressive theme could be taught to extinguish or punish them. Someone who wishes to increase imagery of success and mastery could encourage this by positive reinforcement. The reinforcer could be a high-frequency activity, a tangible reward, or even a covert thought or fantasy itself.

Why did the development of behavioral self-control programs help confirm behavior therapists' interest in cognitive processes? Because many theorists found that describing self-control procedures purely in terms of conditioning processes was cumbersome, unsatisfactory, and unnecessary. The conditioning view was championed by Skinner (1953), who discussed self-control from a behavioristic vantage point, placing the term within quotation marks in his chapter heading for the topic. Acknowledging that a complete theory of human behavior must deal with the facts that people make choices and have some degree of self-determination, Skinner made the point that one can study people's behavior while they do these things. He argued that people control their own behavior in the same way that behavior is always controlled—by altering variables, like reinforcement, that influence behavior (Goldiamond, 1976; Skinner, 1953).

Although he recognized that self-control is an important fact to be reckoned with, Skinner maintained his emphasis on the control of behavior by the external environment. Referring to the behavior involved in self-control, Skinner wrote, "Eventually it must be accounted for with variables lying outside the individual" (1953, p. 229). But the behavior therapists who found self-control programs relevant to many problems presented by outpatients realized that these methods involved more than just conditioning. When clients themselves judge whether their behavior meets the requirements for reinforcement, and when they deliver reinforcement to strengthen their own behavior, it is hard to view this as a passive conditioning process. Clients' own appraisal of the situation interacts with their behavior and with the environment. Accordingly, the use of self-control procedures called attention to clients' cognitive processes and, in that sense, self-control techniques have contributed to the development of cognitive-behavioral therapy.

Summary

The origins of behavior therapists' interest in cognitive techniques and mechanisms are found in Bandura's (1969) theoretical work, in the development of covert conditioning procedures, in studies of placebo and expectancy effects, and in the use of self-control and self-management strategies. Bandura's (1977a, 1977b) later work on social learning theory has provided a strong theoretical basis for several behavioral interventions that take account of cognitive procedures and processes.

Basic Concepts

Social Learning Theory

Albert Bandura (1977b) developed *social learning theory* as a conceptual approach that combines conditioning and learning principles with ideas from observational learning and research on expectancy. In introducing his theory, he begins by criticizing the traditional psychodynamic approaches to understanding personality and behavior. Agreeing with many of the points made by Skinner (1953), Bandura finds it useless to look for the causes of behavior entirely inside the individual. For example, traditional personality theorists might argue that people bite their fingernails because of self-directed hostility. The behavior is caused by a motivational force in the person. But how do we know that the force exists? Presumably, because the people in question bite their fingernails. This is unsatisfactory, because the force is inferred from the behavior without any independent confirmation of its existence.

In any event, Bandura has pointed out, motivational forces inside people cannot explain the great variety of responses people display in different situations. A student may always be late for class. To infer from this that there is a generalized drive, or even trait, of tardiness means that one would expect the student to be late for soccer games, dates, and favorite television shows also. But this may or may not be the case.

Bandura's colleague Walter Mischel (1968) has provided a wealth of data to indicate that people tend to be consistent in their behavior over time in the same situation, but do not necessarily behave the same way in different situations. This is compatible, of course, with the idea of stimulus control and with Guthrie's (1935) hypothesis that people tend to repeat their previous behavior in the same situation. Yet Bandura also finds problems with concepts such as stimulus control. He certainly agrees that it has been productive to analyze behavior in terms of discriminative stimuli and reinforcers. Behavior that used to be seen as the product of unconscious motives has been shown to be influenced by environmental events. But viewing behavior as the product of external stimuli goes too far the other way: "It implies a one-way control process which reduces individuals to passive respondents to the vagaries of whatever influences impinge upon them" (Bandura, 1977b, p. 6). He criticizes the phrase *stimulus control* because it is not the stimulus that has changed so as to become controlling; rather, it is the person who has changed, because he or she has learned to expect certain results if a given stimulus appears.

Operant learning theorists recognize that people and animals can guide their behavior by judging overall patterns of stimuli over long time periods, and classical conditioning theorists acknowledge the role of cognitive factors such as expectancy in learning associations among stimuli (Rescorla, 1988). Bandura has suggested that it is fruitful to examine those cognitive factors. Having established that it is not useful to view people as being pushed around by unconscious motivational forces, Bandura argues that it is no more useful to view people as being buffeted around randomly by the environment. Why not conclude, then, that behavior is the joint product of the person and the environment?

If behavior is assumed to be determined separately by the environment and by personal factors in the individual, there is no recognition that the person and the environment influence each other. But even a behaviorist such as B. F. Skinner (1953) would accept the interaction of person and environment. As we have shown, in his discussion of self-control, he acknowledged that people can alter the environment that alters their behavior. It is more helpful to see behavior as the result of factors in the individual and factors in the environment, working in interaction.

How, then, is Bandura's view different from Skinner's? It is the nature of the interaction that is seen differently in operant learning theory and social learning theory. To Bandura, it is not enough to say that behavior is simply produced by a coalition of person and environment. Behavior itself is one of the interacting determinants. Behavior, the person, and the environment all influence, and are influenced by, each other. This interactional view, known as *reciprocal determinism*, gives more prominence to processes within the individual that influence, and are influenced by, behavior and environment. These include self-adjusting and symbolic processes, those that operate when one engages in self-control activities and talks to one's self covertly about one's situation and behavior. They are the same processes that allow people to learn vast amounts of information without having to go through the trials and errors of direct experience. That is, self-adjusting and symbolic processes allow us to learn by observation.

Observational Learning

Observational learning, or *modeling,* is given great prominence in Bandura's view of behavior change processes. Taken together with classical conditioning and operant learning, observational learning constitutes a form of "third force" that Bandura has contributed to behavior therapy. He has pointed out that it is hard to imagine how people could grow up to learn the language and customs of their society, within a lifetime, only by selective reinforcement: "One does not teach children to swim, adolescents to drive automobiles, and novice medical students to perform surgery by having them discover the appropriate behavior through the consequences of their successes and failures" (Bandura, 1977b, p. 12).

According to Bandura (1971), practically all of the learning that people can acquire through their own direct experience could also be acquired vicariously through modeling (that is, secondhand by observing someone else). The person watches someone else engaging in the behavior of interest and observes the consequences of the behavior to the model.

Modeling can have three principal effects: observational learning effects, inhibitory and disinhibitory effects, and response facilitation effects.

Observational Learning Effects.   The observer of the model may acquire a new behavior pattern by learning to combine previously learned responses in new ways. Most new behaviors are combinations of existing responses available to the person, but this does not necessarily mean that one is dealing with something trivial. After all, learning to play a piano concerto is a new combination of a variety of previously learned finger movements (Bandura, 1971). (Similarly, writing the Great American Novel would just be a matter of combining words already known into some appropriate sequence.) Bandura's view is that an observer can combine response elements into the new pattern at a symbolic level, which is possible because of the information conveyed by the model's behavior and its consequences.

Inhibitory and Disinhibitory Effects. Modeling can also encourage or discourage the observer's production of behavior already learned. The important element here is the consequence of the model's behavior to the model. Seeing somebody being stung by hornets after stumbling into their nest would probably deter you from doing the same thing. That would be an *inhibitory effect*. A *disinhibitory effect* is the result when a socially fearful child enters a playground after seeing a friend do so with rewarding consequences.

In a classic study of modeling, Bandura (1965) showed children a film in which an adult demonstrated the aggressive behaviors of hitting and kicking an inflatable doll. The children saw one of three versions of the film. In one version, the adult's aggression produced reinforcing consequences; in the second, the aggression was punished; and in the third, no consequences of the behavior were shown. Next, the children were given the opportunity to interact with the doll. Those that had seen the model being punished showed less aggression toward the doll than did the children who had seen the other versions of the film. Bandura confirmed separately that all of the children had *learned* the aggressive responses through watching the films, because they all hit or kicked the doll when an attractive incentive was given. But the point was that the children only *displayed* the aggressive behavior that they had at their command when the model had suffered no negative consequences for doing so (Craighead, Craighead, Kazdin, & Mahoney, 1994).

The disinhibitory effects of modeling have been studied in some treatment applications in which the aim is to reduce a client's anxiety. In this context, certain characteristics of the model are particularly important. A *mastery* model would be someone who displays no anxiety at all, moving effortlessly through a poised performance and showing complete mastery of the situation. A *coping* model would be someone who, like the fearful client, shows some anxiety at first, yet demonstrates how to deal with the situation satisfactorily despite some unease (Mahoney, 1980). In most applications of this kind, a coping model would seem more appropriate than a mastery model; in fact, the results of some studies have confirmed that coping models have a more therapeutic effect on the client (Mahoney & Arnkoff, 1978).

Response Facilitation Effects. People may be encouraged to perform socially accepted behavior by observing others "breaking the ice." The idea here is not that the behavior was inhibited in a general way or that the person did not know how to make the correct response; rather, the idea is that other people's behavior and its consequences can indicate the appropriateness of certain behavior in the particular context. For example, people who hesitate before beginning to applaud at the end of a concert until someone else starts to clap are presumably waiting to see if it is "all right" to do so.

Processes within Modeling. Observational learning is influenced by four processes. When they are operating to full effect, the most efficient learning occurs. First, *attention* is important. People will attend to the behavior of a model when it is worthwhile to do so, and therefore incentives are important. Second, *retention* of the modeled information is aided by imagery and verbal coding. Because of the amount of information that can be condensed into words, verbal coding is especially helpful. Third, *performance* of the learned behavior requires putting together the appropriate motor movements from the information gained by modeling. This immediately points up a limitation. Someone unskilled at playing a musical instrument will probably not gain sufficient information to reproduce the performance simply by watching an accomplished musician play a piece. The component skills of making the right muscle movements will have to be practiced. Nevertheless, modeling is important, as many would-be musicians who have had a human tutor as well as a book can testify. Finally, *motivation* determines whether the person will actually employ the behavior that has been modeled. Providing reinforcing consequences for imitation is usually helpful.

Self-Efficacy

An important component of social learning theory is the concept of *self-efficacy* (Bandura, 1977a, 1994, 1995). The concept developed as a result of Bandura's application of social learning theory to an understanding of clinical anxiety disorders. Most behavior therapists had agreed that classical conditioning and operant learning processes are involved when a client develops anxiety in a situation. As in the case of Susan B., whose phobia of spiders was described in Chapter 2, the assumption was that classical conditioning explains the development of anxiety, which in turn motivates the client's avoidance behavior. However, this theory has been contradicted by several experimental findings. One problem is that clients like Susan may continue to avoid their phobic situation even after their anxiety has substantially declined (through systematic desensitization, for example). If anxiety motivates avoidance, why does Susan continue to avoid spiders after her anxiety has been reduced?

Social learning theory predicts that the client's *expectations* play the central role in anxiety and avoidance. For example, despite the successful reduction of her phobic anxiety, Susan still may not trust herself to deal with real spiders because she is not sure she has all the needed skills at her command—she still lacks a realistic expectation of personal effectiveness, or self-efficacy, in the situation. She may be confident that her heart will not pound rapidly when she confronts a spider, but she may still doubt her ability to stand her ground if one crawls over her foot. Bandura's prediction is that any treatment that encourages an accurate sense of self-efficacy will be therapeutic.

An important distinction has to be made between procedure and process. In self-efficacy theory, the *process* through which behavior change operates is chiefly cognitive, whereas the *procedure* that may be necessary to activate that process will usually be behavioral (Wilson, 1982). For example, clients may successfully overcome phobias through a process of positive change in self-efficacy expectations, but the best method for achieving this change is likely to be a behavioral technique rather than a therapy based on verbal persuasion. The most effective way of instilling a strong sense of personal efficacy is through *mastery experiences* (Bandura, 1994, 1995). According to this theory, the mastery experiences fostered by the graduated real-life practice procedure provided Susan with the information necessary to increase her self-efficacy (and, thus, to reduce her avoidance of spiders). We will return to the topic of self-efficacy in Chapter 7 in our discussion of anxiety disorders.

Clinical Implications

Social learning theory provides behavior therapists with a conceptual framework for integrating treatments involving cognitive modification. Before reviewing the major cognitive treatment interventions, we will briefly focus on specific applications of observational learning principles to assertiveness problems, snake phobia, and test anxiety.

Assertiveness Training

Since the early work of Wolpe and Lazarus (1966), behavior therapists have routinely used modeling in combination with role-playing or behavior rehearsal to help certain clients develop social skills. (See the transcript of part of a treatment session with Frank T., presented at the end of Chapter 1, for an example.) Working in this tradition, Richard McFall and his colleagues conducted a series of studies of assertiveness training in order to establish essential treatment components (McFall & Marston, 1970; McFall & Lillesand, 1971; McFall & Twentyman, 1973).[2] Most people agree that appropriate self-assertion includes expressing feelings and opinions in a straightforward manner, insisting on being treated fairly and equitably by others, and refusing unreasonable requests (Dow, 1994).

In application to assertion in college volunteers, the modeling component proved less important to treatment effectiveness than the client's actual rehearsal of assertive responses with coaching and feedback from the therapist. This is consistent with research findings indicating that unassertive individuals usually *do* know what to say and how to say it. The problem is that the person typically focuses on inhibitory and discouraging self-statements in situations calling for self-assertion, such as "I might hurt the other person's feelings if I truly speak my mind," or "What if I try to be assertive but make a mess of it and end up looking foolish?" (Schwartz & Gottman, 1976; Thorpe, 1975). If the model simply demonstrates assertive responses (such as, "No, thank you, I do not wish to buy a new insurance policy today!"), this will not necessarily address the client's negative self-statements. Yet, when the client actually practices making assertive responses, the unhelpful self-statements often decline automatically and are replaced by more constructive cognitions. Both behavior rehearsal *and* a cognitive restructuring procedure that included the modeling and rehearsal of appropriate self-statements have proved successful in studies of assertiveness training (Thorpe, 1975; Thorpe, Freedman, & Lazar, 1985; Thorpe, Freedman, & McGalliard, 1984).

Snake Phobia

Several variations are possible within modeling. The procedures can be broadly divided into those involving live models (the person demonstrating the behavior is present with the client), symbolic models (the client watches a film or videotape of the model), and imaginal or covert modeling (the client imagines observing a model). All can be helpful, as indicated in the following examples.

Bandura, Blanchard, and Ritter (1969) treated snake phobia in a sample of volunteers who were randomly allocated to different experimental conditions. Subjects' fear levels were assessed before and after the treatment by means of a behavioral-avoidance test similar to the one used by Lang and Lazovik (1963; see Chapter 2). The volunteers also rated their attitudes toward snakes on several dimensions and completed a questionnaire surveying common fears. The treatment conditions were as follows.

In *symbolic modeling*, clients viewed a film showing people engaging in progressively more challenging encounters with snakes. The clients followed a procedure similar to systematic desensitization in which they relaxed during the film presentation and controlled the anxiety level produced by the material by stopping and reversing the film as necessary. In *participant modeling*, the clients took part in a procedure that combined the active guidance of a live model with graduated real-life practice. They observed the model handle the snake in various steps graded in their anxiety-provoking potential. Eventually, the clients learned to handle the snake themselves, with the model demonstrating at each step, then guiding the person as they performed the exercises together. Another group of clients received *systematic desensitization* in the usual fashion, imagining encounters with snakes in a graded hierarchy while relaxing deeply. A final group (test-retest) took part in the assessments but received no treatment.

The results, as assessed by the behavioral test, were that the test-retest participants showed no behavior change; systematic desensitization and symbolic modeling were clearly helpful in reducing the phobia; and participant modeling was strikingly successful, with 92 percent of the subjects completely relieved of the phobia. The attitude scales showed a similar pattern of findings. Live and symbolic modeling were both effective but in differing degrees. Notice that both of the modeling conditions in this experiment required participants to look at either filmed or live snakes; desensitization subjects, who imagined snakes, received no modeling. Another conclusion from this study, then, is that real-life exposure to snakes is highly therapeutic; symbolic and imagined exposure to snakes brings intermediate results; and no exposure brings no benefit at all.

Test Anxiety

In a study on covert modeling, Harris and Johnson (1983) treated 63 test-anxious students. The five experimental conditions included a test-retest group that received no treatment. The other students received eight 60-minute treatment sessions. The two chief treatment groups followed a *covert modeling* procedure, but one included academic imagery and the other did not. In other words, people in the covert modeling/nonacademic imagery group practiced developing fantasies in which they pictured themselves acting competently. The activity did not involve academic performance. People in the covert modeling/academic imagery group practiced imagery of personal academic success. The two other groups were subgroups that received relaxation training in addition to the other procedure for the group. Unfortunately, students in the test-retest group actually got worse (their grade point averages dropped) while the others received their treatment. All other participants improved, but the groups with nonacademic imagery did better than the others.

In conclusion, several forms of modeling have developed from Bandura's work, and they have proved helpful in numerous applications. More studies of modeling will be reviewed in the later chapters dealing with specific disorders.

Summary

Bandura's social learning theory emphasizes the reciprocal determinism among behavior, personal factors, and the environment. Rather than advocating treatments involving verbal persuasion, Bandura has demonstrated the wide range of applicability of observational learning methods. Social learning theory provides a theoretical context for cognitive-behavioral therapy.

Treatment Procedures

Now that we have outlined developments in behavior therapy that inspired an interest in cognitive processes, and given an overview of Bandura's social learning theory and his work on modeling, we will complete this chapter with a description of treatment techniques designed to help clients change their thinking patterns. We have used Bandura's work to provide a theoretical foundation for our discussion of cognitive modification techniques, but it is important to note that he emphasizes cognitive theoretical *processes,* not cognitive treatment *procedures,* in therapeutic change. Bandura does not place a high priority on treatments based on verbal persuasion, rational disputation, or self-statement modification; he favors procedures such as participant modeling that involve behavioral performance, on the grounds that they enjoy stronger empirical support.

Terminology is a problem. It is tempting to use *cognitive therapy* as a term for these approaches, but cognitive therapy is associated specifically with Beck's approach (Beck, 1976, 1995; Beck, Rush, Shaw, & Emery, 1979; Beck & Weishaar, 1995). Another possible generic name for these approaches is *cognitive restructuring*, but this term has been used chiefly by Lazarus (1995) in the context of his multimodal therapy. The phrase *cognitive-behavioral therapy,* as used by Meichenbaum (1995), is in common use and we shall use it as a general term in this chapter.

Meichenbaum, Ellis, Beck, Lazarus, and Goldfried are important figures in cognitive-behavioral therapy whose work on theory and technique has enriched the field. Their treatment techniques are described next.

Meichenbaum's Cognitive-Behavioral Therapy

Self-Instructional Training

Originally described as *cognitive-behavior modification (CBM),* Donald Meichenbaum's approach, summarized in a major book published in 1977, was stimulated by a couple of unexpected findings from two of his research projects. One study, his doctoral dissertation work, involved teaching inpatients with schizophrenia to talk appropriately in one-on-one conversations. By contrast with some of the studies we will review later in this book, this intervention produced lasting results that generalized to other settings. What was particularly interesting was the method used by some of the patients to produce the appropriate behavior. They repeated to themselves the instructions that had been given them by the experimenter ("give healthy talk," "be relevant," etc.). In effect, the patients were using helpful self-instructions to guide their behavior appropriately (Meichenbaum, 1977). Encouraged by this unexpected finding, Meichenbaum went on to develop this technique, originally known as *self-instructional training,* and to apply it to impulsive children and other clinical groups (Meichenbaum & Goodman, 1971).

Another important research finding emerged when Meichenbaum and his colleagues attempted to correct a flaw in Paul's (1966) study of treatments for speech anxiety. Recall from Chapter 2 that Paul had compared systematic desensitization (SD) with the psychodynamic insight therapy normally practiced by the therapists in his study. Although he had described SD precisely, so that other researchers could easily replicate the procedures in their own work, the insight therapy was described only in the most general way. The reason for this lies largely in the nature of insight therapy techniques, which are hard to specify clearly in practical terms; yet, the fact remained that it was unclear what, exactly, SD had been compared with in the Paul study. Meichenbaum, Gilmore, and Fedoravicius (1971) sought to conduct a better test of SD versus insight. They selected a form of insight therapy that could be defined quite clearly and devised an experimental version of it to compare with SD. The insight therapy in question was then known as *rational-emotive therapy (RET)* (Ellis, 1962), an approach widely viewed as involving insight but which has its roots in philosophy rather than in psychoanalysis.

The treatments in the Meichenbaum (1971) study were conducted in groups, not in individual treatment sessions, and the experimental version of RET, labeled *self-instructional training* in the study, replaced the insight therapy. Otherwise, the procedures were very similar to Paul's. The results, however, were quite different, in that both treatments were effective and produced impressive results. There was even an indication that self-instructional training might be especially useful in treating generalized, rather than specific, social anxiety. Meichenbaum and his colleagues had discovered a procedure that was as effective as a popular behavioral technique, but that relied on persuading people to alter their views on their situation rather than on anxiety reduction or direct behavior change.

Self-instructional training has been applied to speech anxiety, impulsivity in children, and inappropriate behavior in patients with schizophrenia (Meichenbaum, 1977). In all of these applications, the results were impressive and often showed greater generalization than the results of operant learning procedures. Initially, Meichenbaum emphasized the *insight* aspect of the procedure. In the speech anxiety study, for example, the therapists dealt mostly with the subjects' unhelpful beliefs and explained to them that thinking along discouraging lines could itself create anxiety. During a pretreatment speech before a group of people, conducted as a test of anxiety, the subjects had had private trains of thought like these: "What if I make a mess of this speech? I know I'm no good at speaking; this is just going to be a horrible experience. Why can't I be normal?" In therapy sessions, clients were urged to realize that it was distinctly unhelpful to think along such lines. Later in the treatment, and in an unstructured way, the therapists began to suggest alternative, helpful attitudes, such as, "Even if I'm not the world's greatest public speaker, I can give it my best shot and hope for the best. After all, what's the worst that can happen?" Meichenbaum's later work emphasized clients' rehearsal of helpful, encouraging attitudes of this kind.

Stress Inoculation Training

The success of treatment based on altering self-instructions, and the strong indications that it led to generalized improvement in coping skills, encouraged Meichenbaum (1977) to pursue the idea of a "preventive" treatment. Rather than aiming treatment at a specific problem that had already developed, he sought to devise a procedure that would equip clients with the skills needed to forestall potential problems. He labeled the new method *stress inoculation training SIT.* (This is one of the procedures that was used with Martin, the client with anxiety attacks whose treatment was briefly noted at the beginning of this chapter.)

The SIT procedure progresses through three phases. In the *educational* phase, the client is given an explanation of the role of unhelpful thinking patterns in producing and maintaining unpleasant emotions and dysfunctional behavior. In the *rehearsal* phase, the client practices making coping self-statements designed to help deal with stressful events. In the application phase, the client practices using the coping skills while confronting actual stressors. An example of a real stressor used in the training is the cold pressor test, in which the participant immerses a hand and arm in ice-cold water for as long as possible (that is, until the discomfort becomes unbearable). After rehearsal training, volunteers were able to keep their arms immersed in the water for significantly longer periods than people who had not received the training, indicating that the procedure increases people's resilience in tolerating stressful stimuli.

One helpful application of stress inoculation was its use in anger control (Novaco, 1975). As in other applications of stress inoculation, the rehearsal phase is divided into four elements: preparing for a stressor, confronting and handling a stressor, coping with the sense of being overwhelmed by the stressor, and self-congratulation after having dealt with the stressful experience. Novaco's subjects were angry young men who were easily provoked into aggression. An example of a stressor for one client was another man looking at him in an unfriendly way. Typically, the client would rapidly become consumed by thoughts of being judged, belittled, and put down by the other man, and the usual result was a fistfight and an arrest for disorderly conduct.

The new self-statements that the client would practice in therapy were similar to the following:

1. *Preparing* (when about to enter a bar, for example): "I can develop a plan to deal with this situation so that I won't lose control."
2. *Confronting* (another man looks at him insolently): "I can handle this without losing my cool. I won't give him the satisfaction of getting upset."
3. *Feeling overwhelmed* (the man picks a fight with him): "Even now, I can still cope. It's a strong provocation, but I can relax and defuse this situation. All I need do is keep a cool head."
4. *Self-congratulation* (leaving, after having handled the situation): "I handled that really well, considering that I have had such a problem with this. Wait till I tell my therapist!"

Constructive Narrative

Recently, Meichenbaum (1995) has commented on the metaphorical nature of the theories that are used to explain behavior change. For example, he suggested that the first common metaphor in the field was *conditioning*, in which theorists viewed clients' cognitions as subject to the same laws as overt behaviors. Next came *information processing,* in which cognitions were seen as operating similarly to computer software programs. The latest metaphor is that of *constructive narrative*, in which clients came to be viewed as "narrators, storytellers and makers of meaning" (Meichenbaum, 1995, p. 149). Using this metaphor, therapists help their clients to alter their stories, to reframe stressful events in their lives, to "normalize" their experiences, to develop a "healing theory" of what happened, and ultimately to build new "assumptive worlds" and new ways to view themselves. Treatment based on this model has elements in common with contemporary brief psychodynamic therapy, and Meichenbaum is optimistic about the potential for the ultimate integration of psychodynamic and cognitive-behavioral therapy.

Ellis's Rational Emotive Behavior Therapy

Albert Ellis (1962) developed his psychotherapeutic technique in the 1950s under the original name of *rational-emotive therapy (RET)* (see also Ellis, 1988; Ellis & Harper, 1975; Walen, DiGiuseppe, & Dryden, 1992). (A form of RET was used in the treatment of Martin, the client mentioned at the beginning of this chapter.) Although Meichenbaum's work helped to bring RET to the attention of behavior therapists in the early 1970s, Ellis worked entirely independently of behavior therapy at first, and his approach was usually bracketed with psychoanalysis as an insight therapy. This is ironic, because Ellis had been trained in psychodynamic therapy initially yet rejected it after growing more and more dissatisfied with its poor practical results. His work on RET sprang from his earlier interest in philosophy, particularly the work of the Stoics (early Greek and Roman philosophers like Epictetus and Marcus Aurelius). They had put forward the view that people can more or less put up with any adversity without undue sorrow. The technique? Acknowledge, they argued, that it is not *events* that disturb people. It is, instead, their *view* of those events that makes for misery or unhappiness (or, for that matter, pleasure or joy).

Ellis's therapy aims at persuading clients to dispute the unhelpful views that make then anxious, depressed, or angry. Although the approach is most closely identified with the rational disputation of irrational ideas, Ellis (1979) has claimed that his technique not only involves cognitive modification but also embraces most of the techniques of behavior therapy, especially real-life activity assignments, self-management procedures, and homework exercises. For this reason, he has renamed the approach *rational emotive behavior therapy (REBT)* in his most recent writings (Ellis, 1995).

Ellis characterizes his philosophy and technique as follows:

> *REBT is a cognitive-emotive-behavioristic method of psychotherapy uniquely designed to enable people to observe, understand, and persistently dispute their irrational, grandiose, perfectionistic* shoulds, oughts, *and* musts. *It employs the logico-empirical method of science to encourage people to surrender magic, absolutes, and damnation; to acknowledge that nothing is sacred or all-important (although many things are exceptionally unpleasant and inconvenient); and to gradually teach themselves and to practice the philosophy of desiring rather than demanding and of working at changing what they can change and gracefully putting up with what they cannot. (Ellis, 1995, p. 194)*

In the traditional REBT format, the therapist begins with the disturbing emotion presented by the client. To Ellis, this is the emotional *consequence*, the last step (C) in a progression of three (A, B, and C). Clients tend to believe that C is caused by A, which is the *activating event* that triggers the sequence. As examples of A and C, imagine that an inconsiderate driver joins the road in such a way that the client has to slam on the brakes in order to avoid an accident. The client flies into a rage. The behavior of the first driver is A; the client's rage is C. The client believes that A causes C. Ellis, however, would urge the client to reject that idea and realize that it is B, not A, that causes C. What is B? It is the *beliefs* that the client entertains about A.

Ellis argues that these beliefs are of two kinds, rational (rBs) and irrational (iBs). The *rational beliefs* include the following: "I don't like this; I would prefer this not to have happened. I would like to change this situation if only I could. However, practically, I cannot do that; and, since I do not control everything that happens in the world, I shall work on putting up with it as gracefully as possible. I can cope with this if I put my mind to it." If the client left it at that, the resulting emotion would probably be irritation, annoyance, and displeasure, rather than rage or blind fury. Irritation is fairly easy to cope with, but rage is not. Rage and fury would probably be the result of the *irrational beliefs,* which go something like this: "It is essential that I always get what I want. Therefore, it must not happen that I get inconvenienced, or not treated the way I like. But I just *did* get inconvenienced. This situation, then, is an impossibility—an unheard-of crisis that cannot be withstood or handled. In other words, the other driver should not have done that; something that should not have happened actually happened, it's a terrible state of affairs; because it's terrible, more than just bad, I cannot possibly stand it (or stand for it)."

The therapist moves to D in the progression, the *disputation* of irrational beliefs, pointing out that these beliefs are unrealistic and unhelpful. To challenge the damaging beliefs, the therapist will ask the client to confront questions such as: "Why *must* things go the way you want? (You might *prefer* things to be a certain way, there's no problem with that; but why *must* they be the way you want?) Why is it *terrible* if things do not go your way? (Awkward, yes; inconvenient, yes; a pain in the neck, yes; but hardly terrible!) And why can you not *stand* it? (It takes a bit of putting up with, granted; you don't like it, sure; it gives you a bit of a workout to put up with it, admitted; but you *can* stand it!)"

Ellis advocates his technique as applicable to practically any problem, because the client is always displeased or dissatisfied with something. That means that REBT can be applied to the client's negative emotional state, whatever it is, by identifying and disputing the irrational beliefs about the situation. In fact, according to Ellis, everyone is prone to think irrationally. In U.S. society, people are generally raised in such a way that they tend to believe statements such as, "I must always be loved and approved of by people" or "Any failure is disastrous." Such beliefs are echoed in nursery rhymes, television commercials, and popular songs. Many behavior therapists are sympathetic to Ellis's views but remain cautious about the scientific standing of REBT.

Ellis' (1979) description of REBT as including the whole of behavior therapy certainly makes it a holistic approach, but it also makes it extremely hard to test. (How can one test an approach that encompasses every technique in behavior therapy?) Some empirical findings have been very encouraging. Trexler and Karst (1972) found REBT effective with speech-anxious students, for example. In another study, three variants of REBT were compared with relaxation training plus counseling, and with no treatment, in 50 Community Mental Health Center outpatients (Lipsky, Kassinove, & Miller, 1980). Measures of rational thinking, neuroticism, depression, and anxiety showed that REBT brought greater benefit than the other conditions. This study is important because it dealt with genuine clients who had sought therapy, not with student volunteers. Finally, REBT was the subject of a recent critical appraisal by a team of philosophers and psychologists who have examined its conceptual and empirical standing (Bernard & DiGiuseppe, 1989). Some of the contributors to that volume concluded that Ellis has overstated the level of empirical support and scientific validation enjoyed by his method (Haaga & Davison, 1989; Meichenbaum, 1995), and others find fault with its conceptual bases (Lazarus, 1989), but the tone of these evaluations of REBT is generally positive.

Beck's Cognitive Therapy

The other leading cognitive-behavioral approach to have developed independently of behavior therapy is the *cognitive therapy* of Aaron T. Beck, a psychiatrist who is best known for his work on depression. The theory, technique, and empirical standing of cognitive therapy have been detailed in several books and chapters (Beck, 1976, 1991/1995; Beck, Emery, & Greenberg, 1985; Beck, Rush, Shaw, & Emery, 1979; Beck & Weishaar, 1995; Dobson & Shaw, 1995; Freeman & Reinecke, 1995). This work is discussed more fully in Chapter 8.

Cognitive therapy and rational emotive behavior therapy have some features in common. Both were developed in the 1950s, both involve exploring unhelpful beliefs, and the originators of both were trained in psychodynamic therapy. Beck rejected psychoanalytic theory because he did not agree with the notion that depressed clients displayed retroflected hostility (or "anger turned inwards"). His experience with depressed outpatients led him to see the potential of exploring, and changing, unadaptive belief systems. This is achieved not only by a form of rational disputation, as in REBT, but also by encouraging the client to attempt specific "experiments" in real life to help challenge the faulty assumptions. For example, a depressed woman whose boyfriend had left her concluded that no one could like her, let alone love her (see the case of Mindy, noted in the first few pages of this book). At the urging of the therapist, she made a deliberate attempt to meet 10 people in one week, in order to find out experimentally how many of them would reject her. Predictably enough, she was not rejected by all of these people, and the results of that experiment were used as data with which to challenge the general, negative assumption she had made. Central to Beck's cognitive therapy model are three fundamental concepts, to which we turn next.

The Cognitive Triad

When a client is in a depressive episode he or she typically dwells on negative or pessimistic thoughts about the self, the world, and the future (e.g., "I am no good; the situation is bleak and dispiriting; and there's no hope of it changing for the better"). Self, world, and future form the *cognitive triad* of negative thoughts that require examination in every case of depression (Beck & Weishaar, 1995; Freeman & Reinecke, 1995).

Cognitive Schemas

Beck noticed that depressive clients tend to interpret their experiences on the basis of absolute beliefs, such as "I am unlovable." Such beliefs were labeled by Beck as *cognitive schemas*.[3] Any event that could possibly be relevant to such a belief would immediately be interpreted in terms of the schema (Beck, 1991/95). For example, if Mindy were in a depressive episode, and her boyfriend did not call her in the evening as promised, she would conclude that this was irrefutable evidence of her unlovableness. Beck's view is that such schemas are only active during episodes of disturbance, as in a depressive episode, and are dormant between episodes. A schema could develop early in life in response to a significant event; for example, when your best friend moves out of state when you are seven years old you could conclude "Whenever you really get to like someone, they desert you." According to the theory, if a similar event occurs later in life, it could precipitate a depressive episode.

Cognitive Distortions

Clients experience specific *cognitive distortions* during depressive episodes. Beck lists several of these, each of which, like *selective abstraction*, refers to an exaggeration of the negative aspects of a situation (further examples are described in Chapter 9). For example, a depressive client had been dreading her annual performance evaluation at work, and she told her therapist how it went at their next therapy session. "I knew it would be awful, and it was," she said. The therapist asked for more details. "I have a terrible telephone manner," she replied through her tears. The therapist eventually elicited the following.

The work performance evaluation had 10 parts, dealing with such matters as punctuality, general professionalism, work output, interpersonal effectiveness, and so forth. Each of the ten parts could be rated out of 10 points. The client had received 10 out of 10 on 9 items, but on the last the supervisor had said: "I had to find something for you to work on, but your performance has been so good that it was difficult. Perhaps you could try to terminate phone calls from customers a little quicker; you're too polite with them sometimes!" This was the "awful" event that had so troubled the client—a work performance evaluation that had been 97 percent perfect!

According to Beck's model of depression, the scene is set by the development, early in life, of a negative schema concerning loss, personal worthlessness, or the like. This schema is triggered in later years with the occurrence of a relevant event. The client enters a depressive episode, and the cognitive triad and the various cognitive distortions emerge. Treatment is focused on gently challenging the negative thoughts and encouraging the client to test the pessimistic assumptions empirically.

Several studies have provided support for Beck's theoretical postulates. The general idea that certain thinking patterns correlate with certain mood states has been substantiated in a series of investigations. LaPointe and Harrell (1978) developed a questionnaire on thoughts and feelings and tested it with a college population.

A later version of the questionnaire (Harrell, Chambless, & Calhoun, 1981) presented volunteers with vignettes about common situations involving frustrations or disappointments; the students indicated which thoughts and feelings they would likely have if they were in the situation in real life. For example, a vignette might read, "Suppose you entered one of your paintings in an art contest. You had high hopes of winning first prize, but you did not even get an honorable mention" (after Harrell et al., 1981). Next, the participants would indicate how likely it would be for them to experience each of a group of feelings and each of a group of thoughts. The feelings were angry, suspicious, anxious, depressed, and concerned. An example of a thought that most often correlated with a "depressed" feeling was: "I may as well give up on art. I knew, deep down, that I would fail. I seem to fail at most things, in fact. It's hardly worth trying anything any more."

This study was repeated with psychiatric inpatients and outpatients as well as with two "normal" groups (Thorpe, Barnes, Hunter, & Hines, 1983; Thorpe, Parker, & Barnes, 1992). The same relationships between thoughts and feelings were found in all groups, but the clients and patients endorsed the negative thoughts and feelings more strongly than students and hospital staff members. The results were consistent with Beck's hypothesis that each feeling has a corresponding group of thoughts or ideas (Beck, Laude, & Bohnert, 1974). Experimental work on cognitive therapy with depressed clients is reviewed in Chapter 9.

Lazarus's Cognitive Restructuring

The *multimodal therapy (MMT)* of Lazarus (1973, 1976, 1995) was introduced briefly in Chapter 1. Lazarus recommends that clinicians attend to seven modalities of client functioning in assessment and treatment, modalities whose initials spell out the acronym BASIC I.D.: Behavior, Affect, Sensation, Imagery, Cognition, Interpersonal Relations, and Drugs/Diet. Among these, Lazarus has given some prominence to the *cognitive* modality. As examples of *cognitive restructuring,* Lazarus (1995) cited: "Changes in dichotomous reasoning, self-downing, overgeneralization, categorical imperatives, non sequiturs, and excessive desires for approval" (p. 341). By including cognition in his list of modalities, Lazarus helped put cognitive procedures "on the map" within behavior therapy.

The actual techniques Lazarus has used in cognitive restructuring seem very similar to REBT and to cognitive therapy. For example, Lazarus (1973) helped a client deal with distressing thoughts like "I am inferior, evil, and deserve to suffer" by means of rational disputation and *corrective self-talk* (p. 409). Like Beck, he also addresses errors in the *form* of the thinking as well as in the content. In other words, the clients' overgeneralizations would be handled in therapy by examining the illogic involved in detail so that the client understands the error and how to correct it. Lazarus would also include in the cognitive modality areas of ignorance or misinformation, such as a client's lack of knowledge about sexuality. This form of cognitive restructuring has been described by Wolpe (1958, 1982, 1990) as *correcting misconceptions.*

Goldfried's Coping and Problem Solving

The cognitive-behavioral orientation owes a great deal to the work of Marvin Goldfried (1980) as well as to the other theorists noted earlier. Taking a broader perspective than most others, Goldfried suggests that clients need more than specific solutions to particular problems. A client who is afraid of cats could be treated by systematic desensitization, for example, to have the fear "removed." But this would not necessarily give the client the skills needed to handle any other anxieties that might happen to arise in the course of a rich and varied life. Instead of treating specific issues one by one, why not teach the client how to solve problems in general? This would involve teaching the client *coping skills.*

D'Zurilla and Goldfried (1971) have described the general use of problem solving as a therapeutic strategy. It has potential applications in many areas of client functioning. It involves encouraging the client to adopt an active attitude toward a life problem so that he or she can step back and think about it, define it, generate alternative solutions, make a decision, and try it out. The approach has some similarities with the self-instructional training technique that Meichenbaum and Cameron (1973) used to improve the attention, thinking, and language use of inpatients with schizophrenia. That approach had involved teaching the clients to stop, think ahead, remind themselves of the task at hand, and so on. We shall review problem-solving applications in later chapters, particularly in Chapter 14.

Goldfried's (1980) use of coping skills training encompasses anything from physical health and fitness to dealing with the larger community. He focuses on four areas in particular: problem solving, relaxation, cognitive restructuring, and communication skills. In his discussion of relaxation, for example, he criticizes systematic desensitization for placing the client in such a passive role. Instead of carefully protecting the client from anxiety, Goldfried argues, the therapist would do better to encourage the client to accept anxiety and learn to cope with it during the treatment session. This would equip him or her far better for the real world. Peter Lewinsohn's psychoeducational group approach to teach coping skills to individuals at risk for depression is consistent with Goldfried's model (Hollon & Carter, 1994).

Summary

The various cognitive restructuring procedures have a great deal in common with one another, and the theorists who presented them agree in giving greater responsibility to the client for self-management and in rejecting the idea that clients have to be treated as passive consumers of the healing powers of the therapist. We will review evidence bearing on the effectiveness of these methods in later chapters.

Chapter Summary

Behavior therapists were inspired to examine cognitive techniques and processes by the theoretical work of Bandura and by the development of covert conditioning, treatments capitalizing on clients' expectancies, and self-control and self-management programs. Bandura's social learning theory embraces the three key variables of behavior, personal factors, and the environment. In this model, behavioral procedures are viewed as effective methods for influencing cognitive factors, like self-efficacy, that are among the mainsprings of behavior. Observational learning processes are at the root of effective therapy methods such as participant modeling.

Procedures aimed at altering clients' thinking styles include cognitive-behavior modi-fication, rational emotive behavior therapy, cognitive therapy, cognitive restructuring, and coping and problem-solving training. Therapists who use these cognitive restructuring tech-niques believe that clients are able to take more responsibility for their own self-manage-ment, and do not need to be "cured" in a passive sense by the therapist.

Endnotes

1. Not the real name of an actual client, of course. This example is drawn from three or four clients, one of whom participated in the study that was mentioned.
2. Later work by this group is discussed in Chapter 14.
3. Taken from the Greek word *schema* (singular). The Greek plural is *schemata,* but Beck uses *schemas* (1991/95, pp. 304–305).

Chapter 5

Research Methods
in Behavior Therapy

One of the chief characteristics of behavior therapy is its commitment to scientific evaluation. The main targets of study are (1) identifying the origins of problem behavior, (2)
assessing the effectiveness of behavioral treatments, and (3) describing the processes of
behavior change (Levis, 1982). These targets can be pursued in routine clinical work with
individuals and in broader research studies to test general hypotheses about behavior therapy.
Sometimes experimental work with an individual can shed light on general issues in the
field; this approach, *single-subject*[1] *methodology*, has been a distinctive contribution of
behavior therapists from the beginning (Shapiro, 1966; Yates, 1970). When clients or patients take part in research to test hypotheses about treatment in general, important ethical
issues are raised.

Ethical Issues in Research

There is always the potential for conflict between advancing knowledge through research
and risking discomfort or harm to the participants (American Psychological Association,
1982). Concerns about possible negative effects are multiplied when the participants are
members of vulnerable groups, such as the mentally retarded. Some of the potential problems "failure to obtain informed consent, concealment and deception, exposure to stressful
procedures and possible harm, invasion of privacy, withholding of potentially beneficial
experiences from members of a control group . . . raise important ethical issues" (American Psychological Association, 1982, p. 17).

In the United States, behavior therapists who are psychologists follow the *Ethics Code*
of the American Psychological Association (1992), which clearly insists that the welfare of
the participant always takes priority: "This Code . . . has as its *primary goal* the welfare
and protection of the individuals and groups with whom psychologists work" (p. 1599;

emphasis added). To guarantee this, researchers must take steps to implement appropriate protections for participants, and ensure that they are fully informed about possible risks and benefits, that they freely decide whether to take part, and that they are assured of their right to withdraw at any time without penalty. It is expected that participants will emerge unharmed from the study, preferably having received definite personal benefit. Following the Ethics Code guarantees at least a minimal level of protection to participants, but researchers still need to take responsibility for continuing to educate themselves further about the ethical conduct of research (Sieber, 1994).

Behavior Therapy Research and Clinical Practice

It is unrealistic to expect all clinical practitioners to be active research investigators, yet it is possible for behavior therapists to produce important research data in their routine clinical work (Barlow, 1980; Wilson, 1981). Several methods are available for this purpose. Those described later in this chapter include clinical series, single-case experiments, multiple baseline designs, and crossover studies. Single-case experiments are especially suitable for use in a clinical setting (Barlow & Hersen, 1984; see also Craighead, Craighead, Kazdin, & Mahoney, 1994; Kazdin, 1994).

Some general questions about therapy can be answered only by studies of groups of clients, however. Examples are What causes social withdrawal in patients hospitalized for schizophrenia? Which treatments are generally most helpful for people with anorexia nervosa? How does systematic desensitization work? Each of these questions requires investigation with more than one participant if the researcher hopes to generalize the findings to other people. Ideally, the therapist/researcher would study people similar to those to whom the results will be applied, such as a series of outpatients referred for routine therapy (e.g., Lipsky, Kassinove, & Miller, 1980) or inpatients hospitalized for depression (e.g., Dobson & Shaw, 1986). Where this is not possible, the researcher can conduct an *analogue study*, a study of a sample of people with mild disorders who were recruited specifically for the experiment. An example would be a group of college students with fears of snakes, when the research topic is to discover the "active ingredients" in systematic desensitization (e.g., Davison, 1968a).

In this chapter, we will describe the chief research methods used in behavior therapy. First, we will outline some of the issues concerning scientific methods in general.

Scientific Methods

There are many avenues to knowledge, and the scientific approach is just one of them. The choice of method is influenced by the scholar's goals. If the scholar is a psychoanalytic therapist who wishes to study symbolic meanings, the preferred method might be more similar to techniques of literary criticism or deciphering ancient languages than to experimental science (Cheshire, 1975). Valid as such approaches may be in the service of that particular goal, they clearly differ from the scientific approach that has been a distinctive feature of behavior therapy. Gordon Paul (1969) characterizes that approach as follows: "It seems generally agreed . . . that all scientific research consists of a special way of answering questions such that the knowledge obtained, and the *means* by which the knowledge was obtained, are public, demonstrable, reproducible, and communicable" (p. 35; original emphasis).

Skinner (1953) noted that science is unique among avenues to knowledge in that it makes cumulative progress. Proponents of behavior therapy argue that its strong commitment to a scientific approach has been the single-most important factor in its success. It is largely the work of behavior therapists that has dramatically improved the quality and quantity of psychological treatment research in recent years (Wilson, 1981).

Key Principles

Scientific goals include description and explanation. Scientific methods vary from one field of study to another, but there are some common elements. These have been summarized by Anderson (1966) in a list of 6 "rules" or *key principles:* operational definition, generality, controlled observation, repeated observations, confirmation, and consistency. The first four deal with description, the last two with explanation.

Operational Definition

Psychological research involves studying *variables*. Logically enough, a variable is anything that can vary, such as participants' clinical status as clients or students, their anxiety level, or the frequency with which they display disruptive behavior. In order to communicate to others exactly how a researcher defines such variables in his or her studies, the researcher specifies how he or she decided on someone's clinical status, anxiety level, or disruptiveness. For example, in a study of depression in clinical and nonclinical settings, *clinical status* might be defined by the participant's location (e.g., inpatients were those participants who were receiving treatment in a state hospital ward; outpatients were clients of a Community Health Health Center; and students were members of an Introductory Psychology class at the college). Similarly, in a study of social phobia among students, *anxiety level* might be defined by the person's score on a 30-item true/false questionnaire on social anxiety, and in a study of hyperactivity in first-graders, *disruptiveness* might be defined by the number of times within a five-minute observation period that a child was out of his or her seat in the classroom, as agreed upon by two independent raters. These examples all reflect some level of *operational definition,* which means defining concepts by describing the actual techniques of measurement used in the study (Gold, 1984).

To take one of Anderson's examples, a researcher might measure anxiety by means of the skin conductance response, a pattern of changes in the electrical conductance of the skin of the participant's hand, as measured by a polygraph. The operational definition of anxiety involves specifying the operations involved in identifying anxiety in the study, as follows: Attach two electrodes to the palm of the participant's nondominant hand; pass a tiny, undetectable current through the electrodes; and measure the skin's conductance by means of a microammeter. Anxiety could be defined as a given proportionate increase in conductance, as measured by the above procedure (Anderson, 1966). (In the Results section of the journal article describing the study, the researcher would specify the actual level of the current in microamperes and would supply the make and model number of the electrodes and the polygraph.)

Without operational definition, it could easily be unclear to readers of the research report exactly what was meant by "anxiety" in a study like this. As you will see in a later chapter, it makes a great deal of difference whether anxiety is defined by a questionnaire score, by observation of the person's behavior, or by recording skin conductance, because results can vary widely depending on the definition used. The fact that discrepant results are produced by these varied methods can have significant implications for theory and treatment of a disorder (Barlow, 1988; Lang, 1985; Street & Barlow, 1994).

Generality

The principle of operational definition illustrates the value of being specific in scientific description. Yet, "being specific" can have its disadvantages. A behavior therapist who tests a new treatment for depression with a group of outpatients would like to apply the results to other clients who were not in the research sample, for instance. Researchers have to be careful not to exaggerate the generality of their findings. In therapy outcome research, in particular, there is the danger of assuming, incorrectly, that the clients and therapists in the study are typical of all other clients and therapists (Kiesler, 1966; Martindale, 1978). The principle of *generality* reminds the researcher to collect data so that the conclusions reached may safely be generalized to other situations. In the example of the depression study, generalization would be increased by selecting a representative cross-section of depressed people[2] for the investigation. The researcher could identify all new clients referred for treatment of depression to a community clinic, and invite every third one to take part in the study, making sure that the participants include females and males and a wide range of age groups, ethnic identifications, and education levels.

Before being ready to accept that a new treatment is helpful for most people with a particular disorder, clinicians would want to see some evidence that the treatment has helped a certain number of people. Within a particular study, statistical methods are used to assess the likelihood that behavior change due to treatment really is a notable trend rather than a chance result. But how many studies with favorable results are necessary before a new treatment technique is generally accepted? The recent controversy about *eye movement desensitization and reprocessing (EMDR),* reviewed in Chapter 8, partly involves a dispute about the appropriate generalization of research findings (Greenwald, 1996).

Controlled Observation

Making observations is a vital part of any research project, but observation in itself does not guarantee that the results will be intelligible. *Controlled observation* refers to (1) standardizing the conditions of observation (e.g., to ensure that the different participants all respond to the same set of stimuli or that different research associates follow the same protocol in making behavioral ratings) and (2) regulating the variables in the study so as to narrow the list of factors that may be operating. Controlled observation permits one to make clear conclusions about which variables have an effect on participants' behavior.

For example, if a patient is admitted to a hospital for treatment of schizophrenia, it is possible to conduct experiments to test the effectiveness of different interventions. If a particular medication is administered for a trial period and then withdrawn, researchers may be able to detect changes in the patient's behavior coinciding with changes in the treatment. Controlled observation is operating here because the medication, the variable of interest, is altered deliberately by the experimenter. However, it is also important to account for other variables that may be associated with the treatment. If taking medication also involves lengthy conversations with a sympathetic staff member about such matters as the patient's current symptoms, medication side effects, or general adjustment to life on the ward, then it is always possible that the conversations themselves may be responsible for any therapeutic improvement. Controlling the "conversation" variable by dispensing the medication with only minimal social contact would test the idea that the conversations were responsible for the patient's changed behavior.

Repeated Observations
The hypothesis that a given variable has an effect on behavior receives additional support (at least, it escapes being contradicted) each time the predicted effect is observed. If a psychologist has the idea that contingent praise might reinforce speaking in a mute inpatient, it is likely that more than one observation would be required to settle the matter. If the patient spoke once following a single reinforcement trial, it is possible that the speech was a random event. But if, after a long series of observations, it was shown that every time the reinforcement contingency was in effect, the patient produced coherent speech, the psychologist would justifiably be more confident that the reinforcement was responsible. Yet, although repeated observations are necessary to establish that the behavior change is a dependable phenomenon, not a random event, they are not sufficient to confirm the truth of the particular theory the researcher is testing.

Confirmation
Predictions derived from a theory have to prove successful if the theory is to survive. Consider the theory that people with phobias of dogs have received a form of classical conditioning, so that dogs have become conditioned stimuli for anxiety. A prediction from this theory is that therapy based on extinction will prove effective. In fact, therapy of this kind *is* effective, so the theory survives so far.

Unfortunately, successful predictions are not sufficient to *confirm* the theory from which they are drawn. The fact that treatment based on extinction works is *consistent* with a conditioning explanation of specific phobias, but does not verify it. Aspirin works as a treatment for headaches, but in itself that proves nothing about the causes of head pain. It certainly does not prove that headaches are caused by aspirin deficiency, for example (Marks, 1981a, 1981b).

Even hundreds of successful predictions from a theory cannot confirm its truth definitively, but a single *unsuccessful* prediction may be enough to disprove it. As Anderson (1966) explained it, if one assumes that rain always results in the streets being wet, then observing that the streets are wet *could* mean that it is raining—but it could also mean that there is a burst water pipe under the pavement. Observing that the streets are *not* wet, by contrast, clearly proves that it is not raining. To take a clinical example, if a behavior therapist claimed that all bizarre behavior is caused by reinforcement, someone could disprove that idea simply by finding one patient who displays bizarre behavior without having had that reinforcement history. It seems to run counter to common sense, but by far the most helpful information is gained when observations are able to contradict theories in this way. As a general scientific strategy, trying to disprove a theory is more informative than seeking to sustain it (Mahoney, 1977; Mahoney & DeMonbreun, 1977).

Consistency

Finally, the principle of *consistency* applies when scientists have to fit new findings into the context of other information from controlled research. If two results contradict each other, then the assumption is that one of them must be false. Attempting to understand discrepant findings can advance knowledge by pointing the way to new research and to new ways of thinking about the problem. For example, in an analogue study, Davison (1968a) found that the full systematic desensitization "package" was necessary to reduce a specific phobia; yet, in a study with clinic clients, Gillan and Rachman (1974) showed that the relaxation component was unnecessary. These contradictory findings can be reconciled by considering the different participant groups in the two studies and by recognizing that results from student volunteers cannot always be generalized to clients in clinical settings.

Correlational and Experimental Approaches

Regardless of the specific research method used, the researcher seeks to test a hypothesis by observing a relationship between variables. The hypothesis is stated in the clearest terms possible and refers to the specific observations to be made. As an example, consider the following hypothesis about the role of self-statements in producing or maintaining depression: "There is a positive relationship between depressive thoughts and depressive symptoms, so that clients whose reported self-statements are rated as pessimistic by independent clinicians will tend to have high scores on the Beck Depression Inventory." Scores on the depression inventory constitute the measure of depression. The researcher would provide an operational definition of pessimistic thoughts by specifying the procedures followed in making the ratings.

For example, the clients keep a daily diary of their thoughts, recording them in the form of self-statements; the researcher randomly selects five self-statements per day from each diary; the self-statements are presented to two trained raters who are not informed of clients' depression scores; the raters independently assign a score from 1 to 5 to indicate the "pessimism level" of each thought; the scores of the two raters are averaged; and so on. When the data have been gathered, statistical methods are used to assess the likelihood that a genuine relationship between the variables has been discovered.

Correlational studies and experiments both involve making systematic observations. *Correlational studies* involve observing events that occur independent of the activity of the researcher, but *experiments* involve deliberately altering a variable so as to determine its effect on another. This procedural difference—whether or not the researcher manipulates one of the variables—is very important in determining the conclusions that may validly be drawn from the study.

In the study of pessimistic self-statements and depressive symptoms, the researcher could use correlational or experimental methods. With the *correlational method*, the researcher could select samples of people whose depression scores vary and then assess their self-statements. In one study, participants were drawn from four groups: inpatients in a psychiatric hospital, outpatients of a Community Mental Health Center, staff members at the hospital, and college students enrolled in psychology courses (Thorpe, Barnes, Hunter, & Hines, 1983; Thorpe, Parker, & Barnes, 1992). Scores on the depression inventory were highest among the inpatients and lowest among the students, as predicted. Next, a questionnaire was administered that asked participants to rate a series of thoughts they might have in response to frustrating experiences. The thoughts included some that had been previously rated as pessimistic. A strong association was found between pessimistic thoughts and depression scores.

The problem with a correlational study like this is in how to interpret the results. Finding a link between the two variables does not prove that one causes the other. It is possible that depression causes pessimistic thinking, or that pessimistic thinking causes depression, or that both are caused by something else. The experimental method usually allows stronger conclusions about causes and effects.

In an *experiment,* the researcher would not only measure the level of pessimistic thoughts and depressive symptoms, but would actually alter or manipulate one of these variables. The variable manipulated by the experimenter is known as the *independent variable (IV)*; the participant's responses constitute the *dependent variable (DV)*.[3] The independent variable is deliberately altered so as to gauge its effect on the dependent variable.

An experiment to test the effects of self-statements on depression would involve actually altering clients' self-statements. Studies on this topic have shown that cognitive modification of this kind is effective as treatment for depression (Rush, Beck, Kovacs, & Hollon, 1977). It is also possible to reverse the variables and manipulate the depression level to assess its effect on self-statements. This was done in a quasi-experimental study by Dobson and Shaw (1986), who hypothesized that some self-statements ("schema-based cognitions") were always present in people who have been depressed, whereas other self-statements ("automatic thoughts") were present only during an actual episode of depression. The researchers assessed different groups of inpatients and waited two weeks while the patients received state-of-the-art treatment. Depressed patients who had improved with treatment showed significant changes in automatic thoughts, whereas schema-based cognitions were unaffected, as had been predicted. This study involved manipulating the depression variable by providing active treatment. As a result the researchers could be confident in attributing the changes in self-statements to the change in level of depression.

Testing Theories of Etiology

It is difficult to determine the *etiology,* or causes, of a disorder, because the important events have already occurred before the client consults a therapist. Researchers have often used the correlational approach to indicate which variables are associated with clinical disorders, but, of course, cause/effect relationships cannot be established in this way. Some researchers have employed experimental methods to answer questions about etiology. This involves using experimental procedures to produce behavior that simulates a true disorder.

The students of Jean-Martin Charcot (1825–1893), the famous French physician whose work on hypnosis influenced Freud, once tricked him with a simulation of hysteria. They hypnotized a normal volunteer and gave her posthypnotic suggestions that resulted in her displaying hysteria-like symptoms. This demonstration impressed Charcot and gave him the idea that perhaps "real" hysteria had a psychogenic origin (Davison & Neale, 1990; see also Hergenhahn, 1992; Porter, 1991). Watson and Rayner (1920) created phobia-like behavior in Little Albert through classical conditioning, as described in Chapter 1. The results of their study led the authors to speculate that naturally occurring phobias develop in the same way. Ayllon, Haughton, and Hughes (1965) deliberately induced the "bizarre behavior" of broom carrying in a chronic inpatient by positive reinforcement. Without revealing the origins of the broom carrying, they asked psychoanalytically oriented colleagues to comment. To the great amusement of Ayllon and his associates, the psychoanalytic colleagues made interpretations of the patient's attachment to the broom, which ranged from regal scepter wielding to phallic symbolism. Ayllon and his colleagues argued instead that bizarre behavior could be understood in terms of reinforcement.

In all of these examples, behavior similar to a symptom of a mental disorder was deliberately produced by experimental procedures, suggesting that perhaps real clinical disorders have a similar origin. As discussed in the previous section on confirmation and successful predictions, none of these demonstrations confirms anything definite about the origins of clinical disorders (Cheshire, 1975; Marks, 1981a, 1981b). Nevertheless, behavior analogues of this kind are helpful in generating hypotheses, and they do show possible mechanisms for the development of disorders (Maher, 1966).

Given that it is impossible to confirm a hypothesis in a study (Borkovec & Bauer, 1982), the best way to proceed in testing theories of etiology is to try to falsify them. If self-statements of a certain kind do, indeed, cause depression, then we would expect to see a correlation between these two variables. Finding a strong correlation would not confirm the theory, but failing to find a significant correlation could cast doubt on it.

Assessing the Effects of Treatment

In a classic article, Paul (1967) urged behavior therapists and other mental health professionals to conduct outcome studies in the field of psychological treatment. Recognizing that psychotherapy, in general, had been severely criticized for its ineffectiveness, he reviewed the literature and concluded that more information from well-designed studies is needed. When clinicians did conduct research, this usually consisted of investigations into the content of therapy sessions, rather than on the effects of the course of therapy on the client's adjustment. When treatment effectiveness *was* the topic studied, all too often the wrong questions were asked, such as this impossibly broad question: Does psychological treatment work? Paul's famous appeal for the study of specific factors in therapy was: "In all its complexity, the question towards which all outcome research should ultimately be directed is the following: *What* treatment, by *whom*, is most effective for *this* individual with *that* specific problem, and under *which* set of circumstances?" (Paul, 1967, p. 111; original emphasis).

Agreeing with Paul, Borkovec and Bauer (1982) stressed the importance of establishing cause/effect relationships between treatment procedures and therapeutic behavior change. The best way to do this is to focus sharply on a battery of specific measures of improvement, rather than making global statements about the client's overall level of psychological adjustment. The specific measures should tap the client's presented problems as well as the particular behavioral changes that the treatment was intended to modify. Behavior therapists have not always thoroughly assessed the psychometric properties of their measures, but researchers have been paying more attention to this issue in recent years (Freund, Steketee, & Foa, 1987; Nelson, 1983). Ideal psychotherapy research programs consist of series of studies, each one designed to try to falsify a hypothesis. Every hypothesis tested will have therefore survived attempts to disprove it in earlier studies (Borkovec & Bauer, 1982). Programmatic research of this kind has been favored by several prominent behavior therapists in recent years— for example, the work of David Barlow (1988) and Isaac Marks (1987) on panic disorder and agoraphobia; of Edna Foa on posttraumatic stress disorder (Foa, Riggs, Massie, & Yarczower, 1995; Rothbaum & Foa, 1992a, 1992b); of Gail Steketee (1994) on obsessive-compulsive disorder; and of Neil Jacobson and his colleagues on behavioral couples therapy (Jacobson, 1992; Waltz & Jacobson, 1994).

Analogue versus Clinical Research

Most behavior therapists are clinical psychologists, whose graduate education has a strong research component. However, relatively few practicing behavior therapists regularly contribute research reports to the professional journals. Instead, academic psychologists have produced much of the research on behavior therapy, particularly in the case of interventions for nonpsychotic outpatients. Particularly in the 1960s and 1970s, this resulted in a large number of "analogue" treatment studies in which the participants are not clients or patients, but student volunteers recruited from psychology courses. Many behavior therapists question whether the results of such studies can be generalized to clinical settings. The status of analogue research has been a controversial matter.

Analogue research with student volunteers has some definite advantages when compared to research in clinical settings. It usually permits greater experimental control (Kazdin & Wilson, 1978). The participants in analogue research are readily available, they may be favorably disposed toward research, they form a relatively homogeneous group, and, potentially, large numbers of students may be recruited at once, permitting random assignment to experimental conditions. In any event, there is a sense in which all behavior therapy research is "analogue," in that researchers wish to generalize the results to routine clinical service settings. This remains true, no matter how similar the research setting is to the environment of a clinic in the community.

The chief problem with analogue research with student volunteers is in knowing when the results can be generalized to clinic settings (Emmelkamp & Mersch, 1982; Rosen,

1975). The answer to this question is reminiscent of Paul's (1967) plea for specificity: It depends on the disorder. Emmelkamp (1979) has noted that the most common phobia that clinicians deal with is agoraphobia, but there are no analogue studies of students with this disorder. Studies of students with fears of snakes or small animals have not been helpful in pointing the way to effective treatment of agoraphobia (Marks, 1987; Mathews, 1978). However, there *are* strong similarities between student volunteers with social anxiety and clients with social phobia, and these two groups respond similarly to treatment (Emmelkamp, Mersch, & Vissia, 1985). Thus, it is possible, in this context, to generalize results from students to clients. Emmelkamp and his colleagues did take the important step of actually finding out, experimentally, which analogue results can be generalized to clinical practice.

In recent years most researchers in academic settings have studied clients and patients from clinical settings. For example, the five influential researchers noted in the previous section (Barlow, Foa, Jacobson, Steketee, and Marks)—a group comprising one social worker, one psychiatrist, and three psychologists—all have academic affiliations, yet they conduct their research exclusively with client populations. In a parallel development, more work by practitioners is being represented in at least some professional journals. The journal *Cognitive and Behavioral Practice*, published by the Association for Advancement of Behavior Therapy, was established in 1994 with a two-person editorial team, one primarily a researcher and the other primarily a clinician. Manuscripts submitted to the journal are reviewed by two practitioners and a researcher. The aim of the new journal is to help "bridge the gap between the general findings of empirical research and the complex and specific challenges of daily clinical practice" (Davis & Peterson, 1994, p. 1).

We turn next to the specific methods available for assessing the effects of treatment: case histories, clinical series, single-case experiments, multiple baseline designs, crossover studies, and group (or between-groups) designs.

Case Histories

The oldest and most obvious way of demonstrating the effects of treatment is to provide a detailed, narrative account of the course of therapy with a client. Freud's (1909/1955) report on Little Hans is an example of a case history of this kind. Case histories can be useful in describing interesting clinical phenomena, illustrating the use of a technique, suggesting new ideas, and even disconfirming a hypothesis.

Guttmacher and Nelles (1984) provided a single-case report in which they were able to cast doubt on a theory concerning panic disorder. Medical researchers had shown that clients with frequent panic attacks would show symptoms of panic when injected with a sodium lactate infusion. People with no history of panic attacks did not typically respond in that way. Clients with panic disorder who had been successfully treated with medication did not react to the sodium lactate, either (Appleby, Klein, Sachar, & Levitt, 1981). Such findings led many clinicians to assume that panic disorder is entirely a medical matter, involving biological processes exclusively. Guttmacher and Nelles (1984) showed that a client with panic disorder who had been treated by behavior therapy, not medication, also failed to respond to the sodium lactate infusion, whereas she *had* done so prior to treatment. The demonstration was especially convincing because the client had taken part in a larger project in which the researchers conducting the tests were "experimentally blind," kept in ignorance of which treatment, if any, the clients had received. Finding just this one example of suppression of lactate-induced panic in a client treated by behavior therapy was enough to disprove the hypothesis that only medical treatment could do this.

Case studies are seldom as informative as the example just given, however. There is no replication of findings in a case study, so the results may or may not apply to another client. Stern and Marks (1973) described the case history of a woman with obsessive-compulsive problems together with marital difficulties. Her compulsive rituals concerning cleanliness did not improve with the usual behavioral treatment, but this problem *and* the marital disharmony improved dramatically with behavioral couples therapy. Generalizing from this one case history might have led behavior therapists only to offer couples therapy to their maritally distressed compulsive clients, omitting specific techniques targeting the obsessions and rituals. However, a later study of 12 clients with co-existing anxiety problems and marital difficulties produced contradictory results: Behavioral treatment of the obsessive-compulsive problems improved both the anxiety disorder *and* the marital problems (Cobb, McDonald, Marks, & Stern, 1980). Unless they can disconfirm a hypothesis, case histories have little value in testing the general effectiveness and applicability of therapy.

Clinical Series

In a clinical series, the clinician reports on a succession of clients who have received the same treatment. Wolpe (1958) gave an example when he described the use of treatment on reciprocal inhibition principles with 210 outpatients, and the well-known work of Masters and Johnson (1970) on the treatment of sexual dysfunction was based on clinical series methodology. The clinical series has the advantage over single-case histories in providing for repeated observations, or replications, with several clients. Clinical series methodology is also a helpful alternative to between-groups designs when it is inappropriate or undesirable to place some participants in untreated control groups. In serious medical disorders, for example, it could be unethical to withhold potentially beneficial treatment even for a brief period. Research on the artificial heart as a substitute for a real organ transplant has rested on the use of clinical series methodology.

There are problems with the clinical series, of course, and the chief of these is that clinicians can never know what would have happened if the people in the study had received a different treatment, or even no treatment—their scores on the variables of interest might have looked no different. Without a comparison with at least one other procedure, the results of a clinical series cannot shed any light on how well the treatment under study would have compared with another treatment.

The results of a clinical series in behavior therapy are shown in Figure 5–1. The graph shows the results of a study of home-based treatment for agoraphobia, with the client's spouse serving as cotherapist (Mathews, Teasdale, Munby, Johnston, & Shaw, 1977). Many clients with agoraphobia experience such intense discomfort when away from home that they remain entirely housebound, so that number of hours spent away from home serves as

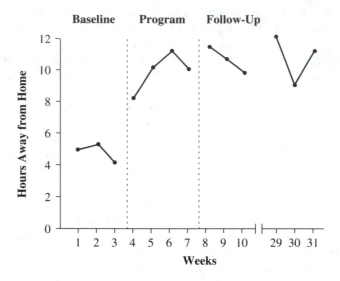

FIGURE 5–1   Average Number of Hours Spent Out of the House Each Week by 12 Agoraphobics Before, During, and After a Home-Based Treatment Program

Source: From Matthews, A., et al., A home-based treatment program for agoraphobia. *Behavior Therapy, 8,* 915–924. Copyright © 1977 by the Association for Advancement of Behavior Therapy. Reprinted by permission of the publisher and the author.

a useful index of therapeutic progress. The idea in the Mathews study was to facilitate transfer of therapeutic progress to real-life situations.

The graph in Figure 5–1 plots time (successive weeks of the study) on the horizontal axis (abscissa), and the average number of hours spent outside the house each week on the vertical axis (ordinate). The number of hours represented by each point on the graph is the average for the 12 clients. During the period of baseline measurement before treatment started (weeks 1 to 3), the average number of hours spent outside was 4 or 5 per client per week. During the period of active treatment (weeks 4 to 7), the average number of hours spent outside ranged from about 8 to 11. This number held up reasonably well during a follow-up period of no treatment (weeks 8 to 10), although the trend seemed to be for clients to spend less time outside as time went on. Finally, an extended follow-up assessment after treatment had ended (weeks 29 to 31) seemed to show that clients were still staying away from home at least 8 hours per week.

As a clinical series, this study did not include a control group of any kind (although the period of baseline measurement before treatment began does show how the clients were doing without therapy). Nonetheless, the results from this investigation could be compared at least informally with the results of other studies. The authors were able to show not only that the home-based treatment was as effective as other behavioral treatments as assessed immediately afterwards but also that the clients went on to make further progress on their own initiative.

Single-Case Experiments

Despite the problems with case histories, it is possible to study the treatment of an individual client systematically so as to provide scientifically respectable data. In a *single-case experiment,* structured observations of an individual client's response to treatment may be made, provided that the clinician is able to manipulate the key variables. This approach did not begin with behavior therapy. Eugen Bleuler (1857–1939), the Swiss psychiatrist who introduced the term *schizophrenia*, described how he took over from another psychiatrist in the treatment of an inpatient with frequent, severe episodes of agitation accompanied by hallucinatory experiences. Bleuler rapidly intervened with a focused treatment method at the beginning of every episode, and eventually the periods of agitation were eliminated: "Attempts at interrupting the treatments demonstrated that the improvement was not purely coincidental" (Bleuler, 1911/1950, pp. 480–481). The treatment used so effectively in this case was hypnosis.

Despite that isolated reference to single-case methodology with hypnosis, the type of treatment that lends itself especially well to this method is an operant learning program in which a particular behavior, occurring at a low frequency before treatment, is targeted for improvement, and positive reinforcement is used to increase the frequency of the behavior. An example could be encouraging a mute inpatient to speak. The most common experimental approach is to alternate periods of active treatment (or reinforcement) with periods of *baseline measurement,* or observation without treatment (extinction, or the absence of reinforcement). This allows the clinician to determine (1) whether the reinforcement program is working, and, if so, (2) whether the client's behavior continues at the improved level after the reinforcement has been discontinued.

Several terms have been used for such studies, including *reversal designs* (because, when a period of treatment is followed by a period of no treatment, the behavioral contingency is reversed from reinforcement to extinction); *withdrawal designs* (because the active treatment intervention is withdrawn in certain phases of the study); *N = 1 studies* (because there is only one participant); and *ABAB designs* (baseline measurement, indicated on a graph by "A," alternates with treatment, indicated by "B") (Hersen, 1982).

This methodology can be used whenever the clinician is able to measure a potentially high-frequency behavior relevant to the client's problem. Direct observation, continuous measurement, and clear criteria for change are all necessary (Hayes, 1981). In a typical ABAB study, the clinician records the data on a graph, with the frequency of the behavior of interest on the vertical axis and the passage of time on the horizontal axis. Events correlated with time, the introduction and removal of treatment episodes, form the independent variable; changes in the frequency of the client's behavior constitute the dependent variable. First, there is a period of baseline measurement without treatment (designated "A" on the graph). Next, treatment is provided for a given amount of time or number of sessions ("B"). Treatment is then suspended while the observations continue ("A" again), and, finally, treatment is reinstated ("B"). Statistical methods for evaluating therapeutic change in an individual client are available (Christensen & Mendoza, 1986), but usually the clinician may see at a glance whether the treatment has been effective.

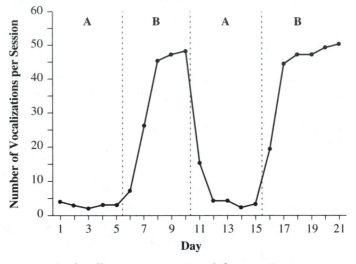

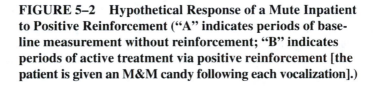

A = baseline measurement (no reinforcement)

B = positive reinforcement contingent on vocalization

FIGURE 5–2   Hypothetical Response of a Mute Inpatient to Positive Reinforcement ("A" indicates periods of baseline measurement without reinforcement; "B" indicates periods of active treatment via positive reinforcement [the patient is given an M&M candy following each vocalization].)

The hypothetical data depicted in Figure 5–2 show the following. On days 1 to 5 ("A"), no treatment is given; the client's behavior is simply observed and the number of vocalizations recorded. It can be seen that the client made very few vocalizations on days 1 to 5. On days 6 to 10 ("B"), a period of active treatment ensued; any vocalization by the client produced an M&M candy. The number of vocalizations increased from 3 to about 10 on the first day, then rapidly went to 25 or 30. On days 11 to 15 ("A"), there was a reversal to baseline measurement without reinforcement, the client's vocalizations rapidly dropped again. Finally, on days 16 to 20 ("B"), treatment was again introduced, and the client's vocalizations again rapidly increased.

Single-case research methodology is convenient for clinical settings and allows clinicians to conduct meaningful research without having to assemble a large sample of participants at one time. The technique quickly produces objective information, and clinicians can efficiently compare different techniques in a single client. Evaluating treatment effectiveness in this way is desirable ethically as well as scientifically, because unhelpful procedures may be rapidly identified and abandoned. If the target behavior increases as soon as the treatment intervention begins, and immediately decreases when the treatment is withdrawn, this is quite a convincing demonstration that the treatment was responsible for the improvement.

There are some problems with single-case research, however. If the behavior change in the first period of treatment is irreversible, then the behavior will not "revert to baseline levels" when treatment is withdrawn. This is ideal from the perspective of the client and the therapist, of course, but puzzling to the researcher, who may not be convinced that it really was the introduction of treatment that accounted for the change in behavior. Another factor, such as a significant life event, coinciding with the introduction of treatment, could have been responsible for the change. Generally, the ABAB type of design is most helpful to the researcher when the client's behavior increases when treatment is introduced and decreases when it is withdrawn. It is clear in that case that treatment was the important element. However, restricting studies to problems that are easily reversible by discontinuing treatment risks trivializing behavior therapy (Kahn, 1977). The ideal treatment would be relatively irreversible and would have positive effects that readily generalize to other problems.

Early studies of behavior therapy for specific phobias used ABAB designs, and an example is given in Figure 5–3 (Leitenberg, Agras, Thompson, & Wright, 1968). This is a

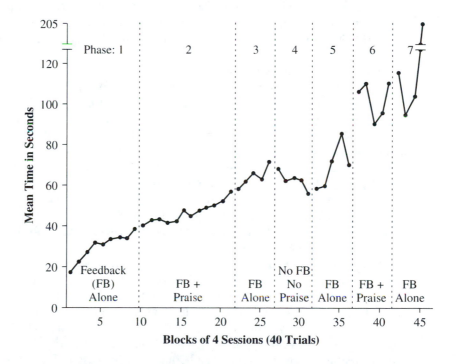

FIGURE 5–3   Duration of Self-Exposure to a Knife by a Phobic Patient as a Function of Feedback, Feedback Plus Praise, and No Feedback or Praise Conditions

Source: From Leitenberg, H., et al., Feedback in behavior modification: An experimental analysis in two phobic cases. *Journal of Applied Behavior Analysis, 1,* 131–137. Copyright © 1968, Society for the Experimental Analysis of Behavior, Inc. Reprinted with permission.

complex example in several ways. First, it is not strictly an ABAB design, because there is only one period of baseline observation without treatment, and that occurs in Phase 4, some time after the study began (Block 30, "No FB, no praise"). Also, there are two different treatments, feedback (FB) and praise, sometimes presented alone, sometimes in combination. Finally, the behavior being studied—measured as the length of time the client could look at a knife—did not clearly reverse at any point, except during that one period of no treatment/baseline measurement. If "A" is used for no treatment, "B" for feedback, and "C" for praise, then the sequence shown in Figure 5–3 consists of the 7 phases B, B + C, B, A, B, B + C, B. Complex as this example is, it does illustrate the versatility of the method.

Multiple Baseline Designs

The *multiple baseline* study is a type of single-case experiment, although it can involve more than one participant. In a multiple baseline study, more than one behavior is measured. This method can be used to study the treatment of a single client with more than one problem or several clients with the same problem. A study of several problems in one client is known as a multiple baseline *across behaviors;* a study of several clients sharing a given problem is known as a multiple baseline *across clients* (Kazdin, 1994).

Multiple Baseline Across Behaviors

Consider a client who overeats, whose social skills are poor, and who is anxious in social situations, leading to avoidance of parties, job interviews, or group activities in general. For each problem, the therapist selects a convenient measure that is valid and quantifiable. Each of the three measures is arbitrarily scored on the same scale (0 to 10, for example) and in the same direction, so that scores of 10 represent the highest level of problem severity (excess weight, minimal social skill, and extreme anxiety) and scores of 0 reflect no problem at all. The therapist measures the three problem behaviors at intervals during a period of baseline measurement, so as to determine the stability of each behavior before treatment. As in other single case experimental designs, behavior measurement continues throughout the study so that changes due to the introduction and removal of specific treatments may be assessed.

After the introduction of treatment, several outcomes are possible. Suppose that the first technique implemented is a self-control program to promote exercise and restrict excessive eating. The technique could improve the problem to which it is primarily addressed, and it might even result in improvement in problems not directly targeted. The client may acquire some wide-ranging skills in the self-control program, and as a result, develop greater self-confidence about solving problems, leading in turn to feeling more at ease in social situations. Successful weight loss could itself increase the client's sense of attractiveness, encouraging greater social participation, which in turn could reduce social anxiety. Alternatively, of course, treatment may be completely ineffective. All of these possible outcomes would be plainly visible on the graph recording the three problem behaviors.

Figure 5–4 gives an example of a multiple baseline study across behaviors in one client (Brownell, Hayes, & Barlow, 1977). This is a complex figure because it depicts three different behaviors, two types of assessment measure, and three phases of the study. This adult male client had two problem behaviors: exhibitionism (as in the case of Frank in Chapter 1) and sexual interest in his stepdaughter. The therapists treated this client by covert sensitization. His response to treatment was assessed in two ways. The "card sort" was a self-report method in which he selected, from a stack of index cards with typed descriptions, those that matched his current level of sexual arousal to the inappropriate

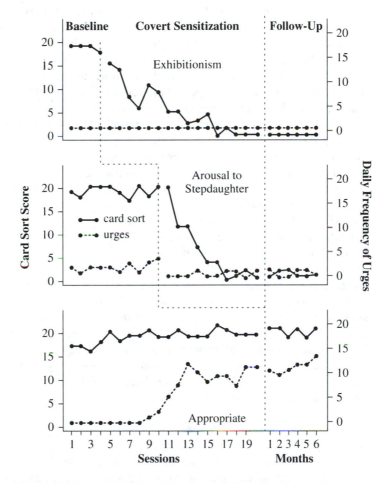

FIGURE 5–4   Card Sort Ratings of Sexual Arousal in Response to Appropriate and Inappropriate Stimuli, and Daily Frequency of Sexual Urges in a Paraphilic Male Treated by Covert Sensitization

Source: From Brownell, K., et al., Patterns of appropriate and deviant sexual arousal: The behavioral treatment of multiple sexual deviations. *Journal of Consulting and Clinical Psychology, 45,* 1144–1155. Copyright © 1977 by the American Psychological Association. Reprinted by permission of the author.

stimuli (people he might expose himself to, and his stepdaughter). The "daily frequency of urges" reflected the number of times per day he experienced the desire to engage in inappropriate sexual behavior. Both card sort (solid line) and daily frequency of sexual urges (dotted line) data are recorded on the graphs in Figure 5–4. Each of the three graphs depicts the course of a specific behavior. In addition to the inappropriate behaviors that were the targets of treatment ("exhibitionism" in upper graph; "arousal to stepdaughter" in middle graph), the therapists measured the client's appropriate sexual interest in his wife ("appropriate arousal" in lower graph).

The three graphs in Figure 5–4 may be interpreted as follows. They all share the same horizontal axis, which records time (sessions 1 to 19, then months 1 to 6). The two upright axes record card sort scores (left upright axis) and daily frequency of urges (right upright axis). At the top of the upper graph are three headings: baseline, covert sensitization, and follow-up. The left part of all three graphs illustrates the "card sort" and "urges" curves for the baseline period (the initial period of measurement, but no treatment). The dotted line that separates the baseline period (to the left) from covert sensitization (to the right) is staggered. This indicates that the baseline period for exhibitionism (the upper graph) consisted of the first 5 sessions, and the baseline period for arousal to stepdaughter (middle graph) was the first 10 sessions (appropriate arousal, lower graph, was never treated, so the period of baseline measurement extends across all sessions).

After session 5, the exhibitionism was treated by covert sensitization (the part of the graph between the two upright dotted lines), but the arousal to stepdaughter was not treated until session 10. This allows one to see whether applying covert sensitization to the client's exhibitionism had any effect on his arousal to his stepdaughter. It looks as if it did not—covert sensitization seems to start working as soon as it is introduced, but only for the behavior to which it is directly applied. Interestingly, the appropriate arousal appears to increase as the arousal to the stepdaughter decreases. The upright dotted line to the right, with the sessions to the left and the months to the right, separates the treatment phase of the study (covert sensitization) from the follow-up phase, and indicates that no treatment was provided for 6 months after the sessions ended (the part of the graph to the right of the line). The researchers continued to monitor the three behaviors (exhibitionism, arousal to stepdaughter, and appropriate arousal) throughout the study. The fact that describing Figure 5–4 takes so much time is a good indication of the wealth of information that can be encapsulated in graphical form!

Multiple Baseline Across Clients

A special advantage of the *multiple baseline across clients* is not simply that there are replications with several clients but that it allows the possibility of having varying lengths of initial baseline measurement in different clients. For example, consider the case of five cigarette smokers who wish to quit (see Figure 5–5). Each client records the number of cigarettes smoked each day during a period of baseline measurement. For the first client, the baseline period is one week; for the second, two weeks; for the third, three weeks; and so on. Treatment is introduced at the end of the particular baseline period selected for the client. If each client begins to show behavior change as soon as treatment is introduced, despite the fact that treatment began at different times for different people, therapists can be more confident that treatment was responsible for the change, not an external event that happened to coincide with it.

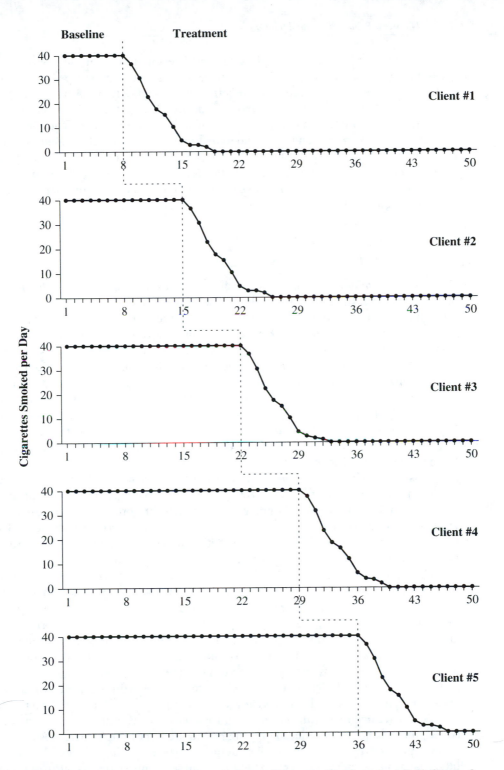

FIGURE 5–5 **Hypothetical Data for Five Cigarette Smokers in a Self-Control Program: Multiple Baseline across Clients**

In Figure 5–5, a separate graph is shown for each client, but the horizontal axis gives the same time line for all of them. Number of cigarettes smoked per day is marked on the vertical axes. The graphs to the left of the staggered dotted line portray each client's rate of smoking during the baseline period, and to the right of the staggered line, each client's rate of smoking once treatment has started. As you can see, in week 2, client 1 has already begun to respond to treatment, while the other clients are still in the baseline period. By week 3 both clients 1 and 2 are in the treatment phase. By week 6, all clients are receiving treatment. In this idealized figure, each client immediately responds positively to treatment as soon as it is introduced. Unfortunately, the data obtained in an actual smoking cessation study would probably not look quite as dramatic (see Chapter 13).

Crossover Studies

The *crossover study* is a combination of single-case experimental methodology and the between-groups design. As in the single-case designs, it is particularly well suited to clinical settings in which appropriate referrals are intermittent, and in which it is unethical to withhold treatment or to use no-treatment control groups. Crossover studies also allow clinicians to gain maximal information from each participant. In the typical crossover study, the researcher wishes to test two treatments to determine which is more effective. Each client receives both treatments and each treatment is given in a block of a fixed number of sessions. Problem assessment is made before and after each treatment component. Clients are randomly assigned to one of the two treatment sequences, so that the order of the treatments is counterbalanced across clients. A client who receives Treatment Y first will cross over into the Treatment Z condition halfway through the study; the reverse happens for the client who began with Treatment Z.

Crossover studies give results that can be looked at case by case (to see if a client does better with Treatment Y or Treatment Z) or between groups. A comparison of the two groups (the Y/Z group and the Z/Y group) shows whether the order in which the treatments were given makes a difference to the outcome. A problem with crossover studies is that by the end of the study, each client has received both treatments, so that later follow-up assessments cannot gauge any separate effects of the treatment components.

The report by Cobb and colleagues (1980) on treating coexisting anxiety and marital problems, mentioned earlier, was based on a crossover study (see Figure 5–6). Figure 5–6 shows the following. Clients' target problems, scaled on the upright axis of the graph, were their phobic or obsessive behaviors, rated on a 9-point (0 to 8) scale. The horizontal axis indicates the passage of time in weeks during the study (the right section of the figure, under the heading "pooled," is really a separate graph, showing the effects of the two treatments with the results of all clients pooled together).

In this study, all 10 clients received both treatments, but in different orders. Look at the upper curve first. These 5 clients started with an average problem rating of 7 on the 0 to 8 scale. They received *marital treatment* for 10 weeks and were then reassessed, but the target problems had been reduced only slightly (dotted line). Next, there was a 12-week follow-up period (no treatment was given during this stage), ending at week 22, again with little change in the target problems. At week 22, these clients started a course of *exposure*

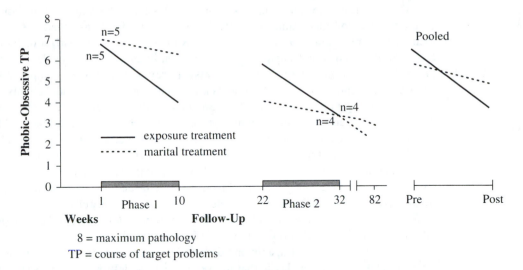

8 = maximum pathology

TP = course of target problems

FIGURE 5–6   Ratings of Phobic-Obsessive Target Problems in Response to Exposure and Marital Treatment in 11 Clients.

Source: Adapted from Cobb, J., et al., Marital versus exposure therapy: Psychological treatments of co-existing marital and phobic-obsessive problems. *Behavioral Analysis and Modification, 4,* 3–16. Copyright © 1980 by Urban and Schwarzenberg, Inc. Reprinted with permission.

therapy for 10 weeks and were then reassessed, and the target problems had been substantially reduced to 3 or 4 on the scale (solid line). Finally, there was a follow-up period of no treatment lasting for several months; the graph shows that the clients continued to improve.

Now consider the other 5 clients. Like the first group, they began the study with target problem ratings of about 7. This group began with *exposure treatment*, which reduced the target problems considerably in 10 weeks (solid line). There was little change during a 12-week follow-up, nor after 10 weeks of *marital therapy* (dotted line), possibly because there was little room for further improvement at that point. These clients also were followed up several months later. All clients in the study had improved significantly by the time they had completed both treatments, but the graph shows that most of the improvement was produced by exposure treatment (the solid lines for each group).

Group Designs

The *between-groups experimental design* is popular in behavior therapy outcome research whenever an adequate sample of clients is available. The treatment variable can be manipulated by randomly assigning clients to different treatment conditions. Suitable measurements of the problem behavior, before and after treatment and at various follow-up intervals, can indicate the amount of improvement and whether or not any improvement persists over time.

The simplest between-groups experimental design is the nonfactorial group design with untreated controls (Paul, 1969). Participants are randomly assigned to either a treatment or a no-treatment condition, as in the study of systematic desensitization by Lang and Lazovik (1963) noted in Chapter 2. Statistical techniques applied to the data from clients' pretreatment and posttreatment assessments can reveal whether they improved beyond chance levels, and whether treated clients improved more than untreated clients.

A simple comparison of a treatment method with no treatment can only assess the difference between *some* treatment and *no* treatment, because one could not tell from the results what would have happened if a different treatment had been used. Lang and Lazovik (1963) found that systematic desensitization was significantly more helpful than no treatment, but one does not know if they might have found the same results with psychoanalysis or client-centered therapy. If the objective of the research is to show that a particular treatment technique, such as systematic desensitization, is highly effective, then additional comparison groups need to be included in the experiment. Often, a good comparison condition to use is another therapy technique of known effectiveness.

Paul's (1966) study of insight and desensitization treatments for speech anxiety, described in Chapter 2, is a classic that has served as a model for many later studies. It has been as valuable for its illustration of good research methodology as for its specific conclusions on treatment effectiveness. Paul demonstrated the use of multiple measures of outcome, including a performance-based behavioral test, physiological monitoring, and self-report questionnaires. He randomly assigned participants to experimental groups, which consisted of two experimental conditions (insight and desensitization), an attention-placebo condition, and no treatment. In order to guard against experimenter bias, Paul selected as therapists local practitioners whose orientation was nonbehavioral. Finally, he used a follow-up assessment of participants' progress to assess the durability of therapeutic change. Some data from this study are shown in Figure 5–7.

Inevitably, between-groups methodology is not foolproof. If the researcher omits a no-treatment control group, it is unclear whether the treatments and placebo conditions used actually improve on the natural recovery rate without treatment. If more participants leave treatment early from one group than another—that is, if there is differential client attrition—the remaining participants form a biased sample that might produce misleading results. Even in a well-designed study in which each therapist treats clients in more than one treatment condition, there is still the possibility that the results may not validly be generalized beyond the particular therapists who took part. Finally, the pre-treatment assessment may influence clients' scores on the posttreatment assessment over and above any effects of the therapy being tested.

Partial Pretest Designs

Sometimes, the most important process of behavior change in a study is a *nonspecific* factor that operates in all treatment conditions. One such factor is the reactive effect of pretesting. In studies of therapy for anxiety disorders, for example, pretreatment assessment may include observing a client's behavior in a phobic situation. The problem raised by this is that exposure to this situation may be therapeutic! In that case, the experimenter has confounded two factors—the pretesting, and the therapy technique used in the study itself—either of which could be responsible for any therapeutic improvement. This prob-

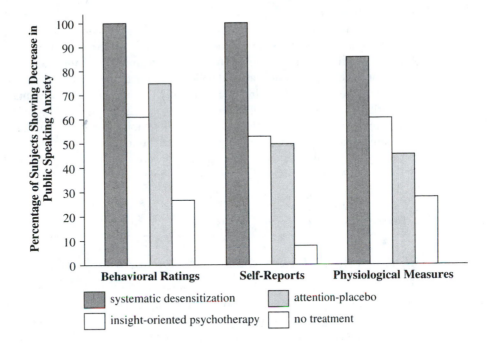

FIGURE 5–7   Percentage of Participants in Each Group in Paul's (1966) Study Showing a Decrease in Anxiety at Posttreatment Assessment

Data from Paul, 1966; adapted by Spiegler, M., *Contemporary behavioral therapy.* Copyright © 1983 by Mayfield Publishing Co.: Palo Alto, CA. Reprinted by permission.

lem can be overcome by use of a partial pretest design, in which only half of the clients in each condition are pretested. This allows statistical analysis of the interaction between pretesting and treatment (Paul, 1967b, 1969).

Constructive and Dismantling Strategies

To test the possible effects of two or more subprocedures within a treatment technique, constructive or dismantling strategies may be used. For example, the technique of systematic desensitization could be dismantled into its components: relaxation training, imagining a hierarchy of feared items, pairing the relaxation with the imagined scenes, and the client signaling the therapist to pause when anxiety arises. Clients in one experimental condition could receive relaxation only; clients in the next could imagine scenes from the hierarchy without relaxation; others could follow the complete procedure. This approach allows researchers to assess the importance of elements within therapeutic procedures. One difficulty with the method is that it is hard to give equal treatment time to clients in all conditions when a subprocedure takes only a fraction of the time taken by the full procedure.

Factorial Designs

A final variant within between-groups designs is the factorial study, in which experimental conditions are formed by manipulating the presence or absence of treatment variables. Rational emotive behavior therapy for procrastination, for example, might involve two treatment factors: disputing irrational beliefs and practicing nonprocrastination in various "homework" exercises. Four treatment conditions could be formed by manipulating the two variables: (1) no disputing and no homework, (2) disputing, but no homework, (3) homework, but no disputing, and (4) disputing and homework. This design permits statistical comparison of the four conditions, as usual; but it also allows further analysis of the factors by comparing pairs of groups. The two groups that disputed irrational beliefs could be compared with the two that did not, for example.

Evaluating Processes of Behavior Change

Efficacy versus Mechanism of a Treatment Procedure

Once a behavior therapy technique has been shown to be effective, researchers usually wish to find out exactly what it is about the technique that is responsible for its effects. No-treatment control groups are insufficient for this purpose (Jacobson & Baucom, 1977). The history of research on systematic desensitization gives an example of the move from questions of efficacy to questions of mechanism (Kazdin & Wilcoxon, 1976). The dismantling strategy has been used extensively here (Davison, 1968a), but none of the obvious procedural factors within the technique has been shown to be vital (Wilkins, 1971).

Some theorists argue that the essentials of effective treatment are found not in specific procedural elements but in broad behavior change processes that may be found in any therapeutic approach. Bandura's (1977) concept of *self-efficacy* is an example. Self-efficacy research typically involves a combination of experimental and correlational methods. Not only is the target behavior assessed in the different treatment groups, before and after the intervention, but also the level and strength of clients' self-efficacy is assessed within treatment. Observing a close covariation between behavior change and changes in self-efficacy expectations gives information consistent with Bandura's theory.

Similarly, Lang's (1979, 1985) *bio-informational theory* of emotional processing includes the hypothesis that fear-reduction therapy is successful only when it activates a relevant cognitive network. This activation can be detected by observing specific changes in physiological activity, such as increases in heart rate and skin conductance. Bio-informational theory has inspired studies in which heart rate is measured during treatment as an indicator of emotional processing. Unless the heart rate actually changes, the therapeutic effects of a procedure cannot be attributed to emotional processing (Hecker & Thorpe, 1987).

Nonspecific Factors

Psychological treatment is a complex enterprise that requires a social interaction between a client and a therapist. There is a multitude of potentially important variables in the situation. Although clinicians tend to believe that their procedures are the most important element, there are many variables in the client, in the therapist, and in their interaction that could be responsible for the success of therapy. This poses problems for the researcher who wishes to identify the vital elements of therapy. Even in the relatively straightforward example of pharmacological or drug treatment, it is well known that factors independent of the chemical properties of the pill may influence therapeutic improvement; the *placebo effect* has been studied for years as a confounding psychological factor.

Examples of nonspecific factors have been cited by Borkovec and Bauer (1982) as follows:

> *Depending on the specific issues under study, one may need to control for such factors as general therapeutic contact independent of therapy content . . . individual differences in the expectation of therapeutic success . . . the relative credibility of the treatment package . . . or the demand characteristics for improvement . . . which might spuriously favor one treatment over another. (p. 143)*

The study of nonspecific factors has been hindered by disagreement about definitions. Sometimes, *nonspecifics* refers to "factors inadvertently inherent in the therapeutic relationship rather than to the specific behavior change techniques employed" (Wilson, 1980, p. 283). At other times it refers to any procedures that are common to all experimental conditions in a between-groups study, so that such factors are not specific to any one condition but are present in all of them. Examples of such nonspecific factors are behavioral avoidance tests and client self-monitoring of target behaviors. The effects of assessment procedures common to all groups in a study can be tested, of course, by including a no-treatment group in which pre- and posttreatment assessment is carried out in the same way as in the experimental groups.

It is usual to include a *placebo group* in addition to a no-treatment group in order to allow for the various potential nonspecific variables attributable to therapist-client interaction. Other terms for placebo groups are *attention-placebo, relationship controls, expectancy controls,* and *nonspecific control* groups (Jacobson & Baucom, 1977). Researchers continue to study alternative aspects of therapy as possible explanations for outcomes that appear to favor specific behavioral procedures. These alternative aspects include differences in the credibility of treatment, in clients' expectancy levels, and in the demand characteristics of an experimental situation. Nevertheless, difficulties arise because the definition of nonspecifics is still governed by ignorance (Wilkins, 1983).

Treatment Credibility

Experiments on treatment effectiveness include a variety of extratherapeutic ingredients, such as "attention to the problem, presence of an interacting therapist, presumed generation of expected improvement, faith, hope, and sometimes charity" (Borkovec & Bauer, 1982, p. 146). Attempts to control for such factors have often failed because placebo conditions have not been seen as credible by subjects. This problem, Borkovec and Bauer have noted, impaired much of the early research on systematic desensitization, because researchers had not ruled out the possibility that a vital factor in the technique is that it is viewed as a highly plausible treatment by clients. That alone *could* account for its success. Because of this, it is important for researchers to ensure that their nonspecific treatment conditions are as credible to clients as the experimental treatments.

Demand Characteristics

Research participants are inevitably involved in a social setting—in this case the laboratory or research clinic—in which there are likely to be many unspoken rules for appropriate conduct. Stanley Milgram (1974) demonstrated, in his studies of "obedience to authority," the chilling power of demand factors—the prestige of the experimenter or of the institution, for example—to justify cruelty that would seem unheard of in other contexts. In the context of treatment research, demand characteristics may include the implied expectation that treated participants are supposed to show improvement after treatment (Bernstein & Nietzel, 1977).

Demand characteristics of the research setting may be especially important in analogue studies. It has been shown that demand characteristics influence approach to a snake in a behavioral-avoidance test, for example. People who had indicated significant fear of snakes were drawn from two samples: students satisfying a course requirement and volunteers for a treatment program. They were asked to approach, touch, and handle a harmless snake. Two levels of demand were compared: *Low,* in which the test was introduced as a measure of fear, and *High,* in which the test was presented as a way of acquiring physiological records of fear while people handled snakes. The high demand condition produced greater approach and less fear, especially in the college students (Bernstein & Nietzel, 1974). Even in this seemingly objective assessment of fear, a behavioral-avoidance test, demand characteristics can have a significant effect on the results.

A study with children showed that clinical interventions that appear to work because information is given may, in fact, have their effect through social mechanisms (Rosenfarb & Hayes, 1984). To illustrate this, showing children that dogs are harmless by means of a modeling procedure not only gives information but also arouses social motivation. That is, the children realize that other people now *know* that they have been told dogs are harmless! In the experiment, children with fears of the dark were treated either by modeling or by self-instructional training methods. Half of the children knew that the experimenter was aware of their treatment; the other half believed that the experimenter did not know. Children in the "public" condition, in which they knew others were aware of their treatment, improved significantly more than children in the alternative condition.

Comments

Studying issues such as expectancy and demand characteristics has been helpful in pinpointing what actually benefits the subjects in treatment research projects. However, it is important to keep goals in perspective. If the goal of the research is to identify specific active elements within therapy, appropriate controls for confounding variables need to be made. If the goal is to identify the most effective treatments, however, actually identifying such treatments is a significant practical achievement, whether or not some of the effective components have to do largely with expectancy and faith.

Concluding Remarks

Behavior therapy has inspired significant advances in treatment outcome research methodology. The work of influential figures such as Marks (1981b, 1987) and Paul (1966; Paul & Lentz, 1977) has been distinguished not only by its important theoretical and practical results but also by the effectiveness of its research technique. Research design has itself become an active topic within behavior therapy, so that it is common for studies on assessment of inter-observer agreement, the design of appropriate control groups, and the like to be the focus of influential articles reported in behavior therapy journals. Progress in research methodology has accompanied theoretical progress in understanding clinical disorders. For example, difficulties in selecting appropriate measures of anxiety in research studies led to the adoption of multiple assessment procedures which, in turn, prompted the development of newer theories (Lang, 1985). It is the emphasis on treatment evaluation within behavior therapy that has been responsible, above all, for the significant progress that has been made in extending the understanding of psychological disorders and their treatment. The extent of this progress will be assessed in later chapters.

Chapter Summary

One of the distinctive features of behavior therapy is its commitment to experimental hypothesis testing in clinical work. When clients or patients take part in research programs to test the effects of therapy procedures, important ethical issues are raised. Guidelines for ethical research practice have been codified by the American Psychological Association and other professional groups.

Scientific work in psychology generally involves attending to the issues of operational definition of variables, generality of results, controlled observation, repeated observation, confirmation of findings, and consistency. The conclusions that may validly be drawn from research vary, depending on whether correlational or experimental methodology is used. In the correlational approach, the scientist observes variables in the natural world and assesses the nature of their relationship. In the experimental approach, the scientist alters one variable to assess its effect on another. The scientist who uses the experimental approach is in a better position to evaluate possible causal relationships between one variable and another. In behavior therapy, the correlational approach is often used to understand the origins of disorders, whereas the experimental approach is usually chosen to evaluate the effects of therapy.

Behavioral researchers have to choose between analogue and clinical research, and among various possible research designs, all with particular advantages and disadvantages. These research designs include case histories, clinical series, single-case experiments and multiple baseline designs, crossover studies, and group designs. In evaluating behavior change processes that underlie treatment effectiveness, researchers often wish to rule out the effects of nonspecific factors, such as the demand characteristics of the experimental situation.

Endnotes

1. Until recently, *subject* was the preferred term for participants in psychology experiments. It is currently more appropriate either to be specific and describe the people actually involved (e.g., students or clients) or to use *participants* to show greater respect for their personal autonomy (American Psychological Association, 1994).

2. Many behavior therapists would object to using diagnostic labels, such as depression, to define a target problem, as discussed in later chapters. A thorough behavioral assessment often reveals very different behavior patterns in people whose problems received the same diagnosis (Wolpe, 1990).

3. The IV is controlled by the researcher, independent of the participant; scores on the DV are dependent on the participant's behavior.

Chapter 6

Behavioral Assessment

Ellen W., a 43-year-old lawyer, referred herself for treatment of depression. During the intake interview, Ellen revealed that her relationship with her husband had soured during the past year and that frequent fighting had given way to stony silences and mutual avoidance. The onset of Ellen's depressive symptoms occurred six months ago, when she reported "giving up hope" that her marriage could improve. Her feelings of dysphoria and hopelessness had become so severe that she was losing sleep and failing to maintain her once active workload.

Steve R., a 30-year-old graduate student, was referred by a local judge for treatment of severe binge drinking. Steve actually reported drinking very little during most days of the week. He was performing well in his graduate program and was successfully maintaining his heavy workload of research and teaching responsibilities. On weekends, however, he typically met his friends at a local bar and consumed between 5 and 8 drinks on each occasion. These experiences led to multiple arrests for driving while intoxicated, and hence to the court referral.

Robert W., a 65-year-old surgeon, consulted a psychologist for evaluation of "stress and anxiety." Following the death of a critically ill patient, Robert began developing symptoms of anxiety such as insomnia, tension, and excessive rumination about the quality of his surgical skills. His anxiety symptoms were especially acute in his work environment, where he reported fearing that he would make a mistake. Because his hands shook noticeably and his concentration was impaired, it became very difficult for Robert to conduct surgery. Although Robert had experienced the deaths of many patients in his long career, recent losses in his own life (the deaths of his father and brother, both during the past year) had left him feeling emotionally vulnerable.

The concerns of Ellen, Steve, and Robert are among the most common that are brought to the attention of psychotherapists. In order to design effective treatments, the therapist must carefully assess the nature, context, and development of each person's emotional and behavioral difficulties. A thorough and well-conducted assessment will guide selection of specific intervention techniques and establish the groundwork for evaluating therapy progress and outcome. Thus, behavioral assessment is a vital part of behavior therapy.

Behavioral assessment developed rapidly during the 1970s, after initially lagging behind behavior therapy. Today, behavioral assessment is a rich and varied subfield of behavior therapy that continues to grow at a rapid pace. In this chapter, we provide an overview of behavioral assessment with adult clients. Assessment of children's problems is a specialized topic and is dealt with in Chapter 15.

Traditional Approaches to Assessment

Behavioral assessment grew both from the need to establish a system for classifying problems and processes behaviorally, and from dissatisfaction with psychodynamic formulations and traditional diagnostic classification. Assessment of psychological disorders has had a long and varied history. Currently, there are many different approaches to the evaluation of psychological symptoms. Behavioral assessment can be seen in context by reviewing other approaches briefly here.

Syndrome-Based Diagnosis

Syndrome-based diagnosis is the oldest and most influential assessment approach. It owes a great deal to Emil Kraepelin (1856–1926), a German psychiatrist who pioneered modern approaches to classification. The central assumption is that certain signs or symptoms tend to cluster together in clinically meaningful ways to define syndromes,[1] or psychological disorders. For example, it is typical for symptoms of dysphoria to co-occur with negative thoughts about oneself, disturbances in activity level, sleep, and appetite, guilt feelings, and perceptions of hopelessness. Collectively, these symptoms define the syndrome of depression. The criteria for identifying syndromal groupings is expert judgement: the consensual opinions of experienced clinicians, based on careful observations of case material.

The *Diagnostic and Statistical Manual of Mental Disorders,* Fourth Edition (American Psychiatric Association, 1994) presents the classification system most widely used in the United States today. Commonly known as the *DSM-IV,* this is an example of diagnostic classification based on the syndromal approach. We will use this classification — from this point in the book onward, simply referring to it as *DSM-IV*—to aid communication, but we will occasionally remind you of some of the problems that *DSM-IV* poses for the behavioral assessment and treatment of particular problems or disorders.

There are many advantages to syndrome-based diagnosis. First, clients' problems do tend to fall into meaningful clusters. When this is the case, the cluster of problems is a suitable treatment target. Indeed, outcomes can be better when the cluster is seen as a distinct disorder than when it is seen as a collection of isolated issues. Second, a single diagnostic term summarizes a great deal of information, facilitating communication between professionals with disparate backgrounds. Third, grouping clinical symptoms into syndromes facilitates research into the causes, correlates, and treatment of various disorders (Klein & Riso, 1995).

One major disadvantage of syndromal diagnosis is the tendency for syndromal groupings to become reified, or treated as though they represent actual "disease" entities (First, Francis, Widiger, Pincus, & Davis, 1992). Furthermore, categorical systems lose many of their advantages if different syndromal groupings have high degrees of co-morbidity, or diagnostic overlap, which is clearly the case with the *DSM-IV* (Klein & Riso, 1995).

Some of the criticisms of *DSM-IV* (and of psychiatric diagnosis as a whole) have even wider implications. One criticism focuses on the drawback that some diagnostic labels seem aimed at particular groups of people and not others, and may therefore be used to discredit broad categories of individuals (such as political dissidents, ethnic minorities, and women). Benjamin Rush (1745–1813), pioneer of American psychiatry and signatory of the Declaration of Independence, introduced the diagnosis *anarchia,* a "form of insanity" affecting people who were unhappy with the new political structure of the United States (Brown, 1990). Similarly, the disease *drapetomania*, identified by Dr. Samuel Cartwright in 1843, was seen only in African slaves and its symptoms involved a "compulsion to run away." African Americans were also supposedly vulnerable to *dyaesthesia aethiopica,* a disorder in which the psychopathology involved "paying no attention to property" (Brown, 1990). More recently, critics of an earlier version of the *DSM-IV* chided its authors for gender bias because it retains several diagnoses that seem to reflect negative stereotypes of women (Kaplan, 1983/1995). However, the proponents of classification point out that there are also many diagnoses reflecting negative stereotypes of men (Williams & Spitzer, 1983/1995)—which may or may not be of any comfort to the critics!

Another broad criticism of diagnosis is that, in their attempt to collect clusters of symptoms into categories, the classifiers sometimes make decisions that are quite arbitrary. This criticism has been expressed as follows:

> At the current state of psychiatric knowledge, grouping patients according to selected properties rather than in terms of their total phenomenology is analogous to classifying a car by observing any four of the following eight properties: wheels, motors, headlights, radio, seats, body, windshield wipers, and exhaust systems. While an object with four of these properties might well be a car, it might also be an airplane, a helicopter, a derrick, or a tunnel driller. (Chang & Bidder, 1985, p. 202; cited by Brown, 1990)

These critics would rather deal holistically with the human being involved than focus on a set of problems. This is ironic, since another disadvantage of diagnosis is that it can be mistakenly applied to *people,* not to problems. Agoraphobia, for example, is a disorder encompassing anxiety about traveling far from home; fear of crowded, public places; and panic attacks; and the diagnostic label is properly applied to the set of problems, not to the person. When a *person* is described as "an agoraphobic," then he or she is being defined and labeled in terms of a disorder, surely a dehumanizing practice!

Empirically Based (Dimensional) Classification

Rather than rely on the opinions of expert clinicians, dimensional approaches to classification involve the use of statistical techniques to identify groupings of interrelated symptoms. Data are derived from symptom-rating scales or questionnaires completed by large numbers of individuals. Multivariate statistical techniques such as factor analysis or cluster analysis are used to reveal dimensions or clusters of discrete problem behaviors that tend to be highly intercorrelated. Behavior therapists have tended to favor dimensional over syndromal approaches to classification, because a client's behavior can be rated along a continuum rather than placed in one or another category (Quay, 1986).

Eysenck (1966) has been a leading defender of dimensional classification. His empirically derived personality dimensions of neuroticism and extraversion have led to predictions about the suitability of behavior therapy for particular clients. Generally, he has argued that it is a mistake to ignore individual differences, as some behavior therapists do. He wrote,

> *No physicist would dream of assessing the electrical conductivity, or the magnetic properties, or the heat- resisting qualities of random samples of matter, or "stuff in general"; [he or she] would insist on being given carefully purified samples of specified elements . . . much energy was spent on the construction of [the] table of the elements, precisely because one element does not behave like another. Some conduct electricity, others do not, or do so only poorly; we do not throw all these differences into some gigantic error term, and deal only with the average of all substances. (Eysenck, 1966, p. 2)*

Eysenck has used this argument to justify classifing people's personality characteristics. Some clients (introverts) are more conditionable than others, for example. According to Eysenck, people with high conditionability are especially prone to develop anxiety disorders, and this has implications for behavior therapy.

However, there are disadvantages to classifying personality and psychopathology on dimensional scales. Methods like factor analysis encourage the view that people's behavior can be described entirely in terms of stable dispositions such as traits. This can be misleading, and in fact contradicts the usual assumptions made by behavior therapists, who have always stressed the importance of the immediate environment of conditioned, discriminative, and reinforcing stimuli in understanding human behavior. Because of the workings of behavioral contingencies and reinforcement processes, behavior tends to be *situation specific* rather than reflecting enduring traits within the person.

Traditional Psychodynamic Approaches

In psychodynamic approaches to assessment, personality is defined by inferred, underlying constructs such as unconscious intrapsychic dynamics. These underlying features are seen as stable aspects of individuals that produce consistency in a person's behavior across different situational settings and across time. The purpose of assessment is to identify these unconscious dynamics and to provide a diagnostic label if they are pathological (e.g., causative of behavior disorders) in nature. A person's response to an assessment instrument is rarely of interest in its own right. Rather, it is viewed as an indirect manifestation of personality traits or dynamics that cannot be directly observed. For example, a person's responses to ambiguous test stimuli such as pictures or inkblots may indicate the presence of unconscious motivational conflicts causative of the client's presenting problem. Assessment of personality traits or unconscious motives may lead to a diagnosis, with general clues for treatment. However, there is little direct relationship between traditional psychodynamic assessment and treatment (Goldfried & Kent, 1972).

Defining Features of Behavioral Assessment

Behavior therapists carefully examine the nature of their clients' problems and the critical factors that influence them. In concert with factors that exist "within" a person—such as patterns of psychophysiological, cognitive, or affective responding—contextual factors in the environment are seen as major determinants of behavior. Thus, in contrast with more traditional views of personality and psychopathology, individual behavior is not viewed as inherently stable across different life situations. Furthermore, a client's overt responses to assessment instruments are of interest in their own right, and must be sampled as extensively and accurately as possible. Finally, in contrast with traditional approaches, a primary function of behavioral assessment includes selection of appropriate treatment techniques and evaluation of treatment progress and outcome. In fact, assessment can be viewed as the first stage of behavioral therapy.

However, behavioral assessment is hardly a static or even well-defined enterprise (Cone, 1988). From the time of its initial development, behavioral assessment has broadened significantly in scope. Many of these changes remain controversial. Thus, we will begin with a brief overview of the development of behavioral assessment, then consider current conceptualizations and controversies.

Development of Behavioral Assessment

Behavioral assessment emerged during the 1960s, partly as a reaction to weaknesses inherent in traditional models of assessment (Kanfer & Saslow, 1969). Syndromal diagnosis and psychodynamic procedures (such as projective tests) were criticized because of their limited scientific validation and limited usefulness in suggesting treatment approaches.

Early approaches to behavioral assessment were idiographic—tailored to the unique features of each case. Consistent with the emphasis on conditioning and learning principles, assessment focused on specific behavior in specific surroundings. During this early period, behavioral avoidance tests (Lang & Lazovik, 1963) and observational measures of problem behavior in specific environmental contexts were developed.

Behavioral assessment continued to expand during the 1970s. This decade has been called the "honeymoon" period in the development of behavioral assessment because it was marked by great optimism and conceptual confidence (Nelson, 1983). Approaches to the behavioral assessment of specific psychological disorders proliferated. Innaugural issues of two journals, *Behavioral Assessment* and *Journal of Behavioral Assessment,* were published. However, during the late 1970s, behavioral assessment entered a self-critical phase that Nelson (1983) has referred to as the "period of disillusionment." The idiographic emphasis of the early behavioral assessment techniques represented a potential strength, but was taken too far. If assessments are truly unique to each case, then generalizations between clients with similar features are impossible. Leading behavior therapists argued that behavioral assessment must meet traditional psychometric standards such as reliability, validity, and standardization (e.g., Goldfried & Linehan, 1977). Lack of standardization of materials and procedures makes cross-study comparisons impossible. "Norms" provide useful standards for decisions about who needs therapy and can help therapists set treatment goals. Finally, normative standards provide objective indices for evaluation of outcome.

Similar concerns were voiced over concepts of situational specificity. It is advantageous to start with the idea that behavior may be situation specific. But if behavior is *always* specific to particular situations, then how can therapists make convincing generalizations about their clients' problems?

Gradually, the idiographic, situationally focused approach of earlier approaches to behavioral assessment has given way to a broader, transactional view of psychological disorders. Assessment techniques have broadened accordingly, much to the approval of many behavior therapists and to the chagrin of others.

Current Conceptualizations and Controversies

How has the field of behavioral assessment broadened in response to earlier criticisms? First, there is much greater appreciation of the complexity of factors that converge to potentiate and maintain behavior disorders (Haynes, 1990). For example, cognitive and affective physiological responses account for much of the variance in the onset, maintenance, and cessation of behavior disorders (Parks & Hollon, 1988). Incorporating affective and cognitive variables into behavioral research and treatment has required significant broadening of assessment options.

Similarly, dynamic, multivariate models of setting and response interrelationships have greater explanatory power than static, univariate models (Haynes, 1991; Mash & Hinsley, 1990). In explaining why a particular person develops a behavior disorder at a particular time, it is common to find bidirectional interrelationships between responses, persons, and settings (Haynes & O'Brien, 1991). For example, in the case of Ellen W. (described earlier), the onset of her depressive thoughts and feelings was related to the "setting" variable of marital maladjustment. Once she began to experience depression, her relationship with her husband deteriorated even more, exacerbating her perceptions of hopelessness. Likewise, in the case of the anxious surgeon, a string of personal loss experiences sensitized him to feelings of vulnerability, and he personalized the death of a patient. Anxious, ruminative fears about his own competence interfered with his surgical skills. His shaky behavior in the operating room elicited critical reactions from others and increased self-criticism, which led to a more generalized anxiety reaction.

At the same time, many of the core assumptions underlying behavioral assessment have remained unchanged. For example, there is widespread agreement that functional analyses of problem behavior should be conducted using minimally inferential assessment tools (Cone, l988). Furthermore, it is widely assumed that modifying setting and response variables associated with the problem behavior will lead to improved functioning (O'Brien & Haynes, l993).

A related issue concerns the changing role of "traditional" diagnostic categorization in behavioral assessment. During the initial development of behavioral assessment, traditional diagnostic labels were rejected outright as useless or even harmful. The reigning diagnostic system at that time, an earlier edition of the *Diagnostic and Statistical Manual* (American Psychiatric Association, 1968), was vaguely formulated and thus unreliable. However, the manual was completely revised in 1980, and diagnostic criteria were specified in concrete behavioral terms. In the latest revision, the *DSM-IV,* empirical studies in the published literature have been used to develop and refine diagnostic categorizations (First et al., l992). Thus, many current behavior therapists have begun to incorporate syndromally based diagnosis into their assessment practices.

There are a number of ways that syndromally based systems can be useful to clinicians who practice behavioral assessment. They may provide an initial step in identifying diagnostic classes that can be further differentiated in functional analysis. As First and associates (1992) stated, "They act as a modular unit—DSM-IV providing the frame and behavior analysis a more finer grained and more specific picture of the particular problem confronting the patient" (p. 304). Furthermore, diagnostic systems such as the *DSM-IV* facilitate communication with other professionals who do not share the behavioristic viewpoint (Nelson & Barlow, l981). However, Krasner (l992) has offered a dissenting opinion. He has argued that efforts to integrate syndromal classification and functional analysis represent a weakening of behavioral assessment. As a result, behavioral assessment is in danger of losing its "root identity," particularly the strong emphasis on assessing social contextual factors related to the onset and maintenance of disordered behavior. This issue remains controversial.

Functions of Behavioral Assessment

Behavioral assessment is an essential part of behavior therapy. How does behavioral assessment actually facilitate the conduct of behavior therapy? There are five main functions:

- Description of problem
- Identification of controlling variables
- Evaluation of adaptive significance
- Selection of treatment
- Evaluation of outcome

Description of Problem

The most obvious first step in behavioral assessment is to obtain a clear description of specific problems that the client would like to change. Often, when clients seek psychotherapy, they present vague descriptions of their problems such as, "I just don't get much pleasure out of life anymore," "I feel tense and wound up a lot," or "I just can't seem to get along with my mate/child/parents." The therapist's task is to encourage the client to "translate" these complaints into specific problems amenable to change. For example, the person who complains of relationship problems may be referring to verbal arguments that tend to recur and are organized around specific conflict issues. The frequency, duration, and intensity of the problem are then pinpointed in order to determine the severity of the problem. One client may describe mild arguments with a spouse that last for a few minutes and occur once or twice a month; another may describe daily fights involving shouting and physical violence.

Identification of Controlling Variables

Once a specific problem (or set of problems) is identified, the next step is to examine the types of antecedent and consequent stimuli that could be maintaining it. This is the essence of functional analysis. Kanfer and Saslow (1969) have proposed a conceptual model, the S-O-R-C-K model, which helps guide clinicians through the stages of assessment. *S* refers to *stimuli*—antecedent events or discriminative stimuli—that function to cue the problem behavior. *O* refers to the *organism*, or the characteristics of the individual that cannot be directly observed but may play a role in perpetuation of the problem (for example, biological predisposition to behave impulsively or dysfunctional thoughts which precipitate depressive feelings). *R* refers to *responses* or behaviors identified by the client as problematic. *C* refers to the immediate *consequences* of the behavior, and *K* signifies *contingencies* or *current schedules* of reinforcement.

Thus, a comprehensive analysis of "controlling" variables must include analysis of precipitating events (which may be characteristics of specific situational contexts), individual predispositions that the client brings to the situation, current environmental variables, and the types of positive and negative consequences which help maintain the problem. For example, in the case of Steve R.'s binge drinking (described earlier), overconsumption of alcohol (*R*) was confined to bar settings (*S*) and resulted in states of drunkenness (*C*). When Steve arrived at the bar, he typically reported having thoughts such as "It's been a stressful week—I deserve to have a good time tonight" (*O*). This pattern of behavior was strongly positively reinforced by the presence of friends, who drank with him and shared "good times" (*K*). Arrests for driving under the influence served as punishing consequences (*K*).

Evaluation of Adaptive Significance

How does the problem behavior affect the person's ability to function effectively in different life contexts? In order to evaluate this important issue, the clinician might use criteria such as comparison of the problem with some "normal" standard; danger to self or others; and impairment of social, occupational, or personal functioning (Kazdin, 1985).

Selection of Treatment

There is no general behavioral model for selecting an appropriate treatment strategy. If a client identifies more than one problem, it is necessary to decide which specific problem behaviors should be changed first. There are no absolute rules for selecting among alternative treatment goals, but useful guidelines have been offered by several clinicians. For example, Nelson and Hayes (1979) have suggested the following criteria for selecting among various treatment targets:

- Dangerousness to self or others
- Behaviors that are highly irritating to others
- Behaviors that are easiest to change (in order to increase the client's feelings of hopefulness and sense of personal efficacy)
- When behaviors exist as part of a sequential chain, those at the beginning of the sequence should be altered first

After alternative problems have been prioritized, assessment data can be used to develop a therapy that has a high probability of success. In guiding the choice of treatment, primary considerations are the nature of the client's problem and the nature of the controlling variables. For example, in the case of Ellen W. (described earlier), it would be a mistake to treat her depressive symptoms without addressing issues of marital maladjustment.

Evaluation of Treatment Progress and Outcome

The final assessment function involves evaluation of treatment progress and outcome. According to Barlow, Hayes, and Nelson (1984), evaluation of treatment effects can be addressed to three different questions: (1) Is the treatment being implemented successfully? (2) Is the treatment effective in alleviating the client's presenting problems? and (3) What are the implications of the treatment effects for clinical science? Reflecting the idiographic emphasis, early behavioral approaches to treatment evaluation involved single-subject designs that were focused on discrete target behaviors. In line with the broadening conceptual paradigms in behavior therapy, current approaches have emphasized the need to treat multiple target behaviors and to assess outcome from many different perspectives (Farrell, 1993). Finally, it is essential to show that treatment effects generalize across different situations and across time (Barrios, 1988).

Behavioral Assessment Methods

Having discussed some general features of behavioral assessment, we now turn to specific methods used to collect data. Behavior therapists tend to use multiple assessment techniques, although the exact nature and number are determined by the unique features of each case.

Behavioral Interviews

Among behavior therapists, the behavioral interview is almost universally employed to gather information concerning problem behavior (Guevremont & Spiegler, 1990). The therapist's general goals are twofold: (1) to establish a warm, supportive, and trusting relationship with the client and (2) to achieve detailed information about the nature, development, and current context of the client's stated problems. This information allows the clinican to develop a preliminary model of controlling factors related to target behavior, and to select settings and methods for assessment and variables for treatment evaluation and design (Haynes, 1990).

1. *Establish a good relationship.* Although behavior therapy is generally time limited and problem focused, this does not preclude the necessity of establishing good rapport with clients. General characteristics of successful therapists have been detailed elsewhere (e.g., Egan, 1982). Good relationship-building skills involve the ability to show respect and caring to the client, the ability to listen carefully and to be empathically responsive to the client's distress, and the ability to present oneself as genuine. These therapist skills are necessary to the success of *any* form of psychotherapy. In addition, successful behavior therapists must possess good structuring skills and strike a balance between allowing clients to ventilate painful feelings and getting detailed information about the problem behavior. All of these qualities require excellent judgement and interpersonal skill, typically achieved through advanced training.

2. *Achieve adequate information about the client's presenting problems.* The information-gathering procedure has been likened to a funnel (Hawkins, 1979) in that, initially, a wide range of life events are discussed, narrowing to more specific information as the interviewer progresses. The therapist attempts to obtain a picture of the "whole" person in his or her social milieu. The following areas are usually assessed:

a. *Psychosocial adjustment.* Psychosocial adjustment reflects the number, type, and severity of emotional or behavioral problems, at the present time and in the past, and the quality of the client's social relationships. Past history is usually explored, although not in the detail achieved by psychodynamically oriented practitioners. Information about the client's overall history of social adjustment is obtained, subdivided into areas such as relationships with family, friends, intimate partners, teachers/employers, and co-workers.

b. *Academic and vocational adjustment.* General information about the client's history of academic and vocational achievement is also obtained, including present level of vocational success and satisfaction and relevant information about school achievement.

c. *Medical.* Pertinent medical information may be obtained, such as past/present histories of serious illnesses and/or hospitalizations. Frequently, clinicians also inquire whether close relatives have had histories of severe psychological and/or physical disorders.

d. *Assets.* The client's assets are carefully assessed. These might include quality of the client's social support system and/or special areas of competence such as high intelligence or good social skills.

e. *Motivation.* Clinicians ask how the client has tried to handle the problem in the past, and how well these efforts have succeeded. It is important to ascertain the strength of the client's motivation to change and whether the client has positive expectancies that change can occur, since these cognitive factors affect how hard people will try (Bandura, 1986). For example, a therapist might ask: How would your life be different if _____ were no longer a problem for you?

Through skilled questioning and possibly the use of other assessment techniques, the therapist and client narrow the focus to one or more well-defined problems. The therapist probes to achieve clear descriptions and examples. Once specific problems have been identified as appropriate for treatment, the therapist moves to an explanation of potential "controlling variables."

Behavioral interviews provide a wealth of information that is used in treatment planning, implementation, and evaluation. However, despite the widespread use of this assessment tool, there is a dearth of information about the reliability and validity of behavioral interviews (O'Brien & Haynes, 1993).

Structured Interviews and Rating Scales

Structured interviews and rating scales were designed to provide differential diagnoses of clients' presenting problems and to assess the severity of symptoms associated with diagnostic categories (Morrison, 1988). Questions refer to the duration, content, course, and severity of specific symptoms. Examples of better-known instruments include the Schedule for Affective Disorders and Schizophrenia (SADS; Endicott & Spitzer, 1978); Diagnostic Interview Schedule (DIS; Robins, Heltzer, Croughan, & Ratcliff, 1988); and the Structured Clinical Interview for the DSM (SCID; Spitzer & Williams, 1985).

Structured interviews have several advantages. They are reliable, inexpensive, and fairly easy to administer, and they allow modest flexibility in interview content. However, they have important disadvantages as well, particularly for behaviorally oriented clinicians. Structured interviews require lengthy administration times (e.g., the SADS takes between 1½ and 2 hours to administer). Moreover, these instruments do not provide information about contextual factors related to problem behavior: Diagnosis alone is insufficient for treatment formulation (Persons, 1991). Finally, the validity of most structured interview formats has not been adequately established (Wixted, Morrison, & Rinaldi, 1993). Use of structured interviews is typically confined to clinical situations where a precise diagnostic label is required, such as treatment studies of individuals who suffer from the same type of disorder.

Questionnaires

Frequently, self-report checklists and questionnaires are used during the initial stages of therapy to identify the range and intensity of the client's presenting problems. Behavioral self-report questionnaires have focused on observable phenomena such as the frequency and type of undesirable behaviors. Unlike self-report questionnaires employed in traditional assessment, behavioral questionnaires are highly problem focused. For example, the Wolpe and Lang (1969) Fear Survey Schedule consists of 72 items on which clients rate the degree of fear corresponding to different situations or objects. More recently, in line with the "cognitive revolution" in behavioral therapy, questionnaires have been designed to assess the type and frequency of maladaptive thoughts (Parks & Hollon, 1988; Smith, 1989). For example, on the widely used Beck Depression Inventory (see Chapter 9), clients assess the frequency of self-critical and suicidal thoughts.

Self-report questionnaires are advantageous because they cover a wide range of clinical disorders and they are easily administered, quick, and inexpensive. Because of these practical virtues, they are frequently used in screening and in evaluations of treatment progress and outcome. Limitations include the possibility of distortion, bias, or misinterpretation in the client's responses; lack of attention to situational specificity; and, in many cases, questionable validity (O'Brien & Haynes, 1993). For these reasons, data derived from self-report questionnaires should always be supplemented with other sources of information about the client's problem.

Analogue Techniques

Analogue techniques involve asking the client to respond to contrived situations in the clinic or laboratory that are similar to real-life problem situations. A range of media and techniques have been used, including paper and pencil responses to written scripts, asking the client to attend to audiotaped or videotaped situations, asking the client to enact problematic social interactions in the consulting room, or asking the client to assume various roles of persons involved in troubling social exchanges. For example, McFall (1977) assessed interpersonal skills of adults by asking them to respond to a contrived script, and Lang and Lazovik (1963) have assessed avoidance behavior in phobias by devising behavioral avoidance tests. Analogue techniques may be very useful in generating hypotheses about the nature of the client's problems. However, the degree of correspondence between contrived stimuli and real-life problems they represent may not be great and has rarely been tested by clinicians (Nay, 1986). For this reason, analogue methods should be used cautiously and supplemented with other sources of information about the problem at hand.

Self-Monitoring

Self-monitoring involves recording aspects of one's own behavior for use in treatment. Self-monitoring is especially helpful in the case of low-frequency events, which would be difficult to observe independently. If the presenting problem involves some sort of "private event," such as cravings or dysfunctional thoughts, self-monitoring is one of the only means available for assessment.

Traditionally, clients have been asked to compute frequency counts of discrete behaviors that are short in duration (such as number of drinks taken or cigarettes smoked). A variety of assessment tools have been used, including written diaries, mechanical counters, and timing devices. If a given response occurs very frequently, the client might be asked to record behavior only during certain time periods each day. In the case of behaviors that are not discrete, such as studying, exercising, practicing, or writing, the client may be asked to record the time spent on the activity each day. Finally, clients may be asked to keep daily records of negative thoughts that are keyed to certain life situations. For example, recording immediate cognitive reactions to upsetting situations can help one assess dysfunctional thought patterns relevant to anxiety or depression.

If self-monitoring is to be successful, the target behavior must be carefully defined and the client must be adequately trained. The advantages of self-monitoring are many:

- It can be can be carried out anywhere.
- It permits sampling of low-frequency private events, such as illicit drug use or sexual behavior.
- It promotes insight into how one's own behavior is related to situational and other factors.
- Simply asking someone to monitor his or her behavior may promote positive change (although this is a disadvantage of the technique as well).

Potential drawbacks of self-monitoring include noncompliance, reactivity, and inaccuracy. In trying to circumvent noncompliance, it is important that the therapist selects a recording method appropriate to client's problem, trains the client in self-monitoring techniques, then follows up with phone or mail contacts (Ciminero, Nelson, & Lipinski, 1977). The reactivity problem is a more difficult one. When individuals self-record their own behavior, it tends to change in frequency. Generally, positive target behaviors tend to increase in frequency under self-monitoring, whereas negative target behaviors tend to decrease (Ciminero et al., 1977). Finally, when independent checks of self-monitored data have been conducted, many investigators have reported poor accuracy. Thus, the assessment function of self-monitoring is hampered by problems of reactivity and inaccuracy, particularly in situations where pretreatment baseline data must be obtained (Bornstein, Hamilton, & Bornstein, 1986). For these reasons, self-monitoring should be used with caution and supplemented with other forms of assessment data.

Direct Observation

Direct observation of problem behaviors in natural settings (such as homes, schools, or residential treatment facilities) played an important role in the initial development of behavioral assessment (Foster & Cone, 1986). The greatest advantage of *in-vivo* observation is that problem behavior can be observed in its customary situational context, leading directly to hypotheses about possible controlling variables. For example, direct observation of bizarre, inappropriate behavior on the part of someone hospitalized with schizophrenia may reveal that the patient gains a lot of attention from the staff for this behavior. This hypothesis can be directly tested, using behavioral treatment methods.

However, the many potential limitations of *in-vivo* observation preclude its widespread use in clinical practice. The following drawbacks are most salient:

1. *Reactivity.* Perhaps the greatest drawback of observational methods is reactivity to the presence of the observer (Foster, Bell-Dolan, & Burge, 1988). People tend to behave differently when they know that they are being observed by others. Research suggests that reactivity effects are greater under some conditions than others. For example, studies of individuals in residential treatment facilities have revealed little evidence for reactivity to observation, whereas studies of normal families and the families of boys referred for behavior problems have revealed strong reactivity effects (Romanczyk, Kent, Diament, & O'Leary, 1973). Reactivity problems can be minimized by decreasing the intrusiveness of the observers and by scheduling an adaptation period that allows the individual(s) to habituate to the presence of the observer.

2. *Reliability of observations.* Reliability refers to how well two independent observers can agree on descriptions of the same phenomena. Typically, this requires intensive training. Diverse factors have been found to affect reliability, including the complexity of social behaviors and interactions under observation, observers' awareness that a reliability assessment is being conducted, observer fatigue, and the tendency for observers to "drift" from the original coding criteria over time (Taplin & Reid, 1973). Scheduling unannounced reliability checks and allowing sufficient rest periods may help attentuate these problems.

3. *Validity of observations.* Validity refers to how well the observational system measures what it is intended to measure. Validity is influenced by many factors, including the comprehensiveness of the coding system, the number of observations conducted, and the extent to which different situations relevant to the problem behavior are adequately sampled (Foster et al., 1988).

4. *Cost-efficiency.* Direct observation is expensive and time consuming. This impracticality has been a critical obstacle to frequent use of observational methods in general clinical practice.

Psychophysiological Recording Methods

Psychophysiological recording methods are used to assess patterns of physiological responding relevant to behavior disorders or health problems. Common assessment targets have included cardiovascular responses, respiratory activity, gastrointestinal activity, electrodermal activity, cortical activity, and muscular activity (Sturgis & Gramling, 1988). Psychophysiological measures have proven useful in assessments of diverse clinical problems, particularly fear and anxiety, problems of sexual arousal, and health-related disorders. However, interpretation is complex, because psychophysiological data are influenced by many different types of individual, setting, and procedural variables (Kallman & Feuerstein, 1988). For example, like observational measures, these measures are reactive to situational variables that are completely irrelevant to the problem behavior (Farrell, 1993). Moreover, the reliability and validity of many psychophysiological measures have not been well established (Kallman & Feuerstein, 1988). Finally, these measures require specialized equipment and expertise, which limits their practicality.

Case Illustrations

Having surveyed the various methods of behavioral assessment, we will now return to the three individuals whose problems were briefly described in the beginning of this chapter. In each case, it is clear that behavioral assessment provided a firm foundation for the selection and evaluation of treatment interventions.

THE CASE OF ELLEN W.

Ellen W., the 43-year-old lawyer who presented concerns about depression, was interviewed and asked to complete a brief rating scale of depressive symptoms. Her scores on the rating scale placed her in the moderately depressed range, and her responses to the interview revealed that marital maladjustment had precipitated her depressive symptoms. Hence, she and her husband were asked to come in for an interview together. During the interview, they discussed their marital concerns and (independently) completed standardized questionnaires designed to assess the severity of their marital dissatisfaction.

In addition, the therapist used an analog technique in which the couple discussed their most heated conflict issues while being observed from behind a one-way mirror. The marital evaluation revealed that the couple had poor conflict resolution skills. For example, during the heat of "battle," Ellen would quickly lapse into blaming statements about her husband's behavior, and he would respond by retreating into stony silence. At the same time, both individuals were willing to work on their marriage. They participated in 12 sessions of behavioral couples therapy designed to improve the general quality of their relationship and to teach them effective conflcit resolution skills. Following therapy, the couple reported significantly higher levels of marital satisfaction (they were now in the "normal" range of satisfaction) and Ellen's depressive symptoms remitted completely.

THE CASE OF STEVE A.

Steve A., the court-referred binge drinker, was interviewed and asked to complete several standardized self-report questionnaires about his drinking problems. In addition, he was asked to self-monitor his drinking behavior for two weeks, noting the situational context of urges to drink and his associated thoughts and feelings. These data revealed that Steve's drinking was completely confined to bar situations, where he drank in the company of friends. Gaining relief from stress was a recurring theme. The assessment also revealed that Steve had many strengths: He was intelligent, motivated to change, and socially resourceful. His goal was to modify his intake of alcohol to no more than two drinks on one occasion.

The therapist helped Steve develop a self-control program that would allow him to achieve his light drinking goal. In addition, because Steve felt stressed by his heavy workload, he was taught cognitive and behavioral techniques for dealing with stress arousal. These included increasing his level of exercise, engaging in daily periods of relaxation, and cognitive restructuring. Steve achieved his light drinking goal within three months, and had maintained progress one year later.

THE CASE OF ROBERT W.

Robert W., the anxious surgeon, was interviewed and given several symptom checklists to complete. In addition, he was asked to keep a diary of his anxiety symptoms for two weeks, noting the types of situational contexts and cognitive reactions that were associated with his feelings of anxiety. Assessment revealed that Robert was an extreme perfectionist who experienced high levels of tension on a daily basis. Typically, his tense and focused demeanor did not interfere with his work. However, he reported feeling "emotionally undone" by the recent deaths of loved ones, which sensitized him to fears about his own vulnerability and competence. Robert's diary revealed that he was engaging in many different types of cognitive distortions about his professional competence.

Thus, a therapy plan was developed, focusing on (1) cognitive restructuring exercises, (2) homework assignments focused on gradual reimmersion into surgery (e.g., he was asked to assist other physicians at first, then gradually reassume more control), and (3) general tension reduction skills (cognitive exercises, aerobic exercise, and relaxation). All of these interventions were framed as ways of helping him become more productive and "in control." After three months of treatment, his anxiety symptoms had decreased to normative levels, and he reported no difficulties in assuming full work responsibilities.

Chapter Summary

Behavioral assessment is a vital component of behavior therapy. Early approaches to behavioral assessment focused on identifying the types of controlling variables that were related to discrete problem behaviors occurring in particular situations. Over time, the field has broadened to encompass standardized measures, and multiple measures of problem behavior that may include cognitive or affective responses. In contrast with other approaches to assessment, the chief function of behavioral assessment is to facilitate behavioral therapy. Behavioral assessment is used to (1) develop clear and specific descriptions of presenting problems, (2) identify variables related to the onset and maintenance of these problems, (3) evaluate the severity of the client's problems, (4) identify effective treatment options, and (5) provide a means of evaluating treatment implementation, progress, and outcome. Methods of behavioral assessment cover a wide range of techniques and situational contexts. They include behavioral interviews, structured interviews and rating scales, self-report questionnaires, analog techniques, self-monitoring techniques, direct observation, and measures of psychophysiological responses.

Endnote

1. In the original Greek, *syndrome* literally means "running together."

Applications with Specific Problems and Disorders

This next section, Chapters 7 to 17, describes applications of behavior therapy to particular clinical issues and problems. Our presentation will show that behavior therapy is applicable to the broad sweep of mental health problems affecting children and adults; inpatients and outpatients; and individuals, couples, and families. Throughout this section, we integrate case examples (often from our own clinical work), reviews of research findings, and surveys of the important theoretical formulations.

Each chapter of Section III covers behavior therapy as applied to a major problem area, such as anxiety, depression, or disorders of childhood. This allows us to explain, for each set of disorders, such matters as the historical development of behavior therapy applications, the variety of conceptual formulations, and the range of potentially suitable therapeutic techniques. We could have organized the section with each chapter focused on a specific treatment method, but that would require considering each major disorder within each chapter. Using problem areas (rather than techniques and procedures) as an organizing principle helps us to communicate better with instructors and students familiar with the typical Abnormal Psychology course. Consistent with our discussion in Chapter 6, this form of organization also helps us to build a bridge between behavioral assessment and the *DSM-IV* classification. Finally, we are able to discuss the specific assessment strategies, research designs, and treatment interventions that have proven appropriate in the context of each problem area.

One drawback to organizing chapters by disorders is that we risk giving the misleading impression that every clinical problem has a matching behavioral treatment technique, to be used in all cases. That would run counter to proper behavioral practice, in which each treatment plan is based on an individual behavioral analysis. For example, you will see that empirical research strongly supports the use of exposure with response prevention to help clients with compulsive rituals, and panic control therapy to treat panic disorder. But that does not necessarily mean that all clients will benefit from the same, generic treatment plan. One of our current clients, whose *DSM-IV* disorder is Panic Disorder with Agoraphobia, was offered the "standard" treatment regimen initially, but he is making far better progress after detailed assessment suggested a cognitive-behavioral intervention to reduce his sense of shame in social situations.

Behavior therapists use research findings on treatment effectiveness judiciously, bringing empirically validated techniques into play when they match the particular pattern of issues presented by the client. It would be inappropriate and unethical to ignore a research-validated "treatment of choice" in formulating a treatment plan and making recommendations to a client. But unthinkingly choosing a treatment technique from a list approved for the particular disorder would be a technical, not a professional, activity that could do clients a disservice. Behavior therapists not only know how to implement therapeutic techniques but they also make professional judgments on which procedures to employ with particular clients. This section of the book is designed to make you aware of the spectrum of conceptual, empirical, and procedural matters relevant to the behavioral assessment and treatment of each disorder.

C h a p t e r 7

Anxiety Disorders

Diana's panic disorder had dominated her life since her college days. On her thirtieth birthday she decided that she had had enough of it. Her family physician had helped her a few years earlier with prescribed medication, but Diana was disappointed when her problems returned almost as soon as she stopped taking the drug. She was not opposed to medication in itself; it had practically saved her life when she had had asthma as a child. But she was determined to deal with her anxiety disorder by psychological methods if at all possible, and she asked for an appointment with a behavior therapist.

Diana told her therapist that her major concern was the unpredictable attacks of panic. These always began with the sudden sensation of being unable to catch her breath, but her symptoms rapidly mounted, so that within a minute, she would feel a surge of additional sensations: racing heart, nausea, dizziness, and a sense of unreality and detachment from her surroundings. Diana's secondary concern was that, as a result of her panic attacks, she had begun to avoid certain situations. As she put it, it was bad enough having a panic attack in the comfort of her own home, but the prospect of having one when she was eating in a restaurant, attending a concert, or sitting on a bus was just too scary for her to risk it.

Diana's treatment proceeded well, but slowly. Although she was no longer troubled by asthma, she was not willing to practice various exercises to help her confront her anxiety about being out of breath—exercises such as holding her breath, sucking air through a straw, or even mild aerobic routines, like running in place for a few minutes. Instead, Diana followed a program of cognitive therapy and graduated real-life practice, systematically confronting feared external situations until the severity of her panics had been reduced considerably.

Over the holiday season, though, Diana had a major setback. Visiting a friend's house, she had encountered the smoke from a scented candle, which immediately precipitated an asthma attack, her first in years. At the emergency room she was given the standard, medically appropriate treatment—an injection of medication designed to open her breathing passages. But the medication contained a significant amount of adrenalin, which, on top of the original asthma crisis, triggered a major panic attack. Fortunately, the story ended happily when Diana resumed her behavioral treatment, this time actively confronting her fear of breathlessness. Within a few months she was panic free and no longer avoiding situations because of anxiety.

Most people have experienced anxiety as a response to the threat of danger: the car sliding out of control down an icy hill, an unfamiliar dog baring its teeth in a menacing way, even news of a natural disaster. Even situations without the threat of physical danger can trigger anxiety: the employer unsmilingly calling you into the office, or the endless expanse of row upon row of faces looking up as you begin an important speech. Perhaps still more unsettling is the sense of tension and "nerves" that may spring up for no apparent reason. Whatever the cause, anxiety has affective, behavioral, and cognitive components: People feel, act, and think anxiously. Take the example of Larry, the mill worker who feared public speaking (see Chapter 2). When speaking, he felt tense, jittery, and nauseated; he could not make eye contact with his audience, he stumbled over his words, he wanted to run from the room; and his thoughts focused on being ridiculed or rejected, embarrassing himself before his friends, and failing to cope adequately with the situation.

Generally, anxiety is viewed as a clinical problem if the client is intensely distressed or disabled by it. It is certainly distressing to experience panic attacks or other intense anxiety episodes. It is certainly disabling when anxiety leads to avoidance of routine activities, so that one cannot work or socialize. And it is certainly distressing and disabling when anxiety arises in harmless situations or in any or all situations (Mahoney, 1980; Wilson, Nathan, O'Leary, & Clark, 1996).

Behavior therapists have paid a great deal of attention to disorders in which anxiety is prominent. The traditional term for any disorder of this kind was *neurosis,* originally defined by the Scottish physician William Cullen (1710–1790) "as all those preternatural affections of sense and motion . . . which do not depend upon a topical affection of the organs, but upon a more general affection of the nervous system, and of those powers of the system upon which sense and motion more especially depend" (Hunter & MacAlpine, 1963, p. 475).

In other words, neuroses are disturbances of experience and behavior that are hard to explain and that are caused not by biological abnormalities but by *something* generally wrong in the nervous system. What that something is varies according to one's theoretical viewpoint. Behavior therapists usually object to the term *neurosis* today because it has strong associations with psychoanalysis and it implies that anxiety is rooted in unconscious conflicts. For similar reasons, the term appears only parenthetically in the *DSM-IV*. But the term is sometimes used in the writings of behavior therapists to refer to a large group of problems commonly treated in outpatient clinics. Examples are compulsive rituals, obsessional thoughts, hysterical fits, phobias, tics, conversion reactions, nocturnal enuresis, reactive depression, and sexual dysfunctions (Stampfl & Levis, 1967). *Causes and Cures of Neurosis* was the confident title of one of the most significant early books on behavior therapy (Eysenck & Rachman, 1965). What were once called *neuroses* now appear in the *DSM-IV* under a variety of headings, one of which is *anxiety disorders*, the topic of this chapter and the next.

The DSM-IV Classification

The anxiety disorders are grouped into 12 categories in the *DSM-IV.* These include categories for medically related and substance-induced anxiety, together with a category for anxiety problems that do not fit into the other 11. We will focus on 9 anxiety disorders in this book, 7 in this chapter and 2 in the next: Panic Disorder Without Agoraphobia, Panic Disorder With Agoraphobia, Agoraphobia Without History of Panic Disorder, Specific Phobia, Social Phobia, Obsessive-Compulsive Disorder, and Generalized Anxiety Disorder (this chapter), and Posttraumatic Stress Disorder and Acute Stress Disorder (Chapter 8).

Panic Disorder

Before describing this disorder[1] it is necessary to define the *panic attack,* which is not a disorder in itself but the major feature of panic disorder. The *DSM-IV* criteria[2] for a panic attack may be paraphrased as follows:

CRITERIA FOR A PANIC ATTACK

A definite period of intense fear or distress with at least 4 from the following list of 13 symptoms, each of which develops rapidly and reaches a peak within 10 minutes:

- Racing or pounding heart, or palpitations
- Sweating
- Trembling or shaking
- Feeling of shortness of breath
- Feeling of choking
- Chest pain or discomfort
- Nausea or abdominal distress
- Feeling faint, dizzy, or light-headed
- Feelings of unreality or detachment
- Fear of losing control or going crazy
- Fear of dying during the attack
- Unusual bodily sensations
- Chills or hot flushes

In *panic disorder* the client has recurrent, unpredictable panic attacks, at least one of which has been followed by one month or more of worry about having further attacks (or about their consequences). These panic attacks must not be the result of medical problems, drug use, or another mental disorder. Panic disorder takes two forms: *Panic Disorder Without Agoraphobia* and *Panic Disorder With Agoraphobia.* These are defined by the presence or absence of *agoraphobia*, not a diagnostic category itself but a feature of certain anxiety disorders. The criteria for agoraphobia are paraphrased next:

CRITERIA FOR AGORAPHOBIA

- Anxiety is experienced about being in situations that would not allow easy escape if panic symptoms arose (e.g., as being far from home, being in crowded public places, and using public transportation).

- The client avoids these situations, or, if not, experiences marked distress if a trusted companion is not present.
- The anxiety symptoms are not better explained by a different disorder.

The *lifetime prevalence* of a disorder is cited as the percentage of people who have the disorder at some point during their lives. Panic disorder (with or without agoraphobia) has a lifetime prevalence of 1.5 to 3.5 percent, and is more common in women than in men (American Psychiatric Association, 1994; Lucas, 1994).

Phobias

A *phobia* (named from *Phobos,* a Greek god who could frighten his enemies) chiefly involves persistent, irrational fear of a specific situation or object, resulting in a strong desire to avoid it. The individual recognizes that the fear is exaggerated or unreasonable, but nevertheless feels unable to control the phobia. In 1812, Benjamin Rush defined a phobia as "a fear of an imaginary evil, or an undue fear of a real one" (Hunter & MacAlpine, 1963, p. 669).

Agoraphobia Without History of Panic Disorder
The term *agoraphobia* derives from the Greek word for "place of assembly" or "market place," not from the Latin word from which we get "agriculture" (Marks, 1970; Thorpe, 1994). Confusion on this point has led many people to associate agoraphobia mistakenly with fear of open spaces such as fields. Instead, the chief feature of agoraphobia is concern about suddenly having embarrassing or crippling symptoms, but not to the extent of actually experiencing panic attacks (if the person has panic attacks, then Panic Disorder With Agoraphobia is the appropriate label). The concern about the sudden onset of distress leads to a strong fear of being in a situation without the possibility of help, or escape, if the symptom should arise. The *DSM-IV* criteria for agoraphobia as a symptom cluster are listed in the preceding section. When the person has agoraphobia but has never had a panic attack, the diagnostic label is *Agoraphobia Without History of Panic Disorder.* Here are the criteria for the disorder:

DIAGNOSTIC CRITERIA FOR AGORAPHOBIA WITHOUT HISTORY OF PANIC DISORDER

- The person has agoraphobia associated with the fear of having panic-like symptoms.
- The person's problems have never met the criteria for Panic Disorder.
- The problems are not caused by medical problems, drug use, or another mental disorder.

The highest estimates of the lifetime prevalence of agoraphobia range from 3 to 6 percent (Weissman, 1985), but these figures are probably too high. Many more women than men have agoraphobia. Almost all people who who seek treatment for agoraphobia have Panic Disorder With Agoraphobia (American Psychiatric Association, 1994).

Social Phobia
In *Social Phobia* the person is distressed by pronounced anxiety about being observed in a critical way by others, coupled with the fear of doing something embarrassing. The person

almost always experiences anxiety in such situations and often avoids them, interfering significantly with social or work activities. This category is essentially a grouping of specific phobias that have in common a theme of social-evaluative anxiety. Common examples are fears of public speaking, interviewing for a job, and eating in a restaurant.

Nearly 350 years ago, in his famous book *Anatomy of Melancholy*, Robert Burton (1651–2/1898) gave a description of social phobia that applies just as well to some clients today: "Many lamentable effects this fear causeth in men, as to be red, pale, tremble, sweat, it makes sudden cold and heat to come over all the body, palpitation of the heart, syncope, &c. [etc.]. It amazeth many men that are to speak, or show themselves in public assemblies, or before some great personages" (p. 172). Men and women seek treatment for social phobia at approximately equal rates; prevalence estimates vary widely (American Psychiatric Association, 1994; Marks, 1987).

Specific Phobia

Any phobia of a particular object or situation, not better described as agoraphobia or social phobia, fits the category of *Specific Phobia*. Typical specific phobias are fears of small animals or insects; of heights, darkness, or confinement; and of blood, injury, and illness. Perhaps the most common specific fear among people, in general, is the fear of illness or disease, but clients rarely seek therapy for this. (The diagnosis of specific phobia is only given if the problem interferes significantly with the person's life.) To take another historical example, in the 1650s in England Sir Kenelm Digby described King James's phobia of naked swords:

> *He could not see one without a great emotion of his spirits. . . . I remember when he dubbed me Knight, in the ceremony of putting the point of a naked sword upon my shoulder, he could not endure to look upon it, but turned his face another way, insomuch, that in lieu of touching my shoulder, he had almost thrust the point into my eyes, had not the Duke of Buckingham guided his hand aright. (Haggard, 1929/1946, p. 347)*

Estimates of the prevalence of specific phobia have varied greatly, depending on how severe the problem has to be in order to be counted as a phobia. Phobias are common among people in general but rarely cause significant disability (American Psychiatric Asociation, 1994). Little Hans's fear of horses (Chapter 1), and Susan B.'s fear of spiders (Chapter 2), would be classified as specific phobias.

Obsessive-Compulsive Disorder

The essential problems in *Obsessive-Compulsive Disorder* are (1) worrisome, intrusive thoughts, ideas, or images that the client resists; or (2) an urge to repeat a ritual or stereotyped behavior of some kind while realizing that this is unreasonable and unnecessary. The disorder is equally common in women and men, and has a lifetime prevalence of about 2.5 percent (American Psychiatric Association, 1994; Weissman, 1985).

One of our clients with obsessive-compulsive problems was a 14-year-old boy who had to do most things exactly three times. If he opened the refrigerator door, he had to open and close it three times. He could not walk past a window inside his house without looking out of it three times. He could not say why he felt he had to do this. If he only looked twice before passing the window, he had to go back and look three times.

Another client, Michael H., was a student of literature who was unable to study for important doctoral-level examinations because of his obsession with contamination. He worried endlessly about microscopic particles of filth infecting his skin if he touched anything that was not perfectly clean. As a result, he could not bring himself to touch the books that he needed to read in order to succeed in his graduate studies. Michael, as well as his whole household, engaged in elaborate cleansing rituals. He spent hours each day repeatedly washing his hands until they were red and raw. When he spoke to his therapist on the telephone, Michael had to get his father to hold the receiver for him because it may have been contaminated. Michael was treated successfully, and he eventually passed his exams. (We will describe his treatment later in the chapter).

Generalized Anxiety Disorder

Generalized Anxiety Disorder refers to a pattern of persistent, exaggerated anxiety and worry about one's general life circumstances. The client finds it hard to control the worry, and shows such symptoms as restlessness, concentration difficulties, muscle tension, and sleep disturbance. The anxiety pattern causes definite distress or clear impairment in social or occupational functioning. The lifetime prevalence of Generalized Anxiety Disorder has been estimated at 5 percent, with roughly equal numbers of men and women seeking treatment. From 55 to 60 percent of Generalized Anxiety Disorder clients are female (American Psychiatric Association, 1994).

Causes of Anxiety Disorders

In the following sections, we will describe conditioning, cognitive, and integrative theories that attempt to explain how clients develop anxiety disorders.

Conditioning Theories

Animal Models of Anxiety

The most obvious laboratory analogue of anxiety is the classical conditioning of fear in animals, but first, it is helpful to mention a couple of less familiar phenomena. For example, obsessive-compulsive disorder has a parallel in several animal studies (Mineka, 1985). Dogs subjected to high levels of shock during avoidance learning often displayed stereotyped behavior patterns with little apparent anxiety. Rats developed "fixations" in another group of studies. They had to jump from a pedestal toward one of two doors. One door would fall open, and the rat would land safely inside, but the other would be locked, so the rat would bump its nose and fall into a net. If the experimenter placed a particular mark on the open door, such as a plus sign, the rats would readily learn to jump toward it, even if the location of door with the plus sign (the door that would fall open) varied from trial to trial. But when the experimenter placed the sign on the doors randomly, so that sometimes the plus sign was on the open door and sometimes on the locked one, it was impossible for the rats to learn the discrimination. Their behavior became stereotyped; they would adopt a policy of always jumping toward the left door, for example, whatever the sign indicated (Yates, 1962).

In her own studies, Mineka (1985) has shown that monkeys under stress also display stereotypic and ritualistic behavior. These laboratory responses are very similar to the behavior of obsessive-compulsive clients. In both the lab and the clinic, this behavior involves a stereotyped pattern that has no bearing on what actually happens next.

Mineka (1985) has also pointed out that *experimental neurosis* (see Chapter 2) is a perfect prototype for generalized anxiety disorder. Discovered by Pavlov and others under certain experimental conditions involving conflict, experimental neurosis consists of a group of symptoms in the animals including agitation, rapid heart beat, hypersensitivity, distractibility, and helplessness (inability to perform previously learned responses). Similar phenomena are seen when monkeys and chimpanzees are separated from their parents. This *separation protest* in human and nonhuman primate infants is very similar to symptoms of panic disorder and generalized anxiety disorder (Hecker & Thorpe, 1992).

Classical Conditioning

Recall that in Chapter 1 we described the famous demonstration of fear conditioning in Little Albert by Watson and Rayner (1920). Partly as a result of this study, behavior therapists became interested in classical conditioning as a way of describing how some anxiety disorders might arise. If a client's anxiety problem arose through classical conditioning, then he or she acquired the fear of some nondangerous object accidentally, simply because it was associated with a stimulus that triggers fear or alarm. The case of Susan B. in Chapter 2 illustrates this. Spiders were not originally dangerous or fear-provoking for her, but when they were paired with the frightening experience of being locked in a shed, they became fear provoking simply because they had become attached to her alarm reflex. For Susan, spiders had become conditioned stimuli for fear.

The treatment techniques described in Chapter 2 were inspired by classical conditioning principles. Wolpe's (1958) systematic desensitization developed from a complex blend of theories, but it also fits the simpler classical conditioning view that extinction of anxiety will take place when the client confronts the feared situation. The various other exposure treatments also developed from basic research on extinction processes, and they all provide a systematic method for the client to follow in confronting feared stimuli.

The classical conditioning explanation of anxiety could apply when the client fears something in particular, as in phobic and obsessive-compulsive disorders. But it is more difficult for classical conditioning principles to accommodate panic disorder and generalized anxiety disorder, because they do not involve specific stimuli. Wolpe suggested that even in generalized anxiety disorder, the client may fear a particular stimulus without realizing it—because the stimulus is so common it is almost always present (such as light and shade contrasts, walls, etc.). But there is an obvious problem with this—one that applies to the conditioning theory of anxiety in general: Why does the client's anxiety not extinguish naturally? Any time the client experiences the feared situation without an aversive event taking place, there is the real-life equivalent of a laboratory extinction trial, and one would expect the anxiety (the conditioned response) to weaken. Why does this not happen in specific phobias, for instance, if the conditioning view is correct?

Two-Factor Theory

Mowrer (1947, 1960) tried to explain why anxiety does not seem to extinguish in the way predicted by classical conditioning theory. He did this by arguing that classical conditioning is only one of two factors operating. In *two-factor theory* the first factor is the classical conditioning of anxiety, and the second factor is the operant learning of escape and avoidance behavior. In other words, first, anxiety is acquired by classical conditioning, when a previously harmless stimulus is paired with an accidental aversive event. Second, because the situation elicits a conditioned response of anxiety on future occasions, the client understandably wishes to escape or avoid it, thus reducing the anxiety.

Applying two-factor theory to Susan B's phobia, she first became afraid of spiders because they were paired with a horribly traumatic event, and second, from that point on, she always avoided spiders because coming into contact with one immediately aroused overwhelming anxiety. But, since Susan is not locked in a shed every time a spider appears, why does her conditioned anxiety not extinguish after she has seen a few spiders under nonthreatening circumstances? The answer is that for extinction to occur, the spider would have to be present for more than a brief moment (Wilson, 1973). Susan's avoidance and escape behavior reduce her anxiety in the short run, but also have the effect of protecting her anxiety from extinction.

Rachman (1971, 1976) argued that obsessive-compulsive disorder is similar to phobias, and two-factor theory applies to both. Obsessional thoughts are similar to phobias in being conditioned stimuli that elicit anxiety. The client's ritualistic or compulsive behavior serves as an escape response that protects the obsessions from extinction.

Criticisms of Conditioning Explanations of Anxiety

Classical conditioning and two-factor theory provide convenient explanations of some anxiety disorders, and they have even inspired the development of effective treatments. But there are many difficult questions about anxiety disorders that conditioning theories cannot answer, requiring one to go further afield for convincing explanations. Some of the problems are the following:

- Animals can learn to avoid aversive stimuli without having been exposed to classical conditioning (Herrnstein, 1969; Herrnstein & Hineline, 1966; Hineline, 1977).
- Levels of fear and avoidance behavior are often at odds with one another in phobic clients (Rachman & Hodgson, 1974).
- The victims of major natural disasters do not necessarily develop new fears, despite having been subjected to highly anxiety-provoking experiences (Rachman, 1977).
- Many clients with phobias cannot recall having had an aversive experience with the situation or object they fear (Marks, 1987).
- Conditioned fear is very difficult to produce in humans in laboratory experiments, and there are many contradictory findings (Harris, 1979).

- People do not become phobic of random stimuli but tend to fear some things—such as spiders, heights, and darkness, rather than others—such as houses, trees, and electrical appliances (Marks, 1969; Seligman, 1971). (Why did Susan B. become phobic of spiders, not of backyard sheds?)
- People often develop phobias of stimuli they have never experienced directly. (Many people who have never even taken a flight describe themselves as afraid of air travel!)

There are some counterarguments. Seligman (1971) proposed that, even though people fear some things more than others, classical conditioning could still operate when phobias do arise. He put forward the concept of biological *preparedness*, suggesting that the stimuli that are prominent in phobias and obsessions are those that would always have been potentially threatening to humans. Prepared stimulus-response connections are biologically important, are easily conditioned, and are slow to extinguish. Experimental evidence on this notion, however, has produced mixed conclusions (Ohman, Erixon, & Lofberg, 1975; Silva, Rachman, & Seligman, 1977). In any event, although conditioning is one possible pathway to fear, there are several others, including observing other people, watching movies, and reading books (Rachman, 1977). Perhaps researchers would do better to focus less on how anxiety develops through conditioning, and more on how it fails to extinguish in certain individuals (Marks, 1981b).

Behavior Therapy Techniques and Conditioning
Despite the deficiencies of conditioning as an explanation of anxiety disorders, behavioral techniques inspired by conditioning have been very successful. The most obvious example is systematic desensitization. Why criticize the theory when the practical results of applying it are so impressive? One answer is that refinements to the theory could lead to further improvements in the effectiveness and efficiency of therapeutic techniques. For example, Wolpe (1958) made several theoretical assumptions when he designed his experiments on cats and developed systematic desensitization. Because of these assumptions, he designed his studies without certain control groups, failing to test the separate effects of feeding and gradual exposure. If he had included a control group of cats that were not fed during extinction, Wolpe could have found that the feeding was irrelevant to anxiety-reduction and therefore that the concept of reciprocal inhibition was unnecessary (Wilson & Davison, 1971).

The results of clinical studies have also called into question the idea that gradual approach is necessary in therapy for situational anxiety problems. Marks (1981) developed successful treatments for agoraphobia and obsessive-compulsive disorder by drawing from Baum's (1970) studies of *blocking* in animals. Rats that had been conditioned to fear environments in which they had been shocked were confined there, without the opportunity to escape, after the aversive stimuli had been removed. This technique of blocking, otherwise known as *response prevention* because the escape response is physically prevented, was highly successful in promoting the extinction of the conditioned anxiety. Confrontive exposure to conditioned stimuli during extinction is more helpful than Guthrie's (1935) *toleration* method, or the technique of gradual approach to feared stimuli (Wilson, 1973).

The clinical equivalents of the blocking procedure are the exposure methods, exposure *in vivo* (in real life) and exposure with response prevention—the client remains in contact with highly feared stimuli without escaping, for prolonged periods if necessary, until the anxiety declines. Clients with agoraphobia, for example, are asked to spend 90 minutes or more in crowded shopping malls without retreating at the onset of anxiety. Obsessive-compulsive clients are asked to confront the stimuli that normally provoke them to ritualize, but this time without performing the ritual. In either case, preventing the escape or avoidance response allows the client to confront the feared situation. In clinical practice, these methods have been highly successful (Marks, 1981), as we will outline below.

Cognitive Theories

Theorists have not found it easy to assemble a convincing explanation of phobias, obsessions, and rituals in conditioning terms. It has been even more difficult to explain panic disorder and generalized anxiety in those terms, because there is no obvious situation or stimulus connected with these fears. These and other difficulties prompted behavior therapists to pay attention to social learning and cognitive factors in accounts of human behavior (Basic Behavioral Science Task Force, 1996). Since the early 1970s theorists such as Bandura, Beck, and Lang have incorporated cognitive events, particularly clients' *expectations*, into their formulations of anxiety disorders. As in the case of conditioning theories, these cognitive-behavioral accounts seek to explain not only the development of disorders but also the effectiveness of therapeutic procedures.

Social Learning and Self-Efficacy Theory

Arguing that a stimulus-response learning view of behavior is needlessly restricting and limited, Bandura (1977b) pointed to factors within the individual that intervene between the stimulus input and the response output. His *social learning theory* rests on the assumption that psychological functioning involves a continuous interplay among external stimuli, behavioral responses, and mediational processes in the person. Rescorla and Solomon (1967) concluded that, even though classical and operant conditioning involve different experimental procedures, a common process may underlie both. Bandura has suggested that the most likely common process is the development of expectancies about what will happen and what the individual can do about it. This theory is highly relevant to anxiety disorders because the laboratory prototype for neurotic behavior, experimental neurosis, arises when people or animals lose their ability to predict or control events (Mineka & Kihlstrom, 1978).

Bandura (1977a) has argued that the general expectation that a situation is dangerous easily explains the client's fear and avoidance behavior. Fear does not cause avoidance (as in two-factor theory); both fear and avoidance are caused by something else, the expectation. This view is helpful for a couple of reasons. First, it can explain the lack of correlation between measures of fear and measures of avoidance in phobic clients, because one of these responses could change independently of the other if the central expectation of danger has not been altered. Second, it suggests that treatment will be successful only when it leads to a change in the client's expectations.

The concept of *self-efficacy* (Bandura, 1977a, 1994, 1995) fits especially well when a given situation is associated with fear and defensive behavior. The chief expectations relevant to a phobia, for example, are the client's sense of (1) What would I need to do to handle this situation satisfactorily? (an *outcome expectation*) and (2) Can I do it? (an *efficacy expectation*). In this model, effective psychological treatments are those that develop or strengthen the client's expectations of personal effectiveness. Efficacy expectations could be derived from the person's own performance accomplishments, from observing others, from verbal persuasion, or from observing one's state of emotional arousal (Bandura & Adams, 1977). The more dependable the source of information, the greater will be the change in self-efficacy. In the case of a phobic individual like Susan B., actual behavioral accomplishment would be a better way of increasing self-efficacy than verbal persuasion. Hence, it would be more therapeutic for Susan to learn to handle real spiders than for her to be encouraged not to think so negatively about them.

Studies of self-efficacy theory involve seeking correlations between efficacy expectations and actual behavior. There should be agreement between (1) the client's expectations about successfully handling the situation and (2) his or her behavior, such as level of avoidance, when confronted by the real stimuli (Bandura, Adams, Hardy, & Howells, 1980). Experimental evidence is highly consistent with Bandura's prediction here (e.g., Biran & Wilson, 1981). It might seem surprising that, while Bandura's theory is so "cognitive," he nevertheless predicts that enactive, performance-based "behavioral" treatments will be more helpful than direct attempts to change the client's thinking patterns. Commenting on this, Wilson (1982) stressed how vital it is to draw a distinction between *procedure* and *process*. The most helpful therapeutic techniques or procedures are behavioral, but the central change process is cognitive. For example, *participant modeling* is a procedure emphasizing behavioral elements (the model demonstrates the desired behavior and the client tries to imitate this), but the central process involves changes in the client's outcome and efficacy expectations.

Self-efficacy theory has been criticized by some theorists. Borkovec (1978) argued that, since the data on the correspondence between self-efficacy and performance are correlational, it is difficult to prove that changes in self-efficacy cause the therapeutic progress. It is equally plausible that changes in self-efficacy simply reflect changed behavior. Eysenck (1978) suggested that it is unnecessary to add cognitive elements to the original learning model of anxiety, and that Bandura has merely translated a conditioning view into cognitive language.

Theories from Cognitive Therapy

Because they involve external cues that can be viewed as eliciting stimuli, phobias and compulsions initially received more attention than other anxiety disorders from conditioning-oriented behavior therapists (Foa & Kozak, 1985). But the development of cognitive restructuring therapies led to an emphasis on *internal* cues, such as sensations of emotional arousal or thoughts of impending catastrophes. Best known for his work on depression (see Chapter 9), Aaron Beck has been a prominent advocate of the view that the client's thoughts or cognitions are the most important element in emotional disorders (Beck, 1995; Beck & Weishaar, 1995). Beck's cognitive theory of the causes and treatment of depression has also been applied to the anxiety disorders, especially to panic disorder (Beck, 1985a; Beck, Emery, & Greenberg, 1985; Clark & Beck, 1988).

Recall that in panic disorder, the client experiences a sudden, unexplained surge of anxiety that rapidly culminates in a terrifying panic attack. The panic attack begins with a bodily sensation that would be perfectly understandable in normal circumstances. The client suddenly gets up from a chair and feels a little faint for a second or two, or is momentarily startled by the sound of the doorbell, or runs to catch a bus and then notices the sensations of a pounding heart and flushed face. The client then interprets these sensations as meaning something terribly uncontrollable, like a serious disease. These alarming interpretations arouse further anxiety, producing a vicious circle in which normal sensations ultimately escalate into a panic attack. The development of such *catastrophic misinterpretations* of routine bodily sensations is central to the cognitive theory of panic disorder (Clark, 1986).

Paulette, a client treated by one of us, described her panic attacks as beginning with a warm feeling in her face. As soon as she arrived for her first interview, Paulette looked worried and asked if the therapist thought it was very warm in the office. He replied that yes, it was rather warm. Paulette breathed a sigh of relief and said, "Thank goodness! I thought I was having a panic attack!" The therapist asked how she would have reacted if he had said no, it was really rather cool in the office. She replied, "Then it would have been a panic attack!" The therapist followed up with, "Then whether you have a panic attack or not depends on whether I tell you it is warm or cool in here!" and went on to point out that the panic attack was obviously a *combination* of (1) certain sensations and (2) her thoughts about them—whether her flushed face made sense or not in the context. An interesting byproduct of Paulette's anxiety about warm sensations in her face was that there was one place in which she could never have a panic attack—a ceramics store where she had weekly pottery classes. The store was always extremely warm because the kiln was operating most of the time. If the client ever felt panic sensations beginning when she was in the store, she automatically attributed them to the heat of the room, and her anxiety disappeared at once!

Paulette and the therapist adopted Clark's (1986) treatment approach. She made a point of deliberately altering her attitudes to changes in how her body felt. For example, she practiced saying to herself, whenever she began to feel panic arising, "Perhaps it's just warm in here."

The client is assumed to have two kinds of cognitions about anxiety sensations. One kind, the *cognitive schema* (see Chapter 4), is a general belief similar to a lasting personality trait—for example, the belief that unfamiliar bodily feelings are likely to be symptoms of some dreadful disease. The other, *automatic thoughts,* are the immediate thoughts that spring to mind when a new sensation is noticed, such as, "Oh, no! Here it comes! Another awful panic attack!"

Finally, cognitive therapy hypotheses have been applied to obsessive-compulsive disorder, "the archetypal example of a cognitive disorder in the neuroses" (Salkovskis, 1985, p. 571). At one level, OCD is a cognitive disorder in that there may be specific memory deficits. Clients whose compulsions involve repeated checking easily confuse memories of having *performed* an act with memories of having *imagined* performing the act (Ecker & Engelkamp, 1995). But at another level, OCD is a cognitive disorder in that these clients' thoughts and beliefs are central to their disorder. Obsessional thoughts are seen as cognitive stimuli that produce other cognitions as responses. These responses are negative automatic thoughts linked to clients' beliefs that they are responsible for eliminating any risk of harm to themselves or to other people (Salkovskis, Richards, & Forrester, 1995).

One of our clients, Peter, an administrator in his fifties, had obsessional thoughts about having left things in an untidy or dangerous condition. He might be driving his car, for example, and suddenly have the thought that he might have seen a nail on the side of the road a couple of miles back. "If I don't go back and check, and—if it was indeed a nail—remove it, then someone could get a flat tire, lose control of their car, and die." So he would turn his car around and drive back to look for the possible nail. The obsessional thought was the intrusive idea about the nail; the automatic thoughts were that he would be to blame for an awful catastrophe if he did not at least check the situation.

According to Rachman (1978), it is not remarkable that the client has occasional *intrusions,* because everyone does to one degree or another. What is unusual is that the client goes on to have automatic thoughts, like "I must check," which are related to exaggerated beliefs about personal responsibility. These beliefs, not the intrusions themselves, lead clients to check or perform rituals. This implies that cognitive therapy for obsessive-compulsive disorder should not concentrate on the intrusive thoughts but on the automatic thoughts produced by the intrusions, and the general dysfunctional beliefs—the cognitive schemas—underlying those automatic thoughts.

If people with OCD have an exaggerated sense of personal responsibility for avoiding possible harm, then one would expect that they would take fewer risks than most people. This hypothesis was tested by Steketee and Frost (1994), who developed and standardized an inventory of everyday risk-taking among college students. Participants indicated the likelihood that they would engage in each of the listed behaviors (e.g., double-parking your car in Boston for 10 minutes) on a 1 ("never") to 5 ("I would definitely do this") scale. This and other similar scales were administered to 23 outpatients with obsessive-compulsive disorder. As predicted, the outpatients reported significantly lower risk taking than a non-clinical college sample matched for age.

Integrative Theories

Some theories of the causes of anxiety disorders are not easily classified in either conditioning or cognitive terms. One example is Peter Lang's (1979, 1985) *bio-informational theory,* primarily a cognitive theory with firm links to experimental psychology, reviewed in the next chapter. Another is the model of *complex agoraphobia* by Goldstein and Chambless (1978), whose integrative theory of agoraphobia addresses clients' personality styles and interpersonal relationships as well as conditioning events. In their view, agoraphobia has four chief elements:

1. The client fears panic attacks rather than particular places.
2. The client tends to lack self-sufficiency, independence, and assertiveness.
3. The client finds it hard to understand the source of emotional feelings when they arise.

4. The client lives in a climate of interpersonal conflict when the symptoms first appear.

These elements interact to produce agoraphobia. Goldstein and Chambless suggested that the disorder may develop as in this example: The client is a woman who feels trapped in an unsatisfactory marriage. She wishes to leave but lacks sufficient independence and personal autonomy to make this a realistic possibility. She also finds it difficult to be assertive and to express her feelings openly to her husband, so she attempts to cope with a bad situation. Imagine that she and her husband have a disagreement at breakfast, bringing to the fore all of the marital problems. Later in the day, when out in public, she feels tense but does not know why. She suddenly has a panic attack when waiting in line somewhere. As a result of the experience, which she does not understand, she later avoids situations in which she fears that a panic attack may arise.

Goldstein and Chambless (1978) argued that waiting in line may remind the client vaguely of her sense of being trapped in her bad marriage. As a result, emotions similar to those that arose during the argument earlier in the day appear again. Not realizing their real source, the client attributes the feelings to some personal deficiency, such as the possible onset of a severe mental illness, and a cycle of panic attacks has begun. Goldstein and Chambless also pointed out that, because the client now cannot leave the house due to her anxiety, the development of agoraphobia successfully resolved her conflict concerning leaving the marriage—by making leaving impossible.

Behavioral Assessment of Anxiety

Behavioral researchers and clinicians have been unable to identify the perfect index of anxiety. Simply asking clients to describe their anxiety does not take into account how their behavior looks to an observer. Observing clients' performance when they are anxious neglects assessment of their bodily functioning during emotional arousal. And measuring changes in clients' heart rates or muscle tensions by psychophysiological monitoring equipment does not allow for the attributions they make concerning their feelings—whether they label a quickened pulse as a sign of fear or of enthusiasm, for example. As a result, behavior therapists have abandoned the search for a single, ideal measure of anxiety and have instead tried to measure the affective, behavioral, and cognitive aspects of anxiety, as recommended by Lang (1968). Measuring these three domains of functioning has usually involved using the assessment techniques of interviews and questionnaires (self-report, subjective, or cognitive aspects), behavioral observation (behavioral or performance aspects), and psychophysiological monitoring (autonomic or emotional aspects). This *triple response mode* assessment has been a feature of most research studies in this area, although it may not be as widely used in routine clinical practice.

Clients are understandably most concerned about their subjective experiences of anxiety. Clinicians normally assess how clients feel by means of *structured interviews* and *self-report questionnaires* or inventories. A widely used structured interview protocol is the Anxiety Disorders Interview Schedule–Revised (ADIS-R; Di Nardo & Barlow, 1988). Self-report questionnaires for anxiety disorders include the Fear Questionnaire (Marks & Mathews, 1979), the Anxiety Sensitivity Index (Reiss, Peterson, Gursky, & McNally, 1986), and several others aimed at specific anxiety disorders (see Hecker & Thorpe, 1992; Street & Barlow, 1994). Clients may also be asked to confront anxiety-provoking situations so that their behavior and physiological responses may be monitored. For example, *behavioral avoidance tests* have been commonly used in the assessment of phobias (see Chapter 2).

Typically, the degree of association among measures from the three response modes is not very impressive. Similarly, treatment interventions often alter the three response systems at different rates. These observations led Lang (1985) to recommend that all three systems be measured routinely in clients with anxiety disorders. Following the work of Rachman and Hodgson (1974) on this topic, behavior therapists have continued to examine the *asynchrony*, or lack of common variation, in the three systems measurement of anxiety. Barlow, Mavissakalian, and Schofield (1980) recommended that treatment should continue until anxiety has been reduced on all three measures. They described a client who made impressive improvements after a treatment program for agoraphobia. She showed excellent progress as assessed by her self-report and by her observed ability to enter and remain in phobic situations, but her heart rate was still high during the behavioral test session. Nevertheless, she pronounced herself satisfied and terminated treatment early. (The other clients in the study made slower progress but improved on all three measures.) At a follow-up assessment one month later, this client was the only one to have relapsed.

Sometimes, the poor correlations among different measures of anxiety are the result of confusing the technique of measurement with the assessment question being asked, as illustrated by an example from an agoraphobia treatment study (Burns, 1977; Thorpe & Burns, 1983). During the assessment phases of the study, each client was asked to try walking as far away from the research clinic as possible before the onset of anxiety. (There was a set route of 4,240 feet from the clinic to the back of a department store in a downtown area; how far the client actually got was measured in feet.) Clients also gave self-report ratings of their anxiety level on a 0 (low) to 4 (high) rating scale. High levels of anxiety would be indicated by the client not being able to get very far from the clinic (e.g., 500 feet) and by reporting intense anxiety (e.g., 4) on the rating scale. Several clients showed high anxiety on the behavioral avoidance measure but low anxiety on the self-report measure. In other words, a client might not get very far from the clinic (only 100 feet: high anxiety) but would report little fear on the rating scale (1: low anxiety).

Apart from being further evidence of the asynchrony of anxiety responses, these findings could indicate that different questions were being asked in the different response modes (Cone, 1979). Clients who did not walk very far may have reported little anxiety because they stopped before anxiety arose, therefore encountering very few phobic stimuli. But clients who walked much further, thus showing less behavioral avoidance, might have described feeling more anxious because there were many more feared stimuli along the way. Although the behavioral test and the self-report ratings were both intended as measures of anxiety, in fact different *questions* were being asked with these different measures. One question (behavioral test) was "How far did you walk?" and the other (self-report ratings) was "How anxious did you feel?" Not only were the assessment modalities different, but so were the questions asked, accounting for the discrepancy. If the same question had been asked in the two modalities, the correlation could have been very high. For example, clients could be asked How far did you walk? The answer through the self-report method could be "About 100 feet." The answer through behavioral observation (a research assistant observing how far the client actually traveled) might be very similar (Thorpe, 1989).

Behavioral Treatment of Anxiety Disorders

Phobias

Systematic Densensitization
In the 1960s analogue research showed that *systematic desensitization (SD)* is helpful in treating college students with specific phobias, but a more challenging test is to apply the technique to clients with agoraphobia in clinical settings. Compared with snake phobia and public speaking anxiety, agoraphobia is far more severe, generalized, disabling, and difficult to treat (Marks, 1981).

An initial case report of behavior therapy for agoraphobia-like symptoms described a favorable outcome, but the chief method used was not SD but graduated real-life practice (Meyer, 1957). The results of SD with clinical series of agoraphobic clients were disappointing. Only minimal therapeutic gains were made, and even those were achieved only after a large number of treatment sessions that sometimes went on for more than a year (Cooper, Gelder, & Marks, 1965; Marks & Gelder, 1965; Meyer & Gelder, 1963). The results of controlled comparisons of SD with traditional psychotherapy were no more impressive. Gelder and Marks (1966) treated 20 agoraphobic clients by "behavior therapy" (SD, graduated real-life practice, and, for some clients, assertiveness training) or by traditional psychiatric interviews concentrating on the clients' current interpersonal issues. Some of the clients were taking minor tranquilizers or antidepressant medication. Clients, therapists, and independent clinicians completed rating scales before, and at various times after, treatment. Results indicated that all clients made similar progress. After an average of 20 weeks of therapy, there were no "cures" from either treatment, and most clients continued to have significant problems. Similar results were obtained by Gelder, Marks, and Wolff (1967) in a study of 42 clients with various phobias.

One of the most thorough studies of SD with phobic clients was conducted by Gelder, Bancroft, Gath, Johnston, Mathews, and Shaw (1973). Some 36 clients with agoraphobia, social phobia, or specific phobias were given 15 sessions of treatment in as many weeks. Clients were randomly distributed among three treatment conditions: SD, imaginal flooding, and "associative psychotherapy" (a placebo-control condition in which clients made free associations to phobic imagery). The last four sessions of treatment were devoted to real-life practice in phobic situations. Clients were assessed before and after treatment and again six months later. Imaginal flooding and SD were both more helpful than associative psychotherapy on various measures of outcome. Clients with agoraphobia did especially poorly with associative psychotherapy.

A problem with this study is that the real-life practice sessions were given to all clients before the posttreatment assessment, so one cannot tell how effective SD and imaginal flooding would have been without the graded practice. In a second report on this study, the authors made the comment that improvements in clients' estimates of future anxiety (similar to a self-efficacy measure) appeared only after real-life practice had begun (Mathews, Johnston, Shaw, & Gelder, 1974).

Other studies of SD with phobic clients concentrated on the role of various procedural elements. In a study of 24 clients, semi-automated desensitization (with the anxiety hierarchy presented by a prerecorded narrator) proved as effective as the normal SD procedure, but neither technique brought a great deal of benefit (Evans & Kellam, 1973). In a small sample of eight phobic clients, Benjamin, Marks, and Huson (1972) tested SD with and without the muscle relaxation component, and found relaxation unnecessary. A larger-scale study by Gillan and Rachman (1974) also showed that in 32 clients with agoraphobia and specific phobias, SD was helpful with or without relaxation. Both procedures were more helpful than desensitization to a hierarchy of fear-irrelevant items.

Despite the great deal of attention that was paid to SD in early reviews of behavior therapy, there is a consensus that, used alone, it is of limited value in treating commonly presented phobias (Marks, 1981). It remains useful in the treatment of some specific and social phobias, especially when the feared events are difficult to replicate in real life (such as criticism by an employer). Nevertheless, SD has been generally supplanted by techniques with an *in-vivo* component, like participant modeling or exposure *in vivo,* especially for agoraphobic avoidance.

Graduated Real-Life Practice

Experiments on *graduated real-life practice* (also called "graded practice") with phobic clients often used single-case research methodology. Several studies of this kind were conducted by a team of researchers in Vermont in the late 1960s (Agras, Leitenberg, Barlow, & Burlington, 1968; Leitenberg, Agras, Thompson, & Wright, 1968). One consistent finding was that it is helpful for clients to enter phobic situations repeatedly until fear arises. These researchers also noted that several behavioral techniques, such as systematic desensitization and operant shaping, include the common elements of designating the behavior to be changed, presenting learning tasks in small increments, and measuring behavior continuously so that changes are observable to client and therapist. Leitenberg and colleagues (1968) tested the hypothesis that the "feedback of progress" element may be important to graded practice methods. Two clients with simple phobias took part. Both clients were women in their fifties; one had claustrophobia and the other had a phobia of knives.

The client with claustrophobia progressed through three treatment phases in which feedback was sequentially presented, withdrawn, and presented again. Within each phase the client entered a small, closed room two to four times per day for six days. She was told, "Come out of the room as soon as you feel the slightest discomfort or anxiety, and you are to go back only after you rest a while" (Leitenberg et al., 1968, p. 132). In feedback conditions, the client was asked to use a stopwatch to time and then record the duration of each stay in the room. She was aware that an automatic timer operated whenever the door closed, and she was given the explanation that her use of the stopwatch was to serve as a check on the accuracy of the timer. In the no-feedback phases, she was told that the stopwatch was broken. The findings were that there was a practice effect in each of the three phases, because the client tended to spend progressively longer times in the room, but the increases were far more marked in the phases with feedback. At a follow-up assessment three months later, the client reported that she had maintained the treatment gains in her daily activities at home. Behavioral observations in the room used in treatment, and in the hospital elevator, confirmed that there had been no relapse.

The second study, with the client who feared contact with sharp knives, also involved gradual exposure with or without feedback. The element of praise from the therapist for specific, gradual improvements was added. The client progressed well overall, but praise produced no incremental effects (a graph of this client's responses appears in Figure 5–3 in Chapter 5).

In the treatment of agoraphobia, the Vermont team was able to show that feedback on progress from the therapist and praise for specific accomplishments do provide added benefit (Agras et al., 1968). Contingent praise was shown to be effective as reinforcement because clients made progress in either distance walked from the clinic or time spent away from the clinic, depending on which criterion was used for reinforcement. Essential elements in a successful program for agoraphobic clients are practice in real phobic settings (Leitenberg, Agras, Edwardes, Thompson, & Wincze, 1970) and therapist feedback on progress, especially in the early stages of treatment (Leitenberg, Agras, Allen, & Butz, 1975).

After a few initial sessions, graduated real-life practice can be continued by the client with only minimal contact with the therapist, who can serve as consultant or "troubleshooter." Several European studies provided evidence on the effectiveness of this approach. In the Netherlands, Emmelkamp (1974) conducted a controlled trial of four procedures with 20 agoraphobic clients: flooding (imaginal plus real-life exposure), self-observation (graduated real-life practice), the combination of flooding plus self-observation, and no treatment. Each client had 12 90-minute treatment sessions. All three treatments produced marked improvement on several measures, but the no-treatment condition did not.

It is hard to imagine clients going through any form of exposure treatment without the therapist recommending real-life practice (self-exposure homework) between treatment sessions. Self-exposure instructions to agoraphobic clients, with minimal therapist contact, were more therapeutic than treatment sessions devoted to a discussion of social life events and problem-solving strategies (McDonald, Sartory, Grey, Cobb, Stern, & Marks, 1979). Similar results were produced in crossover studies with agoraphobic clients by Emmelkamp and his colleagues (Emmelkamp & Ultee, 1974; Everaerd, Rijken, & Emmelkamp, 1973).

An important development in the treatment of agoraphobia was the use of home-based treatment programs derived from graduated real-life practice techniques. These programs included the active involvement of the spouse or other significant person whenever possible (Goldstein & Chambless, 1978; Hafner, 1982). The home-based treatment program of Mathews and his colleagues (Mathews, Teasdale, Munby, Johnston, & Shaw, 1977; Mathews, Gelder, & Johnston, 1981) was as helpful as the most successful of the clinic-based programs, and with greater economy of the therapist's time. Clients and companions were given manuals that explained the treatment, gave instructions for self-paced exposure, and provided tips for the companion on managing problems as they arise. Results from a clinical series of 11 clients were extremely encouraging, not only in the short-term impact of treatment but also in the continued improvement of the clients in the following six-month period. Jannoun, Munby, Catalan, and Gelder (1980) obtained similar results in a more large-scale study.

In Spain, 31 agoraphobic clients followed regimens of self-exposure treatment with or without the tranquilizer alprazolam (Xanax), or took alprazolam with or without exposure. All conditions produced clear improvement except the alprazolam condition. Clients who took the medication fared less well than the others during a six-month follow-up interval (Echeburua, de Corral, Garcia Bajos, & Borda, 1993). Finally, a British study of 99 clients with agoraphobia, social phobia, or specific phobias showed that six hours of self-exposure instruction together with daily homework produced significant and enduring gains that were not increased by adding nine hours of therapist-aided exposure (Al-Kubaisy, Marks, Logsdail, Marks, Lovell, Sungur, & Araya, 1992).

Imaginal Flooding and Exposure In Vivo

Beginning in the late 1960s clinical researchers explored the rapid treatment of phobias by confrontive, prolonged exposure to feared stimuli. Boulougouris and Marks (1969) treated four phobic clients with imaginal flooding and prolonged real-life practice, obtaining impressive results. In a crossover study comparing imaginal flooding with systematic desensitization, Boulougouris, Marks, and Marset (1971) showed that flooding was generally the more effective in a sample of phobic clients. Flooding was particularly helpful to the agoraphobic clients.

In another crossover trial with a sample of phobic and obsessive-compulsive clients, Greist, Marks, Berlin, Gournay, and Noshirvani (1980) asked the participants (1) to confront or (2) to avoid feared situations for one week. In the confronting condition, clients were advised to remain in the feared surroundings for as long as it took for their anxiety to diminish, for hours if need be. In the avoidance condition, clients were recommended to take a break from anxiety and steer well clear of fear-provoking situations. The problems dealt with in the 19 clients were compulsive rituals, agoraphobia, social phobia, and specific phobias of wasps, spiders, ants, enclosed spaces, and incontinence (losing control of one's bladder or bowels). Treatment-related changes consistently favored the confrontation condition.

Clinical researchers have compared several possible procedural variations to find out which factors in the exposure treatment of phobias are most important.

Relevant versus Irrelevant Fear Stimuli.   An advantage of imaginal flooding is that the client can be asked to imagine a variety of stimuli, including those difficult to present in real life. For theoretical reasons, researchers have studied the effects of presenting stimuli unrelated to the client's phobia in imaginal flooding. What would be the effect of presenting scenes that would be frightening to anyone, not just people with specific phobias? If flooding only works when relevant stimuli are used, then extinction may be the process operating, because extinction requires that the client confront conditioned stimuli. But if flooding to irrelevant fear stimuli were effective in reducing specific fears, then a process other than extinction must be at work.

Watson and Marks (1971) sought evidence on this point by treating 20 phobic clients by imaginal flooding. This was a crossover study in which clients had eight 50-minute sessions of each treatment. In one condition, clients were exposed to phobia-relevant imagery.

In the other, they were "flooded" to horrific imagery of fearful situations unrelated to their specific phobias. For example, clients would listen to vivid descriptions of being eaten alive by a Bengal tiger that had escaped from its cage at the zoo. Both procedures were effective in reducing phobic anxiety, as assessed by clinical ratings and by physiological monitoring during phobic imagery. One interpretation is that extinction was operating in the relevant fear condition, and another process in the irrelevant fear condition, because different patterns of autonomic responding were associated with improvement within each treatment phase (Marks, 1972).

Brief versus Prolonged Exposure.   In treating phobic clients by exposure *in vivo*, it is more helpful to provide a few long treatment sessions than several short ones (Stern & Marks, 1973). In this study the overall treatment time was held constant, so that clients had either a single two-hour session or four half-hour sessions. Treating a group of people with specific phobias of spiders, Mathews and Shaw (1973) found the same effect with imaginal flooding. All clients were given a single, prolonged treatment session, but some clients imagined spider scenes continuously throughout the session, while others had a series of briefer trials. Continuous flooding was significantly more therapeutic.

These findings in favor of prolonged exposure are consistent with more than one theory of the process operating in successful treatment. *Extinction* could be facilitated by prolonged contact with the conditioned stimulus with repeated evocation of the conditioned response (the anxiety). This is true as well for *habituation*, an elementary learning process marked by a lessening of the response after it has been made repeatedly in a session. Extinction applies only to learned responses, but habituation applies to learned and unlearned behavior. Watson and Marks (1971) suggested that habituation may have been operating in the irrelevant fear conditions in their study. Finally, *emotional processing*[3] following activation of a fear network would also be facilitated by prolonged exposure to anxiety-eliciting stimuli (Hecker & Thorpe, 1987).

Imaginal Flooding versus Exposure In Vivo.   The Stern and Marks (1973) study included a comparison of imaginal and *in-vivo* exposure. Exposure *in vivo* was particularly effective with prolonged sessions, but it was also clearly superior in effectiveness to imaginal flooding, whether this was brief or prolonged. Similar results emerged from a study of 19 Dutch agoraphobics who were treated with imaginal, *in vivo*, or the combination of imaginal plus *in vivo*, exposure (Emmelkamp & Wessels, 1975). All clients had four 90-minute treatment sessions; exposure *in vivo* was the most effective procedure.

Another study on this topic with 36 English agoraphobic women showed no clear differences between imaginal and *in-vivo* exposure (Mathews, Johnston, Lancashire, Munby, Shaw, & Gelder, 1976). Some clients followed imaginal procedures, some had exposure *in vivo*, and there was a combined treatment group. This was an ambitious study in which clients had 16 90-minute treatment sessions. It is likely that, with that amount of exposure, all techniques were able to exert their maximum impact.

Virtual Reality Graded Exposure.   Barbara Rothbaum and her colleagues have used computer-generated, virtual reality environments in exposure treatment for people with a specific phobia of heights (acrophobia). The procedure is described as *virtual reality graded exposure (VRGE)*. The technology involves real-time computer graphics, body tracking devices, and visual displays. Clients wear a head-mounted display with an electromagnetic sensor, so that the virtual environment changes in a realistic way with head and body motion (Rothbaum, Hodges, Kooper, Opdyke, Williford, & North, 1995).

Using VRGE, 17 acrophobic students received treatment in seven 35- to 45-minute exposure sessions (Hodges, Kooper, Meyer, Rothbaum, Opdyke, de Graaff, Williford, & North, 1995). These clients were exposed to three environments: an elevator, a series of balconies, and a series of bridges. The open elevator was presented as located on the inside of a 49-floor hotel; the participant would actually hold on to a waist-high rail that was depicted as a guard rail. The goals of the study were to find out if (1) the simulated environment was realistic and (2) anxiety could habituate under these conditions. Both goals were clearly reached. The "sense of presence" was such that clients produced a range of anxiety symptoms that included nausea and actual vomiting in one participant. Treated participants showed significant improvement on measures of avoidance and anxiety, whereas a waiting-list control group showed no change.

Individual versus Group Exposure Treatment.   Clients often ask their therapists to introduce them to other clients with the same problem, so that some comfort can be drawn from knowing someone else struggling to overcome similar difficulties. There is also the potential advantage of being able to compare notes with other clients on successful strategies for confronting feared situations. Before data were available on this topic, some behavior therapists were concerned that bringing two or more phobic clients together for their treatment would run the risk of their demoralizing each other or developing a "group panic" as they alarmed themselves more and more about their shared problem. Alternatively, if the success of treatment depends more on exposure principles than on qualities of the therapeutic relationship, there is no reason not to conduct treatment in groups. This could have advantages in economy of professional time and in the potential for clients to help each other.

Half-a-dozen studies in the 1970s comparing group with individual exposure treatment in phobic clients confirmed that group treatment brings added benefits (for reviews, see Thorpe & Burns, 1983; Thorpe, Burns, Smith, & Blier, 1984). Treatment for agoraphobic clients was improved when they were treated together with other sufferers who lived in the same neighborhood (Sinnott, Jones, Scott-Fordham, & Woodward, 1981). These clients tended to use each other's homes as targets for practice expeditions, and the extra social contact encouraged clients to try harder.

Cognitive-Behavioral Therapy

Analogue studies with student volunteers showed that cognitive modification procedures are potentially effective treatments for anxiety problems (Emmelkamp, 1979). Researchers working with clinical phobias had also been encouraged by the effects of adding cognitive restructuring techniques to behavior therapy (Mathews & Rezin, 1977; Mathews & Shaw, 1973). What are the results, then, of controlled experiments to compare cognitive interventions with exposure treatment for phobic clients? The answer is that it depends on the type of phobia.

Emmelkamp, Kuipers, and Eggeraat (1978) reported a crossover study with 21 agoraphobic clients who received group sessions of exposure *in vivo* and a combination of various cognitive restructuring procedures. Clients improved significantly more with exposure than with cognitive treatment. Other studies with agoraphobic clients added cognitive restructuring procedures to behavioral techniques, without appreciable effects on outcome (Thorpe & Burns, 1983; Williams & Rappoport, 1983).

Similar results were obtained for simple phobias. Biran and Wilson (1981) treated clients with fears of heights, darkness, or being confined. Graduated real-life practice ("guided practice") was compared with a battery of cognitive restructuring methods that included relabeling of emotional feelings, elements of rational emotive behavior therapy, and stress inoculation. Guided practice was clearly more efficient and effective in the study than the cognitive treatment package. The practical implications are clear. If a client has a fear of heights, it is far more helpful for him or her to practice walking on the roof of a high building with the therapist than to dispute unhelpful attitudes in the therapist's office.

In studies of social phobia, cognitive modification procedures have produced more encouraging results. Not only are cognitive interventions as helpful as performance-based behavioral treatment for social phobia but there is also evidence that results from student volunteers are very similar to those observed in clinic clients with this disorder (Emmelkamp, Mersch, & Vissia, 1985; Emmelkamp, Mersch, Vissia, & van der Helm, 1985). In these studies, Emmelkamp and his colleagues noticed that some kinds of cognitive restructuring may be more helpful than others. The impression is that it is more helpful to focus on removing self-defeating or negative self-statements than to try to promote "positive thinking." A review of 12 studies of cognitive-behavioral treatment and 9 studies of exposure treatment for social phobia revealed, however, that these techniques are equally effective (Feske & Chambless, 1995).

Summary

In the treatment of phobias, direct exposure to relevant stimuli, whether accomplished in gradual steps or at full-flooded intensity, is generally more helpful than systematic desensitization and cognitive modification methods. In the case of social phobia, cognitive restructuring does bring significant benefit. Prolonged exposure *in vivo* is especially valuable in treating agoraphobia. Theorists are still unsure exactly why these procedures work, and the results of studies of treatment effectiveness are consistent with more than one theory.

Obsessive-Compulsive Disorder

Behavioral treatment of obsessive-compulsive disorder (OCD) has paralleled the treatment of phobias in some ways, because, in both disorders, the client is more anxious in some situations than in others. In a case like Michael H., the literature student with contamination fears, the obsessional thoughts are triggered by an external stimulus event, such as the sight of a doorknob in a public building. His prolonged hand-washing rituals can be seen as attempts to escape from the feared situation, which, in his case, is feeling contaminated. This is very similar to a phobic disorder, because there is an external feared stimulus together with problem behavior in the client representing an attempt to escape or avoid.

However, some obsessions are prompted more by internal than external stimuli, and these obsessions are not as easy to formulate in situational terms. Many clients with OCD fear their own impulses, for example, or worry a great deal about the idea that they might think blasphemous thoughts. Salkovskis (1983) described a 23-year-old man who had obsessional ruminations about people being violent toward him. He attempted to neutralize these disturbing thoughts by repeating the exact thoughts, internally, an even number of times, but as soon as he did this, the thought would return, and he had to repeat the process. Each episode of this kind lasted from 15 minutes to 3 hours. Cases like this are different from phobias in that the important stimuli are internal, so different treatment methods have been necessary. This section contains a brief review of behavioral treatments for OCD.

Systematic Desensitization

Several case studies have described the application of systematic desensitization (SD) to obsessional thinking. Worsley (1970) outlined the treatment of a 24-year-old woman who was greatly troubled by sharp knives and scissors, and by the idea that she might harm someone with them. Treatment consisted of SD, with the relaxation component assisted by the use of short-acting barbiturate medication. After the SD sessions, the client progressed to real-life exposure to knives. During the course of five months, 23 treatment sessions were held. The client responded well to treatment and was still free of obsessions at a follow-up visit two years later. Although many case studies like this have been reported, a comprehensive review of OCD treatment, completed after the popularity of SD had declined, revealed no controlled studies of this technique in application to OCD (Beech & Vaughan, 1978).

Exposure with Response Prevention

When external stimuli evoke compulsive rituals, therapists can advise clients to confront these stimuli without ritualizing. This procedure, *exposure with response prevention,* is parallel to exposure treatment with phobic clients in that the situation is confronted without escape or avoidance (Stanley & Wagner, 1994). Michael H., referred to earlier, was treated by this method. A particular problem for him was any sense of stickiness on his hands, so that he was unable to use adhesives of any kind. The worst situation for him would be to handle plastic electrical insulating tape. The therapist asked Michael to consent to a two-hour therapy session in which he would make his hands sticky with electricians' tape and then refrain from handwashing for the duration. Michael agreed to this plan, and in the course of this long session, his subjective rating of anxiety gradually decreased to a minimal level. Several sessions of this kind were held before his behavior changed significantly in everyday life.

Modeling has also proved useful in combination with exposure and response prevention. The therapist demonstrates an appropriate behavior sequence while the client looks on, providing an opportunity for the client to acquire adaptive coping skills. It can be surprisingly helpful to show the client what a reasonably normal hand-washing procedure looks like, for example. Modeling, exposure, and response prevention can be a particularly powerful technique combination (Rachman & Hodgson, 1980).

Marks (1981) reviewed a large number of studies that confirm the validity of this approach. It was even helpful in an unusually complex case reported by Lelliott and Marks (1987). The client was a 24-year-old man who worked, when he was employed, as a warehouse clerk. He had described a seven-year history of compulsive rituals, delusional beliefs, and auditory and visual hallucinations. The chief element in the obsessive-compulsive problem was the client's belief in a "Power" that brought him luck, as long as he engaged in various rituals.

The obsession began with what seems to have been a hallucinatory experience in which the client thought he saw a shadowy figure in a doorway. At the same time, the client heard a voice say, "Do the habits and things will go right." The Power came to reside in the client's electric guitar, which he kept carefully in a closet and hid from other people for six years. Some of the compulsions involved twiddling the guitar's control knobs in a ritualistic way. Despite numerous hospitalizations and much traditional psychotherapy, together with a regimen of tranquilizing medication, the client had shown little improvement. However, he did respond extremely well to a 16-week program of exposure *in vivo* and self-imposed response prevention. The rituals improved, the delusional beliefs disappeared, and the hallucinations were greatly reduced in frequency. The client was still symptom free two years later.

Treatment Variations

As in the case of phobias, researchers have investigated the effects of different treatments and technique variations on OCD. Emmelkamp, van der Helm, van Zanten, and Plochg (1980) compared exposure with response prevention with cognitive interventions for obsessive-compulsive clients and obtained the same results that had been found in the treatment of phobias: The performance-based exposure treatment was significantly more effective than cognitive restructuring procedures. The importance of using relevant obsessional theme material in imaginal flooding was also tested. In a crossover study with six OCD clients, Emmelkamp and Giesselbach (1981) confronted clients with either obsession-relevant material or imagery of ordinary frightening experiences. In this case, the results were different from those of Watson and Marks (1971) with phobic clients: Only the real obsessional material in flooding led to improvement.

We noted early in this section that some obsessions are triggered by internal cues. In cases like this, it is difficult to identify a suitable stimulus with which to confront the client in therapy. Salkovskis (1983) described the treatment of the obsessional ruminator who tried to neutralize thoughts of violence by repeating them exactly to himself, covertly. The obsessional thoughts of violence were the stimuli, and the neutralizing thoughts (repeating the obsessions in a ritualistic way) were the responses. Treatment would involve having the client confront the stimuli without making the responses—very difficult to do in this case. Salkovskis succeeded in treating this client by preparing an audiotape of the client voicing his unpleasant thoughts, and then playing the tape back repeatedly! This treatment may have worked because the exposure could proceed without the escape response (the neutralizing thoughts) being made. The client did not have time to neutralize each thought as it was expressed on the audiotape, because the stimulus tape was under the control of the therapist during these treatment sessions—and the therapist kept the tape running without pause.

Maintenance of Gains from Behavioral Treatment

Exposure with response prevention is accepted as an effective short-term treatment for obsessive-compulsive disorder, and most clients continue to do well years after the termination of treatment (Stanley & Wagner, 1994; Steketee, 1993). However, several studies indicate a relapse rate of 25 to 30 percent. In a study of 43 adults treated for obsessive-compulsive disorder, the relationship was examined between various measures of social support and clients' clinical status nine months after treatment. Level of social support in general did not predict relapse, but empathy and positive communications from others predicted maintenance of treatment gains. Negative family interactions, especially the type of displayed anger and criticism that has been examined in the "expressed emotion"[4] literature, were correlated with relapse (Steketee, 1993).

Body Dysmorphic Disorder

Formerly known as dysmorphophobia (literally, "bad shape fear"), *body dysmorphic disorder* is described in the *DSM-IV* not as an anxiety disorder but as a somatoform disorder involving a pathological preoccupation with an imagined or exaggerated defect in personal appearance. (Body dysmorphic disorder is not diagnosed if the person has anorexia nervosa or a gender identity disorder, both of which may involve body image distortions or marked concerns about appearance.) Although people with body dysmorphic disorder have obsessional thoughts about their appearance and may engage in checking and other rituals, it is not classified as a type of obsessive-compulsive disorder. Nonetheless, behavioral treatment plans for body dysmorphic disorder usually look very similar to those recommended for obsessive-compulsive disorder (Neziroglu & Yaryura-Tobias, 1993), and this and other *obsessive-compulsive spectrum disorders* share a similar functional analysis: "Anxiety increases in response to obsessive-like ideas (illness, appearance) and is reduced by specific behaviors (medical consultation, testing, purging, exercise)" (Steketee, 1994, p. 615).

As an example of body dysmorphic disorder, consider a client who was evaluated by one of us a few years ago. She was a married woman in her twenties who was convinced that one of her legs was fatter than the other. Her concern about this led her to spend a significant part of each day in measuring her thighs, looking at herself in the mirror, and practicing exercises specifically designed to correct the supposed defect. Despite attempts at reassurance by the family physician and the husband, the client's concerns persisted and led to her being referred for behavior therapy. Because the problem had many elements in common with obsessive-compulsive disorder (obsessional preoccupations with body shape and ritualistic checking and exercising in response to these obsessions), the therapist suggested a treatment plan involving exposure with response prevention. For example, the client could practice standing before the mirror until she started worrying that her legs looked wrong, then stay there—deliberately refraining from measuring, checking, or exercising—until the subjective discomfort declined. The client was unimpressed, however, saying that she had no need of therapy because her concerns about her body were justified.

Hypochondriasis

Classified as a somatoform disorder, *hypochondriasis* can also be seen as an obsessive-compulsive spectrum disorder. The client is obsessed with the thought that he or she has a morbid illness, and repetitively seeks medical reassurance to the contrary. Salkovskis and Warwick (1986) showed that exposure with response prevention can be an effective treatment. The client confronts the feared stimuli (certain bodily sensations, reading medical magazines, or listening to other people describing their medical symptoms) without ritualizing (seeking reassurance). It is important for therapists to enlist the support of people who have provided past reassurance to the client, ensuring that everyone involved follows the treatment plan and stops giving repeated reassurance (Emmelkamp & Bouman, 1991).

Summary

Research results from the treatment of obsessive-compulsive disorder (and OCD spectrum disorders) are similar to those from phobic disorders. Exposure with response prevention is the preferred treatment whenever the client can identify the external stimuli that trigger rituals. Cognitive modification procedures have yet to prove themselves effective with OCD. When the cues for obsessions are internal, it is harder to confront the client with the stimulus and prevent the ritual, especially when the ritual itself is internal (neutralizing thoughts). As Salkovskis (1983) has shown, therapists have to use ingenuity in such cases.

Generalized Anxiety Disorder

The most common of the anxiety disorders (Weissman, 1985), *generalized anxiety disorder (GAD),* poses a challenge for behavioral treatment because it is not linked to particular situations or characteristic behavior patterns. Together with various somatic symptoms of anxiety, the client experiences a series of worrying thoughts or images. This aspect of the problem invites exploration by cognitive therapists, but the worrying thoughts are not as organized or systematic as in obsessive-compulsive disorder, making them difficult to deal with. Hence, specific treatments that have been successful in other applications—systematic desensitization, exposure *in vivo*, stress inoculation—cannot be applied meaningfully. Behavior therapists have typically armed the generalized anxiety client with as many coping strategies as possible, chiefly drawn from techniques of relaxation training and rational emotive behavior therapy.

Wolpe (1973) recommended *thought-stopping* to disrupt prolonged worrying, and several case reports have illustrated the use of this technique. The therapist asks the client to begin worrying, and to do so in earnest for a few minutes. The client signals the therapist when the worrying is definitely in progress. A few seconds after the client's signal, the therapist suddenly shouts "Stop!"—preferably slapping a hand on a desk or table at the same time. The usual effect is for the client to be surprised and startled—and for the worrying thought pattern to be disrupted. When the client tries to resume worrying, it is often difficult to reinstate the original thoughts. Nonetheless, client and therapist proceed with the technique. Eventually, the client, not the therapist, shouts "Stop!" when the worrying is in progress, and later still, the client practices the technique covertly. The utility of this thought-stopping technique is supported by a variety of illustrative anecdotal reports, but compelling experimental data are lacking (O'Brien, 1979).

Since the 1980s, however, more attention has been paid to generalized anxiety by clinical researchers, and some preliminary information is now available to guide the practitioner. Behavior therapy for GAD has been hindered by the lack of a clear behavioral analysis or formulation of the typical case. In a review of theory and research, Deffenbacher and Suinn (1987) proposed a model of the disorder that suggests four suitable intervention targets:

1. Taking control of any stimuli that elicit generalized anxiety or worry
2. Reducing fear in general by employing any or all available techniques
3. Controlling autonomic arousal, not only to reduce anxiety in general but also to dismantle vicious circles that arise when the client is alarmed by signs of high arousal
4. Changing negative cognitions

These treatment strategies all have some empirical support.

Stimulus Control

Applying *stimulus control* methods involves helping the client limit the situations and occasions for the problem's occurrence. The target of this approach has been the client's tendency to worry most of the time and in practically all situations. Theoretically, it is assumed that if the client has usually worried in various places, then those places have come to set the occasion for worrying. In operant learning terms, those situations have become discriminative stimuli. Borkovec, Wilkinson, Folensbee, and Lerman (1983) applied this technique by asking clients to set aside a half-hour "worry period" each day; to keep track of worrying thoughts when they arise; each time a worrying thought emerges, to postpone worrying about it until the designated time; and then to worry as thoroughly as possible during the appointed half-hour period. The technique has proved successful, but it is not entirely clear why.

Flooding and Exposure Methods

Although Deffenbacher and Suinn (1987) recommended that the methods normally used in phobias and obsessive-compulsive disorder be applied to generalized anxiety disorder, they found little encouragement in the literature for doing so. These methods make sense only when the GAD client has anxieties clearly focusing on particular themes, such as the threat of becoming seriously ill at any moment. Clinicians have often used systematic desensitization and other exposure methods in cases like this, but controlled experiments are lacking.

Anxiety Management Training

The best-known application of relaxation training in this context is the *anxiety management training* of Suinn and Richardson (1971). Clients are trained in relaxation in the usual manner. Next, they are taught to notice when they become tense, and then to use the feelings of tension as a cue to relax. As the treatment program progresses, the therapist presents anxiety- arousing scenes for clients to imagine, and they apply relaxation to reduce these feelings of anxiety. The therapist gradually makes the presented scenes more challenging, while slowly reducing his or her influence on clients' efforts to relax. In a test of this technique, Jannoun, Oppenheimer, and Gelder (1982) treated 27 GAD clients. Anxiety management training was presented as a self-help program. Significant anxiety reduction was achieved, as measured by clients' and independent clinicians' ratings. Improvements had been maintained at a follow-up assessment three months after treatment.

Relaxation training alone can be of significant benefit to generalized anxiety disorder clients. Lehrer (1978) treated 10 GAD clients with four sessions of relaxation training and compared them with 10 untreated GAD clients. Additional comparison groups included 20 nonclients, 10 of whom had relaxation and 10 of whom did not. Results were that the treated GAD clients were similar to the nonclients on important measures after treatment.

Cognitive-Behavioral Therapy

In a study with Community Mental Health Center outpatients, rational emotive behavior therapy (REBT) proved more effective than relaxation with a sample of 50 adults who appeared to have had general anxieties (Lipsky, Kassinove, & Miller, 1980). The clients' problems were labeled as "adjustment reaction" or "neurosis," so this study was not an investigation of generalized anxiety disorder specifically. Ramm, Marks, Yuksel, and Stern (1981) treated 12 generalized anxiety clients by what they described as "anxiety management training." The techniques used, however, involved self-statement modification. In six one-hour treatment sessions, clients learned to adopt either positive or negative self-statements concerning their problems. Results were not very impressive, but both groups improved at similar rates. One month after treatment, the measures no longer showed a significant improvement from pretreatment levels. Later studies have produced somewhat more encouraging results for cognitive interventions for generalized anxiety (Barlow, Rapee, & Brown, 1992).

Combined Treatments

The most helpful behavioral treatment approach for generalized anxiety disorder has been the combination of relaxation training with some form of cognitive modification procedure. A prospective between-groups study of GAD clients was reported by Woodward and Jones (1980). Clients were randomly distributed among four treatment conditions: cognitive restructuring (a combination of rational emotive behavior therapy and self-instructional training), systematic desensitization (including the use of coping imagery), the combination of cognitive restructuring and SD, and no treatment. The combined treatment group was clearly the most successful intervention; clients in this condition made clinically significant improvement, whereas those in the other conditions showed little therapeutic change.

The combination of relaxation training and cognitive modification has also been found therapeutic by Barlow and his associates (Barlow, Cohen, Waddell, Vermilyea, Klosko, Blanchard, & Di Nardo, 1984). One component of this study was a comparison of somatic and cognitive treatments for GAD in five clients; another four GAD clients served as an untreated control group. The somatic treatments were progressive relaxation training and electromyograph biofeedback, a technique in which clients could observe monitored changes in muscle tension (in this case, the frontalis muscle of the forehead) and thus learn to reduce the tension. The cognitive treatment procedure was derived from stress inoculation and cognitive therapy methods. Treatment took place during 18 sessions. Treated clients improved significantly, whereas untreated clients did not, on many measures, including reductions in frontalis muscle tension, heart rate, self-report of state anxiety, and clinicians' ratings of problem severity.

A later study by this group focused on 65 carefully diagnosed generalized anxiety disorder clients who were treated by relaxation, cognitive therapy, or the combination of both techniques (Barlow, Rapee, & Brown, 1992). A waiting-list control group provided a baseline for comparison. The active treatments all produced modest therapeutic gains, but clients in these conditions showed significant improvement as compared with the control group participants; the gains persisted over a two-year follow-up interval. Most clients were left with residual anxiety, and there was a substantial dropout rate during the study, yet treated participants used less prescribed medication during the follow-up.

Summary

Generalized anxiety disorder has been most successfully treated by a combination of relaxation training and cognitive restructuring procedures. The cognitive modification techniques are easier to apply when the client has distinct themes for his or her worry and anxiety. However, when the client cannot identify clear themes, cognitive restructuring can be aimed at helping the client adopt constructive coping attitudes (Meadows & Barlow, 1994).

Panic Disorder

Panic disorder was not treated as a separate diagnostic category until 1980 (American Psychiatric Association, 1980). Its separation from the other anxiety disorders was partly the result of the influential work of Donald Klein (1981) on the *pharmacological dissection* of anxiety disorders. He had found that medications normally used to treat depression (the antidepressants) are effective in reducing panic attacks, but they have little impact on the client's anticipatory anxiety about having a panic attack. Conversely, minor tranquilizers are helpful in treating generalized or anticipatory anxiety, but they do not block panic attacks. These observations suggested that panic disorder is a distinct syndrome that should be separated from generalized anxiety disorder. Before 1980, the behavior therapy literature relevant to panic disorder is found in articles on generalized anxiety disorder and agoraphobia (Ley, 1987). The behavioral literature on panic disorder itself begins in 1984.

Waddell, Barlow, and O'Brien (1984) described the treatment of three men with panic disorder. Two of the clients had had their first panic episode during an illicit drug experience. The treatments were cognitive restructuring and relaxation training, the number of treatment sessions ranging from 12 to 17 in the three clients. The research design was a multiple baseline across clients, so each client's treatment began at a different time. As gauged by decreases in the number and duration of panic attacks, the program was successful at least up to a three-month follow-up assessment. However, there was an increase in "background" or generalized anxiety in two of the clients. Barlow and associates (1984), cited in the previous section on generalized anxiety disorder, treated 11 clients with panic disorder. Of the group, 5 clients were treated by a combination of relaxation, biofeedback, and cognitive-behavioral therapy; 6 served as a waiting-list control group. Parallel to the results with the GAD clients, the results for panic disorder clearly favored the treated clients, who improved significantly on all major measures; waiting-list clients did not show improvement. On the criterion of self-monitored panic attacks in both panic disorder and GAD groups, all 10 of the treated clients improved, whereas 4 of the 10 untreated clients actually got worse.

Theoretical interpretations of panic disorder have combined the somatic and cognitive aspects of the disorder, justifying treatment by relaxation or biofeedback and cognitive approaches. Theorists assume that panic attacks develop because, first, there is a bodily reaction similar to anxiety (whether it was actually triggered by biological factors[5] or by external stimuli), and, second, the client interprets this in a catastrophic fashion (Hecker & Thorpe, 1992; Thorpe & Hecker, 1991). To take the hyperventilation idea as an example, examining both bodily reactions and catastrophic interpretations leads to two logical treatment approaches. First, the client can be told that his or her symptoms are understandable in terms of overbreathing or hyperventilation. This information allows the client to construe the bodily sensations as a normal reaction to hyperventilation, rather than as an unexplained attack of anxiety. Second, the client can be trained to control his or her respiration so that episodes of hyperventilation are less likely to occur.

In a study of respiration control for clients with panic disorder, Clark, Salkovskis, and Chalkley (1985) treated 19 people who had panic attacks and anticipatory anxiety. The clients had been selected from a larger sample of people with panic disorder because their symptoms were consistent with the hyperventilation interpretation. Clients were given a rationale and explanation that encouraged them to interpret the sensations of anxiety as the result of hyperventilation, and they were trained in respiration control. After two weeks of treatment, there were significant reductions in panic frequency and in the self-report of anxiety. Further reductions took place within six-month and two-year follow-up intervals, although the results here may have been partly due to extra treatment given in the interim. No exposure treatment was given in the study, but behavioral-avoidance tests served as an index of improvement for these clients.

Panic Control Treatment

Since 1989, the essential techniques used in the psychological treatment of panic disorder have been cognitive restructuring, exposure to somatic cues, and breathing retraining, collectively referred to as *panic control treatment* (Beck & Zebb, 1994; Rapee & Barlow, 1991; Street & Barlow, 1994). The treatment component receiving most emphasis is *exposure to somatic cues*, or deliberately producing and confronting the bodily sensations that the client associates with panic.

The theory is that panic disorder does not reflect anxiety about external situations such as public places, crowds, or heights. Instead, it reflects anxiety about certain bodily sensations such as dizziness, light-headedness, and muscle tension. If the client is anxious about crowds, the therapist would normally recommend exposure therapy—confronting crowds until the anxiety declines. Similarly, if the client is anxious about the sensation of light-headedness, the therapist could recommend exposure therapy—confronting the feeling of light-headedness until the anxiety declines.

Diana, the client whose fear of breathlessness returned dramatically after an asthma attack was triggered by the aroma of a scented candle, was treated in this manner. She and the therapist considered several possible methods—spinning around in a swivel chair to produce dizziness, stationary running to increase the heart rate, and breathing through a straw to induce a sense of smothering. They settled on voluntary hyperventilation as the most appropriate way of re-creating the essential sensations she experienced during a panic attack. Within treatment sessions, Diana would deliberately draw rapid, shallow breaths for two minutes at a time, automatically producing an array of symptoms, including dry mouth, numbness and tingling in the fingers, light-headedness, and muscle tension. By deliberately reproducing and confronting the sensations of being out of breath, Diana was able to reduce her anxiety through normal exposure mechanisms.

The *cognitive restructuring* component of panic control treatment is a form of cognitive therapy, applied to the client's implicit schemas construing panic sensations as signs of catastrophic illness (Clark, 1986). Through this type of intervention, Diana was able to recognize that, despite the discomfort and distress associated with breathlessness, there was no evidence that she had to be incapacitated by her symptom. In fact, she was able to remind herself that she had always survived everything that had ever happened to her!

David Barlow and his colleagues conducted a large-scale treatment outcome study to compare four conditions: the panic control treatment package (PCT), relaxation training, PCT plus relaxation training (combined treatment), and a waiting-list control (Barlow, Craske, Cerny, & Klosko, 1989). The three active treatments brought significant benefits as measured by panic frequency reduction and general improvement on a battery of measures. The PCT and combined conditions were most successful overall, and significantly more clients terminated treatment early from the relaxation condition. Two years after the conclusion of treatment, clients in the PCT condition were faring best, 80 percent of them remaining free of panic attacks (Street & Barlow, 1994).

There are indications from a Canadian study that panic control treatment may be delivered economically to clients with reduced therapist contact. Some 21 clients with panic disorder were treated over 17 weeks, 10 clients (therapist-directed) meeting the therapist each week and 11 ("reduced therapist contact") working from a treatment manual, having seven irregularly scheduled clinic sessions and 8 impromptu telephone calls from the therapist. Both treatment conditions brought significant and lasting benefit that persisted at least one year after treatment (Cote, Gauthier, Laberge, Cormier, & Plamondon, 1994).

Summary

When a client's panic disorder does not include agoraphobia, the panic control treatment of Barlow and his colleagues is highly recommended. When a client's panic disorder does include avoidance of agoraphobic situations, the panic control treatment is also recommended, but exposure *in vivo* can also be used to reduce anxiety in specific situations. Panic control treatment involves a double-barreled attack on the somatic and cognitive aspects. The somatic components of panic are addressed by exposure to somatic cues, relaxation training, and respiratory control or breathing retraining. The cognitive component is addressed by various forms of cognitive-behavioral therapy, chiefly Beck's cognitive therapy. The use of these approaches in the 1990s has significantly improved the outlook for clients with panic disorder.

Chapter Summary

Initially, behavior therapists focused most of their attention on the anxiety disorders linked to specific situations, like phobias and some obsessive-compulsive patterns. Exposure treatments drawn from learning theory concepts proved successful and seemed to work because of the extinction of conditioned responses and avoidance behavior. The need to address nonsituational anxiety, as in generalized anxiety disorder and panic disorder, encouraged behavior therapists to develop treatments based on cognitive restructuring and on exposure to somatic cues. Barlow's panic control treatment—combining cue exposure, cognitive restructuring, and breathing control—represents a dramatic advance in treatment effectiveness, bringing renewed hope to clients with panic disorder.

Endnotes

1. Our section headings do not follow the *DSM-IV* exactly. We prefer to use the terms that behavior therapists favor in their writings, and these are not always exactly the same as the *DSM-IV* labels.
2. *Criteria* are specific, identified factors that must be present (or, sometimes, absent) if the particular label is to be validly used. *Criteria* is the plural, *criterion* the singular.
3. Emotional processing is discussed with bio-informational theory in the next chapter.
4. See Chapter 14.
5. One possibility is hyperventilation, which could account for all of the somatic symptoms associated with a panic attack (Ley, 1987).

Chapter 8

Posttraumatic Syndromes

Craig, a middle-aged man who owns a small construction business in northern New England, sought therapy two years after he was seriously injured in a propane gas explosion. One bitterly cold morning in January, he got up early to inspect a house site. An industrial propane gas heater ran day and night inside the foundation to keep the newly poured cement above freezing. On this particular morning, as happened occasionally, the burner flame had gone out. Confident in the fail-safe system that automatically shut off the propane when the flame died, Craig relit the burner. But the cut-off valve had failed, and the cellar was inches deep in heavier-than-air propane. The resulting explosion practically blew Craig out of the foundation. In a dream-like state, his clothes and hair on fire and the skin peeling from his hands, he managed to drive himself five miles to the nearest emergency room.

Craig eventually made an excellent physical recovery, but he has suffered severe psychological problems ever since. He has relived that drive to the emergency room twice a week for two years in his recurrent nightmares. Each nightmare is an exact replay of the original drive, complete with the original sensations, feelings, and even the precise thoughts he had at various stages along the route. The nightmare ends with the look of horror on the face of the nurse who greeted him as he staggered through the doors of the hospital. Craig can no longer work because of his extreme irritability, his poor concentration, his preoccupation with images of the explosion, and his strong startle reaction at any unexpected sound. He keeps to himself and has lost contact with his many friends. A recent television news item about an explosion at an oil depot led him to run from the room in a cold sweat.

Sharon is a woman in her twenties who was victimized in childhood by repeated sexual abuse from a close male relative. She was practically kept prisoner in the house for years. Eventually she escaped and lived on the streets, abusing alcohol and various illicit drugs. The escape was only partial, because Sharon's lifestyle increased her vulnerability to further victimization by men. Her treatment began when she entered a residential program for recovering substance abusers. Other clients and staff members soon noticed that Sharon found it extremely difficult to participate in group therapy when the topic of sexual abuse arose (as it does all too frequently).

Sharon was also extremely reluctant to enter a room when men were present. She was terrified when a new staff member, a man, joined the unit; she was convinced for a time, despite objective evidence to the contrary, that he was the man who had abused her. On one occasion, she was drying dishes in the kitchen when the telephone rang; she was so startled by the sudden sound that she screamed and dropped the plate she was holding, which shattered on the floor. Sharon often came downstairs in the early hours of the morning to talk to the night staff after a nightmare had disturbed her sleep. Recently, she was puzzled to find among her possessions children's toys and messages in childish handwriting. Sharon was unable to account for their presence among her belongings. She loses track of time, and finds herself in unfamiliar neighborhoods with no recollection of how she got there. The other day a person she does not know approached her on the street and greeted her warmly, as if they were close friends.

Wayne celebrated his fiftieth birthday by traveling out of town alone, taking a room in a cheap motel, and locking himself in with a 12-pack of beer and some rented videotapes. The Department of Veterans' Affairs has paid for his weekly psychotherapy sessions for over 12 years. Every time they meet, Wayne and his current therapist make wry jokes at the surprisingly large number of references that the news media make to Vietnam every day of the year. Wayne's tour of duty in Vietnam ended 25 years ago, but for him, the war is still going on to this day. He can barely handle life outside an institution. He shuns people and prefers to drive around in his truck most of the day. Dealing with authority in any form terrifies him. His chief phobia is of the local V.A. hospital, which he refuses to visit, even for needed health care. The appearance of an official government letter in his mailbox causes instant panic.

Stimuli reminiscent of combat—gunfire in the woods in hunting season; a car backfiring; hot, humid weather; or, worst of all, a helicopter passing overhead—evoke intense fear. Occasionally Wayne has dramatic, waking hallucinations of the Viet Cong, who either are hiding in the trees near his home talking to each other, or are present in large numbers in the local supermarket so that every face he sees while shopping seems that of a southeast Asian.

Wayne's sleep has been disturbed for years, despite state-of-the-art pharmacotherapy and behavior therapy interventions. When he does sleep, he is usually awakened by his nightly "movie reruns" of combat experiences, precise replays of actual incidents from the war. Recently, his dreams have changed in character and are more like the "normal" surrealistic dreams that most of us experience. Themes of guilt are prominent in Wayne's newer-style dreams. Instead of dreaming about the enemy throwing grenades into his tank or about bayoneting an enemy soldier, he dreams of the police arriving at his present-day home and arresting him for murder.

In the previous chapter we discussed four of the five major anxiety syndromes: panic disorder, phobias, obsessive-compulsive disorder, and generalized anxiety disorder. In this chapter we shall cover the other important syndrome, posttraumatic stress disorder.[1] Conceptually, this differs from the other anxiety disorders in two chief ways. First, in one sense, it is simpler to understand, in that it is easy to identify the obvious stressful event that triggered the onset of the disorder in the individual client. Second, it is a more complex disorder, because it combines many features of the other anxiety disorders. We shall explain these points in the following paragraphs.

Origins of the Disorder

Everyone would agree that the anxiety disorders described in the previous chapter cause great emotional distress and behavioral disability in a large number of people, rightly drawing sympathy and motivating one to find effective treatments. Yet these disorders still strike one as obviously "abnormal"; avoiding crowded shopping malls, suddenly becoming terrified for no apparent reason, engaging in lengthy and elaborate cleansing or checking rituals, and worrying endlessly about everyday hassles are problems that seem illogical, senseless, counterproductive, and self-defeating. Arguably, the main reason most people would find these disorders puzzling is that they cannot understand *why* individuals develop them.

Behavior therapists usually explain anxiety disorders as understandable extensions of "normal" experience and behavior, and as the product of routine behavioral processes such as conditioning, modeling, or the development of certain expectations. With most clients, however, it proves very difficult to point to the actual conditioning events or modeling experiences that gave rise to such persistent distress (Marks, 1981a, 1981b, 1987).

In that context, posttraumatic stress disorder (PTSD) is far easier to understand. By definition, it is triggered by an extremely stressful experience or series of experiences—military combat, life-threatening natural disasters, rape, prolonged abuse in childhood—well beyond the range of stressors people would normally expect to encounter. In the aftermath of such experiences, some people develop chronic patterns of fear, avoidance, and other problems that cluster together as a distinct anxiety disorder. Strictly speaking, because not *all* people exposed to traumatic events develop PTSD, the complete cause has not yet been identified. "More accurately, we know the proximal event that activates the disorder in vulnerable individuals" (Barlow, 1988, p. 499). Nonetheless, experts agree that everyone who has PTSD has been subjected to an identifiable traumatic stressor, and that without that experience the anxiety disorder would not have arisen. Although the client's current anxiety symptoms seem unnecessary because the trauma has passed, at least there is no mystery about their origin in extremely terrifying, real-life events.

Complexity of the Disorder

Clients who develop PTSD are doubly unfortunate. First, they were traumatized by the original stressor or stressors. Second, they have developed an anxiety disorder after (sometimes, long after) the traumatic event has passed. In the aftermath of trauma, clients continue to be troubled by unwanted memories, flashbacks, and nightmares; they are distressed by and avoid reminders of the event; they severely limit their lives and activities; and they experience a generalized pattern of heightened sensitivity to threatening stimuli. Like Sharon, at the beginning of this chapter, some clients have *dissociative episodes* in which the usual sense of continuity in one's memory, personality, habits, and even identity is strangely disrupted.

The complexity of the disorder is challenging to behavior therapists. It is fairly easy to understand why Wayne, the traumatized combat veteran, breaks into a sweat at the sound of gunfire, because classical conditioning processes clearly apply. But what about his recurrent nightmares, his tendency to jump out of his skin whenever a door slams, his wariness of other people, and his high level of general emotional arousal? As a result of his combat experiences, Wayne now seems to have all the anxiety disorders at once. As if he has a specific phobia, he dives for cover at the sound of a helicopter passing overhead. As if he has generalized anxiety disorder, he is tense, jumpy, and "nerved up" continuously. As if he has obsessive-compulsive disorder, he broods and dwells on his problems and is troubled by intrusive thoughts and images of combat that he tries to resist.

There are two approaches behavior therapists can take with such a complex, multifaceted syndrome. First, each specific problem (e.g., generalized anxiety, fear of particular stimuli, avoiding people) could be the target of a specific treatment intervention (e.g., relaxation training, graded practice, social skills training), as in the multimodal approach (Lazarus, 1989). Second, a complete theory could be constructed to explain how the various anxiety elements fit together in PTSD, and then a treatment approach that follows logically from that theory could be developed and tested. With either approach, treatment outcome research can show empirically how effective behavioral treatments are with PTSD. But there are many advantages of developing an overall understanding, rather than using a piece-meal approach. With a theory that successfully integrates all elements of the disorder, more focused and efficient treatments may possibly be designed. It is also possible that the insights derived from an overarching theory may allow clinicians to give people advice on how to avoid developing PTSD in the aftermath of trauma.

History of the Concepts

Distinct patterns of psychological distress following exposure to terrifying experiences have been described for centuries (Saigh, 1992a). Table 8–1 provides a summary of the different terms used to describe these syndromes in the last hundred years or so.

Current Classifications

Although most behavior therapists have been unimpressed by the use of diagnostic categories to classify mental health problems, recent research and practice have usually followed

TABLE 8–1   Chronological Listing of Terms Describing Posttraumatic Syndromes in Response to Various Extreme Stressors

- COMPENSATION NEUROSIS (1879; various traumatic experiences)
- HYSTERIA (1881; so-called concussion of the spine)
- NERVOUS SHOCK (1882–85; various traumatic experiences)
- ERICHSEN'S DISEASE (1889; one form of the traumatic neuroses)
- SCHRECKNEUROSE (1896; house fires, railroad accidents, natural disasters)
- shell shock[1] (1914–18; military combat; originally referring to a neurological syndrome following physical trauma from bursting shells)
- shell concussion (1940; military combat; term replacing the original usage of "shell shock")
- SHELL SHOCK (1940; military combat; referring to the stress-related, psychological syndrome)
- TRAUMATOPHOBIA (1942; various traumatic experiences)
- POST-TRAUMATIC MENTAL COMPLICATIONS (1943; Coconut Grove Fire)
- WAR NEUROSIS (1943; military combat)
- COMBAT NEUROSES (1945; military combat)
- GROSS STRESS REACTION (1952, *DSM-I*; military combat or civilian catastrophe)
- PHOBIC ANXIETY DEPERSONALIZATION SYNDROME (1959; overwhelming anxiety, including anxiety connected with physical illness)
- CHRONIC COMBAT FATIGUE (1962; military combat)
- TRANSIENT SITUATIONAL DISTURBANCE (1968, *DSM-II*; overwhelming environmental stress)
- PHYSIONEUROSIS (1969; military combat)
- RAPE TRAUMA SYNDROME (1974; rape; acute and long-term phases distinguished)
- DELAYED STRESS RESPONSE SYNDROME (1975; military combat)
- POSTTRAUMATIC STRESS DISORDER (1980, *DSM-III*; stressor evoking significant distress in anyone; acute vs. chronic or delayed subtypes)
- POST-TRAUMATIC[2] STRESS DISORDER (1987, *DSM-III-R*; psychologically distressing event outside the range of usual human experience, examples specified; acute subtype dropped)
- POSTTRAUMATIC STRESS DISORDER (1994; DSM-IV; "extreme traumatic stressor," examples specified; acute subtype reinstated)
- ACUTE STRESS DISORDER (1994; *DSM-IV*; "extreme traumatic stressor" but different symptom cluster from PTSD)

Sources: American Psychiatric Association, 1952, 1968, 1980, 1987, 1994; Barlow, 1988; Foa, Steketee, & Rothbaum, 1989; Katz, 1994; Saigh, 1992a; Trimble, 1981

1. Syndromes in lower-case lettering were originally thought to be neurological disorders with physical causes.
2. Note the hyphen.

the *DSM* diagnoses of the American Psychiatric Association (for ease of communication with other professionals, if nothing else). As we discussed in Chapter 6, some disorders do consist of coherent clusters of specific problems running together as syndromes, justifying the use of diagnostic labels for distinctive patterns of problems. As suggested by the experiences of Craig, Sharon, and Wayne at the beginning of this chapter, the posttraumatic anxiety disorders are good examples of syndromes of this kind, because very similar patterns of problems can be seen in men and women of varied ages and lifestyles who encountered widely differing traumatic stressors. Three diagnostic categories are recognized currently: the two *DSM-IV* categories *posttraumatic stress disorder (PTSD)* and *acute stress disorder* (American Psychiatric Association, 1994) and *disorder of extreme stress, not otherwise specified (DESNOS)* (Katz, 1994; Sato & Heiby, 1991).

Posttraumatic[2] Stress Disorder (PTSD)

PTSD describes a characteristic pattern of problems experienced by a subset of those people who have been subjected to extreme, emotionally traumatic[3] stress. Unlike the anxiety disorders described in Chapter 7, PTSD, by definition, is precipitated by actual traumatic or life-threatening events such as those experienced by Craig, Sharon, and Wayne. What makes PTSD a disorder is the set of distressing, impairing, and disabling symptoms that follow exposure to the stressor.

The person's situation and problems must conform to six specified criteria before the *DSM-IV* diagnosis of PTSD is given (American Psychiatric Association, 1994):

1. Exposure to an extreme stressor and reacting with intense fear or emotional trauma
2. Continued reexperiencing of the event in the form of nightmares, flashbacks, or intrusive imagery
3. Continued avoidance of reminders of the event coupled with reduced emotional responsiveness ("psychic numbing")
4. Continued symptoms of emotional activation or arousal
5. Persistence of significant symptoms beyond one month
6. Significant distress or impairment in social or occupational functioning

Some authors have argued that the typical PTSD syndrome is even more complex than the *DSM-IV* suggests. From 60 to 75 percent of combat veterans receiving treatment for PTSD also have substance use disorders at some point (Abueg & Fairbank, 1992; Foy, Osato, Houskamp, & Neumann, 1992). High rates of depression and general distress also typically accompany PTSD (Nishith, Hearst, Mueser, & Foa, 1995; Saigh, 1992a; Sato & Heiby, 1991; Steketee & Foa, 1987), raising the question that the disorder may be too narrowly defined in the official classification.

Acute Stress Disorder

Acute stress disorder is similar to PTSD but occurs within one month of exposure to the stressor and it is short-lived, not lasting more than four weeks. The person with acute stress disorder also has at least three *dissociative* symptoms (such as memory loss for the traumatic event or a sense of numbing or detachment) (American Psychiatric Association, 1994). As this is a new category at the time of writing, published research devoted to acute stress disorder is currently lacking.

Disorder of Extreme Stress, Not Otherwise Specified

This disorder, abbreviated as DESNOS, was proposed for inclusion in *DSM-IV* (Sato & Heiby, 1991) but did not appear in the published manual. It is described as "an extreme variant of PTSD characterized by [a] motivationally complex pattern of traumatization and extreme personality and somatic changes beyond those routinely seen in PTSD" (Katz, 1994, p. 555). DESNOS is the possible consequence of the most extreme forms of traumatization, such as concentration camp experiences or chronic childhood abuse. Victims of DESNOS have more symptoms than are required for the diagnosis of PTSD, including personality changes, dissociative episodes, self-mutilation, and suicide attempts. DESNOS may, in turn, set the scene for the development of borderline personality disorder and dissociative identity disorder (formerly known as multiple personality) (Harvey & Herman, 1992).

In summary, three posttraumatic anxiety syndromes are recognized at present. But two of them, acute stress disorder and DESNOS, have received relatively little attention from clinical researchers as yet. PTSD remains the best-known and most extensively researched syndrome, and therefore it will be the focus of this chapter. Remember, however, that behavior therapists, as a group, are not committed to the *DSM* as the only way of describing mental health problems. For that reason, some of the material we will present does not conform precisely to *DSM* formulations of PTSD.

Behavioral Theories of PTSD

Any theory of the causes of PTSD has to explain the three chief symptom clusters: *intrusion* (flashbacks, nightmares, and even hallucinations of traumatic stimuli), *constriction* (avoidance of stimuli related to trauma, psychic numbing, and limiting one's life and activities in general), and *hyperarousal* (exaggerated startle reflex, difficulty in falling asleep, and high heart rate and blood pressure) (Herman, 1992). In seeking explanations for any disorder, behavior therapists often find a helpful starting point in the familiar processes of classical conditioning, operant learning, modeling, and the modification of cognitions such as expectancies and attributions. Explanations of PTSD in terms of conditioning mechanisms, cognitive and emotional processes, and biological factors have all been considered.

Conditioning Mechanisms

Because all clients with PTSD have been exposed to trauma, there is the obvious possibility that classical conditioning mechanisms are involved in the disorder. Potentially traumatic events such as explosions, assaults, and witnessing sudden death can readily be seen as aversive unconditioned stimuli, allowing the operation of classical conditioning when these are paired with other stimuli that happen to be present. For example, the sights and sounds of houses under construction were so routine to Craig before the propane explosion that he would have laughed at the idea of fearing any of them, but since the accident, his heart pounds at the sound of hissing gas or the smell of wet cement. In classical conditioning terms, the explosion is an unconditioned stimulus (UCS), automatically producing alarm, fear, and pain as unconditioned responses (UCR). The previously neutral smell of wet cement, paired with the explosion (UCS), becomes a conditioned stimulus (CS), now capable of evoking a conditioned response (CR) like those elicited by the explosion.

Level of Exposure to Traumatic Stimuli

If classical conditioning is to hold up as an explanation of PTSD, one would expect the disorder to arise chiefly in people exposed to the most intense and frequent traumatic stimuli. David Foy and his colleagues explored this in studies of military combat veterans, looking for any differences between those who developed PTSD and those who did not. Veterans with and without PTSD gave information on several dimensions of their functioning at three time periods: premilitary (education, occupation, family functioning, and family history); military (court martials, discharge status, length and nature of military duty, and—especially important—length and severity of exposure to combat); and postmilitary. The results were that level of combat exposure was far more significant than premilitary adjustment in predicting PTSD severity.

Later work confirmed that exposure to high levels of combat was the strongest predictor of PTSD, but in veterans with relatively low combat exposure, level of family psychopathology correlated with PTSD rates. Consistent with these findings, studies by Zahava Solomon and her colleagues in Israel showed that veterans who had experienced adverse life events (particularly disturbances in social relationships) in the three months preceding their exposure to combat were more likely than others to develop PTSD (Foy, Osato, Houskamp, & Neumann, 1992; Foy, Resnick, Sipprelle, & Carroll, 1987).

Similar results are found in studies of female rape victims. High levels of general psychological distress are typically seen in victims of sexual assault, and as many as 29 percent develop PTSD (Kilpatrick, Saunders, Amick-McMullen, Best, Veronen, & Resnick, 1989). Consistent with the literature on combat veterans, there is a strong correlation between the severity of rape events and subsequent PTSD rates (Foy et al., 1992; Saigh, 1992b).

These results suggest that high exposure to traumatic stimuli is enough to make anyone vulnerable to PTSD. The military studies show that someone who encountered relatively low levels of combat would also need to have experienced other vulnerability factors, such as the presence of psychological problems in the family, before being at risk for the disorder. The general finding that the level and extent of trauma exposure is the strongest predictor of PTSD is consistent with classical conditioning as an explanation for at least some symptoms of the disorder (Foy et al., 1992; Marks, 1987).

Two-Factor Theory of Fear and Avoidance Learning

Some behavior therapists suggest that two-factor theory applies perfectly to PTSD (Keane, Zimering, & Caddell, 1985). Remember that this theory suggests that (1) previously neutral stimuli take on the power to elicit anxiety when, through classical conditioning, they are paired with aversive unconditioned stimuli; and (2) the formerly neutral but now noxious conditioned stimuli *remain* aversive because the person (understandably) steers clear of them, protecting the conditioned anxiety response from extinction. Classical conditioning is the crucial process in creating anxiety; clients' learned avoidance is the vital factor in maintaining it.

We can illustrate two-factor theory as an explanation of PTSD by applying it to the cases of Craig, Sharon, and Wayne, noted earlier in the chapter. Receiving serious injuries in a sudden explosion, being subjected to prolonged and repeated sexual abuse, and seeing one's buddies killed in combat while under fire from the enemy can obviously be seen as aversive unconditioned stimuli. Any other prominent stimuli noticeable at the time, however harmless or insignificant, could, in the future, provoke distress or alarm through classical conditioning (pairing with the traumatic stimuli). Stimuli that were repeatedly paired with traumatic events should elicit longer-lasting conditioned responses. Craig reacts with aversion to the smell of wet cement; Sharon is ill at ease in small rooms and when a bearded man is present; and Wayne dives for cover when he hears a helicopter. Each client's conditioned fear of these stimuli tends to continue indefinitely because the client avoids them, never confronting them long enough for extinction to set in (Fairbank & Brown, 1987).

Evaluation of Conditioning Mechanisms in PTSD

Research confirms that high trauma exposure is associated with high prevalence and severity of PTSD, consistent with conditioning explanations. Case examples also provide what seem to be clear illustrations of classical conditioning in clients with PTSD. But there are several problems with classical conditioning and two-factor theory as explanations of this disorder, as noted by Edna Foa and her colleagues (Foa, Steketee, & Rothbaum, 1989).

Conditioning Only Explains Some Elements of PTSD.   Although two-factor theory does explain the fear, avoidance, and generalization of distress following a traumatic event such as rape or military combat, it can only explain some of the typical features of PTSD (Foa et al., 1989). Anxiety and avoidance triggered by trauma-related stimuli are important aspects of the disorder, but PTSD also includes reexperiencing or intrusion, constriction of one's life through psychic numbing and hyperarousal (American Psychiatric Association, 1994; Herman, 1992). Two-factor theory does not easily explain why Craig no longer works or sees his old friends, why Sharon startles when the telephone rings, and why Wayne has recurrent nightmares of combat scenes.

Why Don't Flashbacks and Nightmares Provide Therapeutic Exposure?   Foa and her colleagues raised the interesting question: "If exposure results in decreased anxiety, why don't the reexperiences of the trauma reported by PTSD sufferers result in decreased symptomatology?" (Foa et al., 1989, p. 157). In other words, why does Wayne still have traumatic nightmares about combat, 25 years after his tour of duty in Vietnam, when such extensive exposure should have weakened his conditioned anxiety responses? Keane, Zimering, and Caddell (1985) proposed some answers to this question as it relates to combat veterans. Perhaps the repeated nightmares and flashbacks fail to reduce distress because they do not include enough relevant stimuli. Why does the reexperiencing not include enough relevant stimuli? Perhaps clients do not recall everything because they try to suppress their memories; because, through embarrassment, they keep their memories and painful emotions to themselves; and because critical traumatic episodes took place under conditions of abnormally high excitement that never recur in civilian life.

Despite these ingenious counterarguments, conditioning mechanisms appear to provide only a partial explanation of the PTSD syndrome, with some difficult questions about its causes remaining unanswered.

Cognitive and Emotional Processes

Cognitions and Attributions

In Chapter 4, we described cognitive restructuring procedures that stemmed from research establishing links between certain thinking patterns and corresponding emotional states. These thinking patterns can range from fleeting self-statements in which one comment to one's self on aspects of the immediate situation ("Oh, no, the test is on Friday and I haven't started studying yet!"), to lasting attributional styles, consistent attitudes that one brings to a variety of events ("Even when the going gets rough, I usually come through pretty well when I'm under pressure"). In Chapter 9, we will show that the study of attributional styles has proved especially helpful in understanding depression, because some people who are vulnerable to depressive mood states typically blame negative events (quite unfairly) on enduring, across-the-board personal shortcomings. This has positive implications for treatment via cognitive therapy in which the client can learn to adopt more constructive attitudes.

Recent research on clients with PTSD shows that their self-statements and attributional styles are well worth examining. Studies of Israeli combat veterans revealed that those who developed PTSD were more likely than the others to ascribe negative events to external, uncontrollable causes (Mikulincer & Solomon, 1988; Saigh, 1992b; Solomon, Mikulincer, & Flum, 1988). In the case of rape victims, those who attributed the rape to a *particular* facet of their own behavior were less prone to later depression than were those who attributed the crime to lasting flaws in their own personalities (Foy et al., 1992).

As you will see in Chapter 9, the typical pattern of attributions in depression differs from that seen in PTSD clients, who are more troubled by the unpredictability and uncontrollability of external aversive events, shaking the foundations of their sense of security. As Ronnie Janoff-Bulman expressed it in her aptly titled book *Shattered Assumptions: Towards a New Psychology of Trauma:*

> At the core of our assumptive world are abstract beliefs about ourselves, the external world, and the relationship between the two. More specifically, and most simply, I propose that our three fundamental assumptions are:
>> The world is benevolent
>> The world is meaningful
>> The self is worthy. (Janoff-Bulman, 1992, p. 6)

When an individual is terrorized by a traumatic event, there is a sudden, profound alteration in his or her fundamental assumptions on a scale that Janoff-Bulman compares to a scientific revolution. Such a tremendous cognitive change—an attitudinal upheaval in which the world abruptly becomes dangerous and threatening—could explain PTSD clients' psychic numbing and hyperarousal. However, this conception of PTSD still does not account for clients' reexperiencing of trauma.

Janoff-Bulman's formulation of PTSD in terms of shattered assumptions has elements in common with the original *learned helplessness* model of depression, derived from animal studies in the 1960s. Proponents of learned helplessness theory claim that such patterns as passivity and psychic numbing following uncontrollable, negative events result from a generalized expectation that nothing one can do makes any difference (Peterson, 1994). An expanded learned helplessness model put forward in the 1970s encompasses clients' attributional styles (Abramson, Seligman, & Teasdale, 1978) and comprises the following hypotheses: People inevitably seek explanations for uncontrollable, aversive events, and such explanations vary along three dimensions: responsibility (internal/external, or the event's being one's own fault versus someone or something else's), persistence over time (stable/unstable), and stability across situations (global/specific).

Individuals who lose self-esteem in the most persistent and pervasive ways make internal, stable, and global attributions for the aversive, uncontrollable event ("I have always managed to put myself in the wrong place at the wrong time"; "If there's any kind of trouble waiting to happen, I'm guaranteed to be the one to find it"). Individuals who are less self-critical and experience less distress make external, unstable, and specific attributions ("The idiot who led us into this ambush has to be the one officer in the whole army who knows nothing about the conditions on this highway") (Foa et al., 1989).

Bioinformational Theory and Emotional Processing

The emotional processing model of Foa and Kozak (1986) stems from Lang's (1979, 1985) *bio-informational theory,* which construes anxiety as a memory network of propositionally coded information (see Chapter 7). These propositions fall into three groups: (1) stimulus information, (2) response information, and (3) meaning information. This network of propositions is a program for escape and avoidance behavior—a program that is "run" when the individual is presented with information that matches elements of the fear network.

For example, Susan B., whose phobia of spiders was described in Chapter 2, has a memory network concerning spiders, a network that may be activated in several ways. Suddenly seeing a spider would certainly be likely to activate this network and all of its propositions, including Susan's fund of stimulus information about spiders (such as their size, activity level, and hairiness), relevant response propositions (such as her running away, perspiring, heart pounding rapidly), and meaning elements ("This situation is highly dangerous"). Susan's "spider" network could also be activated, though probably to a lesser extent, whenever her heart pounds rapidly, because that is also part of the network. So even running up the stairs could activate Susan's fear network to a degree, if the sudden exercise accelerates her heart rate.

Clients are not always able to state the information in a fear network directly, as in the preceding example. Clinicians can study information processing in subtle ways that do not depend on the client's ability to verbalize the information. In the Stroop color-naming paradigm, for example, subjects look at words printed in different colors and are asked simply to name the colors, ignoring the meanings of the words. But emotionally significant words tend to slow the client's color-naming response, giving rise to a useful technique for discovering which words may be associated with trauma—simply identify those words that produce the longest hesitations before the color is correctly named. Several studies have demonstrated the validity of this technique in evaluating trauma-relevant themes in combat veterans and rape victims with PTSD (McNally, 1995).

Foa and Kozak (1986) argued that fear reduction requires two procedures: (1) activating the fear network; and (2) providing new information that alters the network. Activation of a fear network can be detected by such methods as measuring the client's heart rate (to see if it accelerates) and asking him or her to give subjective ratings of discomfort. Successful progress in treatment is indicated when the client shows emotional activation at three stages: (1) initial activation of the fear network in a treatment session, (2) reduction of fear during treatment sessions, and (3) reduction of fear across treatment sessions.

Habituation of fear due to successful emotional processing leads to new, benign information being incorporated into the network. For example, Susan may overcome her phobia if she participates in several sessions of imaginal exposure in which the spider network is initially activated, her fear is gradually reduced during a treatment session, and at least some fear reduction persists between sessions. Eventually, new meaning elements are added (e.g., "I used to feel helpless when faced by a spider, but now I have learned that I can remain calm and cope easily").

Foa and colleagues (1989) argued that concepts of bio-informational theory and emotional processing provide a necessary supplement to conditioning accounts in explaining PTSD. Especially important is the meaning element, because *perceived* threat is more important in PTSD than actual threat. The therapeutic techniques used in emotional processing overlap considerably with the procedures normally used in behavior therapy to treat anxiety disorders (Hecker & Thorpe, 1987).

Biological Factors

Neurobiological theories of PTSD in adults are drawn from studies of aversive conditioning and learned helplessness in animals. Repeated exposure to inescapable shock leads to depletion of the neurotransmitters norepinephrine and dopamine. Norepinephrine depletion becomes a conditioned response to stimuli signaling aversive events, and this possibly accounts for the psychic numbing seen in PTSD. For example, Sharon enters a room and sees a bearded man, to her an aversive CS; the CR is a reduced level of certain neurotransmitters; and this, in turn, leaves her feeling emotionally numbed (together with a sense of helplessness). However, depletion of neurotransmitters could eventually lead to increased sensitivity to stimulation in the receiving neurons, and that might explain the vivid nightmares and excessive startle reflexes associated with PTSD (Van der Kolk, 1987). A problem with this line of research is that the aversive events used to induce learned helplessness alter a number of brain chemicals directly, making it difficult to point to a particular neurotransmitter as mediator of the effects of uncontrollability (Peterson, 1994).

There is evidence that repeatedly eliciting acute fear causes excessive stimulation of the neural networks of the limbic system, the brain's "emotional center." Neurologists would predict that loss of function and lessened inhibition would follow from the automatic *healing* process that takes place in the central nervous system. Emotional numbing, increased startle reactions, and flashbacks and nightmares could all be consistent with the overstimulation, then healing, of certain brain areas (Kolb, 1988).

Finally, biological interpretations of PTSD receive some support from recent research on the tragic issue of child sexual abuse. Significant changes in hormone and neurotransmitter levels have been found in female victims. These developments are the subject of increased research attention at present (DeAngelis, 1995).

Integrative Theories

Each of the theories summarized thus far explains some aspects of PTSD, but an overall perspective on the disorder that neatly accounts for all of its features is still needed. Based on their extensive research review, Foy and associates (1992) described the necessary and sufficient conditions for *developing* the disorder; Barlow (1988) and Jones and Barlow (1992) presented a holistic view both of the origins of the disorder and of its particular constellation of problems and symptoms.

David Foy and his colleagues proposed the following:

> *Overwhelming trauma in conjunction with an immediate stress reaction (conditioned emotional response) constitute the necessary and sufficient conditions for acute PTSD symptoms to occur. Trauma can occur from three routes. Direct personal experience and observational experience, such as witnessing the death or near-death of another person, comprise the two most obvious mechanisms. However, recent work with PTSD in war-traumatized children demonstrated that "vicarious" experience, such as learning about the death of a loved one, can also elicit PTSD reactions. (Foy et al., 1992, p. 42)*

Whether acute stress develops into the chronic, PTSD pattern depends on the presence of additional biological, psychological, or social factors that increase vulnerability to developing the full-blown disorder. Consistent with this are the findings we reviewed earlier in the chapter, showing that military veterans who were exposed to moderate levels of combat were more likely to develop PTSD if they were *also* dealing with family problems at home or if their families had a history of mental disorders.

Barlow (1988) suggested that *anxious apprehension* operates in all anxiety disorders. Anxiety disorders arise when a biological vulnerability to stress (possibly genetically transmitted) is activated. Stress-producing negative life events activate the vulnerability and trigger *alarm reactions*. The stressful event (and possibly the alarm as well) is construed as unpredictable and uncontrollable. Chronic anxiety may be activated, and anxious apprehension becomes focused on a particular type of stimulus (external stimuli, bodily sensations, or certain thoughts, for example). Vulnerability to anxiety may be reduced by social support or by a sense of control or mastery. Because the process, once begun, can be self-perpetuating, factors that instigate anxiety also maintain it (Jones & Barlow, 1992).

Jones and Barlow (1992) argued that the development of anxious apprehension is the essential element causing the disorder. The conditioned stimuli that were paired with traumatic events not only cause fear and avoidance but they also lead clients to develop distorted thoughts and markedly negative mood states, leading to a "downward spiral" of symptomatology:

> *If the vulnerabilities line up correctly, an individual will experience the over-whelming true alarm [the original traumatic stressor] and subsequent learned alarms [responses to conditioned stimuli] as unpredictable, uncontrollable aversive events. The individual will react to these events with chronic over-arousal and additional cognitive symptoms of hypervigilance to trauma-re-lated cues. . . . Since the original alarm contained many strong arousal-based components, the existing chronic overarousal combined with a hypervigilance to arousal that might signal the beginning of a future alarm would ensure a succession of learned alarms and associated traumatic memories. (Jones & Barlow, 1992, p. 156)*

Cognitive-Behavioral Treatment

Although clients with PTSD necessarily have a set of problems that match the diagnostic criteria, considerable variability from client to client is still possible. There is a wide vari-ety of original traumatic stressors, of levels of exposure to them, and of clients' clusters of specific problems that pose methodological difficulties for treatment outcome researchers (Rothbaum & Foa, 1992a). Usually, each study focuses on a group of clients who were traumatized in the same general way. For example, a study might focus either on rape victims or on combat veterans, but not both.

Behavioral treatments for PTSD fall into two groups: exposure techniques and anxiety management techniques:

> *Exposure techniques are used when the disorder involves excessive avoidance and treatments are intended to activate and modify the fear structure. AMT [anxiety management training], on the other hand, is used when anxiety per-vades daily functioning. In this case, there is no need to activate the fear as much as manage it. In PTSD, both specific fears and general chronic arousal are among the defining characteristics. . . . Therefore, both exposure techniques and AMT may be applicable in the treatment of the disorder. (Rothbaum & Foa, 1992a, p. 90)*

Exposure techniques include systematic desensitization (SD) and imaginal flooding. The principal *anxiety management techniques* are relaxation training, breathing re-train-ing, and the various forms of treatment based on cognitive restructuring, such as rational emotive behavior therapy, cognitive therapy, and stress inoculation training (Fairbank & Brown, 1987; Rothbaum & Foa, 1992a). All of these techniques are consistent with the major theoretical models of PTSD. Conditioning and emotional processing models both predict that exposure methods, allowing appropriate confrontation of traumatic material, would reduce unnecessary anxiety and avoidance. The emotional processing model further predicts that cognitive restructuring procedures would also help clients beneficially alter the meaning component of trauma-related material.

Reducing Fear and Avoidance

Selection of appropriate treatment targets can be a controversial matter. Clearly, a client who was the victim of sexual abuse in childhood, and who has developed PTSD as a result, does not wish—and would not be encouraged—to learn to see abuse as innocuous. Unlike the other anxiety disorders, PTSD is not based on irrational assumptions. It is only the presence of *current* distress and impairment, continuing to disrupt the sufferer's life after the trauma has passed, that leads clients and therapists to view PTSD as a disorder needing treatment.

Military Combat Veterans

Imaginal flooding potentially has several advantages for theme-relevant exposure because it is flexible and allows repeated presentation of stimuli. Case studies in the early 1980s showed that imaginal flooding can be therapeutic for combat veterans with PTSD, but usually additional techniques such as relaxation training and anger management were included, complicating interpretation (Foy, Donahoe, Carroll, Gallers, & Reno, 1987). Follow-up assessment has shown that therapeutic improvement, as measured by specific anxiety symptoms and improved adaptive functioning, lasts at least one year after treatment (Keane & Kaloupek, 1982).

Fairbank and Keane (1982) used imaginal flooding in the treatment of two Vietnam veterans who had intrusive thoughts, nightmares, and flashbacks of traumatic combat-related scenes. One client, treated 11 years after combat, had had a 5-year history of flashbacks and nightmares. Treatment was provided daily for two hours per session, involving imaginal flooding to significant scenes from combat such as the following:

> *The subject listened to the screams of an enemy combatant whom he shot and killed during a night ambush attack upon enemy troops . . .*
>
> *While on routine river patrol the subject viewed the drowning deaths of two small children who fell from a sampan into a river . . .*
>
> *The subject observed medical corpsmen examining the badly decomposed body of a drowned American soldier. (Fairbank & Keane, 1982, p. 500)*

The anxiety produced by the scenes used in treatment rapidly declined to zero, and there was some generalization of treatment effects from one traumatic memory to another. However, when therapeutic generalization occurred, it was only to scenes similar to those used in treatment; there was little, if any, positive generalization to dissimilar scenes—a finding that was sustained in the results from the treatment of a second veteran.

In this second study, physiological monitoring of the client's heart rate and skin conductance confirmed that his anxiety was reduced only in respect of scenes actually presented during flooding. Later research has shown convincingly that heart rate in response to audiotaped sounds of combat is extremely helpful in the assessment of PTSD in combat veterans. Increases in heart rate beyond an arbitrary threshold reliably identified 88 percent of combat veterans and 70 percent of combat veterans with PTSD, and showed only a 10 percent false positive rate (Blanchard, Kolb, Gerardi, Ryan, & Pallmeyer, 1986). Similar results hold for clients whose PTSD followed their involvement in motor vehicle accidents (Blanchard, Hickling, Taylor, Loos, & Gerardi, 1994).

Two 1986 studies used systematic desensitization (SD) with combat veterans. One study compared SD plus electromyographic (EMG) feedback with no treatment and found the treatment package superior in reducing specific PTSD symptoms; clinical gains were maintained over a two-year follow-up interval. The other showed that six months of SD to trauma scenes brought significant clinical gains. Another, uncontrolled 1986 study showed that EMG biofeedback training with progressive muscle relaxation training produced general symptomatic improvement in six combat veterans with PTSD (reviewed by Rothbaum & Foa, 1992a).

Keane, Fairbank, Caddell, and Zimering (1989) compared imaginal flooding with no treatment (a waiting-list condition) in 24 Vietnam veterans with PTSD. Treated veterans were significantly more improved than untreated participants after 14 to 16 imaginal flooding sessions, as assessed by therapist ratings and several standard psychometric instruments. Notable improvement was seen in the reexperiencing, anxiety, and depression components of the disorder, but not in psychic numbing or social avoidance. Of the 11 treated participants, 7 showed clinically significant improvement.

Rape Victims

Systematic desensitization, imaginal flooding, stress inoculation training, and cognitive therapy have all been found helpful in studies of rape victims with PTSD (Steketee & Foa, 1987). Case studies and clinical series in the late 1970s showed that SD can be effective in reducing anxiety and depression and in improving sleep patterns and social adjustment. For example, 14 sessions of SD produced improvement in social adjustment and reduced anxiety in 17 sexual assault victims in a 1983 study (reviewed by Rothbaum & Foa, 1992a).

Imaginal flooding was used with a 22-year-old single woman who had been the victim of incest trauma (Rychtarik, Silverman, van Landingham, & Prue, 1984). Five 90-minute sessions of imaginal flooding were given. Behavioral, psychophysiological, and self-report measures all showed improvement by follow-up assessment on major treatment targets. Results generalized to current life stress, also, but some problems emerged nevertheless, including complications from the client's substance use disorder. In a comment on this case report, Kilpatrick and Best (1984) urged caution in selecting appropriate treatment targets, making the point that therapists have to be very careful not to give the client the impression that it is irrational to be traumatized or even upset by sexual abuse. Nevertheless, experts recommend that this caution should not deter therapists from encouraging their clients to confront vivid, graphic details of their traumatic experiences when therapeutically necessary (Rothbaum & Foa, 1992b).

Frank, Anderson, Stewart, Dancu, Hughes, and West (1988) reviewed studies of the typical course of the symptoms of rape trauma syndrome and concluded that there are three typical sequential reactions: short-term, intermediate, and long-term. The *short-term reaction* consists of a broad range of generally distressing symptoms that include somatic complaints, nightmares and sleep disruption, generalized anxiety, depression, and impaired social functioning. The *intermediate reaction* arises between three months and one year postassault and consists of depression, impaired social functioning, sexual dysfunction, and rape-specific anxiety. The *long-term reaction* one year and more after the rape, involves anger, reduced enjoyment of life, hypervigilance concerning danger, and sexual dysfunction.

Victims typically show very high scores on various measures of distress during the short-term reaction, but the usual pattern is of marked improvement without treatment by one year after the assault, with most of the improvement occurring in the first three months. In fact, several researchers who have attempted to evaluate the possible contributions of behavior therapy to the recovery process have found very few victims in need of treatment three months after the trauma. This observation raises methodological and ethical issues. On the one hand, since most victims do fine after three months without treatment, is it ethical to provide interventions that no one has yet shown to be effective? On the other hand, is it ethical to withhold treatment because of the absence of data on effectiveness, when it might be helpful? *DSM-IV* does, after all, recognize acute stress disorder in which significant symptoms are experienced within one month of the trauma and last only a few weeks. In practice, clinicians are understandably reluctant to withhold treatment from recent rape victims even if improvement would probably result with or without intervention (Frank et al., 1988).

In their retrospective investigation, Frank and her colleagues took two approaches. First, they examined their assessment and treatment outcome data from early versus late treatment seekers. Second, they compared the improvement rates of (1) treated victims in their own studies and (2) untreated, but repeatedly evaluated, victims from studies at other sites. "Immediate treatment seekers" were those 60 participants who sought treatment within an average of 20 days of the assault; "delayed treatment seekers" were the 24 who appeared for treatment four months or so postrape. The "nonvictimized controls" were 29 friends of the other participants who had not been victimized themselves. Treated participants were randomly assigned to SD or cognitive therapy conditions.

The results were as follows. Delayed treatment seekers showed greater distress pretreatment (higher levels of trait anxiety particularly) than immediate treatment seekers. Participants showed significant general improvement with treatment; SD and cognitive therapy were equally effective; and immediate and delayed treatment seekers did not differ in level of symptomatology posttreatment. From 67 to 75 percent of treated participants showed clinically significant improvement as determined by comparison with the nonvictimized controls. The immediate treatment seekers were more depressed and anxious initially than the untreated victims at the other sites; three or four months later, treated and untreated groups did not differ on the measures of depression, state anxiety, or fear (Frank et al., 1988). Although the rape victims in the study were not formally diagnosed, it seems likely that their problems might have qualified as PTSD. The fact that SD and cognitive therapy brought significant therapeutic benefit to these victims attests to the potential value of cognitive-behavioral interventions in this application.

A study of 37 rape victims supported the therapeutic value of stress inoculation, assertion training, and supportive psychotherapy plus information giving, each delivered separately in six sessions of group treatment (Resick, Jordan, Girelli, Hutter, & Marhoefer-Dvorak, 1988). Some of the participants gave data before and after a waiting period of six weeks before they received treatment. No changes were seen during the waiting period, but significant overall improvement was noted after group therapy. There were no between-group differences, but the authors observed that only the supportive psychotherapy group did not show clear pre- to posttreatment change. Resick and associates suggested that their results (no group differences, all showing improvement) fit current formulations of behavior change in terms of expectancy modification and emotional processing, rather than extinction of anxiety. Specifically, all interventions, including the supportive/information-giving condition, could have helped clients change the meaning element of their experiences, whereas only stress inoculation and assertion training were aimed at specific behavioral and cognitive changes (Resick et al., 1988).

Survivors of Transportation Accidents

Emotional trauma following involvement in transportation accidents has been a common form of PTSD. A classic psychiatric study of the 1960s focused on the survivors of a marine explosion that caused nine deaths at sea (Leopold & Dillon, 1963). Several accounts of the emotional aftermath of railroad accidents appeared in the 1800s in the United States and Europe, one of which (in England in 1865) received particular attention because its survivors included the novelist Charles Dickens. Apparently, he behaved calmly during the accident and was able to give help to two other passengers, but the incident had an emotional effect on him, as his description shows: "I was in the carriage that did not go over the bridge, but which caught on one side and hung suspended over the ruined parapet. I am shaken but not by that shock. Two or three hours' work afterwards among the dead and dying surrounded by terrific sights, render my hand unsteady" (quoted by Trimble, 1981, p. 28).

McCaffrey and Fairbank (1985) have described controlled case studies of clients whose PTSD developed following motor vehicle accidents. One client, a 28-year-old woman, had had four car accidents within a few months. She self-monitored trauma relevant dreams and nightmares and recorded subjective distress ratings at three-hour intervals each day. Relaxation, imaginal flooding, and self-directed exposure *in vivo* led to clinical improvement sufficient to allow her to return to driving without undue anxiety.

Eye Movement Desensitization and Reprocessing

This latest behavioral technique to be introduced as an intervention for PTSD deserves to be covered in its own section. In the late 1980s, Francine Shapiro described *eye movement desensitization (EMD)* as a new, brief treatment for posttraumatic stress disorder (Shapiro, 1989). Treatment focuses on specific traumatic memories. The client attends to three things at once: an image of the memory, negative evaluations of oneself or of the trauma, and the physical elements of the anxiety experienced. At the same time, the therapist elicits a series of repeated rapid, jerky, side-to-side eye movements ("saccades") by asking the client to follow the therapist's moving finger. During treatment, clients provide ratings of how anxious they feel and how strongly they believe in the thoughts that accompany their traumatic memories.

The author tested the procedure informally with 70 people, then conducted an experiment with 22 people who were either sexual assault victims or Vietnam veterans. Her conclusions were: "A single session of the eye movement desensitization (EMD) procedure was sufficient to desensitize completely subjects' traumatic memories and dramatically alter their cognitive self-assessments" (Shapiro, 1989, p. 212).

Shapiro cited the example of a 63-year-old female rape victim whose problems, 15 months after the trauma, included intrusive thoughts, forgetfulness, flashbacks, and nightmares. In a single 50-minute session, the therapist treated three memories of the rape (the sudden arrival of the attacker, forced oral-genital contact, and forced sexual intercourse). The client's original self-statement concerning the memories of rape was "I'm overwhelmed," but she and the therapist agreed to aim at replacing it by the self-statement "It's over" (Shapiro, 1989, 215). During the session the client's subjective ratings of distress declined from 10 (maximum anxiety) to 0 (no anxiety), and at the same time her acceptance of the desired self-statement "It's over" increased to the maximum level. Three months later, the client reported complete and lasting improvement.

The EMD technique was discovered accidentally and was not derived deliberately from theoretical hypotheses. Shapiro has speculated that the rapid eye movement (REM) stage of sleep, associated with dreaming, may reflect the same process as EMD—a process in which troubling emotional material is desensitized. Several biological bases for the procedure have also been proposed (Rothbaum, 1992; Shapiro, 1989, 1991a). As yet, the theoretical processes underlying EMD have not been definitively identified, but Shapiro has stressed the central importance of cognitive change during the procedure. This, together with increasing evidence of its broader applicability to many disorders in which emotion is prominent, led to its being renamed *eye movement desensitization and reprocessing (EMDR)* (Shapiro, 1991a).

Soon after that, Shapiro (1991b) cautioned professional readers against employing the technique without obtaining specialized training, details of which could be had by writing to her. In her 1989 paper, she had indicated that 60 to 70 percent of traumatic memories could be desensitized from the information presented in that article; in 1991, she gave a figure of 50 percent, but added that "in the other cases, untrained clinicians place the client at risk, e.g. experiencing ocular problems, retraumatization, suicidal reactions, etc." (Shapiro, 1991b, p. 188).

The need for professional people to obtain specialized training from the originator of a procedure makes EMDR unique in the history of behavior therapy, and this has understandably drawn strong criticism (Baer, Hurley, Minichiello, Ott, Penzel, & Ricciardi, 1992; Fish, 1992; Rosen, 1992). Descriptions of other behavior therapy techniques have always been in the public domain to professionals in order to allow experimental replications, one of the hallmarks of behavior therapy. Shapiro's assertion that, as of 1992, EMDR was still in "this very awkward, 'experimental limbo' state" (Shapiro, 1992, p. 114) offered little reassurance to professionals that the specialized training was worth buying, yet those who have received the training have given "satisfied customer" testimonials (Beere, 1992; Lipke, 1992; see also Abruzzese, 1995).

Experimental data on the results of EMDR, as employed by clinicians trained in the procedure by Shapiro, have been available since 1993. In a study of 30 male Vietnam veterans with PTSD, EMDR produced significantly greater reductions than an exposure-control condition in subjective ratings of discomfort to images of trauma, but psychological tests and physiological measures did not reveal group differences (Boudewyns, Stwertka,

Hyer, Albrecht, & Sperr, 1993). EMDR and exposure-control participants received two 90-minute treatment sessions aimed at each veteran's most disturbing traumatic memory; control participants received standard inpatient PTSD treatment for 14 days. There was no follow-up assessment, so information on overall outcome for these clients is lacking. The study is useful in showing that EMDR produces greater subjectively rated change within treatment sessions than a condition allowing equal exposure to trauma-related imagery. Nonetheless, such subjective ratings could have been influenced by demand characteristics of the situation, as the authors note.

Similar results were obtained by Jensen (1994) in a study of 25 Vietnam veterans with PTSD. The two therapists had been trained by Francine Shapiro. Subjective distress was successfully reduced during the two treatment sessions, but overall improvement in the disorder was not found. Jensen concluded that EMDR cannot be recommended as a treatment for PTSD in Vietnam combat veterans.

Hassard (1995) studied a clinical series of 27 pain clinic patients who described traumatic memories or flashbacks; 13 of these patients actually had PTSD. All participants received EMDR, in addition to normal pain clinic procedures, and showed reduction of subjective distress during treatment sessions. The number of treatments given varied across participants, with a mode of four sessions. Of the 27, 7 patients dropped out of treatment before completion, but the others made good progress. Some return of symptoms was noted subsequently, and at a three-month follow-up, 12 patients were still doing well. A case report by this author had previously illustrated the successful application of EMDR to fear of a surgical operation coupled with negative body image in a 37-year-old woman with a congenitally damaged hip (Hassard, 1993).

Merckelbach, Hogervorst, Kampman, and de Jongh (1994) studied 40 normal volunteers to see if EMDR inhibits aversive images any more than does a control condition of finger tapping. These researchers obtained essentially null findings except for a tendency for aversive images to be less intense over time in both conditions. Several methodological limitations of this analogue study prevent it from adding much to the understanding of EMDR.

In summary, EMDR has been used to treat PTSD and other disorders, including pain syndromes and body image disturbance. Many reports are anecdotes, case studies, or clinical series, but a few controlled studies have been reported at the time of writing, with several more awaiting publication. EMDR can produce rapid reduction in subjective distress during treatment sessions, but evidence that it successfully treats major disorders, including PTSD, is lacking. Further research on efficacy and mechanisms of treatment, together with increased clinical use of the technique, may be prompted by the appearance of Shapiro's book on EMDR (Shapiro, 1995).

Treatment of Nightmares

The previous sections have covered treatment methods chiefly designed to reduce the subjective distress and avoidance prompted by traumatic stimuli associated with PTSD; this section deals with interventions aimed at eliminating a key clinical feature of the disorder, recurrent nightmares.

Normal and Abnormal Nightmares

The occasional experience of a frightening or distressing dream is probably familiar to everyone. Nightmares of this kind are a common phenomenon of little or no clinical significance (Eccles, Wilde, & Marshall, 1988). Some people, however, have recurrent nightmares—sometimes a single nightmare that is repeated in exact detail on successive occasions—distressing enough to warrant seeking professional help. Although there is no general consensus on the causes of nightmares, behavior therapists have speculated that they express fears and anxieties evident in the individual's waking life (Eccles et al., 1988). Consistent with this view, several clinicians have reported that when an individual with a specific phobia is troubled by nightmares on that theme, successfully treating the phobia usually guarantees elimination of the nightmares (Bergin, 1970; Geer & Silverman, 1967; Thorpe, 1971). Even when the theme of the nightmare has no obvious parallel in waking life, desensitization or exposure therapy to dream content can be therapeutic (Eccles et al., 1988).

The recurrent nightmares experienced by clients with PTSD are of a different class from those frightening dreams that can disturb anyone's sleep from time to time. Furthermore, the nightmares associated with PTSD tend to be even more intense, harrowing, realistic, and persistent than phobic nightmares. Hartmann (1984) offered the following classification, based on sleep laboratory research. The *night terror* (also known as "incubus attack," "terror attack," or "stage 4 nightmare") is common in young children. Night terrors abruptly awaken the sleeper early in the night in a state of panic or terror, with screaming, confusion, and disorientation, but no recollection of having been dreaming (Blanes, Burgess, Marks, & Gill, 1993). *True nightmares* (also known as "dream anxiety attacks") "are long, vivid, frightening dreams, which awaken the sleeper and are usually clearly recalled" (Hartmann, 1984, p. 5). They take place during rapid eye movement or REM sleep, and their themes usually involve threats to "survival, security, or self-esteem" (Blanes et al., 1993, p. 37). On awakening, the sleeper quickly becomes alert and oriented and can recall the dream content. Chronic posttraumatic nightmares, or simply *traumatic nightmares,* are more like nightmares than night terrors, but the content is repetitive—more similar to a vivid, actual memory than to a fantasy or dream. Traumatic nightmares (TNs) can include the dreamer's imagery, speech, thought, and emotion. Laboratory research has shown that TNs typically occur within an hour or two of falling asleep, whereas ordinary nightmares usually arise some hours later.

Traumatic nightmares are extremely common in burn victims, especially children. Individuals with the clearest and most serious cases of PTSD have the most exact memories during their nightmares. Usually, TNs disappear a few weeks after the traumatic event that caused them. Hartmann's (1984) view is that normal dreaming helps one deal with and integrate traumatic memories, but if the individual avoids the traumatic theme material in waking life, it becomes *encapsulated* and this is associated with the development of frequent TNs.

Behavioral Interpretations of Dreams and Nightmares

Because it is difficult to imagine any subject more mentalistic and less behavioral than dreaming phenomena, dreams and nightmares seem an especially odd choice of topic in a book on behavior therapy. After all, the early behavior therapists developed their approach partly in opposition to the mentalistic ideas of psychoanalysis, and sought to anchor their theories and techniques firmly in objective data and observable behavior. Nonetheless, behavioral theories of dreaming have been put forward.

Writing in a behaviorally oriented publication, Seligman and Yellen (1987) argued that dreaming involves three elements: (1) internal, disconnected bursts of hallucinatory visual activity; (2) internal, unrelated emotional episodes; and (3) cognitive attempts to integrate the visual hallucinations and emotional episodes, thus bringing meaning to the dream. The visual and emotional experiences probably result from random neural and hormonal processes during sleep. Seligman and Yellen predicted that dreams should contain two types of visual information: Vivid, detailed, and unexpected material (from the hallucinatory bursts), and less vivid, less detailed, yet more predictable "secondary visual imagery" (from the cognitive synthesis).

For example, Seligman and Yellen cited a dream in which the dreamer was standing at the end of the Royal Crescent in Bath, England, when an enormous fir tree, the size of a skyscraper, suddenly appeared. This tree was described in unusual detail. Then the dreamer looked at the houses, but it was unclear whether they were Tudor or Georgian; they eventually appeared as Georgian, as would be expected. The surprising fir tree was described in great detail (the product of a neural, visual burst); the predictable Georgian houses were indistinct (the product of secondary visual imagery from the cognitive synthesis or integration).

Seligman and Yellen (1987) noted that dream theories fall into two classes. In "movie" theories the dreamer begins by somehow constructing the script of a dream that is then played before the passive viewer. Freud proposed that dreams originate in a disturbing, unconscious wish (the hidden or "latent" content)—material that is transformed by a censor into distorted, but more acceptable, images (the apparent or "manifest" content). In "improvisationist" theories (like that of Seligman and Yellen) the dreamer integrates and makes sense of a series of bursts of random mental activity as the dream progresses.

The authors were able to produce some experimental data consistent with their theory. First, they predicted that the most vivid images in a dream would be the most unexpected (because they result from bursts of random visual activity) and that the least vivid images would be predictable from the dream's plot (because these result from the dreamer's attempts at cognitive integration). Some 60 college volunteers described 114 recent dreams in detail and rated them for vividness. Independent raters scored the dream descriptions for surprisingness of content versus predictability from the plot or story-line. As predicted, imagery vividness and surprise value were strongly correlated.

Second, Seligman and Yellen predicted that dreamers who were good at integrating random stimuli when awake would also be good at constructing dream plots from the visual and emotional bursts encountered when asleep. Here, 17 college volunteers reported 63 dreams, and independent judges rated the dream descriptions for coherence (a coherent dream formed a well-constructed story; an incoherent dream was a series of disconnected events). The 17 participants were also shown a series of seven unrelated color slides in the laboratory and were asked to construct a story about the sequence of slides as they were presented. The independent judges rated the stories for coherence. Strong correlations were found between coherence of dream content and integration of the color slides into a meaningful story, lending support to the hypotheses that dreamers play a vital role in making sense of their dream material, and that there are individual differences in ability to organize it coherently (Seligman & Yellen, 1987).

Treatment of Recurrent Nightmares

The Seligman and Yellen theory has implications for understanding and treating recurrent nightmares. Any dream is partly influenced by "residue" from the previous day's events. (For example, if you have been reading a Stephen King novel, scenes of spooky old houses on the fog-bound coast of Maine may predominate in your residue.) But there may also be longer-lasting residues. In recurrent dreams, some "remote residue" that may have endured for years (such as having been briefly separated from one's parents in a crowded airport at the age of 8) may have become connected with the cognitive integration that the dreamer constructed during the original dream. If the same visual burst occurs in later dreams, material from the original cognitive integration may also be evoked, accounting for the recurrent dream.

Palace and Johnston (1989) described a *dream reorganization* therapy for recurrent nightmares that was drawn from the Seligman and Yellen (1987) theory. Previous case studies had provided some support for two behavioral approaches to recurrent nightmares: systematic desensitization to anxiety-provoking dream content and cognitive modification by means of "rehearsal of neutral, absurd, confrontational or triumphant dream endings" (Palace & Johnston, 1989, p. 220). The dream reorganization approach is a combination of three procedures: systematic desensitization, rehearsal of coping self-statements, and story-line alteration.

Palace and Johnston argued that the Seligman and Yellen theory suggests two important stages for intervention in recurrent nightmares. First, the secondary visual imagery, caused by the cognitive integration contributed by the dreamer, could be deliberately controlled by means of guided imagery techniques practiced when awake. Second, the emotional episodes, which, in the case of nightmares, always involve distressing emotions like fear or terror, could be replaced by feelings of relaxation, well-being, or triumph by means of systematic desensitization as a counterconditioning tactic. Adding coping self-statements to the desensitization could help change the cognitive integration or meaning brought to the dream by the dreamer. From that point, the new, less threatening cognitive integration is stored, and reappears when the same visual bursts next arise in sleep (Palace & Johnston, 1989).

These authors illustrate the use of dream reorganization with the case study of a 10-year-old boy who developed posttraumatic problems after two accidents. First, a car hit and seriously damaged the family home; afterwards, the client began to sleep in his parents' room, and it was extremely difficult to break him of this habit. Second, 18 months later, the boy and his parents were involved in an automobile accident; the client started sleeping with his parents again and continued to do so until treatment was sought 6 months later. Although he would try to sleep alone, each night the boy would go to his parents' room after being awakened by recurrent nightmares of bad people trying to hurt him, and sounds of squealing tires and cars crashing.

The therapist and client constructed a 10-item anxiety hierarchy consisting of elements in the nightmare. The sequence of treatment techniques used was as follows: Progressive muscle relaxation training and systematic desensitization to the hierarchy items; rehearsal of coping self-statements that were also added to the desensitization hierarchy; and guided rehearsal of "mastery" responses to dream elements, such as:

> As [the bad guy] reaches into the black bag with his deformed hands, and hurls an axe into the air, you transform into Jake Rockwell who wears a cast iron exoframe armed with artillery. You coolly call Crystal on your wristcom to send down the heavy assault system, and fire the freeze machine, automatically freezing in space the bad guy and his axes. The intruder is arrested. (Palace & Johnston, 1989, p. 223)

Some 16 sessions of treatment successfully eliminated both problems, the nightmares and the refusal to sleep alone, and these gains had persisted when a follow-up assessment was conducted six months beyond the termination of treatment.

Marks (1981, 1987) described the successful treatment of a recurrent nightmare of 14 years' duration by *rehearsal relief,* a procedure similar to dream reorganization. The client was a 45-year-old woman who had been hospitalized for treatment of depression and compulsive checking rituals. Shortly before her scheduled discharge from the hospital, she revealed that every three months she had a stereotyped nightmare that would awaken her at 1 A.M., keep her awake the rest of the night, and make her so tense that she could not go to work the next day. In the dream the client killed her despised (actually deceased) mother, "whose dead eyes then bored into her terrifyingly" (Marks, 1987, p. 393).

During a single session, the client described the nightmare in vivid detail, three times, to an audience of mental health professionals in the hospital unit. Her description was accompanied by intense emotion, and at the end of the account of the dream, she yelled, "My bloody mother. She always wins." Afterwards, encouraged by the therapist, she wrote about the nightmare three more times, giving the dream a triumphant, victorious, and gruesome ending in which the client bloodily destroyed her mother. The total length of treatment was three hours; the nightmare had not recurred during a follow-up interval of three years.

Marks (1981) suggested that rehearsal relief has three possible therapeutic components: systematic exposure to threatening stimuli; "abreaction" (emotional reliving of an experience) in confronting the intense emotion evoked by the dream; and therapeutic mastery, a form of expectancy modification in which the meaning of the dream is altered in a benign direction. Marks found examples of therapeutic mastery in reports from the 1930s on the Senoi, an isolated group within present-day Malaysia who maintained a tradition of dream interpretation. Adults would reassure their children that anxiety-provoking dreams, such as those involving falling, really reflect positive and constructive communications from the spirit world, and can safely be approached rather than avoided. Any danger encountered while dreaming should be confronted head-on, with the help of the dream images of one's friends if necessary, because "dream characters were bad only as long as one was afraid and retreated from them, and would continue to seem bad and fearful as long as one refused to come to grips with them" (Marks, 1981, p. 7). This advice, clearly based on the exposure principle, is just as helpful today for Westerners troubled by bad dreams, as Marks (1987) and Palace and Johnston (1989) have shown.

Chapter Summary

Craig, Sharon, and Wayne, like other clients with PTSD, experienced one or more traumatic stressors and later developed a syndrome consisting of reexperiencing the trauma, emotional withdrawal or psychic numbing, and increased general tension. It is easy to identify the event that triggered the disorder, but it is difficult to explain all the complex features of PTSD, which seems to combine the symptoms of all the anxiety disorders. Mental health professionals recognize three posttraumatic anxiety syndromes today, but PTSD is the most familiar and has been researched extensively. Classical conditioning and two-factor theory seem useful explanations for the fear and avoidance aspects, and data on level of trauma exposure in clients with PTSD are consistent with conditioning explanations, but they cannot explain all features of the disorder. Attributional styles, learned helplessness, and emotional processing have all been shown to be useful explanatory concepts in PTSD. David Barlow and his colleagues have proposed that PTSD can be understood as the development of anxious apprehension about learned alarms, an alternative to accounts in terms of conditioning.

Behavioral treatments for PTSD fall into two groups: exposure methods and anxiety management training. Systematic desensitization and flooding have been successfully applied to the psychological problems of combat veterans, rape victims, and survivors of automobile accidents. Cognitive restructuring methods have also been found helpful for rape victims. The controversial new technique of eye movement desensitization and reprocessing is helpful in reducing subjective distress in the short term, but its benefits in treating the full-scale disorder have yet to be demonstrated. Recurrent and traumatic nightmares may be treated by exposure methods, by dream reorganization, and by rehearsal relief.

Endnotes

1. As you will see later in the chapter, there are three distinct posttraumatic anxiety syndromes, but we focus on posttraumatic stress disorder because it is the most prevalent, the best understood, and the most representative syndrome.
2. *Posttraumatic* was hyphenated in the *DSM-III-R* (American Psychiatric Association, 1987).
3. The Greek word *trauma* refers to a wound or injury. In mental health work, the term usually refers to an *emotional* wound. Someone with PTSD not only experienced an unusually severe stressor but also reacted with intense fear at the time (and, following that, developed the anxiety disorder). Some writers view PTSD as a disorder that follows traumatic stress; others view it as a "chronic stress disorder following trauma" (Keane, Zimering, & Caddell, 1985, p. 11). For an extended discussion, see Heimberg (1985), Keane (1985), Rachman (1985), and Saigh (1985).

$$Chapter \quad 9$$

Depression and Suicide

During an initial psychological evaluation, Mr. S., age 64, sat slumped in his chair with a sad expression. His hands and body shook continuously. Mr S. made only fleeting eye contact and seemed to have a very difficult time responding to questions. Questions asked of Mr. S. often had to be repeated or rephrased. When he did respond, there were long pauses between the question and his answer. Although Mr. S. had enjoyed a long career as a successful attorney, he was currently unemployed due to the severity of his symptoms. Mr. S. complained that for the past two months, he had lost interest in all activities that usually gave him pleasure, such as exercising, working, and seeing friends. He felt that he had no energy, and spent this time sleeping or reading at home. Mr. S. reported that he constantly ruminated on feelings of worthlessness and guilt, which impaired his ability to concentrate on even menial tasks. He admitted that he often fantasized about suicide, but did not plan to act on his fantasies.

Depression has been called the common cold of psychopathology (Seligman, 1973), due to its high prevalence in the general population. Most normal individuals experience temporary periods of sadness, self-blame, or apathy. However, as in the case of Mr. S., the clinical syndrome of depression represents a composite of interrelated problems in emotional, motor, social, and biological areas of functioning. Depression is one of the most subjectively painful psychological disorders. If sufficiently severe, it can be incapacitating and life threatening.

During the past two decades, there has been an explosion of interest in cognitive–behavioral treatment of depression. It is one of the most vital areas of behavior therapy. This chapter will be restricted to a discussion of unipolar depression because most relevant behavioral research and therapy has focused on that disorder. Finally, because suicidal ideation and behavior are frequently associated with depression, behavioral interventions with suicidal clients also will be considered.

Behavioral Assessment of Depression

Behavioral assessment of depression occurs in several stages. First, it is necessary to conduct a detailed analysis of presenting symptoms. Prominent symptoms must be carefully described, along with descriptive features such as frequency, severity, and duration. It must be determined whether depression is the primary problem, and, if so, the severity and type of depression must be evaluated. Next, a highly individualized functional analysis is conducted, in which specific patterns of thought, behavior, and interpersonal interactions are identified as potential depression-maintaining variables. These maintaining variables serve as targets for behavioral intervention. Finally, progress in symptom remission and adaptive functioning is monitored throughout therapy, until client and therapist mutually agree that termination is appropriate.

Clinical Features of Depression

The *DSM-IV* currently lists three depressive disorders: Major Depressive Disorder (characterized by one or more major depressive episodes); Dysthymic Disorder, a somewhat milder form of depression that tends to be chronic; and Depressive Disorder Not Otherwise Specified, used to code disorders with depressive features that do not meet criteria for Major Depression or Dysthymia. A *major depressive episode* is characterized by dysphoric mood (persistent and prominent feelings of sadness, irritability, and/or hopelessness) and/or loss of interest in normal activities. The onset of symptoms represents a marked change in the individual's normal mood and behavior. At least five of the following symptoms must be present almost daily for two weeks or longer:

- Depressed mood most of the day
- Markedly diminished interest or pleasure in all, or almost all, activities
- Significant weight loss or decreased appetite
- Insomnia or hypersomnia
- Psychomotor agitation or retardation
- Fatigue or loss of energy
- Feelings of worthlessness or excessive guilt
- Diminished ability to think or concentrate and/or indecisiveness
- Recurrent thoughts of death, or suicidal ideation

A positive diagnosis requires that these symptoms cause significant emotional distress and cannot be accounted for by bereavement, medication, cognitive (organic) disorder, or physical illnesses. Major depressive episodes may have associated psychotic features, but schizophrenia must not be present. Finally, there must be no evidence of bipolar disorder, defined by periods of mania or hypomania that may alternate with periods of depression. The essential feature of *Major Depressive Disorder* is the presence of one or more major depressive episodes. Major depressive disorder is twice as common in adult females as in males (American Psychiatric Association, 1994).

Dysthymic Disorder is diagnosed when dysphoric mood or loss of interest in normal activities has persisted for two years or longer. At least two of the following symptoms must have been present during this period:

- Depressed mood for most of the day, for more days than not, for two years
- Presence of two or more of the following during the depressed moods:
    - Poor appetite or overeating
    - Insomnia or hypersomnia
    - Low energy or fatigue
    - Low self-esteem
    - Poor concentration, indecisiveness
    - Feelings of hopelessness

Dysthymic disorder differs from major depressive disorder in that the depressive symptoms are milder and, because of their chronic nature, do not seem different from the individual's "usual" way of functioning. Nonetheless, these symptoms cause significant emotional distress, and often impair the quality of the individual's social or occupational adjustment. The case example of Ms. G. illustrates the features of dysthymic disorder following a major depressive episode:

THE CASE OF MS. G.

Ms. G., age 23, sought psychotherapy because she felt "weak, dependent, and incapable of coping well with stress." Three years earlier, she became involved with a man who was much older than herself. When he suddenly broke off the affair, Ms. G. "dropped out of life." She stopped attending her college classes, began eating and sleeping excessively, and became disinterested in all of her prior activities. Her depressive reaction was so severe that she left school altogether and returned home to be cared for by her mother. She was able to return to school after a few months, but continued to suffer from depressive symptoms. Ms. G. viewed herself as inferior to others, unworthy of love, unattractive, and incapable of producing positive changes in her own life. She was able to function adaptively at work and school, but nonetheless felt almost continuously distressed. Her mood was markedly unstable, with depressive affect predominating. She also was prone to worrying and overreacted to minor life stresses, particularly those involving interpersonal conflicts with her new boyfriend. Ms. G. was a highly intelligent person who derived pleasure from achievement and possessed good interpersonal skills. These considerable assets were denied or downplayed by her.

Diagnostic criteria for depression and dysthymia may not apply to members of all cultural groups, because cultural factors have a profound effect on how people experience and report feelings of emotional distress. Somatic expressions of depression are more prevalent in non-Western societies (Marsella, 1979). For example, in Chinese culture, depression tends to be expressed in somatic terms such as tiredness, diffuse aches and pains, and gastrointestinal or cardiovascular symptoms, rather than with dysphoric mood or self-deprecation (Kleinman, 1986). Kleinman's case of Q.Z., a 40-year-old factory worker, is illustrative. Q.Z.'s presenting symptoms included chronic dizziness, headache, weakness, and fatigue. She also complained of insomnia, poor appetite, difficulty concentrating, and experienced recurrent thoughts about death. These symptoms apppeared to be precipitated by multiple and escalating stresses in her life (Kleinman, 1986).

Assessment of Depression

Clinical Interview and Clinician Rating Scales

The clinical interview is the starting point for differential diagnosis of depression. Interviewing depressed individuals is difficult and can be distressing to the interviewer (Beck, 1967). Depressed individuals tend to be socially unresponsive and have difficulty concentrating. Overt expressions of emotional pain and hopelessness, such as crying or slumped posture, are common. Typically, there are long latencies between interviewer questions and the depressed person's responses to them. Therefore, the interviewer must be patient and show a high degree of clinical sensitivity and skill. For example, it is necessary to check out the depressed person's reactions to specific statements or questions, because the client may misinterpret their meaning. In addition, the interviewer must be alert to the possibility of suicidal thoughts and behaviors. Potential suicidal intent or ideation should be openly discussed in a matter-of-fact but caring way (Freeman & Reineke, 1993; Linehan, 1981).

A number of structured clinical interviews have been developed for differential diagnosis of depression. These instruments vary in terms of breadth of content, length of administration time, and psychometric soundness (Rehm, 1988). The most commonly used interview methods are described here.

The *Schedule for Affective Disorders and Schizophrenia (SADS)* is a semi-structured interview format that has been widely used in research. Based on answers to careful questioning about their current and past functioning, individuals are categorized according to the research diagnostic criteria (Spitzer et al., 1978). The item content of the SADS covers symptoms of mood disorders and schizophrenia. Information about the individual's symptoms and adaptive functioning is categorized according to the following temporal framework: present week, "worst" period of the recent problem, and historically throughout life. Although the SADS is a lengthy procedure (requiring one to two hours to administer, depending on the patient's mental state), it provides a comprehensive and reliable tool for differential diagnosis of major mental illness.

The *Diagnostic Interview Schedule (DIS)* (Robins, Helzer, Croughan, & Ratliff, 1981) was developed for use in large-scale epidemiological surveys. Symptom information is obtained for five different time frames: within the last two weeks, the last month, the last six months, the last year, and prior to the last year. Psychometric properties of the DIS appear to be adequate (Robins et al., 1981).

The *Hamilton Rating Scale for Depression (HRSD)* (Hamilton, 1960) consists of 17 variables rated on four- or five-point scales. The emphasis of the scale is on behavioral and somatic symptoms of depression. However, a 24-item version of the scale was developed after 1960 to incorporate cognitive items such as feelings of worthlessness and hopelessness. The HRSD is reliable, shows moderate correlations with other measures of depression, and is sensitive to change in depressive symptoms (Shaw, Vallis, & McCabe, 1985). Because the major emphasis of the scale is on somatic features of depression, the HRSD is most applicable as a measure of depression severity within inpatient populations.

Finally, the *Feelings and Concerns Checklist* (Grinker et al., 1961) consists of 47 items rated on zero- to four-point scales. Item content is almost exclusively focused on verbal and cognitive behaviors associated with depression.

Self-Report Measures

Self-report measures of depression are frequently used as auxiliary diagnostic measures and as tools for assessing the depressed individual's progress over the course of therapy. They are also widely used to screen research participants and to assess psychotherapeutic outcome. Self-report measures are typically brief and easy to administer and score. However, there is only a modest correlation between self-report and behavioral measures of psychopathology (Franks & Wilson, 1978; Rehm, 1988). Also the possibility of response distortion or bias is inherent in any self-report questionnaire. Thus, self-report measures should always be supplemented with other measures, particularly in situations requiring accurate differential diagnosis. Descriptions of widely used self-report measures of depression follow.

The *Beck Depression Inventory (BDI)* (Beck et al., 1961) is the most frequently used self-report measure of depression. The BDI consists of 21 items representing cognitive, affective, behavioral, and biological features of depression. Each item is self-rated according to a zero- to three-point scale of severity. The questionnaire is psychometrically sound and has been used extensively in research and clinical work as an index of depression severity.

The *MMPI Depression Scale (MMPI-D)* (Hathaway & McKinley, 1951) has been frequently used to assess depression. The MMPI-D Scale consists of 60 true/false items with heterogeneous content, and taps a range of depressive symptoms.

The *Center for Epidemiological Studies Depression Scale (CES-D)* (Radloff, 1977) was designed as a population survey instrument. The CES-D contains 20 items, self-rated on a zero- to three-point scale, and covers symptoms of depressed mood, hopelessness, psychomotor retardation, loss of appetite, and sleep disturbance. The CES-D has good psychometric properties (Radloff, Weissman, et al., 1977), and appears to be an excellent measure for the purpose it was intended: screening depressive symptoms in large groups of people.

The *Depression Adjective Checklist (DACL)* (Lubin, 1967) is a brief, reliable measure of depressed mood. The DACL has seven different parallel forms that were derived from adjectives that best differentiated normal from depressed individuals. Although the DACL is a good measure of negative mood, it does not tap other important depressive symptoms. Therefore, its usefulness in diagnostic situations is limited.

Finally, the *Pleasant Events Schedule (PES)* (Lewinsohn & Libet, 1972) is a list of 320 events and activities rated on three-point scales according to frequency and perceived pleasantness. It is based on the assumption that depressed individuals engage in fewer positively reinforcing activities than others. The PES is most useful as a means of identifying behavioral deficiencies associated with depression. Analysis of PES responses can help the clinician target pleasurable activities that can be gradually increased in frequency. As with other self-report scales, the main drawback of the PES is the possibility that depressed individuals may not accurately assess their activity levels.

Observational Methods

Observational measures have been rarely used to assess depressive symptoms. Many studies are based on single cases involving hospitalized individuals. For example, Williams, Barlow, and Agras (1972) developed an observational checklist for assessing severity of depression in hospitalized patients. The *Ward Behavior Checklist (WBC)* targets overt behaviors such as smiling, talking, motor activities, and time out of the room every half hour. Scores on these four scales were found to be highly intercorrelated, and were summed into a global scale of depression severity. The global scale of the WBC had high reliability and high correlations with other measures of depression. However, because the measure was developed on severely depressed inpatients, its usefulness with other depressed populations is questionable.

A unique approach to the observational assessment of depression was taken by Lewinsohn and his colleagues (e.g., Robinson & Lewinsohn, 1976). They developed a complex coding system for the overt verbal behavior of depressed individuals. For example, the number of verbal initiations to other people was targeted, as well as the person's latency to respond to the initiations of others. This coding system has been used in home observation and in group therapy settings. Similar measures have been developed by Fuchs and Rehm (1977), and by Hautzinger, Linden, and Hoffman (1982).

In summary, observational measures are potentially valuable means of assessing overt motor and verbal behaviors associated with depression. However, they are more appropriate as research than clinical tools, because no standard set of behavioral codes has been developed. Furthermore, in comparison with alternative measures such as clinician ratings or self-report scales, observational techniques are extremely cost-inefficient, requiring large amounts of time from staff members.

Interviews with Significant Others

Interviews with significant others are frequently used in the assessment of depressive symptoms. If the client is severely depressed, family members or friends may even be primary informants. In addition to offering another perspective on the client's behavior, these interviews can help the clinician assess the extent of interpersonal stress in the client's life (e.g., do family members seem hostile and blaming or supportive? To what extent is the patient's depression tied to interpersonal stressors such as marital or parent/child conflict?) and the willingness of family members to become involved in treatment, if appropriate.

Functional Analysis

Subsequent to a confirmed diagnosis of depression, a functional analysis is conducted to identify environmental, interpersonal, and/or psychological factors related to specific depressive symptoms. In order to accomplish this important goal, some form of symptom monitoring is almost always used. Typically, the depressed client is asked to keep detailed daily records of mood fluctuations and to record the stimulus context of each entry. These records are carefully examined in therapy sessions. Once a sufficient number of entries has been gathered, the therapist and client look for patterns of experience that appear to "set off" depressive symptoms. In doing so, targets for intervention are identified.

The functional analysis is clearly the first stage in the behavioral treatment of depression. However, different behavioral theorists emphasize different types of "controlling variables" in their functional analyses. For this reason, detailed discussion of functional analysis will be integrated into each different treatment model presented. Major behavioral and cognitive-behavioral models of depression are outlined below.

Major Treatment Models

Lewinsohn's Behavioral Model of Depression

Conceptual Basis

Lewinsohn's behavioral model of depression is based on Bandura's social learning theory (Bandura, 1977). Depression is viewed as a person-behavior-environment transaction. This means that depressive feelings and behavior are precipitated by changes in the environment; once activated, depressive behaviors elicit negative reactions and consequences, resulting in a vicious cycle effect. According to Lewinsohn, a low rate of response-contingent positive reinforcement and/or a high rate of aversive experience precipitates depression. Thus, when a person's behaviors result in few positive outcomes or a high rate of negative consequences, depressive mood, cognition, and behavior are stimulated (Grosscup & Lewinsohn, 1980; Lewinsohn, Youngren, & Grosscup, 1979).

There are many reasons why these changes in reinforcement patterns may occur. Perhaps there are few reinforcers available in the person's environment, due to impoverishment or loss. The depressed person may have skill deficits that prevent rewarding interactions with others. An extremely shy person, or an individual with a severe communication deficit, would fall into this category. Finally, an individual may lose the capacity to experience a potential reinforcer as pleasurable. In this case, it is the person's *perception* of life experiences that has changed, not necessarily the experiences themselves.

Generally, empirical studies have shown that depressive individuals report experiencing fewer pleasant events and more negative experiences than others. Also, as depressive symptoms begin to diminish in frequency and intensity, individuals tend to report more pleasurable and fewer aversive life experiences (Rehm, 1989). However, causal connections between specific environmental changes and onset of depressive symptoms have not been established.

Lewinsohn, Hoberman, Teri, and Hautzinger (1985) proposed a revision of the basic model. The revised model was developed to explain heterogeneity within depressive populations. This model is more specific in regard to the types of stressors that precipitate depression and in regard to cognitive processes that mediate coping behaviors. In particular, strong emphasis is placed on the role of heightened self-awareness in unsuccessful coping with stress. The revised model also takes into account diverse factors that predispose individuals to depression.

Treatment Approach

According to Lewinsohn, experiencing an adequate rate of positive reinforcement is critical to the prevention of depression. Hence, the main goal of treatment is to bolster the depressed individual's ability to seek life experiences that enhance feelings of personal mastery and/or pleasure. If the depressed person is experiencing high rates of aversive life events, these also must diminish in frequency. These goals are primarily accomplished by changing the frequency, quality, and range of the person's activities and social interactions (Lewinsohn & Arconad, 1981). Beyond these general aims, specific treatment goals and strategies are highly individualized. Several characteristics of Lewinsohn's therapy apply to all cases, however. It is a highly structured and time-limited therapy in which the client plays an active role. The average length of treatment is 12 weeks, with a range of one to three months (Lewinsohn & Arconad, 1981). Finally, there are several discrete stages involved in every therapy contact. These are described here.

Initially, a diagnostic assessment phase is necessary for determining the nature, severity, and subtype of the individual's presenting problem. Toward this end, a combination of interview and self-report measures is used (Lewinsohn & Lee, 1981). Next, if depression is the primary problem, a *conceptualization* phase is conducted in which the rationale for treatment is discussed. According to Lewinsohn and Arconad (1981), depressed individuals tend to see themselves as "helpless victims" of forces beyond their control. The purpose of the conceptualization phase is to increase the person's awareness of how closely dysphoric mood is tied to specific events. Through this process, the person's problems are "demystified" and redefined in ways that increase perceptions of hopefulness and control. Once redefined, the individual's depressive symptoms become specific problems that can be solved. Lewinsohn emphasizes that the conceptualization phase is critical to the success of therapy and requires great skill and sensitivity on the part of the therapist. The redefinition of presenting problems must be acceptable to both therapist and client (Lewinsohn & Arconad, 1981).

A *functional analysis* of the person's depressive symptoms must also be conducted, in order to generate specific treatment goals. Lewinsohn's method of functional analysis is comprehensive. Typically, a home observation is conducted in which all family members are observed during mealtime. This is an excellent method of pinpointing negative transactions within the depressed person's immediate social environment. The client is also asked to fill out the *Pleasant Events Schedule (PES)* (MacPhillamy & Lewinsohn, 1982) and the *Unpleasant Events Schedule (UES)* (Lewinsohn, 1975). Both instruments are lengthy (320-item) checklists of events that most people find pleasant and unpleasant, respectively. From the person's responses to the PES and UES, an individualized activity schedule is constructed. This schedule contains 80 events rated most pleasant by the individual and 80 events rated most unpleasant. The activity schedule is used in daily monitoring exercises (described next).

Mood and activity monitoring exercises are used to further develop and refine specific treatment goals. Mood fluctuations are assessed using the DACL (Lubin, 1967), and pleasant/ unpleasant activities are recorded. Clients are taught to graph data from daily monitoring, in order to demonstrate the association between mood and pleasant/unpleasant events concretely. A wide range of methods are typically used to accomplish specific treatment goals. Generally, these strategies fall into three categories:

1. **Change aspects of the environment** that are related to mood fluctuations. Depressed individuals may be directed to engage in specific rewarding activities on a daily or weekly basis and to alter or avoid mood-impairing activities.
2. **Teach the client concrete skills** that can be used to change negative environmental interactions. A depressed parent might be taught parenting skills designed to enhance

parent/child interactions; a shy individual might be given assertiveness training to increase frequency and positivity of social interactions; and so on.

3. Teach the client to enhance the pleasantness and reduce the unpleasantness of person-environment transactions. Clients are frequently given relaxation training, because high anxiety is incompatible with the experience of pleasure and tends to make unpleasant events more aversive. If a depressed client seems incapable of experiencing pleasure, the therapist must facilitate changes in the way the client perceives and interprets social experience. For example, clients may be taught to discriminate between positive/negative, necessary/unnecessary, and constructive/destructive thoughts.

Finally, toward the end of treatment, the client and therapist develop an individualized maintenance/prevention program to enhance treatment generalizability (Lewinsohn & Arconad, 1981).

Treatment Evaluation

Systematic studies of treatment outcome have been conducted (Brown & Lewinsohn, 1984; Sanchez, Lewinsohn, & Larson, 1980; Zeiss, Lewinsohn, & Munoz, 1979). Zeiss and associates (1979) compared three treatments: cognitive training, pleasant activities training, and social skills training. All were short term, time limited, and highly structured. The three treatments were equally effective in reducing depression.

A psychoeducational group treatment program also has been evaluated (Brown & Lewinsohn, 1984). The *Coping with Depression (CWD)* course involves 12 two-hour group sessions spread over eight weeks, with one- and six-month follow-ups. CWD has been compared with individual treatment, and the differences between modalities were small (Bellack, Hersen, & Himmelhoch, 1981; Teri & Lewinsohn, 1986). Given the cost effectiveness of the CWD course, this is a promising finding.

Beck's Cognitive Therapy of Depression

Conceptual Model

According to Beck (1967), predisposition to adult depression is created during childhood. In childhood, the individual develops a *negative self-schema*. This refers to a tendency to view oneself, the environment, and the future in negative ways. During adulthood, this cognitive triad involving self, others, and the future is activated and intensified by negative environmental stressors. There is specificity between the type of stressful events that precipitate depression and the predominant theme of the negative self-schema. For example, an individual who suffered parental loss during childhood would be most reactive to adult stressors involving loss or the threat of loss. Similarly, if the self-schema is organized around the experience of parental criticism, adult failures in achievement would be likely to precipitate depressive reactions. Once activated, the cognitive triad determines all other affective, behavioral, and motivational features of depression.

Arousal of depressive self-judgments is associated with errors in information processing that reflect these "underlying" negative self-schemata. These cognitive errors are described in Beck (1967). *Selective abstraction* refers to focusing on a negative detail, then seeing the whole experience in this light. For example, a depressed person might focus on one negative exchange within an entire conversation and interpret this as a sign of rejection on the part of his or her partner. *Magnification/ minimization* refers to the tendency to overestimate the importance of negative events and underestimate the importance of positive attributes or experiences. Similarly, *overgeneralization* involves the tendency to draw sweeping negative conclusions from a single incident. Finally, *arbitrary inference* involves the tendency to draw conclusions in the absence of clear or sufficient evidence. According to Beck, errors in information processing tend to maintain depressive symptoms. Hence, these errors are prime targets for clinical intervention.

Evidence supporting the cognitive model of depression has been reviewed in several sources (Beck & Rush, 1977; Haaga, Dyck, & Ernst, 1991; Sacco & Beck, 1985). The existence of the cognitive triad in depression has received consistent empirical support. Depressives tend to view themselves, their environments, and the future in a negative light. Also, several studies have supported the idea that depressed individuals possess negative self-schemata (Nelson & Craighead, 1977; Roth & Rehm, 1980). However, the hypothesis that depressed individuals negatively distort aspects of their experience has had weak and inconsistent support. For example, several studies have shown that depressed individuals may actually be *more* realistic than others in their evaluations of social experiences (e.g., Taylor & Brown, 1988). Similarly, the idea that illogical thinking precedes and precipitates other symptoms of depression has not been well established.

Beck's Cognitive Therapy

Cognitive therapy of depression was designed to produce rapid symptom remission through the identification and modification of depression-inducing thought patterns. The typical length of therapy is 16 weeks. Moderate to severe depressives are initially seen twice a week, tapering to weekly sessions after some improvement.

The therapist's role is active and directive. However, Beck has emphasized that effective therapists must be flexible enough to deal with pressing issues and possess good basic clinical skills. Finally, the therapist must maintain an optimistic attitude to avoid adopting depressed clients' characteristic pessimism. At the same time, the client's negative world view must be empathically acknowledged and never directly contradicted. The therapeutic relationship is framed as a team effort, requiring much active participation on the part of the client. The client's personal views are carefully acknowledged, then examined using the technique of *logical empiricism*. This means that the client's personal constructs are framed as hypotheses to be tested out, through dialogue with the therapist and in homework assignments. Initial sessions are devoted to diagnostic assessment. Individuals suffering from unipolar depression without psychotic features are best suited for cognitive therapy. Once depressive symptoms are described in detail, they are redefined within a cognitive framework. A therapy plan is then formulated, based on mutual collaboration between therapist and client.

At the beginning of therapy, behavioral tasks are used frequently. The purpose of these tasks is to quickly mobilize activity on the part of the client. Mobilization of activity helps to break the downward spiral of depressive inactivity, and shows the client that his or her beliefs are different from his or her actual capabilities. Usual targets for behavioral tasks include avoidance behaviors, inactivity, inability to express appropriate emotions, and inability to experience pleasure. All behavioral tasks are presented to the client as "experiments" or exercises that can provide useful information regardless of outcome. Later in therapy, behavioral tasks are chiefly used to test specific dysfunctional beliefs against actual experience.

Self-monitoring exercises also are used from the first session on. These exercises are designed to increase clients' awareness of the link between dysfunctional thoughts and depressive mood and behaviors. Clients are taught to engage in daily monitoring of moods, noting when significant fluctuations occur. A triple-column technique called the *Dysfunctional Thought Record (DTR)* is often used, with entries for mood (type, intensity) and situational context. The client then enters "automatic thoughts," or thoughts that occurred immediately in response to the upsetting situation (e.g., "I have to be perfect"; "I must be liked by everyone"). These thoughts are not immediately available to conscious awareness. Clients must be taught to recognize them.

After the initial sessions, there is a gradual shift in emphasis from concrete behavioral and motivational issues to evaluation of dysfunctional thoughts and their consequences. As clients become increasingly aware of their automatic thought patterns, they begin to achieve some objectivity. The therapist teaches the client to carefully evaluate these thoughts in terms of their accuracy (is there convincing evidence to support them?) and their real-world consequences. Specific therapy methods involve creating real-life "experiments" to test the validity of a belief, considering alternative interpretations of real-life events, and examining automatic thought using the triple-column technique just described.

During the latter stages of therapy, more adaptive cognitive responses gradually begin to replace illogical, "depressogenic" patterns. At this point, supraordinate themes underlying the client's depressive tendencies are identified and challenged. These supraordinate assumptions are global, underlying beliefs which predispose individuals to experience depression under stress. These must be modified in therapy, in order to prevent further episodes of depression. Examples of depressogenic assumptions are listed in Beck (1976) and include: "I can't live without love"; "My value as a person depends on what others think of me"; and so on. Changing such stable and generalized cognitive schemas is not an easy task. In confronting each illogical assumption, clients are challenged to examine the relative advantages and disadvantages of holding the beliefs. "Real-life" experiments are often prescribed as well. For example, a client holds the belief "I must be perfect in everything I do." This person might be told to perform a task in only a "satisfactory" way, then observe the consequences (Beck et al., 1979). Thus, the course of cognitive therapy proceeds from the specific and concrete to the general and abstract (Coleman & Beck, 1981).

Treatment Effectiveness

The effectiveness of cognitive therapy with depressed individuals has received consistent empirical support. Cognitive therapy has proven effective relative to control conditions and has equaled or outperformed alternative treatments such as tricyclic medications. Moreover, cognitive therapy is more effective than medication alone in preventing future episodes of depression (see reviews by Dobson, 1989; Hollon, Shelton, & Loosen, 1991; Robinson, Berman, & Neimayer, 1990). This is an important finding, because drug treatments have potential contraindications. Although pharmacotherapy is the most common treatment for depression, antidepressant medications frequently produce unpleasant physical side effects. In addition, clients who improve with drug treatment may attribute the change solely to the effects of the drug, thus leaving feelings of personal control unaffected or impaired. Finally, antidepressant medications should be prescribed with extreme caution for suicidal individuals, because overdoses of these medications can be lethal.

Rehm's Self-Control Therapy

Conceptual Model

Rehm's self-control model of depression is derived from Kanfer's model of self-regulation (Kanfer, 1970, 1971). According to Rehm (1977, 1988), depressed individuals develop specific self-control deficits when exposed to stressful situations, particularly those involving loss experiences. These deficits involve:

- Selectively attending to negative events (a self-monitoring deficit)
- Attending to immediate rather than delayed outcomes
- Setting perfectionistic standards for self-evaluation
- Making attributions that are consistent with negative expectations
- Engaging in insufficent levels of self-reward and excessive self-punishment

Clinical symptoms of depression are thought to reflect different self-control deficits. For example, pessimistic thinking reflects a deficit in self-monitoring; perfectionism, a deficit in self-evaluation; and helplessness, a deficit in self-attribution (Rehm, 1981). Specific patterns of self-control deficits vary between different depressed individuals.

Self-Control Therapy Program

Time–limited, highly structured group therapy session are used to remediate self-control deficits specified in the model. Clients participate in 6 to 12 90-minute weekly sessions that are highly didactic in nature (Rehm, 1981). The initial focus of treatment is on building awareness of how environmental events affect mood. During this *self-monitoring* phase, homework is liberally used to supplement the therapy sessions. Next, during the *self-evaluation* phase, planning and decision-making activities become the focus of discussion and homework. Clients are taught to set realistic standards for self-evaluation. Also, they are taught to break desirable goals into smaller, more immediately attainable subgoals, and to avoid distant and unattainable goals.

The third phase, *reattribution*, features analysis of self-recorded recent events. Depressive attributions are examined for evidence, and alternative explanations are considered. Finally, during the *self-reinforcement phase,* clients are taught to increase the use of contingent self-reward. Various techniques are used, such as teaching clients to increase their awareness of positive attributes through the use of supportive self-statements. Similarly, clients are asked to generate a "reward menu" of easily accomplished pleasant activities. These are used to reward the accomplishment of more difficult goal-related activities (Rehm, 1981).

Treatment Effectiveness

Studies by Fuchs and Rehm (1977) and by Rehm, Fuchs, Kornblith, and Romano (1979) provided empirical support for the effectiveness of self-control therapy. After only six weeks of treatment, clinically significant reductions in depression were achieved. Further, self-control training was superior to assertion training alone for most depressed clients (Rehm et al., 1979). Finally, treatment gains were maintained at one-year follow-up (Rehm, 1981).

Helplessness, Hopelessness, and Pessimism

Reformulated Learned Helplessness Model

The reformulated learned helplessness model of depression (Abramson, Seligman, & Teasdale, 1979) was proposed as a major modification of Seligman's original helplessness theory of depression (Seligman, 1975). The original model was developed to explain the effects of uncontrollable stress on animal behavior. Similarities were drawn between the behavior of dogs exposed to uncontrollable shock and that of clinically depressed humans. For example, both groups show behavioral passivity in the face of uncontrollable stress. Although the original helplessness model resulted in a large volume of interesting research on stress, coping, and depression, numerous conceptual and methodological inadequacies necessitated the reformulation (see Peterson & Seligman, 1984, for detailed discussion of weaknesses inherent in the former model). Many individuals, for example, are exposed to uncontrollable negative events and do not become depressed.

The reformulated model focused on how individuals attribute meaning to their life experiences. The individual at elevated risk for depression has a depressive attributional style. This refers to a tendency to attribute negative experiences to personal, generalized, and stable aspects of oneself. When individuals with this characteristic cognitive style actually experience negative life events, they become depressed (Peterson & Seligman, 1994). For example, a young woman became depressed after her boyfriend suddenly broke off their affair. When questioned about the meaning she attributed to the break-up, she replied, "It's my fault for being inadequate. I'm not attractive enough to keep a man and I never will be."

Evidence supporting the reformulated helplessness model has been drawn from analogue studies of college students labeled "depressed" on the basis of Beck Depression Inventory cutoff scores. Moreover, clinically depressed individuals also tend to manifest a globally negative cognitive style (Robins & Hayes, 1995). However, it is unclear whether this attributional style is a causal factor in the onset of depressive symptoms. For example, Hamilton and Abramson (1983) found that the "classic" depressive attributional style characterized depressives during their hospital stays, but was no longer present after discharge. Careful review of the evidence has suggested that attributional style is only weakly related to the onset of depressive symptoms (Brewin, 1988; Robins & Hayes, 1995). Once depression begins, however, attributional style is an important maintaining factor, making recovery more challenging (Whisman, 1993).

In recent years, Seligman (1989) has reformulated the helplessness model into a personality theory that highlights pessimism as a vulnerability factor in depression. Pessimism is viewed as a stable individual trait that is formed early in life as a consequence of negative life experiences. Seligman and his colleagues have argued that maintaining a pessimistic orientation to life places people at elevated risk for a wide range of negative life outcomes, including depression, physical illness, and underachievement (Peterson, 1995; Peterson & Bossio, 1991).

Hopelessness: A Third Reformulation

Lyn Abramson, Lauren Alloy, and their colleagues (Abramson, Metalsky, & Alloy, 1989; Abramson & Alloy, 1990) have proposed a third reformulation of the helplessness model; *Hopelessness Theory*. They argue that the original reformulation of learned helplessness theory was related less to depressive phemomenology than to the general phenomenon of helplessness. Thus, the hopelessness model focuses more on depression and less on attributional style. Hopelessness is viewed as a major subtype of depression that is caused by a complex pathway of processes, including stressful life events and negative self-appraisals. The central feature of *hopelessness depression* is the perception that one can never achieve desirable life outcomes (Abramson, Alloy, & Metalsky, 1995).

Therapeutic Implications

There is no systematic model of treatment based on the helplessness model. However, clinical interventions suggested by the model have been discussed (Layden, 1982; Peterson, 1982). Four potential therapy strategies derived from the reformulation have been outlined (Layden, 1982). Of these, *attributional retraining* has the most direct relevance to psychotherapy with depressive individuals. The goal of attributional retraining would be to teach the depressed individual to attribute negative experiences to malleable aspects of oneself or the situation. For example, poor test performance might be viewed as a result of inadequate preparation, not "stupidity." Similarly, positive experiences should be attributed to internal "causes" such as effort, not external factors such as luck or circumstance. Studies have shown that general cognitive therapy with depressive individuals produces substantial changes in explanatory style. Changes in explanatory style, in turn, appear to play an important role in the prevention of relapse (DeRubeis & Hollon, 1995).

Integration of Models and Case Example

Major behavioral models of the treatment of unipolar depression have been reviewed in this chapter. The conceptual bases of these models differ appreciably, but the corresponding therapy programs share many similarities. All programs are highly structured and time limited, and involve careful assessment of presenting symptoms. Targets for intervention are well-defined patterns of behavior and/or cognition. The importance of developing a shared conceptualization of presenting problems, and mutual collaboration in working toward treatment goals, are stressed in all programs. Finally, continuous mood and/or activity monitoring, homework assignments, and specialized skills training are common features of these therapies.

How effective are these different treatment paradigms in relation to each other, and in relation to alternative, nonbehavioral treatments? Results of meta-analytic studies (Dobson, 1989; Steinbruck, Maxwell, & Howard, 1983) have shown that cognitive and behavioral treatments were more effective than drug treatments in alleviating symptoms of unipolar depression. This suggests low variability between different behavioral treatment programs in terms of outcome efficacy. Furthermore, different components of the *same* treatment programs do not appear to selectively impact different types of depressive symptoms (Zeiss et al., 1979).

A more moderately optimistic picture can be drawn from the results of the National Institute of Mental Health (NIMH) *Treatment of Depression Collaborative Research Program* (Elkin et al., 1989). In this large study, four different treatment conditions were compared in relation to their efficacy with (unipolar) depressed outpatients: cognitive-behavioral therapy, interpersonal psychotherapy, imipramine, and pill placebo. Results generally supported the equality of the three treatment conditions. However, Hollon and associates (1992) conducted a major treatment evaluation study in which 107 outpatients with unipolar depression were randomly assigned to either (1) cognitive therapy, (2) drug treatment, or (3) cognitive therapy plus drug treatment. All clients showed significant improvement in their depressive symptoms, but those who received the combined intervention did the best.

Studies of relapse following different types of treatment have provided the most compelling support for the effectiveness of cognitive-behavioral therapy. At one-year (Simons, Murphy, Levine, & Wetzel, 1986) and two-year (Blackburn, Eunson, & Bishop, 1986) follow-up intervals, depressed individuals treated with cognitive therapy or with a combination of cognitive therapy and drugs have shown lower relapse rates than those who received drug treatment alone. For example, Evans and colleagues (1989) compared the following conditions: posttreatment withdrawal of all drug treatment, posttreatment continuation of drug treatment for one year, cognitive-behavioral therapy, and cognitive-behavioral therapy combined with drug treatment (the drugs were withdrawn posttreatment). At two years posttreatment, half of the group whose medications were withdrawn had relapsed, most within the initial four months. Those who continued on medication, and those who received cognitive-behavioral treatment with or without medication, had significantly lower relapse rates.

Finally, researchers have identified several factors that limit the potential effectiveness of cognitive-behavioral therapy with depressed individuals. It is important to emphasize that these factors do not make cognitive-behavioral interventions impossible—just more difficult.

1. *Severity.* Initial severity of depression has been related to poorer outcome (Norman, Miller, & Dow, 1988; Rude & Rehm, 1991). Results of the NIMH collaborative study suggested that cognitive-behavioral therapy may be most appropriate for mildly, but not severely, depressed outpatients. However, recent studies have indicated that cognitive-behavioral therapy can be effective with even severely depressed inpatients (Bowers, 1990; Thase et al., 1991).

2. *Marital and family stress.* The experience of severe marital or family stress has been strongly related to depression. Individuals in distressed marriages tend to experience very high rates of depression (e.g., Beach, Sandeen, & O'Leary, 1990). Having a depressed partner, in turn, places a great burden on the nondepressed spouse, possibly increasing the severity of the couple's distress. Not surprisingly, behavioral couples therapy has been proven to be an effective treatment for depressed individuals (Beach, Whisman, & O'Leary, 1994; Jacobson, Holtzworth-Munroe, & Schmaling, 1989). In fact, behavioral couples therapy and cognitive therapy appear to be equally effective in relieving depression. However, cognitive therapy does not *spontaneously* result in increased marital satisfaction (Beach et al., 1994). Thus, marital and family interventions should be carefully considered in treatment planning with depressed individuals.

   3. *Personality disorders.* Depressed individuals who also have personality disorders tend to be difficult to engage in therapy and show poorer responses to standard treatment than those without personality disorder symptoms (Frank et al., 1991). If personality disorder is present, the therapist must tailor strategies of rapport building and intervention to the features of the disorder (see Chapter 10). Generally, individuals with personality disorders require much longer periods of rapport building and intervention than those with "uncomplicated" Axis I disorders (Beck et al., 1990; Turkat, 1992).

Case Example

The following detailed case example illustrates the use of multiple cognitive and behavioral interventions in the treatment of unipolar depression.

> Following an initial assessment period, Susan K. was seen for 14 sessions of psychotherapy. She was a young, single, 24-year-old woman. Her goals for therapy were to learn how to overcome chronic feelings of depression and to learn how to deal with temptations to overeat. Client and therapist agreed on cognitive-behavioral therapy for her depression. Initial sessions were focused on an introduction to the basic concepts of cognitive therapy: beginning homework on identifying cognitive distortions, identifying her self-schemas and their relationship to her problem-solving style, and identifying self-defeating behaviors and cognitions.
>
> Susan's coping style was carefully assessed, and patterns began to emerge. She tended to look for avenues of escape when confronted with difficult problems or unwanted emotions. This means of escape would vary (e.g., taking drugs, overeating, and behavioral withdrawal were common reactions to stress). At the time of assessment, Susan was unemployed and living with her aunt and uncle in a rural area. She had no means of personal transportation. As her relations with her aunt and uncle seemed to precipitate many of her current feelings of depression and anxiety, assessing these situations became a focal point of initial sessions. Early homework centered on identifying negative thoughts about self via self-monitoring, and identifying pleasurable activities that could be increased immediately. Because of the homework, Susan became better able to identify reasons for depressive feelings when they occurred. For example, in one early session she reported feeling worse over the week, then related this mood state to her perception that her aunt and mother disapproved of her.
>
> Hypersensitivity to the reactions of significant others and the belief that they could control her feelings seemed to be central to her low self-concept and feelings of help-

lessness. Susan described her mother as knowing which "buttons to push." This metaphor was examined and challenged. She was questioned as to how her mother controlled her emotions: Where were these buttons? Did they have a physical reality? Once again, the principle was asserted that it is not the actions of others that cause emotions, but one's cognitions about them. Then cognitions she had concerning certain "looks" or critical statements were examined. When her aunt was looking "sickly and silent," Susan believed that it was because she was displeased with her for not helping enough. The evidence for this belief was examined, and there was none. Alternative explanations were explored, such as the aunt might be truly ill, having a bad day, or upset with her spouse. Susan admitted that all explanations were equally plausible. Furthermore, it was noted that in ambiguous social situations, she tended to draw the most negative and personalized conclusions.

After practicing identifying negative thoughts using the triple column method described in Beck and associates (1979), Susan began to challenge negative cognitions when she caught herself thinking them. Also, in these middle sessions, there was a focus on her family background and relationships. At one point during this period, she began to feel worse. When explored, her mood seemed to be related to an upcoming visit by her mother. She felt very anxious to gain her mother's approval, but constrained in her ability to live up to her mother's expectations. She also had fantasies of making her mother feel happy. Her inability to do this was perceived as a failure ("I should be able to make her feel better; because I can't, I've failed as a daughter"). This belief was challenged. Once more, it was pointed out that people cannot "make" other people feel things.

Her consistent tendency to evaluate her self-worth in terms of her family's approval was examined. Susan still had fantasies of her family becoming like the "Walton" family (e.g., a "normal" family that was loving and accepting of one another. Instead, her own family was distant and argumentative with one another). Susan began to let go of this fantasy and grieved over this loss. Once this had been done, she began to gain a better understanding of how her current cognitive distortions could be related to overconcern with familial approval. As she began to let go of her desire to live up to imagined expectations, she stopped seeing herself as a failure.

During the last stage of therapy, Susan's mother visited. This provided a real test of the gains she had made, as it was her mother's criticism that Susan feared most. At first, she reported feeling easily wounded by her mother's criticisms (example, as reported by client: "Why don't you cook for your brother? If I was in your position, I would have"). These examples were used as opportunities to identify and challenge self-defeating thoughts. Soon, Susan was able to see her mother's critical statements as her mother's problem, not her own. She also discovered that as she became better at ignoring her mother's critical remarks and not taking them to heart, her mother began to be more relaxed and open around her, and criticized her less.

During the final stage of therapy, Susan was mostly depression free and experienced no urges to binge on food. She made plans to attend college, a lifelong goal. During this stage there was also some focus on how to handle future depressive feelings. Advance coping strategies were formulated in the event that Susan began feeling depressed again.

Upon agreement by client and therapist, a brief vacation from therapy was taken. At the end of three weeks, Susan was still successfully challenging self-defeating thoughts and remained depression free. A follow-up session was scheduled for one month later. This was the 16th session of therapy. At that time, Susan had been depression free for almost four months. She reported feeling "great, better than I've been feeling in a long, long time." She reported that her family and friends had complimented her on the positive changes she had made. She also reported feeling greater self-confidence in her ability to succeed at school. Upon termination, she planned to seek therapy in her college community if she began to feel depressed again.

Management of Suicidal Behavior

Experiencing thoughts or fantasies about suicide is a common symptom of depression (see *DSM-IV* criteria for major depressive disorder). However, the majority of depressed individuals do not make suicide attempts. Conversely, not all individuals experience depression prior to their suicide attempts (Pokorny, 1968). Thus, suicidal behavior is much more than just a simple "correlate" of depression. Effective management of suicidal individuals requires specialized assessment and treatment techniques.

Assessment

Because of the immense potential for self-harm, thorough clinical assessments of current risk, and of the client's life situation are essential. During the initial interview, the following areas would be assessed:

- Nature of the presenting problem
- Precipitating stresses
- Family history
- Client's psychological status, particularly whether there are concomitant Axis I and/or II disorders
- Degree of suicidal intent and reasons for wishing to die
- Current life situation and psychosocial adjustment
- Emotional, material, and social resources
- Deterrents to self-harm (What would deter the client from making a suicide attempt?)

In addition to interviewing the suicidal client, interviews with significant others are essential in helping the clinician assess the potential lethality of the client's suicidal ideation or behavior, assess the types of psychosocial stressors and supports in the client's life, and formulate immediate plans for intervention.

Current risk is an index of dangerousness: It involves the likelihood of attempting suicide in the immediate future (Linehan, 1981). Direct indicators of current risk include overt threats, suicide planning or preparation for death, and recent self-injurious behavior. Indirect indices include membership in high-risk populations, negative environmental stressors (particularly experiences of interpersonal loss), hopelessness, the presence of major psychological disorder, and veiled references to death (e.g., "Sometimes I feel that I'd be better off dead"). Factors exacerbating suicidal risk include alcohol or drug abuse, post-traumatic stress disorder, and a history of prior self–destructive behavior (Bongar, 1991; Clark & Fawcett, 1992).

Standard psychological tests (such as the MMPI and Rorschach) are less accurate predictors of suicide risk than specially constructed scales (Farberow, 1981). For example, Beck, Kovacs, and Weissman (1975) developed the *Hopelessness Scale* for assessing immediate suicidal risk. The scale contains 20 items reflecting negative attitudes toward the future and general pessimism; it has been found to predict suicidal behavior among depressed individuals (Beck, Steer, Kovacs, & Garrison, 1985). If the client's level of hopelessness is high, the therapist must deal immediately with the possibility of suicidal behavior. Similarly, Patterson and associates (1983) have developed the *SAD PERSONS Scale,* a clinical checklist for professionals based on 10 risk factors (reflected in the acronym). Finally, Linehan, Goodstein, Nielsen, and Chiles (1983) developed the *Reasons for Living Inventory.* The questionnaire involves self-ratings of how important various reasons for living would be if the respondent was considering suicide.

The aforementioned assessment techniques provide useful information concerning suicidal risk, but there are no clear guidelines for the clinician. Linehan has compared therapy with acutely suicidal patients to "walking a tightrope, in that the clinician must continually balance the need for an active, caring response against the need to refrain from reinforcing suicidal behavior" (1981, p. 258). The balance depends on a clinically astute assessment of current risk.

Once suicidal behaviors have been clearly identified, a functional analysis must be conducted to identify appropriate targets for intervention. Potential targets for analysis include suicidal ideation and imagery, planning, verbalizations, and/or self-injurious acts (Linehan, 1993; Freeman & Reineke, 1993). It is particularly important to analyze the client's motives for self-harm. Does the client wish to escape from pain? Alteratively, is suicidal behavior meant to communicate anger or disappointment to others, or does some combination of motives exist? Analysis of suicidal motives helps to guide the clinician's response. For example, if the client's primary motive is to "escape" from pain, feelings of hopelessness can be focused on. If the primary motive is to influence the feelings or behaviors of other people, alternative ways of communicating and problem solving can be explored.

Treatment Strategies

Crisis intervention must be conducted if the client is acutely suicidal. During this phase, the therapist is very directive in giving detailed concrete instructions regarding crisis management. These instructions may involve emergency hospitalization. The decision to hospitalize is likely if there is a high degree of current risk, severe concurrent psychopathology, loss of capacity for self-care, and/or extreme psychosocial stress (Yufit & Bongar, 1992).

Even when the immediate crisis has abated, risk of suicide must be continuously assessed. Linehan (1981, 1993) has recommended that the therapist coordinate with community crisis services, make short-term antisuicide contracts with the client that are kept up to date, and coordinate with the client's physician to prevent overprescription of psychotropic medications.

Linehan (1981, 1993) has provided detailed suggestions for long-term behavioral therapy with suicidal clients. Before formal interventions are initiated, careful attention should be paid to the development of a supportive therapeutic environment. Specific long-term interventions vary according to the needs of the client, but center on learning cognitive and behavioral skills necessary for constructive real-life problem solving.

Suggestions for cognitive therapy with suicidal individuals have been published in several volumes (Beck et al., 1979; Freeman & Reineke, 1993). Beck and his colleagues have recommended that the therapist enter into a dialogue with the client, discussing the pros and cons of living. The therapist may even elicit a list of reasons for living, which could be put into writing. Beck and associates see feelings of hopelessness as underlying most suicidal behavior (Beck et al., 1985). In order to reduce feelings of hopelessness, the "evidence" in support of them must be carefully examined. Once the client sees that there are other ways of viewing upsetting situations, these situations can be reframed as potentially solvable problems. For example, general problem-solving approaches to upsetting life situations can be reviewed, practiced, and applied to new situations as they arise. If the client lacks basic skills that are necessary for effective problem solving (e.g., assertiveness, anger control, anxiety management), these skills must be acquired in therapy. The latter stages of therapy are exclusively oriented to prevention of further depressive and suicidal behavior. Termination of therapy is achieved gradually, with an explicit "open door" policy should further problems arise (Freeman & Reineke, 1993).

Finally, management of suicidal patients is highly stressful for the therapist. According to Bongar (1991), the chances of losing a client to suicide are 1:5 for psychologists and 1:2 for psychiatrists. Most mental health professionals have not been trained to cope with the actuality of suicide in their clients. Losing a client to suicide is emotionally devastating and can precipitate extreme reactions and cognitive distortions in the therapists (Bongar, 1991). Therapists with suicidal clients should actively seek out peer support and consultation, as well as legal advice in the event that the client does attempt suicide (Bongar, 1991; Linehan, 1993). Advance preparation is a key to effective coping behavior on the part of the therapist.

Chapter Summary

Depression is a relatively common disorder characterized by problems in emotional, cognitive, behavioral, social, and physiological functioning. Prominent symptoms include dysphoric mood, loss of interest in normal activities, negative thoughts about self, and hopelessness. Depressive disorders are classified according to the severity and chronicity of these symptoms.

Assessment and treatment of depressive disorders is a vital area of behavior therapy. A variety of interview and self-report instruments have been developed to aid in the identification and evaluation of depressive symptoms. Behavioral models of depression include Lewinsohn's low positive reinforcement model, Beck's cognitive model, Rehm's self-control model, and Seligman's reformulated helplessness model. Although the conceptual emphases of these models differ, therapy programs based on these models share many similarities. Treatment programs are highly structured, time limited, and typically involve continuous mood and activity monitoring, frequent homework assignments, and individualized training in cognitive and behavioral coping skills. Outcome research indicates that these programs can be highly effective in alleviating depressive symptoms.

Suicidal behavior is frequently associated with depression, but not invariably so. Specialized assessment and treatment techniques are needed to effectively manage suicidal behavior. Important aspects of assessment include careful evaluation of current and long–term risk, and analysis of appropriate targets for interventions. Short-term crisis intervention is often necessary. Longer-term behavioral management involves creating a supportive therapeutic environment in which the client learns cognitive and behavioral skills necessary for more effective coping and problem solving.

Chapter 10

Personality Disorders

Sarah, age 29, was hospitalized after ingesting a near-lethal dose of antidepressant medication. Her suicide attempt was precipitated by a confrontation with her employer, who threatened to fire her if she could not restrain her frequent, angry outbursts toward co-workers. Sarah described herself as a "moody" person. Her greatest wish was to be in a secure, happy relationship with a man. Instead, she related a long history of stormy affairs that didn't work out. Her relationships with family members and co-workers were equally stormy. She suffered from frequent episodes of panic and depression that were centered on the theme of being alone and unloved. During these episodes, she sometimes gained temporary relief by cutting her skin repeatedly with a kitchen knife.

During his initial contact with a therapist, Mr. A. sat rigidly in his chair and made only fleeting eye contact. Pale and thin in appearance, his voice and demeanor were devoid of emotional expression. Mr. A. was self-employed and lived alone with his three cats. He described himself as a "loner who prefers it that way—other people just don't interest me." Although he saw his parents and brothers on major holidays, he related that as long as he could remember, he had preferred his own company. Mr. A. sought treatment because he was concerned about recent episodes of insomnia and depression. He expressed no interest in becoming more socially active.

Molly, age 31, sought treatment because she felt "lonely and depressed" most of the time. The only child of two alcoholic parents who tended to abuse her physically and emotionally during their drinking episodes, Molly had concluded from an early age that she was "bad" and "inferior." Although she wanted to have friends and love relationships, she had avoided both since adolescence. She felt convinced that she was unworthy of love and attention from others, and that if she tried to engage others in friendship, they would quickly become aware of her flaws and reject her.

Personality disorders are defined by the DSM-IV as long-standing patterns of experience and behavior that lead to emotional distress and/or impaired cognitive, behavioral, and interpersonal functioning. Because the personality disorders reflect long-standing maladaptive behavior patterns that can occur together with other clinical problems, they are unlike the other disorders we have discussed so far, and they are coded differently in the *DSM-IV.* Disorders such as Major Depressive Disorder or Panic Disorder with Agoraphobia are coded as *Clinical Disorders* on *Axis I,* the first of five axes or dimensions used in the *DSM-IV.* The personality disorders and *Mental Retardation* are coded separately on Axis II to ensure that clinicians will not overlook the possibility that they are present, because they so often coexist with other disorders. (Axes III, IV, and V cover medical problems, psychosocial and environmental problems, and a global assessment of functioning, respectively.) As shown by the symptom patterns of Sarah, Mr. A., and Molly, personality disorders are quite diverse in nature and encompass a broad range of life situations.

It is remarkable that a chapter on personality disorders is included in the second edition of this text. Until recently, behavior therapists have questioned the very existence of pervasive, long-standing personality characteristics or "traits" (e.g., Mischel, 1968). Dating from several early psychoanalytic cases like Anna O. (Breuer & Freud, 1895/1955), the psychotherapeutic literature on treatment of personality disorders has been dominated by psychoanalytic and psychodynamic formulations (e.g., Goldstein, 1985; Gunderson, 1984; Kernberg, 1948; Masterson, 1985). However, with the publication of Millon's seminal book on the social learning foundations of personality disorders (Millon, 1981), behavioral (Linehan, 1993; Turkat, 1990) and cognitive-behavioral (Beck & Freeman, 1993; Freeman, Pretzger, Fleming, & Simon, 1990; Pretzger & Fleming, 1989; Young & Swift, 1988) models of the conceptualization and treatment of personality disorders have been proliferating. Perhaps more than any other clinical application, this is a sign of the growing flexibility of cognitive-behavioral conceptualizations and therapies.

Personality disorders account for the largest class of psychological disorders. Exact prevalence rates are difficult to determine, but most clinicians agree that they are very common (Turkat, 1992). For example, over 50 percent of patients who participated in the field trials for an earlier *DSM* met diagnostic criteria for one or more personality disorders (American Psychiatric Association, 1980). Clients with personality disorders account for a large proportion of individuals who do not respond well to psychotherapy (Beck et al., 1993). Thus, developing effective treatment strategies for these individuals is an important and timely issue. However, there are several features of these disorders which make them special challenges for clinicians:

1. Most individuals with personality disorders do not refer themselves for treatment of the personality disorder itself. They are either unaware of it, do not consider it to be a problem, or feel reluctant to change (Beck et al., 1993; Turkat, 1992). Rather, individuals with personality disorders come to the attention of mental health professionals because they have developed one or more Axis I disorders, or because their behavior is disturbing to family members, friends, or work associates (Turkat, 1990). Diagnosis and treatment are complicated because individuals may present with overlapping personality disorders and with acute-onset Axis I disorders. Given these complexities, it is not surprising that personality disorders have been difficult to diagnose reliably (APA, 1980; Turkat, 1990).

2. The unwillingness of personality-disordered individuals to change poses a formidable barrier to therapy. Thus, in relation to more "standard" behavioral treatment protocols, effective treatment of personality-disordered individuals generally requires a much longer period of relationship building before intervention can be attempted. Failing to do so may precipitate premature termination of therapy, or in some cases, a severe emotional crisis in the client (Freeman et al., 1990).

3. Because personality disorders represent long-standing patterns of behavior and experience, they require more time to treat than most "uncomplicated" Axis I disorders. This poses a challenge to behaviorally oriented clinicians, who tend to work in structured, efficient, and time-limited ways. Even so, behavioral treatment of personality disorders is very cost effective relative to psychodynamic therapies. For example, Beck and colleagues (1990) have estimated that cognitive-behavioral therapy with personality-disordered individuals requires between one and three years, compared with an average of five to seven years for the psychodynamic therapies.

There has been relatively little controlled research on the treatment of personality disorders. However, a growing body of literature, primarily derived from uncontrolled case studies, has shown that cognitive and behavioral approaches can be quite effective with some forms of personality disorder (APA Task Force Report on the Treatment of Personality Disorders, 1989; Freeman et al., 1990). These approaches are summarized next, in relation to each different personality disorder that is currently recognized in the *DSM-IV.* Traditionally, personality disorders have been grouped into three broad clusters—A, B, and C—based on shared descriptive similarities.

Cluster A Disorders

Individuals who manifest Cluster A personality disorders are often described as odd or eccentric. They tend to lead solitary lives, preferring to maintain few, if any, close personal relationships. Cluster A disorders have been subgrouped into three categories: Paranoid Personality Disorder, Schizoid Personality Disorder, and Schizotypal Personality Disorder. Because individuals with these disorders rarely refer themselves for treatment, little is known about cognitive-behavioral intervention aside from individual case reports.

Paranoid Personality Disorder

The central themes of *Paranoid Personality Disorder (PPD)* are distrust of others' motives and hypersensitivity to negative social evaluation. Distrust of others tends to be pervasive, extending across many different situations. For example, individuals with PPD may feel that others are quick to harm or exploit them, and they tend to be preoccupied with doubts about the loyalty of family members, friends, and associates. Because they fear that self-disclosure will result in harm from others, individuals with Paranoid Personality Disorder tend to keep their feelings self-contained, and generally avoid social relationships. They may choose to follow a self-sufficient lifestyle. Some paranoid individuals have grandiose fantasies about power and rank. Although individuals with PPD are not psychotic, they may experience brief psychotic episodes under stress.

Not surprisingly, individuals with PPD tend to have poor social relationships. Other people tend to describe them as hostile, guarded, cold, argumentative, rigid, and hypercritical. Paranoid individuals are constantly alert for signs of hostility and tend to "read" threatening meanings into neutral or benign statements or situations. If they perceive that they are being attacked, paranoid individuals are quick to react angrily and tend to bear grudges. Ironically, these tendencies create a self-fulfilling phrophecy: Increasing guardedness and hostility on the part of the paranoid individual elicits negative reactions from others, which confirm the initial distortion that "people are out to get me" (American Psychiatric Association, 1994; Beck et al., 1990).

According to criteria listed in *DSM-IV,* four or more of the following characteristics must be present for a diagnosis of PPD:

- Suspects, without sufficient basis, that others are exploiting, harming, or deceiving him or her
- Is preoccupied with unjustified doubts about the loyalty or trustworthiness of friends or associates
- Is reluctant to confide in others because of unwarranted fear that the information will be used maliciously against him or her
- Reads hidden demeaning or threatening meanings into benign remarks or events
- Persistently bears grudges (e.g., is unforgiving of insults, injuries, and slights)
- Perceives attacks on his or her character or reputation that are not apparent to others and is quick to react angrily or counterattack
- Has recurrent suspicions, without justification, regarding the fidelity of spouse or sexual partner

It is important to note that paranoid-like traits may be adaptive in highly threatening environments. Thus, Paranoid Personality Disorder should not diagnosed when individuals have a history of extreme policial or sociocultural exploitation (e.g., members of persecuted minority groups; political refugees). A diagnosis of PPD is only warranted when these suspicions appear to be distortions, and when they are inflexible, maladaptive, pervasive, and long-standing (American Psychiatric Association, 1994).

Paranoid personality disorder has been poorly researched (Thompson-Pope & Turkat, 1989). Individuals with this disorder rarely refer themselves for psychological treatment, and when they do, it is usually for other problems (Weintraub, 1981). Because of their high levels of distrust, it is extremely difficult to engage individuals with PPD in psychotherapy.

Even so, Turkat (1990, 1992) believes that individuals with PPD can be successfully treated with behavior therapy. Based on his own clinical experience, he has proposed two target areas for intervention. The first, hypersensitivity to criticism, could be treated using standard anxiety management techniques (e.g., the individual could be desensitized to a graduated hierarchy of threatening situations). The second area, poor social skills, could be treated using modeling, coaching, and role-playing techniques combined with careful analysis of the paranoid individual's social interactions.

For example, Turkat and Maisto (1985) described the treatment of Mr. E., a client with PPD. The authors hypothesized that Mr. E. had developed hypersensitivity to negative social evaluation without acquiring good social skills. For example, his attempts to gain approval from others often elicited criticism, which would exacerbate his long– standing tendency to engage in social withdrawal and paranoid rumination. Turkat and Maisto selected behavioral interventions focused on the goals of decreasing Mr. E's anxiety about social evaluation and improving his social skills. Little attention was given to his paranoid cognitive style *per se.*

In another case, a 37-year-old woman with PPD was treated using multiple behavioral interventions. Dating from her experience of abuse as a child, she had great difficulty trusting others. At the time of referral, she reported interpersonal problems that were linked to her tendency to look for signs of rejection, and to explode in anger when she found them. She received 15 months of behavioral treatment focused on fear of social criticism, anger control, and social skills training. At termination, she had achieved marked improvements in her social and vocational functioning (Turkat, 1992).

In contrast with the behavioral approach just described, Beck, Freeman, and their associates (Beck et al., 1990; Freeman et al., 1990) have proposed a cognitive conceptualization of Paranoid Personality Disorder. They view the main dysfunction in PPD as an automatic assumption that other people are dangerous, untrustworthy, and malicious. As a result of this maladaptive cognitive style, individuals with PPD tend to experience impaired self-efficacy. One of the author's cases illustrates the self-perpetuating nature of this maladaptive belief–social feedback cycle (Freeman et al., 1990). Gary, a radiologist in his late 20s, sought treatment for chronic anxiety and insomnia. After seven sessions focused on the initial presenting problems, the therapist "discovered" that Gary had PPD. Based on his experiences growing up in an extremely adverse family environment, Gary believed that people were basically malevolent and would try to hurt him if they had the opportunity. Thus, he reasoned that his best defense was to remain hypervigilant for signs of impending attack. This assumption had a strong negative impact on his social relationships: He avoided closeness with others and was quick to react aggressively to small perceived slights. Naturally, his behavior tended to provoke hostility and distrust from others, reaffirming Gary's initial assumptions and fears.

According to Beck, Freeman, and their associates, one must challenge these assumptions because they produce experiences that confirm the paranoid mindset. Initially, however, the most important step in treatment is to establish a collaborative relationship with the paranoid client. Beck and colleagues recommend a straightforward acknowledgment of the client's distrust of the therapist, combined with careful attention to the types of moment-to-moment distortions that paranoid individuals may make. Once a collaborative relationship has been achieved, the primary strategy in cognitive therapy is to increase the client's feelings of self-efficacy, so that he or she does not need to ruminate about vulnerability to attack. This can be done in two ways. First, if the client is capable of handling social situations skillfully, but overestimates the degree of threat involved, the therapist can try to promote more realistic appraisal of situations using cognitive therapy techniques such as guided discovery. If the client does not have sufficient social skills, skills training must supersede other treatment objectives. Finally, cognitive interventions can be used to challenge and restructure the paranoid individual's dysfunctional assumptions about self and others (Freeman et al., 1990).

The cases of Ann and Gary, described in Freeman and colleagues (1990), illustrate successful cognitive-behavioral treatment of individuals with PPD. Ann, a woman in her mid-30s, sought help for problems of tension, fatigue, and irritability. She was convinced that her office co-workers were trying to harm her directly or trying to turn their supervisor against her. The therapist asked her to focus on how much danger was really inherent in her work situation. For example, she perceived that co-workers were making noise and dropping things just to annoy her. With skillful questioning from the therapist, she acknowledged that she was perceiving much more risk than was actually present. In addition to helping her appraise the "evidence" more realistically, the therapist engaged in stress management and assertiveness training, and in improving Ann's communication with her husband. At the termination of therapy, Ann was still interpersonally guarded, but less likely to overreact to minor provocations, and more assertive. Because of these changes in her behavior and outlook, her relationship with her husband improved.

Freeman's treatment of Gary, whose symptoms were described earlier, required a somewhat different approach. Following initial rapport building, the therapist concentrated on improving Gary's self-efficacy, especially his tendency to chronically and unrealistically berate this own abilities. Next, his dichotomous view of untrustworthiness was challenged. The therapist encouraged him to test out his assumptions about trustworthiness more directly—for example by setting up carefully planned "experiments." Consequently, Gary took calculated risks and discovered that most people were less malevolent than he had initially assumed. This led to a revised "world view" that there were benevolent and indifferent as well as some malevolent people. The therapist also encouraged him to change his interpersonal style, so that hostile reactions from others were not so readily provoked. This was accomplished by coaching him in assertiveness and communication skills.

In the final phase of treatment, the therapist tried to improve Gary's empathic understanding of others by using role reversal and by asking him to anticipate how others would be affected by his behavior. He discovered that irritating behavior in other people was not always motivated by malicious intent. At termination, Gary reported experiencing only situational stress and anxiety (e.g., before major exams). He reported feeling more relaxed around friends and colleagues, and better able to consider his girlfriend's point of view when conflicts arose.

Schizoid Personality Disorder

The central feature of *Schizoid Personality Disorder (SPD)* is pervasive detachment from social relationships. Schizoid individuals spend most of their time alone and do not *desire* close relationships. They tend to show a restricted range of emotion, appearing cold and detached to others. They seem indifferent to praise or criticism, and evidence little interest in sex. Schizoid individuals seldom marry, but may be gainfully employed if they are allowed to work in isolated conditions. Although schizoid individuals appear quirky or odd to others, they are not psychotic. However, under acute stress they may experience brief, reactive psychotic episodes.

The following diagnostic criteria for Schizoid Personality Disorder are listed in the *DSM-IV* (at least four must be present):

- Neither desires nor enjoys close relationships, including being part of a family
- Almost always chooses solitary activities
- Has little, if any, interest in having sexual experiences with another person
- Takes pleasure in few, if any, activities
- Lacks close friends or confidants other than first-degree relatives
- Appears indifferent to praise or criticism from others
- Shows emotional coldness, detachment, or flattened affectivity

Individuals with SPD rarely refer themselves for treatment (Turkat, 1990). When they do come to the attention of mental health professionals, it is usually because their behavior is disturbing to others or because they have developed an Axis I disorder (Beck et al., 1990). As with Paranoid Personality Disorder, these characteristics create a formidable barrier to treatment. It is unlikely that therapy will be effective unless the individual is motivated to change (Liebowitz, Stone, & Turkat, 1986). For example, Beck and associates (1990) described the case of a schizoid man who acknowledged that he was a "misfit" and that he was capable of socially appropriate behavior, but had no desire to change. In such cases, there is little that therapists can or should do.

Based on their own case studies, Beck and associates (1990) have made several recommendations for conducting therapy with schizoid individuals. They caution that the therapist must not impose his or her own agenda on the client, and must postpone comments on the client's atypical social behavior until a sound working relationship is established. Initial goals usually focus on the client's presenting problems, which may include acute episodes of depression, anxiety, or psychosis. For example, Beck and colleagues (1990) described the cognitive-behavioral treatment of Jack, a 28-year-old schizoid man who referred himself for treatment of depression. Jack had no friends and expressed little desire for relationships with others. He had led a lifelong solitary existence, but had nonetheless managed to maintain steady employment. Initially, he was treated for depression using cognitive-behavioral techniques. Progress was slow, but his depression eventually remitted. Therapy shifted to a focus on social skills training and increasing Jack's level of social involvement. Eventually, he was able to ask a woman out on a date, but he felt little pleasure in the relationship. At this point, Jack chose to terminate therapy.

Schizoid individuals tend to show little understanding of appropriate interpersonal relationships. As Freeman and associates have commented, "It is as though the therapist were explaining human interactions to a Martian, newly arrived on our planet and completely naive about humans" (Freeman et al., 1990, p. 174). Typically, schizoid individuals are inexpressive, and the therapist must work hard to solicit feedback from them. It is difficult for therapists to maintain a warm, supportive demeanor vis-à-vis these clients because of their profound unresponsiveness. If these barriers can be surmounted, there are several possible targets for therapeutic change: improving the client's social skills, using structured exercises and feedback; helping the client to experience more frequent positive emotions; and attempting to change dysfunctional thoughts using reasoning. With difficulty, persistence, and some motivation on the part of the client, it is possible to improve the social skills of schizoid clients and to increase their rate of social interaction. However, profound changes are unlikely because schizoid individuals will continue to be socially aloof and show little capacity for warm, empathic relatedness (Beck et al., 1990; Freeman et al., 1990).

Schizotypal Personality Disorder

Of all the personality disorders, *Schizotypal Personality Disorder* is most severe in relation to the level and pervasiveness of cognitive, emotional, and behavioral impairment. Schizotypal individuals tend to show pervasive and long-standing problems with social skills, acute discomfort with interpersonal relationships, and cognitive, perceptual, and behavioral eccentricities. To meet *DSM-IV* criteria, at least five of the following characteristics must be present:

- Ideas of reference
- Odd beliefs or magical thinking
- Unusual perceptual experiences
- Odd thought and speech patterns
- Suspiciousness
- Inappropriate or constricted affect
- Odd, eccentric behavior
- Lack of friends or confidants
- Social anxiety that stems from paranoid fears

Although the diagnosis requires that these patterns must not exclusively occur during the course of schizophrenia, a major mood disorder, or pervasive developmental disorder, most schizotypal individuals seek treatment for Axis I disorders. The difference between schizophrenia and Schizotypal Personality Disorder appears to be a matter of degree (Freeman et al., 1990), as shown by the following case vignette:

> Mary, a 48-year-old single woman, was referred by a local social service agency. She appeared physically disheveled and she initially shrank from contact with the therapist. Mary had lived alone most of her life, eking out a marginal existence on the streets. She had drifted from different group homes to homeless shelters. The staff at the shelter was concerned because she seemed disabled by fear that others people could "read" her thoughts.

Literature on the behavioral treatment of schizotypal personality disorder is sparse. Turkat (1990) described the behavioral treatment of a schizotypal woman. He hypothesized that her schizotypal symptoms were generated by a lack of confidence in her own judgment skills; for example, she would consider many bizarre ideas because she lacked the ability to critically evaluate them. The client was taught observational and descriptive skills, such as how to distinguish between description and inference and how to test the validity of an idea. Once she achieved these skills, her schizotypal symptoms diminished markedly.

The bizarre thought patterns of Schizotypal individuals make cognitive therapy difficult. However, Beck and associates (1990) believe that schizotypal individuals often desire better social relationships. Treatment goals would be similar to those of working with schizophrenics: decreasing levels of anxiety and inappropriate social behavior and increasing adaptive social skills. Establishing a sound therapeutic relationship is the first step in treatment. Beck and associates (1990) recommend that therapists keep sessions highly structured and identify one small goal to be accomplished each time. The client's level of social responsiveness can be improved using social skills training, ideally carried out in a group therapy setting.

In line with Turkat's approach to treatment, clients can be encouraged to look for objective evidence in the environment to evaluate their thoughts. Bizarre thoughts can be labeled *symptoms,* and clients can be taught to discount them. Finally, because schizotypal individuals tend to be severely impaired, they may require assistance with the practical aspects of daily living: how to seek and maintain steady employment, stable housing, and a workable social network. Given the severity of the disorder, dramatic changes in the schizotypal individual's functioning are unlikely. With steady and patient guidance, however, schizotypal individuals can gradually improve their coping behavior and the quality of their social and vocational adjustment.

Cluster B Disorders

Individuals with Cluster B personality disorders manifest symptomatic behavior that is dramatic, erratic, and/or impulsive. They tend to have difficulties with emotional regulation, show little evidence of empathic concern for others, and have great difficulty maintaining stable, satisfactory interpersonal relationships.

Antisocial Personality Disorder

The central feature of *Antisocial Personality Disorder (ASPD)* is a pervasive, long-standing disregard for the rights of others. Individuals with ASPD lack remorse for hurting others, and tend to blame other persons or circumstances for their mistakes. They are impulsive and irresponsible, and appear to lack the ability or motivation to plan ahead. Antisocial individuals have poor frustration tolerance: When their immediate needs are thwarted, they are quick to respond with irritability or anger. ASPD tends to be a very long-standing disorder. Most individuals with this disorder evidence conduct problems before the age of 15, and many begin showing signs of the disorder in early childhood (McMahon, 1994).

Diagnostic criteria for Antisocial Personality Disorder include at least three of the following *(DSM-IV):*

- Failure to conform to social norms with respect to lawful behaviors
- Deceitfulness (e.g., repeated lying, use of aliases, conning others)
- Impulsivity or failure to plan ahead
- Irritability or aggressiveness
- Reckless disregard for the safety of self or others

- Consistent irresponsibility (e.g., failure to sustain consistent work or to honor financial obligations)
- Lack of remorse, as indicted by being indifferent to or rationalizing having hurt, mistreated, or stolen from another

Because they tend to blame others for their misfortunes, antisocial individuals rarely refer themselves for treatment. Rather, someone else has pressured them into change—employers, the courts, teachers, parents, or spouses. For example, Turkat (1994) described the case of a 31-year-old man who admitted himself to an inpatient unit. He told staff that he wanted to "get in touch with his feelings." Actually, it appeared that he was seeking refuge from jail, due to his illegal activities. The client had a 20-year history of cocaine abuse, and manufactured and sold street drugs. He admitted that he got into frequent street fights and that he engaged in extremely impulsive behavior (e.g., hopping a plane to the Carribean for lunch, even though he had insufficient funds to cover the trip). He had a long and extensive arrest record, dating from adolescence. When offered intensive inpatient treatment for his ASPD, he elected, instead, to discharge himself and face a lengthy prison term.

In his review of the antisocial personality disorders, Turkat (1990) proposed two primary target areas for behavioral intervention. First, the therapist could attempt *anger management training.* This could be accomplished by asking the client to generate a list of situations that made him or her extremely angry, pairing imaginal exposure to these situations with competing responses that reduce levels of arousal (e.g., pleasant imagery; relaxation). Second, the therapist could engage in *impulse control training.* After the client has generated a list of situations in which he or she is likely to behave impulsively, competing responses could be trained using systematic distraction. For example, distraction strategies might involve doing mental arithmetic or turning on loud music (Turkat, 1990).

Beck, Freeman, and their associates (Beck et al., 1990; Freeman et al., 1990) view cognitive therapy as a way of improving the moral and social adjustment of individuals with ASPD. Antisocial individuals act impulsively on the assumption that moral constraints do not apply to them, producing consequences that are self-defeating and harmful to others. They tend to overestimate likelihood of success and minimize negative consequences of their behavior. Engaging them in therapy is extremely difficult, however. Beck and Freeman suggest framing therapy in ways that are consistent with the client's self-interests. For example, ASPD clients could be told that cognitive therapy offers a way of evaluating situations that might be interfering with what *they* want.

Antisocial individuals typically deny personal responsibility for their behavior, but Beck and colleagues suggest that their symptoms can be "objectified" as a serious problem that has negative, long-term consequences for the individual. If a treatment contract is achieved, Beck and Freeman suggest training in constructive decision making: identifying situations with problems/tensions, reviewing options and evaluating advantages and disadvantages of various choices, and helping the client anticipate the interpersonal consequences of his or her actions. Finally, an open, nondefensive demeanor on the part of the therapist, combined with extensive use of guided discovery, minimizes resistance.

Beck and colleagues (1990) described the successful treatment of two different antisocial individuals. The first case involved a 34-year-old welder who voluntarily admitted himself to an inpatient unit for treatment of alcoholism and wife battering. His history of conduct problems began before age 15. As an adult, chronic patterns of aggression, irresponsibility, and violation of others' rights were evident. He received 18 sessions of therapy for violent behavior toward his family; alcohol treatment was concurrent. The client was asked to carefully analyze the types of family stresses that triggered his violent behavior—they were minor family stresses, such as hearing his children arguing, which he would personalize and immediately attribute to his wife's mismanagement. His anger toward his wife would build until he would explode in violence.

These "triggering" stresses were carefully examined in the light of the kinds of distorted interpretations he was making, and the pros and cons of different action choices. The client had a good response to therapy. He became less irritable and more friendly and positive with others. His family was able to remain together, and the incidents of battering did not recur.

The second case involved a 29-year-old man who was in trouble for chronic stealing. The client was described as handsome and charming. The therapist engaged him in discussions about the pros and cons of impulsive stealing. With careful guidance, he was able to think through options and potential consequences, and to realize that his impulsive behavior cost him too much in the long run. Consequently, he was able to generate and act on more constructive strategies.

Borderline Personality Disorder

Individuals with *Borderline Personality Disorder (BPD)* show marked problems in many different areas of functioning. They have unstable self–images and are often preoccupied with fears of being abandoned. These fears make it very difficult for them to maintain stable, close relationships. Consequently, long-standing difficulties with relationships are very common. Borderline individuals show emotional instability and dysregulation: inappropriate and intense anger, depression, anxiety, and suicidal threats and behavior are common reactions to stress. For example, Freeman and associates (1990) described the case of a young woman who was performing competently in an advanced training setting. At the end of each day, however, she would lapse into a severe depression and struggle with impulses to slash herself with broken glass. These impulses and feelings were so transient that her supervisor was unaware that she had serious emotional problems. Finally, the difficulties that borderline individuals have with self-regulation extend to impulse control, as well, in that clients with BPD often report evidenced by problems with impulsive spending, overeating, substance abuse, and reckless behavior.

Accurate diagnosis of BPD is difficult. There is no "prototypical" pattern of symptoms found in all borderline individuals, and BPD often coexists with other personality disorders and with many different Axis I disorders (Millon, 1981). To meet current diagnostic code *(DSM-IV),* at least five of the following characteristics must be present:

- Frantic efforts to avoid real or imagined abandonment
- A pattern of unstable and intense interpersonal relationships (client alternates between extremes of devaluation and overidealization)
- Identity disturbance: markedly and persistently unstable self-image

- Impulsivity in at least two areas that are potentially self-damaging (e.g., overspending, sex, substance abuse, reckless driving, binge eating)
- Recurrent suicidal behavior, gestures, or threats, or self-mutilating behavior
- Affective instability due to a marked reactivity of mood
- Chronic feelings of emptiness
- Inappropriate, intense anger or difficulty controlling anger
- Transient, stress-related paranoid ideation or severe dissociative symptoms

BPD has received far less attention in cognitive-behavioral literature than in psychodynamic writings. Recently, however, there have been several cognitive-behavioral formulations of BPD (Beck et al., 1990; Freeman et al., 1990; Linehan, 1993; Millon, 1981, 1987; Young & Swift, 1988). For example, Young (Young & Swift, 1988) developed a cognitive-behavioral approach to borderline personality disorder labeled *schema-focused cognitive therapy*. He hypothesized that stable, maladaptive patterns of thought can develop during childhood and foster behaviors that tend to reinforce them. Maladaptive cognitive schemas organized aroung issues such as abandonment/loss, mistrust of others, and unlovability are thus carried into adulthood, increasing the likelihood of borderline symptoms.

According to Turkat (1990; Turkat & Maisto, 1984), borderline individuals have a basic deficit in problem-solving ability. The nature of the problem-solving deficit varies from case to case. For example, some individuals are unable to see the "middle ground" in problem situations, others feel overwhelmed by intense anxiety or anger. Turkat (1990) outlined a behavioral treatment method whereby borderline individuals receive training in concept formation and problem solving. Based on individual case studies, these treatment strategies have been successful with even severely impaired borderline clients (Turkat, 1992).

Linehan (1993) has developed a behavioral treatment for borderline individuals called *dialectical behavior therapy (DBT)*. The DBT model evolved from her extensive clinical work with borderline women who had histories of suicidal behaviors. Linehan's model highlights emotional disregulation as the key feature of BPD. She has hypothesized that individuals at risk for BPD are born with an emotionally vulnerable temperament style that transacts with an adverse ("invalidating") family environment. The result is an individual who experiences chronically high arousal but lacks the capability to regulate it. Thus, sudden mood shifts, depression, anxiety, and overexpression or underexpression of anger are common features of the borderline emotional experience. Linehan has challenged the commonly held view that the predominant affect of BPD individuals is anger. Rather, she believes that much of the borderline individual's erratic behavior stems from feelings of panic or hopelessness. Moreover, these feelings are partly rooted in the extremely stressful life experiences that borderline individuals tend to report. According to Linehan, "Borderline individuals usually have good reasons for wanting to be dead" (1993, p. 125). A primary motive for their suicidal behavior is escape from pain.

Linehan has strongly emphasized the importance of taking time to establish a supportive working relationship with the borderline client, which she has called "creating a context of validation." Focusing too early on change recapitulates invalidating environment of the borderline individual's childhood experience. (The only possible exception to this is if the client enters therapy actively suicidal—then crisis intervention must be carried out). Steps in creating a "validating" therapeutic environment include active listening, reflection of feelings, and direct validation of the client's experience. These behaviors are intended to communicate to the client that his or her behavior makes sense in its current context. Ideally, active rapport building will facilitate the first critical step in therapy, agreeing on the goals of treatment.

Validation and problem-solving techniques are the core of DBT, and all other strategies are built around them (Linehan, 1993). Training in problem solving involves the standard elements of teaching the client to carefully describe the problem, helping him or her to generate, evaluate, and implement possible solutions; and helping the client to link problem-solving strategies with real-world outcomes. Other key interventions involve strengthening the client's social skills and helping him or her to increase behaviors that are related to a positive quality of life.

Linehan's DBT is one of the few cognitive-behavioral interventions for personality disorder that have been systematically evaluated. In a controlled outcome study, 24 women diagnosed as having BPD with suicidal tendencies were randomly assigned to receive DBT, and 23 were assigned to receive "treatment as usual" in their home communities. Treatment extended over a one-year interval. Results clearly favored the DBT intervention. During the course of therapy, women who received DBT interventions had fewer suicide attempts or ideation, lower dropout rates, and fewer hospitalizations than controls. At termination, they received higher ratings on global adjustment and perceived themelves as more competent in areas of emotional control and interpersonal problem solving than women who received alternative treatments. Finally, the superiority of DBT over standard treatment was maintained at an 18-month follow-up (Linehan, Heard, & Armstrong, 1994).

In contrast with the behaviorally focused models of Turkat and Linehan, Beck, Freeman, and their associates have proposed that the cognitive assumptions of borderline clients are primary targets for intervention. According to Beck and colleagues (1990), borderline individuals suffer from three mutually reinforcing problems. First, their basic cognitive assumptions about themselves and others ("I am unlovable", "I am unacceptable", and "The world is dangerous") are erroneous. Borderline individuals tend to view themselves as helpless in a threatening world, vacillating between autonomy and dependence. These assumptions lead to hypervigilance and guardedness, which in turn reinforce views of personal powerlessness and vulnerability. The second problem is that borderline individuals tend to engage in dichotomous thinking, in that they perceive situations and other people as either good or bad, black or white with no middle ground. Dichotomous thinking can lead to abrupt mood changes such as panic and dysphoria. Finally, borderline individuals have weak identities: In close relationships, it is difficult for them to separate their own feelings and experiences from those of others. These three problems create a self-reinforcing system that is resistant to change.

The first goal in cognitive therapy is to establish an effective working relationship with the borderline client. Borderline individuals present many difficulties for therapists: They tend to mistrust the therapist, are prone to dramatic mood shifts which may include angry outbursts, and often engage in impulsive self-destructive behavior. They have difficulty formulating clear goals and they fear and resist sudden change. Cognitive-behavioral therapists cannot work in their "customary" way with borderline clients—onducting business as usual could result in premature termination, and may even precipitate a severe emotional crisis (Freeman et al., 1990). Rather, therapists must take a collaborative, strategic approach based on guided discovery. For example, power struggles are diminished if the therapist allows the client to have an active role in formulating and setting treatment goals.

Noncompliance and impulsive behavior can be dealt with by acknowledging the client's power to resist and by exploring the pros and cons of different action strategies. Behavioral experiments are effective for testing the validity of the client's social interpretations, and for gradually increasing more adaptive social behaviors. All of these interventions tend to foster a progressive "chipping away" of maladaptive beliefs and behaviors over time.

Intense emotional reactions to the therapist must be dealt with immediately and directly, using a calm, methodical approach. Crises, emergency calls, and requests for special arrangements are especially prominent in initial sessions, and Freeman sees these as "tests" of caring. The therapist must set clear limits and consistently abide by them. Because borderline clients are so challenging to treat, Freeman and associates recommend that the therapist consult with unbiased colleagues for advice and for personal support. Finally, termination must be handled cautiously, because it may evoke fears of abandonment. Termination should be planned for at least three months in advance, with gradual tapering of sessions (Freeman et al., 1990).

A case example from Beck and colleagues (1990) illustrates successful cognitive therapy with a borderline client.

> Joan, a married woman in her mid-30s, referred herself for treatment because she had too little motivation for looking for work. She reported experiencing frequent panic attacks, depression, anger, and history of conflict with bosses. Joan believed that those in authority would mistreat her and that she was helpless against their power. She was always on alert for danger and harmful treatment from others, and suffered from poor self-esteem and a weak sense of identity. She procrastinated in her job hunt because of fear of ill treatment, and her procrastination fed back into her poor self-concept.
>
> Joan was seen weekly for five months. In therapy, she was quick to assume that the therapist was trying to manipulate her, but she couldn't express her feelings assertively, and so her anger would build. The therapist was alert for signs of anger (such as clenched fists, flushed face) and carefully analyzed situations in the session that seemed to elicit them. When explosive anger occurred, the therapist tried to clarify the situation immediately and even admitted making mistakes when appropriate. This contradicted the client's view of authority figures as all-powerful and malevolent.
>
> As trust in the therapy relationship grew, the therapist challenged Joan's view that trust in others was all or nothing. Her view of herself as helpless was challenged by reviewing evidence in her past performance that supported her competence. At termination, the client reported no problems with mood swings, anxiety, or depression. She had overcome her tendency to procrastinate and had found a good job. Joan's attitude

toward authority was far more flexible than at intake, and she reported feeling more comfortable in her marriage.

Histrionic Personality Disorder

The key feature of *Histrionic Personality Disorder (HPD)* is dramatic self-presentation. Individuals with HPD tend to behave and dress in ways that attract attention—for example, through self-dramatization, theatricality, and/or inappropriate sexually seductive or provocative behavior. Their style of speech and thinking is highly emotionally toned and impressionistic. Individuals with HPD often appear to be quite warm and charming, but these qualities tend to be superficial: Genuine empathic concern for others and deep expressions of feeling are lacking.

For example, Freeman and associates (1990) described a case of a 31-year-old woman with HPD. Her reasons for entering therapy were vague (e.g., getting her life together). She was a recovering alcoholic who also presented with symptoms of depression, anxiety, and social isolation. Her manner of dress was unconventional. During the session, her mood tended to fluctuate from one strong emotion to another, such as from anger to sadness to brightness. When describing others, she assumed their voices and mannerisms. Her speech style contained a lot of hyperbole. For example, she tended to repeat adjectives three or four times for emphasis and she cast her difficulties in the most dramatic light possible (e.g., by referring to the break-up of a romantic relationship as her "death").

DSM-IV criteria for diagnosis of HPD include the following characteristics (at least five or more must be present):

- Is uncomfortable in situations in which he or she is not the center of attention
- Displays inappropriate sexually seductive or provocative behavior to others
- Displays rapidly shifting and shallow expression of emotions
- Consistently uses physical appearance to draw attention to self
- Has a style of speech that is impressionistic and lacking in detail
- Shows self-dramatization, theatricality, and exaggerated exression of emotion
- Is suggestible—easily influenced by others or circumstances
- Considers relationships to be more intimate than they actually are

Little has been written about behavioral treatment of individuals with HPD. According to Brantley and Callon (1985), treatment should be based on an individual case formulation—standard social skills training would fail with histrionic clients. As a case in point, Turkat (1990) has reported mixed results using social skills and empathy training with HPD clients. For example, one 29-year-old woman was unable to comply with Turkat's recommendation of social skills training. She attended therapy only sporadically, and continually brought in new crises, each demanding immediate resolution (Turkat, 1992).

Cognitive formulations center on the histrionic individual's vague, impressionistic cognitive style (Beck et al., 1990; Freeman et al., 1990). This style of thinking reflects lack of cognitive integration, which makes the individual vulnerable to fears of rejection. Cognitive therapy is especially appropriate for HPD individuals because it offers a systematic way of improving one's thinking. Initially, however, there are barriers to therapy that must be surmounted before effective work can transpire. The systematic, logical approach inherent in cognitive therapy conflicts with the dramatic and unfocused style of the histrionic individual. Thus, it is necessary to help the client focus attention on one issue at a time. The therapist must strive to work collaboratively, using guided discovery, in order to surmount potential resistance.

Finally, as with borderline clients, histrionic clients often require clear and consistent limit setting. For example, Freeman and associates (1990) reported a case in which a 31-year-old client asked for a special fee. The therapist explained the fee structure and told her he would help her find a lower fee elsewhere if necessary. Accumulating a large bill, a characteristic pattern of the client in past therapy relationships was correctly seen as countertherapeutic. The therapist set the limit that if the client was two sessions behind in her fees, he would wait until she was caught up before resuming. This rule was tested once, and the therapist stood firm despite dramatic and tearful pleas for a session. Subsequently, the client behaved more adaptively.

Another barrier to treatment is that histrionic clients do not tend to stay in therapy long enough to make significant changes. Rather, they tend to lose interest and drop out early. Thus, a key therapeutic issue involves making certain that treatment goals are personally meaningful, and helping the client "operationize" them ("How would you know if you were a better _____?").

Finally, loss of stimulation and excitement can be threatening to the HPD client. The therapist can try to circumvent this by scheduling part of the session for dramatic retelling of traumatic events and the rest for working on treatment goals. In addition, the client can be encouraged to channel sensation seeking into constructive outlets such as drama or sports. If necessary, the therapist can schedule traumas weekly, in order to help the client confront them. This intervention involves asking the client to select a certian time of the day/week to "give in" to strong feelings (Freeman et al., 1990).

Once a good working relationship has been established, cognitive interventions can be pursued. Histrionic individuals tend to react emotionally, then feel out of control. Because of their vague and distractible cognitive style, histrionic clients need careful shaping to be able to monitor their automatic thoughts. Once clients have learned to identify their automatic thoughts, use of a thought sheet can help to interrupt panic reactions by cueing them to stop and explore problem-solving alternatives. Freeman and colleagues (1990) emphasize that it is important to focus on mental images as well as thoughts, because histrionic individuals tend to have vivid imaginations.

In addition to helping the histrionic client stop and think through problem situations, treatment goals often involve improving interpersonal relationships. Histrionic individuals tend to use emotional outbursts to manipulate interpersonal conflict situations. Assertiveness is often new to them and can be used to explore constructive ways of getting what they want (Beck et al., 1990).

The overall goal in cognitive therapy is to increase the client's sense of self-efficacy by setting up situations where he or she can achieve competence. With histrionic clients, progress toward this goal is slow and unsteady, requiring at least one to three years of weekly sessions. For example, Beck and colleagues (1990) described the treatment of one female client who was unable to work due to severe depression and agoraphobia. There was rapid, early remission of the most acute Axis I problems, but lasting changes in her HPD required three years of treatment. At termination, the client was asymptomatic and had made remarkable improvements in the quality of her psychosocial adjustment (Beck et al., 1990).

Narcissistic Personality Disorder

The central theme of *Narcissistic Personality Disorder (NPD)* is grandiosity. Individuals with NPD have strong needs for constant admiration. They show little capacity for empathy, often using others for self-motivated gains. Narcissistic individuals believe that they are entitled to special privileges. They may engage in compulsive striving for wealth or recognition but take little satisfaction in their acccomplishments. Narcissistic individuals usually seek treatment when they develop an Axis I disorder or when they experience serious problems with work or intimate relationships. Depression is a common reason for self-referral, because narcissistic individuals have low tolerance for discomfort. Narcissistic depression usually centers on the discrepancy between the client's grandiose desires and reality: Unmet expectations, especially the "shortcomings" of others, are common themes (Freeman et al., 1990). Substance abuse, particularly with "high-status" drugs such as cocaine, is common among narcissistic clients because it provides immediate relief from discomfort and a sense of power.

Current diagnostic criteria for Narcissistic Personality Disorder *(DSM-IV)* include five or more of the following characteristics:

- Grandiose sense of self-importance (exaggerates achievements, talents)
- Preoccupaton with fantasies of unlimited success, power, beauty
- Belief that self is special—can only be understood by others who are special
- Need for excessive admiration
- Sense of entitlement—unreasonable expectations of favorable treatment
- Socially exploitative (takes advantage of others to achieve own ends)
- Lacks empathy—unwilling to recognize/identify with feelings of others
- Envious
- Arrogant, haughty behavior and attitudes

As with other Cluster B disorders, accurate assessment of NPD is difficult. The narcissistic client may present with features of other personality disorders, especially the Histrionic, Antisocial, and Borderline disorders. The individual's behavioral presentation may offer some of the strongest clues to the disorder. Narcissistic clients tend to have a sense of personal entitlement in negotiating therapy relationships. Often, they appear hyperconcerned about their physical appearance as evidenced by meticulous attention to dress and grooming. Narcissistic clients respond poorly to feedback. They may assume a haughty stance toward the therapist, perhaps even demeaning or challenging the therapist's credentials. Conflicted intimate relationships are commonly reported.

Narcissistic individuals tend to have unrealistic expectations for their partners, and difficulties in their lives are typically blamed on the shortcomings of other people. They often show a strong commitment to work, but with the goal of achieving personal recognition, wealth, and/or power. Relationships with authority figures tend to be rocky, because narcissistic individuals resent being in subordinate positions.

For example, Beck and associates (1990) described the case of David, an attorney in his early forties who sought treatment for depression. The client presented as socially outgoing. He was meticulously groomed and frequently called the therapist's attention to the expensive quality of his clothing and possessions. David was the only son of a successful businessman. He described getting anything he wanted by provoking his parents to give in. He worked extremely hard in law school, motivated by fantasies of personal success and recognition. Divorced with one child, he blamed his ex-wife for not living up to his expectations; he rarely saw his child or paid support. At the time of referral, David's dysphoric moods were precipitated by interactions with co-workers and family who did not treat him with the deference he felt he deserved. He could not accept criticism from others and felt irritated with those who made requests of him.

Little has been written about the behavioral treatment of individuals with NPD. Turkat (1992) described the case of a 22-year-old woman who had experienced chronic difficulties getting along with others. She reported throwing frequent temper tantrums and appeared to be lacking in empathy for others. She reported playing a game with herself about picking up attractive men in bars. Her resulting long string of impulsive, unsatisfying sexual liasons was seen by the therapist as a problem with sensation seeking. Thus, the focus of therapy was on developing control over her impulses to engage in sensation seeking. The therapist observed that the client did not tend to generate guilt feelings on her own but was capable of experiencing guilt when the consequences of her behavior were pointed out. She was trained to self-induce guilt, using a graded hierarchy of situations involving sensation seeking. Following 36 sessions of treatment, the client was described as asymptomatic, happily married, and productively employed.

Beck, Freeman, and their associates (Beck et al., 1990; Freeman et al., 1990) have hypothesized that NPD reflects dysfunctional cognitive schemas that are rooted in early messages from significant others about the client's uniqueness and importance. As adults, narcissistic individuals continually scan the environment for signs of their superiority and tend to feel angry or dysphoric when social transactions fail to confirm their grandiose expectations.

It is necessary to pay careful attention to the developing therapy relationship. Achieving mutual agreement toward therapy objectives may be difficult with narcissistic clients, because they tend to challenge authority and may view therapy as a "competitive game." Beck and associates (1990) emphasize that confronting the client in the early stages of therapy is a sure path to failure. Rather, the therapist must work *with* narcissistic patterns. For example, Freeman et al. (1990) described the case of a 64-year-old surgeon whose wife had suffered a major depressive episode. The woman's depression was tied to feelings of helplessness vis-à-vis an overdemanding spouse, and marital therapy was strongly recommended. Her husband refused to participate, and when his refusal was challenged, he demeaned the therapist's credentials and status. His cooperation was ultimately achieved when treatment (focused on helping the man to respond differently to his wife) was reframed as a way of improving his ability to meet his own needs in the marital relationship.

Another potential barrier to treatment is that narcissistic clients often expect special privileges from their therapists. For example, Beck and associates (1990) described the case of a 42-year-old client who used empty office space in the therapist's suite to make personal phone calls and gave the therapist's secretary personal photocopying assignments. As with all clients in the Cluster B group, it is neccessary to set firm, consistent limits early in therapy and to consistently enforce them.

Once a satisfactory working relationship is achieved, cognitive interventions could be tailored to three major target areas (Freeman et al., 1990):

1. *Grandiosity.* Cognitive techniques could be used to adjust the client's distorted beliefs about self and others. Narcissistic clients tend to automatically compare themselves with others, using "all or nothing" thinking. Alternative beliefs may include self-statements such as "No one ever owes me anything in life"; "Other people have needs and opinions that matter"; and "I don't need constant attention from others to be happy."

2. *Hypersensitivity to evaluation.* Classic desensitization techniques could be used to help the client feel less anxious about receiving critical feedback from others. In the advanced stages of the hierarchy, the client could be instructed to ask directly for social feedback, beginning with the "safest" prospect and progressing to individuals who may be somewhat critical. In addition, narcissistic individuals can learn to be more discriminating in attention to evaluation, rather than compulsively focusing on any type of social feedback without regard for its importance.

3. *Empathy training.* During the final stages of treatment, the therapist can attempt to promote greater empathic responsiveness in the client. For example, in Beck and colleagues' (1990) treatment of David, whose symptoms were described earlier, the client's presenting complaints centered on problems with moodiness and on difficulties with work colleagues and with his spouse. David's automatic thoughts reflected classic narcissistic beliefs about his own importance. Shifting the focus of attention from himself to others helped to redirect him. Role-plays/reversals were useful in helping him to achieve this shift in consciousness, as were behavioral experiments ("Observe something unique about other people"). Taking the perspective of others was made personally meaningful by showing how the responsiveness and cooperation of others could be helpful to him.

Cluster C Disorders

Individuals with Cluster C disorders tend to suffer from pervasive problems with anxiety. Unlike the Anxiety Disorders described in Chapters 7 and 8, however, individuals with Cluster C personality disorders manifest additional, long-standing problems with self-schemas and interpersonal functioning that make these disorders quite challenging to treat.

Avoidant Personality Disorder

Individuals with *Avoidant Personality Disorder (APD)* tend to have long histories of extreme discomfort with others, fear of negative social evaluation, and social shyness. Avoidant individuals are very cautious about taking risks and are unlikely to become socially involved unless they are certain of being accepted. Avoidant individuals desire friends, yet typically have few. Their loneliness is maintained by intense fears of rejection and feelings of inferiority. Avoidant individuals are easily hurt and tend to greatly exaggerate risks to self-esteem involved in ordinary activities. They tend to be chronic worriers, ruminating about the possibility of negative social evaluation. For example, Freeman and associates (1990) described the case of a 29-year-old woman who self-referred for "fear of people." She had avoided most social relationships since adolescence, due to strong fears that no one would accept her. She was extremely self-critical and certain that if she trusted other people she would get hurt.

Criteria for the diagnosis of Avoidant Personality Disorder *(DSM-IV)* include the following characteristics (four or more must be present):

- Avoids occupational activities that involve significant interpersonal contact
- Unwilling to get socially involved unless certain of being liked
- Restrained in intimate relationships
- Preoccupied with social criticism
- Socially inhibited (fear mediated)
- Sees self as socially inept, inferior
- Reluctant to take risks or to engage in new activities

It is important to distinguish individuals with APD from those with social phobias, because avoidant individuals often seek treatment for Axis I disorders. Turner, Beidel, Danen, and Keys (1986) found that individuals with APD and social phobia could be reliably distinguished from one another. There were equal levels of anxiety between the groups, but those with APD had poorer social skills. Clients with APD require a longer period of therapy than those with social phobia, and much greater attention to building a trusting relationship with the therapist.

The sparse behavioral literature on treatment of APD has focused on anxiety management and social skills training (Turkat, 1990). Alden (1989) conducted a 10-week group treatment for individuals with APD. Clients were assigned to one of four groups: (1) graduated exposure to anxiety-provoking situations using progressive relaxation; (2) interpersonal skills training; (3) exposure and skills training plus additional emphasis on developing intimate relationships; and (4) no treatment. Clients in all three intervention groups fared better than controls, but the magnitude of improvement did not bring clients up to normative comparison levels. The fact that the treatment groups lasted only 10 weeks may account for the modest degree of positive change.

According to Freeman and Beck (Beck et al., 1990; Freeman et al., 1990), social skills training is not sufficient for avoidant individuals; cognitive interventions are also needed to challenge their dysfunctional beliefs. Avoidant clients tend to have automatic thoughts organized around themes such as "I am defective and unlikable." Their method of coping is to avoid threatening situations. Avoidant individuals have difficulty evaluating others' reactions—they may misread neutral social cues as evidence of rejection, and discount positive feedback. For example, Beck and colleagues (1990) described the case of Jane, a young client with APD who was raised by an abusive parent. Jane had internalized and generalized her mother's abusive treatment of her. As an adult, she still expected to be mistreated by all others. She was highly self-critical and tended to look for signs of disapproval in her social transactions. Because of her strong belief that she was unlikable, she had few friends. She was underemployed and too fearful to take steps to improve her position.

Because of their extreme discomfort with social evaluation, avoidant clients tend to distrust therapists and often terminate therapy prematurely. Trust builds slowly and with great difficulty. Initially, the client should be allowed to maintain a safe distance from therapist, due to his or her acute discomfort (Freeman et al., 1990). The client may test the therapist's propensity for rejection before deciding to open up. Avoidant clients should be encouraged to discuss their fearful thoughts about the therapist during their sessions.

Cognitive interventions are difficult because, by definition, avoidant clients tend to avoid thinking about things that cause negative emotion. The therapist can start by discussing situations that cause slight anxiety, then slowly build the client's tolerance for discomfort. Role-playing is useful, because avoidant clients have trouble identifying their negative thoughts. Finally, clients can be encouraged to develop a continuum of interpersonal trust, rather than viewing trust as an "all or none" phenomenon.

If the avoidant client has skills deficits, social skills training must be part of therapy: Training should be focused on reducing levels of social anxiety, increasing the client's ability to "read" nonverbal cues, and on helping the client develop skills in areas such as conversational methods, assertiveness, sexuality, and conflict management (Beck et al., 1990). It may be helpful to instruct the client to act as if he or she had had a certain quality, such as social confidence. Although very anxiety provoking for the client, moving the client to group therapy after a period of individual work offers a safe environment for practicing new skills. It also helps facilitate the transition from individual therapy to termination.

Finally, *relapse prevention* should be part of the final stages of therapy, because avoidant clients can easily become symptomatic again (Freeman et al., 1990). The frequency of sessions should be "faded" well before termination, to allow the client time to engage in new experiences. Following the relapse prevention model, difficulties in the period following termination should be predicted and prepared for. With careful attention to rapport building and with patient guidance, avoidant clients can make considerable gains in therapy (Beck et al., 1990; Freeman et al., 1990).

Dependent Personality Disorder

Individuals with *Dependent Personality Disorder (DPD)* have difficulty making everyday decisions without advice and reassurance from others. They tend to feel uncomfortable when they are alone, and often report intense fears of being abandoned by significant others. Depression, anxiety, somatic concerns, and substance abuse are common co-occurring problems (American Psychiatric Association, 1994; Turkat, 1992).

The following are diagnostic criteria for Dependent Personality Disorder *(DSM-IV;* at least five characteristics must be present):

- Difficulty making everyday decisions without a lot of reassurance from others
- Needs others to take responsibility for most major areas of life
- Difficulty expressing disagreement with others—fear of loss of support
- Difficulty initiating things on own
- Excessive in seeking nurturance and support
- Feels helpless when alone
- When close relationships end, urgently seeks another
- Is unrealistically preoccupied with fears of being left to care for self

There is very little literature on the behavioral treatment of individuals with DPD. Turkat has reported success using anxiety management procedures with dependent individuals (Turkat, 1992; Turkat & Carlson, 1984). For example, Turkat (1992) described the treatment of a 29-year-old woman whose anxiety and depression were precipitated by recent interpersonal losses (death of her grandmother; relocation of her sister). Although there was no evidence to support her fear, the client engaged in chronic anxious rumination that her boyfriend would leave her. She was treated with behavioral anxiety management procedures based on a graded hierarchy of situations involving emotional abandonment. The successful treatment required 29 sessions, and no relapses were reported over a 5-year period.

Beck, Freeman, and their associates (Beck et al., 1990; Freeman et al., 1990) have focused on the types of cognitive assumptions that dependent clients make about themselves and the world. According to these authors, dependent clients have two basic assumptions: They view themselves as helpless and inadequate and they view the world as dangerous and unpredictable. Thus, they subordinate their needs to those of someone who will take care of them. The idea of being competent and autonomous is frightening, because it implies potential loss of significant relationships. Dependent individuals commonly fear that competence will lead to abandonment.

The dependent individual's symptomatic behavior is pervasive enough to be manifest in therapy. Early on, the client should be allowed to engage in some dependent behavior, although the therapist should not be tempted to "take over" (Beck et al., 1990). Working toward goal setting is a major issue—the therapist should gradually shape more autonomy in agenda setting using guided discovery and socratic questioning.

A structured, collaborative approach can be used to help dependent clients build confidence in autonomy. Gradually, they can be encouraged to take more active roles in dealing with problem situations. As therapy progresses, progress toward goals can be used as evidence of the client's competence (Beck et al., 1990). In addition, dichotomous views of one's own competence can be challenged by setting up behavioral experiments. For example, Beck and associates (1990) reported the treatment of a married woman who was convinced that her husband would react negatively to her assertion. As part of an experiment, she tried asking for more support and received a positive response. However, it cannot be assumed that significant others will always support the client's attempts to change. Marital or family therapy may be required as an adjunct to individual treatment.

Naturally, termination is an extremely threatening issue for dependent clients. Termination should be prepared for well in advance by moving the client from individual therapy to a group setting, by "fading" the frequency of therapy sessions, and by offering booster sessions as needed (Freeman et al., 1990).

Obsessive-Compulsive Personality Disorder

Individuals with *Obsessive-Compulsive Personality Disorder (OCPD)* tend to be rigidly overconcerned with orderliness, perfectionism, and control. They are preoccupied with making the "right" decisions and tend to lose sight of their original goals in anxious rumination about details and nuances. Consequently, and ironically, they may have considerable difficulties with work productivity. Interpersonal relationships also tend to be difficult, because individuals with OCPD experience discomfort with intimacy. Problems with procrastination and chronic anxiety often motivate OCPD clients to seek therapy (Turkat, 1992).

Diagnostic criteria for Obsessive-Compulsive Personality Disorder are as follows (*DSM-IV*; at least four must be present):

- Preoccupation with rules, details, lists, organization, schedules such that point of major activity is lost
- Perfectionism interferes with task completion
- Excessively devoted to work and productivity, to exclusion of leisure and friendships
- Overconscientious, inflexible regarding morality, values
- Unable to discard worn-out objects, even those with no sentimental value
- Reluctant to delegate
- Miserly spending style toward self and others—hoards money for future "catastrophes"
- Rigid and stubborn

It is important to distinguish OCPD from Obsessive-Compulsive Disorder (OCD). Individuals with OCPD do not tend to experience true obsessions and compulsions. Indeed, they consider their compulsive thinking and behavior adaptive, because they believe that it facilitates productivity and goal orientation. In contrast, individuals with OCD *cannot* control their obsessive-compulsive rituals, and experience them as intrusive and noxious (American Psychiatric Association, 1994).

Little has been written about behavioral intervention with clients who experience OCPD. Turkat (1992) has found behavioral anxiety management training to be productive with some OCPD clients. For example, Turkat (1992) treated a 59-year-old woman who suffered from chronic, stress-related vomiting. He found that the vomiting was secondary to her intense fear of being out of control. Behavioral anxiety management training was used to treat her fear of loss of control. Following three months of treatment, the client was asymptomatic in all domains.

It may seem counterintuitive that cognitive therapy would be helpful with individuals who "think too much," but Beck, Freeman, and their associates (Beck et al., 1990; Freeman et al., 1990) have made a strong case for the efficacy of cognitive therapy with OCPD clients. Because clients with OCPD are overwhelmed by multiple tasks and "should" messages, their thought patterns are disorganized and lacking in internal structure. The content of obsessive individuals' thoughts is often irrational, reflecting their strong tendencies to engage in dichotomous thinking. For example, typical self-statements of OCPD individuals include:

- "This must be done perfectly";
- "I must avoid mistakes to be acceptable";
- "To make a mistake equals failure, and failure is intolerable"; and
- "It is dangerous to lose control" (Beck et al., 1990).

One potential barrier to treatment is the strong desire of OCPD individuals to avoid mistakes. Clear goals must be set early in therapy, and the difficulty that OCPD clients may experience over goal setting provides an initial window into their self-defeating thought patterns. Rapport building is difficult because obsessives are socially rigid and uncomfortable. According to Freeman and colleagues (1990), therapy should be business-like and problem focused. Helping OCPD clients engage in agenda setting, prioritizing, and focusing on one topic at a time tends to reduce their anxious rumination and indecisiveness.

Real-life problems can be dealt with using problem-solving techniques such as analyzing the situation in detail, considering the pros and cons of different action choices, and trying out the most promising solution. Because symptoms of anxiety and depression tend to co-occur with OCPD, it is necessary to help the client manage them. Training in relaxation or meditation may be helpful. To counter chronic worrying and rumination, the therapist might instruct the client to ruminate for a designated period of time and note the results, or provide a certain time of each day (week) for rumination. Activity scheduling could be used to elevate the client's mood and to decrease procrastination. Finally, behavioral experiments may help the client dispute certain dysfunctional beliefs.

Beck and colleagues (1990) decribed the successful cognitive treatment of a 45-year-old engineer. His presenting complaints centered on concerns about severe, stress-related muscle pain in his back, neck, and shoulders. From childhood, the client reported experiencing chronic anxiety over not living up to the expectations of others, particularly those of his hypercritical mother. Although he was married, he reported feeling uncomfortable with intimacy, and had no close friends. In therapy, he was asked to monitor his experience of pain using an activity schedule. He was able to pinpoint stresses that were associated with increased pain: having tasks to do and coping with novel social situations. His increased tension in relation to assigned tasks reflected extreme perfectionistic standards. Even in mundane situations such as doing the dishes, he worried that his ability to carry out the task was unacceptable.

Through the use of "guided discovery," the client came to understand that he had internalized his mother's unrealistic expectations and unsupportive attitude. He gathered evidence to support an alternative belief that he was able to perform tasks competently. For example, he conducted behavioral experiments such as asking directly for evaluative feedback. He found that his procrastination had caused most of the problems, not inadaquate performance of the task *per se*. The client also spent some time working on decreasing his social anxiety—this, too, was connected to his fears of being unacceptable. The therapy required 15 sessions. At termination, the client reported experiencing much less muscle pain. Six months later, he was pain free. Furthermore, he had spontaneously generalized his coping skills to new situations (such as making a public speech).

Chapter Summary

Treatment of individuals with personality disorders represents one of the newest frontiers for cognitive–behavioral therapists. Long the province of psychoanalytically oriented theorists and practitioners, cognitive-behavioral models of the development and treatment of personality disorders have proliferated during the past decade.

Personality disorders are defined by long-standing patterns of maladaptive cognition, emotional regulation, and behavior. In the current version of the *DSM (DSM-IV)*, there are 10 different personality disorders, grouped into three categories. All personality disorders share several features that make them special challenges in treatment. Most individuals with personality disorders tend to refer themselves for treatment of coexisting Axis I disorders and/or problems getting along with significant others, not treatment of their personality disorder. Because of their unwillingness to change such long-standing aspects of their behavior and experience, it is very difficult to engage individuals with personality disorders in treatment.

Short-term, goal-oriented behavioral techniques are inappropriate for this population. Generally, establishing rapport with personality-disordered clients is a lengthier process than with other clients, often requiring special strategies keyed to the features of the particualr disorder. Likewise, cognitive-behavioral treatment of personality disorders usually requires between one to three years of treatment that is "tailored" to the features of the disorder. The literature on cognitive-behavioral treatment of personality disorders is relatively sparse and is based primarily on uncontrolled case studies. However, this emerging body of work is thoughtful and encouraging, in that most forms of personality disorder are amenable to cognitive-behavioral treatment. There is a great need for further development of cognitive-behavioral methods for these disorders and, especially, for controlled studies comparing the efficacy of different types of cognitive-behavior interventions with individuals who share the same disorders.

Chapter *11*

Behavioral Couples Therapy and Treatment of Sexual Dysfunctions

The scene is a therapist's office in a community mental health center in a mill town in New England. The cast of characters comprises two therapists (a man and a woman) and two clients (a man and a woman, a married couple). The story so far is that Jay and Essie Fawley have become extremely dissatisfied with their relationship and have recently considered divorce as a solution. However, they thought they would give counseling a try first, so they made an appointment by telephone. The scene begins with a somewhat tense silence as clients and therapists wait for someone to begin. Pam, one of the therapists, leans forward and smiles at the Fawleys.

"We understand from what you said on the phone that you have been having problems in your relationship," she begins. "Would you like to tell us more about it?"

Jay Fawley looks at his wife, then says to Pam, "Well, I'll tell you, if she won't. She had this affair, see, with a guy at work--we both work at the mill--and she says it's all over, but she still talks to him!"

"How am I supposed to work in the same place without talking to the people I work with?" responds Ms. Fawley. "You're so jealous all the time, it's no wonder I had a little fling. If you would show some trust and stop spying on me all the time maybe I wouldn't need to find other people to talk to."

"How am I supposed to trust you when you go off and have an affair? Why should I believe you when you say it's all over? You didn't tell me the truth the first time, so why should I believe you now?"

"See what he's like?" Ms. Fawley looks toward the male therapist for sympathy. "Just because of one mistake, I'm going to have to listen to his interrogations all day,

256

every day. It's all we ever talk about. If I'm five minutes late from something, he thinks I've been with him [the other guy]. If that's what our marriage is going to be like, we might as well divorce."

"So I'm supposed to trust you without question, after you made a fool of me in front of all my buddies — everyone at the mill knows all about it — and not only that, but you go on seeing him, going off to lunch with all the office people, smiling at him, and dressed to kill all the time. Anyway, can you people get her to understand my point of view, or are we just wasting our time?"

The therapists could tell immediately that working with the Fawleys was likely to present a challenge, but this opening was not too bad a start. The clients had rapidly let the therapists know about at least one important issue concerning their relationship, and they had each conveyed something of their attitudes toward their situation and their expectations of each other. They had also given brief descriptions of some of the behavior each observed in the other and disliked (he spied on her and "interrogated" her, she spent time with the other man and was "dressed to kill"). In addition, there were several indications of the mixed feelings each partner had about the situation. Essie had first justified her "fling," then referred to it as a "mistake," suggesting some ambivalence; and Jay did not make it quite clear whether he was more upset at being embarrassed before his buddies or jealous of the other man. The therapists, a social worker and a psychologist, were both behavior therapists, and they negotiated a treatment plan with the Fawleys based on behavioral couples therapy. We shall return to this clinical illustration later.

Behavior therapists are mental health professionals—clinical and counseling psychologists, psychiatrists, social workers, and others—and of necessity they deal with a variety of problems, not all of them major psychiatric disorders. Clients often present problems with their intimate relationships as the chief clinical issue. In the first section of this chapter, we will describe behavioral assessment and therapy for troubled relationships. In the second section we shall outline behavioral interventions for a representative sample of disorders of sexual functioning.

Behavioral Couples Therapy

Some 90 percent of Americans enter into that legally recognized, long–term, sexually exclusive intimate male/female relationship known as marriage at some point in their lives (Epstein, Evans, & Evans, 1994). Other adult relationships include cohabiting male/ female couples, gay male couples, and lesbian couples. In some jurisdictions, gay and lesbian marriages are legally recognized, but it is more common for such relationships not to be sanctioned by the general community (Balaguer & Markman, 1994). All of these intimate relationships understandably tend to assume central importance in each partner's life, and it is clear that each partner is a significant part of the other's environment. Dissatisfaction with one's relationship with an exclusive partner may therefore cause considerable distress, and when dissatisfaction arises, one or both partners may seek professional help to improve the troubled relationship. *Behavioral couples therapy* is the term for the combination of treatment interventions behavior therapists employ when working with distressed couples (Waltz & Jacobson, 1994). Because so many intimate relationships are heterosexual marriages, they have been the focus of most behavior therapy research to date. But behavioral couples therapy is just as applicable, of course, to any distressed relationship.

About half the marriages contracted in the United States in the 1970s can be expected to end in divorce (Block, Block, & Gjerde, 1988; Epstein et al., 1994). If divorce and single-parent families are now commonplace, why do clients seek help for their troubled relationships, and how do therapists justify the time spent trying to help them? A review of the statistics on divorce suggest that its effects are often "devastating" (Stuart, 1980, p. 8). Divorced people die younger than married people, and are more likely to commit suicide or to die from coronary disease, certain cancers, and automobile accidents. Couples who eventually divorce tend to be unsupportive parents to their children for years beforehand, and children are more likely to display various problems when parents function poorly or their relationship is distressed (Block et al., 1988; Sanders & Dadds, 1993; Stuart, 1980).

These statistics are drawn from correlational studies, and there are limits to the conclusions one can make. It is possible that people who are already prone to develop cancer or to drive recklessly may be the ones who get involved in shaky marriages for some reason. Similarly, it is always possible that problem children put a strain on marriages, thereby causing the marital distress, and not the other way around (Franks, 1987). Whether or not divorce causes all these problems, most therapists conclude that it is worthwhile to try to help couples stay together, provided that each partner has at least some commitment to the relationship. A large majority of adults, even those who have been divorced more than once, agree; 90 percent view marriage as a desirable condition (Epstein et al., 1994; Stuart, 1980). Couples therapy is especially justified when sexual difficulties are present, because general problems in the relationship need to be addressed first to develop an adequate level of trust (Jehu, 1984; Stuart, 1980).

Development of Behavioral Couples Therapy

The first reports of behavior therapy for relationship problems were narrowly focused on changing behavior in one partner. For example, Goldiamond (1965) used stimulus control procedures to help a husband reduce his troublesome thoughts about his wife's infidelity. The relationship as such was not the target of treatment. However, the precise application of learning principles to problems in relationships was an important innovation at the time (Weiss & Wieder, 1982).

The second stage in the development of behavioral couples therapy involved two trends. First, the operant learning-based approaches used to manage problem child behavior in the home were extended to help troubled couples. Second, learning principles were combined with procedures from family therapy (Alexander & Barton, 1976). The experimental literature on treatment outcome, however, was devoted largely to studies of communication training, problem solving, and contingency contracting (Bennun, 1987). Although the techniques were often effective, coherent theoretical guidelines were lacking because behavioral couples therapy was a loose federation of operant learning, social exchange, and systems theory concepts (Weiss & Wieder, 1982).

In 1976, behavioral couples therapy entered a third phase (Weiss & Wieder, 1982) characterized by an emphasis on communication training and on cognitive restructuring procedures (Jacobson & Margolin, 1979; Margolin & Weiss, 1978). Treatment became more holistic, addressing a broad range of issues and employing an array of treatment techniques. The importance of the cognitive element of attributional change was stressed (Dattilio & Padesky, 1990; Jacobson & Margolin, 1979). Previously neglected by behavior therapists, the couple's relationship itself became more of a focus.

A fourth phase was marked by the introduction of an integrative approach by Neil Jacobson and his colleagues that incorporates strategies to promote "acceptance of partner" (Jacobson, 1992). The intent is to balance acceptance with the traditional goal of behavior change. Rather than simply prescribing the form of communication training producing the best average outcomes in group studies, therapists base their interventions on a unique functional analysis, or behavioral assessment, of the particular couple's communication patterns. Each partner is encouraged to tolerate negative behavior in the other, and to develop greater self–care so as to become less dependent on the other. Although the idea of acceptance is not new, this model is innovative in integrating the goals of change and acceptance: "As we discovered in our work with couples, whether we like it or not, many people cannot be helped unless they can be taught to accept and embrace those parts of themselves that cannot be changed" (Jacobson, 1992, p. 505).

Theoretical Origins of Behavioral Couples Therapy

The various psychological theories underlying mental health interventions can be divided into four groups: psychoanalysis, trait theory, situationalism, and interactionalism (Stuart, 1980). *Psychoanalysis* was discussed in Chapter 1 as the view that human behavior is largely determined by the obscure machinations of a dynamic unconscious. *Trait theory* involves discovering enduring personality characteristics by using statistical methods to group behavior ratings or questionnaire responses into meaningful clusters. *Situationalism* means explaining behavior by examining the person's prior experience in the given situation, assuming that what the person does depends on what behavior was reinforced or punished previously in the same context. *Interactionalism* is the view that behavior, the environment, and the person's cognitive appraisal of them interact to produce psychological functioning (Bandura, 1986, 1994). Situationalism and interactionalism are most consistent with behavioral couples therapy. Situationalism, consistent with operant learning approaches, is the concept behind the techniques of behavioral contracting, stimulus control, and behavior exchange. Interactionalism is consonant with social learning theory, and underlies the procedures that emphasize communication, reattribution, and problem solving.

Stuart (1980) pointed out the key differences between traditional psychoanalytic therapy and behavior therapy as applied to relationship problems. As a psychoanalytic trainee he was taught that because everyone is different, therapists have to spend a great deal of time thoroughly understanding each client's uniqueness before therapy can begin. Further, because clients have sole access to the inner knowledge essential to remedying their problems, therapists were advised to give the client the central role in the treatment. It was assumed that, because people contain within themselves the materials necessary for improvement, clients gain more from the right kind of relationship with a therapist than from specific behavior change techniques.

Rejecting these assumptions, Stuart (1980) developed an alternative approach. Acknowledging that clients understand their situation well, he pointed out that they are not necessarily experts on how to *solve* their problems. He wrote, "We are more alike than different, and . . . the process of relieving marital distress is generic, so that treatment can be offered as an action program, with significant change being accomplished in the very first session" (Stuart, 1980, p. xii).

Rejecting unconscious motivation does not mean that behavior therapists are naive about their clients' attitudes toward therapy. Behavior therapists recognize, for example, that a client may enter therapy not with a view to learning how to make positive changes for the sake of the relationship, but rather with the aim of earning some sort of Certificate of Mental Health from the therapist. Consider the Fawleys, introduced at the start of this chapter. In the first few minutes of their first therapy session, Jay and Essie each indicated clearly that they were not particularly interested in being confronted with their *own* contributions to the problem. "See what he's like?" said Essie. "Can you people get her to understand my point of view?" asked Jay.

While it is clear that clients sometimes have hidden (and not-so-hidden) agendas, traditional therapists' attempts to delve into clients' "real" issues often seem undisciplined and haphazard. Behavior therapists have provided an alternative by bringing to couples therapy the methodological rigor of operant learning (Stuart, 1980). It is not inconsistent for behavior therapists to develop structured treatments for their clients' presented problems while remaining aware of the "process issues within the system" (Bennun, 1987, p. 4).

In the 1960s, it was popular to refer to marriage counseling as "a technique without a theory" (Gurman, 1980). Even so, few distinctive treatment procedures were available. The growth of family therapy and behavior therapy were important in the development of marital therapy because they encouraged the essential notion that what goes on *between* people is as important for therapy as what goes on *within* them (Gurman, 1980). In dealing with interactions among people, theorists have found several versions of interactionalism helpful. These include systems theory and social exchange theory.

Systems Theory

An intimate relationship may be seen as a network of interacting forces that maintain a certain equilibrium. Homeostasis, achieved by a set of self-regulatory mechanisms, can preserve the balance in a marriage just as a thermostat can regulate a home heating system. A husband may accept his wife's returning home from work late, provided that she tolerates his casual attitude toward household chores, for example. A change in one component of the system is likely to affect another component. If the wife begins to complain vigorously about her husband's untidiness at every opportunity, it is likely that this will have an effect on his behavior. He could counterattack by criticizing his wife's tardiness, or he could comply with her request for him to change his ways.

Whatever he does will reflect the operation of forces that preserve equilibrium. He may do nothing for fear that his wife might escalate the level of unpleasantness, for example (Stuart, 1980).

Assortative mating is one way to maintain equilibrium in a marital relationship (Hafner, 1977). A couple displaying this pattern have chosen each other as marital partners because each sees the other as having a similar level of mental health. A woman with an anxiety disorder, for example, marries a man who is prone to depression, because having a husband without problems might throw the spotlight on her difficulties, and she would suffer from the comparison. He, in turn, chooses her as a mate for similar reasons; her anxiety gives him a useful role as a trusted companion, deflecting attention from his own issues. A system like this would be thrown into imbalance if one of the partners received successful therapy. A systems theorist would predict that, if a therapist treated the wife's anxiety without making allowance for the equilibrium of the system, another problem would emerge somewhere else. The husband could enter a severe depressive episode—one that would improve only when the wife relapsed—or he could subtly (or not so subtly) resist his wife's improvement and become uncooperative when she requests his support.

Alternatively, successful treatment of the husband's depression could affect the system. If the husband were no longer troubled by depression and its consequences, the wife's difficulties could come to the fore as a problem for the marriage. She might be under pressure to solve her problems, too, because the husband may now wish to spend more time on outside activities with his renewed interest in life. The increased pressure could worsen the wife's anxiety, or she could protect herself from the unfavorable comparison by increasing his depression in some way.

Many behavior therapists reject systems theory and assortative mating concepts because of a lack of empirical support (Emmelkamp & Gerlsma, 1994), but anecdotal examples can be found in agoraphobia research (Cavallaro, 1987). A participant in one of our studies was a married woman whose severe agoraphobia kept her housebound. The therapists made a home visit to begin the evaluation and initiate treatment. The client's husband had chosen not to be involved in the session, but he hovered in the background, sometimes interjecting comments. The client was able to whisper to the therapists that her husband was a recovering alcoholic who did not want her leaving the house without him. He was afraid that she would leave him for another man. She felt obliged to stay in the relationship, because she feared that he would start drinking again if she left him. Yet, she had decided to make a determined effort to overcome her agoraphobia so as to have more personal autonomy.

When the therapists presented the rationale for behavioral treatment to the client, the husband intervened, telling the therapists not to "upset her" by suggesting that she take on unreasonable challenges. The client said she did not view these as such, but the husband persisted, eventually asking the therapists to leave against the wishes of the client. Future attempts to contact the client were all unsuccessful, because the husband intercepted his wife's mail and telephone calls and told the therapists she did not wish to hear from them. It was evident that he liked the situation just the way it was, having an agoraphobic wife who was, of necessity, dependent on him.

Social Exchange Theory

Behavioral couples therapy owes a great deal to *social exchange theory* (Kelley & Thibaut, 1978; Thibaut & Kelley, 1959). Thibaut and Kelley's (1959) original book was intended as a comprehensive text on small group behavior, not as the presentation of a coherent theory. The authors called attention to the complexity of social interaction, recognized by social psychologists since the early 1900s. Social interaction is a reciprocal phenomenon in which each person involved presents stimuli to the other and responds to stimuli from the other. "Each subject's behavior is at the same time a response to a past behavior of the other and a stimulus to the future behavior of the other" (Thibaut & Kelley, 1959, p. 2). For this reason, it is difficult to study social interactions experimentally.

In analyzing social interaction and its consequences, Thibaut and Kelley (1959) focused on the results of particular encounters in dyads (groups of two people). They began by describing the interdependency of two people as each tries to obtain the most satisfaction from the relationship. The consequences for a member of a dyad can be divided into *rewards* and *costs*. Some relationships are more satisfying than others, and the same is true for interactions within a relationship. Consistent with learning principles, it is expected that more satisfying interactions will be repeated, while less satisfying ones will be avoided. The results of an interaction can be described in terms of the rewards and costs for each person involved. If the costs exceed the rewards, it seems likely that the person will leave the relationship or seek to end the particular interaction. But whether the person leaves or not depends on the *comparison level,* which refers to (1) the standard the person uses to assess how satisfactory the relationship is and (2) the standard the person uses in deciding whether to remain in a relationship.

Take the example of Jay and Essie Fawley, the distressed couple introduced earlier. For Essie, the rewards in the relationship include the availability of a faithful husband who seems to adore her despite her peccadillos. The costs include Jay's jealousy, his persistent questioning about her relationships with her co-workers, and his efforts to restrict her social life. For Jay, the rewards include being married to an attractive person whom he loves, and the costs are the feelings of shame and rejection he suffers as a result of Essie's infidelity. For each partner, the rewards and costs seem equally balanced, because the Fawleys were vacillating between seeing a divorce attorney or a couples therapist.

At this point, the concept of comparison level becomes relevant. Essie may still choose to continue the marriage even if her interactions with Jay lead to more costs than rewards. She has to consider the expected costs and rewards of the *alternatives*. Obtaining a divorce has its own costs, financial and emotional, which might even be worse than the costs of interacting with Jay every day. Whether the relationship is maintained or not depends on the "*jointly* experienced outcomes [being] above each member's CLalt [comparison level for alternatives]" (Thibaut & Kelley, 1959, p. 23).

> *Perhaps it seems overly cynical, placing too much emphasis on the short-term bargaining or trading nature of some of these relationships . . . the point should be made, however, that whatever the gratifications achieved in dyads, however lofty or fine the motives satisfied may be, the relationship may be viewed as a trading or bargaining one. (Thibaut & Kelley, 1959, p. 37)*

The rewards that can be derived from relationships can be based on similarities or differences in the partners. Participants in a study of adolescent friendships displayed both patterns. One pair of friends said they liked each other because they both prefer to be rowdy and to have a noisy environment. Another pair had a friendship based on opposites. A chose B because B was energetic, breezy, and dramatic, so that her self-confidence spilled over on to A. At the same time, B preferred A because A was quiet and shy and confided in her, treating her like an older sister. The authors concluded that "for a dyadic relationship to be viable it must provide rewards and/or economies in costs which compare favorably with those in other competing relationships or activities available to the two individuals" (Thibaut & Kelley, 1959, p. 49).

Research supports the prediction of social exchange theorists that relationships involving *reciprocity* will be relatively harmonious (Epstein et al., 1994; Waltz & Jacobson, 1994). That is, partners in stable relationships do what they do because of the rewards they expect to obtain from each other, and therefore exchange positive reinforcement at a high rate. Distressed relationships, by contrast, are typified by low rates of positive exchange (Epstein et al., 1994; Weiss & Wieder, 1982). Reciprocity is contrasted with *coercion,* which, like low rates of exchange of positive reinforcement, is associated with marital distress. Coercion involves negative exchange, or the use of aversive stimuli such as nagging and threats, in an attempt to gain positive outcomes from the other party (Waltz & Jacobson, 1994).

The person whose behavior is controlled by coercion is also controlling the coercing partner. For example, the wife's nagging may stop the husband's excessive drinking, at least when he is in her company. His compliance reinforces her nagging. At the same time, her suspension of nagging reinforces his compliance. An illustration of this is given by Patterson (1969): "Listen to Aunt Maud's complaints about her wayward bowels and you avoid the hurt silence which will follow if you neglect to do so. In such a situation, behaviors of both the "deviant" individual and [the] audience-responder are being mutually maintained" (p. 365). Combined with operant learning principles, systems theory and social exchange theory were important influences on the conceptual development of behavioral couples therapy.

Assessment of Troubled Relationships

Identifying the characteristics that differentiate between distressed and nondistressed couples has helped researchers develop suitable measures of relationship distress (Waltz & Jacobson, 1994). These measures have the potential for identifying troubled relationships and evaluating the effectiveness of treatment. We assume that encouraging distressed couples to behave more like nondistressed couples would be therapeutic in helping them to resolve their problems.

Two studies by Jacobson, Waldron, and Moore (1980) revealed several systematic differences between distressed and nondistressed couples. All participants' daily ratings of satisfaction were influenced by the partner's behavior, but distressed and nondistressed couples differed in the *type* of behavior in the partner that made for satisfaction. In happily married couples, pleasing behavior on the part of the spouse was clearly associated with satisfaction. In the distressed couples, it was the absence of displeasing behavior that led to greater happiness. The difference in behavioral exchanges between distressed and nondistressed couples was not simply in the amount of pleasing behavior, it was in the type of reinforcement that was effective. Nondistressed spouses responded with pleasure to rewarding behavior, but were not particularly troubled by punishing stimuli from the partner. Distressed spouses, by contrast, reacted strongly to punishing stimuli and responded in kind (Jacobson et al., 1980).

Distressed and nondistressed couples also vary in the attributions, or cognitive appraisals, they make of behavior in the partner. Distressed spouses are significantly more likely to judge the displeasing behavior of the partner as global and stable, but the pleasing behavior as specific and unstable (Camper, Jacobson, Holtzworth-Munroe, & Schmaling, 1988). For example: "When asked why his partner did not smile at him when she got home from work, a distressed husband might say, 'Because she's an irritable person and she's always trying to get me down,'" and a nondistressed husband would be more likely to say, "Because she had a bad day' " (Waltz & Jacobson, 1994, p. 170). Research has also shown that distressed couples tend to have few shared recreational activities and experience difficulties in communication and problem solving (Bennun, 1987).

Assessing behavior in relationships is a difficult and complex task. *Direct observation* poses the problems of determining which behaviors to assess, and deciding where a given behavior begins and ends during a prolonged interaction. Because many of the most important interactions are private, direct observation is sometimes not possible at all. Using *self-report questionnaires* creates the possible problems of biased or self-serving reporting, minimizing or exaggerating symptoms, and dealing with *two* sets of questionnaires, one from each partner. If the two partners give inconsistent responses (e.g., one reports that there are never any disagreements on financial matters, but the other reports that they fight about money all the time), does the clinician simply add the two scores and take the mean, or treat the partners as two different clients?

Recognizing these difficulties, behavior therapists usually take a multimodal approach in assessing troubled relationships. Self-report questionnaires, behavioral observation (by the partners in the natural environment and by trained independent observers in laboratory simulations), and even psychophysiological monitoring of heart rate, have all been used in research (Kelly & Halford, 1995; Weiss & Wieder, 1982).

Self-Report Questionnaires

Several questionnaires on marital adjustment are available, but many have been criticized for their lack of clear theoretical basis and their questionable psychometric properties (Spanier, 1976). Traditionally, the most familiar among psychotherapists of all orientations was the *Marital Adjustment Scale (MAS)* of Locke and Wallace (1959). Inventories used in behavioral research on troubled relationships include several developed by Robert Weiss and his colleagues. The *Willingness to Change Questionnaire* (Weiss, Hops, & Patterson, 1973) assesses each partner's desire for change in the other and is consequently helpful for treatment planning. The *Marital Status Inventory* (Weiss & Cerreto, 1980) is designed to gauge the seriousness with which the partners have contemplated divorce. The *Maudsley Marital Questionnaire (MMQ)* has been used by researchers at the Institute of Psychiatry in London, both as an outcome measure in studies of behavioral couples therapy and as an ancillary measure in studies of behavioral treatment of anxiety disorders. Devised by Crowe (1978), the MMQ has a short form of nine items on marital satisfaction and compatibility, each rated on a 0 to 8 scale.

Another inventory that has been popular in treatment outcome research is the *Dyadic Adjustment Scale (DAS)* developed by Spanier (1976). The DAS is a 33-item scale that was derived from extensive factor-analytic work. The four subscales, with examples of questions from each, are:

- *Dyadic satisfaction* ("How often do you or your mate leave the house after a fight?")[1]
- *Dyadic cohesion* ("How often do you laugh together?")
- *Dyadic consensus* ("To what extent do you disagree on handling family finances?")
- *Affectional expression* ("To what extent do you agree on demonstrations of affection?")

Spanier has argued that the DAS is more helpful than earlier inventories because it can include "any nonmarital dyad which is a primary relationship between unrelated adults who are living together" (1976, p. 16). The DAS and the MMQ have both been used in studies of behavioral couples therapy reviewed below.

Observational Measures

The *Spouse Observation Checklist* (Weiss & Perry, 1979) has been used extensively in research trials and in clinical practice. Spouses record pleasant and unpleasant aspects of their day-to-day relationship, recording the frequency of specific behaviors by means of wrist counters and giving evaluative ratings via checklists.

The best-known observational measure is the *Marital Interaction Coding System (MICS)* (Hops, Willis, Patterson, & Weiss, 1971). The coding system is applied to videotaped simulations of marital conflict resolution. The partners discuss a topic important to their relationship for 15 minutes, and the videotape of the discussion is reviewed by independent raters, who code the verbal and nonverbal behaviors displayed. Although 30 behavior codes may be used, in many investigations the researchers focus on 2 or 3 categories.

Psychophysiological Monitoring

In distressed couples, behaviors from different domains of measurement improve at different rates. Kelly and Halford (1995) treated five married couples with a combination of procedures, including behavior exchange, communication skills training, problem-solving training, conflict management strategies, and cognitive restructuring of unhelpful attributions and beliefs. The researchers monitored changes in behavioral, cognitive, and psychophysiological (heart rate during marital communication) domains, citing evidence that all three response domains discriminate between distressed and nondistressed couples. The results were that *behavior* improved consistently and rapidly, *cognitive* changes were variable but sustained, and *heart rate* showed no consistent reduction. Kelly and Halford concluded that the asynchrony of responses in the three domains might explain the limited effectiveness of treatment for some couples, and recommended further investigation of the psychophysiological domain in behavioral couples therapy.

Comments on Assessment

Most behavior therapists can find fault with self-report measures because they are vulnerable to various kinds of bias. Clients may distort their responses in an attempt to present themselves in a favorable light, for example. Observing actual behavior overcomes some of these difficulties. But finding problems with self-report questionnaires does not mean that observational assessment must be better by default. It is true that the ratings of unbiased, independent researchers who view videotapes of couples interacting can provide objective information. However, videotaped interactions are still susceptible to bias and distortion. The partners may present themselves as favorably as possible, whether they are responding to a questionnaire or communicating about their relationship in front of a camera. Furthermore, observational assessment of this kind may also be lacking in relevance. In typical research studies, all couples are placed in the same situation for observational assessment, regardless of their particular problems. An observational coding system may measure communication problems, for example. This makes sense for partners who really agree much of the time but do not realize this because of their poor communication. However, it may miss the point for couples who communicate loud and clear but cannot negotiate or compromise (Jacobson, 1985, 1992).

Techniques of Behavioral Couples Therapy

The principal techniques of behavioral couples therapy are behavior exchange, communication skills training, and problem-solving training. Ideally, the therapist establishes a collaborative working relationship with the couple so that all three are "on the same side," teaming up to improve the relationship. In practice, each partner in a distressed couple tends to focus initially on convincing the therapist that the other is at fault. The Fawleys' therapists spent a great deal of time in persuading Jay to focus on changing *his* behavior for the sake of the relationship, and Essie on changing hers. By the time that was actually accomplished, the therapists knew that a positive conclusion was in sight.

Behavior Exchange

Consistent with the finding that nondistressed couples exchange positive reinforcement at a high rate, the aim of *behavior exchange* is to encourage each partner to do things that please the other (Waltz & Jacobson, 1994). At its simplest, behavior exchange can take the form of a *behavioral contract*, a formal agreement to exchange particular behaviors (Stuart, 1980). Each partner agrees to do something specific in return for something specific from the other—a *quid pro quo* agreement. For example, the Fawleys' therapists could monitor an arrangement in which Jay agrees not to act like a prosecuting attorney for a day, provided that Essie does not go out for lunch with the "other man." The theory is that each partner's behavior serves as a reinforcer for the behavior of the other. Generally, however, it is preferable to use more holistic contracts in which the aim is a shared goal, rather than a series of particular individual goals. This usually takes the form of a *good faith* contract in which each person expects the other to make changes but does not wait for the other to behave differently before going ahead with his or her own changes. This technique requires negotiation, of course, and therapists may need to help couples do this appropriately.

Stuart (1980) described the use of *caring days* to build commitment to the marriage. Using the caring days technique, the partners begin to act *as if* they care for each other a great deal (whether or not this is actually how they feel). Therapists stress the point that each partner needs to make a wholehearted effort, quite independent of the other. Each partner records preferences as to what the other could do to show caring. The ideal caring behaviors are positive, specific, small (can be performed at least once a day), and not the focus of the most highly charged conflict. The negotiation skills learned during these caring days can be applied in future behavior exchanges.

Communication Skills Training

Couples commonly cite problems in communication when they bring their relationship problems to a therapist, suggesting that *communication skills training* would be a logical treatment intervention. The idea is that, if only each party could express feelings, thoughts, and opinions clearly and effectively, then many apparent problems would be revealed to be mere misunderstandings.

To return to the example of Essie and Jay: In some ways, of course, there is no problem with communication. Essie is quite capable of telling Jay that his interrogations displease her, and he, likewise, leaves no room for doubt that he objects to her having illicit affairs. Nevertheless, both could benefit from communication skills training at another level—that of emotion or feelings. Jay "tells" Essie, verbally and nonverbally, that he does not want her to spend time with another man. Yet he only hints at how he *feels* about her behavior. We can only guess that he may feel hurt, rejected, ashamed, and so on. On the assumption that he does have feelings like these, Jay could learn, in therapy, to express them more fully by means of communication skills training. The expectation is that this would be very helpful to his relationship with Essie. The ideal progression would be like this:

Jay: (*before* communication training) How am I supposed to trust you? You made a fool of me, and you keep doing it. You ought to change. Why do you keep making me feel angry? Why are you doing this to me?

Jay: (*after* communication training) You are free to do as you like, of course. But I want you to understand how I feel. When you spend time with him, I feel hurt and rejected. I care for you so much, the idea of losing you to someone else is a real threat to me. I admit I feel bad when the guys taunt me at work over you and him. But that doesn't hurt half as much as the idea of losing you.

Assuming that those are, indeed, Jay's true feelings, it would be more helpful for him to state them clearly than simply to criticize Essie for her behavior. Essie may or may not change her ways as a result of Jay's emotional honesty, but at least she knows where he stands emotionally, and he is doing his part to facilitate greater openness.

The usual ground rules in communication training are:

- *Do* speak for yourself.
- *Do* assume responsibility for your own feelings.

- *Do* stay with present issues.
- *Do not* speak for the partner.
- *Do not* blame the partner for "making" you feel a certain way.
- *Do not* repeatedly bring out carefully saved examples of past illogical or undesirable behavior in your partner (Gurman, 1980).

Common techniques in communication training are modeling, coaching, behavior rehearsal (role-playing), and feedback from the therapist, together with extensive explanation and discussion of the treatment rationale.

Problem-Solving Training

In the context of behavioral couples therapy, *problem-solving training* is aimed at helping couples gain the skills needed to resolve areas of disagreement. These skills include (1) defining problems in the relationship, (2) proposing solutions, (3) suggesting compromises, and (4) being willing to accept responsibility (Weiss & Wieder, 1982). Typically, the steps involved are (1) define the problem and (2) negotiate a solution (Waltz & Jacobson, 1994).

It is not clear from the research literature that distressed couples actually have more difficulty with problem solving than do nondistressed couples. Yet, there is a difference in the pattern of problem solving in the two groups. Nondistressed couples can usually settle on an agreement in a negotiation phase that follows exploration of their differences. Distressed couples, by contrast, tend to continue to disagree in the negotiation phase; instead of gradually coming together on a solution, they keep proposing new ideas. Both groups, then, can propose solutions and suggest compromises, but the distressed couples cannot complete the important final task of settling on a mutual agreement (Gottman, 1979). The treatment techniques offered by the therapist include behavior rehearsal, feedback, and homework assignments (Weiss & Wieder, 1982).

It is often difficult, in practice, to separate problem-solving training from other forms of communication skills training, so the distinction is rather arbitrary. Blechman (1980) described a family approach to problem-solving training based on contingency contracts, so the boundaries between these three popular elements in behavioral couples therapy (behavior exchange, communication skills training, and problem-solving training) are not sharply defined.

Applying problem-solving training to the troubled relationship of Essie and Jay would involve, first, persuading each of them to recognize the problems as perceived by the other. Essie would be asked to understand that, whatever the true rights and wrongs of the case, it bothers her husband a great deal for her to go to lunch with the man with whom she had an affair. Jay would be encouraged to recognize that, from Essie's point of view, it is highly unpleasant for her to be confronted continually by detailed questions on how she spent each minute of the day. Mutual acknowledgment of these areas of distress could lay the foundation for some suggestions as to what to do to alleviate these concerns. These suggestions could, in turn, lead to agreement on a joint policy concerning these issues. For example, Jay could agree to stop badgering Essie with questions and to go out to dinner with her more often. For Essie to go out with him willingly, particularly if she was "dressed to kill," might remove some of

Jay's causes for extreme jealousy. This kind of solution could easily be expanded into a behavior exchange agreement, with each partner doing something specific, by arrangement, for the benefit of the other (and of the relationship).

The following selective review of empirical findings illustrates several behavioral couples therapy techniques.

Studies of Treatment Effectiveness

Behavioral couples therapists have developed a holistic approach to treatment in which couples are taught behavior exchange, problem-solving, and communication techniques. Because research showed that behavioral contracts often had short-lived effects, some behavior therapists argued that communication and problem-solving skills should be developed before the partners proceed to behavior exchange agreements (Patterson, Hops, & Weiss, 1975). More recently, behavior exchange has been recommended as an ideal *first* step, because it can rapidly increase positive feelings and thus make it easier to work on problems (Waltz & Jacobson, 1994).

In a preliminary study, Jacobson (1977) treated 10 distressed couples, divided into experimental and control groups. Couples in the experimental group received several sessions of behavior therapy, in which they learned problem-solving and behavior exchange principles. The behavioral contracts were good faith agreements in which each partner tried to make positive changes, regardless of the other's behavior. The control group couples were placed on a waiting list while the others received their treatment. The self-report and observational measures used in assessment were the Marital Adjustment Scale (MAS) and the Marital Interaction Coding System (MICS), both described earlier. Verbal and nonverbal responses were videotaped as the partners discussed a topic germane to their relationship, and the videotapes were later coded on dimensions of *rewardingness* and *problem solving*. On all measures, the couples who had received behavior therapy were significantly more improved than the waiting list couples.

The design of the study permitted analysis of single cases within each group. Observational data collected by each spouse in the home gave results consistent with the group data analyses. A one-year follow-up assessment with self-report data indicated that the improvement had been maintained. Limitations of the study were that Jacobson himself conducted all the treatment sessions, only a few couples were treated, and these were solicited by advertisements as opposed to seeking treatment spontaneously.

In a second study, Jacobson (1978) investigated the treatment of 32 couples, who were randomly distributed among four experimental conditions. Two of these involved behavior therapy, the third was a placebo condition, and the last was a waiting list. This time, three therapists treated couples in each treatment condition. The therapists did not differ in their impact on the treatment, as assessed by the couples' outcome data. The behavior therapy conditions both included problem-solving training, but differed in the type of behavior exchange agreement used. One of these was the good faith type of contract, as in the previous study; the other was the *quid pro quo* type, in which each partner's behavior change served as a reinforcer for that of the other. The behavioral treatment conditions did not differ from each other, but they brought significantly more benefit than the other conditions. On the four measures used (the MAS, another self-report inventory, and two behavioral dimensions—positive and negative—from the MICS), the behavioral conditions were significantly more effective than no treatment. On three of the four measures, the behavioral conditions were significantly more effective than the placebo condition (which had been rated as credible by the couples).

Reciprocity counseling was compared with *discussion-type counseling* in a partial cross-over study of 55 distressed couples (Azrin, Besalel, Bechtel, Michalicek, Mancera, Carroll, Shuford, & Cox, 1980). Discussion-type counseling meant encouraging clients to describe their problems, their beliefs about the origins of the problems, and their suggestions for remedying the situation. No particular recommendations for action were made by the therapists. Reciprocity counseling comprised three procedures: stimulus control, reinforcement exchange, and communication training. The *stimulus control* procedure involved making partners aware of the positive reinforcement they exchange, achieved by having the partners make lists of reinforcers exchanged and by concentrating questions in interviews on positive interactions rather than on problems. The *reinforcement exchange* component consisted of behavioral contracting, with written requests and agreements. *Communication training* was specifically focused on verbal reinforcement; the partners made a point of exchanging compliments and statements of appreciation. Partners also learned to make positive requests so as to facilitate reinforcement. Four 90-minute treatment sessions were given.

The results clearly favored reciprocity counseling. The three self-report measures all indicated significant improvement for the reciprocity counseling couples, but not for the couples in the discussion condition. Half of the discussion couples chose to receive reciprocity counseling at the end of the study, and they responded as well as the other reciprocity counseling couples. Unfortunately, about 11 couples in each condition terminated their participation after only one session. Couples who dropped out could not be distinguished from the treatment completers on any pretreatment measure.

All three of the popular behavioral couples therapy components were studied in an experiment by Baucom (1982). The study investigated 72 maritally distressed couples who were distributed among four conditions: (1) problem-solving training, communication training, and contracting; (2) problem-solving training and communication training; (3) contracting; and (4) waiting list. Couples were treated in 10 weekly sessions of 60 to 90 minutes each. The contracting procedures were of the *quid pro quo* variety. Assessments consisted of self-report (MAS) and observational (MICS) ratings. Results of this ambitious study revealed no difference in the three behavioral treatments, but all were significantly more helpful than no treatment. Generally, the treated clients who returned follow-up questionnaires three months after treatment indicated that they were still doing well.

Jacobson (1984) compared behavior exchange with communication and problem-solving training in a between-groups study. Because behavior exchange is aimed at increasing the frequency of positive interactions, Jacobson predicted that it would produce rapid results but might not equip couples to offset problems in the future. By contrast, communication and problem-solving techniques should be helpful in the long run in preventing problems from getting out of hand but probably would not produce dramatic change right away. He predicted that the standard combination of all three techniques would produce the best outcome, strong immediate effects, and lasting results. In fact, the conditions were equally effective in the short term. At a follow-up assessment six months later, 44 percent of the behavior exchange couples, but none of the problem-solving/communication training couples, had relapsed. Couples who had had the complete treatment showed an intermediate relapse rate of 11 percent.

In a subsequent article, Jacobson and Follette (1985) stressed the importance of assessing the clinical significance of therapeutic change. This has the two aspects of determining (1) whether treatment-related changes persist and (2) how many couples actually reach a normal level of functioning after treatment. Researchers added 24 new couples to the 36 of the prior report (Jacobson, 1984), so that the results from 60 couples could be analyzed. As before, the conditions were behavior exchange, communication plus problem-solving training, the combination of all three techniques, and a waiting list. The therapists were five graduate students who proved equally effective in the study. The clients were young, well educated, and moderately distressed. The observational measure was a videotaped communication assessment, and the self-report questionnaire used was the Dyadic Adjustment Scale (DAS) of Spanier (1976).

The behavior exchange condition included specific homework assignments and supplementary techniques to foster desirable cognitive changes. In the communication and problem-solving training condition, couples were trained in conflict resolution and practiced the skills at home. Therapists used modeling and behavior rehearsal procedures and encouraged the couples to become self-sufficient so that they could be their own therapists. As assessed by stringent criteria of clinical and statistical significance, the behavioral procedures emerged clearly superior to the control condition. However, improvement rates had declined by the time of the six-month follow-up assessments. This result was almost entirely due to relapse patterns in the behavior exchange clients. Therefore, on clinical and statistical criteria, the complete treatment package is clearly more helpful than behavior exchange training alone.

One year after treatment, the group differences were not distinct, with about one-third of couples showing deterioration of their earlier improvement. Although the difference between behavior exchange and the other conditions was no longer significant on the dependent measures, couples who had received the complete package were most likely to be happily married and not separated or divorced (Jacobson, Follette, Follette, Holtzworth-Munroe, Katt, & Schmaling, 1985).

Results of a Meta-Analysis

A broad-ranging study by Hahlweg and Markman (1988) had the objectives of comparing the results of behavioral couples therapy in European and American studies, and comparing behavioral couples therapy with *behavioral premarital intervention (BPI),* a program designed to offset marital problems before they start. The Hahlweg and Markman report represents an analysis of analyses, or a *meta-analysis,* identifying and reviewing the relevant studies and reworking the statistics to combine the results into a single, overall analysis.

The authors located 17 behavioral couples therapy studies and seven prevention (BPI) studies. The BPI studies had all been conducted in the United States, but the other studies allowed a cross-cultural comparison. General conclusions from the statistical meta-analysis were that behavioral couples therapy is more effective than no treatment, and this difference persists during varying lengths of follow-up. The same results held for European and American studies. Not only was treatment more helpful than no treatment but it was also significantly superior to a placebo condition. The BPI approach, intended as a cognitive-behavioral preventive measure to steer couples away from marital distress, emerged from the meta-analysis as clearly more helpful than no treatment. Techniques aimed at preventing distress are becoming popular among behavioral couples therapists because they are easier, cheaper, and less intensive than treatment delivered after major problems have arisen (Sullivan & Bradbury, 1996).

Distressed Relationships, Anxiety Disorders, and Depression

Couples Treatment and Anxiety Disorders.   Cobb, McDonald, Marks, and Stern (1980) treated 11 clients with coexisting anxiety disorders and marital problems. We have already noted this study in Chapter 5 (see Figure 5.6). The background for this study was a case report by Stern and Marks (1973) of a woman with obsessive-compulsive disorder who improved only when the therapists addressed her marital problems specifically. The Cobb and associates' (1980) study was an extension of the case report, and was designed to assess the contribution of behavior therapy aimed at the marital problems of clients who also had anxiety disorders. Treatment sessions included both partners in each case. Some couples received contract marital treatment and some followed exposure procedures for the anxious partner with the spouse as cotherapist. After a 12-week follow-up assessment a crossover design was followed in which each couple was given the alternative treatment. The results contradicted those of the original case report and showed that exposure treatment successfully relieved the anxiety and the marital problems, whereas the marital therapy had effects on the marital relationship only.

Similar results were obtained in a study of obsessive-compulsive disorder treated by exposure with response prevention. Half of the 54 participants reported marital distress before treatment. After treatment, 42 percent of these were no longer maritally distressed, although their relationships had not been the target of treatment (Riggs, Hiss, & Foa, 1992).

There is a substantial literature on the role of behavioral couples therapy in the treatment of anxiety disorders in general and agoraphobia in particular (Barlow, 1988; Emmelkamp & Gerlsma, 1994; Goldstein & Chambless, 1978; Hafner, 1982). General conclusions are that behavioral couples therapy does not serve as effective treatment for anxiety disorders, but behavior therapy for anxiety disorders sometimes relieves distress in relationships. Behavioral couples therapy will often be necessary as a component of the treatment plan for many anxious clients.

Couples Treatment and Depression.   Behavioral couples therapy does not directly improve anxiety disorders, but there is evidence that it may reduce depression. Maritally distressed couples in which the wives had depressive disorders were treated either by a typical behavioral couples therapy package or by individual cognitive therapy (other participants were assigned to a waiting list). Both treatments improved the depressive symptoms, but the couples treatment improved both the depression and the relationship (Beach & O'Leary, 1992). Behavioral couples therapy is an effective treatment for depression occurring in the context of marital discord (Beach, Whisman, & O'Leary, 1994).

Behavioral Couples Therapy and Family Therapy

Recently there have been attempts to combine behavioral couples therapy with other approaches, such as strategic family therapy (Bennun, 1987). A combination of couples therapy and family systems therapy has been described as especially helpful to the families of terminally ill medical patients (Cohen & Cohen, 1981). Taking a behaviorally oriented family therapy approach has brought great benefit in the treatment of aggressive children (Patterson, 1982). This particular version of interactionalism has led to an understanding of child aggression in terms of ineffective punishment strategies of the parents (Wells, 1984). More generally, *behavioral family intervention* has become accepted as a comprehensive intervention for children who are behaviorally and emotionally disturbed and their parents (Sanders & Dadds, 1993). Based on improving parenting by the appropriate use of operant learning concepts, behavioral family intervention helps parents avoid inadvertently reinforcing problem behavior in their children. Sanders and Dadds gave this example of a "reinforcement trap" occurring when Sam, age 7, wants to continue watching TV instead of obeying his mother and going to bed:

Sam: (starting to cry) No, it's not fair.

Mother: Come on, I'll read you a story. Get up and brush your teeth. (Mother starts to pick up the child.)

Sam: (starts to scream and cry) Just let me watch this show, then I promise to go to bed, I promise.

Mother: All right, just to the end of this show and then you're off to bed with no fuss. Do you hear me? (yelling)

Sam: Yes, Mom. (Sanders & Dadds, 1993, pp. 21–22)

Sam's noncompliance is reinforced by his mother (he can continue watching TV, and his mother stops making demands). The mother's giving in and relaxing her demands are reinforced by Sam (he stops screaming, and agrees to the new rule). We would predict that Sam would continue to protest and his mother would continue to yield on future occasions. Behavioral family intervention is a useful expansion of behavioral couples therapy when parents are distressed by problematic interactions with their children.

Summary

Like other mental health professionals, behavior therapists view marriages and other exclusive relationships as worth saving. The principal techniques of behavioral couples therapy are behavior exchange, communication skills training, and problem-solving training. These appear to be of comparable effectiveness but best delivered as a package. Behavioral couples therapy has been shown to be more helpful than certain nonbehavioral treatments and no treatment. Recent emphasis on acceptance and on preventive interventions may lead to treatment innovations that will improve long-term outcomes.

Postscript

Eventually, Jay and Essie Fawley were successfully treated by means of a behavioral couples therapy approach centered on communication skills and problem-solving training. It was not easy, and the therapy progressed for many weeks. The therapists brought in some concepts from rational emotive behavior therapy as a component of treatment. The problem-solving treatment component involved negotiation, which was very difficult for Jay in particular. He could only participate effectively after he came to the realization that there was no reason—however much he disliked what Essie did—that she *must* behave differently. By learning to alter his wishes from demands to preferences, Jay was able to act in a less controlling way. This encouraged Essie to make changes of her own for the sake of the relationship. Without realizing it, Jay had anticipated behavior therapists' current emphasis on acceptance by over a decade!

Behavioral Treatment of Sexual Dysfunctions

Mental health professionals recognize several disorders of human sexual behavior. In this section, we will focus on those that take place in the context of consenting adult relationships. The sexual disorders most often presented by distressed couples are the *sexual dysfunctions*, in which the partners are troubled by an unfulfilling erotic relationship. Sexual dysfunctions have been defined as "physiological, cognitive-affective, or behavioral problems that prevent an individual from engaging in or enjoying satisfactory sexual activity, intercourse, or orgasm" (Friedman, Weiler, LoPiccolo, & Hogan, 1982, p. 653).

The DSM-IV *Classification of Sexual Disorders*

Three groups of sexual disorders are described in the *DSM–IV: sexual dysfunctions, paraphilias,* and *gender identity disorder.* Couples with sexual dysfunctions are unable to achieve a satisfying sexual encounter at least some of the time. Sexual dysfunctions may be the result of a medical condition or of substance use, but our focus is on those attributable to psychological factors.

In *paraphilias* (literally meaning "unusual likings"), an individual is attracted by unacceptable sexual fantasies or activities, usually concerning inappropriate choices of the target for sexual activity. Nonconsenting partners, nonhuman partners, and inanimate objects are the chief examples. Clients with exhibitionism, for example, are males who derive their sexual pleasure chiefly from exposing their genitals to unsuspecting strangers. In fetishism, a nonliving object, such as an item of intimate female apparel, is the target of interest. There are several such paraphilias, some of which have been discussed in earlier chapters to illustrate the applications of specific behavioral treatment techniques.

Gender identity disorder (listed separately from the dysfunctions and paraphilias) has two components: "strong and persistent cross-gender identification" and "persistent discomfort about one's assigned sex or a sense of inappropriateness in the gender role of that sex" (American Psychiatric Association, 1994, pp. 532–533). Clients with gender identity disorder wish to live or be treated as members of the other sex, or believe that they have the essential characteristics of the other sex, despite nature having endowed them with the features of their biological sex. The person usually feels that nature has played a cruel trick by endowing him or her with the wrong genitalia and other physical sex characteristics. Gender identity disorder is not to be confused with having a gay or lesbian sexual orientation. For example, men and women who do *not* have gender identity disorder may prefer biologically opposite-sex or same-sex sexual partners. Men and women *with* gender identity disorder may prefer biologically opposite-sex or same-sex sexual partners.

Sexual Dysfunctions

The *DSM-IV* classification of sexual dysfunctions is based on the known characteristics of the sexual response cycle. Sexual functioning in humans has been carefully researched and reported by a number of investigators. The best known of these are William Masters and Virginia Johnson, a research team who based their initial conclusions on laboratory studies of nearly 700 people (Masters & Johnson, 1966, 1970), and Helen Singer Kaplan (1974). The most significant finding from naturalistic research is that men and women respond to sexual stimulation similarly, and a standard sequence of four stages can be identified in the sexual response cycle of men and women (LoPiccolo, 1994; Mahoney, 1980).

The *desire* phase refers to the onset of a desire for sexual activity on a given occasion, and it includes thoughts and fantasies about the activity. In the *excitement* phase, feelings of sexual pleasure coincide with a series of characteristic physical responses, which include penile erection in the male and vaginal lubrication in the female. The phase of *orgasm* includes, physically, the ejaculation of semen by the male and contractions in certain muscles surrounding the vagina in the woman. These events go together with a sense of release from sexual tension and a climax of pleasurable sensations. The *resolution* phase involves a sense of relaxation and general well-being.

Problems may arise at any point in this cycle, although it is hard to find examples of problems at the resolution phase. The problems most commonly brought to the attention of clinicians are those that make sexual intercourse painful, difficult, or impossible. Representative *DSM-IV* sexual dysfunctions are briefly listed and described here:

DSM-IV SEXUAL DYSFUNCTIONS (partial list)

Note that each of these problems is only viewed as a disorder if it causes "marked distress or interpersonal difficulty" (American Psychiatric Association, 1994, pp. 498–522). These problems are only diagnosed as sexual dysfunctions if they are recurrent or persistent, and when a separate psychiatric or medical disorder cannot explain the symptoms better.

Sexual Desire Disorders
- Hypoactive Sexual Desire Disorder (deficient or absent sexual fantasies or desire)
- Sexual Aversion Disorder (aversion to genital contact with a sexual partner)

Sexual Arousal Disorders

- Female Sexual Arousal Disorder (inability to maintain adequate genital lubrication/swelling during sexual excitement)
- Male Erectile Disorder (inability to maintain an adequate penile erection during sexual excitement)

Orgasmic Disorders

- Female Orgasmic Disorder (absence of, or delay in, orgasm following a normal sexual excitement phase)
- Male Orgasmic Disorder (absence of, or delay in, orgasm following a normal sexual excitement phase)
- Premature Ejaculation (ejaculation of semen with minimal sexual stimulation, before the client wishes it)

Sexual Pain Disorders

- Dyspareunia (genital pain associated with sexual intercourse, not caused by another sexual dysfunction)
- Vaginismus (involuntary spasm of vaginal muscles, interfering with sexual intercourse)

Assessment

About 20 percent of couples in stable marriages report sexual dysfunction, but it is not known how many of these seek treatment (Marks, 1981). As in other applications of behavior therapy, accurate assessment is important, not just of the sexual dysfunction itself but also of clients' intimate relationships. Therapists prefer to work with the couple, even if only one partner first arrives at the clinic to present a problem. However, some clients seek treatment for sexual dysfunctions when they are not currently in a relationship, sometimes attributing the lack of a relationship to the dysfunction.

For example, one of our clients wanted his arousal disorder resolved before he asked another woman for a date, so as to avoid embarrassment if they became sexually involved. This opens up other areas requiring assessment, such as the client's general social skills and his or her beliefs about relationships. For instance, the therapist might ask, "Must you always be perfectly sexually functional to avoid rejection? Would it be terrible to discuss your embarrassment about your arousal disorder with a potential sexual partner?" Other areas for assessment are essential for goal-setting, as indicated in the following quotation:

> *A preliminary decision has to be made concerning the appropriateness of a program of behavioral treatment focused upon the sexual dysfunction rather than some other form of intervention . . . to alleviate a relevant organic problem or a marital therapy to reduce partner discord. Subject to this decision, the goals . . . are determined by the client and partner according to their own wishes and values, but in consultation with the therapist. (Jehu, 1984, pp. 231–232)*

Cognitive-Behavioral Theories

Psychoanalytic therapists traditionally regarded sexual dysfunctions as the offshoot of unconscious conflicts, established early in personality development. Behavior therapists have criticized this view because psychoanalysis has not produced convincing data, the theory itself is partly based on discredited prescientific views of human sexuality, and, in any event, many forms of dysfunction result from faulty expectations and incomplete education about sexuality. Accordingly, treatment based on insight into unconscious dynamics would miss the point entirely (Friedman et al., 1982).

Following the early work of Wolpe (1958), who thought of sexual dysfunctions as the result of conditioned anxiety, behavior therapists concentrated on helping clients remove their fears of sexual activity. Masters and Johnson (1970) identified the immediate factors maintaining dysfunction as performance anxiety, and taking the role of "spectator" rather than that of participant. Lack of information and poor communication about sex were also seen as important causal factors.

Sexual dysfunctions have been attributed to a variety of causes, including underlying psychopathology (such as anxiety, depression, and personality disorders), victimization by sexual abuse, and other interpersonal, cognitive, and conditioning factors (Gold & Gold, 1993; Letourneau & O'Donohue, 1993; Morokoff, 1993). In most research samples, a large majority of women who were sexually abused in childhood report experiencing sexual dysfunctions as adults (Jehu, 1987; Morokoff, 1993). Although posttraumatic stress disorder following rape or other sexual assault clearly accounts for sexual dysfunction in many victims, convincing evidence that desire or arousal disorders are *generally* caused by anxiety is lacking (Barlow, 1988; Everaerd, 1993). This may seem paradoxical, because treatments known to be effective for sexual dysfunctions appear to follow anxiety-reduction principles (LoPiccolo, 1994).

Cognitive-Behavioral Treatment

Generally, behavioral treatment consists of reducing discomfort and training sexual skills in a graduated program involving both partners together. Ideally, the partners assume mutual responsibility for the problem. Therapists give information about sexuality and teach the couple to communicate about sexual feelings. The partners set aside time for sexual activity and engage in graduated practice to decrease anxiety and reduce pressure to "perform," taking graded steps toward more difficult assignments (Marks, 1981; Masters & Johnson, 1970).

Several specific techniques of therapy for sexual dysfunctions have been described and evaluated (Friedman & Chernen, 1987; Leiblum & Pervin, 1980). In a typical Masters and Johnson program for a heterosexual couple, the partners are treated together by a male/female therapist team. Take the example of a male partner who cannot maintain penile erection during sexual activity, and a female with arousal disorder whose lack of vaginal lubrication makes sexual intercourse difficult. Clients with such problems often develop a "fear of fear" pattern that becomes self-perpetuating. When the problem develops, a partner may become preoccupied with it, and look forward to the next sexual encounter with anxiety. The client's self-statements here may include

"What if it doesn't work out properly tonight? I hope this isn't going to be yet another failure." This preoccupation in itself will be likely to interfere with the client's relaxation and ability to enjoy sexual stimulation. The client takes on the role of spectator, carefully assessing each sensation during the encounter to see if his or her performance is satisfactory. Any information that suggests that arousal is not taking place as planned can lead quickly to increased worry and physical tension, thus disrupting the sexual response (Friedman & Chernen, 1987).

To combat this self-perpetuating cycle, therapists ask clients to adopt a *sensate focus,* concentrating positively on their sexual sensations during intimate times with the partner. To reduce performance anxiety, the therapists advise the partners to go home, to undress and go to bed (at the appropriate time), and to enjoy kissing, hugging, and caressing each other *without any attempt at intercourse.* The therapists are careful to stress the ban on intercourse for the week. In following this plan, the partners have no reason to fear the effects of their dysfunctions, because it is not necessary for the man to have an erection or for the woman to experience swelling or lubrication. In other words, there is no pressure to perform, and the partners can begin to associate sexual stimulation with relaxation, pleasure, and peace of mind. From this point, a gradual progression can be made toward intercourse over the weeks. This program is very similar to graded practice or *in-vivo* desensitization programs used to treat anxiety disorders (Friedman et al., 1982).

A variation on this procedure for the man with erectile disorder is as follows. The therapists give the couple the paradoxical directive that the man should *avoid* having erections for a while, so that the partners can enjoy sensual pleasures without intercourse. They can progress to the point at which the man lies on his back, the woman sits astride him, and then she pushes his flaccid penis into her vagina. The therapists tell the couple that this works best when the man does not have an erection. Removing the anxiety, worry, and threat of "failure" in this way can soon lead to the man's being unable to avoid penile erection under these circumstances (LoPiccolo, 1994).

Other specific techniques may be used to deal with premature ejaculation and vaginismus. The *pause procedure* is used for men with premature ejaculation (LoPiccolo, 1994). The partner stimulates his penis until orgasm approaches, then stops. When orgasm is no longer imminent, the partner resumes the stimulation, and the procedure is repeated. Clear communication between the partners is necessary, of course, for the technique to succeed, and this is beneficial to the relationship in any event. The stimulation may be manual, oral, or the partners may begin intercourse and stop making pelvic movements when the man's sensations indicate approaching orgasm. One variation of this is described by Masters and Johnson as the *squeeze technique*, in which the partner is taught to suppress the man's ejaculation physically by compressing part of the penis. This is done at the point of "orgasmic inevitability." The effect of the pause procedure and the squeeze technique is to help the man gradually prolong the amount of stimulation he can tolerate before orgasm occurs.

In the treatment of vaginismus, the female client may learn to tolerate the insertion of a graded series of vaginal dilators. Initially, she implements this herself in private. At the appropriate time, the partner may be included in this gradual progression, first stimulating her manually. At each point, the woman suspends the activity if discomfort arises. As in the treatment of premature ejaculation, progressing through a series of graded exercises leads eventually to physical and psychological acceptance of the desired sexual activity (Beck, 1993; LoPiccolo, 1994).

Studies of Treatment Effectiveness

The early work of Masters and Johnson (1970), while of immense clinical importance in pointing the way to appropriate interventions, has been criticized for using clinical series methodology, excluding experimental comparisons with control groups. The participants were not representative of all dysfunctional clients because of the expense and duration of the program (Friedman et al., 1982; Marks, 1981). Other criticisms have addressed the absence of adequate definitions and assessments of dysfunction (Friedman & Chernen, 1987).

Controlled treatment studies have been reviewed by Friedman and Chernen (1987), Jehu (1984), Marks (1981), O'Donohue and Geer (1993), and others. Some of the highlights are as follows. Mathews, Bancroft, Whitehead, Hackman, Julier, Gath, and Shaw (1976) studied 36 couples. In half of the couples, the woman had presented the problem initially, and in the other half the man had initiated the treatment. Couples were divided into three treatment conditions: (1) systematic desensitization (SD) plus counseling about anxiety, (2) therapy based on the Masters and Johnson procedures, and (3) a home-based Masters and Johnson program in which therapists and clients had contact by mail. After this 12-week program, assessments were made by an independent assessor and by the therapist. A four-month follow-up assessment was also conducted. Results were that SD was the least helpful technique and directed counseling plus practice was the most helpful, as gauged by increased female sexual enjoyment and a greater frequency of sexual intercourse. It was marginally more helpful to have two therapists rather than one in the Masters and Johnson procedure.

Three studies were reported by Everaerd (1977). In the first, 48 women had sought therapy, chiefly for orgasmic disorder. Four experimental conditions were formed to compare SD, the Masters and Johnson approach, the combination of the two, and no treatment. After 12 treatment sessions, all treatments had proved superior to the no-treatment condition. The same results were seen at follow-up assessment six months later. In the second study, 42 couples in which the woman had orgasmic disorder were treated. Two treatments were compared: "behavioral Masters and Johnson therapy" and communication skills training. The Masters and Johnson approach was more successful in the short term, but at the six-month follow-up the conditions were equal. The third study was another investigation to compare SD with the Masters and Johnson techniques. This time, the focus was on men with either arousal disorder or premature ejaculation. Results were generally unimpressive, but at the six-month follow-up, improvement from the Masters and Johnson program just reached statistical significance.

Another study showed that directed masturbation added significant benefit to the effects of sexual skills training in women with orgasmic disorder (Riley & Riley, 1978). The superior effects of directed masturbation were still present one year after treatment. When this technique was presented to the clients who had initially received only sexual skills training, most of them made significant further progress.

Studies of clinical series from the 1970s to the 1990s have provided support for the

Masters and Johnson techniques. Both the squeeze and the pause techniques have been helpful in the treatment of premature ejaculation in over 50 couples in four studies. The outlook for arousal problems in men and for orgasmic disorder in women was less encouraging than for other dysfunctions (Friedman & Chernen, 1987), but recent studies of rational emotive behavior therapy have shown it to be helpful (Everaerd, 1993). Success rates approaching 100 percent have been reported for vaginismus (Beck, 1993).

Treatment of sexual dysfunctions in gay and lesbian couples has its own increasing literature, and there are some special considerations that therapists new to this area have to inform themselves about (McWhirter & Mattison, 1980). Nevertheless, the principles of successful therapy are similar in all intimate relationships. The same goes, of course, for the more general relationship difficulties we have discussed under the heading of behavioral couples therapy. People in gay or lesbian partnerships may feel especially isolated if relationship problems arise. Couples distress is challenging enough even if the person is "out" and has a supportive community of friends and relatives, but not everyone is in this situation (Dattilio & Padesky, 1990). When relationships dissolve, lesbians are more likely than gay men to maintain a friendship with the former partner because they tend to belong to close-knit social networks (Kelley & Dawson, 1994).

Chapter Summary

Behavioral couples therapy has progressed through a series of stages that began with attempts to change specific behaviors in individual partners. Borrowing from systems theory and social exchange concepts, behavior therapists developed more holistic treatment programs that typically include behavior exchange, communication skills training, and problem-solving training. These methods have all received empirical support and appear to be equally effective (behavior exchange in the short term and the other methods with more lasting impact). The treatment of sexual dysfunctions in people in intimate relationships includes education, communication training, and specific methods designed to reduce performance anxiety. The problem-oriented methods pioneered by Masters and Johnson include graduated practice and specific procedures like the squeeze technique. Such methods have generally received support from studies with clinical series and group design methodology.

Endnote

1. Some questions are scored in reverse, of course.

Chapter *12*

Obesity and Eating Disorders

Sarah, age 15, was 5'4" but weighed only 71 pounds. During the past five months, she had severely restricted her food intake and had begun a strenuous program of aerobic exercise, dropping 40 pounds. Despite the strong concerns of her parents, teachers, and friends, she refused to gain back any of the weight and continued exercising and restricting her food intake. Although listless and emaciated, she adamantly claimed that the only problem was that she was "too fat," and that once she got her "sloppy habits under control," things would be alright.

Christina, age 20, referred herself to a college counseling center because she felt depressed. During an intake interview, she revealed that she had a four-year history of binging on high-calorie "junk foods" then forcing herself to vomit. During these binges, which occurred on a daily or near-daily basis, she consumed as much as 3,000 calories. She felt distressed by these binge-purge episodes, but believed that she could not control them.

In recent decades, there has been an explosion of interest in cognitive and behavioral therapies for eating-related problems. Current behavioral approaches to the treatment of obesity, anorexia nervosa, and bulimia nervosa are discussed in this chapter. As illustrated by the symptom pictures of Sarah and Christina, anorexia nervosa and bulimia nervosa are established psychiatric disorders. However, obesity is a medical problem characterized by excess body fat and is not associated with elevated rates of general psychopathology (O'Neil & Jarrett, 1992; Stunkard & Wadden, 1992). Obesity and the eating disorders are discussed together because clinical management involves changing eating-related thoughts and behaviors, and on making lifestyle changes necessary to maintain treatment successes. Also, although they do not suffer from an "established" psychological disorder, many obese individuals do suffer emotional distress because of their condition and because of the social stigmatization they endure as a result of it (Friedman & Brownell, 1995).

Obesity

In 1967, Stuart published the results of a behavioral treatment study in which obese women were successfully treated using behavior therapy principles. This pioneering report stimulated the rapid development of other behavior therapy programs for *obesity*. Today, these programs are so popular that behavioral techniques have been integrated into national self-help programs (such as Weight Watchers). Ironically, the popularity of behavioral treatments has reinforced misconceptions concerning the nature of obesity (Brownell, 1981). For example, a common misconception is that obesity is a "food addiction," or a habit disorder reflecting overconsumption of food coupled with periodic binge eating. However, research has shown that obese people do not necessarily eat more than others (Wooley, Wooley, & Dyrenforth, 1979) and that there does not seem to be an "obese eating style" involving rapid consumption of food (Garner, Rockert, Olmsted, Johnson, & Coscina, 1985; Stunkard & Kaplan, 1977). Similarly, although many obese individuals do experience binges (Fairburn & Wilson, 1993), others do not.

A second misconception is that obese people are "stimulus bound," in that overeating is strongly cued by environmental conditions such as having ready access to favorite foods. Although this notion has served as a springboard for many behavioral treatment programs, it has received inconsistent scientific support (Rodin, 1980). A final misconception is that obesity is a simple behavior problem reflecting excessive food intake and inadequate energy output. However, in recent years, important scientific work has been done on genetic and biochemical contributions to the development of obesity. These contributions are currently acknowledged by behavior therapists, especially in regard to metabolic processes that help maintain obesity (Brownell & Wadden, 1991). In short, obesity is a highly complex problem with interactive biological, psychological, and social origins. Losing weight and keeping it off is anything but a simple task.

Defining Obesity

Defining obesity is more difficult than it would seem. The most commonly used criterion is that of excess body weight, defined in relation to deviation from a population standard based on height and gender, such as the norms found in the Metropolitan Life Insurance Tables (1983). For example, individuals whose weight exceeds at least 20 percent of their "ideal" weight are considered moderately obese; by this standard, approximately one-fourth of men and women in the United States are obese (Kuczmarski, 1992). However, obesity is a measure of body fat, not body weight. Precise measures of body fat are difficult and expensive to obtain. For example, one way of assessing body fat is to measure skinfold thickness at several different body sites using caliper instruments.

A different issue related to the definition of obesity is: Who should be treated? Wooley and Wooley (1984) have written, "It is very hard to construct a rational case for treating any but massive, life-endangering obesity" (p. 191). They point out that people live in a weight-obsessed society that fosters rigid standards of physical attractiveness for women. At worst, these standards may help promote life-threatening eating disorders such as anorexia nervosa; otherwise, they foster negative, unrealistic self-evaluation in women and social rejection of overweight individuals. In other words, some investigators see mild obesity as a social problem, not a significant health risk.

Most behavioral clinicians would not agree that mildly to moderately overweight individuals be turned away from therapy. However, it is essential to carefully assess the client's motives for weight loss, including the costs and rewards of following a treatment regime (Brownell, 1991; Craighead, 1985). Treatment may not be in the best interests of all individuals.

Assessment

Behavioral assessment of obesity should be comprehensive and multimodal. The client's functioning in all spheres of life must be assessed, so that appropriate treatment goals can be set. Assessment targets include the following areas of functioning (Craighead, 1985; Williamson, Davis, Duchman, McKenzie, & Watkins, 1990):

1. The overall physical health of the client, assessed in a medical evaluation
2. A carefully evaluated weight history including weight fluctuations throughout the years and past attempts to lose excess pounds
3. Personal goals for weight loss
4. Energy balance, which is typically assessed by asking the client to keep a detailed record of daily calorie intake versus activity expended for one to two weeks
5. An assessment of eating habits, using self-report questionnaires that are supplemented by self-monitoring of daily food intake and exercise (Self-report measures such as the Master Questionnaire [Straw, Straw, Mahoney, Rogers, Mahoney, Craighead, & Stunkard, 1984] and the Eating Inventory [Stunkard & Messick, 1985] have proven useful as measures of eating habits.)
6. Adequacy of psychological and social functioning, assessed in behavioral interviews and possibly supplemented with information from others who are closely acquainted with the client (such as family members or employers) (Evidence of severe psychopathology or marital/family discord would be critical in making initial or later treatment decisions.)

Behavioral Treatment of Obesity

The success of behavioral treatment programs for obesity has been documented in over 100 controlled studies (Bennett, 1986; Brownell & Wadden, 1986). Most behavioral programs promote slow but steady weight loss. Behavioral weight loss programs typically involve multiple intervention components carried out in weekly, small group sessions. Common treatment components are described next.

Self-Monitoring

Clients keep detailed daily records of everything they eat, along with the time and setting of consumption. Self-monitoring increases awareness of maladaptive eating patterns and is a critical aspect of weight control programs (Baker & Kirschenbaum, 1993).

Stimulus Control

Stimulus control involves modifying the environment so that weight loss is facilitated. Usually, the amount and accessibility of food is limited. For example, clients may be asked to put leftovers away immediately following meals and to refrain from purchasing "binge foods." Clients may also be asked to restrict their eating to specific settings, such as the dining room.

Modification of Eating Behavior

If maladaptive eating behaviors are present, clients may be asked to reduce the speed of food consumption, the size of their bites, and/or the frequency and size of daily meals. Instructing obese clients to slow their eating rate (by increasing the length of their meals) appears to accelerate weight loss (Spiegel, Wadden, & Foster, 1991). In addition, maladaptive behavior chains such as eating in response to loneliness or boredom can be identified and changed.

Modest Calorie Restriction

A balanced diet involving modest calorie restriction is frequently prescribed, along with nutritional education. Severe calorie restriction should be employed with extreme caution and only under intensive medical supervision, because it can by physically harmful and does not promote long-term maintenance of weight loss (Brownell & Wadden, 1991).

Self-Reinforcement

Rewards are used to encourage compliance with treatment recommendations. Craighead (1985) suggested that clients set up separate self-reward systems for behavior change goals and for weight loss goals, because weight loss is frequently a slow and unsteady process.

Effectiveness of Standard Programs

The "standard package" behavioral program—primarily consisting of self-monitoring, stimulus control, and self-reinforcement—became a widely used weight-loss intervention in the late 1970s. These 10- to 12-week programs have consistently resulted in average weight losses of 11 pounds (Brownell & Wadden, 1986; Foreyt, 1987). More recently, other components have become increasingly common additions to weight-loss treatment programs, because many individuals either regain the weight (Brownell & Jeffrey, 1987) or fail to benefit from standard behavioral interventions (Kirchenbaum, 1988). These components are described here.

Exercise

Physical exercise is becoming central to the treatment of obesity (Dishman, 1991). Increased energy expenditure has been correlated with long-term success in maintaining weight loss (Brownell, 1984; Craighead & Blum, 1989). However, the reasons for these positive effects are unclear. Research attention has focused on the metabolic effects of exercise, particularly the assumption that metabolic rate increases during exercise and remains elevated for a period of time after exercise. Evidence supporting this assumption has been contradictory: Some studies indicate that exercise increases metabolic rate in obese individuals, whereas others show a suppression effect (Brownell & Jeffery, 1987). Studies of the long-term effects of exercise on metabolic rate are needed. Positive effects of exercise on weight maintenance could reflect a host of nonbiological factors, as well. For example, engaging in an exercise program could enhance many different aspects of psychological well-being, such as relaxation, sense of personal control, and energy level. The consensus among behavior therapists is that moderate exercise should be part of all behavioral weight-loss programs, if not in the very beginning, then later in treatment (Brownell & Jeffery, 1987).

Encouraging obese clients to *comply* with exercise programs is a separate and challenging issue for the therapist. Compliance has reportedly been a major problem in initial studies of exercise and weight loss (Dishman, 1991). Jeffery and his colleagues (1984a, 1984b) have researched methods of encouraging obese clients to comply with exercise. They found that financial incentives for compliance increased initial weight losses by approximately 30 percent relative to behavioral treatment without incentives. Brownell and Stunkard (1980) have recommended that physical exercise programs involve routine activities that can be casily integrated into the client's normal lifestyle, such as walking, climbing stairs, or performing vigorous household tasks.

Cognitive Restructuring

In recent years, cognitive restructuring interventions have been added to some behavioral treatment programs. The first step is to identify negative internal monologues that interfere with treatment compliance. Mahoney and Mahoney (1976) identified five types of negative self-statements common to individuals attempting to lose weight. For example, some clients felt that it was impossible for them to lose weight because their weight was "determined" by physical factors beyond their control. Once these negative internal monologues are pinpointed, coping self-statements are substituted and rehearsed. However, as yet, treatment programs with strong emphasis on cognitive restructuring have not proven superior to more traditional programs (Collins, Wilson, & Rothblum, 1986; Mahoney et al., 1977).

Relative Effectiveness of Behavior Therapy

Treatment studies reported in the mid-1980s have shown larger average weight losses than the standard package programs discussed earlier (Brownell & Jeffrey, 1987). For example, in 1986 the average weight loss (based on multiple studies) was 22 pounds, in contrast with the typical 11-pound loss reported by earlier investigators. Brownell and Jeffery attribute these apparent improved results to a combination of factors, including increased emphasis on exercise, social support, and relapse prevention. Also, weight-loss programs have become *longer* over time—an important consideration because longer periods of treatment appear to enhance weight loss (Fitzgibbon & Kirschenbaum, 1993; Perri, Nezu, Patti, & McCann, 1989).

How do behavioral therapies fare relative to alternative treatments for obesity, such as pharmacotherapy? Although appetite-suppressant drugs have been widely used in the treatment of obesity, behavioral and pharmacological treatments have rarely been compared. In an exemplary study, Craighead, Stunkard, and O'Brien (1981) examined the relative effectiveness of three treatments: behavior therapy, drug therapy, and combined behavior and drug therapy. Treatment subjects were 145 individuals who met criteria for clinical obesity (at least 60 percent above normal body weight). These individuals were assigned to one of four treatment conditions: (1) multicomponent behavior therapy ("standard package"); (2) medication only (fenfluramine), administered in a group setting to control for the effects of social contact with other obese individuals; (3) combined behavioral and medication treatment; and (4) no-treatment control. Patients in each treatment group lost significant amounts of weight. However, at one year posttreatment, patients in the behavior therapy condition had retained their losses to a greater degree than those in the medication condition. Surprisingly, combining medication and behavior therapy did not enhance long-term maintenance. These findings have been replicated by other investigators (Brownell & Stunkard, 1980; Craighead & Agras, 1991; Marcus et al., 1990).

Long-Term Maintenance of Weight Loss

Behavioral modification programs promote at least short-term weight loss in many obese individuals. Furthermore, attrition rates in behavioral programs are significantly lower than in medication-only or self-help programs (Wilson & Brownell, 1980), and behavioral therapy programs promote better long-term maintenance of weight loss than medication programs (Craighead & Agras, 1991). However, even in the "best" behavioral treatment programs, long-term maintenance is highly variable across individuals. Overall, clinically significant weight losses do not tend to be maintained (Brownell & Jeffrey, 1987). For this reason, long-term maintenance is the most important issue in the treatment of obesity.

Efforts have been made to identify psychological and social factors that promote long-term maintenance of weight loss. Correlates of successful weight maintenance include close self-monitoring of food intake (Baker & Kirschenbaum, 1993; Wing & Jeffery, 1989), including exercise in weight maintenance programs (Craighead & Blum, 1989; Gormally et al., 1980; Katahn, Pleas, Thackery, & Wallston, 1982), increasing the strength of one's efficacy expectations (Gormally, Rardin, & Black, 1980), and increasing the length of treatment (Perri et al., 1989). According to Brownell and colleagues (1986), relapse involves a typical sequence of events: (1) a precipitating event, perceived as stressful by the individual; (2) associated negative emotions, such as depression, anxiety, or anger; (3) negative self-referent thoughts, such as guilt or self-deprecation; and (4) collapse of self-management behaviors. For example, Rosenthal and Marx (1981) examined the causes of initial "slips" among dieters. They followed a group of dieters posttreatment and analyzed the immediate precipitants of failures to follow daily calorie allotments. Negative mood states such as anxiety and depression were associated with initial slips in 48 percent of the sample. The remaining slips were precipitated by troubling interpersonal interactions.

In relapse prevention training, clients are taught to identify high-risk situations and to learn skills needed to cope with them. Rosenthal and Marx (1978) piloted a relapse prevention program for dieters based on Marlatt's (e.g., Marlatt & Gordon, 1985) general program. Compared with with dieters who followed a standard behavioral treatment program, the relapse prevention group lost more weight at follow-up and had significantly fewer relapses. In a large, controlled study of relapse prevention for obesity, Perri, Shapiro, Ludwig, Twentyman, and McAdoo (1984) also reported superior long-term maintenance in relapse prevention groups, but only when relapse prevention training was combined with "standard" behavior therapy and with extensive posttreatment contact by phone and mail. Thus, relapse prevention appears to be a potentially helpful treatment adjunct for obese individuals.

In addition to relapse prevention training, other methods could be effective in promoting maintenance of weight losses. Increasing the length of treatment has significant positive effects on the amount of weight loss; programs that run for six months or longer report much greater averge weight losses than the typical 10- to 15-week programs (Beliard et al., 1992). Finally, individuals should be matched to treatments that best fit their particular problems, levels of motivation, and expectations regarding treatment (Brownell & Wadden, 1991). Behavioral treatments may be optimal for some obese clients and contraindicated for others. Identifying these important individual difference characteristics may ultimately lead to greater and more long-lasting treatment successes, preventing the heartbreak and demoralization of relapse.

Anorexia Nervosa

Anorexia nervosa is a potentially fatal eating disorder involving self-starvation, fear of obesity, and obsession with thinness. Anorexia nervosa is not a simple disorder involving too little food intake. Rather, it is a complex problem with interactive psychological, social, and physiological components. Thus, as with obesity, multicomponent assessment and treatment programs are required.

Clinical Features

The clinical features of anorexia nervosa have been well defined. Anorexia nervosa occurs between the ages of 10 and 40, with an average age range of 17 to 18 years. Over 90 percent of cases occur in females. Anorexia nervosa is currently subdivided into restricting type (those who dramatically restrict food intake) and binge eating/purging type (those who restrict their food intake but engage in periodic binge eating, followed by self-induced vomiting or use of laxatives). The following diagnostic criteria are listed in the *DSM-IV:*

- Refusal to maintain body weight over a minimum normal weight for age and height (body weight at least 15 percent below expected weight)

- Disturbance of body image, exemplified by perceiving self as too fat even though underweight, and/or denial of seriousness of current low body weight
- Intense fear of gaining weight or becoming obese
- In postmenarcheal females, amenorrhea (absence of three consecutive menstrual cycles)

Anorexic individuals are preoccupied with food but intensely afraid of becoming obese. Body weight is controlled by severe calorie restriction, often coupled with compulsive exercising and/or purging after meals. Although this bizarre disorder is rare in the general population, its prevalence may be as high as 1/100 among late adolescent and young adult women (American Psychiatric Association, 1994). The course of the disorder is highly variable. Anorexia nervosa may be unremitting until death, episodic, or characterized by a single episode with return to normal weight. Over 10 percent of people with anorexia eventually die from the effects of self-starvation or from physical complications associated with starvation (American Psychiatric Association, 1994; Halmi, 1980).

Assessment

Anorexia nervosa is a multifaceted disorder requiring comprehensive assessment. A number of specialized assessment tools have been developed for this population. The *Eating Disorder Examination (EDE)* (Fairburn & Cooper, 1993) is a comprehensive, widely used structured interview protocol for assessing eating disorder symptoms and their social and physical sequelae. Self-report questionnaires such as the *Eating Disorders Inventory (EDI)* (Garner, 1991) have been widely used in the assessment of eating disorders. The following components should be part of any assessment protocol (Garner, 1991; Williamson, 1990; Wilson, 1993).

Physical Functioning
A general medical workup is required, due to the potentially severe medical complications of anorexia nervosa (Comerci, 1990; Halmi, 1980). In addition, body weight should be measured precisely, using a sensitive scale with small weight gradations (Brownell, 1982).

Functional Analysis of Behavior
A detailed functional analysis of anorexic behavior must be carried out, including dieting history and daily patterns of food restriction; features of food consumption (type, quality, setting); the pattern, frequency, and methods of purging; and specific beliefs or fears about weight gain (Fairburn & Cooper, 1993; Garner, 1991). To achieve this end, clients are asked to keep a daily diary of all eating-related behaviors.

Psychological and Social Functioning
Past and present social and psychological adjustment should be assessed. Evidence of depression and suicidal ideation/intent are the most serious indicators of acute psychological distress. Disturbed family functioning also appears to play an important role in the devel-

opment and maintenance of anorexia nervosa (Minuchin, Rosman, & Baker, 1978; Russell, Symukler, Dare, & Eisler, 1987). Finally, the presence of social skills deficits and/or social anxiety may play a role in maintaining isolation from peers.

Primary versus Secondary Symptoms

Many of the anorexic client's symptoms may be directly attributable to the effects of starvation (Shafer & Garner, 1995). Psychological changes such as impaired concentration, emotional lability, irritability, and dysphoria are common reactions to severe and prolonged caloric restriction (Keys, Brozek, Henschel, Michelson, & Taylor, 1950). Thus, if these symptoms are noted, it is difficult to state the direction of effects. Olmsted, Davis, Garner, Eagle, and Rockert (1991) have shown that clients' responses to brief, psychoeducational treatment may be a good assessment tool. Many anorexic clients show considerable improvement in their psychological functioning with weight restoration.

Behavioral Treatment of Anorexia Nervosa

Effective treatment of anorexia usually requires hospitalization, because of the potential severity of associated medical complications. Behavioral treatment of anorexia is frequently used, and has been described in many clinical reports. In the majority of cases, operant conditioning procedures have been used to directly promote weight gain. However, systematic desensitization has also been employed to treat fear of gaining weight, and social skills training approaches have been used to improve the social adjustment of some anorexic individuals. The newest treatment approach has been to apply cognitive-behavioral interventions to modify maladaptive beliefs and self-perceptions that people with anorexia typically espouse.

Operant Procedures

Operant conditioning procedures have been used to promote weight restoration in anorexic individuals. The vast majority of studies have been carried out in hospital settings with severely anorexic patients. The typical procedure is to reward weight gain and/or appropriate eating behavior, and to ignore or remove rewards for weight loss. For example, Garfinkel, Kline, and Stancer (1973) carefully established baseline weights for hospitalized anorexic patients. A daily weight gain of at least one-half pound was then required in order to achieve special hospital privileges. Despite methodological problems that are inherent in many of these studies (e.g., uncontrolled single-case designs with inadequate long-term follow-ups), positive reinforcement of weight gain typically leads to rapid short-term weight restoration (Agras & Kraemer, 1984; Bemis, 1987). However, generalization of treatment gains to the home environment is problematic, due in part to the difficulties involved in careful monitoring of anorexic symptoms. Also, psychosocial factors that could be maintaining anorexic symptoms (such as distorted beliefs or troubling family interactions) are not dealt with in this form of behavior therapy. Thus, operant procedures are useful as an initial step in the treatment of severely ill anorexic patients, but other interventions are needed to ensure treatment generalization and maintenance.

Systematic Desensitization

Some behavioral clinicians have defined the central feature of anorexia as fear of gaining weight. Thus, systematic desensitization has been used to reduce "weight phobia," with resulting short-term gains in weight (Lang, 1965; Ollendick, 1979; Schnurer, Rubin, & Roy, 1973). However, as with operant treatment procedures, only one feature of this complex disorder is addressed. Broader coping skills must be provided to promote long-term improvement and enhanced psychosocial adjustment.

Cognitive Restructuring

Approximately one-third all treated anorexic patients have poor outcomes. Even in weight-recovered patients, abnormal eating patterns and distorted beliefs about thinness tend to persist (Garfinkel & Garner, 1982). These data suggest the need for cognitive interventions in anorexia nervosa. Garner and Bemis (1982) have outlined a cognitive-behavioral model of the development and maintenance of anorexia. They suggest that the belief "I must be thin" is a way of coping with normal developmental crises of early adolescence. Early dieting successes promote a sense of mastery and efficacy in the preanorexic individual. Initially, there is social reinforcement for dieting success. By the time that social praise turns to concern over the girl's increasing emaciation, the complex of anorexic beliefs and behaviors may have become "functionally autonomous" or self-reinforcing, so that weight loss becomes the sole pleasure bringing relief from unhappiness. Thus, the central belief to be challenged in therapy is the equation of thinness with self-worthiness.

This model leads directly to a cognitive-behavioral treatment program. Garner and Bemis have emphasized that although anorexia shares components with depressive and phobic disorders, it is a unique disorder requiring a unique treatment approach. Major steps in their treatment program are as follows:

1. *Relationship building.* People with anorexia typically deny that they are ill and generally are unwilling participants in treatment. "Standard" cognitive-behavioral treatment programs have not been designed to handle this level of resistance. Thus, the first stage in therapy is relationship building, facilitated by honesty, warmth, supportiveness, and a nonjudgmental attitude on the part of the therapist. The anorexic individual should be informed that her experience will be guiding the course of therapy. Although her distorted beliefs should not be directly challenged, the therapist may point out that the usefulness of these beliefs will be examined in therapy.

2. *Education.* The client should receive didactic infomation about the symptoms, risks, and course of anorexia. This information helps to redefine anorexia as a psychological disorder rather than a unique and heroic characteristic of the individual client. Also, some negative symptoms (such as irritability and weakness) can be reattributed to the effects of starvation.

3. *Weight stabilization.* Weight restoration is a necessary and even life-saving aspect of treatment. The therapist's difficult job is to accomplish this goal without destroying the therapeutic relationship. Potentially helpful interventions involve framing hospitalization as a way of achieving control over upsetting symptoms, acknowledging the panic that most

anorexic patients feel at the prospect of gaining weight, telling patients exactly what to expect, and setting upper limits on weight gain.

4. *Behavioral interventions.* Traditional behavioral interventions may be helpful during the initial stages of therapy. Examples include behavioral rehearsal, scheduling pleasant events, and modeling of normal eating behaviors.

5. *Cognitive interventions.* A thorough assessment of distorted cognitions is essential. Beliefs should be identified using self-monitoring exercises and clearly specified so they can be examined in therapy. Therapists should never directly contradict these beliefs or argue over values. Rather, the client can be framed as a "collaborator" who tests the usefulness of these beliefs against her own experience. For example, if the client believes that social acceptance is related to weight status, then real-life experiments can be designed to test the validity and usefulness of this idea.

Family Interventions

Family therapy may be an important adjunct to individual treatment of the anorexic client. In many previous reports, problematic family interaction styles (e.g., overprotection, lack of effective conflict resolution, inappropriate parent/child alliances) have been linked with symptoms of eating disorders in young, female family members (Minuchin, Rosman, & Baker, 1978; Vandereycken, Kog, & Vanderlinden, 1989). Possible foci for intervention include offering family members psychoeducational information about the nature of eating disorders, helping parents develop adaptive ways of responding to their anorexic children, and challenging inappropriate family beliefs about eating and health (Vandereycken et al., 1989).

Summary and Case Illustration

In conclusion, treatment of anorexia nervosa must encompass not only the goal of weight restoration but also maladaptive assumptions about self-worth in relation to weight and to generalization of treatment gains to the client's broader psychosocial environment. Due to high relapse rates, long-term posttreatment follow-up is essential. The following case example, provided by Harris and Phelps (1985), illustrates a thoughtful and comprehensive approach to the management of anorexia:

> L., a 22-year-old female with a primary diagnosis of anorexia nervosa, was voluntarily admitted to an inpatient ward. L. was five feet tall and weighed 72 pounds on admission. She had been engaging in severe caloric restriction combined with excessive exercising and episodes of binging and purging. L. had a history of dieting that began in late adolescence. Six months prior to admission, she began dieting more strenuously in response to the stressful life changes of moving away from home and assuming a demanding job. At the time of admission, L. was binging and vomiting twice a week, followed by severe caloric restriction on other days. L.'s family described her as responsible, independent, and socially successful, with a long history of superior academic achievement.
>
> L. was hospitalized for nine weeks. The initial focus of treatment was on weight restoration. A contingency management plan was developed whereby privileges were

earned for achieving a daily one-half pound weight gain and lost for weight decrements. L. was weighed daily and placed on a 3,000 calorie diet, divided into four meals plus snacks. She also participated in a group token economy program, in which points were lost for violating house rules and gained for meeting ward expectations. These programs resulted in steady weight gains. The second phase of treatment focused on cogitive-behavioral training in effective problem-solving. L. was taught to identify risky thoughts and feelings (such as urges to binge and purge), describe alternative ways of coping with them, evaluate the short- and long-term consequences of each coping strategy, then select a course of action. L.'s therapist also engaged her in extended discussions of the pros and cons of maintaining her eating disorder. It was emphasized that giving up her eating disorder meant that she must endure temporary discomfort. Finally, during the last two weeks of treatment, discussions of problem-solving focused on difficulties that might be encountered post-discharge.

L. showed good compliance with all aspects of treatment, and achieved her target weight (105 pounds) after seven weeks. Follow-up sessions were scheduled to ensure maintenance and generalization of changes made during hospitalization. Treatment sessions were scheduled twice weekly for a period of time immediately after discharge, gradually tapering to meetings held at six-month intervals. Long-term goals not only encompassed weight maintenance, but also increasing the quantity and quality of social activities with family and peers. Twenty months after discharge, L. was maintaining her weight and was not engaging in binge/purge episodes. She had also established an independent residence, an achievement that had been difficult for her before hospitalization,and was maintaining positive relations with family and friends. (Harris & Phelps, 1985, pp. 277–287)

Bulimia Nervosa

The core symptoms of *bulimia nervosa* are uncontrollable binge eating followed by self-induced purging. Bulimia nervosa is a heterogeneous disorder that can occur in clients who present at normal weight, with obesity, or with anorexia nervosa. Bulimia nervosa is currently recognized as a separate disorder in *DSM-IV.* Although binge/purge cycles are the most obvious identifying feature of bulimia, many investigators believe that the most prominent feature is a "morbid" fear of fatness combined with extreme sensitivity to weight gain (Fairburn, Cooper, & Cooper, 1986). The following diagnostic criteria are listed in *DSM-IV:*

- Recurrent episodes of binge eating, defined as either eating larger than normal amounts of food within a discrete time period and/or perceiving that one has lost control over eating during the binges
- Recurrent, inappropriate compensatory behavior in order to prevent weight gain, such as self-induced vomiting, use of laxatives or diuretics, strict dieting, or excessive exercise
- Self-evaluation is unduly influenced by concern with body shape and weight
- A minimum of two binge eating episodes per week for at least three months

Binge eating episodes are experienced as uncontrollable and excessive. During these episodes, there is rapid consumption of large quantities of food. For example, it is not unusual for people with bulimia to consume between 5,000 to 10,000 calories during each binge episode (Fairburn, Cooper, & Cooper, 1986). Most people with the disorder practice self-induced vomiting after these binges. A minority use laxatives or diuretics as purgative agents. People with bulimia are aware that this pattern of eating is abnormal and often express fear over not being able to stop voluntarily. Depressed mood, especially following the binge/purge episodes, is a common associated feature of bulimia. Bulimia nervosa is associated with a host of medical complications, including dental erosion, electrolyte imbalance, cardiac arrhythmias, and kidney malfunction (Williamson, Cubic, & Fuller, 1992).

Bulimia usually begins in late adolescence or early adulthood. Over 90 percent of cases have involved females. The course may be chronic, or intermittent with episodes of bulimia (followed by normal eating) over a period of many years (American Psychiatric Association, 1994).

One common treatment approach has been to combine "standard" behavioral interventions with cognitive restructuring to provide a broad spectrum cognitive-behavioral program. For example, Fairburn (1984) has developed a cognitive-behavioral approach to the treatment of bulimia nervosa. The central target of this approach is the client's overconcern with body size as a basis for self-evaluation. Following a conceptualization phase during which the client is assured that she will retain responsibility for therapy, the client engages in daily self-monitoring of all food intake. The client is also asked to restrict eating to three to four planned meals, with no restrictions on the type of foods eaten. The purpose of this intervention is to disrupt the cycle of overeating and vomiting.

Because relapses are common in the treatment of bulimia, coping strategies for dealing with initial lapses (recurrences of binge patterns) are developed in advance. The active support of family and friends is also enlisted.

During the second stage of therapy, irrational beliefs about body shape and weight are identified. Tbe usefulness and validity of these beliefs are then challenged, and alternative coping strategies are discussed. Finally, a treatment maintenance program is developed. Active planning for coping with lapses is continued, and clients report progress during monthly or bimonthly visits.

Overall, bulimic individuals have shown a positive response to treatment programs such as Fairburn's (Craighead & Agras, 1991). However, there tends to be great individual variability in responsiveness to treatment, and relapse rates are high (Fairburn et al., 1986). For example, Kirkley, Schneider, Agras, and Bachman (1985) conducted a controlled study in which bulimic patients either received broad spectrum cognitive-behavior therapy (CBT) or "nondirective" therapy. Treatment sessions extended for 16 weeks. The CBT group had fewer dropouts and higher reductions in rates of binging/vomiting than controls at the end of treatment. However, three months later, the superiority of the behavioral treatment was gone, due to high relapse rates.

An alternative behavioral treatment approach involves *exposure with response prevention (ERP)* Rosen & Leitenberg, 1984). Vomiting is viewed as a compulsive behavior pattern that reinforces binging by providing temporary relief from the fear of weight gain. The immediate goal of treatment, then, is to prevent vomiting from occurring after binge eating episodes. Later stages of treatment focus on the prevention of binge episodes altogether. For example, Leitenberg, Gross, Peterson, and Rosen (1984) exposed five bulimic clients to highly anxiety-arousing thoughts and images during a series of therapy sessions. Normal "binge foods" were supplied, and clients were told to eat as much as they wanted but to refrain from vomiting afterwards. In-session eating was associated with high anxiety during early sessions, but gradually diminished over time. The majority of the clients benefited from treatment. Similar reports have been submitted by Wilson (1984) and by Rossiter and Wilson (1985). Thus, ERP merits further research attention as an effective treatment for bulimia.

Research on the effectiveness of combining ERP and "standard" CBT has yielded conflicting findings. Leitenberg, Rosen, Gross, Nadelman, and Vara (1988) compared four groups: (1) ERP, clinic setting only; (2) ERP, multiple settings (clinic, restaurant, home); (3) standard CBT but no exposure; and (4) waiting list controls. All treatment groups showed improvement, and there was no particular advantage to multisetting ERP. However, those who received CBT only showed less reduction in vomiting at postreatment and at follow-up than those who received exposure-based treatment.

In another major treatment evaluation study, Agras, Schneider, Arnow, Racburn, and Telch (1989) reached different conclusions. They compared the following groups over a four-month period: (1) self-monitoring and nondirective therapy, (2) CBT alone, (3) CBT plus ERP, and (4) wait list controls. Only the CBT alone group showed significant reductions in purging behavior. Interpretation of findings from these two research groups is difficult because they used different protocols for both the ERP and the CBT interventions. Pending additional comparative studies, one can only conclude that both types of treatment show promise, but neither has been proven to be superior in the treatment of bulimia nervosa.

Another important treatment issue involves the addition of antidepressant drugs to behavioral treatment. Antidepressants have proven superior to placebo trials in reducing symptoms of bulimia nervosa, with reductions of 64 to 91 percent in binge eating (Craighead & Agras, 1991). However, relapse typically occurs when medication is withdrawn (Pope, Hudson, & Yurgeless-Todd, 1983). Are there any relative merits of combining drugs and CBT in the treatment of bulimia nervosa? Mitchell and associates (1990) conducted 12-week trials of the following treatment groups: (1) imipramine (an antidepressant) alone, (2) imipramine plus CBT, (3) CBT plus drug placebo, and (4) drug palcebo alone. Individuals in all treatment groups did better than those who received drugs alone. Adding antidepressants to CBT did not affect eating behavior, but did reduce negative mood states (anxiety, depression) associated with bulimia nervosa. Those who received antidepressant medications had higher drop-out rates than those who received placebos, presumably due to the unpleasant side effects of the drug.

Finally, factors related to long-term treatment success versus relapsing should be explored. For example, Wooley and Kearney-Cooke (1986) found that role relationship problems in bulimic individuals' families of origin are critical maintaining factors. As with anorexia, a flexible, multifaceted treatment approach appears to be necessary in order to promote long-term treatment gains. Garner (1994) has provided a good example of such an approach. He described the treatment of J., a 24-year-old college student who suffered from bulimia nervosa.

For months prior to referral, J. engaged in between 1 to 10 binge-vomiting cycles per day, and had been trying to restrict her food intake. During these cycles, she would consume large quantities of sweet, fatty, food; immediately afterward, she felt dysphoric and engaged in self-induced vomiting and use of laxatives. J. felt distressed with her body, which she believed was extremely fat (she presented at normal weight for her age and height). These weight concerns had been present since childhood. At the time of referral, she reported significant depressive symptoms with suicidal ideation, anxiety, low self-esteem, and social insecurity. Following a comprehensive assessment, initial sessions were devoted to individual cognitive-behavioral therapy.

Treatment goals were to help the client learn to monitor shifts in mood and in corresponding binge/purge cycles; to help her separate her self-worth from her body weight; and to help her develop better problem-solving skills for coping with family stresses. Because different family stresses were present (for example, a multigenerational history of anorexia; inappropriate attitudes about eating and health), family therapy sessions were conducted for two months. Following the family sessions, the focus of therapy shifted to the client's relationship with her boyfriend. Following one year of treatment and numerous relapses, the client was able to refrain from binging/purging for three months, and therapy was terminated.

Binge Eating Disorder

Initially described by Stunkard (1959), *Binge Eating Disorder* refers to a pattern of maladaptive eating in individuals who do not fit criteria for either anorexia nervosa or bulimia nervosa. Recently, Fairburn and Wilson (1993) have devoted considerable attention to this eating disorder subtype. In the *DSM-IV*, Binge Eating Disorder would be diagnosed when there are compulsive binges but no compensatory behaviors or food restriction. (Binge eating disorder is not yet an official *DSM* diagnostic category. It is listed in *DSM-IV* among criteria sets deserving further study.)

Chapter Summary

Obesity is a highly complex problem with biological, psychological, and social origins. Behavioral treatment programs have typically involved multiple intervention components such as self-monitoring, stimulus control, modest calorie restriction, and self-reinforcement. More recently, physical exercise and cognitive restructuring interventions have become important additions to "standard" treatment programs. Behavioral treatment programs have consistently resulted in significant short-term weight losses. However, obesity tends to be a chronic problem with high relapse rates. Thus, explicit attention must be given to relapse prevention and to other means of promoting long-term maintenance of weight loss.

Anorexia nervosa is a potentially fatal eating disorder involving self-starvation, fear of obesity, and obsession with thinness. Most people with anorexia are adolescent or young adult females. Behavior therapy for anorexia has primarily focused on weight restoration.

Contingency management programs have consistently resulted in short-term weight restoration. However, relapse rates are relatively high, and generalization of treatment gains remains a problem. For this reason, weight restoration should be the initial goal of treatment, followed by broader spectrum interventions to improve the client's psychological and social functioning.

Bulimia nervosa, also prevalent among young women, involves recurrent episodes of binge eating followed by self-induced vomiting or other purging methods. Both broad spectrum cognitive-behavioral interventions and combined exposure/response prevention programs have shown promise as behavioral treatments for bulimia. Because bulimia tends to be a chronic problem, explicit attention should be given to relapse prevention and to long-term maintenance of treatment gains.

Chapter 13

Addictive Disorders

Mr. J., a 47-year-old unemployed sales manager, was referred to an inpatient unit for treatment of severe alcohol dependence. Although Mr. J. had been drinking heavily since his teenage years, recent family difficulties had precipitated an exacerbation of drinking that resulted in the loss of his present job and two convictions for driving under the influence. Upon admission to the hospital, Mr. J. appeared severely depressed. He related that he felt hopeless and that he had been thinking seriously about suicide.

Ms. S., a 21-year-old college student, referred herself to a university counseling center for treatment of problem drinking. Ms. S. reported that she grew up in a family where all of the adults engaged in frequent, heavy drinking. Ms. S. typically drank 4 or 5 glasses of beer or wine each day. She reported drinking as many as 12 glasses of beer or wine on weekends, usually in party situations. Recently, she experienced her first blackout, and felt very scared by it. Ms. S. appeared to be an intelligent and insightful person. She felt alarmed that she might follow her parents' paths to a lifetime of heavy drinking, and wished to reduce her daily intake to one or two drinks during meals only.

Treatment of addictive disorders has achieved central importance in the field of behavior therapy. Addictive disorders encompass a wide range of maladaptive behavior patterns, including alcohol and drug abuse, smoking, gambling, and overeating. However, as Brownell (1982) has noted, there are important commonalities between all addictive behavior patterns. Addictive behaviors provide immediate short-term gratification that leads to chronic long-term maladaptation. Physical health and psychosocial adjustment are adversely affected. Addictive behavior patterns have no simple etiology. Rather, multiple biological, psychosocial, and environmental risk factors interact in complex ways to cause and maintain addictive disorders. Finally, addictive disorders are resistant to change. Relapse rates are very high across the entire spectrum of addictive disorders. Furthermore, about two-thirds of all relapses occur within the first

90 days following treatment (Marlatt & Gordon, 1985). Behavioral approaches to two major addictive problems—alcohol dependence and abuse and nicotine dependence—are discussed in this chapter.

Alcohol Abuse and Dependence

As with all substance use disorders, a distinction is made between alcohol abuse and alcohol dependence *(DSM-IV)*. In order to be labeled *alcohol dependent,* an individual must show physiological signs of addiction. The most typical indicators are *tolerance,* in which increasingly larger amounts of alcohol are required to produce the same effect, and physiological *withdrawal reaction*s upon cessation of drinking. It is noteworthy, however, that a substantial minority of alcohol-dependent individuals never experience clinically significant levels of withdrawal. *Alcohol abuse* refers to a pattern of excessive alcohol use that persists despite attempts to stop and is associated with impaired physical, social, and/or vocational functioning *(DSM-IV)*.

Alcohol is the most widely abused drug in the United States. An estimated 10.5 million Americans are alcoholics (National Institute on Alcohol Abuse and Alcoholism, 1990), and four times as many are problem drinkers (Institute of Medicine, 1990). The consequences of alcohol problems are disastrous and wide ranging. Alcohol dependence is associated with serious health problems such as malnutrition, liver and pancreatic damage, and brain damage, and is a risk factor for other chronic diseases (IOM, 1990; Schukit, 1995). Alcohol dependence and abuse are associated with family conflict and violence (O'Farrell, 1995), impaired social and vocational functioning (IOM, 1990), and severe developmental disabilities in infants born to alcoholic mothers (NIAAA, 1990). Finally, half of all highway fatalities and homicides are associated with severe intoxication (McCord, 1992). In short, the negative effects of alcohol abuse and dependence are so extensive that they are virtually inestimable.

Causes of Alcoholism

No single cause of alcoholism has been identified. Studies have suggested that genetic predisposition may be a risk factor for alcoholism (Schukit, 1994). For example, family incidence studies have consistently revealed that alcoholism tends to run in families, but this is weak evidence for a genetic contribution *per se*, due to the effects of shared social experience. In a now classic study, Goodwin, Shulsinger, Hermansen, Guzew, and Winokur (1973) provided stronger evidence for a genetic link to alcoholism. The authors examined alcoholism rates in adopted sons whose biological fathers were alcoholics and contrasted them with alcoholism in adopted sons of nonalcoholic biological fathers. Adopted sons of alcoholics were three times more likely than controls to have serious drinking problems. Results of subsequent adoption studies (Cadoret, Cain, & Grove, 1981; Cloninger, Bohman, & Sigvardsson, 1981) have supported these findings.

If there is a genetic predisposition for alcoholism, then what exactly is inherited? Specific vulnerabilities have not been identified, but abnormal metabolism of alcohol and physiological insensitivity to the effects of alcohol have been suggested as possibilities (Schukit, 1994).

In addition to biological risk factors, social learning factors play an important role in the development and maintenance of alcoholism. Many alcoholics do not have family histories of alcoholism. Furthermore, members of certain ethnic groups, notably Jews and Chinese, have much lower alcoholism rates than others. In both ethnic groups, overconsumption of alcohol is viewed negatively, and drinking is condoned in special circumstances such as religious or social rituals (Heath, 1987). Similarly, Vaillant (1983) has reviewed longitudinal studies of life history differences between alcoholics and nonproblem drinkers. Family backgrounds that tolerated adult drunkenness have consistently differentiated these groups.

Traditional versus Behavioral Models of Treatment

Fostered by the rapid growth of the Alcoholics Anonymous movement, the traditional (or "disease") model of alcoholism (Jellinek, 1960) has dominated service delivery in the United States. Alcoholism is viewed as a symptom of an underlying disease, marked by loss of control over drinking behavior (Morse & Flavin, 1992). Biological determinants are seen as the most salient causes, and once an individual loses control over drinking, it is assumed to lead to progressive deterioration. For this reason, abstinence is viewed as the only acceptable treatment goal, and treatment typically involves an intensive period of hospitalization during which the individual achieves total abstinence (Marlatt, 1992).

In contrast, behavioral models emphasize that alcohol problems comprise a *continuum* of socially acquired behavior patterns maintained by a potentially diverse range of internal and external conditions (Marlatt & Donovan, 1981; Marlatt, 1992). Behavioral models do not exclude physiological vulnerabilities to alcoholism. However, physiological vulnerabilities are viewed as one "internal" factor relevant to problem drinking, not a sufficient cause.

Early behavioral models of alcoholism focused on specific learning mechanisms involved in the acquisition and maintenance of problem drinking. For example, a great deal of early research focused on the *tension reduction hypothesis*. According to this theory, individuals begin drinking as a means of coping with stress and tension, and drinking is increased and maintained because it reduces distress. In a classic experiment, Conger (1951) showed that alcohol can relieve fear in animals subjected to an approach avoidance situation in which they were shocked for eating. Subsequent studies have shown that there is no simple relationship between drinking behavior and reduced distress. Rather, the relationship between drinking and tension reduction depends on many factors, including individual social learning histories, the amount of alcohol consumed, expectations about the effects of drinking, and the social context of drinking (Sher & Levenson, 1983).

Clearly, other learning mechanisms besides negative reinforcement may be involved as well, such as social modeling of excessive drinking, positive reinforcement of drinking by others, and specific deficits in self-regulatory skills. Finally, cognitive factors (such as expectancies concerning the outcome of drinking) and social skills deficits figure prominently in current behavioral models of alcoholism (Marlatt & Donovan, 1981; Sobell & Sobell, 1993).

Assessment

Assessment of alcohol problems should be comprehensive and multimodal. According to Marlatt and Donovan (1988), it is essential that the client and therapist understand how abuse is embedded in broader life circumstances. Typically, the following areas are assessed using interviews, questionnaires, and direct samples of behavior (Miller, Westerberg, & Waldron, 1995; Sobell, Toneatto, & Sobell, 1994):

- Type and severity of the client's alcohol problem
- Specific patterns of use (detailed accounts of quantity, frequency, and patterning of use)
- Associated psychiatric problems
- Negative consequences of use
- Quality of social and vocational functioning
- Activities that compete with substance use
- Family history
- Medical complications of use
- Motivation for change

Although the most comprehensive assessment is conducted at intake, drinking behavior should be monitored throughout treatment and at posttreatment intervals. Techniques and issues relevant to the assessment of alcohol problems are described here.

Structured Interviews

Structured interview protocols provide a broad-band assessment of alcohol problems and their physical and social sequelae. One widely used interview format is the *Comprehensive Drinker Profile (CDP)* (Miller & Marlatt, 1984), an easily scored, reliable format that can be used with inpatients and outpatients. The CDP consists of an extensive series of questions concerning typical patterns of consumption, alcohol-related life problems, motivation for treatment, medical history, and expectancies regarding the probable outcome of treatment.

An alternative interview format is the *Addiction Severity Index (ASI)* (McClellan et al., 1992). The ASI has eight subscales: life problems, medical; legal, employment, alcohol, other drugs, family/social, and psychiatric. The ASI has good psychometric properies (Kosten, Rounsaville, & Kleber, 1983).

Style of Interview. The manner in which the interview is conducted has an important impact on the client's motivation to change. In traditional alcohol treatment programs, it has been common for therapists to use a highly confrontational approach. However, behaviorally oriented therapists has eschewed this style in favor of a more collaborative, respectful, and supportive approach. Motivation is seen as the product of an interaction between the client and those around him or her. *Motivational interviewing* (Miller & Rollnick, 1991) is the opposite of a confrontational approach in that the therapist tries to elicit concerns from client, avoids arguing with the client, and frames interventions in ways that support the client's sense of self-efficacy. Although motivational interviewing is a relatively new concept in the behavioral literature, there is some empirical support for its use. In a study of clients undergoing treatment for alcohol problems, Miller, Benefield, and Tonigan (1993) found that the more confrontational the therapist, the more the client resisted.

Self-Report

Self-report measures have been used extensively in the assessment of alcohol problems. The client's self-report provides the basis of the functional analysis of drinking behavior. *Self-monitoring* techniques can be very helpful in achieving a detailed assessment of drinking behavior and can also be used to measure treatment progress. Typically, the client is asked to record the exact amount of alcohol consumed; the date, time, and setting of ingestion; and thoughts and feelings occurring prior, during, and after the drinking incident. These data should be kept for two weeks (to provide a baseline assessment) and throughout treatment/follow-up. Instruments such as the *Grid* (Miller & Marlatt, 1984) or the *Timeline Followback* (Sobell & Sobell, 1992) can aid in self-monitoring. Self-monitoring has proven to be an extremely useful assessment tool, but it is nonetheless subject to potential limitations such as patient noncompliance or distortion of assessment data.

A number of *self-report questionnaires* have also been developed to assess problem drinking. For example, the *Alcohol Use Inventory* (Wanberg & Horn, 1983) consists of 140 forced choice questions divided into 22 different scales. This questionnaire has good psychometric properties and is particularly useful in achieving a functional analysis of drinking behavior. Similarly, the *Michigan Alcoholism Screen Test* is a widely used questionnaire consisting of 25 forced choice items (Selzer, 1971). The *Alcohol Dependence Scale (ADS)* (Skinner & Horn, 1984) provides a psychometrically sound tool for assessing the severity of the client's drinking problem, particularly whether there is evidence of dependence. Finally, the *Alcohol Expectancy Questionnaire (AEQ)* (Brown, Goldman, Inn, & Anderson, 1980) may be useful in treatment planning, because it has been found to predict relapse at one-year follow-up (Brown, 1985).

Other self-report instruments have been developed to assess the impact of drinking on the client's level of physical and social functioning. For example, the *Drinking Problems Index* is a 17-item questionnaire designed to measure alcohol-related problems (cite). Similarly, the *Drinker Inventory of Consequences* (Miller, Tonigan, & Longabaugh, 1994) consists of five scales that assess alcohol-related problems: physical health, social responsibility, intrapersonal, impulse control, and interpersonal.

Although self-report instruments can be reliable and valid for use in clinical settings (Zung, 1979), they are subject to many different sources of distortion. However, clients with alcohol problems do seem capable of accurately reporting their behavior under certain circumstances (Babor, Stephens, & Marlatt, 1987). Reliability can be improved by avoiding retrospective accounts and by providing "anchors" to help the person put substance use in temporal or situational context. Thus, self-report measures should be used in conjunction with other sources of information, and should not be administered to patients when they are intoxicated or undergoing withdrawal. Biomedical markers of use—derived from breath, urine, saliva, and blood tests—may be used to supplement the client's report (Litten & Allen, 1992). Likewise, collateral reports from significant others and/or objective records (hospital, jail, employment) may be used to supplement self-reported information about life functioning.

Analogue Measures

Finally, problem drinking has been assessed using analogue measures. Researchers have tried to simulate drinking environments such as bars and living rooms in controlled settings. For example, Miller, Sobell, Sobell, and Schaefer (1971) turned a hospital dayroom into a cocktail lounge, replete with wet bar. The number and types of drinks ordered, size of sips, and pace of drinking were then recorded. Similarly, Miller, Hersen, Eisler, and Elkin (1974) developed a taste-rating test to assess the reinforcement potential of drinking. Alcohol was made contingent on pressing a lever. The number of lever presses was then used as an index of reinforcement value. Because analogue measures are used in highly controlled settings, they have primarily served as research tools for understanding specific patterns of problem drinking.

Gender-Related Issues

Women problem drinkers present a special assessment challenge. Women reach higher peak blood/alcohol levels than men, and peak blood/alcohol levels vary significantly throughout the menstrual cycle (Jones & Jones, 1976). Because of these changes, it is difficult to achieve a stable baseline assessment. Finally, use of oral contraceptives dramatically slows alcohol metabolism (Jones & Jones, 1976). Therefore, any factors affecting estrogen levels should be carefully assessed (Miller, 1982).

Antidipsotropic Medications

Antidipsotrophic medications such as disulfiram (Antabuse) induce acute nausea when combined with alcohol. Disulfiram has been extensively prescribed for alcohol-dependent individuals who are attempting to achieve abstinence. Individual responses to disulfiram treatment have been highly variable (Miller, Brown, Simpson et al., 1995). According to Fuller (1995), the ideal candidate for disulfiram treatment is a middle-aged, alcohol-dependent male who has relapsed, has some degree of social stability, and is not significantly depressed. For example, in a large (controlled, blinded, multisite) study, disulfiram treatment did not add significantly to counseling in affecting abstinence rates. However, in subgroup of men who were older, socially stable, and not significantly depressed, use of disulfiram was related to significant reduction in drinking days (Fuller et al., 1986). Even with "optimal" candidates for treatment, disulfiram should always be part of a comprehensive treatment program, and careful, continuous screening is necessary because of risk of toxicity (Fuller, 1995).

Behavioral Treatment Programs

Behavioral treatment programs involve combinations of interventions that are tailored to the needs and life situation of the client. The goal in all programs is to reduce or eliminate alcohol consumption and to promote positive coping skills that help facilitate the client's social and occupational adjustment.

Aversion

Aversive conditioning techniques have been frequently used to treat alcohol dependence. *Chemical aversion* involves the repeated pairing of Antabuse (disulfiram), a nausea-inducing drug, with alcohol ingestion during the patient's hospital stay. The rationale for this procedure is straightforward: Pairing noxious experiences with alcohol ingestion is hypothesized to produce conditioned aversion to the taste and smell of alcohol. Chemical aversion conditioning tends to suppress alcohol ingestion for the first few months after treatment (Rimmele, Howard, & Hilfrink, 1995). However, chemical aversion has serious drawbacks as a therapy tool. It is extremely unpleasant for the patient. It is an expensive intervention, due to the need for continual medical supervision. Finally, its long-term effectiveness has not been sufficently investigated. Other methods are needed to ensure generalization of treatment gains to the client's natural environment.

Physical aversion, typically carried out with electric shock as the aversive stimulus, also has been used in the treatment of alcoholism. Not surprisingly, electrical aversion is associated with high attrition. Moreover, it is generally not effective in reducing problem drinking (Miller et al., 1995). Finally, there are serious ethical issues involved in the use of painful or physically coercive interventions, especially when alternative methods have proven effective. Therefore, use of physical aversion cannot be justified as a treatment for alcohol problems (Rimmele et al., 1995).

Covert sensitization is an alternative aversive method that has been used to treat alcoholism (Clarke & Hays, 1984; Rimmele et al., 1995). In this technique, clients are first put into a state of relaxation, then instructed to imagine a drinking episode. A detailed, vivid description involving the onset of nausea and vomiting is immediately given. For example, Rimmele and colleagues (1995) instructed a client to imagine that the sight, smell, and taste of beer elicited acute nausea. The following is part of the imaginal scene that they helped the client construct:

> *Now greenish bile is in your mouth and running into the sink. Your eyes are watering and your nose and throat are burning. You can still taste the beer, and you try to spit that taste out as well. The stench from the sink is almost unbearable—the sour odor of vomit, half–digested food, and beer. The smell triggers another heave in your stomach, but there is nothing left to come up. Still, your stomach continues to churn and heave. (Rimmele et al., 1995, p. 141)*

This technique is safer, less intrusive, and less expensive than chemical aversion and provides the patient with a coping tool that can be used in any setting. Unfortunately, controlled studies have provided only mixed support for the effectiveness of covert sensitization with alcohol dependent clients (e.g., Miller et al., 1995). According to Rimmele and associates (1995), when procedures for covert sensitization are well defined, it can result in significant reductions in drinking. However, the success of this technique depends heavily on the individual's ability to generate and sustain vivid imagery. Finally, covert sensitization is not a unidimensional treatment; it should always be combined with other interventions in treatment of alcohol problems.

Cue Exposure and Response Prevention

Recently, there has been a resurgence of interest in cue exposure therapy (CET) with alcohol-dependent clients (Drummond, Tiffany, Glautier, & Remington, 1995). Cue exposure techniques are intended to reduce alcoholics' reactivity to alcohol cues (Monti et al.. 1987; Niaura et al., 1988; Rohsenow et al., 1990). In controlled settings, clients are presented with cues for consumption, then prevented from engaging in consumption of alcohol. A wide range of cues may be relevant: the sight, smell, and/or taste of alcohol; the time of day when alcohol is usually ingested; sensations upon ingestion; or even moods and thoughts that tend to preceed drinking episodes.

In most programs, the sight and smell of alcohol have been used as cues, because they are powerful elicitors of cravings and easy to manipulate in controlled settings. Hierarchies of cue situations are established, usually on basis of relative urge to drink (Monti et al., 1993) or cue-elicited salivation (Rohsenow et al., 1994). According to Rohsenow, Monti, and Abrams (1995), at least 6 to 7 40- to 50-minute sessions are needed to reduce reactivity to alcohol cues. Cues can be presented imaginally, or *in vivo*. Among alcoholics, *in-vivo* exposure is more effective in reducing urges to drink than imaginal exposure (Rankin, Hodgson, & Stockwell, 1983).

Traditionally, the rationale for CET has been based on classical and operant conditioning models. Cue exposure interventions are believed to extinguish cravings for consumption, which have been conditioned to drug cues (Hammersley, 1992; Pomerleau, 1981). However, explanations based on cognitive social learning theory are also quite plausible. For example, presentation of alcohol cues could influence a host of cognitive processes such as attributions, outcome expectancies, self-efficacy, and motivation (Monti et al., 1989; Tiffany, 1995). Moreover, individual differences in responsivity to drug cues are strongly affected by a diverse range of factors, including level of dependence, affective states, and high-risk familial and personality factors (Rees & Heather, 1995).

How effective is cue exposure therapy in reducing cravings for alcohol? Single case studies of cue exposure treatment date from 1970s (Rohsenow et al., 1995). At present, however, only a few CET interventions have been conducted using controlled group designs. Monti and associates (1993) randomly assigned 34 alcohol dependent male clients in a VA inpatient unit to receive either CET or no additional treatment. The experimental group received six individually administered CET sessions on consecutive days. Controls received no additional treatment, just daily evaluations of the urge to drink. Clients in the CET group were exposed to their customary beverage until they reported reduced urge to drink. They were asked to imagine their most difficult "trigger" situations, then practice coping techniques (e.g., passive delay; thinking about negative consequences; substituting other, nonalcoholic substances; pleasant imagery). Results strongly favored the CET intervention: Relative to controls, clients in the CET group had a higher rate of abstinence and increased use of coping strategies three to six months posttreatment.

In another study, Drummond and Glautier (1994) assigned male alcoholic inpatients to a CET group, and controls to a relaxation training group where they also received very small doses of cue exposure. Clients in the CET group were asked not to drink. Alcohol was presented for 40-minute sessions on 10 weekdays. Six months later, men in the CET group reported higher latencies to resist heavy drinking and consumed less alcohol than controls. Thus, although further controlled studies are needed, CET appears to be a promising addition to comprehensive treatment programs for alcohol problems.

Contingency Management

In many previous reports, contingency management techniques have been linked to reduced rates of problem drinking (Miller, Hersen, Eisler, & Watts, 1974). Moreover, contingency management has been used successfully in a variety of treatment settings, including research laboratories, hospitals, and natural environments. Typically, a formal contract is established between therapist and client, specifying (1) concrete goals for behavior change and (2) consequences for lapsing versus sticking with the contract.

Although contingency contracting has been an important part of most behavioral treatment programs, it has several potential drawbacks. A high degree of ongoing therapist supervision is required. It is difficult to determine the occurrence of target behaviors and to identify effective reinforcers for treatment compliance. Finally, although contingency contracting often leads to short-term cessation of addictive behavior patterns, relatively little research has been done on the long-term maintenance of these gains (Sobell & Sobell, 1982).

Skills Training

The experience of negative emotional states, interpersonal conflict, and direct or indirect social pressure to drink have been identified as significant risk factors for alcoholic relapse (Marlatt & Donovan, 1981). In order to stabilize positive gains made in treatment, clients must learn how to cope effectively with all of these risk experiences. In addition, some clients may need to develop entirely new social networks that are supportive of their attempts to achieve sobriety. Hence, coping and social skills training is an important addition to behavioral treatment packages (Monti & Rohsenow, 1995). Skills training is conducted in small groups, and can be used in both inpatient and outpatient settings (Chaney, 1980). Initially, the specific nature of each client's coping skill deficits must be identified through careful behavioral assessment. Role-plays that encompass high-risk situations in the patient's natural environment (e.g., having an intense fight with one's spouse; being pressured to take "just one" drink at a party) are constructed, and modeling and group reinforcement are used to shape adaptive responses to these situations.

A diverse range of skills can be targeted for improvement. Assertiveness training interventions are primarily focused on coping with direct social pressure to drink. Social skills interventions focus on increasing clients' competence in conversation, listening, giving and receiving feedback, and conflict resolution. General problem-solving and job skills training are also options, if they are applicable to the client's needs. Finally, if high rates of anxiety accompany drinking, anxiety reduction skills must be taught and practiced, particularly in relation to situations that "trigger" drinking episodes. Assessing and treating anxiety should be part of any comprehensive treatment program for alcohol problems (Stockwell, 1995).

Relapse Prevention

Relapse rates are very high across the spectrum of addictive disorders (Marlatt & Gordon, 1985; Chiauzzi, 1991). The nature of the posttreatment environment plays a powerful role in long-term treatment outcomes (Tucker et al., 1991). Thus, *relapse prevention* is widely viewed as the most important challenge in addictions treatment. Marlatt (Marlatt & Gordon, 1985) has developed a general model of factors involved in the relapse process. Marlatt's model whas been extremely influential in sparking the development of relapse prevention programs. According to Marlatt, individuals who voluntarily change addictive habit patterns experience a sense of perceived control as long as abstinence is maintained.

Relapse is likely to be precipitated by exposure to high-risk situations, such as experiencing social pressure to drink, interpersonal conflict, or negative emotional states. If the individual's coping resources are ineffective in these situations, an initial "slip" occurs. Whether the first lapse is associated with total relapse depends on the individual's perceptions of the lapse and emotional reactions to it. Individuals who are at risk for total relapse experience strong self-blame following the initial lapse and conclude that they are failures for lapsing. This phenomenon is known as the *abstinence violation effect (AVE)* and is viewed as a central factor in the process of total relapse.

The goal of Marlatt's relapse prevention program is to prevent total relapsing by preparing clients, in *advance,* for the possibility of a lapse. The cornerstone of relapse prevention involves teaching the client coping skills that can be directly applied to high-risk situations. These might include problem-solving skills for managing high-risk situations, rehearsing relapses in advance, and/or relaxation training to counteract high anxiety. Cognitive restructuring techniques are also employed to counteract the abstinence violation effect. Initial lapses are reconceptualized as single events, not disastrous indications of complete failure. Finally, lifestyle changes may be initiated in order to reduce levels of stress in the patient's environment and to increase the amount of pleasurable experiences incompatible with addictive behavior patterns. A detailed program of relapse prevention for recovering alcoholics is outlined in Donovan and Cheney (1985).

Annis has proposed a model of relapse prevention that differs from Marlatt's model in relation to the conceptualization and prevention of relapse episodes. Annis and colleagues developed the *Inventory of Drinking Situations (IDS)* to assess specific contexts of heavy use (e.g., negative mood states; interpersonal conflict; social pressure to drink) (Annis et al., 1987). Based on clients' responses to the IDS, a hierarchy of risk situations is developed and used as the basis for graduated *in-vivo* exposure. Next, coping responses in relation to the risk situations are evaluated. Annis and Davis (1987) found that clients who were helped to identify and anticipate high-risk situations achieved lower drinking rates and higher levels of self-efficacy than those who did not receive relapse prevention.

There have been few controlled studies of the effectiveness of relapse prevention (RP) programs (Dimeff & Marlatt, 1995). The first controlled study was conducted by Chaney, O'Leary, and Marlatt (1978). Men who were assigned to a relapse prevention group made greater improvement and had less severe lapses than controls who were assigned to an "insight-oriented" group. In a Finnish study, Koski and Jannes (1990) found that individuals assigned to an RP group made better long-term progress than those who received psychodynamic, family systems, or traditional behavioral interventions. Allsop and Saunders (1989) found that clients who were randomly assigned to a preformance–based RP group had better outcomes than those who experienced verbally mediated RP or traditional treatment. On the other hand, Sobell and Sobell (1993) found that participation in RP was unrelated to the maintenance of light drinking goals among problem drinkers. Finally, Ito, Donovan, and Hall (1988) assigned alcohol-dependent male inpatients to RP or interpersonal therapy groups. Although the results favored RP intervention (they drank on fewer days, completed more aftercare), these differences were not statistically significant, perhaps because of their small sample sizes.

It is difficult to evaluate the effectiveness of relapse prevention programs because of the limited number of controlled studies, and because RP interventions have typically been part of comprehensive treatment "packages." Clearly, there is a great need for attention to relapse issues in the treatment of alcohol dependence and abuse. Much additional work needs to be done on the types of subject and treatment variables that affect drinking outcomes in RP programs.

Marital and Family Therapy

Because conflicted marital relations are frequent concomitants of alcohol problems, behavioral couples therapy (BCT) is an important treatment component (O'Farrell, 1995). Comprehensive treatment programs have been developed for couples when one partner has a serious drinking problem (Miller & Hersen, 1976; O'Farrell & Cowles, 1989). For example, O'Farrell's program is entitled *Counseling for Alcoholic Marriages (CALM)* (O'Farrell, Cutter, & Floyd, 1985). During the initial stages of treatment, interventions focus on motivating the client to seek treatment, reducing use, and reducing danger to self/family members. Next, interventions are focused on improving family communication and supporting long-term abstinence. The following case example, provided by Hay (1982), illustrates the successful use of broad-spectrum interventions in a situation where *both* partners had serious drinking problems.

A middle-aged couple who had been married for 29 years referred themselves for treatment. They reported that their relationship had deteriorated over the past five years. Both were extremely heavy drinkers. They were struggling with the life cycle transition of having more time together after their grown children had left home.

Each partner was asked to monitor his or her own drinking behavior and feelings of marital dissatisfaction on a daily basis. Marital satisfaction was extremely low for both partners. Daily drinking patterns for each partner were identified, with a focus on high-probability situations for heavy consumption. The husband drank excessively in response to work stressors, whereas the wife drank in response to interpersonal conflict with her mate and to being in the company of friends who drank. Separate consumption reduction and coping skills training goals were developed for each partner. Within 10 weeks both partners had met their individual consumption reduction goals, and maintenance plans were developed. At this point, conjoint marital treatment (seven sessions) was initiated. Goals of marital therapy included enhancing the couple's communication and problem solving and increasing the number and enjoyability of shared activities. Although the couple's marital satisfaction had remained low during the alcohol treatment phase, marital therapy was related to steady increases in positive feelings about the marriage. At one year follow-up, positive changes in drinking behavior and marital satisfaction were maintained.

Adding BCT to individually focused behavioral treatment has consistently promoted higher rates of abstinence and enhanced marital satisfaction (O'Farrell, 1995). For example, McCrady and colleagues (1991) found that clients who received BCT in addition to behavioral interventions for problem drinking had fewer marital separations, higher levels of marital satisfaction, and better drinking outcomes than those who received alcohol-focused treatment alone. Likewise, O'Farrell and associates (1992) found that alcohol abusers who received individual counseling plus BCT were significantly improved on measures of marital and drinking outcomes. Unfortunately, however, these advantages faded after two years. Thus, during the second phase of the CALM project, O'Farrell added a relapse prevention component. The results were encouraging: Combining RP and BCT was associated with long-term improvements in marital satisfaction and drinking behavior (O'Farrell et al., 1993).

Controlled Drinking
The most controversial issue in contemporary alcohol treatment concerns specification of treatment goals. Total abstinence has long been considered the only legitimate treatment outcome. However, the notion of controlled drinking involves learning self-moderation of drinking behavior. In an early study, Sobell and Sobell (1978) reported that at least some chronic alcoholics can learn to moderate their drinking. Their controlled drinking group consisted of chronic alcoholic inpatients who were taught to moderate their drinking behavior through discrimination training. For example, patients were shocked for drinking too fast or drinking too much at one time. Patients in the treatment group also were given problem-solving and assertiveness skills training.

At six-month and one-year follow-up intervals, progress of the controlled drinking group exceeded that of chronic alcoholic inpatients who had total abstinence as a goal and were shocked for consuming any alcohol. However, a heated controversy arose over a 10-year follow-up investigation of the controlled drinking group conducted by Pendery, Maltzman, and West (1982). These authors found that many individuals who had received controlled drinking treatment continued to drink excessively and had distorted the extent of their drinking in follow-up interviews. The Sobells were even accused of scientific fraud by one member of the follow-up research team, but these charges were found to be completely invalid by a group of independent investigators (Marlatt, 1983).

Moderation is currently seen as a reasonable goal for problem drinkers. Controlled drinking is most appropriate for younger (age 40 or less) problem drinkers who have been drinking excessively for less than 10 years and are not physically dependent on alcohol (Miller & Hester, 1980; Sobell & Sobell, 1993). Sobell and Sobell (1993) have provided the following rationale for developing specialized services for problem drinkers:

1. For alcohol abusers, outpatient interventions are as effective as inpatient treatment (Edwards, Orford, et al., 1977; Pittman & Tate, 1969). Furthermore, no differences have been found between "lay" interventions and inpatient treatment as effective therapies for alchohol abusers (Heather, 1989; IOM, 1990). Other studies have shown that alcohol abusers respond equally well to less intensive versus more intensive outpatient treatments (Hall & Heather, 1991; IOM, 1990; Kazdin & Bass, 1989). Thus, in contrast with alcohol dependent clients, alcohol abusers are capable of responding positively to minimal interventions.

2. The issue of progressivity (e.g. Jellinek, 1960) lacks empirical support. Only 25 to 30 percent of problem drinkers show progressive deterioration. An episodic pattern of problem drinking is most typical.

3. Problem drinkers score low on measures of alcohol dependence (Heather, Kisson-Singh, & Fenton, 1990). Moreover, in relation to alcohol-dependent individuals, problem drinkers are younger and have better psychosocial adjustment, fewer serious health consequences, and higher levels of education and social and economic resources.

Clearly, problem drinkers differ from alcohol-dependent individuals in many significant ways. The Sobells have argued that traditional inpatient treatment may be "overkill" for problem drinkers, reducing their motivation to comply with treatment (Sobell & Sobell, 1993). Outpatient programs that focus on issues of self-management seem more appropriate for this population. Two such programs are described here.

Behavioral Self-Control Training (BSCT) (Hester, 1995) is a well-known outpatient treatment program for nondependent problem drinkers. BSCT involves seven steps that occur in order:

1. Setting limits on the number of of drinks per day (the recommended upper limits are 12 drinks per week for men and 7 per week for women)
2. Self-monitoring of drinking (the client is instructed to fill out information on each drink before consuming it [date/time/ type/amount of alcohol/ place/ who with])
3. Changing the rate of drinking by switching from stronger to weaker drinks, favored to less favored drinks, gulping to sipping, and/or spacing drinks across time
4. Refusal strategy training, conducted using role-plays of refusal situations
5. Setting up reward systems for compliance (e.g., congratulatory self-talk and/or tangible, tailor-made rewards
6. Identifying antecedents to overdrinking, accomplished by asking the client to monitor situational factors and feeling states that are associated with urges to drink heavily
7. Coping skills training (the client is asked to list the most desirable effects of drinking [e.g., relaxation; feeling more at ease socially, etc.] and then to then brainstorm other ways of getting them)

The effectiveness of BSCT has been demonstrated in over 309 controlled clinical trials. Problem drinkers do respond positively to BSCT interventions, sustaining nonproblem drinking over long periods (Hester, 1995). Similar effects have been achieved for those who choose either abstinence or moderate drinking as treatment goals.

Guided Self-Management Therapy (Sobell & Sobell, 1993) is an outpatient-based treatment program for problem drinkers. It is described as a treatment program for those who self-identify as problem drinkers, do not have severe problems, and want to take responsibility for self-change. Steps in the program are as follows:

1. *Screening/Assessment.* Careful screening is necessary to select those individuals who may optimally benefit from this form of treatment. A comprehensive assessment of the client's drinking behavior, history, health, and psychosocial adjustment is conducted. Clients who are frequent, heavy drinkers (i.e., 12 drinks or more on an average of five days per week) and/or those who show evidence of dependence are excluded. A detailed functional analysis is conducted to identify high-risk situations for problem drinking. Based on self-monitored data supplemented with the Inventory of Drinking Situations (Annis & Graham,1988), typical "triggers" for problem drinking are identified (e.g., Does the client primarily imbibe while alone and angry or dysphoric? With others in rowdy party situations? In response to particular life situations?).

2. *Intervention procedures.* Goals are set for a prospective six-month period. The need for flexibility in setting treatment goals is strongly emphasized. Generally, it is recommended that the client does not have more than three drinks on four days, avoids drinking in high-risk situations, has no more than one drink per hour, and exercises a "thinking period" of 20 minutes before taking a drink. About 1/4 of the Sobells' clients have chosen total abstinence as a goal. Treatment interventions involve extensive use of self-monitoring, didactic reading, and problem-solving and relapse prevention skills (Sobell & Sobell, 1993).

Thus far, outcome evaluations of guided self-management therapy have been promising. In the year following treatment, clients who took part in this program achieved a 54 percent reduction in the total amount of drinking, and significantly reduced the number of their heavy drinking days (Sobell & Sobell, 1993). Further evaluations are needed to determine whether these positive effects hold up over longer periods of time. The following case examples illustrate the successful application of guided self-management therapy (Sobell & Sobell, 1993).

> In the first case, a 31-year-old mother of two was referred for heavy drinking related to negative mood states. The client reported that she had been drinking for about 10 years. Her pattern was to consume wine when alone, in response to feelings of anger or dysphoria. She wished to confine drinking to social occasions. In order to achieve her goals, she planned to solicit more household help from her family, schedule "private" time for herself, increase her rate of exercise, and cut out caffeine. The client had an excellent response to therapy: During the course of one year, she increased her abstinent days by 79 percent, and reported no heavy drinking days.
>
> In the second case, a 28-year-old man reported problems with heavy drinking related to positive mood states. He fit a "good times" profile of problem drinking in that he drank excessively on weekends, always in the company of others. His goals were to reduce alcohol consumption to no more than two drinks on two days per week, and to drink only during meal times. He was able to realize his light drinking goals within one year.

According to the Sobells, "These examples clearly illustrate that problem drinkers not only can take responsibility for dealing with their own problems, but that they can be quite creative and ingenious" (1993, p. 153).

Cognitive Therapy

In a recent volume (Beck, Wright, Newman, & Liese, 1993), Aaron Beck and colleagues outlined a cognitive therapy model of the treatment of substance abuse. According to Beck and colleagues, dysfunctional beliefs play an important role in the sequence of addiction. There are many different types of maladaptive beliefs that "feed" the addiction cycle. First, *global* maladaptive beliefs ("I am unlovable/helpless/vulnerable") interact with life stressors to increase anxiety, dysphoria, anger. *Anticipatory* beliefs involve the conviction that drinking will lead to feelings of pleasure. Eventually, anticipatory beliefs may lead to the view that alcohol is necessary for relief from pain. *Permissive* beliefs ("I deserve it"; "It will be OK just this time"; "I'm too strong to get addicted") allow the individual to rationalize use. Finally, *relief-oriented* beliefs are associated with fear and helplessness ("Withdrawal will be intolerable"; "I am helpless against my craving"), thereby increasing the likelihood that addictive behaviors will continue. Cognitive therapy is a way of reducing the self-defeating nature of addiction by replacing maladaptive beliefs with those that promote self-efficacy and control.

The first challenge in cognitive therapy is to build a trusting relationship without colluding with the client's maladaptive thoughts and behaviors. As with all forms of cognitive therapy, Beck and colleagues (1993) advise appealing to the client's positive self-esteem, and "disarming" with humility and empathy. If confrontation is necessary, it must be honest, direct, and diplomatic. For example, Beck and colleagues (1993) described the case of a male client who had clearly been drinking heavily just prior to a therapy session. Previously, a rule had been set that no therapy would be conducted if the client arrived in an inebriated or drug-intoxicated state. The limit was respectfully enforced by the therapist, despite denying, sarcastic, and angry reactions from the client.

Once a positive therapeutic alliance has been established, clear goals are set in order to gain a sense of direction and to foster hope. Guided discovery and homework "experiments" are used to illustrate the roles that automatic beliefs play in the cycle of addiction. The ultimate goal of treatment is to replace addictive beliefs with those that involve positive control. For example, the client might learn to "talk back" to cravings with self-statements such as "If I wait out this craving, it will go away", or "I will feel strong if I resist." Another important part of treatment involves helping the client manage life problems such as family or marital dysfunction, chronic daily stressors, legal difficulties, and/or medical complications of use. As Beck and colleagues have observed, these problems tend to plague substance abusing individuals, and can easily trigger substance use by overwhelming the person's tolerance for discomfort. Increased use, in turn, exacerbates the nature of these problems, leading to a vicious cycling effect. For example, in the case of a client named Dee, stresses included being a single parent to her infant son, having her employment and personal freedom restricted by maternal responsibilities, and coping with the baby's irritable temperament. The use of positive coping imagery was helpful in redirecting the client's drug cravings (Beck et al., 1993). Finally, relapse prevention is presented as part of the CT framework. Following Marlatt's general model, the nature of the client's beliefs and responses to high-risk situations are viewed as central to the prediction and control of relapse.

Community Reinforcement Approach

The *Community Reinforcement Approach (CRA)* is a broad-spectrum behavioral treatment program for substance abuse problems (Azrin et al., 1982). The emphasis of CRA is on building self-esteem through positive reinforcement, not confrontation. A detailed functional analysis is conducted to identify typical "triggers" for drinking, and contexts for nondrinking. Rather than pressing the client to adopt a treatment goal of total abstinence, *sobriety sampling* is used to establish a treatment contract. In sobriety sampling, the client is asked to commit to abstinence for a mutually agreed upon period, often 90 days. During this trial period, use of disulfiram is an option. The CRA offers a menu of interventions that are tailored to the client's needs and life situation. All clients receive training to enhance the effectiveness of their communication, problem-solving, and drink refusal skills. Other interventions focus on helping clients find and keep gainful employment, build a supportive social/recreational network, and/or improve the quality of their marital relationships. Finally, relapse prevention is conducted as a means of consolidating and stabilizing positive treatment gains (Smith & Meyers, 1995).

The Challenge of Informed Eclecticism

As shown in this chapter, behavioral approaches to the treatment of alcohol problems are quite diverse. Moreover, clients show diversity in the types and severity of their drinking problems. Finally, clients differ appreciably in their backgrounds and current life situations, and these differences interact meaningfully with treatment goals and interventions. Clearly, behavioral treatment packages must be multidimensional and keyed to the special needs of the client. For this reason, Miller and Hester (1995) have proposed that behavioral clinicians adopt an *informed eclecticism model* of treatment. Informed eclecticism implies that there is no single approach that works with all alcohol problems and that the clincian must be trained to use a broad range of interventions that are uniquely fitted to each different case. However, in order to actualize this objective, behavior therapists must establish clearer criteria for matching clients to appropriate interventions (Miller & Hester, 1995).

Nicotine Addiction

The harmful effects of tobacco on the U.S. population exceed those of all other abused substances combined (Solberg & Kottke, 1992). In the United States, approximately one-third of the adolescent and adult population use tobacco (CDC, 1992). Long-term cigarette smoking is associated with lung cancer, emphysema, cancer of the larynx and esophagus, and cardiovascular and cerebrovascular diseases, chronic obstructive and other lung diseases, ulcers, and maternal and fetal complications (USDHHS, 1990). Those who have never smoked but are chronically exposed to tobacco smoke are at elevated risk for lung cancer and heart disease (Garland, Barrett-O'Connor, Szaret, Criqui, & Wingard, 1985). For these reasons, smoking has been called the largest preventable cause of death in the United States (USDHHS, 1989). As Prochaska, Diclemente, Velicer, & Rossi (1993) stated, "Of the people alive in the world today, an estimated 500 million will die from the use of tobaccco. Even a moderate breakthrough in our ability to help people quit smoking could prolong and improve millions of lives" (p. 399).

Over 80 percent of those who smoke wish to stop (American Psychiatric Association, 1994). However, it is very difficult to quit smoking. At 6 to 12 months posttreatment, most smoking cessation programs have modest abstinence rates of 15 percent to 20 percent (Lichtenstein & Brown, 1982; Zelman et al., 1992).

Cigarette smoking is an addiction: Repeated smoking builds physiological tolerance to nicotine, and withdrawal symptoms occur when the individual ceases to smoke (Schacter, 1978). Tolerance is manifest by the absence of nausea, dizziness, and other symptoms despite the ingestion of substantial amounts of nicotine. Cessation of nicotine produces a well-defined cluster of withdrawal symptoms that occur within two hours of abstinence. These include intense cravings for cigarettes, drowsiness, anxiety, dysphoria, insomnia, irritability, impaired concentration, decreased heart rate, increased weight gain and increased appetite (American Psychiatric Association, 1994). Most withdrawal symptoms abate within one month, but weight gain, hunger, and cravings may last for six months or longer (Hughes, Gust, Skoog, Keenan, & Fenwick, 1991).

Smoking is a multifaceted addictive disorder: It is learned in diverse settings, highly practiced on a daily basis, and reinforced by a variety of physiological, psychological, and social factors (Lichtenstein & Brown, 1982). For example, smoking is associated with the experience of pleasure and relaxation in many different settings. Nicotine is a psychostimulant that produces unpleasant withdrawal symptoms upon abrupt cessation. Finally, smoking is correlated with interpersonal attractiveness in media advertisements and is widely modeled by other individuals.

Assessment Issues

As with addictive disorders, in general, it is essential to conduct a comprehensive assessment of the client's addictive behavior patterns, current life situation, and personal and social strengths and weaknesses. Suggestions for content areas to be included in the initial assessment are outlined later in this chapter.

Relatively few scales have been designed to assess nicotine dependence (Sobell et al., 1994). The most frequently used scales include the *Fagerstrom Test for Nicotine Dependence* (Fagerstrom et al., 1991) and the *Revised Tolerance Questionnaire* (Tate & Schmitz, 1993). Both are short self-report instruments. However, a single question may provide the best current index of dependence. Pomerleau and associates (1990) have found that latency to the first cigarette after waking ("After you wake up, how many minutes pass before you have your first cigarette?") is strongly predictive of dependence.

Smoking behavior is typically assessed using self-monitoring techniques. Two dependent measures have been derived from self-report data to indicate treatment progress: *smoking rate,* or daily frequency of cigarette consumption, and *smoking abstinence.* Although abstinence measures are less susceptible to the reactive effects of self-monitoring than smoking rate measures, they can be easily distorted. For these reasons, physiological measures of smoking (based on breath or blood samples) should be used to corroborate self-monitoring data whenever possible (Lichtenstein & Brown, 1982).

Behavioral Intervention Techniques

As with treatment of alcohol problems, behavioral interventions for smoking usually involve multicomponent treatment "packages." Specific techniques that often comprise these programs are described here.

Aversion Techniques

Aversive methods have been frequently used in behavioral interventions for smoking (Raw, 1978). These methods differ according to the type of aversive stimulus used to eliminate smoking. Electrical aversion involves the pairing of electrical shock with smoking behavior. Although this method may temporarily suppress smoking, it does not produce long-term abstinence (Russell, Armstrong, & Patel, 1976). Furthermore, use of electrical aversion requires specialized equipment and supervision and it is extremely unpleasant for the client.

Covert sensitization has also been used in smoking control programs. Covert sensitization eliminates many of the practical and ethical problems inherent in electrical aversion. However, at best, only modest gains in smoking reduction have been achieved relative to placebo controls (Lichtenstein & Danaher, 1976). Thus, the effectiveness of covert sensitization as a smoking reduction technique requires more conclusive support.

Finally, *satiation* and *rapid smoking* techniques involve the use of cigarette smoke itself as the aversive stimulus. Satiation is carried out in the home setting. Clients are simply instructed to double or triple their baseline smoking rates. Although satiation is effective when it is part of a multicomponent treatment program (Best, Owen, & Trentadue, 1978; Delahunt & Curran, 1976), it is difficult to monitor and control.

Rapid smoking is conducted in the laboratory or clinic setting. Clients are instructed to smoke continuously, inhaling frequently until tolerance is reached. Although early reports suggested that rapid smoking was a highly effective treatment technique (Danaher, 1977), studies have provided mixed reports of effectiveness (Lichtenstein & Brown, 1982). Investigators have also questioned whether serious physical side effects might be produced by rapid smoking. Although nicotine poisoning does not result from rapid smoking, potential cardiac complications remain a serious concern. For this reason, rapid smoking should always be used in a medical setting and should be restricted to healthy young adults with no family history of cardiovascular disease.

Cue Exposure

Cue exposure treatment (CET) represents a new direction in the behavioral treatment of nicotine addiction (Brandon, Piasecki, Quinn, & Baker, 1994). Typical cues involve holding a cigarette, generating smoking imagery, or observing live or videotaped smoking by others (Niaura et al., 1992). There has been relatively little research on the effectiveness of CET with smokers. Early reviews have been disappointing, failing to show that CET is superior to any other treatment in reducing smoking (Brandon et al., 1994). However, these conclusions must be tentative, given that the available studies have used small numbers of participants. Furthermore, cue exposure has been used as a singular treatment for smoking, whereas most investigators agree that multicomponent packages are essential. Thus, further research is needed to determine the contribution of CET to multicomponent smoking cessation programs.

Nicotine Fading

Nicotine fading involves the gradual reduction of nicotine intake by switching cigarette brands. Brands with significantly less nicotine are introduced on a weekly basis, until abstinence is achieved. This smoking reduction method has not received much research attention. Available studies suggest that nicotine fading may have limited effects on total abstinence (Glasgow & Bernstein, 1981). However, this method does promote switching to brands that contain low levels of tar and nicotine, and long-term maintenance of these changes has been demonstrated (Lichtenstein & Brown, 1982).

Nicotine Gum

Use of nicotine gum appears to enhance the client's ability to stop smoking (Fagerstrom & Melin, 1985; Lam et al., 1987). For example, Jarvis and associates (1982) found that during the first two months of smoking cessation, withdrawal symptoms such as hyperirritability, cravings, and hunger were rated less severe by those receiving nicotine gum than by controls. The use of nicotine gum must be combined with instructions and a clear rationale, because the gum does not completely eliminate cravings and other withdrawal symptoms (Jarvis, 1989).

Case Example

The following case example, drawn from O'Hara (1994), illustrates the difficulties involved in treatment of nicotine addiction.

> The client was a 49-year-old man who had begun smoking at age 17. He had desired to quit his pack-a-day habit for over 20 years. He had tried nicotine gum and abstinence. During the withdrawal period, he experienced intense cravings for nicotine and began substituting food for the nicotine. He set a "quit date," and prepared for it by getting a prescription for nicotine gum and by changing his smoking routine. His withdrawal symptoms peaked 48 hours after quitting. During the first week of abstinence, he experienced intense cravings for nicotine combined with fatigue, insomnia, dysphoria, and irritability. Although the intensity of the withdrawal symptoms abated after a few weeks, the client relapsed after 5 weeks of abstinence. During a 3-month follow-up visit, the therapist reframed his experience as a partial success, in that he was able to remain abstinent for 5 weeks. After some hesitation, the client accepted the therapist's assessment and indicated that he might be willing to try again.

Innovative Multicomponent Interventions

It is clear that new approaches to the treatment of nicotine addiction are needed. Prochaska and his colleagues have argued that smoking cessation programs should be based on knowledge of how people quit on their own, not on how professionals *assume* that they change (Prochaska & DiClemente, 1983). His research studies have revealed distinct stages that smokers pass through in the self-change process (DiClemente et al., 1991). In a large controlled study, Prochaska and associates (1993) found that a combination of interactive computer feedback about the client's progress and didactic self-help information matched to the individual's stage in the change process produced promising long- term quit rates.

Another innovative approach to smoking cessation involves carrying out interventions in peoples' work sites. Worksite interventions have been shown to reach larger numbers of people and to produce higher quit rates than clinic-based interventions (Fisher, Glasgow, & Terborg, 1990). For example, Jason, McMahon and colleagues (1995) randomly assigned 1,492 smokers to one of the following conditions: (1) studying a standardized self-help manual, (2) studying a self-help manual plus receiving monetary incentives for each day of abstinence, or (3) studying the manual, receiving monetary incentives, and attending 6 weekly group meetings plus 14 booster sessions of multi-component cognitive-behavioral interventions (e.g., strategies for identifying and changing smoking patterns, relaxation, contracting, self-visualization). Smokers who participated in the multicomponent intervention had higher long-term quit rates than those in the control conditions.

Long-Term Maintenance

The most urgent issue in the behavioral treatment of smoking is promoting long-term maintenance. Although smoking cessation programs have relatively high success rates, most smokers resume their habit within a few weeks or months of quitting. What factors predict who will remain abstinent? This a complex question, involving a diverse range of personal and environmental variables. Increased levels of stress have been linked to elevations in smoking and to relapse following smoking cessation (Baer & Lichtenstein, 1988). The presence of concurrent psychological disorders may also play a significant role in nicotine addition. For example, Glassman (1993) reported that half of individuals who made repeated, unsuccessful attempts to quit smoking suffered from major depressive disorder.

Characteristics of the immediate environment, such as whether other family members or friends smoke (Morgan, Ashenberg, & Fisher, 1988) and characteristics of the broader social environment affect vulnerability to nicotine addiction. For example, in recent years, the most elevated rates of smoking have occurred in women and minorities (Fiore, Novotny, Pierce, et al., 1989). Finally, a host of cognitive variables have been found to predict successful smoking cessation: intrinsic motivation (Curry, Wagner, & Grotham, 1990), expectancies for the usefulness of nicotine gum in relieving withdrawal symptoms (Gottlieb, Killen, & Marlatt, 1987), and self-efficacy for quitting and maintaining abstinence (Haaga & Stewart, 1992).

A relapse prevention program for smoking has been developed by Shiffman, Read, Maltese, Rapkin, and Jarvik (1985). Their program is based on Marlatt's relapse prevention model (described earlier). According to this model, the greatest single cause of relapse is failure to cope adaptively in a relapse crisis. Hence, active planning for relapse crises is at the core of this treatment approach. The adequacy of each client's coping repertoire is carefully assessed, and high-risk situations for relapse are identified. The most powerful method of promoting maintenance involves *relapse crisis debriefing:* circumstances surrounding the client's most recent relapse crisis are carefully reviewed, and alternative coping skills are taught. Relapse crisis debriefing provides an ideal context for teaching coping skills. Steps in the debriefing assessment include identification of the high-risk incident; identification of the relapse precipitant; identification of thoughts and feelings that occurred during the relapse crisis; and, finally, identification of thoughts and feelings which occurred as consequences of the lapse.

Following the relapse crisis debriefing, strategies for coping with high-risk situations are taught. These might include simple strategies such as avoiding and escaping from high-risk situations, use of distraction, and/or use of delay to "wait out" cravings for cigarettes. More elaborate coping skills involve the use of cognitive restructuring or self-verbalization techniques, as well as behavioral skills such as relaxation or assertion.

Chapter Summary

Behavioral assessment and treatment of addictive disorders should be multimodal and formulated in terms of current knowledge about the development and maintenance of specific addictive problems. A wide variety of behavioral interventions have been used to treat addictive disorders, including aversion methods, contingency management, discrimination training, and training of diverse coping skills. Although behavioral intervention programs have been associated with short-term improvements, relapse rates are very high across the entire spectrum of addictive disorders. Thus, issues of relapse prevention and long-term maintenance must be explicitly dealt with in therapy.

Chapter 14

Cognitive-Behavioral Interventions for Chronic Disorders

George F. and Esther F. are mental health professionals[1] and researchers who have spent decades improving treatment programs for people with chronic mental illnesses such as schizophrenia. In 1964 George was struck by the long-term dependency of psychiatric inpatients, created by the regimented social organization of hospitals. In a controlled experiment, he compared the traditional ward structure (managed by the staff alone) with a ward managed jointly by staff and patients. In the jointly managed ward, the patients formed small problem-solving groups that made decisions about daily living. The small groups functioned effectively without staff leadership. Money and passes were used to reinforce positive behavior change. The unit with joint management and small groups produced significantly greater improvement than the traditional unit in patients' social behavior, self-esteem, and general morale.

The small group program brought many benefits, but it did not improve people's long-term adjustment in the community after discharge from the hospital. George therefore established problem-solving groups in community settings outside the hospital. The pioneers of this program, randomly selected from a larger group of inpatient volunteers, formed the first unit in the community, naming the setting and the program "the Lodge." Before they left the hospital, they had practiced dealing with daily living matters and resolving possible problems that could arise. A mental health professional was on hand to provide support as needed. As the Lodge members tried to start a business (a janitorial service) in the community, there were several failures, but these produced immediate feedback and became constructive learning experiences. Outside consultants gave advice on legal matters, accounting and bookkeeping, and food preparation. The mental health professional was eventually replaced by someone from the community. The Lodge became self-supporting and self-governing, and severed its links with the hospital and the mental health system.

Meanwhile, the patients who had been randomly assigned to traditional community placements (e.g., day hospital treatment, outpatient psychotherapy) were significantly less likely to stay employed, more likely to return to the hospital, and were being treated at much greater expense. George and Esther extended their work to include individualized community programs with the same commitment to client empowerment (Fairweather & Fergus, 1993).

Definitions of psychological therapy often imply that it involves voluntary outpatients working with professional providers in dyadic relationships. For example, traditional psychotherapy has been described as "an interpersonal process" to bring about changes in areas "which have proven troublesome to the person seeking help from a trained professional" (Strupp, 1978). A recent series of videotapes by the American Psychological Association demonstrating 12 forms of psychotherapy focuses entirely on therapist/client pairs in an outpatient setting. But, as shown in the introductory example, the psychotherapy that is often delivered to people with schizophrenia and other chronic and severe disorders is not limited to therapist/client partnerships. It is more likely to include (1) inpatient, group home, and therapeutic community settings; (2) service providers other than mental health professionals; and (3) interdisciplinary teams of providers, especially in inpatient settings.

It is true that one-on-one behavior therapy does take place in hospitals. Clients with anorexia nervosa often have to be admitted to a hospital ward to allow therapists to gain control over life-threatening food refusal. Clients with depression may need therapists available round the clock to head off suicide attempts. Obsessive-compulsive and severely phobic clients are sometimes admitted to hospital units so that behavior therapy can be implemented intensively over a couple of weeks. Yet, this form of inpatient therapy is really just an extension of the typical outpatient work. The clients are still "clients" in a meaningful sense, if they have chosen to team up with a therapist to work on personal goals. The situation of the person who is institutionalized with a severe and chronic mental disorder is usually quite different.

Involuntary Hospitalization and Patients' Rights

Major disorders like schizophrenia, autistic disorder, severe and profound mental retardation, and some of the problems associated with brain damage often lead to hospitalization, not only for more intensive treatment and supervision but also because the sufferer cannot always be trusted to act safely in society. Several such disorders involve *psychosis,* implying bizarre symptoms, severe impairment of behavioral functioning, and extremely poor judgment.

This situation creates important ethical problems. People in the community who are disturbed by the behavior of the psychotic person will, understandably enough, want the mental health professionals to take over and remedy the problem. However, the proposed "patient" may wish to have nothing to do with the local psychiatric hospital and its staff. Under these circumstances, people deemed by a court to pose a serious threat of harm to themselves or to others because of a mental disorder may be hospitalized involuntarily for a limited period. However, this does not deprive patients of their civil rights. Involuntarily hospitalized patients' rights include:

- The right to appropriate, state-of-the-art treatment
- The right to treatment in the least restrictive setting consistent with the safety of the patient and the community
- The right to *refuse* treatment
  (Stromberg et al., 1988)

Mental health professionals cannot avoid the ethical problems of hospitalizing people against their will simply by refusing to do so. Severe civil penalties can be imposed when a provider fails to take steps to protect citizens from a dangerous patient. Protecting citizens may often mean referring the proposed patient for emergency, involuntary hospitalization (Stromberg, Schneider, & Joondeph, 1993).

Not all people with schizophrenia and other severe disorders are hospitalized against their will, of course. But schizophrenia itself impairs people's judgments, so how can one rely on a patient's informed consent to treatment, or on a patient's ability to participate in treatment planning with a behavior therapist? This is not the only issue that distinguishes the hospitalized patient with a severe disorder from the usual outpatient. Hospital treatment does not commonly involve just one-on-one contact with a therapist. Treatment is assumed to include the whole "therapeutic milieu," meaning the entire ward context of other patients and professional and paraprofessional staff members. The patient does not have a unique relationship with a therapist that he or she has sought out. Instead, the "therapist" is a large team of people who come and go daily with changes of shift. In addition to psychiatrists, psychologists, social workers, psychiatric nurses, and paraprofessional mental health workers, this team may include occupational therapists, teachers, activity aides, and vocational counselors whose mission is not specifically to diagnose and treat the *DSM-IV* disorder but to play a part in a much broader overall treatment plan.

It is clear, then, that many psychiatric inpatients are in a very different situation from typical outpatients. Inpatients are surrounded by a large treatment team. They have varying degrees of restriction on their movement about the hospital buildings, grounds, and community. They suffer from severe problems that are still poorly understood and lead to impairments across the whole range of behavioral functioning. Finally, they often live in state hospitals with barely adequate financial support and staffing, and built in an architectural style described by one administrator as "Early Halloween."

To return to appropriate definitions of *psychotherapy,* here is a recent one that does fit better in the context of severe disorders in hospital settings:

> *We can define intentional psychotherapeutic activities, no matter what their form, as efforts that are made to guide and control the "underlying reorganizing process[es]" necessary to restore (and refine) the individual's capacity to participate in normal social relationships. Since that capacity has both intrapersonal and interpersonal aspects, therapeutic measures might focus primarily on problems in one or the other or both of these areas. (Orlinsky & Howard, 1995, p. 6)*

In this chapter, we will describe the contributions of behavior therapy to the treatment of psychiatric patients with chronic problems. Despite the pessimism that often surrounds this topic, we are happy to report that among the psychological therapies normally applied to outpatients, cognitive and behavioral interventions have recorded impressive successes in this area. The development in recent years of behavioral, milieu, and community treatment programs has contributed to a much improved outlook for the seriously disturbed psychiatric inpatient.

Diagnoses and Typical Problems

Schizophrenia

The best-known chronic mental illness is *schizophrenia*. Experts have disagreed about its important characteristics for a century. In Europe, Emil Kraepelin (1855–1926) compared schizophrenia to a dementia occurring early in life, and associated it with a progressive deterioration of functioning with a very poor outlook for improvement. Eugen Bleuler (1857–1939), who first used the term *schizophrenia,* had a broader view of the disorder and did not restrict the diagnosis to poor prognosis cases. Generally, Europeans favored Kraepelin's definition and Americans preferred Bleuler's, and as a result, schizophrenia was the predominant diagnosis for the problems of psychiatric inpatients in the United States for decades. Since 1980, U.S. diagnostic criteria for schizophrenia have been closer to Kraepelin's than to Bleuler's. The *DSM-IV* criteria may paraphrased and summarized as follows:

- Evidence of two or more of these characteristic symptoms over a significant time span: delusions, hallucinations, disorganized speech, bizarre behavior, dulling of emotional responsiveness
- Impairment in work performance, social relationships, or self-care
- Continuous signs of disturbance for at least six months
- Not associated with a different major psychiatric disorder, with substance abuse, or with a medical condition that could explain the symptoms

When they occur in schizophrenia, *hallucinations* are typically auditory and "are usually experienced as voices, whether familiar or unfamiliar, that are perceived as distinct from the person's own thoughts" (American Psychiatric Association, 1994, p. 275). *Delusions* are faulty beliefs that may be bizarre (believing that someone is controlling one's thoughts with an X-ray machine) or nonbizarre (believing that one is under surveillance by the Central Intelligence Agency). *Disorganized speech* reflects disordered thought processes, as evidenced by using made-up words (neologisms), failing to make abstractions or to get beyond the most literal meanings of words (concrete thinking), linking words that rhyme (clang associations), and incoherence or a disconnected quality in the person's train of thought (loose associations) (Neale & Oltmanns, 1980; Lenzenweger & Gottesman, 1994).

Mental Retardation

In *mental retardation*, the client has multiple problems in adaptive functioning related to significantly low intelligence, evident before adulthood. Typical problems in adaptive functioning are impoverished social and daily living skills, difficulties with communication, and limited independence and social responsibility. Specific problems such as self-injurious behavior can also arise. A formal definition is:

> Mental retardation *refers to substantial limitations in present functioning. It is characterized by significantly subaverage intellectual functioning, existing concurrently with related limitations in two or more of the following applicable adaptive skill areas: communication, self-care, home living, social skills, community use, self-direction, health and safety, functional academics, leisure, and work. Mental retardation manifests before age 18.* (American Association on Mental Retardation, 1992, p. 1)

The authors of that definition caution diagnosticians to make allowance for (1) differences in communication, (2) cultural and linguistic diversity, (3) community environments lacking appropriate supports, (4) clients having strengths in other areas of functioning, and (5) the expectation that functioning will improve with appropriate supports over a sustained period. The *DSM-IV* definition of mental retardation overlaps almost entirely with this definition.

Suitable Treatment Targets

Behavior therapy for people with schizophrenia or mental retardation has usually been aimed not at the disorders but at specific problems in behavioral functioning. For example, programs to help clients communicate better often take the same form, regardless of the diagnosis. Similarly, behavioral treatment of elderly inpatients focuses on particular issues such as negative mood states, social withdrawal, obsessions, or grief rather than on diagnostic syndromes (Richards & Thorpe, 1978).

In current formulations, schizophrenia and most forms of mental retardation are viewed as multiply determined syndromes with strong genetic and biological underpinnings (Bellack & Mueser, 1994; Lenzenweger & Gottesman, 1994). This certainly does not imply that behavioral interventions are inappropriate, but it does mean that one no longer seeks the ultimate causes of these disorders in such psychological factors as faulty parenting, unfortunate conditioning experiences, or adopting unhelpful self-statements. Instead, behavior therapists focus on helping clients cope with these chronic disorders by complying with regimens of prescribed medication, confronting interpersonal stress constructively, and developing coping skills (Bellack & Mueser, 1994).

Appropriate treatment targets have changed over the years with changes in the service delivery system. In the 1950s, people with schizophrenia vegetated in overcrowded state institutions and were supervised and cared for rather than being actively treated. When behavioral approaches were first introduced in the early 1960s, behavior therapists tried to improve specific areas of patients' functioning, such as coherent speech—an appropriate form of intervention at the time. By the late 1960s, behavior therapists were using reinforcement principles on entire ward populations to counteract the negative impact of the institutional routine. By the 1980s, when far fewer people with chronic disorders were routinely housed in state hospitals, social skills training for individuals in community settings became the norm (Bellack & Mueser, 1994). The following sections provide an outline of this progression of suitable treatment targets and methods.

The Social Breakdown Syndrome

When a client with schizophrenia is treated in a hospital setting, the more dramatic features of the disorder (bizarre delusions, absurd and incomprehensible speech, etc.) are often relatively short-lived. Comprehensive treatment with medication and psychosocial interventions typically improves the client's functioning enough to allow discharge within a few weeks. It is common for people with schizophrenia to live in the community for months at a time in between fairly brief periods of hospitalization (Gottesman, 1991; Neale & Oltmanns, 1980). Unfortunately, patients who were first admitted before modern treatments were available tended to require continuous hospitalization, and some of those admitted today need lengthy stays despite the best efforts of staff members to discharge them. When a patient has been continuously hospitalized for more than a few months, the main problems are less likely to be the florid symptoms of acute schizophrenia than the effects of having been institutionalized and out of circulation for so long. Years of adapting successfully to the hospital environment have created a new problem—the problem of institutionalization, sometimes called the *social breakdown syndrome* (Paul, 1969).

Some of the problems of institutionalization were recognized in the early 1800s. In 1816, John Reid, a London physician, commented that asylums were "'nurseries for and manufactories of madness' rather than hospitals for recovery and cure" (Hunter & MacAlpine, 1963, p. 723). Reid argued that

- Mental illnesses can be infectious, not through biological mechanisms but through "sympathy" (or, in modern terms, social learning influences).
- Mental illnesses grow and flourish in institutions because of "the idea that [the patients] are supposed to be insane" (or through expectancy effects).
- Depriving the patients of rational, sympathetic conversation, and subjecting them to "coarse and humiliating" treatment, are the very reverse of the appropriate interventions (Hunter & MacAlpine, 1963, pp. 723–724).

Why did so many patients become "long-stay chronic hospital residents" (Paul, 1969, p. 82)? The characteristics of the individual patients were less important than features of the hospital environment itself in producing the social breakdown syndrome. The problem was not that hospital staff members were uncaring; typically, staff members looked after the patients' needs very well. Patients were given a balanced diet, their medical needs were attended to, and their personal care and hygiene were closely supervised. Hospital barbers and beauticians helped take care of patients' appearance, activity aides provided opportunities for constructive occupations, and ward staff members assisted patients in shaving or cutting their fingernails.

The problem with taking care of patients' needs so fully is that, under these circumstances, people easily lose their initiative, their independence, and their ability to fend for themselves. Dependency, withdrawal, and inability to take personal responsibility for activities are the result (Paul, 1969). "Custodial" care looks after patients but fails to teach them survival skills for the outside world, so they remain dependent on the institution.

Paul (1969) argued that long-stay patients who had become institutionalized needed rehabilitation focused on resocialization, instrumental role performance, reduction of bizarre behavior, and establishing a supportive relationship with a roommate in the community. In other words, suitable treatment interventions would help people learn social skills, self-care, and work or household management skills. They needed to learn to behave conventionally enough that concerned people would not return them to the hospital. Finally, patients were likely to need a capable person from whom to draw support in issues of everyday living.

Suitable Treatment Methods

By the late 1960s, it was clear that the most promising treatments for institutionalized patients were milieu therapy, social learning therapy, and special aftercare procedures in the community.

Milieu Therapy

Usually operating within a "therapeutic community," *milieu therapy* contrasts significantly with the traditional image of custodial care. In a therapeutic community, patients are expected to interact with one another, to encourage each other to become more active and engaged in the life of the community, and to learn to take personal responsibility for behaving in constructive, goal-oriented ways. There is more freedom than in a traditional ward, because staff members do not make all the decisions—patients are urged to discuss issues among themselves and decide on aspects of the ward routine. In a therapeutic community in England in the 1960s, for example, patients made group decisions on how to resolve conflict over which television station to watch, how to respect the rights of smokers and nonsmokers on the unit, and what was an appropriate bedtime. In the late 1960s, research findings on the effectiveness of milieu therapy were inconclusive (Paul, 1969).

Social Learning Therapy

Behavior therapy programs in inpatient settings are often known as *social learning therapy*. Based on learning principles, social learning therapy is usually aimed at the group of patients on a particular ward rather than at a series of individual patients. This is justified by the fact that patients with the social breakdown syndrome tend to share a common list of problems, including social withdrawal and apathy.

The most familiar example of social learning therapy as applied to whole wards of patients is the *token economy*[2] (Ayllon & Azrin, 1968). In the token economy, operant learning methods are used to reinforce specific types of desired behavior. The token economy is so named because the chief reinforcer used is the token, which may be anything from a plastic poker chip to a special card impressively emblazoned with the crest of the hospital. What makes these tokens worth earning is their value when traded in for "backup reinforcers"—any of a variety of rewards, which include candy, cigarettes (in the early programs), even trips to the movies. Token reinforcement is immediately consequent upon the desired behavior, but the exchange of tokens for backup reinforcers usually takes place much later.

As outlined at the beginning of this chapter, Fairweather (1964) described a treatment program that combined elements of the token economy with features of a therapeutic community, such as patient-led problem-solving groups. Initial research findings from token economy and social learning programs were extremely encouraging, with no negative effects reported (Paul, 1969).

Special Aftercare Procedures

Even the most effective psychological treatments will fail in the long run if they are abruptly discontinued when the patient leaves the hospital. Successfully rehabilitating long-term inpatients requires special *aftercare* arrangements in which patients progress through a community program, an extension of the hospital, before final discharge (Fairweather & Fergus, 1993; Paul, 1969; Paul & Lentz, 1977). In an initial study, patients discharged to a "community lodge" in which they formed a supportive group stayed outside the hospital much longer, and were far more likely to be gainfully employed, than patients discharged to the community in the traditional way (Fairweather, Sanders, Cressler, & Maynard, 1969). The patients in this study were not as chronic or regressed as in other studies, however (Davison, 1969).

Treatment Techniques and Empirical Findings

Theoretical Background

The principles of reinforcement, extinction, and stimulus control are always influencing people's behavior. Behavioral contingencies are already at work in a psychiatric hospital ward, whether or not a behavior therapist has deliberately arranged a specific reinforcement program. Consider some examples. The first is drawn from a book by Schaefer and Martin (1969).

> *The administrator of a hospital for patients with mental retardation was alarmed at the number of "headbangers" in the institution. Many of the patients had developed a pattern of deliberately banging their heads against the wall. This behavior was obviously harmful, because the patients' heads were often bleeding after such episodes. No fault could be found with the treatment staff. In fact, they were unusually sympathetic and caring people. Whenever a patient started headbanging, a nurse would hasten to offer comfort and would even give the patient candy or chocolate. However, this treatment did not reduce the amount of headbanging. The patients tended to start banging their heads whenever they saw a nurse arriving with a supply of candy. (Schaefer & Martin, 1969, pp. 47–48)*

Faced with a problem like this, behavior therapists would not discourage the nurses from being sympathetic, and would not want them to stop giving candy to patients. But one certainly *would* suggest that the nurses *reschedule* their offerings of candy and sympathy! It is quite clear that bringing candy and words of comfort only when someone bangs their head on the wall creates a behavioral contingency of positive reinforcement. We would advise the nurses to offer reinforcement at any time *other than* when the patients are banging their heads, thus placing the headbanging under extinction and positively reinforcing incompatible behavior.

The next example comes from one of our experiences when working as a psychologist in a psychiatric hospital.

Dick was a mute patient, assumed to be hearing impaired, who had lived on Ward C2 for many years. He communicated either by making grunting noises or by staring earnestly at the onlooker, flapping his hands vigorously in front of his face. What could be reinforcing this bizarre behavior? The mental health worker who led the treatment team on the unit did not know.

"Look," he said, as we entered the ward. "Let's see what you psychologists make of our Dick over here. Oh . . . he isn't doing it right now. Wait a minute. Hey, Dick!"

Dick's attention was still elsewhere. The team leader went up to him and attracted his attention.

"Hey, Dick! How are you today?" he asked, looking at his patient unexpectantly.

"Ar! Gug!" replied Dick, and started waving his hands energetically.

"There you are!" said the team leader, smiling triumphantly. "That's what he does! That's how you talk to us, isn't it, Dick?"

The team leader and several of the other people present made no attempt to hide their amusement.

To a behavior therapist, the smiles, the attention, the expectant looks could all be seen as powerful stimuli controlling Dick's behavior. Whenever he did something bizarre, people paid attention to him. When he did not, people largely ignored him. When people looked at him expectantly, Dick's hand flapping was almost certainly followed by their smiles of appreciation. The initial attention and expectant looks had become discriminative stimuli. The hand flapping was the operant behavior being produced by the patient. The smiles, laughter, and words of encouragement that followed Dick's behavior were positive reinforcers. After years of exposure to this contingency, even the arrival on the ward of a familiar staff member was enough to encourage Dick to grunt and flap his hands.

If stimulus control and positive reinforcement contingencies are indeed operating here, what treatment plan would we recommend? First, moving Dick to a new ward with different therapists could remove many of the stimuli that were influencing his behavior. The research reviewed later in this chapter shows that simply a change of ward can promote improved social behavior even before new treatments are implemented. It seems quite likely that removing stimuli that control the undesired behavior is responsible. Furthermore, there is the principle of extinction. If Dick's hand flapping had been reinforced continually, then removing the reinforcement (the smiles of appreciation) wouldlead fairly rapidly to extinction of the behavior. That was the treatment plan adopted for Dick's problem behavior.

All staff on the ward were asked to stop encouraging Dick to act inappropriately. Whenever he flapped his hands, staff members were to look away and pay no attention. However, whenever he tried to communicate appropriately (looking calmly toward someone while making a vocal noise[3] of any kind), staff members were to smile and greet him. This strategy brought quite promising results, initially. Dick showed a dramatic decrease in his bizarre behavior. This behavior only returned when a staff member from another unit visited Dick's ward for the first time in weeks. On entering the ward, the staff member loudly yelled at Dick, started flapping his own hands in front of his face, and shouted, "Hey, Dick! What's the matter with you? Aren't you going to 'talk' to me? Go on! Flap your hands! There you go, that's my old Dick!" This interaction was very amusing for the visitor, but it was not very therapeutic for Dick—not, at least, if the long-term goal was to equip him what all the skills needed to communicate effectively in the outside world.

A final example concerns the role of operant learning in physical rehabilitation (Greif & Matarazzo, 1982). The context was a rehabilitation ward in which patients often became inordinately demanding of the nurses. One focus for such demands in units of this kind is pain medication, usually delivered (within certain prescribed limits) on request. The patients' requests for medication and attention had become excessive, and the nurses were frustrated by the demanding nature of these requests. A behavior therapy consultant suggested that, ironically, the patients' inappropriate behavior was being reinforced by the nurses' attention. The only way for patients to gain attention from a nurse was to complain of discomfort and to ask for medication, so that was what they did, and that was what was being reinforced. The remedy? Suggest to the nurses that they approach and talk to patients when they are *not* complaining of a problem (in addition to responding in the usual way to reasonable requests, of course). In addition, the nurses could ask the physician to prescribe medication "by the clock" rather than on request, so that a request for medication does not become an operant behavior that is reinforced by social interaction. Such straightforward remedies are often dramatically successful and improve the quality of staff/patient interactions.

Treatment of Specific Behavior Problems

In the early years of behavior therapy, its practitioners were eager to provide an alternative to the "disease model" of schizophrenia and other severe disorders (Curran, Monti, & Corriveau, 1982). Instead of aiming treatment at a disease presumed to underlie the various signs and symptoms, behavior therapists dealt with specific behavioral problems. Examples of treatment targets have been delusional speech, hallucinations, ritualistic behavior, distressing thoughts, anxiety, nonassertive behavior, towel hoarding, and glass breaking. Typical treatment procedures have been positive reinforcement, extinction, feedback, modeling, self-monitoring, self-administered punishment, time out, systematic desensitization, stimulus satiation, and aversive conditioning with covert processes (Curran et al., 1982). A few examples will illustrate the advantages and disadvantages of treatment programs of these kinds.

Speech Problems

A popular focus in schizophrenia has been speech problems. these include mutism (the patient does not speak at all), delusional speech, and disorganized speech. The general approach has been positive reinforcement for appropriate speech. Isaacs, Thomas, and Goldiamond (1960) tried to reinstate speech in two patients who had been mute for 14 and 19 years. One of them was visibly attracted by a stick of gum that had accidentally fallen from a psychologist's pocket. The therapists seized the opportunity and used the gum as a reinforcer. After careful shaping of speech sounds by reinforcement, the patient was able to answer direct questions in group therapy sessions, but only when the original therapist asked the questions!

Ayllon and Haughton (1964) tried to reduce delusional speech in three patients. The researchers used a reversal design to study the effects of reinforcement. Staff members recorded a series of conversations for 15 to 20 days pretreatment. Then reinforcement was introduced. This consisted of listening, showing interest, and giving candy or cigarettes. Reinforcement was made contingent on either "neutral" or "psychotic" talk, depending on the phase of the study. As expected, reinforcement increased the rate of whichever behavior was the target at the time.

Other studies reviewed by Curran and colleagues (1982) showed that in 10 inpatients with paranoid schizophrenia, corrective feedback from the therapist was sometimes helpful and sometimes distinctly unhelpful. Positive reinforcement, by contrast with feedback, was generally more therapeutic. Irrational speech was successfully reduced during treatment sessions with four chronic patients. The therapists simply stopped talking and ignored the patients when they spoke irrationally.

The interventions described here were all successful within the limits of the particular studies. However, there was very little generalization of treatment effects from one therapist to another, from the therapist's office to the ward, or even from one time of day to another. In one study, a patient's delusional speech improved in therapy sessions but got worse on the ward. In these early studies, there were few attempts to assess patients' behavior at extended follow-up intervals. The behavioral techniques used were implemented precisely and produced clear control of the behavior, but generalization across situations and over time, perhaps not surprisingly, was very poor.

Hoarding and Stealing

An early study by Ayllon (1963) demonstrated the successful treatment of three problems in a 47-year-old woman who had been hospitalized for nine years for chronic schizophrenia. Ste stole food, she hoarded towels in her room, and she wore excessive amounts of clothing at one time (such as six dresses, two dozen pairs of stockings, and several sweaters). To encourage her to stop stealing food from other patients in the dining room, the ward staff would remove the patient from the dining room whenever she attempted to steal. Removing her from the dining room meant that she had to miss her meal. Two weeks of this approach was sufficient to eliminate the stealing entirely. This had the beneficial effect of allowing the staff to maintain the patient on a needed, medically prescribed diet.

The patient's towel hoarding led her to keep from 19 to 29 towels in her room, instead of the usual 1 or 2. Nurses had to remove towels from the room periodically to maintain the ward supply. Therapy followed the principle of *stimulus satiation,* a concept drawn from laboratory studies indicating that responses typically weaken when the reinforcing stimulus is made too abundant. Accordingly, instead of *removing* towels from the patient's room, staff members started carrying them *into* her room. When the number of towels in the room exceeded 600, the patient began to carry towels out herself. She gave every sign of being tired of them, because she said, "Take them towels away. I can't sit here all night folding towels" (Ayllon, 1963, p. 57). Eventually the patient was keeping just 1 or 2 towels in her room.

The patient problem, wearing enormous amounts of clothing, was treated by making the patient's access to the dining room contingent upon her fully clothed weight falling below a certain limit. At first, she was allowed to wear over 20 pounds of clothes, but this allowance was gradually reduced. The patient gradually discarded more and more clothes until she was typically wearing about 3 pounds of clothes.

Ayllon's treatment of this individual was highly innovative at the time, when a typical intervention would have focused on interpreting the unconscious dynamics underlying her problems. In discussing his findings, Ayllon pointed out that:

- Beneficial changes occurred within a short period of time.
- The therapeutic gains persisted for months.
- No new problems emerged to take the place of these bizarre behaviors.
- Improvement in these specific bizarre behaviors was accompanied by a more positive general social adjustment.

In fact, the patient's relatives were more willing to take her away from the hospital for visits, for example, now that she no longer looked, as they put it, like a "circus freak."

These illustrations of the use of operant learning to remedy specific problems show that psychological treatment can be rapidly effective. The treatment techniques involved are not very complicated, and they can be delivered by staff without extensive training. Similarly, treatment is typically brief, and therefore a small investment in time may make a significant contribution to a patient's rehabilitation. The disadvantages of such approaches are seen mainly in their applications to delusional speech and mutism, when therapists have to take special measures to promote therapeutic generalization. This usually involves conducting the treatment in several situations, requiring intensive work by a team of therapists. But when all the patients on a ward have similar problems, it can be economical and efficient to design wardwide treatment programs.

Wardwide Treatment Programs

The Token Economy

The *token economy* was developed by Ayllon and Azrin (1965, 1968). Their initial studies, reported in 1965, demonstrated that token reinforcement could be effective in increasing "healthy" behaviors such as taking care of personal hygiene and attending work therapy assignments (Davison, 1969).

A study of a wardwide program by Fairweather (1964) did not address the token economy as such. He compared two hospital treatment programs. One was the conventional hospital regimen of custodial care. The other program was conventional treatment with the addition of patient-led problem-solving groups, meeting for two hours each day. Fairweather's hypothesis was that the patients' chief problem was lack of social skills, so he predicted that the milieu-style group therapy would be more beneficial than custodial care. The milieu program included an incentive system in which patients received increasing allowances of money from their personal accounts in return for progress through a series of functional steps. Money and off-ward pass privileges were made contingent on appropriate social and self-directed behavior. The program lasted for 27 weeks. Assessments were made throughout the study and at a six-month follow-up. Compared with traditional treatment, the milieu/reinforcement intervention was associated with more social interaction, less pathological behavior, reduced use of medication, shorter hospital stays, and longer intervals before rehospitalization. However, patients in the two conditions did not differ in their hospital readmission rates in the long term.

The work of Ayllon and Azrin (1965, 1968) largely consisted of developing and testing operant learning procedures. There were no large-scale experimental comparisons of one type of ward regimen with another. An important general finding was that contingent presentation of tokens for desired behavior was more effective in increasing response rates than simply giving the same number of tokens noncontingently. Ayllon and Azrin used reversal or ABAB designs, in which periods of contingent reinforcement alternated with periods of noncontingent reinforcement. The authors showed that only contingent reinforcement was effective in maintaining patients' on-ward work assignments, and in influencing their choice of initially preferred and nonpreferred jobs.

Unfortunately, this demonstration was based on flawed methodology because two variables were confounded. Not only were patients switched from contingent to noncontingent reinforcement but they were also told that they would be getting "a vacation with pay." Telling the patients that they were getting a vacation might have influenced their behavior independent of the actual change in contingency (Kazdin & Bootzin, 1972; Peck & Thorpe, 1971). Bandura (1969) has also pointed out that modeling effects may have been an important influence in that some patients simply imitated the behavior of others, regardless of the operant learning contingency. These criticisms may help us understand the otherwise disappointing finding that behavior could so easily revert to baseline levels after 18 months of successful therapy (Peck & Thorpe, 1971).

A study by Schaefer and Martin (1966) did demonstrate the superiority of contingent to noncontingent tokens in a group of severely regressed, chronic patients. There was no confounding of extinction with instructions in this study.

A series of studies by Roger Baker, John Hall, and their colleagues in Britain have addressed the issues of contingent reinforcement versus extinction (noncontingent tokens), and token economy versus milieu-style programs. In one demonstration, the authors selected seven male patients aged 48 to 50 for special study (Baker, Hall, & Hutchinson, 1974). These men had all been described as having schizophrenia, and they had been in the hospital continuously for a mean of 17 years.

The patients' treatment regimen progressed through a series of phases over 39 weeks. This was an "additive" treatment study in which each component, once begun, continued throughout the entire project. First, the patients were moved to a new ward—a smaller, better furnished unit with a higher than usual staff/patient ratio. In this first phase, no new treatment was introduced (six weeks). Second, a stimulating activity program was introduced. Patients went on trips into the community, took part in an active occupational therapy program, and took responsibility for individual tasks (three weeks). Third, tokens were freely given to the patients to trade for necessities and luxuries. The tokens were not contingent on behavior (seven weeks). Fourth, tokens were made contingent on desired behavior (shaving, making one's bed, arriving on time for meals, etc.). Emphasis was placed on spontaneous social interaction and on neat appearance. This phase lasted for 14 weeks. Finally, there was a one-week posttreatment assessment period and a final follow-up assessment two months after patients had returned to their original wards.

The results were that clear changes were seen in patients' appropriate dressing and social interaction, but these changes had occurred *before* the introduction of token reinforcement. Two months after treatment, patients were again as socially withdrawn as they had been pretreatment. The authors attributed this largely to problems in rater reliability and to the reinforcement of inappropriate behavior by staff members on the patients' original wards. The authors concluded that "the patients have undoubtedly improved as a consequence of this programme [but] there was little evidence that a specific token contingency was the main factor in changing the patients' target behaviour" (Baker et al., 1974, pp. 380–381).

Building on their earlier work, Hall, Baker, and Hutchinson (1977) conducted an experimental study of 18 patients with chronic schizophrenia who were assigned to token economy and control treatment wards. In a thoughtful commentary, the authors pointed out that there are several factors other than token reinforcement that can promote behavioral improvement in a new program. These include:

- Changing the ward environment
- Specifying goals
- Creating a more meaningful environment
- Increasing the amount of social stimulation
- Giving feedback
- Mobilizing positive attitudes and expectations in the staff

Operant learning theorists would predict that even such a simple matter as moving patients to a new ward could bring improvement. By leaving the old ward, patients are no longer exposed to the various stimuli that previously set the occasion for bizarre behavior. Other changes that can coincide with setting up a new program have more obvious effects. In some programs, staff members were prompted to obtain more social work input so as to facilitate the expected increase in patient discharges and consequent need for aftercare planning. Adding professional resources and developing high expectations of success also entail confounding a study of token effectiveness (Kahn, 1977).

The 18 patients in Hall and associates' (1977) study were divided into six matched groups of three. In each group, one patient remained on the original ward, while the other two went to the new program. These 12 patients were assessed in a three-month baseline period. Next, the 12 were further divided into a token group and a control group. The token economy treatment lasted for one year. In the token group, appropriate behavior was immediately followed by verbal praise, explaining why the behavior was reinforced, and by the delivery of tokens. In the control group, appropriate behavior was immediately followed by praise and explanation but not tokens. Instead, tokens were given, not contingent on behavior, but at fixed times. Token and control patients were all housed on the same ward during the study. Ward behavior rating scales and psychiatric ratings were the chief measures used, and these were repeated at intervals. The outcome of this ambitious and well-controlled study was that no difference could be detected between token and control patients on the various measures. In general, patients improved on social functioning, appearance, and engaging in important routine behavior without prompting. There was evidence that token reinforcement had positive, immediate effects, but in the long run the same overall improvement was seen in both patient groups. Social behavior was the area most responsive to treatment.

It is important to remember that token *and* control patients did receive reinforcement. The only difference in procedure was the addition of *token* reinforcement in one group of patients. Both groups received contingent praise, or social reinforcement, for specific desired behavior.

Another study by this group (Baker, Hall, Hutchinson, & Bridge, 1977) produced similar findings. These authors also examined the pattern of treatment-induced changes, to see whether the token economy had more of an impact on specific behaviors or on the patients' psychopathology in general (the "symptom picture"). The conclusion was that "the token economy improved patients in withdrawal and social behaviour but did not change symptomatology" (p. 391). This finding was confirmed in two other British studies of the token economy. Specific behaviors such as work habits, self-care skills, and social participation increased, but the cognitive and affective symptoms of schizophrenia (delusional speech, emotional incongruities, etc.) were unchanged (Fraser, McLeod, Begg, Hawthorne, & Davis, 1976; Mumford, Patch, Andrews, & Wyner, 1975).

The Token Economy versus Milieu Therapy

The most comprehensive and large-scale study of social learning therapy in an institution was conducted in the United States by Paul and Lentz (1977). The authors sought to improve treatment practices, in general, for chronic psychiatric inpatients. In their book, they describe three major projects and over 20 small-scale studies. This important research is conveniently summarized in a special review by Hartmann and Barrios (1980).

One of the major projects was an experimental comparison of a token economy with a milieu therapy program. A second major study was a comparison of these token economy and milieu programs with a matched group of patients in a traditional hospital ward program. Some 84 patients were studied for 4½ years, and there was a follow-up assessment 1½ years later. As patients were discharged from the hospital after treatment, similar patients from other units took their places. During the stage of active treatment, 90 percent of the token economy patients and 50 percent of the milieu patients improved. The better the staff were at following the correct procedures, the greater was the improvement in the token economy patients. However, for milieu therapy patients, the results were better when the staff did not stick faithfully to the prescribed procedures. At the 1½ year follow-up assessment, Paul and Lentz (1977) observed that over 90 percent of the token economy patients were still living in the community. For the milieu therapy and standard treatment groups, the figures were over 70 percent and under 50 percent, respectively.

The third major study was an experimental comparison of two methods of after-care treatment (implemented after patients left the hospital). This project was only partially successful. Overall, the Paul and Lentz (1977) research was remarkable for its careful attention to assessment. Among the many smaller studies reported in the book were experiments on the effects of medication and on how long it took patients to get used to the observers who made behavioral ratings. There was a great diversity of outcome measures, chiefly entailing careful observation of specific behaviors in patients and staff. The monitoring of staff behavior was continuous throughout the project. The research was clearly successful, overall, in showing that social learning therapy, and, to a lesser extent, milieu therapy, were substantially more effective than traditional hospital treatment. The authors also showed that the new programs were more cost effective than traditional treatment. Nevertheless, behavior therapists have been disappointed by the lack of general interest in these findings, and these studies have never been replicated (Bellack & Mueser, 1994). Traditional hospital programs continue to be the norm in most state hospitals (Wilson, 1982), and professional ignorance, lack of resources, and theoretical differences still create barriers to the adoption of behavioral interventions in psychiatric hospitals (Corrigan & Liberman, 1994; Yoman, 1996).

Social Skills and Problem-Solving Techniques

Token economy and milieu therapy programs have been notably successful, and both can improve the interpersonal functioning of inpatients with schizophrenia in such areas as general social participation, taking responsibility for activity, and learning to deal with potential areas of conflict with other people. Community-based milieu programs, particularly the aftercare lodges described by Paul and Lentz (1977) and Fairweather and Fergus (1993), show even greater promise for developing social skills for life outside the hospital or institution. Yet, clinicians wish for even more powerful techniques for helping patients to gain the level of interpersonal skill, social judgment, and conflict-resolution ability necessary for successful functioning in the community. Even the most successful wardwide programs can only reinforce new combinations of existing behavior patterns, and may not do enough to equip patients to deal successfully with the social complexities of community life outside the hospital (Curran, Monti, & Corriveau, 1982). From the 1970s onward, researchers have examined teaching social and problem-solving skills to people with schizophrenia as the principal treatment plan.

Social Competence
Contemporary interest in helping people with schizophrenia to socialize more effectively began with the work of Zigler and Phillips (1960) on *social competence*. Problems or deficits in social skills are central to the development (and persistence) of schizophrenia (Trower, 1995). Consider the example of Jim O., an 18-year-old high school dropout treated by one of us a few years ago.

Jim had always been teased by his peers, probably because he was strongly tied to his family (his social worker described it as "enmeshed") and avoided going out whenever possible. He had always found it hard to talk to people who were not in his immediate family. As he described it in the first therapy session, he tried to act "normally," but did not know how. For example, he said, he went into a corner store to buy a newspaper. Another customer was already at the counter, so Jim waited. While waiting, he tried hard not to look nervous or odd. He looked at a magazine rack, he carefully studied a display of candy, and continually tried to look "normal." Another customer came in, and Jim had to solve the problem of exactly where he should stand so as to be a normal person waiting in line. Getting too close to the person at the counter would look weird, Jim thought, but standing too far away might also appear odd. He carefully adjusted his position until it seemed just right. He began to feel that he was, indeed, handling this situation quite normally. At that point, however, he noticed that the other customers and the storekeeper were looking toward him, smiling. Jim felt extremely uncomfortable and left abruptly. He thought it likely that the people in the store were talking about him as he ran down the road.

Jim did not display many of the signs and symptoms of schizophrenia; in fact, most of his problems could have been construed as social phobia. Yet Jim, his relatives, and his therapist were all concerned that his problems were increasing. There was a family history of schizophrenia, and Jim's anxious preoccupations with what people were thinking about him had already extended to the point of delusion, in that he often found a sinister personal significance in the most trivial external event.[4] If he were waiting in line and another person sneezed, Jim would be likely to conclude that the sneeze meant something, like "I know you're crazy, Jim, you can't hide it from me!"

Therapy to train Jim in social skills seemed most appropriate. Jim had acknowledged two things. First, he did not know how to act. Second, he kept a running commentary going on his activity—a commentary that was not particularly helpful. He would think, "Am I standing in the right place? I *know* they think I'm weird. They can tell just by looking at me. A normal person wouldn't even *think* about where to stand in a store, he'd just do it. I am truly messed up." A treatment plan with behavioral and cognitive elements seemed ideal. According to the Zigler and Phillips (1960) view, it is the lack of social abilities that leads to psychopathology, not the other way around. Hence, equipping Jim with social skills and a series of more helpful self-statements might prevent a hospitalization for schizophrenia.

Conceptualization of Social Skills

Early psychoanalytic and ego psychology theories assumed that all people are able to socialize effectively—unless problems in the personality structure intrude on functioning (Bellack & Morrison, 1982; Curran, 1981). Such problems would be viewed as enduring traits such as repressed hostility, and the appropriate remedy would be to resolve the underlying issues, not to change specific responses.

By contrast, behavior therapists construe social behavior in the same way that they construe any behavior—as the result of specific learning experiences as moderated by the individual's appraisals of them. To a behavior therapist, *social skills* refers not to a generalized trait but to a set of situation-specific and response-mode specific behaviors. As an example of situational specificity, a client may have no trouble giving a speech before a large group, yet become tongue-tied during a one-on-one job interview. As an example of response-mode specificity, two clients anxious about asking someone for a date could show different specific reaction patterns. One might be aware of a pounding heart and sweaty palms, yet still be able to interact in a relatively poised way. The other might feel oppressed by a series of negative self-statements, yet somehow remain fairly calm and relaxed physically (Dow, 1994). Because social skill does not reflect a unitary, global trait, behavior therapists assess a client's particular pattern of problems, designate specific targets for treatment, and implement a program tailored to that individual's precise requirements.

Social Skills Training Techniques

Initially, behavior therapists were encouraged by the book *Behavior Therapy Techniques* by Wolpe and Lazarus (1966), which explained the principles of assertiveness training and related social skills training concepts. Today, *social skills training (SST)* describes a particular group of techniques, including instruction, modeling, behavior rehearsal, praise, prompts, coaching, feedback, reinforcement, and homework assignments (Curran et al., 1982; Trower, 1995). SST is suitable for some chronic inpatients, but it is more appropriate, in general, for outpatients (like Jim O.) or for hospitalized patients who may expect realistically to be discharged to the community. Even in these people, for whom the outlook for significant improvement seems promising, the typical course of treatment may last over six months.

The techniques of SST are commonly applied to specific aspects of social behavior. These include starting a conversation, paying a compliment, criticizing someone's behavior, expressing feelings, and listening attentively. The chief component of SST is the combination of modeling with behavior rehearsal (role-playing). Also important is some form of cognitive restructuring to help the person maintain a constructive perspective on the situation. In the case of Jim O., it was helpful to have him practice speaking forthrightly and self-confidently in simulated real-world situations, but it was also helpful to encourage him to focus on the right set of cognitions. Instead of dwelling on how odd he must appear to other people, he learned to adopt a more encouraging view of his situation, such as: "Why worry what other people think? If they don't like me, that's their problem, not mine. Let me just concentrate on what I want to do here." The interactionalist social learning theory of Bandura (1977) applies very well to SST.

Models of Social Skills Training

Bellack and Morrison (1982) described four theoretical models of SST: a skills deficit model, a conditioned anxiety model, a cognitive-evaluative model, and a faulty discrimination model.

The *skills deficit* model, the most popular, rests on the assumption that the client does not know what to do or how to do it socially. It leads to a response acquisition approach in which the client proceeds through a hierarchy of training exercises that include instructions, role-playing, feedback and praise for progress, modeling, and real-life practice.

Behavior therapists subscribing to the *conditioned anxiety* model assume that the client has the appropriate skills but does not put them into practice because anxiety has an inhibiting effect. Techniques such as systematic desensitization would apply here. Related to this, Piaget and Lazarus (1969) described *rehearsal desensitization* as a procedure that combines skills training with anxiety reduction. Therapist and client proceed through a hierarchy of role-play items, carefully graded for degree of anxiety elicited. It combines elements of systematic desensitization with the role-playing procedure.

Therapists following a *cognitive-evaluative* model also cite anxiety as an important issue, but they assume that the client needs to abandon unproductive trains of thought that deter him or her from interacting appropriately. The client may know what to say and may make suitable judgments as to when to say it, but nevertheless remains silent. Faced with a persistent door-to-door salesperson whose product is overpriced and of no interest to the person, the usual goal would be to say "no" in a socially appropriate fashion. If that were, indeed, the goal, it would be clearly *unhelpful* to think, "I had better say 'yes', or I'll hurt his feelings. I'd probably mess it up anyway if I tried to say 'no.'" Instead, the patient could learn to adopt an alternative attitude: "Remember, it's my perfect right to refuse. Even if I don't carry it off perfectly, better to try than to be a doormat for everybody" (Thorpe, 1975). Research by Schwartz and Gottman (1976) demonstrated that, in the case of assertive behavior, people usually know what to say and how to say it. The problem is not lack of skill, but focusing upon an unhelpful set of self-statements.

The *faulty discrimination* model is particularly appropriate to people with schizophrenia because it follows directly from one of the behavioral theories of that disorder. Charles B. Ferster, an influential operant learning researcher who collaborated with Skinner on some important early projects, argued that schizophrenia may develop because the person fails to learn to attend to people as vital stimuli. As a result, the person withdraws from people. When contact with people is inescapable, the person does not know how to "tune in" to them and interact appropriately. The right behaviors may be available, but the person does not know which responses to select. The treatment that follows from this formulation is often known as *problem-solving training (PST)*, a version of which was described in the discussion of behavioral couples therapy. Role-playing is used extensively in PST, together with efforts to clarify the client's thoughts about the situation.

For example, one client was faced with an uncooperative landlord who refused to fix a faulty heating system. The therapist invited the client to practice a suitable interaction, with the therapist taking the role of the landlord. The patient began the interaction by saying: "I'm going to report you to the housing department, and if they don't take care of you, I have some friends who will." The therapist interrupted and asked: "If you were to start out that way, how would the landlord probably feel?" The client was able to reflect on the possible consequences of beginning the conversation in that threatening manner, and began to learn to develop more appropriate judgment in such situations.

Another example of faulty discrimination was seen in a session one of us had with an outpatient client.

Timothy T. was living in an apartment under the close supervision of the city's housing department. Now in his early thirties, he had spent about 10 years in the state hospital after having been found not guilty of a violent crime because of diminished criminal responsibility due to a mental illness. Timothy's problems had features of schizophrenia, a dementing cognitive disorder, and mild mental retardation, and experts had disagreed as to which of the three was the most appropriate label. He had been living in the community, somewhat marginally, for two years. Timothy was particularly vulnerable to "flying off the handle" when provoked by anyone. A few days before the therapy session, he had been disturbed by loud music from a neighboring apartment late at night. One month previously, the neighborhood had been shaken by a multiple murder. A man had shot and killed four of his relatives after he had been annoyed by their refusal to turn down their stereo system at night. Mindful of this, Timothy's first conversational gambit when he approached the neighbors was: "You'd better turn that noise down. You wouldn't want what happened on State Street to happen here, would you?"

Timothy was surprised at the neighbors' reaction, which was to display considerable alarm and call the police. Luckily for Timothy, the officers called to the scene knew him well, and judged that the likelihood of his acting dangerously now was minimal. But they strongly suggested that he discuss the incident with his therapist! The treatment session was spent in a largely successful attempt to show Timothy that there were more appropriate ways to ask people to make less noise than to threaten, however indirectly, to murder them.

Research Findings on Social Skills and Problem-Solving Training

Following guidelines set by Goldfried and D'Zurilla (1969), Goldsmith and McFall (1975) extended laboratory work on assertiveness training to the treatment of psychiatric inpatients. They devised a questionnaire presenting difficult interpersonal situations, and 74 outpatients rated the items for relevance and level of difficulty. Detailed interviews with 16 participants revealed considerable consistency in the ratings. The situations ultimately selected included interactions concerning dating, making friends, interviewing for jobs, and dealing with "more intelligent and attractive" people. Potential areas of difficulty in these situations included being assertive, knowing when to begin and end the conversation, deciding how self-disclosing to be, and handling silences. Further ratings by inpatients helped narrow the questionnaire to 20 items. Staff members role-played the situations, other researchers rated the responses for competence, and a scoring manual was devised.

Goldsmith and McFall (1975) used the situations and scoring manual in a treatment study with 36 inpatients. The patients were randomly distributed among three experimental treatment groups: (1) interpersonal skills training, (2) pseudotherapy control, and (3) assessment only (patients in this group were advised that the practice involved in repeated assessments could be helpful). The skills training patients had three one-hour training sessions with modeling, behavior rehearsal, coaching, and feedback. The pseudotherapy patients followed similar procedures but, instead of receiving training concerning response alternatives, they explored their feelings. The outcome was that skills training was more successful than assessment only, as measured by patients' self-report. As assessed by ratings of audiotaped role-plays, skills training was clearly superior to both the other conditions. Pseudotherapy and assessment-only conditions did not differ from each other. The same results were seen with a simulated real-life test. A follow-up assessment eight months after treatment did not include enough patients to allow statistical comparison of the treatments, but about a quarter of those patients who were reassessed had required readmission to the hospital.

Goldstein, Sprafkin, and Gershaw (1976) described a *structured learning therapy* that overlaps considerably with other versions of SST. The authors criticized token economy and milieu therapy programs for not extending patients' improvement to the world outside the hospital. To address this problem, they proposed the structured learning therapy package, which included not only the familiar modeling, role-playing, and social reinforcement elements but also *transfer training* aimed at promoting generalization of the effects of treatment to the patients' lives in the community after leaving the hospital. Preliminary studies revealed some encouraging findings, but the newly acquired skills did not always carry over to community settings. Goldstein and associates addressed this by assigning "homework" exercises in a series of easy steps, with each assignment carefully selected as likely to produce rewarding consequences in real life.

Citing evidence that hospitalized psychiatric patients have problems with "interpersonal problem-solving cognition," Siegel and Spivack (1976) described a *problem-solving therapy* program for chronic patients. Their program involves a series of training exercises which may be grouped under the headings of :

- Problem identification
- Goal definition
- Solution evaluation
- Evaluation of alternatives
- Selection of the best solution (Kendall, 1987)

Problem identification is an important element. Siegel and Spivack show a series of color slides depicting people in various situations, and ask patients questions about the slides to ensure that they have attended to them appropriately. Another element of the program attempts to train *attentiveness* to other people. Therapists first show patients a color slide of a group of people, then present a different slide including one person from the first slide among a group of different people. The patient is asked to identify the person common to both slides. Other program elements include learning to assess the *emotions* displayed by people in magazine pictures and learning to ask intelligent questions in a guessing game.

Pilot work by Siegel and Spivack (1976) indicated that the exercises were relevant, held the patients' interest, and were pitched at an appropriate level of difficulty. A study of seven chronic patients in a postdischarge aftercare program showed that an average of 14 sessions were needed to complete the training. The guessing game seemed particularly helpful as an antidote to thought disorder and deserves further examination. A second pilot study produced some evidence that patients' ability to think of suitable solutions to imagined real-life problems improved.

Hansen, St. Lawrence, and Christoff (1985) used a multiple baseline design to demonstrate that problem-solving training was helpful to seven chronic patients in a partial hospitalization/ aftercare program. The patients met twice weekly in groups. Not only was the program effective within the context of the study but the effects of training also generalized to new situations. Patients' new-found skills, which were shown to be comparable to those of community members, in general, were maintained for at least four months after treatment. A similar study in Australia produced slightly different results. Six chronic schizophrenia patients living in community hostels showed significant clinical improvement after social skills training, but the generalization of gains to the community setting was relatively weak (Payne & Halford, 1990). But in a larger experimental study of 63 similar patients, only those who received social skills training (as opposed to attending a discussion group) showed any improvement in functioning in the community (Hayes, Halford, & Varghese, 1995).

A recent review indicates that social skills training brings lasting benefit to people with schizophrenia in several specific areas, including:

- Nonverbal behaviors (smiling and eye contact)
- Conversational skills
- Assertive responses
- Independent living skills
- Job interviews
- Job maintenance skills (Bellack & Mueser, 1994)

Transfer of these benefits to patients' daily lives in the community cannot be guaranteed unless therapists take special steps to enhance this generalization.

The current trend in equipping people with the skills they need to function outside the hospital is to begin by assessing the demands of the community environment, not the patient's general social abilities. Trying to increase patients' general level of social skill, trusting that this will enable them to cope with any environment, seems more consistent with psychoanalytic than behavioral formulations. By contrast, an appropriate behavioral strategy is "instead of starting with the skills and hoping they will generalize, we should start with the role setting and work out which skills are necessary" (Trower, 1995, p. 73). This is especially important when the inpatient with schizophrenia is discharged to a family setting with high rates of *expressed emotion*, meaning "high rates of criticism, hostility, and emotional overinvolvement exhibited by relatives toward family members who suffer from mental illness" (McNally, 1994, pp. 2–3).

People discharged to homes with high levels of expressed emotion are especially vulnerable to relapse, so improving family interaction may help the person with schizophrenia avoid rehospitalization (McNally, 1994; Suinn, 1995). More detailed investigation of expressed emotion has shown that the *attributions* made by family members are especially important in predicting relapse in the family member with schizophrenia. Compared with relatives low in expressed emotion, relatives with high expressed emotion make more attributions concerning mental illness. Within the high expressed emotion group, different attributions are associated with emotional overinvolvement, on the one hand, and criticism and hostility, on the other. Emotionally overinvolved relatives ascribe problems to uncontrollable factors outside the patient. Critical and hostile relatives ascribe problems to factors inside the patient, and assign him or her more responsibility for them. The nature of the attributions is more important than level of expressed emotion in predicting later relapse: The benign attributions of overinvolved relatives correlate with favorable outcomes, whereas the attributions of critical and hostile relatives predict relapse (Barrowclough, Johnston, & Tarrier, 1994).

Comments

Social skills and problem-solving training are obviously relevant to the social problems of certain groups of psychiatric inpatients. These methods seem especially helpful in fostering appropriate adjustment to the community after a period of hospitalization. The specific techniques have some overlap with milieu therapy and, to a lesser degree, with token economy procedures. All of these techniques can be helpful for certain patients. Problem-solving therapy is not suitable for the most acutely disturbed individuals, but it shows great promise as a predischarge intervention to help patients adjust to community living. In the absence of clear research findings in some areas, clinicians can use their experience and ingenuity to determine which therapy is suitable for which patient. It is clear that some hospital programs would be improved if chronic patients could progress through a suitable wardwide program to specific social skills and problem-solving interventions to help make the transition to the community.

Cognitive Therapy and Schizophrenia

Recent reports advocating cognitive therapy for people with schizophrenia emphasize (1) developing a positive therapeutic alliance and (2) engaging patients in their own symptom management. Parallel to this, and prompted by research findings on the attributional styles of patients' relatives, cognitive-behavioral family intervention programs show considerable promise (Goldstein, 1996).

Delusional Beliefs

Several reports describe the successful treatment of patients with schizophrenia by cognitive therapy. The rationale and method are similar to those used in treating depression. Patient and therapist collaborate in testing the hypotheses underlying delusions, for example. Eventually, patients can use the skills learned in therapy to reason themselves out of such beliefs (Alford & Correia, 1994; Chadwick, Lowe, Horne, & Higson, 1994).

These ideas are not entirely new. André du Laurens, physician to Henry IV of France, described a similar approach in 1597. The patient was a man who had decided that he would rather die than urinate, because he imagined "that when he first pissed, all his towne would be drowned." The physicians tried to explain to him that 10,000 people could not contain enough urine to swamp even the smallest dwelling, but the patient was unmoved. Realizing that removing this delusion would require extraordinary measures, the doctors went to considerable lengths to effect a cure. They had the adjacent house set on fire, and persuaded the townspeople to ring all the bells, to shout for help, and to beg the patient to urinate on the fire, as this would be the only way to save the town. Believing that the town was indeed in danger, the patient "emptied his bladder of all that was in it, and was himselfe by that means preserved," meaning that the experience convinced him that he need have no further worries about producing inordinate volumes of urine (Hunter & MacAlpine, 1963, p. 52).

Hallucinations

Treatment of hallucinations has involved strategies to enable patients to make new attributions concerning their experiences. The rationale for cognitive therapy in this context is that auditory hallucinations arise from the mistaken ascription of certain internal events to an external source. These internal events are unwelcome, intrusive thoughts that are accompanied by subvocalization (Morrison, Haddock, & Tarrier, 1995).

Two patients with auditory hallucinations were treated using a focusing strategy, in which they explored the content and meaning of the voices with the therapist. The patients carefully monitored various aspects of the voices, such as their frequency, volume, content, and how much distress they caused. One patient started expressing doubts as to the content of the hallucinations during treatment, using phrases like "I thought I heard them say . . . " or "I think they said . . . " This patient ultimately came to believe that most of the voices were really his own thoughts; those hallucinations that persisted were benign in tone. The other patient showed some fluctuations in his attributions concerning his hallucinations, but in the end showed no change in their frequency (Haddock, Bentall, & Slade, 1993). A second study with six participants reduced both the amount of time spent hearing voices and the distress associated with them in three of the patients (Bentall, Haddock, & Slade, 1994).

The cognitive-behavioral treatment of problems associated with acute schizophrenia is an exciting new development that promises to attract greater attention from professionals in the future. We hope that this development will improve therapeutic outcomes significantly for people with schizophrenia.

Elderly Individuals, Chronic Disorders, and Problems of Later Life

In previous decades, as we have seen, the standard treatment for people with chronic disorders like schizophrenia was a lengthy psychiatric hospitalization. As a result, many patients developed the social breakdown syndrome, then grew old during their stay in the hospital. Clinicians have been divided on whether to view the age of these patients as a special issue. Some clinicians emphasize the special problems experienced by people over the age of 65, including physical illness, loss of mobility, general infirmity, and perhaps even dementia or intellectual decline. Because of such special problems, elderly psychiatric inpatients are often referred to a geriatrics or gerontology unit within the hospital so that specialists can take over their treatment. Other clinicians, including many behavior therapists, do not find it helpful to assign patients to different programs on the basis of age. Passing the age of 65 implies no dramatic change. Behavior therapy is aimed at particular *problems,* not at people at different developmental stages. Research findings in behavior therapy provide no particular reason for dividing hospitalized adults into those over and under a certain age (Richards & Thorpe, 1978).

But what about patients who are first admitted to a psychiatric hospital in later life? Some clinicians advocate specialized programs because the disorders take on new forms.

For example, depression in older patients is more likely to be related to problems with retirement, grief after the death of a spouse, or simply having less to look forward to in life. Anxiety can also be an important issue for older people confronting loss of their physical or mental capabilities. Treatment is likely to be conducted differently with these individuals than with younger clients (Gallagher-Thompson & Thompson, 1995).

Nonetheless, special issues and problems do not necessarily require special programs. For many disorders, the outlook for improvement is good regardless of the patient's age, and there is evidence that assigning older patients to special units can be detrimental. Kahana and Kahana (1970) studied a series of elderly males referred to a state hospital, randomly allocating them either to a regular adult admissions unit or to a geriatrics ward. Interviews, observations, and staff ratings assessed the patients' mental status and social interaction over a three-week period. By the end of the three weeks, the patients in the regular admissions ward had improved significantly more than those housed in the ward for the elderly.

Mental Health Problems in Later Life

Many older people with mental health problems requiring residential treatment go to nursing homes rather than to psychiatric hospitals (Kahn, 1977). By the late 1970s over one million Americans, 5 percent of those over age 65, were living in nursing homes. The probability of anyone *eventually* entering a nursing home is more like 25 to 30 percent (Carstensen & Fisher, in press). Older people are more likely than younger individuals to experience mental health problems, and from 50 to 80 percent of nursing home residents have a diagnosable mental disorder (Gottesman, 1977). Unfortunately, few mental health professionals are available to work with them and the quality of treatment interventions has been poor (Carstensen, 1988; Carstensen & Fisher, in press; Kahn, 1977). It is discouraging to find that so many people will need nursing home care, that so many of them will have psychological problems, and that so few of them will receive adequate psychological treatment. In recent years behavior therapists have paid more attention to the mental health needs of the elderly, bringing more knowledge about effective treatment that we hope will result in more widely available programs.

Promising Areas for Treatment

We began this section of the chapter by referring to people with chronic disorders who have grown old in psychiatric hospitals. This led to a discussion of older people with mental health problems who are *first* admitted for residential treatment in later life. This, in turn, leads naturally to considering older clients in outpatient settings. In the following sections we shall discuss the problems of elderly psychiatric inpatients, nursing home residents, and outpatient clients.

Promising areas for behavior therapy with elderly clients include all the problems that are routinely treated successfully in younger adults. Marital problems, sexual dysfunctions, depression, anxiety, and behavioral medicine issues can be addressed just as meaningfully in those over age 65 as in younger adults. One difficulty here is not so much with the suitability of behavioral treatment, as with *cohort effects* that deter elderly people from seeking therapy. People in their seventies, for example, represent an age cohort. Members of this cohort differ from people in their thirties not only in their chronological age but also in the experiences they have had in life. A 70-year-old man with depression might never have thought of consulting a psychologist when he was 30, whereas a present-day 30-year-old might do so with little hesitation. But the 70-year-old may *still* be unwilling to seek help, even though times have changed. Whatever the reason, it is clear that very few elderly people consult mental health professionals in outpatient clinics, despite the strong impression that elderly people may be especially vulnerable to common psychiatric disorders (Storandt, Siegler, & Elias, 1978).

Cautela and Mansfield (1977) described the use of behavioral procedures like systematic desensitization and other covert therapy techniques for elderly outpatients. The techniques themselves often require little modification, but therapy may take longer with older clients. Current interventions focus on anxiety and depression, and involve modifying unhelpful beliefs and developing constructive activities likely to bring reinforcing consequences. Because of the cohort effects mentioned earlier, older clients tend to be unfamiliar with psychological treatment and need to be "socialized" into therapy. (The therapist carefully explains the assumptions, rationale, and role expectations of the treatment contract). Therapists also need to be aware of possible sensory deficits in the client, and it may be necessary to reduce the pace of treatment somewhat. The recent research literature supports the utility of cognitive-behavioral interventions for depression in the elderly (Gallagher-Thompson & Thompson, 1995).

Much of the literature on behavior therapy with older clients is focused on inpatient and other residential settings. Despite their (potentially) greater access to mental health professionals, even the institutionalized elderly are unlikely to bring their problems to the attention of psychologists. Instead, hospital and nursing home staff members tend to be the ones who present patient problems to mental health professionals. These problems are more likely to be those that interfere with the ward routine—like shouting, complaining, or bed wetting—than problems of greater concern to the individual patient—like nightmares, depression, or obsessions. Elderly patients were seldom included in treatment decisions in a series of studies reviewed by O'Donohue, Fisher, and Krasner (1986).

Not only are elderly people unlikely to seek psychological therapy, whether as outpatients or inpatients, but mental health professionals seem reluctant to work with them in any event (Carstensen, 1988). There is the paradox that "although the geriatric population exhibits more psychological problems than any other generation, it is a fact that deliverers of psychological services seldom come in contact with this high-risk group" (Hussian, 1981, p. 184).

Hussian believes that this is unfortunate and unnecessary. Nursing homes and other residential treatment programs are potentially ideal environments for behavior therapy because the residents do not have to travel to attend therapy sessions, they may be observed round the clock by a multidisciplinary staff who may be trained, if necessary, to follow behavioral procedures, and there is the opportunity for modeling from other residents in the treatment community (Hussian, 1981).

Behavioral Treatment of the Institutionalized Elderly

Behavior therapy has several advantages as a useful psychological approach for elderly inpatients for the following reasons:

- It is usually short-term.
- It emphasizes activity.
- It relies on an individual functional analysis.
- It is not closely tied to psychiatric diagnoses (thus avoiding morbid labels and professional pessimism).
- It is experimental.
- It has clear codes of ethics and accountability.
- Behavior therapists try to make the patient the chief decision-maker, not the staff (Hussian, 1981; O'Donohue, Fisher, & Krasner, 1986; Richards & Thorpe, 1978).

Self-Care

Institutionalized elderly people are generally well cared for by the staff, but this creates the risk that the resident may become dependent upon the staff and the institution (the social breakdown syndrome). Problems with self-feeding, toileting, and even walking may arise, ironically, *because* staff members provide help, limiting residents' opportunities to maintain their independence. A common example is dependence on wheelchairs. Minor injuries in nursing home residents usually lead to the temporary use of a wheelchair. The resident in this situation may enjoy the novelty of not having to walk, and may earn more attention than usual from other people. These factors can operate as reinforcers, of course, so staff members have to be alert to the possibility that the resident may continue to use the wheelchair unnecessarily even if the original injury has been treated successfully (Hussian, 1981). In one study, two elderly residents were found to be able to walk quite well despite their prolonged use of wheelchairs. The therapists simply encouraged the residents to stay away from their wheelchairs and praised them when they did so (MacDonald & Butler, 1974).

Social Behavior

Research programs investigating the token economy and milieu therapy often included elderly patients who had grown old in the hospital. Some studies produced conclusions specific to older inpatients. For example, assertive social behavior was the focus of a study by Weinman, Gelbart, Wallace, and Post (1972). Patients were given one of three treatments over a three-month period: socioenvironmental treatment, systematic desensitization (SD), and relaxation training. In the socioenvironmental condition, patients were encouraged to take part in group activities with a great deal of prompting and reinforcement from staff members. In SD, patients were desensitized to a hierarchy of imagined situations calling for assertive responses. The relaxation condition simply involved relaxation training without desensitization. The results clearly favored the socioenvironmental condition, which was especially effective for the older patients. In the SD group, there was insufficient time to complete the anxiety hierarchies, even with 36 sessions of treatment over three months. Younger outpatients usually complete a course of SD long before this. It is not clear whether the age of these patients, or the fact that their problems had required inpatient treatment, accounted for the length of treatment and its ineffectiveness in this study.

Some effective treatments do not require elaborate attention to theory or sophisticated clinical procedures. Risley and Edwards (1978) increased social interaction at meal times in elderly nursing home residents by means of the following procedure. They got rid of tables that could seat 12 people and replaced them with smaller tables to seat 4 to 6. Conversation increased significantly.

Social skills training (SST) and problem-solving training (PST) have been studied to assess their potential for increasing the social participation of elderly inpatients. Berger and Rose (1977) compared SST with two control conditions, discussion groups and assessment only. Treatment was conducted in three one-hour sessions. SST consisted, as usual, of role-playing, modeling, and coaching concerning responses to social situations. The average age of the participants was 77. As measured by a role-play test, SST was significantly more helpful than the other conditions. Unfortunately, there was little evidence of generalization of treatment effects from this brief program (Hussian, 1981).

Toseland and Rose (1978) compared SST with PST in a group of patients over the age of 55. Social group work was used as a comparison condition. After six 90-minute sessions of treatment, both SST and PST patients had clearly improved their social skills by comparison with the group work patients. These results derived from self-report and role-play assessments.

Cognitive and Emotional Issues

Despite the popularity of cognitive-behavioral approaches in many areas of behavior therapy, cognitive therapy has not been used extensively with older patients. Clinicians may tend to avoid using cognitive interventions with elderly patients because they are often assumed to be declining in intellectual ability. Although there is some substance to this concern, intellectual decline in later life is a complex matter that has been exaggerated and oversimplified (Baltes & Lindenberger, 1988; Storandt, Siegler, & Elias, 1978). In any event, cognitive-behavioral approaches seem ideal for *improving* cognitive functioning, rather than requiring a high level of verbal ability in the first place. The self–instructional strategy training of Meichenbaum (1974) teaches the patient to practice self–statements to help solve practical problems. Similar techniques have been shown actually to increase memory functioning (Hussian, 1981).

For example, one 79-year-old woman asked for therapy because she was concerned about her memory loss; she would arrive downtown and then forget why she had gone there. She became afraid of venturing out alone. The therapist and client developed a program in which they considered every aspect of a trip in advance. The client would rehearse self-statements that encouraged her to attend to particular areas of difficulty, such as: "If I forget what I was going to buy downtown, I can always stop in a store and browse while I collect my thoughts" or "I need to pause and be quite sure it's safe before crossing this intersection." This strategy led to a remarkable improvement (Hussian, 1981).

A study of depression in nursing home residents illustrates the potential for behavior therapy in treating important emotional issues. Hussian and Lawrence (1981) treated 36 residents, all over the age of 60. They were assigned randomly to treatment conditions. These were social reinforcement for activity, problem-solving training (PST), and no treatment. After one week of intensive treatment, these groups were further subdivided. Half of the social reinforcement group now had PST, while the other half continued with social reinforcement. Similarly, in the PST group, half switched to reinforcement, the other half did not. After the first week of treatment, the activity reinforcement and PST residents showed substantially more improvement than the untreated residents. After the second phase of treatment, it was clear that treatment conditions that had included PST produced the best results. The same trend was seen at a follow-up assessment three months later.

Training of Residential Staff and Community Caregivers

Much helpful information with practical relevance can be "given away" by behavior therapists to mental health workers and caregivers in the community (Milne, 1986). A great deal can be accomplished by training direct-care staff in behavior management principles, especially in nursing homes when patients are especially dependent on staff members. Studies have confirmed the beneficial impact on inpatients of the successful, positive modification of staff behavior and attitudes (Graziano & Katz, 1982; Hussian, 1981; Richards & Thorpe, 1978). Training community caregivers in effective behavioral management of the problems of impaired elderly clients has been successful, both in improving client behavior and in enhancing caregiver/client interactions (Pinkston, Linsk, & Young, 1988). Finally, there has been a recent renewal of interest in increasing the capacity of psychologists to work effectively with older inpatients, as reflected in the development of specialized post–doctoral training curricula (Moye & Brown, 1995).

Comments

This brief review of issues in behavior therapy for the institutionalized elderly shows that there are grounds for optimism. Few elderly clients receive behavior therapy; however, the problem is not that the available treatments are inadequate but that clinicians are generally unwilling to try to treat older clients. Behavior therapy is a particularly promising approach in this area, and both research efforts and clinical practice need to be extended.

Chapter Summary

Some severe mental health problems require hospitalization to protect patients from themselves, to provide more intensive treatment, or to protect the community from dangerous behavior. Mental health professionals often prefer to work with outpatients rather than inpatients, but behavior therapists are among those who have developed treatments to rehabilitate the institutionalized mentally ill. Addressing the social breakdown syndrome and other treatment targets identified by Gordon Paul, behavior therapists used methods drawn from operant learning to remedy specific problems such as mutism, hoarding, or bizarre behavior, and general problems such as social withdrawal and dependence on the institution. The token economy represents a significant contribution by behavior therapists to the rehabilitation of long-stay inpatients by using reinforcement procedures with ward groups. Research has shown that social learning-based and milieu treatment programs produce substantial therapeutic benefit with typical chronic inpatients. Social skills and problem-solving training have been helpful in preparing certain patients for discharge to the community.

Traditional therapy programs have segregated older from younger inpatients. Questioning this practice, some behavior therapists have demonstrated that there is no valid reason for placing all elderly patients in special hospital units. Self-care, social behavior, and cognitive and emotional symptoms have all been realistic treatment targets for behavior therapy. Teaching staff members to use behavioral principles can be extremely helpful in improving inpatient therapy for older patients, and teaching similar skills to caregivers in the community can enhance the adjustment of elderly outpatients.

Endnotes

1. The opening clinical illustration for this chapter focuses on providers rather than on clients, allowing us to use their real names.
2. See Chapter 3 for the theoretical background to the token economy, and a later section of this chapter for relevant empirical findings.
3. Behavioral assessment had revealed that Dick was not actually hearing impaired (Peck, 1971). If he had been deaf, it would of course have been appropriate to teach him sign language.
4. This form of delusional thinking is referred to as *ideas of reference*.

Chapter *15*

Behavior Disorders
of Childhood
Assessment and Treatment Planning

Ari, age 13, was referred to an inpatient unit after he attempted suicide by ingesting a large number of aspirin tablets. According to Ari's parents, in recent weeks he had become increasingly despondent over the accidental death of his best friend. He began losing weight, neglecting his appearance, sleeping for excessive amounts of time, and refusing to attend school. Although Ari gave no direct warning of his suicide attempt, he had made veiled references to death using phrases such as "Maybe the world would be better off without me."

Carl, age 4, was referred to a child psychologist for extremely disobedient and defiant behavior. His parents described him as "impossible," relating that he had been very hard to manage since infancy. Carl's behavior problems at home consisted of severe and prolonged tantrums whenever he did not get his way, consistent refusal to comply with his parents' requests, aggression toward his younger brother, harassment of the family dog, and defiance toward all family members. His mother related that she was afraid to take him anywhere in public, because his misbehavior was so extreme and embarrassing. He had been "expelled" from two different preschools for aggressive and disruptive behavior toward peers and teachers. In addition to feeling distressed about Carl's behavior at home, his parents worried that his behavior problems would carry over to his forthcoming transition to kindergarten.

This chapter and the next contain an overview of behavioral approaches to the assessment and treatment of major childhood behavior disorders. It was once believed that childhood behavior disorders represented "downward extensions" of adult disorders (Phillips,

Draguns, & Bartlett, 1975). This belief, called *adultomorphism*, has been strongly discredited. Children's behavior disorders are now recognized as unique and complex problems in their own right. Furthermore, childhood behavior disorders cannot be understood apart from the social and developmental contexts in which they occur.

Defining Child Behavior Disorders

Determining Clinical Significance

Ms. R., a 28-year-old mother of two children, contacted a child psychologist with the following complaint: "My son John will not obey me. When I ask him to do simple things around the house, like picking up his toys, he refuses, becomes angry with me, and often throws a tantrum." What criteria can be used to determine whether John, or any other child, is in need of treatment? Most clinicians rely on multiple guidelines to answer this question. Although no simple or concise answer exists, the following criteria have proven useful.

Deviance from Developmental Norms

Children's normal development is characterized by continuous change and reorganization. This poses a challenge for the child clinician: It is impossible to label a child's behavior as *deviant* without knowing what is normally expected for his or her age group. Some "problem behaviors"—such as fears, negativistic tendencies, and toileting difficulties—are relatively normal for children of certain age groups. Thus, the first question that a clinician would be likely to ask Ms. R. (above) is: "What is your son's age?" Oppositional tendencies in a toddler or young preschool child would present a dramatically different clinical picture from those exhibited by an older child.

The typical growth rate and sequence of children's physical, cognitive, and social skills can be charted and used as an index for defining abnormal development. For example, normal prelanguage and language behaviors in young children of different ages are charted in Table 15–1. The table reflects only the average tendencies of large numbers of children at each specific age period. Failure to conform exactly to these expectations does not mean that the child's development is abnormal. Child clinicians are most concerned about relatively extreme deviations from normative expectations.

Normative comparisons are also essential in designing behavioral interventions for children. Behaviors targeted for change, and intervention strategies used to accomplish change, must be appropriate to the child's developmental level (Kendall et al., 1984). For example, systematic desensitization would not be an appropriate treatment strategy for a fearful preschool-age child, because it requires the use of vivid and complex cognitive imagery. Many preschool children are incapable of generating and sustaining such imagery. Finally, in evaluating the effects of treatment interventions on children's behavior, it is necessary to include untreated comparison groups. This is to ensure that observed behavioral changes are related to the treatment, rather than to normal developmental changes reflecting the passage of time.

TABLE 15–1 Approximate Ages of Normal Prelanguage and Language Behaviors

Age (months)	Comprehension	Production	Pragmatics
0–1	90% respond to bell	Reflexive crying; variable fundamental frequency	
2	Different response to speech/nonspeech	Noncry cooing	
3		Laughs; more vowel than consonant sounds produced	90% smile spontaneously
4	Localizes to sound	Squeals	
5–7		Consonant sounds are increasing	
8–9	Comprehends name; 90% turn to voice	Vocalization increase in response to speech; imitation of some sounds	85% play peek-a-boo
10–13	Looks at objects that mother looks at	90% imitate speech sounds. Inconsistent word usage; produces substantive words (i.e., names of things), nominative words (i.e., names of people), and function words (e.g., no, all gone). Produces words longer than one syllable	90% indicate wants (requests)
	Recognition of familiar words; responds most appropriately to commands or requests one word in length	Language used to label objects; overinclusion and underinclusion of word meanings are common	60% imitate housework
18–22	75% point to named	Produces successive single-word utterances	
20–30	Locates objects mentioned and gives evidence of notice,	Combinations of two-word utterances; present progressive verb form (e.g., I or does what you walking); preposition: in; usually do plural nouns (e.g., books); what questions (e.g., What that?); 90% follow two of three directions	
22–44	Understands prepositions: in, and on; personal pronouns: he, she; questions: what, what—ing, and why; 90% understand: cold, tired, and hungry	/m/, /n/, /w/, /b/, /p/, /fl, and /h/ are produced correctly by 75% of the children tested; produce longer combinations of words; preposition: on; possessive noun (e.g., Mommy's); where questions (e.g., Where Daddy going?)	90% interactive play

(Cont.)

TABLE 15–1   *(Continued)*

Age (months)	Comprehension	Production	Pragmatics
30–50	Understands negative/ affirmative statements; questions: who, whose, and where	/j/, /k/, /m/, /d/./g/, /tn/, are produced correctly by 75% of the children tested; produce articles: a and the; regular and irregular past tense verbs (e.g., walked and fell); who questions (e.g., Who took the dolly?)	

Source: From Gabel, S., and Erickson, M. T., *Child development and developmental disabilities.* Copyright © 1980 by Little, Brown and Company. Reprinted with permission.

Perceptions of Significant Others

Children rarely refer themselves for treatment, nor do they have much influence over treatment decisions. The perceptions and behavioral styles of significant adults in the child's life, usually parents and/or teachers, play a prominent role in evaluation and treatment. As in the cases of John R. and Carl, children are most often referred for treatment because their behavior is disturbing to others. However, adults vary significantly in their expectations for children's behavior, their knowledge of normal developmental processes, and their ability to tolerate conflict (Dix, 1991). These considerations help to make child behavior therapy a unique, complicated, and challenging enterprise.

Situational Influences

Children interact with others in many different life situations, the most significant being home and school. It is not unusual to find that a child's problem behaviors are specific to a given setting, or even a particular situational context within that setting (Mash & Terdal, 1988). A child who shows significant behavior problems in the home may appear problem free in the school environment, or conversely. Relatedly, the type and degree of stress in the child's environment has been strongly linked to the development of problem behavior (Goodyer, 1990; Hetherington, 1984). For example, it is relatively normal for children to manifest short-term emotional disturbance in response to stressful life changes such as hospitalization, the birth of a new sibling, or parental divorce (Rutter, 1983). Hence, children's problem behavior cannot be fully understood apart from the environmental context in which it occurs.

Frequency, Duration, and Persistence

To what extent does the problem behavior interfere with the child's normal adaptive ability? In order to answer this question, clinicians obtain specific information from the referring adult(s) concerning: (1) the daily frequency of the problem behavior, (2) the duration of each problem episode, (3) the long-term persistence of the problem behavior, and (4) the quality of the child's adjustment at home, with peers, and at school. It is relatively common for children to show transient problem behaviors during the course of their development. The child clinician is therefore most strongly concerned about frequent patterns of maladaptive behavior that have persisted for one year or longer.

Classification

Childhood behavior disorders are defined by the presence of multiple problem behaviors that occur together in the same child. Classification systems provide a means for describing the groups of behaviors that define different psychological disorders.

There have been two general approaches to the classification of children's behavior disorders: clinical and empirical. The *empirical* approach involves the use of statistical techniques to identify clusters of problem behaviors that co-occur. The statistical analyses are based on observations or ratings of adult informants. Typically, an adult provides detailed information about the presence and severity of specific problem behaviors in a given child. These responses are quantified, usually on a 0- to 2-point scale (0 = never or rarely occurs; 1 = sometimes occurs; 2 = frequently occurs) for each question. Data are collected for large numbers of children, then statistically analyzed. Discrete problem behaviors that are highly intercorrelated are viewed as comprising "syndromes," or broad dimensions of maladaptive behavior.

Achenbach and his colleagues have reviewed the findings of many different empirical classification studies, representing divergent age groups, settings, and populations (Achenbach, 1985; Achenbach, Howell, Quay, & Conners, 1991). Two dimensions of child maladaptation consistently emerged: the *externalizing* (or *undercontrolled*) dimension, representing problems of aggression, disruptiveness, and impulsivity, and the *internalizing* dimension, representing problems of overanxious, depressed, and socially withdrawn behavior. There is disagreement, however, concerning the type and number of narrower dimensions of problem behavior that may be age-, sex-, and/or situation-specific (Achenbach & Edelbrock, 1983).

The *clinical* or *syndromal* approach to classification represents the consensus judgments of expert clinicians that certain problem behaviors tend to occur together. The *DSM-IV* provides a comprehensive system for classifying disorders of infancy, childhood, and adolescence.

What is the role of diagnostic classification in the *behavioral* treatment of children? Traditionally, behavior therapists have been critical of diagnostic classification. Objections to diagnosis have focused on empirical inadequacies of diagnostic systems (such as poor reliability), lack of attention to situational influences on behavior, lack of relevance to treatment, and and failure to provide normative developmental standards for assessing child deviance (e.g., Kendall, 1987; Mash & Terdal, 1988). The empirical approach to classification is more consistent with the behavioral tradition than clinical approaches. Recently, strides have been made in integrating CBCL data from multiple informants into behavioral treatment (Achenbach, 1993).

Today, the gradual broadening of behavioral assessment that has occurred over time has promoted more flexible attitudes about the use of clinically based diagnostic criteria (Barrios, 1988). Traditional objections to diagnostic classification have applied less to the current *DSM* than to earlier versions. The clinical classification of childhood disorders still has many weaknesses and does not lead directly to treatment planning (Cantwell & Rutter, 1995). However, diagnostic data can serve a useful hypothesis-generating function in the initial stages of assessment by suggesting controlling variables for clinicians to investigate in each individual case (Harris & Powers, 1984; Nelson & Barlow, 1981).

Other criticisms of diagnostic classification involve the negative social and psychological effects that can occur when diagnostic labels are applied to individual children. Labels themselves can negatively bias adult perceptions of children (Foster & Salvia, 1977). Also, having a label such as *hyperactive* applied to oneself could affect self-concept and motivation to change, stimulating a negative self-fulfilling prophecy (Whalen & Henker, 1976). Finally, diagnostic labeling implies that the locus of problem behavior is in the individual child, whereas it is generally accepted that "problems" are socially constructed (Cicchetti, 1989).

Alternatively, it is not always the case that labeling a child's deviant behavior produces negative social consequences. For example, some parents feel relieved when their child's problems are diagnosed, and become more accepting of the child's limitations (Cantwell & Rutter, 1995). Moreover, diagnostic labels facilitate research and effective communication between professionals and, in some cases, help guide appropriate treatment decisions (Mash & Terdal, 1988). Thus, it behooves the child clinician to use diagnostic classification judiciously, and in ways that promote positive change (Wicks-Nelson & Israel, 1991).

Assessment for Behavior Change

Accurate assessment of target behavior is an essential first step in the process of child behavior therapy. Well-planned behavioral assessments lead naturally to the specification of intervention methods. According to Mash and Terdal (1988), child behavioral assessment involves a process of hypothesis testing regarding the nature of the problem, its causes, and the likely effects of various interventions. Specific assessment techniques vary according to the unique features of each case. However, at the minimum, behavior assessment techniques must be appropriate for the child's developmental level, and sensitive to situational influences and variability in children's problem behaviors (Mash & Lee, 1995). Moreover, modern child behavior therapists (following the S-O-R-C-K model, see Chapter 6) typically include multiple target behaviors in their assessments, incorporating overt behaviors, affective-physiological responses, and cogitive-verbal responses into their analyses (Ollendick & Hersen, 1984). Finally, whenever possible, child behavior therapists strive to include reliable and valid assessment procedures that have been standardized on normative populations of children (Mash & Terdal, 1988).

Methods of Child Behavioral Assessment

Methods of child behavioral assessment cover a broad range of techniques. The use of multiple assessment techniques is a distinguishing feature of child behavioral assessment. However, as Mash and Terdal (1988) have warned, this does not mean applying a standard "battery" of techniques to all cases. The number and nature of assessment tools used in any given case is guided by specific features of the referral situation, practical considerations (such as time and availability of key informants), and the extent to which each data source provides unique and sigificant clinical information.

Behavioral Interviews with Parents

Behavioral assessment of children differs from its adult counterpart in terms of the sheer number of individuals who are involved. The assessment process is usually started with the child and his or her parents during the first interview. Both are typically seen individually and together (Ollendick & Cerny, 1981).

In most cases of child behavior therapy, the parental interview serves as the most salient source of assessment information (Swan & MacDonald, 1978). An important therapeutic goal is to establish a warm, supportive relationship with the parents and to enlist the parents as allies in assessment and treatment (Evans & Nelson, 1977). This is crucial because behavior therapy with children is frequently carried out via parental intervention. Another important goal is to obtain highly specific information concerning the parents' views of their child. A "funnel method" of interviewing is useful, in which the therapist first obtains general information about the child's background and family characteristics. This is followed by queries about problems the parent may perceive in the child. Once areas of concern are identified, the clinician obtains specific information about the exact nature of the problem behavior(s), including frequency of occurrence, intensity, episodic duration, environmental antecedents and consequents, and the parents' role in maintaining the behavior. The following is an excerpt from a clinical interview with the mother of a 9-year-old boy:

EXAMPLE OF PARENT INTERVIEWING

Therapist: You sounded quite worried over the phone. Tell me more about your problems with Billy.

Parent: Well, he just hasn't been himself lately. He seems depressed.

Therapist: Depressed?

Parent: Yes, sad, downcast, withdrawn . . .

Therapist: Give me some examples of how he acts when he's depressed.

Parent: He retreats to his room and spends a lot of time alone. His appetite has been poor lately, and his grades have begun to decline. He doesn't bring friends home like he used to. . . . He seems very unresponsive and appears tired. At first, we thought that he had some kind of flu bug, but clearly it's more than that.

Therapist: How often does Billy behave this way?

Parent: Lately quite often. Just about every day. But he doesn't always seem depressed... it comes in spells.

Therapist: What seems to lead up to these spells?

Parent: I'm not really sure. . . . Well, his father and I haven't been getting along well lately, and we've started considering a trial separation. We haven't discussed this with Billy yet, of course. But I have noticed that when we fight and stay cold and distant with one another, Billy tends to withdraw.

Parents are also asked about the child's strengths and skills in other areas, so that appropriate alternative responses for the child can be identified (Gross, 1984). After the problem identification phase, the clinician obtains a historical account of the child's development, beginning with the mother's pregnancy and following through to the present time. This information helps to provide a developmental context for understanding the child's current difficulties. Information about the child's medical, school, and social histories should be included and carefully reviewed. It is also important to obtain a brief family history, as well as information about parental adjustment, marital adjustment, particularly the presence of chronic discord, and the presence and types of family social-ecological stressors and supports (Mash & Lee,1995). Finally, the clinician must assess the parents' willingness to be involved in the treatment process. This can be inferred from direct questioning and by observing how well parents comply with therapeutic "homework" tasks (Gross, 1984).

Although parent interview data represent an important part of the treatment process, they have potential limitations. Several investigators have noted serious problems with parents' retrospective reports of their children's behavior, including low reliability, inaccurate recall, and positive bias (Evans & Nelson, 1977; Hetherington & Martin, 1979; O'Leary & Johnson, 1979). The potential limitations of parent interview data underscore the need for using multiple informants and assessment methods.

Child Interviewing

Clinical interviews with the child alone are usually not conducted unless the child is at least 7 years old. It is difficult to obtain reliable information from preschoolers, due to their limited verbal repertoire (Ciminero & Drabman, 1977; O'Leary & Johnson, 1979). As with all clinical interviews, process (establishing rapport) and content (obtaining information) goals can be differentiated. The importance of establishing a good therapeutic relationship with the child has been stressed by many behavior therapists (e.g., Evans & Nelson, 1977; Roberts & La Greca, 1981). Rapport building is facilitated by a warm, responsive demeanor on the part of the clinician, particularly one that conveys respect for the child; the use of age-appropriate language; and careful phrasing and timing of questions (Kanfer, Eyberg, & Krahn, 1992). Content goals usually involve obtaining the child's view of the presenting problem, along with his or her perceptions of self, sigificant others, and environmental surroundings. Content areas frequently assessed in child interviews are shown in Table 15–2.

Structured and Semistructured Interviews

Structured interviews provide a standardized format for assessing the presence and severity of behavior disorders in school-age children and adolescents. Most structured interview protocols use both child and adult informants, generate *DSM* categories, and have good reliability (Young et al., 1987). Highly structured interviews specify the exact wording and

TABLE 15–2   Current Areas Frequently Assessed in Child Interviews

Areas	Examples of Specific Content
All Ages Referral problem	What does the child think the main problem is? Does the child see the referral problem as a problem? What does the child think will help?
Interests	What does the child like to do (in spare time)? What does the child like to do alone? with friends? with family members?
School	What does the child like best about school? Least? How does the child feel about his or her teachers? What kinds of grades does the child get in school?
Peers	Whom does the child like to play with? Who are the child's friends? What do they like to do together? Who does the child dislike?
Family	How does the child get along with his or her parents? What do they do that the child likes? That makes the child angry? How does the child get along with his or her brothers and sisters? What do they do that the child likes, dislikes?
Fears, Worries	What kind of things is the child afraid of? What kinds of things make the child nervous, jumpy? What kind of things does the child worry about?
Self-image	What does the child like, dislike about himself or herself? What can the child do well, relative to peers? How would the child describe himself or herself?
Mood, Feelings	What kinds of things make the child feel sad? happy? How often do these feelings happen? What kinds of things make the child feel mad? What does he or she do when mad?
Somatic concerns	Does the child have any headaches or stomachaches? Or other kinds of body pains? How often does this happen? What does the child usually do?
Thought disorder Describe them.	Does the child hear things or see things that seem funny or unusual?
Aspirations	What would the child like to do for a living when he or she gets older? What are other things the child would like to do when older?
Fantasy	What kinds of things does the child daydream about? What kinds of things does the child dream about? If the child could have any three wishes, what would they be?
Adolescents Heterosexual relations	Is the adolescent involved in any dating activities? What kinds of dating activities? Are there any restrictions on the adolescent's dating activities? How does he or she feel about them?

(Cont.)

TABLE 15–2   *(Continued)*

Area	Examples of Specific Content
Sex	What kinds of sexual concerns does the adolescent have? What are his or her attitudes toward premarital sex? Do these conflict at all with parents' views? Is the adolescent adequately informed about contraception?
Drug, Alcohol use	What kinds of things has the adolescent ever used to get "high" (e.g., pills, alcohol, pot, glue)? Are other friends involved in these activities?

Source: From Walker, C. E., and Roberts, M. C. (Eds.), *Handbook of clinical child psychology.* Copyright © 1983 by John Wiley and Sons. Reprinted by permission of John Wiley & Sons, Inc.

coding of each question, and are less vulnerable to clinician inexperience than other interviewing techniques (Edelbrock & Costello, 1988). Disadvantages include the lengthy assessment process, and the fact that various protocols may cover only limited diagnostic categories, or more categories than are appropriate to the current case (Costello, 1991). Examples of highly structured scales include the Diagnostic Interview for Children and Adolescents (DICA) (Herjanic & Reich, 1982) and the Diagnostic Interview Schedule for children (DISC) (Cohen, Velez, Kohn, Schwab-Stone, & Johnson, 1987).

Semistructured interview protocols allow more flexibility in the format of the interview and in the phrasing of questions. Examples of semistructured scales include the Kiddie Schedule for Affective Disorders and Schizophrenia (K-SADS) (Ambrosini, Metz, Prabucki, & Lee, 1989), the Child Assessment Schedule (CAS) (Hodges, 1987), and the Interview Schedule for Children (ISC) (Kovacs, 1985). Disadvantages of these instruments include lack of normative data, and inapplicability to clinical situations that require considerable flexibility (LaGreca & Stone, 1992). Finally, with the noteworthy exception of Hodge's CAS, these interviews have not been designed to facilitate rapport with the child or adolescent.

Interview with Teachers

Interviews with a child's teachers are an essential part of the behavioral assessment process. Frequently, teachers are primary referral sources and function as intervention agents if the child's problem behavior extends to the school setting. It is very important for the clinician to develop good rapport with the teacher by showing respect for his or her opinions and by ensuring that the teacher does not feel that his or her performance is being evaluated (Bardon, Benneu, Bruchez, & Sanderson, 1976). Bardon and colleagues also caution the clinician to avoid interfering with normal classroom routines and to avoid behaving in ways that stigmatize the child. Content goals for teacher interviews generally involve obtaining a detailed description of the child's strengths and weaknesses, along with suggestions for intervention (Sattler, 1988). The following content areas are typically assessed in teacher interviews:

1. *Peer relations.* How does child get along with peers? How many close friends does the child have? What is the specific nature of any perceived peer problem (e.g., is the child actively rejected by peers or ignored)? Are problems specific to a given classmate or situation? How long have these problems been present, and what factors were associated with their onset?

2. *Academic behavior.* What are the child's relative strengths and weaknesses in each specific academic area? What is the child's classroom behavior like? How motivated is the child to perform academically?

3. *Relationship to authority.* How does the child behave vis-a-vis authority figures such as teachers and administrators? If problems with authority figures exist, are they person or situation specific?

4. *Teacher's willingness.* Is the teacher willing to get involved in treatment process, if appropriate?

Behavioral Observations

Direct observations of behavior have been important assessment tools for the child behavior therapist. As with behavioral observations of adults, the observations can be carried out in naturalistic or clinic settings.

Naturalistic observations of child problem behaviors have been conducted in a wide range of contexts, including familial, classroom, institutional-residential, and peer settings (La Greca & Stone, 1992). As with adult behavioral observation, target behaviors are pinpointed using a coding system. The usefulness of the observation procedure is determined by the reliability and validity of the coding system (see Chapter 7 for discussion of threats to the validity of coding systems) and the appropriateness of the observational data to the referral question. Finally, most clinicians have the problem of assessing the behaviors of an *individual* child, whereas coding systems are developed on groups. Guidelines for individualized observational assessment have been put forth by Gelfand and Hartmann (1984) and by Evans and Nelson (1986).

It is not always practical for the clinician to observe the child at become or at school. Therefore, structured behavioral observation formats have been developed for use in clinical settings (see Hughes & Hayes, 1978, for a review of these procedures). Typically, the child and his or her parents are brought into a clinic playroom and observed through a oneway mirror. They are usually asked to interact with one another under different task conditions. A good example is the Forehand and McMahon (1981) procedure for observing mothers and their noncompliant children in a clinic playroom. The procedure was developed to clarify maladaptive parent/child interactions relating to extreme noncompliance in 4- to 8-year-old children. The parent/child pair is observed in a toy-filled clinic playroom.

Prior to the observation, the parent is instructed to interact with the child in two different contexts: "Child's Game" and "Parent's Game." The Child's Game is a free-play situation in which the child is allowed to choose and direct activities for the dyad. The Parent's Game is a command situation in which the parent directs the child to perform certain activities. Interaction behaviors are coded from behind a one-way mirror that has been wired for sound. A predetermined category system is then applied to interaction behaviors in each context. A sample data sheet from observation during the parent's game is shown in Figure 15–1. These procedures are less time consuming than naturalistic observa-

SCORE SHEET

Page _____

Child's Name _____

Date _____ Time _____

Coder's Name _____

Session _____ Place _____

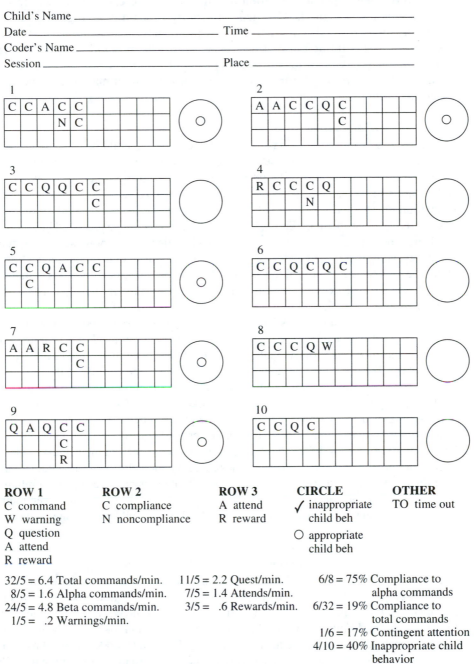

	ROW 1	ROW 2	ROW 3	CIRCLE	OTHER
	C command	C compliance	A attend	✓ inappropriate child beh	TO time out
	W warning	N noncompliance	R reward		
	Q question			○ appropriate child beh	
	A attend				
	R reward				

32/5 = 6.4 Total commands/min.   11/5 = 2.2 Quest/min.   6/8 = 75% Compliance to
 8/5 = 1.6 Alpha commands/min.   7/5 = 1.4 Attends/min.   alpha commands
24/5 = 4.8 Beta commands/min.   3/5 = .6 Rewards/min.   6/32 = 19% Compliance to
 1/5 = .2 Warnings/min.   total commands
                                                                   1/6 = 17% Contingent attention
                                                                   4/10 = 40% Inappropriate child
                                                                          behavior

FIGURE 15–1   Score Sheet

Source: Helping the noncompliant child by R. L. Forehand and R. J. McMahon, copyright © 1981 by Guilford Press: New York. Reprinted by permission of the authors and publishers. Reprinted by permission.

tions and provide a standard situation for clients to be observed in. However, limitations include the possible lack of generalizability to natural settings, as well as the possibility of never observing low-frequency problem behaviors. Hetherington (1984) has suggested structuring these observations so that the possibility of observing targeted problem behaviors is maximized. For example, asking a parent to keep the child on task and away from toys for a given period of time might maximize the chance of observing child noncompliance.

Behavioral Questionnaires

Checklists and dimensional rating scales are widely used in child behavioral assessment. Typically, an adult who knows the child well responds to a set of questions about the presence and frequency of specific problem behaviors or competencies. For example, the Achenbach Child Behavior Checklist/4-18 (CBCL/418) (Achenbach, 1991) a widely used behavioral questionnaire, consists of 113 items representing specific child problems behaviors (e.g., "disobedient in school," "argues a lot," "has strange ideas"). The parent rates the degree to which each item characterizes the child on a 0- to 2-point scale. The number, frequency, and patterning of endorsed items are used to make clinical inferences about the child's behavioral and emotional functioning. In addition, suplementary items include questions about the child's competence in extracurricular pursuits, friendships, and academic performance.

Behavioral questionnaires have begun replacing observations as favored child assessment tools because they are easy to administer and interpret and they require minimal time from the informant. (The Achenbach questionnaire can be completed in approximately 15 minutes.) They provide a standardized index of adult perceptions of the child, which can be used to develop hypotheses about the nature of the child's problem and to evaluate treattnent progress. Disagreement on the part of key informants, such as teachers and parents, could indicate situational specificity in the problem behavior. Finally, problem-specific checklists such as the Conners Rating Scales for Hyperactivity (Conners, 1990) can be used to develop hypotheses about diagnosis and treatment. On the negative side, however, a number of factors may influence the reliability and validity of these quesfionnaires (McMahon, 1984). Furthermore, behavioral questionnaires have been proven reliable for the purposes of group classification (Achenbach & Edelbrock, 1978). However, their usefulness in generating diagnostic classifications of individual children is limited (Achenbach, 1991).

Tests of Intelligence and Achievement

Behavioral assessment of children differs from that of adults in that assessment of the child's cognitive skills is usually an important part of the evaluation process (Newcomb & Drabman, 1995). Standardized tests of intelligence such as the Wechsler Intelligence Scale for Children-Third Edition (WISC-III) (Wechsler, 1991) and tests of achievement such as the Woodcock-Johnson Psychoeducational Battery-Revised (Woodcock & Johnson, 1989) are essential for diagnostic decisions involving mental retardation or learning disabilities. In other clinical situations, these tests provide a standard structure for observing individual differences in behaviors such as frustration tolerance, achievement orientation, performance anxiety, and impulse control. In addition, they provide a general index of the child's adaptive strengths and weaknesses which can be integrated into treatment planning and evaluation (Sattler, 1988).

Child Self-report Questionnaires

A number of child self-report questionnaires have been developed for identifying emotional problems such as anxiety, depression, and low self-esteem (e.g., Finch & Rogers, 1984; Harter, 1994). Items are phrased in age-appropriate language and are usually read to younger children. The reliability and validity of child self-report data are always of concern, so these questionnaires should be used as supplements to other sources of information. However, as Finch and Rogers (1994) have pointed out, psychometrically sound child self-report questionnaires can provide information that is very useful in treatment planning and evaluation.

Self-Monitoring

Self-monitoring procedures have been used to obtain frequency counts of problem behavior and have even been used as intervention techniques (E. S. Shapiro, 1984). Using paper and pencil, stickers, mechanical counters, or other methods, the child or parent is asked to record a clearly defined target behavior. Self-monitoring techniques have been applied to a wide range of target behaviors and situational settings. Potential limitations of self-monitored data include inaccuracy and reactivity. Although it is possible to attenuate potential reactivity effects, self-monitoring techniques should be used very cautiously as sources of baseline data. Clinicians also should ensure that the data are being accurately reported by performing "reliability checks" and by using methods that are easily implemented (Nelson, 1977).

Cognitive-Behavioral Assessment

A variety of techniques have been developed for assessment of specific problems in cognitive and social information processing (Kendall, Pellegrini, & Urbain, 1981). As with all cognitive-behavioral assessment techniques, a central assumption is that children's cognitions mediate overt problem behaviors. The purpose of the assessment, then, is to pinpoint the nature and severity of specific information-processing problems and to provide data that can be used in treatment planning and evaluation. Implicit in the use of these techniques is the acknowledgment that children are not passively shaped by their environments: They respond to a perceived world and play an active role in structuring their own social experiences (Harris, 1985). Examples of cognitive-behavioral assessment techniques include measures of role-taking ability (Chandler, 1973); interpersonal problem-solving ability (Spivak & Shure, 1974); attributional style (Nowicki & Strickland, 1973); and conceptual tempo (Kagan, Rosman, Day, Albert, & Phillips, 1964).

Integrating Assessment and Treatment

A well-conducted behavioral assessment (1) pinpoints the nature of the child's most pressing problems and greatest relative strengths, (2) provides information about current factors in the child and/or the environment that are maintaining the problem, and (3) provides practical information concerning the best means of implementing and evaluating behavior change. In other words, behavioral assessment is the first stage of treatment. No general model has been developed for facilitating the selection of appropriate behavioral interventions (Mash & Terdal, 1988). All behavioral therapies, however, involve two general goals: decreasing the frequency and severity of maladaptive behaviors and increasing the frequency of behavioral assets. Beyond this, clues to the most effective treatment for a given child problem might ideally be drawn from the empirical literature specific to that problem. For this reason, behavioral treatment techniques and modalities specific to different childhood behavior disorders are discussed in the next chapter.

Chapter Summary

Behavior disorders of childhood are unique in relation to adult disorders and cannot be understood apart from the social and developmental contexts in which they occur. When children are referred for treatment, multiple sources of assessment information must be tapped to gain a comprehensive and situationally sensitive picture of the child's behavioral strengths and weaknesses. A well-conducted assessment pinpoints the nature of the child's most pressing problems, provides information about current characteristics of the child or environment that are maintaining the problem, and provides practical information concerning the best means of implementing behavior change.

Chapter 16

Behavior Disorders of Childhood

Specific Treatment Interventions

A comprehensive presentation of childhood behavior disorders is beyond the scope of this book. In this chapter, major childhood behavior disorders will be briefly described, along with behavioral treatment methods specific to the disorder. As discussed in the previous chapter, most childhood behavior problems can be grouped into two broad categories: *internalizing* disorders reflecting high levels of anxiety and/or social withdrawal and *externalizing* disorders reflecting aggression and/or poor impulse control (Achenbach & Edelbrock, 1983; Quay, 1986). A much smaller albeit significant group of problems, such as Autistic Disorder, involve severe and generalized developmental deviations. These disorders typically do not appear in factor-analytic studies because of their rarity in the general population (Quay, 1986).

Internalizing Disorders

Internalizing disorders of childhood encompass a broad range of symptoms, including high levels of anxiety, depression, low self-esteem, social withdrawal, and somatic concerns. These problems tend to cluster together, comprising the second most common pattern of childhood behavior disorders (Quay, 1986).

Anxiety Disorders

Childhood anxiety disorders encompass a large and diverse range of symptoms, including fears and phobias, behavioral avoidance of feared objects and situations, generalized feelings of tension, and somatic complaints. As with the adult anxiety disorders, *anxiety* is defined in relation to the child's perception that certain situations or stimuli are dangerous. Likewise, anxiety reactions are defined by three different response systems: *motor behavior* (trembling, freezing, screaming or crying, avoiding the feared situation); *heightened psychophysiological arousal* (increased heart rate, sweating, muscle tension); and *subjective responses* (thoughts of being harmed, scary images; thoughts of helplessness or inadequacy) (Barrios & O'Dell, 1989; Lang, 1984). However, differences in children's developmental levels strongly affect the assessment and treatment of anxiety. For example, young children have difficulty putting their thoughts, feelings, and mental images into words, or making complex judgments about the rationality of their thoughts.

In the *DSM-IV, Separation Anxiety Disorder* is the only anxiety disorder considered specific to children and adolescents. All other childhood anxiety disorders are diagnosed using adult criteria because it is assumed that they share the same features. Childhood anxiety disorders have not been well researched, and so the validity of this assumption awaits further evidence (Werry, 1994).

Fears and Phobias

Mild, transient fear reactions are very common in childhood (LaPouse & Monk, 1959; MacFarlane, Allen, & Honzik, 1954). Moreover, many children develop one or more *severe* fears during their childhood years (Ollendick, 1983; Rutter, 1989). In evaluating the clinical relevance of these fears, it is essential to adopt a developmental perspective. There are marked age-related changes in the ways that children perceive and experience fear, and in the actual content of fear stimuli. For example, preschoolers commonly fear monsters, animals, separation from parents, and darkness, whereas older children tend to fear social censure and physical injury (King et al., 1989; Miller et al., 1974). Childhood fears persist for variable lengths of time: Some are transient and others may persist for several years or longer (Barrios & Hartman, 1988; Campbell, 1986).

As with adult phobic disorder, childhood fears are deemed *phobias* when the fear is out of proportion to the actual degree of danger involved in the situation. Phobic children attempt to avoid the feared situation or object. In confronting the phobic stimulus, the child may experience feelings of panic, accompanied by psychophysiological reactions such as shortness of breath, nausea, and/or heart palpitations.

Assessment Issues.   During the behavioral interview, the clinician gathers essential information about the nature of the child's phobic reaction and the types of controlling variables that could be maintaining it. The following criteria are often used to evaluate the severity of the child's phobia: level of subjective distress experienced by the child, persistence over time, the degree to which the fear reaction disrupts the child's normal adaptive functioning, and inappropriateness of the fear reaction to the child's developmental level (King, Hamilton, & Ollendick, 1988). In determining how the phobia should be treated, it is essential to assess the quality of the child's adaptive functioning in all relevant contexts and domains. A well-adjusted child with a simple phobic reaction presents a very different clinical picture than that of a child whose phobia co-occurs with multiple, interactive problems.

A number of specialized assessment tools have been developed for evaluating children's anxiety disorders. These include structured interview formats such as the Anxiety Disorders Inventory for Children (Silverman & Nelles, 1988) and the Children's Anxiety Evalu-ation Form (Hoehn-Saric, Maissami, & Wiegand, 1987). Commonly used self-report mea-sures include the Fear Survey Schedule for Children-Revised (FSSC-R) (Ollendick, 1983; Ollendick, Oller, & Yule, 1991), and the Louisville Fear Survey for children (LFSC) (Miller, Barrett, Hampe, & Noble, 1971). Finally, is is important to include *in-vivo* observations of the child's responses to phobic stimuli, whenever possible.

Behavioral Treatment Approaches.   Systematic desensitization has been frequently used to treat childhood fears and phobias. However, controlled research studies on systematic desensitization have focused on children with mild to moderate fears, limiting generaliza-tion of findings to clinical populations (Silverman & Kearney, 1993). Generally, system-atic desensitization is more appropriate for older than younger children because younger children have difficulty generating and sustaining complex mental imagery (Barrios & O'Dell, 1989). Use of *in-vivo* exposure and concrete instructions is strongly recommended with children of all ages (King et al., 1988).

Lazarus and Abramowitz (1962) have developed a variant of SD involving emotive imagery. Instead of engaging in relaxation, the child imagines a positive story involving his or her favorite fantasy hero, then proceeds goes through a graduated anxiety hierarchy "with" the hero. The complexity of the imagery must be adjusted to child's developmental level. Single-case studies have supported the effectiveness of this procedure with fearful children (King, Cranstoun, & Josephs, 1989).

The most widely used behavioral treatment procedures for children's fears are modeling-based interventions (Graziano et al., 1979; Morris & Kratochwill, 1983; Bar-rios & O'Dell, 1989). Unlike systematic desensitization, modeling procedures have proven effective even with very young children. Furthermore, certain procedures can enhance the potential effectiveness of modeling interventions. These include the use of live versus filmed models; use of participant modeling, in which a live model dem-onstrates and guides the child through steps in coping (Rosenthal & Bandura, 1978); and the use of "coping" models, in which the child model originally demonstrates fear, then gradually masters the problem (Meichenbaum, 1971). Thus, modeling-based thera-pies have been proven versatile and effective in the treatment of children's fears. How-ever, most treatment studies have been conducted with subclinical populations; there are few controlled studies on treatment of severe fears in children (Ollendick & Francis, 1988). Also, because modeling interventions usually involve multiple treatment com-ponents (e.g., exposure, contingent reinforcement of coping responses, cognitive im-agery), it is unclear which specific treatment mechanisms account for positive thera-peutic change (Barrios & O'Dell, 1989).

Finally, cognitive restructuring techniques have been used to change children's fear-relevant cognitions. Instructing the child to practice competence- and coping-oriented thoughts in the presence of the fear stimulus can lead to rapid remission of the fearful behavior (Barrios & O'Dell, 1989; Kanfer, Karoly, & Newman, 1975; Graziano, Mooney, Huber, & Ignasiak, 1979). For example, Graziano and associates (1979) used cognitive change strategies with 11 8- to 13-year-old children who had severe night-time fears. Chil-dren were taught to use relaxation techniques, positive imagery, and competence-oriented self-statements when experiencing fear reactions. Practicing these skills every night earned "bravery tokens" from parents that could be cashed in for a hamburger party to celebrate the child's bravery. Children also recorded their tokens in a special book. Most children showed rapid fear remission that remained stable at follow-up.

In a subsequent study, Graziano and Mooney (1980) replicated these findings using a group comparison study with waiting list controls. Thus, preliminary evidence points to the effectiveness of cognitive techniques in reducing children's fears. However, because multicomponent interventions have been used in most studies (e.g., in the Graziano study, relaxation, imagery, self-statements, self-monitoring, and contingency management were used), it is unclear whether self-verbalization alone would be effective in reducing children's fears. Indeed, Ollendick and colleagues found that self-instructional training in the absence of operant-based procedures was not sufficient to reduce children's fears (Hagopian, Weist, & Ollendick, 1990; Ollendick, Hagopian, & Hantzinger, 1994). Additional evidence is needed, but these studies suggest that cognitive interventions with fearful children may be helpful only as part of a comprehensive treatment package.

The following case example, described in Hagopian and Ollendick (1993), illustrates the use of multiple behavioral interventions in the successful treatment of childhood phobia.

> Billy, age 9, was referred by his parents for treatment of severe dog phobia. The onset of his phobia was linked to a traumatic incident in Billy's recent past. Six months earlier, Billy had been attacked on his bicycle by a German Shepard dog, and suffered bite wounds and scratches. He felt extremely distressed by the attack, refused to go near the area where attack occurred, and avoided riding his bike altogether. During the months following the attack, he began to fear contact with all dogs.
>
> A psychological evaluation revealed that Billy was a well-adjusted child with no other significant problems. Thus, treatment focused on the phobia alone, and the therapists decided to employ a combination of systematic desensitization with *in-vivo* exposure and self-instructional training. A behavioral avoidance hierarachy was established: With his parents, Billy was able to walk one block away from the site of the attack. The end goal in the hierarchy was walking by the yard where the attack occurred. Next, Billy was trained in progressive relaxation and in the use of self-instructional training. Billy rehearsed steps in the hierarchy *in vivo,* using his newly acquired coping skills. His parents accompanied him and provided praise and encouragement for positive coping efforts. After 10 sessions, Billy was able to walk or ride his bike by the area where the attack had occurred. He remained symptom free at follow-up (Hagopian & Ollendick, 1993).

Separation Anxiety Disorder

Separation Anxiety Disorder (SAD) is the only anxiety disorder deemed specific to children and adolescents in the *DSM-IV.* Children with SAD experience an excessive, irrational fear of separation from their caregivers. When faced with separation, they feel intensely distressed and tend to worry about being lost, kidnapped, or harmed, or about their parent(s) being hurt or killed. Because it is normal for young children to feel anxious about separation, the child's anxiety must be intense and developmentally inappropriate to meet criteria for SAD.

Approximately 2 to 4 percent of children suffer from clinically significant levels of separation anxiety (Bell-Dolan, 1995). Among children who have been referred for treatment of anxiety disorders, about half receive diagnoses of SAD, and most of these cases involve prepubertal children (Last et al., 1987; McGee et al., 1990). The course of SAD is variable in that symptom levels tend to fluctuate over time, usually in response to increased levels of environmental stress (Bell-Dolan, 1995). There are some suggestions that children with SAD may develop mood or anxiety disorders in adulthood (Ollendick & Huntzinger, 1990).

Current diagnostic criteria for Separation Anxiety Disorder include the following characteristics (three or more must be present) *(DSM-IV)*:

- Excessive distress upon actual or anticipated separation
- Persistent worry about losing attachment figures
- Persistent fear of being lost or kidnapped
- Persistent reluctance/refusal to attend school
- Reluctance to be alone
- Reluctance to go to sleep without being near attachment figure
- Nightmares involving theme of separation
- Physical symptoms when separated

The term *school refusal* is sometimes used synonymously with SAD. However, not all children with Separation Anxiety Disorder refuse to go to school, and many cases of school refusal do not involve anxiety over separation (e.g., the child could fear stressful situations exclusive to the school environment, such as being teased or bullied by peers) (Last & Strauss, 1990).

Treatment.   If school refusal is part of the clinical picture, it is important to get the child back to school as soon as possible (King, Ollendick, & Gullstone, 1990). Using functional analysis, the clinician can pinpoint the apparent reason for the child's refusal to attend school (e.g., Does the child fear separation from a parent? Is the child failing academically and/or being persecuted by peers?). Behavioral interventions are used to reduce the child's anxiety, eliminate positive consequences of avoidance, and reward the child's adaptive coping efforts.

The behavioral treatment literature on SAD is relatively sparse, and most interventions have involved descriptive case reports of anxiety-based school refusal (Lease & Strauss, 1993). Last and Francis (1988) have recommended graduated, *in-vivo* exposure as the most effective approach to treating SAD. In collaboration with the child's teachers and/or parents, the child is instructed to practice each step in a graduated hierarchy of anxiety-provoking situations until feelings of anxiety become manageable.

Because children with SAD tend to worry excessively about the possibility of harm befalling themselves or their loved ones, others have recommended self-instructional training to promote effective coping, more realistic appraisal of stressful situations, and use of self-reinforcement (Kane & Kendall, 1989). For example, Mansdorf and Lukens (1987) used self-instructional training with two children who suffered from anxiety-based school refusal. One child was concerned about separation from the mother; the other was concerned about negative social evaluation. Both children and their parents received training in cognitive restructuring. The children practiced thoughts such as "My mother can care for herself well," whereas the parents replaced fears about their children "falling apart" under stress with coping thoughts such as "He (or she) will gradually learn to handle it." Self-instructional training was combined with graduated exposure to school and with reinforcement of school attendance. Both children resumed school attendance.

Problems inherent in the family context may require additional interventions. For example, parents of children with SAD often report experiencing anxiety and mood disorders (Bernstein & Garfinkel, 1988; Last et al., 1987). Unless the parents' emotional problems can be effectively dealt with, it is unlikely that children will show lasting positive change.

Finally, in treating symptoms of SAD, it is important to adjust treatment interventions to the child's developmental level. For example, younger children have difficulty with self-reinforcement and with imaginal rehearsal.

The following case example illustrates the use of combined behavioral interventions in treatment of SAD (Lease & Strauss, 1993).

Jimmy, age 10, was referred for treatment of school refusal related to separation anxiety. The onset of symptoms occurred during a period of parental separation. Initially, Jimmy felt reluctant to attend school, and feared that his father (now living apart from the family) would be harmed. In time, his concerns generalized to both parents. Even when they resumed living together, he became distressed whenever his parents left home. At the time of referral, Jimmy experienced stomachaches prior to attending school, and appeared sad and withdrawn.

Based on interviews with Jimmy and his parents, an ll-step fear and avoidance hierarchy was established. The least anxiety-arousing situation involved playing outside with other children; the most arousing situations involved going to school on the bus and staying home with his brother while his parents went out for an evening. Treatment was administered in 11 sessions attended by Jimmy and his mother. The primary interventions were *in-vivo,* graduated exposure to situations on the hierarchy coupled with self-instructional training. Jimmy's parents gradually increased the amount of time that they spent out of the house. Each time, Jimmy would practice coping until he indicated that he felt no fear (e.g., "It's only for a short time"; "I can handle this"; "Mom and dad can take care of themselves"). At termination, Jimmy was able to attend school without calling home, stay with a sitter home while his parents went out for an entire evening, go and return from school on the bus, and play with peers for one hour or more. His feelings of sadness and withdrawn behavior were markedly diminished.

Generalized Anxiety
Some children show evidence of pervasive anxiety problems. Once called Overanxious Disorder (American Psychiatric Association, 1987), pervasive anxiety problems in chil-

dren are now diagnosed using adult criteria for Generalized Anxiety Disorder. Children who suffer from GAD show anxiety symptoms that are not focused on a specific object or situation. They tend to ruminate about past or future events, and experience somatic symptoms, low self-esteem, and tension. There is relatively little knowledge about GAD in children, and most of it is is descriptive. Symptoms of GAD appear to be relatively common: Approximately 5 percent of children and adolescents report clinically significant levels of generalized anxiety (Strauss, 1994). Childhood GAD has a gradual onset and overlaps with other anxiety problems and with depression (Last, 1989). There are developmental differences in the associated features of GAD. In a comparison of pre- and postpubertal children with GAD, older children had more symptoms and higher levels of anxiety and depression than younger children, whereas younger children were more likely to receive concurrent diagnoses of SAD or ADHD (Strauss, Last, Lease, & Francis, 1988).

Currently, structured interview schedules provide the most reliable index of GAD in children and adolescents (Strauss, 1994). Additional research is needed to evaluate the usefulness of self-report, parent and teacher questionnaires as measures of GAD, and to assess sytmptoms of GAD in home, school, and peer group contexts (Silverman & Eisen, 1992).

There is a thin literature on behavioral treatment, and controlled studies are lacking. One promising approach involves use of broad-specturm cognitive-behavioral interventions with an emphasis on helping children modify their anxious self-statements into coping self-statements. For example, Kane and Kendall (1989) used a multiple baseline design to evaluate the effect of comprehensive cognitive-behavioral therapy with 9- to 13-year-old children who suffered from OAD. Treatment components involved recognizing anxiety feelings, clarifying cognitions in stressful situations, developing a plan to cope with stressful situations, evaluating the success of coping, modeling and *in-vivo* exposure, and homework assignments. The acronym STOP (scared, thoughts, other, praise) was used to teach children about modifying anxious thoughts. All four children showed impovement on parent, teacher, and self-report ratings.

Obsessive-Compulsive Disorder

Children with *Obsessive-Compulsive Disorder (OCD)* have symptom pictures that are similar to those of adults with OCD. Obsessions are repetitive, intrusive thoughts or images, whereas compulsions are ritualistic behaviors that the child feels compelled to perform. Obsessive-compulsive disorder in children usually involves a combination of obsessions and compulsions, although either can occur alone. One-quarter of children with OCD have co-occuring affective and anxiety disorders (Flament et al., 1988; Swedo & Rapoport, 1989) and/or motor disturbances (Swedo, Rapaport, Leonard, Lenane, & Cheslow, 1989). Boys outnumber girls in cases of OCD by ratios of 2:1 to 3:1 (Swedo et al., 1989).

Symptoms of OCD initially manifest themselves between the ages of 3 and 14 (Rapoport, 1986). Because little data exists, the progosis for childhood OCD is unclear. However, reports indicate that OCD symptoms may be quite chronic. For example, approximately 60 to 70 percent of children with OCD still have symptoms 2 to 7 years after initial diagnosis (Flament, Koby, et al., 1990; Rapoport, 1986).

The presence of discrete obsessive or compulsive behaviors may be normal, especially during certain age periods. For example, children may have elaborate rituals about bedtime or play, or may be extremely preoccupied with certain objects or interests. However, the types of obsessions and rituals that characterize OCD are qualitatively different from those of normal children. For example, checking, touching, and washing rituals are common foci for OCD symptoms, but are rarely seen in normal children (Leonard, Goldberger, Rapoport, Cheslow, & Swedo, 1990). Obsessive-compulsive behaviors are considered clinically relevant when highly disruptive of normal adaptive functioning and/or distressing to the child. Children who receive this diagnosis tend to have higher than average levels of intelligence, active fantasy lives, and a tendency to present themselves as overly mature for their age (Adams, 1973; Judd, 1965).

The most effective interventions for childhood OCD involve graduated exposure and response prevention combined with positive reinforcement for adaptive coping (Francis, 1993). For example, Stanley (1980) successfully employed response prevention and contingency management in the treatment of an 8-year-old girl who had counting and physical arrangement rituals. Treatment was carried out by family members, who verbally prohibited her from engaging in the rituals and changed their own behaviors that had previously reinforced the rituals. Similarly, DiNardo and DiNardo (1981) successfully treated a 9-year-old boy with severe contamination fears, and handwashing and touching compulsions. The boy was given systematic desensitization with coping imagery, and family members were instructed to stop cooperating with his rituals. In both of these studies, symptom remission was rapid and long-lasting, with no evidence of symptom substitution.

Other interventions for children with OCD have involved extinction of adult attention to symptomatic behavior (Francis, 1989) and thought stopping in cases of older children who suffer from obsessive ruminations (Campbell, 1973). For example, Francis (1989) treated compulsive reassurance seeking in an 11-year-old boy who had obsessive thoughts about illness and death. The boy constantly asked his parents for reassurance (e.g., "Am I going to die?" "Do I have a tumor?"). He tried to avoid anxiety-provoking situations such as eating or attending school. At the time of referral, he was described as highly agitated and barely able to complete a day at school. Francis used an ABAB reversal design to evaluate the effectiveness of the intervention. Following a baseline period, the boy's parents were instructed to ignore all requests for reassurance by turning away and/or redirecting the conversation. His symptomatic behavior worsened temporarily, then gradually dropped to zero frequency during the next six days. His symptoms increased dramatically when hen his parents began attending to them again, then returned to zero frequency following the reinstatement of extinction.

Thus, existing case studies indicate that behavior therapy can be effective in treating childhood obsessive-compulsive disorders. More systematic treatment research is needed to determine the optimal components of behavior therapy for these disorders. Pinto and Francis (1993) have outlined three important foci for further treatment efforts. First, it is critical to actively involve families in treatment. Children tend to include family members in their rituals or control family routines by angry outbursts. Second, because OCD symptoms tend to follow a chronic course, relapse prevention training should be integrated into "standard" behavioral treatment protocols. Finally, social skills training may be necessary to help children reintegrate into their peer groups.

Childhood Depression

Children and adolescents do experience depression, and the essential clinical features of childhood depression are widely believed to be the same as in adults (American Psychiatric Association, 1994; Mitchell et al., 1988). However, children do not show some of the serious concomitants of adult forms of depression, such as psychomotor retardation (Kazdin, 1989). Moreover, the age of the child strongly affects the expression of depressive symptoms Young children, for example, find it difficult to attach verbal labels to their thoughts and feelings (Cantwell, 1990). Finally, the associated features of depression differ for adults and children. For example, depressed children frequently manifest concurrent conduct and impulsivity problems (Kovacs et al., 1984; Puig-Antich, 1982). For these reasons, the assumption that adult and childhood depression are "equivalent" is best treated as a working hypothesis.

Estimates of the prevalence of childhood and adolescent depression have been influenced by the nature of the informant, the age of the child, and the type of measures used to assess symptomatic behavior (Kazdin, 1995). Use of strict criteria (such as standardized diagnostic interviews) has revealed that 2 to 5 percent of children and 5 to 8 percent of adolescents suffer from depressive disorders (Kashani, Carlson, et al., 1989; Whitaker, Johnson, Schaffer, et al., 1990). There is a marked increase in depressive symptoms when children mature into adolescence, particularly for girls (Rutter, 1986). The associated features of the disorder also change with age. Adolescents are more likely than school-age children to experience the "classic" depressive symptoms of fatigue, irritability, guilt, and suicidal ideation (Kashani, Rosenberg, & Reid, 1987).

Single episodes of childhood depression tend to last between seven and nine months, but recur over the course of time (Kovacs, 1989). For example, in an 18-year follow-up of depressed children, 60 percent had suffered recurrent epidodes (Harrington, Fudge, Rutter, Pickles, & Hill, 1990).

Assessment Issues.   The clinical picture of childhood depression is complicated because most depressed children experience symptoms of other disorders. As with adults, symptoms of anxiety are the most common concomitants, but depressed children also tend to suffer from co-ocurring symptoms of conduct and attention-deficit hyperactivity disorders (Biederman & Steingard, 1989; Kovacs, Paulaskas, Gatsoni, & richards, 1988). The clinical interview is essential for evaluating the presence and severity of depressive symptoms. Semistructured assessment protocols such as the Kiddie Schedule for Affective Disorders and Schizophrenia (K-SADS) (Chambers et al., 1985) or the Diagnostic Interview Schedule for Children (DISC) (Costello, Edelbrock, & Costello, 1985) are often used in the diagnostic evaluation of childhood depression.

In addition, a number of self-report instruments can be used to reliably assess depressive symptoms in school-age children and adolescents (Reynolds, 1995). These include the

Children's Depression Inventory (CDI) (Kovacs, 1981), the Reynolds Child Depression Scales (Reynolds, 1989), and the Hopelessness Scale for Children (Kazdin, French, et al., 1983). A range of rating instruments for childhood depression also have been developed using parent, teacher, and peer reports (Clarizio, 1995). Finally, assessment of family pathology is essential, given that very high proportions of of depressed children have depressed parents (Hammen, 1991; Kaslow & Racusin, 1990).

Behavioral Treatment of Childhood Depression.   Several different behavioral intervention strategies have been used with depressed children. A number of investigators have focused on improving the quality of the child's social skills (Frame et al., 1992). Many of these reports have involved single- subject designs. For example, Frame, Matson, Sonis, Fialkov, and Kazdin (1982) used social skills interventions to decrease depressive symptoms in a 10-year-old boy who was diagnosed with Major Depressive disorder. The main goal of treatment was to increase the quality of the child's communication competence. Behaviors targeted for improvement included slouching, poor eye contact, mumbling, unresponsiveness, and bland affect. A combination of didactic instruction, modeling, and behavioral rehearsal resulted in significant levels of improvement within five weeks.

A second theme in the behavioral treatment literature has involved use of broad-spectrum cognitive-behavioral interventions, many of which are quite similar to those used with depressed adults. Cognitive-behavioral interventions have been linked to improvement in children's depressive symptoms (Asarnow & Carlson, 1988; Butler et al. 1980; Stark, Reynolds, & Kaslow, 1987). For example, Butler and colleagues (1980) identified school-age children as depressed on the basis of their responses to self-report questionnaires. Depressed children were randomly assigned to one of four groups: (1) role plays of problems relevant to depressed children, (2) cognitive restructuring, (3) attention placebo, or (4) regular classroom activities. Children who experienced the intervention groups showed significant improvements in their depressive symptoms. Similarly, using a group treatment format, Stark, Reynolds, and Kaslow (1987) assigned 9- to 12-year-old depressed children to either self-control training, problem-solving training, or wait list control groups. Following 12 sessions, children in both treatment groups showed significant improvment.

Finally, Lewinsohn's Coping with Depression course (see Chapter 9) has been successfully adapted to the needs of depressed adolescents (Clarke et al., 1992). For example, relative to those who experienced alternative behavioral interventions such as relaxation training, depressed adolescents who had been randomly assigned to the CWD course reported clinically significant changes in depressive symptoms (Clarke et al., 1992).

The third theme in the treatment literature has addressed the need for family- and school-based interventions. Because depressed children and adolescents tend to have depressed and/or highly stressed parents, parental involvement in treatment is crucial. Relatively few interventions have been developed for parents whose children have internalizing problems. Programs should be individualized to the parents' needs. For example, it may be necessary to provide personal therapy to a depressed parent, along with concurrent training in child management skills. As an example of the latter, Stark and associates (1995) have taught parents to recognize symptoms of emotional distress in their depressed children, to assist their children in the appropriate use of problem solving, and to encourage and praise their coping efforts. Conjoint family treatment is another option. Stark and associates (1995) have developed a family treatment program that is designed to ameliorate family patterns (e.g., poor communication and conflict resolution; lack of shared enjoyable activities) that reinforce children's depressive behaviors.

Depressed children may experience many different types of difficulties with peers (Puig-Antich et al., 1985). Moreover, their ability to concentrate and to participate in active learning may be markedly impaired. Thus, social skills interventions to improve peer relationships (Kazdin & Racusin, 1990) and general school-based intervention (Stark & Bookman, in press) are important treatment components.

Social Isolation

Social isolation and withdrawal represent one common form of peer adjustment difficulty. The term *social isolation* carries a broad range of meanings that are essential to specify in designing treatment interventions. For example, some children may prefer solitary activites to group involvement, some may withdraw from peers because of social anxiety, and others may be actively rejected by peers because of their unskilled or negative behavior (Rubin et al., 1989). Depending on the type of criteria used to define isolative behavior, up to 25 percent of preschool children and between 5 and 20 percent of school-age children have difficulties in this area (Harris & Ferrari, 1988).

Longitudinal studies have shown that socially inhibited behavior is fairly stable throughout infancy and early childhood (Kagan, Reznick, & Gibbons, 1989; Moskowitz, Schwartzman, & Ledingham, 1985). Furthermore, patterns of social isolation or withdrawal may forecast long-term difficulties in social competence. For example, socially isolative behavior in early childhood has been found to predict later measures of internalizing problems and low social competence (Hymel, Rubin, Rowden, & LeMare, 1990). Relatedly, Mansin and Masten (1991) found that children who suffered from social isolation in the school-age years tended to have lower social competence than others in adolescence.

Assessment and Treatment Issues.   Precise definitions of social isolation vary, but most center on low observed rates of peer interaction (Rubin, 1985). However, there is some disagreement that rate of interaction is appropriate target for intervention. For example, there is little evidence that rate of peer interaction predicts social incompetece or risk of later problems (Dodge, 1989). This issue could be clarified by defining discrete thresholds for clinically relevant levels of low interaction. For example, Hops and Greenwood (1988) argued that children with extremely low rates of social interaction differ from those with low but normal-range rates. Other common methods for identifying isolated children involve asking classmates and/or teachers to identify children who are ignored or disliked by peers (Dodge, 1989).

The leading behavioral model of peer isolation is a social skills deficit model (Asher & Renshaw, 1981; Hops & Greenwood, 1988). The main assumption of the model is that social isolates possess cognitive and/or behavioral deficits that interfere with their social competence. Thus, a range of social skills training programs have been developed to remediate these deficits. Most of these intervention programs have featured modeling and/

or coaching/instructional techniques. It is imperative that children targeted for social skills training do, in fact, lack definable social skills (Ladd, 1985). Children can be unpopular with peers for many different reasons, not all of them reflecting social skills deficits. Hence, the need exists for careful assessment procedures in subject selection and for process assessments of skill acquisition during the course of therapy (Mize & Ladd, 1990).

An intriguing approach to the treatment of peer isolation involves the use of peers as therapists. Peers have been successfully used to cue and reward socially appropriate behavior in withdrawn children and to serve as models for social skills (Strain & Fox, 1981). Four different types of peer-mediated programs have been used with socially withdrawn school-age children: peer tutoring, peer modeling, group contingency, and peer interaction (Durlak, 1992). In the most successful programs, peer managers have been trained to reinforce a target child's prosocial behaviors or to initiate interaction with isolated children (Kohler & Strain, 1990; Sancoillo, 1987).

Externalizing Disorders

Children are most often referred for psychological evaluation because their behavior is disturbing to others. Hence, it is not surprising that disruptive behaviors such as aggression, impulsivity, and noncompliance are the most common problems that are dealt with by child and family clinicians (Kazdin, Siegel, & Bass, 1990). Three disorders are recognized by *DSM-IV:* Attention-Deficit Hyperactivity Disorder, Conduct Disorder, and Oppositional Defiant Disorder. All of these disorders tend to begin early in life, persist for relatively long periods of time, and are difficult to treat (McMahon, 1994). As shown next, behavior therapists have made considerable strides in the assessment and treatment of these serious and potentially life-long disorders.

Attention-Deficit Hyperactivity Disorder

The primary features of *Attention-Deficit Hyperactivity Disorder (ADHD)* have been well established. One primary characteristic is that of *overactivity.* Hyperactive childen are often described by parents and teachers as "fidgety," "always on the go," "restless," and "accident-prone" (Whalen, 1989). Qualitative features are of paramount importance, in that the overactivity of ADHD children appears disorganized, haphazard, and contextually inappropriate in contrast with the goal-directed behavior of highly active but normal peers. *Attentional problems* comprise the second primary chracteristic of ADHD. Parents of ADHD children complain that they never listen and have difficulty playing alone and sticking to single activities. Teachers complain that they are frequently off task in classroom situations and that they have difficulty following directions and completing assignments. Finally, *difficulties with impulse control* comprise the third core feature of ADHD. Problems of impulse control manifest themselves in diverse situations. The hyperactive child my intrude upon the games of other, have difficulty waiting his or her turn to play, behave in "silly" ways that are situationally inappropriate, interrupt others, or even run into traffic to retrieve a wayward toy.

ADHD is a heterogeneous disorder, in that symptom expression may take many different forms. For example, in the current version of the *DSM (DSM-IV,* 1994), children with ADHD may show predominantly inattentive behavior (Predominantly Inattentive subtype), predominantly overactive or impulsive behavior (Predominantly Hyperactive/Impulsive subtype), or mixed features of all core symptoms. To meet diagnostic code, children must have symptoms of inattention and/or symptoms of hyperactivity and impulsivity that have persisted for at least six months. Symptoms of *inattention* (six or more) include:

INATTENTION

- Often fails to give close attention to details or makes careless mistakes in schoolwork, work, or other activities
- Often has difficulty sustaining attention in tasks or play activities
- Often does not seem to listen when spoken to directly
- Often does not follow through on instructions, and fails to finish school assignments or chores
- Often has difficulty organizing tasks or activities
- Avoids or dislikes tasks that require sustained mental effort
- Often loses things necessary for tasks or activities

Symptoms of *hyperactivity-impulsivity* include (six or more must be present):

HYPERACTIVITY

- Often fidgets with hands or feet or squirms in seat
- Often leaves seat in classroom or in other situations where it is inappropriate
- Often runs about or climbs in situations where it is inappropriate
- Often has difficulty playing or engaging in leisure activities quietly
- Often is "on the go" or acts as if "driven by a motor"
- Often talks excessively

IMPULSIVITY

- Often blurts out answers before questions have been completed
- Often has difficulty awaiting turn
- Often interrupts or intrudes on others

At least some symptoms must have been present before the age of 7. Current symptoms must be present in more than one situation (e.g., home and school), and there must be clear evidence of clinically significant impairment in the child's social, academic, and/or occupational functioning. ADHD occurs in both sexes, but boys greatly outnumber girls by ratios of 6:1 to 9:1 (Barkley, 1990).

Children with ADHD tend to have many different problems of life adjustment. Academic competence and achievement are frequent areas of poor functioning. Relative to normal peers, children with ADHD receive poorer grades, lower achievement test scores and teacher evaluations, and more frequent grade failures and placements in special education classes (Edelbrock, Costello, & Kessler, 1984; McGee & Share, 1988). Disturbances of conduct—defined by aggression, noncompliance, and destructive behavior—frequently co-occur with symptoms of ADHD (Hinshaw, 1987; Szatmari, Boyle, & Offord, 1989). Finally, relative to other children, ADHD children tend to have few friends and experience high rates of peer rejection (Johnston, Pelham, & Murphy, 1985; Whalen, Henker, Dotemoto, & Hinshaw, 1983). Similarly, parents and teachers tend to be more directive and controlling with hyperactive children than with normal children (Mash & Johnston, 1982; Whalen, Henker, & Dotemoto, 1981).

It was once believed that children with ADHD "grew out of it" when they reached adolescence. However, accumulating evidence from follow-up studies of hyperactive children have put this notion to rest. Children with ADHD are at elevated risk for a host of adaptational difficulties in adolescence and adulthood, ranging from problems in self-esteem and social relationships to serious criminality (Klein & Manuzza, 1991; Thorley, 1984; Weiss & Hechtman, 1993). In school-age children with ADHD, the presence of comorbid conduct disorder is the best predictor of negative outcomes in later life (Farrington, Loeber, & VanKammen, 1990).

The following case example illustrates the combined presence of ADHD and serious conduct problems:

> Robert C., age 8, was referred for psychological evaluation due to persistent disruptiveness and impulsivity in the home and at school. Robert presented as an outgoing child who expressed his need for attention by engaging in silly or show-off behaviors. Robert was in constant motion during psychological testing, as evidenced by frequent jumping up to look at test materials, fidgeting with objects, getting out of his seat to look around the room, and chattering at the examiner. Robert was in the average range of intellectual functioning. However, his approach to problem solving was highly impulsive, with little capacity for self-correction in evidence. For example, block designs were constructed quickly and haphazardly, without comparing the standard to his own performance. If this approach did not work, he tended to give up rather than attempt an alternative strategy.
>
> Robert was observed interacting with his mother in a clinic playroom. He switched activities frequently and showed many other signs of distractibility. He chatted constantly at his mother, moved around a great deal, and acted impulsively.
>
> During a separate interview, his mother reported that Robert had shown an extremely high activity level since infancy. At age 5 he was deemed "hyperactive" by a psychiatrist. Robert's behavior problems at school began in first grade, when he started to engage in frequent fighting with peers and classroom disruptiveness. At present, his behavior problems were labeled "severe" by school officials, who were considering suspending him. Robert's mother reported that he was also very difficult to manage at home. Primary problems involved high levels of restlessness, inattentiveness, attention seeking, impulsivity, and disobedience. In addition, Robert occasionally had severe temper tantrums that resulted in the damaging or destruction of household property.

Assessment

The symptoms of ADHD are heterogeneous in nature, extend across multiple settings, and potentially affect many different areas of the child's adjustment. Thus, assessment of children with ADHD must be multimodal, comprehensive, and multicontextual. In addition, symptoms of ADHD are defined in relation to age-inappropriate trends. Because there is pronounced variability in levels of impulsivity, attentional control and activity with increasing age, the diagnosing clinician must be well versed in knowledge of normal developmental variations (Barkley, 1990).

Interviews with parents, teachers, and children are used to clarify the presence of primary and secondary symptoms and the extent to which these symptoms disrupt the child's social and academic adjustment (Pelham & Hinshaw, 1992). Interviews with family members also include a developmental history and careful assessment of family stresses and resources, especially the willingness and competence of parents to engage in treatment. If one or both parents have serious psychological problems, they may require treatment before child-focused interventions are attempted. Some medical disorders have symptoms that are similar to those of ADHD. Thus, a medical evaluation is required to rule out this possibility (Hoza, Vallano, & Pelham, 1995).

Assessment in the school setting includes interviews with teachers, and observations of classroom behavior and peer interactions. For children with academic difficulties, intelligence and achievement tests are also required to pinpoint the nature of the child's most pressing problems.

The assessment of ADHD often involves use of standardized questionnaires that can be completed by teachers and parents. Examples of widely used instruments include the Iowa Conners Teacher Rating Scale (Pelham, Milich, Murphy, & Murphy, 1989) and the Conners Parent and Teacher Rating Scales (Goyette, Conners, & Ulrich, 1978).

Pharmacotherapy

The most widely used treatment for ADHD is pharmacotherapy. Over 70 percent of children with ADHD tend to show behavioral improvements on psychostimulants such as methylphenidate (ritalin), dextroamphetamine (dexedrine) or pemoline (Cylert). A large body of research has shown that children with ADHD who receive psychostimulant medication are better able to focus attention, stay on task, remain in their seat, and refrain from disruptive or annoying behavior than those who do not receive medication (Barkley, 1990). Moreover, treated children become more responsive to peers, teachers, and parents, thereby enhancing their levels of social adjustment (Whalen et al., 1989). However, longitudinal research has shown that treatment with psychostimulant medication has no long-term benefits (Weiss & Hechtman, 1993). In addition, psychostimulant medications often have unpleasant side effects, may promote attributions of helplessness in treated children, and do not "work" for approximately 30 percent of children with ADHD.

Finally, psychostimulant medications are contraindicated for childen younger than 4 years of age because they are relatively ineffective with this age group and because very young children experience more frequent and severe side effects than older children (Barkley, 1990). For these reasons, psychostimulant medication should not be used as a singular treatment for ADHD (*Physicians Desk Reference*, 1994). Psychosocial interventions are necessary, and behavior therapy is considered the nonmedical treatment of choice (Barkley, 1990; Pelham & Milich, 1991).

Behavioral Treatment

Parent Education.   Parent education is a crucial step in the treatment process. The contingency management approach features parent or teacher training as the primary mode of intervention. Parents are viewed as direct "therapists" for their children's maladaptive behaviors; the professional therapist functions as a consultant to the parents. Barkley's (1990) well-known program is conducted in 10 sessions. Initially, parents are given information about the nature, course, causes, and treatment of ADHD. Parenting a child with ADHD is extremely stressful. A primary goal is to dispell inaccurate information and to help the parents accept the child's ADHD as a life-long handicapping condition that requires realistic parental expectations.

Child management training is usually carried out in two stages: (1) the parents are taught to reinforce positive behaviors and to improve the quality of their relationship with the child and (2) the parents are taught to use positive attention/rewards contingently and to ignore or punish maladaptive behaviors such as negativism or noncompliance. Punishment involves use of time out from reinforcement and/or response cost. For example, with response cost punishment, a child might lose tokens such as poker chips for disruptive behavior, aggression, or noncompliance. Tokens can be gained for appropriate play, helping behaviors, and compliance. The net amount of earned tokens is "cashed in" for material rewards and special privledges.

Parents are taught that external cues must be concrete, commands simple and concise, and behavioral consequences (such as reinforcement or punishment) immediate. During the latter stages of therapy, parents learn how to maintain their child's progress, and generalize it to new settings (such as the supermarket). A large body of research has shown that these procedures result in increased child compliance and cooperation, and decreased noncompliance, disruptiveness, and defiance (Barkley, 1990). However, there is little natural generalization to the school setting.

A similar contingency management program should be implemented in the school setting with all relevent school personnel. Barkley (1981) has emphasized that in the school setting, children should be taught rule governed behavior and compliance, not passive conformity such as paying attention or sitting still. In typical programs, children are rewarded for staying on task, completing assignments, and engaging in appropriate group behavior (Pfiffner & O'Leary, 1995). Token rewards such as stickers or poker chips are given immediately, then "cashed in" for tangible treats or privileges when the child returns home. Rewards are lost if the child violates rules that have been clearly designated. Contingency management can be very successful in increasing time on task and in enhancing the child's academic productivity (Barkley, 1989; Werry & Wollershein, 1989).

Self-Instructional Training.   Cognitive-behavioral approaches to the treatment of hyperactivity have focused on self-instructional training (Meichenbaum, 1977) and its variants. Influenced by experimental studies of verbal mediation of overt behavior (Bem, 1967; Luria, 1961; Vygotsky, 1962), Meichenbaum and Goodman (1971) developed a program for remediating cognitive deficits of impulsive children. In the original study, the following steps were performed in individual training sessions (Meichenbaum, 1977, p. 32): (1)

An adult model performed a task while talking to himself or herself aloud (cognitive modeling: "O.K, what is it I have to do? You want me to copy the picture with the different lines. I have to go slowly and carefully). (2) The child performed the identical task while the adult model provided verbal instructions. (3) The child performed the task while instructing herself/himself aloud. (4) The child whispered instructions to herself/himself while performing the task. (5) The child performed the task using covert self-instructions or "private speech."

Over a number of sessions, the range and types of self-statements modeled by the therapist were expanded to include performance-relevant tasks such as defining the problem, focusing attention, self-reinforcement of performance, and self-evaluation. Initial results indicated that impulsive children could be taught to use planful monitoring strategies in approaching different cognitive tasks. Results were maximized when the child engaged in self-instructional rehearsal during the training sessions (Meichenbaum & Goodman, 1971).

Self-instructional training (SIT) targets two central deficits of children with ADHD: inattention and impulsivity. Thus, the advent of self-instructional training approaches was greeted with great enthusiasm, and many variants of the original program have been developed (Kendall & Braswell, 1985; Braswell & Bloomquist, 1991). With clinically diagnosed hyperactive children, however, the results of SIT have been inconsistent. Short-term gains are often reported, but these tend to be limited to specific measures of cognition and attention (Whalen, Henker, & Hinshaw, 1985). Treatment gains tend to be greatest when cognitive training is supplemented with behavioral contingencies, and when SIT is conducted as an interactive process between therapist and child (Kendall & Braswell, 1985). Even so, the following problems remain. Generalization to academic performance is rarely reported, and generalization from cognitive task performance to social-adaptive behavior tends not to occur, even when multiple materials, trainers, and settings have been used (Whalen et al., 1985). Furthermore, there is no evidence for long-term maintenance of treatment gains (Braswell & Bloomquist, 1991). Finally, there is no evidence that cognitive behavior therapy is superior to other, less costly treatment approaches or that it adds "incremental gains" to the effects of psychostimulant medications (Whalen et al., 1985).

Thus, although SIT is a creative and intuitively appealing treatment approach, only limited evidence exists for its effectiveness. Further research should focus on delineating specific child characteristics (e.g., age, cognitive level, attributional style) and treatment characteristics related to generalized positive outcome (Kendall & Braswell, 1985). Braswell and Bloomquist (1991) have recommended that SIT interventions should be part of a comprehensive treatment program that also includes problem-solving training, training in anger and frustration management, social skills training, classroom contingency management, and a range of family-level interventions. Further research is needed to determine whether such a comprehensive approach to the treatment of ADHD produces significant and long-term gains.

Disruptive Disorders

Conduct Disorder (CD) refers to a diverse cluster of problem behaviors involving persistent violations of the rights of others and of major social rules (*DSM-IV,* 1994). Children and adolescents with this disorder often behave aggressively toward people and animals. For example, they may initiate frequent fights; bully, intimidate, or threaten others; or torture animals. In some cases, acts of aggression include rape, assault with a deadly weapon, or homicide. Children and adolescents with CD tend to engage in destructive behavior that results in loss or damage to someone's property—they may vandalize public buildings, set fires, or break up furniture in the family home. Deceitfulness—as evidenced by chronic lying, breaking promises, or stealing—is frequently evident. Finally, children with CD tend to violate important rules set by parents and school officials; for example, they may stay out late, "run away" overnight, or repeatedly fail to attend school. Children with CD tend to lack empathy for others, show poor frustration tolerance, and high levels of irritability.

To meet diagnostic code, three or more of the following criteria must have occurred during the past year, with at least one criterion in evidence during the past 6 months (DSM-IV, 1994):

AGGRESSION TO PEOPLE AND ANIMALS

- Often bullies, threatens or intimidates others
- Often initiates physical fights
- Has used a weapon that can cause serious harm to others
- Has been physically cruel to people
- Has been physically cruel to animals
- Has stolen while confronting a victim
- Has forced someone into sexual activity

DESTRUCTION OF PROPERTY

- Deliberate fire setting with intention of causing damage
- Deliberate destruction of property

DECEITFULNESS OF THEFT

- Has broken into someone else's house, building, or car
- Often lies to obtain goods or favors or to avoid obligations
- Has stolen items of nontrivial value without confronting a victim

SERIOUS VIOLATIONS OF RULES

- Stays out at night despite parental prohibitions, beginning before age 13
- Has run away form home at least twice
- Is often truant from school, beginning before age 13

A second type of disruptive disorder, *Oppositional Defiant Disorder (ODD),* is currently recognized. The central feature of ODD is a chronic pattern of negativistic, defiant, and noncompliant behavior toward authority figures, usually the child's parents. Children with features of ODD are described as stubborn, resistant, irritable, and argumentative. They tend to show frequent temper tantrums, often refuse to comply with their parents' requests, and may make deliberate attempts to be annoying. These patterns are usually evident before the age of 8. Although Oppositional Disorder is listed separately from Conduct Disorder in the *DSM-IV*, it shares features of conduct disorder such as strong disobedience, negativism, and opposition to authority. Children who receive a diagnosis of ODD are also highly likely to be diagnosed with CD (Hinshaw & Lahey, 1993). However, although the majority of children with CD have histories of ODD, most children with ODD do not progress to CD (Lahey & Loeber, 1994).

To meet diagnostic code, at least four or more of the following characteristics must be present during the past six months, to a degree that the child's social or academic functioning is significantly impaired:

- Often loses temper
- Often argues with adults
- Often actively defies or refuses to comply with adults' requests or rules
- Often deliberately annoys people
- Often blames others for his or her mistakes or misbehavior
- Is often touchy or easily annoyed by others
- Is often angry and resentful
- Is often spiteful and vindictive

The prevalence of ODD and CD is between 8 and 12 percent for school-age children and adolescents, depending on the age and gender of the child (Costello, 1990). Boys outnumber girls in cases of ODD and CD by ratios of 2:1 to 3:1 (Quay, 1986).

Associated Problems

Conduct disorders are associated with pervasive problems in the child's social and academic functioning. Children with CD tend to show lower intelligence, achievement, and school adjustment than their normal peers. Reading disabilities are especially prominent. These cognitive and academic problems begin early in life and remain chronic throughout the child's school career (Kazdin, 1987). Children with CD show equally broad-ranging problems in their social adjustment. Conduct problems tend to co-occur with a diverse range of overlapping familial and social-ecological stressors, including poor child management skills, parental psychopathology, marital distress and discord, poverty, and social isolation (Kazdin, 1993; Webster-Stratton & Herbert, 1994).

Moreover, children witrh CD quickly "turn off" their peers with their aggressive and annoying behaviors, resulting in high levels of peer rejection (Coie, Belding, & Underwood, 1988). For example, Olson (1992) found that aggressive children as young as four years of age showed strong and stable levels of peer rejection in preschool. Over time, peers began to counterattack and provoke these children, thereby creating a negative spiral of aggression and rejection. In addition to negative peer relationships, children with CD have poor relationships with their teachers. Young children with ODD symptoms are frequently "expelled" from preschools (Webster-Stratton & Herbert, 1994), and school-age children with CD tend to have conflicted and unsupportive relationships with teachers (Campbell & Ewing, 1990). Not surprisingly, parents and school officials often conflict over the child's behavior problems (Webster-Stratton & Herbert, 1994).

Children with CD tend to present other symptoms of emotional and behavioral malad-justment. There is a high degree of overlap between conduct disorder and ADHD (Moffitt, 1990; Hinshaw et al., 1993). Children with "dual" diagnoses tend to display more severe and persistent antisocial behaviors than those with single diagnoses (Loeber, 1988) and are more likely than others to have fathers with severe antisocial psychopathology. Finally, a significant number of children with CD also qualify for a diagnosis of depressive disorder, particularly during adolescence (Ollendick & King, 1994).

Developmental Course of Conduct Disorder

There are multiple pathways that lead to symptoms of CD in childhood and adoles-cence. The best-known pathway is called the *Early Starter Pathway* (Patterson, Capaldi, & Bank, 1991). As the term suggests, symptoms of CP begin in the preschool or early elementary years and tend to persist throughout into adulthood. The type of problem behavior changes with age, however. In young children, problem behavior most often involves noncompliance, negativism, and temper tantrums—the characteristic symp-toms of ODD. As children mature, symptoms become more serious, and overt signs of CD (fighting, disruptive behavior) become more covert (stealing, lying, fire setting) (Loeber et al., 1993).

Adolescents who have "early starter" histories are at high risk for continuing antiso-cial behavior in adulthood (Kazdin, 1987; Caspi & Moffitt, 1995). As adults, they tend to receive diagnoses of Antisocial Personality Disorder and are vulnerable to broad range of negative life outcomes including attention deficit disorder, poor health, low educational and occupational attainment, marital maladjustment, and problem parenting (Caspi & Moffitt, 1995).

Children who follow the *Late Starter Pathway* begin to show symptomatic behav-ior in adolescence and do not have early histories of conduct problems (Caspi & Moffitt, 1995). Late starters tend to show less serious forms of conduct problems than early starters (Loeber et al., 1993). For example, late starters typically engage in acts of minor delinquency such as stealing or truancy, whereas early starters show a broad range of problems that typically include violence toward other people. By early adult-hood, late starters show a sharp decline in the frequency of their conduct problems. Girls may be more likely to enter late starter pathway to conduct disorder than the early-starter pathway (McGee et al., 1992). Although the frequency of their conduct-disordered behavior declines with age, girls with CP are at great risk for unresponsive parenting and their children tend to show early developmental problems (Serbin, Pe-ters, McAfter, & Schwartzman, 1991).

Assessment Issues

As with cases of ADHD, a thorough asssessment of CD includes information about the child's functioning at home, at school, and with peers. Interviews with parents are essential for gathering information about the child's history and current functioning, and for evalu-ating the presence of associated family problems and stressors. Interviews with teachers and school personnel are essential for evaluating the extent to which the child's conduct problems disrupt his or her social and academic functioning. If academic problems are present, tests of intelligence and achievement are required. Finally, the extent of the child's problems with peers can be assessed in interviews with relevant adults, and in direct observations of peer interactions.

Behavioral Interventions

Four different types of behavioral interventions have been used to treat conduct-disordered children: family-based interventions that highlight parent education and training, school-based interventions, community-based programs, and social skills training. Most of these programs have highlighted "overt" forms of CD (McMahon & Wells, 1989).

Family-Based Interventions.   Leading behavioral formulations of conduct disorder have centered on the role of parent/child interactions in shaping and maintaining high rates of aggressive behavior. For example, Patterson and his colleagues have conducted extensive home and clinic observations of aggressive boys and their families (Patterson, 1976; 1992). Observations revealed that aggressive children were part of a family system in which coercive methods of interpersonal control predominated. Aggressive children engaged in high rates of aversive behaviors such as provocative noncompliance and tantrums, and parents reciprocated with criticisms, threats, and physical punishment. According to Patterson (1976), this pattern of family interactions developed from parental deficits in child management, particularly "giving in" to aversive child behaviors to provide short-term relief. Patterson has also observed that parents of aggressive children provide higher than normal rates of positive consequences for coercive behavior. For example, reasoning with a child during tantrum behavior may serve as a reward (positive attention) which increases the likelihood that the tantrum will be repeated.

In Patterson's treatment program, discrete parenting skills are the major targets of therapeutic change. Parents are initially trained in behavioral recording techniques, so they can effectively monitor their child's behavior at home. Also, parents study a prepared text on child management skills. Training sessions are conducted at home and in the clinic. Therapist "consultants" closely monitor the parents' progress during the course of therapy. If child problem behaviors also occur at school, similar procedures are carried out with teachers.

Forehand and colleagues developed a similar approach to parent training that has been successfully used to treat symptoms of ODD (Forehand et al., 1981; Forehand & Long, 1988). (The assessment phase of this program was described earlier.) Most impressive has been evidence of long-term maintenance of treatment gains. Forehand and Long (1988) contacted 43 families who had participated in parent training 4 to 11 years earlier. Results indicated that families who had received an earlier course of parent training were indistinguishable from controls on a variety of outcome measures.

A unique and highly promising variant of PT has been developed by Webster-Stratton and her colleagues (Webster-Stratton & Herbert, 1994). Their program is designed for young (ages 3 to 7) children and their families. A key feature is the use of videotaped programs of modeled parent skills that are shown to groups of parents whose children have clinically relevant conduct problems. After each videotape, the therapist leads a discussion. Significant improvements in child behavior were obtained with approximately $2/3$ of the sample, and maintained for relatively long periods of time (1 to 3 years) (Webster-

Stratton, 1990). The video modeling intervention has a low individual treatment cost and is accessible to parents with very limited educational backgrounds. Those who failed to benefit from the program tended to have other severe stressors in their lives. For example, Webster-Stratton and Hammond (1990) found that the combination of low SES, single-parent status, and social insularity virtually insured a poor outcome.

CASE EXAMPLE: PARENT TRAINING

Annie C., age 7, was referred to a child psychologist by her mother. Ms. C. reported that Annie was frequently disobedient at home. Specific problem behaviors included talking back to her mother, whining, refusing to comply with requests, tantruming, and engaging in provocative violations of household rules (e.g., hitting her younger sister for no apparent reason). In addition, Ms. C. reported that Annie had been held back in school for poor academic achievement and that Annie was continuing to perform poorly in her academic work.

During the initial interview, Ms. C. provided detailed information about Annie's present and past difficulties. Ms. C. reported that her husband found it easy to gain compliance from Annie. Although he did not use physical punishment, he was much firmer in discipline than his wife. Ms. C. reported that her disciplinary methods involved "reasoning" with Annie after she had refused a request. In general, this method did not result in compliance but rather in escalating arguments and tantrums on Annie's part. Ms. C. felt that she had little influence over her daughter's behavior and that all means of controlling Annie had been exhausted.

Annie was interviewed and administered the WISC-R. She presented as a friendly and cooperative child, and worked hard on the intelligence test. Her scores on the IQ test revealed that she was very bright, functioning in the superior range of intelligence relative to other children her age. Annie and her mother were observed interacting in the clinic in free and structured play. Ms. C. was revealed to be an affectionate and caring but overattentive mother. Annie frequently elicited her mother's attentions through small rule infractions and continually tested her limit-setting abilities. When Ms. C. desired a change in Annie's behavior, she often resorted to requests followed by long explanations. Annie would respond by saying "Yes, but momma. . . . " and give her reason for doing what she wanted. This would be followed by further explanation and counterargument. The usual result would be some sort of compromise or capitulation on Ms. C.'s part. During the observation, Ms. C. seemed to find it almost impossible to ignore her daughter's behavior, so that even squirming and whining would attract her attention.

A treatment plan was devised from the assessment data, with the following goals: Ms. C. would be taught to provide positive attention for desirable behaviors, to ignore inappropriate attention-seeking behaviors, and to use a time-out procedure to control Annie's misbehavior. The rationale behind parent training was discussed with Ms. C., and she agreed to give the program an earnest try. In addition, a token economy was instituted at school for the timely completion of schoolwork. Stars were given for completed assignments which could be turned in for rewards decided on by Annie and her mother.

Initial treatment sessions were spent teaching Ms. C. to attend to and reinforce Annie's positive behaviors. Ms. C. kept daily behavioral records. She reported that in response to the increased attention and praise of positive behaviors, Annie began to seek attention for positive actions.

For example, she began to make her bed without her mother asking. But high levels of conflict between Annie and her mother remained. The next sessions were spent on teaching Ms. C. to ignore inappropriate attention-getting behaviors. For example, Ms. C. reported that Annie would talk with her mouth full at the dinner table and show the food in her mouth on purpose. This behavior was against the house rule. Ms. C. decided to target these attention-getting behaviors for ignoring. She found this part of the program very difficult to carry out, but persisted in her efforts. Finally, in order to deescalate conflict between Ms. C. and Annie, and to help Ms. C. achieve a sense of control, she was taught a time-out procedure. When Annie threw a tantrum, Ms. C. would tell her to sit in a quiet corner of the room for three minutes. Annie was told that if she called out or complained while in the corner, another minute would be added. The first time Ms. C. tried to use time out, Annie screamed and cried but complied. She did call out to her mother to complain, and Ms. C. added another minute to the time spent in the corner. After this initial episode of testing the limits, Annie began to comply with time-out without showing tantrum behavior.

Ms. C. reported an increased sense of effectiveness and decreased conflict between herself and Annie. Subsequent sessions focused on reviewing the skills Ms. C. had learned and applying them to specific situations. In addition, more general parenting skills were developed (such as making requests in a simple, direct manner without resorting to explanations). Once Ms. C. gained confidence in her new parenting skills and applied them diligently, the amount of conflict between herself and Annie decreased sharply. Additionally, Annie's teachers reported an increase in her self-esteem and significant improvements in study habits. Ms. C. reported that her husband also felt that there was considerable improvement in Annie's behavior at home, although he was initially skeptical of therapy and reluctant to finance it. Finally, Ms. C. reported that her relationships with her other children had improved as well.

Termination was mutually agreed upon when it was felt that Ms. C. was able to maintain the skills she had learned and apply them to new situations as they arose. It was agreed that she would return next fall with Annie to prepare for the new school year, and that the therapist would meet with Annie's teacher to help maintain gains she had achieved in school. The entire therapy contract required 11 weekly sessions.

The effectiveness of parent management training with families of aggressive children has been extensively evaluated (McMahon & Wells, 1989; Miller & Prinz, 1990). The benefits of treatment are wide-ranging and affect the entire family system. Children's behavior improves significantly, returning to the level of normal peers in about $2/3$ of treated cases. Improvements in children's behavior persist for at least one year posttreatment, sometimes for longer periods of time. Furthermore, these positive changes generalize to untreated siblings. Finally, there are significant improvements in parents' levels of stress and depression (Kazdin, 1985).

Beyond these generally positive findings, there are characteristics of children and families that predict responsiveness to treatment. Parent management training has been found to be most effective with school-age (6 to 12 years old children. Younger children and adolescents do not appear to benefit as much, although positive treatment responses do occur in these age groups, as well (Patterson et al., 1994). As noted earlier, families that experience severe, interactive ecological stresses such as poverty, single-parent status, and social insularity tend to show the least favorable responses to treatment.

Community-Based Interventions.   Community-based interventions involve efforts to restructure the total living environment of conduct-disordered youth. As an alternative to placing these youth in group homes, some have developed live-in communities that are organized according to behavioral principles. The best known of these programs, Achievement Place, employs a token economy sytstem to help children learn responsibility, academic skills, and appropriate social behavior (Willner, Brankmann, Kirigin, & Wolf, 1978). Benefits of these programs outweigh those of alternative group homes, but positive effects do not appear to extend across time. Two to three years posttreatment, there are few differences between children who particpated in these programs and those who received ordinary community placements (McMahon & Wells, 89).

Problem-Solving Skills Training
As described earlier, children with CD tend to experience high levels of peer conflict and rejection. A substantial body of research has shown that aggressive children have deficits in social-cognitive functioning that help promote and maintain their social difficulties (Dodge, 1993). For example, especially when cues of intent are ambiguous and their self-esteem is threatened, aggressive boys are quick to attribute hostile intent to others (Dodge & Somberg, 1987). More generalized impairments in social problem solving, empathic understanding, and perspective taking also have been found in children and adolescents with CD (Kazdin, 1993).

Thus, skills training programs have been developed to remediate these deficits. Most training programs are conducted in small groups, where children learn a step-by-step approach to solving problems, with increasing attention to "real-life" examples as treatment progresses. Therapists play an active role in these groups by modeling appropriate skills, coaching, setting up role-plays, and providing reinforcement or response-cost punishment. These programs have produced encouraging results in children with CD. For example, Lochman, Lampron, Gemmer, and Harris (1987) developed an Anger Coping program for 9- to 12-year-old boys. Group therapy interventions were carried out in the school setting. Treated boys had lower rates of drug and alcohol involvement, higher self-esteem, and better problem-solving skills than untreated boys, both immmediately after treatment and 2.5 to 3.5 years later (Lochman, 1992).

Another major program has targeted deficient problem-solving skills. Kazdin, Esveldt-Dawson, French, and Unis (1987a; 1987b) developed the Problem-Solving Skills Training (PSST) program for adolescents with CP. This program is broadly focused and includes impersonal, interpersonal, and academic problem-solving skills as targets for therapeutic change. Children who participated in PSST were rated more highly on parent and teacher reports than those who received relationship therapy or attention placebo. Treatment gains were maintained after one year (Kazdin, Bass, Siegel, & Thomas, 1989). However, most children in the treated group were still outside the normal range on measures of problem-solving efficacy. Kazdin and colleagues found that combining PSST wiith parent training increased the number of children within range of normal functioning.

In sum, cognitive-based treatments do appear to promote decrements in aggressive behavior (Kazdin et al., 1992; Kendall et al., 1990). Because of the complexity of skills that are targeted, treatment is more effective with older than younger children (Durlak, Furhman, & Lampman, 1991). However, the magnitude of change is relatively modest, indicating the need for broad-spectrum treatment.

Treatment of CD: The Need for Comprehensive, Long-Term Care and Prevention

It is clear that behavioral interventions can be effective with conduct-disordered children. However, Kazdin (1993) has cogently argued that children with CD suffer from problems in so many different areas of life functioning that there is a need for broad-based, inte-grated treatment that extends for long periods of time. In other words, treatment should be evaluated according to "chronic care" model; short-term interventions are inappropriate with this population.

A second important theme involves prevention. The most serious and intransigent conduct problems begin in early childhood. There is a need to identify children at elevated risk for these difficulties and to intervene before they become chronic. For example, FAST Track (Families and Schools Together) is a large-scale, multisite intervention study designed to prevent the exaccerbation of conduct problems in kindergarten-age chil-dren (CPPRG, 1992). Young children identified as high in externalizing problem be-havior are selected for treatment. These children participate in intensive, long-term interventions that target positive changes in disruptive behavior in home and school settings, social-cognitive skills, peer relationships, academic performance, and col-laboration between parents and school officials. There is great hope that programs such as these will divert significant numbers of children from potential life-long pat-terns of serious maladjustment.

Pervasive Developmental Disorders

The final group of childhood behavior disorders are rare but severe. These disorders are called *pervasive* because they involve marked impairments in all aspects of children's adap-tive competence. Our discussion will focus on Autistic Disorder because it is the best re-searched pervasive developmental disorder.

Autistic Disorder

The earliest clinical description of autism was provided by Leo Kanner (1943). While working in a residential treatment center for severely disturbed children, Kanner noted that a subgroup of children behaved quite differently from those with schizophrenia or mental retardation. These atypical children manifested "extreme autistic aloneness," referring to a profound lack of responsiveness to others; they also manifested severely impaired language development with many peculiarities of speech and an obsessive desire for environmental sameness. Over time, the word *autism* was generalized to many different types of severe developmental disabilities, including mental retardation and schizophrenia. It is now known that infantile autism refers to a unique behavior disorder appearing very early in life. The following criteria have been put forth to differentiate autism from other related disorders (*DSM-IV*, 1994):

QUALITATIVE IMPAIRMENT IN SOCIAL INTERACTION (AT LEAST TWO OF THE FOLLOWING):

- Marked impairment in use of nonverbal behaviors (eye-to-eye gaze, facial expression, body postures, gestures)
- Failure to develop age-appropriate peer relationships
- Lack of social or emotional reciprocity

QUALITATIVE IMPAIRMENT IN VERBAL AND NONVERBAL COMMUNICATION (AT LEAST ONE OF THE FOLLOWING):

- Delay in or absence of spoken language
- If adequate speech is present, marked impairment in ability to sustain social conversation
- Stereotyped, repetitive use of language or idiosyncratic language
- Lack of varied, spontaneous make-believe or social imitative play

RESTRICTED REPETITIVE AND STEREOTYPED PATTERNS OF BEHAVIOR, INTERESTS, AND ACTIVITIES (AT LEAST ONE OF THE FOLLOWING):

- Preoccupation with stereotyped and restricted patterns of interests that are abnormal in intensity or focus
- Inflexible adherance to specific, nonfunctional routines/rituals
- Stereotyped and repetitive motor mannerisms
- Preoccupation with parts of objects

DELAYS IN AT LEAST ONE OF THE FOLLOWING, WITH ONSET BEFORE AGE 3:

- Social interaction
- Language as used for social communication
- Symbolic or imaginative play

Some of these clinical features are illustrated by the following case vignette:

Sam, age 6, was observed in a playroom setting with other adults and children present. Sam sat alone in a corner of the room, repetitively twirling a mechanical toy. He appeared unaware of other people and activities in the room. An adult approached Sam, offering him a toy and said, "Sam, do you want this toy?" Without making eye contact, Sam replied in a toneless voice, "Sam, do you want this toy?" Sam continued playing with the mechanical toy. When an adult insisted that he go into the lunchroom with others, he screamed loudly, thrashed his arms and legs, and resisted physical attempts to move him.

Autistic infants show little evidence of normal attachment and communicative behaviors. For example, normal infants over 3 to 4 months of age anticipate being picked up by extending their arms, and they smile and vocalize to their caregivers. Autisic infants are extremely passive and do not make eye contact or engage in reciprocal communicative exchanges with caregivers. They do not anticipate being picked up and may arch their bodies rigidly or hang limply in response to being held. As the autistic child grows, he or she continues to act as though others were not present but may develop strong attachments to inanimate objects, such as spinning tops. Even minor changes in the social or physical environment may provoke strong emotional protests such as screaming and tantrums. If speech is present in later years, it is often peculiar. For example, as shown ain the example of Sam's behavior, many autistic children show *echolalia,* a tendency to repeat back, verbatim, phrases that are addressed to them.

The clinician must differentiate Autistic Disorder from other developmental disorders with which it shares some features. For example, autistic children are often mentally retarded but have additional behavioral, cognitive, and social features that are unique to the disorder. Similarly, their profound lack of responsiveness to others suggests a possible hearing impairment, but, in fact, autistic children have no known hearing problems. Finally, the early onset of the disorder distinguishes it from schizophrenia, which is rare in childhood. Language disturbance is a key feature of autism: About half of all autistic children never acquire speech (Rutter, 1966).

Autism is a rare disorder, occurring in about 2 to 5 cases per 10,000 (Bryson, Clark, & Smith, 1988). Autism is far more common in boys than girls, by ratios of 3:1 to 4:1. The prognosis for autistic children is generally poor. The strongest predictors of long-term outcome are the child's cognitive level and degree of language impairment. Most children with performance IQs in the 50–60 range or lower will remain severely handicapped (Lord & Rutter, 1995). However, high-functioning autists can be successfully mainstreamed into public school classrooms, provided that the classrooms have good structure and that teachers are prepared to cope with a child who has special needs (Harris et al., 1990). Older autistic children tend to show some improvement over time, in that they generally show more interest in people and fewer ritualistic behaviors (Cantwell, 1989). However, speech and language handicaps remain major problems, and adequate social adjustment is rarely achieved (Rutter et al., 1992).

The causes of autism remain a modern mystery, despite hundreds of research studies. It was once believed that cold, distant parents "caused" autism in their infants, but this "refrigerator parent" theory has been roundly refuted in research (Cantwell, Baker, & Rutter, 1978). Due to the extremely early onset of the disorder and the extent of cognitive impairment, the primary causes of autism are most certainly biological in nature. However, aside from evidence that autism can be genetically transmitted, specific etiological agents remain to be identified (Rutter, Bailey, Bolton, & Lecouteur, 1993).

Behavioral Management

Major treatment advances during the past two decades have been in the area of behavioral management. Although behavior therapy is hardly a "cure" for autism, it has been successful in improving the social adaptive skills of autistic children and in decreasing levels of dangerous or inappropriate behavior. Major targets of intervention involve behavioral skills *deficits*—such as the absence of speech, self-help, and social skills, and behavioral *excesses*—such as self-injurious behavior, tantrums, aggression, and self-stimulatory behaviors (e.g., rocking, spinning, twirling). The steps in setting up a behavioral management program are described here.

Assessment.   Adequate assessment of autistic chddren involves at least three foci: interviews with parents/guardians, examination of the future environments in which the child will most likely function, and psychoeducational assessment of the child's strengths and weaknesses (Luce, 1986; Schopler et al., 1990). It is necessary to obtain precise descriptions of behavioral excesses and deficits in order to arrive at an accurate diagnosis and set up effective interventions. The most challenging aspect of diagnosis is ruling out the many different developmental and medical problems that may mimic symptoms of autism (Lord & Rutter, 1995). The overarching long-range goal would be to promote the highest level of adaptive functioning that the child is capable of achieving, with integration into the community, if possible.

Teaching Adaptive Skills.   Teaching autistic children adaptive skills has been a major focus of behavioral intervention (Schreibman, Charlop, & Kurtz, 1992). Frequent, individually tailored sessions with a high degree of structure seem to promote the highest levels of learning (Clark & Rutter, 1981). Because speech and language deficits are such important features of the disorder, a great deal of work has been put into developing effective language training programs. In a typical program, the therapist begins with simple shaping of speech sounds, then gradually progresses toward words, phrases, and sentences (Lovass, Berberich, & Schaffer, 1966). Initially, the therapist relies heavily on modeling of desired sounds and words, reinforcing the child for correct imitations. Although individual autistic children vary in terms of degree of language impairment, the training process is an arduous one that often requires years of intensive one-to-one sessions. Once the child has made sufficient progress with a personal therapist, it is essential to get parents involved in training so transfer of learning can occur in the home (Lansing & Schopler, 1978).

More recently, the Natural Language Program (NLP) (Koegel, O'Dell, & Koegel, 1987) has been developed to establish speech in functionally mute autistic children and to develop communicative speech in ecolalic children. NLP is conducted during brief, play-based sessions. During each session, the therapist models responses for the child to imitate, and the child is rewarded with praise and access to a toy for attempting to respond. NLP has built-in generalization trials to other settings—in addition, parents are taught to use NLP. Laski, Charlop, and Schreibman (1988) found that following NLP, both mute and ecolalic autists significantly increased their verbalizations.

Even with advances in training technology, speech remains difficult to teach. Rarely do children achieve spontaneous speech that generalizes to new settings (Schreibman et al., 1992). Thus, recent research has focused on teaching language under more natural conditions. For example, parents have been trained to use a time delay procedure at home to increase spontaneous speech. Autistic children were taught to speak spontaneously in response to temporal cues. For example, they were cued to say "Good morning" upon awakening, "May I have a snack?" upon returning home from school, "Good night" before bed time, and so on. These procedures were successful in increasing children's spontaneous speech in a variety of settings.

Other targets for intervention have involved the autistic child's profound unresponsiveness to others. Although early efforts to teach social skills to autistic children were disappointing (e.g., Lovass et al., 1966), recent efforts have been more promising. Charlop, Milstein, and Moore (1989) found that video modeling was effective in promoting cooperative social skills in autistic children and that these skills generalized to new settings. Koegel and his colleagues have developed a program to teach self-monitoring skills to autistic children (Koegel, Frea, & Surratt, 1994). During the pretraining period, target behaviors (skills deficits) are defined using careful functional analysis, and reinforcers are identified. During training, the therapist models desirable behavior and sets clear contingencies for appropriate and inappropriate behaviors. Once the child has acquired a given skill, the amount of time spent self-monitoring is increased, and reliance on prompts is faded. Finally, generalization training is conducted to ensure that the newly acquired skills will be produced in different settings.

The following case example, described in Koegel and associates (1994), illustrates the successful application of these strategies.

Carl was a 7-year-old autistic boy who was placed in a regular second-grade classroom because of his relatively high degree of cognitive functioning. Carl had great difficulty making friends, and was described as extremely socially isolated and unhappy. Observations revealed that Carl's most serious deficit was a lack of responsiveness to questions and other social initiations. In effect, Carl had "extinguished" his peers' social interest by failing to respond to them.

Initially, he was taught to discriminate between responsiveness and unresponsiveness to the therapist's questions. Next, he was given a wrist counter, which he pressed every time he answered a question. He was rewarded every 3 presses. His reward ratio was gradually thinned to 30 presses, and his skills were generalized to the school setting using peers and teachers as prompters. Carl was able to sustain a high level of responsiveness to his peers. Ultimately, he stopped wearing the watch because natural peer interest became more rewarding than the contrived reinforcers.

Suppressing Behavioral Excesses.   Behavioral "excesses" common to autistic children include self-injurious behavior (SIB), tantrums, and behavioral stereotypes such as spinning rituals. Many different methods have been used to eliminate behavioral excesses in autistic children. Simple extinction, carried out by ignoring problem behavior, can be dangerously slow in eliminating self-injurious behavior. The vast majority of interventions have involved some type of aversive treatment, particularly when the target of intervention is self-injurious behavior such as head banging or self-mutilation.

In early reports, electric shock was used to suppress self-injurious behavior that did not respond to less intrusive methods. Brief electric shock is effective in suppressing self-injury, in that it rapidly suppresses self-destructive behaviors, allowing children and therapists to focus on shaping adaptive skills (Lumas, 1977). However, this method of intervention raises serious ethical issues as well as concerns about generalization of treatment effects.

In 1982, a task force for the Association for the Advancement of Behavior Thempy reported on the self-injurious behavior in children (Favell et al., 1982). The report identified the need for careful assessment of problem behavior, reinforcement of adaptive behavior, creating an environment that is not associated with self-injury, careful use of punishment, and ensuring that treatment of self-injury is planned by a professional who builds in generalization training. It was also recommended that human subjects and professional peer review committees be established to insure the rights of the child.

In response to these and other concerns, recent treatment of self-injury has involved the use of less punitive methods (Matson & Sevin, 1995). Accumulating evidence has shown that relatively "weak" punishers can reduce severe behavior problems (Schreibman et al., 1992). Systematic approach to treatment involves risk assessment and management, identification of replacement behaviors and reinforcers for strengthening these behaviors, and use of functional analysis to identify current variables maintaining SIB (Iwata, Zarcone, Vollmer, & Smith, 1994). For example, Iwata, Dorsey, Slifer, Bauman, and Richman (1982) observed occurrences of problem behavior during analogue conditions, and found that it was possible to identify variables associated with SIB and aggression. The motivation for self-injury differed for each child, but tended to fall into three categories: bids for attention, escape from aversive demands, and, self-stimulatory behaviors. This information can help the therapist select an appropriate intervention—for example, an attention-motivated child could receive contingent attention for nonself-injurious behavior. Other examples of this approach include:

1. Offering self-injurious individuals a more interesting environment or reinforcing incompatible behaviors such as the use of toys (Azrin, Besalel, & Wisotzek, 1982; Touchette, Macdonald, & Langer, 1985).
2. Overcorrection, which includes restitution and positive practice (Foxx & Azrin, 1972). Following an inappropriate behavior, the child is required to repeatedly practice an appropriate alternative response or restore the environment to its previous state. Studies have shown that this technique can be effective in reducing self-injurious behavior (Johnson et al., 1982; Wesolowsid & Zawlocki, 1982).
3. Using a varied menu of nonphysical punishments, such as time out, verbal prohibitions, and overcorrection (Schreibman et al., 1992).
4. Teaching children how to self-monitor and control their own behavior. For example, self-monitoring interventions have been used successfuly to decrease behavioral stereotypies (Koegel & Koegel, 1990) and aggression (Benson, 1986).

Other Treatment Issues.   Even in the best educational and behavioral treatment programs, there are limits on how much severely impaired autistic children can achieve. The development of an individualized treatment plan is an important step in protecting the rights of the child and his or her parents (McClanahan & Krantz, 1981). Ethics committees should also be used to monitor the progress of autistic children to ensure that treatment goals are being met in a timely and appropriate manner. Finally, parents should be directly involved in the treatment process. Although parents of autistic children are not "pathogenic" as was once believed, their child's special needs are a source of chronic stress—for example, family members with autistic children report higher rates of depression, somatic complaints, and marital dissatisfaction than others (Harris, 1995). Providing emotional and educational support to these families is of paramount importance. Moreover, parents play a critical role in their child's behavioral rehabilitation. Although autistic children can benefit considerably from individualized training, often there is little generalizability of learning to other settings. Koegel and colleagues (1982) have demonstrated that time-limited parent training is superior to that of extended residential training in promoting generalization of skills across time and treatment settings.

Chapter Summary

One major group of child behavior disorders have high levels of anxiety, depression, and/or social withdrawal as common features. A wide range of behavioral interventions have proven effective in eliminating these problems, particularly modeling-based interventions and those based on gradual, *in-vivo* exposure to fearful situations.

Disorders of attention, impulse control, and conduct comprise a second broad class of childhood behavior disorders. Contingency management programs carried out by parents and/or teachers have proven effective in reducing levels of impulsive, disruptive, or aggressive behavior and in promoting prosocial skills. Newer approaches involve systematic shaping of metacognitive and social cognitive skills that may be effective in preventing maladaptive behavior.

Finally, pervasive developmental disorders such as autism involve severe deficits in nearly all aspects of adaptive functioning, particularly communication skills. Effective management involves systematic shaping of adaptive skills, suppression of self-injurious or other maladaptive behavior patterns, and setting up programs to promote generalization of training to the child's future living environments.

Chapter *17*

Stress, Coping, and Behavioral Medicine

James R., a 59-year-old insurance salesman, was referred to a behavioral medicine clinic for evaluation of risk factors related to essential hypertension. James had dangerously high levels of blood pressure. In addition, he was 50 pounds overweight and was not attempting to lower the amount of salt or fat in his diet. He described his work life as "stressful" and admitted that he was the kind of person who felt impatient to get things done, and that his greatest fault was his "quick temper." Upon his return from work each day, he watched television for four or five hours. As he described it, "I feel so stressed by work that I just need to relax." James's father died of a massive coronary at the age of 61.

Mary W., age 45, was referred to a pain clinic for treatment of chronic back pain. During the past year, Mary's back pain had become so severe that she was confined to her bed for long periods of time. Extensive medical evaluation revealed no specific organic pathology.

Behavioral medicine involves the clinical application of cognitive and behavioral techniques to the diagnosis, management, treatment, and/or prevention of physical illness (Pomerleau & Brady, 1979; Schwartz & Weiss, 1977). As such, behavioral medicine represents a unique integration between psychology, medicine, and related health disciplines. The cases of James R. and Mary W. illustrate two of the many faces of behavioral medicine: management of risk factors associated with chronic diseases and management of chronic pain. This growing area of specialization is founded on "revolutionary" reconceptualizations of health and illness. Thus, current concepts of illness, stress, and coping will be briefly reviewed here, followed by a survey of behavioral medicine intervention techniques and their relevance to specific physical disorders.

Concepts of Illness, Stress, and Coping

Concepts of Illness

Multiple biological, psychological, and social-environmental factors interact in complex ways to cause illness, particularly chronic illnesses such as hypertension, heart disease, and cancer. For example, cancer has been linked to hereditary predisposition, stress, age, diet, smoking, and exposure to environmental toxins (American Cancer Society, 1994). Furthermore, for any given chronic illness, there are multiple causative "paths" that could potentiate the disease (Meichenbaum & Turk, 1982).

This reconceptualization of physical illness is at the core of the field of behavioral medicine. It has replaced previous medical views of illness as resulting from single pathogens (such as germs). It also has replaced previous psychological views that some specific illnesses are produced by intrapsychic factors such as unresolved conflicts (Brantley & Bruce, 1986). The reconceptualization grew in part from shifts in the epidemiological patterning of life-threatening illnesses (Meichenbaum & Turk, 1982). During the course of this century, chronic diseases such as cancer, hypertension, and coronary heart disease have superseded infectious illnesses as leading causes of death (Oyama & Andrasik, 1992).

Concepts of Stress and Coping

Stress is currently viewed as a potential causative or maintaining factor in all physical illnesses (*DSM-IV*, 1994). Models of illness implicating relationships between stress and disease were sparked by the pioneering work of Hans Selye. Selye (1936) defined stress in terms of the *general adaptation syndrome:* nonspecific psychophysiological reactions that are elicited by noxious life changes. A three-stage reaction involving alarm, resistance, and exhaustion characterized responses to stress. The specific nature of the noxious stimulus was not viewed as important. According to Selye, *continuous* exposure to stress (causing extended physiological hyperarousal) resulted in illness.

Selye's important definition helped to popularize the concept of stress. Indeed, current research has demonstrated clear links between stress exposure and vulnerability to illness (Cohen, Tyrell, & Smith, 1991; Stone, Bovberg, & Neale, 1992). Furthermore, researchers have learned that the experience of stress suppresses the natural protective functions of the immune system (e.g., Stone et al., 1993). However, there is controversy over the meaning of *stress.* Is stress mainly a condition of the environment or of the organism? Holroyd and Lazarus (1985) have commented that even in extreme circumstances, the consequences of stress cannot be understood merely in terms of the stressful event. Because worldly events are always imbued with personal meaning, the same event could be viewed as a catastrophe by one individual and as a minor hassle by another. Hence, most current behavioral conceptualizations of stress include *cognitive appraisal,* or an individual's perceptions of a stimulus event.

Another important factor in understanding stress is individual vulnerability. Because of biological predisposition or early sensitization, some individuals are more likely than others to respond negatively to stressful life events (Davidson, 1992). The nature of these vulnerabilities may in part account for the *type* of illness that is developed. For example, Rose, Jenkins, and Hurst (1978) found that air traffic controllers with high blood pressure reactivity were more likely than other controllers to develop hypertension. Similarly, vulnerability to Sudden Cardiac Death is enhanced by exposure to chronic stress and precipitated by the experience of strong positive or negative affect (Lane & Jenkins, 1995).

Characteristics of stressful stimuli also have unique effects on psychophysiological responding. For example, experiencing different negative emotions such as anger and fear has different effects on physiological functions (Levenson, 1992). Similarly, the type and chronicity of stressful stimuli have been linked to different patterns of autonomic, hormonal, and cortical activity (Weiner, 1994).

Finally, it is helpful to bear in mind that the relationship between stress and illness is transactional. Developing a physical illness is a source of stress that increases ones' vulnerability to emotional distress and to other illnesses.

In short, stress is a highly complex concept. In order to fully understand the nature of stress, the individual's biological predispositions and prior learning history must be taken into account, along with immediate cognitive reactions to the stressor and characteristics of the stressful situation itself.

The concept of coping is closely related to that of stress. As Holroyd and Lazarus (1985) have pointed out, health outcomes are the result of effective coping, not just consequences of stressful events. However, there is no widely accepted definition of coping ability. Current definitions of *coping* range from global personality traits to specific behavioral outcomes (Moos & Billings, 1982). The most influential behavioral model of coping has been developed by Lazarus and his colleagues (Lazarus & Folkman, 1984; Folkman, Lazarus, Dunkel-Schetter, et al., 1986). In contrast with models that define *coping* in terms of enduring personality "traits" or characteristics of the situation, Lazarus and colleagues define *coping* as a *process* of managing demands that threaten to exceed the resources of the person.

Optimally effective coping processes change over time, relative to different situational demands. Coping that has had a positive function at one stage of stress management may be inadequate at another. For example, in studies of bereaved parents, Hofer, Wolff, Friedman, and Mason (1972) found that coping behaviors that had helpful functions at one state of grieving (such as denial) had negative consequences at other stages. Moreover, cognitive appraisal of stressors plays a critical role in the definition and management of stressful events. Finally, coping includes not only active attempts to regulate stressful conditions but also "palliative" strategies such as regulating stress-relevant emotions or thoughts.

Coping behaviors can potentially affect health outcomes in several different ways (Rodin & Salovey, 1989). Consistent with Selye's theory, coping behaviors can affect the frequency and intensity of neuroendrocrine responses to stress. Second, coping can affect health outcomes through patterns of illness *behavior:* how the individual deals with symptom reporting, seeking medical help, and treatment recommendations. Third, coping behaviors may affect illness through high-risk behavior patterns such as smoking, drinking, or exposure to environmental toxins. For example, an individual may begin drinking heavily as a coping response to job stress; continued heavy drinking would place the person at risk for seriously impaired health and for experiencing stressful interactions with others. This pattern of maladaptive coping is illustrated by the following case example:

> Michael T. was a 56-year-old midlevel executive in a large corporation. His business was the victim of a hostile takeover by another corporation, and he feared that he might lose his job. Although he hadn't smoked for 20 years, he resumed smoking, and began to drink heavily after work hours. Consequently, his relationships with his wife and children deteriorated, causing him to experience more stress and distress. In addition, he reported feeling exhausted and "paralyzed" at work.

Relatedly, Thoits (1994) has argued that there are certain personality characteristics such as mastery and self-esteem that serve to "select" people in and out of stressful life circumstances. Finally, it is plausible that the ways in which individuals cope with illness can affect the actual course of the illness (Rodin & Salovey, 1989).

Assessment

A thorough medical examination is an essential prerequisite for any further behavioral assessment of stress. Blanchard (1981) has strongly recommended that the nonphysician behaviorist begin with the physician's findings and maintain a close working relationship with the physician. This is because problems dealt with in behavioral medicine involve the existence or threat of real organic pathology. Bypassing this step could have life-threatening consequences for the client.

Behavioral assessment occurs in several stages. As with any behavioral assessment situation, the goals are to identify specific psychological, physiological, and environmental factors associated with the illness. Typically, behavioral interviews are used to achieve this end. Interview formats vary according to the degree of structure and specificity of questions. Unstructured interviews are most appropriate when the client has vague or multiple problems. In addition to achieving a comprehensive analysis of the current problem, it is important to obtain a good history of the person's current symptoms and previous physical problems (Blanchard, 1981). Among other uses, the history helps the therapist distinguish episodic from chronic illness patterns.

Numerous self-report questionnaires have been developed for use in behavioral medicine. These include globally focused instruments, such as Lazarus's (1971) *Life History Questionnaire,* as well as specific problem-oriented questionnaires such as Rosenman's questionnaire for the assessment of Type A behavior (Rosenman et al., 1964).

Direct observations may be used to achieve detailed information about the current problem. Observational data used in medical settings are typically collected by nursing staff. Brantley and Bruce (1986) advised that behavioral observation procedures be clearly specified in order to avoid reliability problems. Also, observation procedures should not interfere with normal job routines. Finally, periodic reliability checks are recommended in order to ensure the adequacy of the procedures.

Self-monitoring is frequently used to obtain detailed accounts of symptoms and their immediate antecedents and consequences. Self-monitoring is a highly cost-efficient assessment tool that can be applied to a broad range of problem behaviors and situations. Furthermore, self-monitoring *must* be used for "subjective" symptoms (such as pain) that cannot be directly observed. Specific methods of self-monitoring should be keyed to the type of presenting problem (Brantley & Bruce, 1986). For example, keeping a daily diary may be most appropriate for episodic symptoms such as asthma attacks, whereas event sampling would be appropriate for high frequency symptoms such as chronic pain. As with all self-monitoring techniques, issues of reactivity, reliability, and compliance are major concerns. A variety of methods have been developed for attenuating these potential problems. For example, periodic reliability checks can be conducted, baseline periods can be lengthened to deal with reactivity, and self-monitoring forms can be mailed on a daily basis to offset problems with compliance.

Finally, psychophysiological measures are used in behavioral medicine to monitor responses such as blood pressure, muscle tension, cortical activity, and autonomic arousal. Physiological measures can provide pretreatment baseline measures of specific physiological responses targeted for change. Also, the patient's responses to various kinds of stressors (such as pain, mental arithmetic, or stressful imagery) can be assessed. Thus, regular monitoring of physiological responsivity to stress could supplement self-report data in evaluations of treatment progress. However, because these methods require high levels of expertise and use of expensive equipment, self-monitoring remains the most commonly used assessment tool.

Treatment Techniques

There are three general situations in which cognitive and behavioral interventions have been applied to physical illnesses. First, specific illness-related problem behaviors may be targets for direct intervention. For example, reducing tension may be indicated for headache sufferers, and reducing elevated levels of blood pressure for cardiac patients. The second situation involves adherence to prescribed medical regimes. Behavioral techniques such as self-monitoring, shaping, and contingency contracting may be used to help clients comply with medical recommendations (Meichenbaum & Turk, 1987). Finally, behavioral interventions have been applied to the prevention of illness. These interventions involve modifying behavioral factors that place an individual at elevated risk for later disease. For example, overeating and smoking are established risk factors for later coronary heart disease. Both high-risk behavior patterns are amenable to direct behavioral intervention. Specific intervention techniques that have been widely used in behavioral medicine are described next.

Relaxation Training

Relaxation training (RT) is frequently used in behavioral medicine to induce muscular and cognitive relaxation. Many different relaxation techniques have been designed. In the United States, progressive muscle relaxation is best known, although physical exercise, meditation, and hypnosis generally result in the same end (Lehrer & Woolfolk, 1984). Progressive reluation is a versatile coping tool that has been applied to many different clinical problems. For example, relaxation training has been helpful in the treatment of hypertension, headache, insomnia, panic disorders, and chronic pain.

Progressive relaxation involves teaching an individual to tense then relax different muscle groups in a systematic manner. Although relaxation can be taught using audio- or videotaped instructions, the best results are achieved with direct therapist/client contact (Lehrer & Woolfolk, 1984). No specialized equipment is needed in order to teach relaxation. An electromyograph (EMG) could be a helpful adjunct because it measures muscle contraction, but it is not absolutely necessary. Steps in relaxation training are as follows (Pinkerton et al., 1984):

1. A conceptual rationale for treatment is provided and discussed in detail with the patient.

2. Baseline assessments of relaxation are taken in the clinician's office or laboratory, using EMG recordings or self-ratings of arousal. Baseline measures are gathered under normal resting, relaxation, and stressful conditions. Once the patient becomes proficient in self-monitoring of target symptoms, relaxation training is begun.

3. The patient is trained to induce states of relaxation by systematically tensing and relaxing each different muscle group, and by discriminating resulting states of tension from those of relaxation. Although training instructions are usually provided by an individual therapist, they also can be provided by audiotape, videotape, or group induction.

4. Patients are urged to practice frequently at home, at least once daily, until relaxation becomes part of their normal routine. Once relaxation under conditions of low stimulation is achieved and highly practiced, levels of stimulation are gradually increased. For example, practicing in the presence of the radio, TV, or other people might be prescribed once practice during quiet conditions has been mastered. Finally, practice during stressful situations (e.g., involving high anxiety arousal) is assigned and made part of the patient's daily routine.

Biofeedback

Biofeedback is a self-regulation technique in which the patient learns to influence psychophysiological processes not typically under voluntary control (Blanchard & Epstein, 1978). One or more of the individual's physiological response processes is "fed back" in the form of a tone, meter, or light display. Special instruments are necessary, such as an electromyograph for measuring muscle tension, an electrocephalograph for measuring electrical activity in the brain, or a blood pressure monitor. Typical clinical procedures are as follows (Pinkerton et al., 1984):

1. The client is provided with a conceptual rationale for biofeedback training. The rationale usually involves discussion of how physical symptoms are related to life stress and how stress arousal can be controlled using biofeedback techniques.

2. An assessment phase is carried out. Specific physiological responses most strongly aroused by stress are identified and targeted for change. If the therapist is unclear about appropriate target symptoms, the individual's responses to stressful stimuli in the laboratory can be used to determine intervention targets. Two- to three-week baseline measures of the target response are then achieved under conditions ranging from relaxation to stressful arousal.

3. In biofeedback control training, the patient reclines in a comfortable chair while a machine provides immediate and continuous feedback of target physiological responses. The patient is then informed of optimal changes in these responses. For example, decrements in blood pressure might be targeted for hypertensive individuals, whereas decrements in muscle tension would be appropriate for tension headache sufferers. The therapist helps the patient to maintain a relaxed posture. Changes in the desired direction are rewarded, until the patient reaches the criterion objective for control set at the beginning of therapy. If one simple physiological response is trained, 4 to 16 office visits are usually required.

4. The next phases involve transfer training: generalization of skills to the natural environment and to higher levels of environmental stress. The first "transfer" task is to maintain the desired response criterion independent of machine feedback. Home practice is critical to the success of this therapy program, and so a detailed home practice schedule is worked out. The next step involves achieving and maintaining the response criterion under average levels of stimulation. Initially, this is done in the office, then at home. Finally, using the same techniques, clients learn to achieve their response criterion under conditions of high environmental stimulation. A maintenance schedule for practice is worked out before the client leaves therapy.

Self-Control Interventions

Self-control interventions are most applicable to behavioral "excesses" such as smoking, drinking, and overeating that place a person at elevated risk for chronic diseases. Self-control techniques involve training clients to manipulate the environment in order to reduce frequencies of maladaptive behavior and to increase levels of adaptive behavior incompatible with the target problems. A unique advantage of self-control training is that patients learn to become their own "therapists." Thus, self-control therapies have a built-in generalization component and are cost effective (Mahoney & Arnkoff, 1978).

At the outset of self-control training, the client is introduced to basic principles of behavior change. The rationale for self-control training is discussed. Next, target behaviors are specified, and the client is given supervised practice in the daily self-monitoring of these behaviors. Therapist and client work together to set specific goals for behavior change. Written contracts, signed by therapist and client, are often used to "formalize" treatment goals. Short-term, behaviorally specific goals are emphasized in these contracts.

Treatment interventions usually involve a combination of stimulus control and self-reinforcement techniques. For example, eating may be restricted to certain times and situations; compliance with these goals is self-reinforced using material rewards or covert self-statements. Once desired self-control behaviors have been achieved, they are strengthened during practice sessions. Prior to termination, these skills are applied to a diverse range of situations in order to promote generalization.

As discussed in Chapters 12 and 13, self-control interventions have been proven effective in the modification of obesity, problem drinking, and cigarette smoking. However, maintaining these improvements has been problematic and requires additional interventions carried out over a relatively long time span.

Cognitive-Behavioral Interventions

Meichenbaum's *Stress Inoculation Training (SIT)* (Meichenbaum, 1977; Meichenbaum & Cameron, 1983) is a multicomponent treatment program for stress-related problems. Cognitive interventions are given primary emphasis. Stress Inoculation Training has been successfully applied to a broad range of problems, including speech anxiety, fears, anger control, social anxiety, pain management, posttraumatic stress, and alcoholism. The training program involves three phases:

   1. First is a conceptualization phase during which the client is provided with a framework for understanding cognitive responses to stress. Situations that arouse stress in the client are revealed using cognitive imagery, and thoughts and feelings occurring in response to the imagery are recorded. Stress Inoculation Training involves exposing an individual to preparatory information describing what it would be like to experience the negative consequences of a stressful situation. The term *inoculation* implies that the person develops coping skills in advance of the feared negative outcome. Through dialogue between therapist and client, the client's awareness of the different components of coping with stress is increased. For example, effective coping involves preparation for confronting a stressful situation, actual confrontation of the situation, and evaluation of the outcome of the situation. Different coping skills are required to effectively handle each component. These concrete cognitive and behavioral coping skills are taught and practiced in the session using imagery and role-playing techniques.

   2. During the second phase, cognitive and behavioral coping techniques are directly applied to the target problem. Relaxation training or social skills training might be used to increase the client's ability to effectively confront a stressful situation. However, the development of effective *cognitive* coping skills is the centerpiece of SIT. The general goal of treatment is to encourage the client to develop a task-oriented, problem-solving view of coping with stress. For example, Meichenbaum and Butler (1982) found that inadequate task performance was mediated by negative self-referent thoughts such as "I am not doing well" and "I will be seen as a failure." The maladaptive nature of this type of thinking is discussed in therapy, using examples from the client's own life. Then, the client is trained in the fundamentals of effective problem solving.

   3. The final phase of treatment involves practicing newly acquired coping skills in the laboratory and in natural situations. Behavioral homework is frequently assigned and graded in terms of difficulty level. The client is treated as a fellow "behavioral scientist" who is setting out to experiment with new ways of thinking and behaving. All stress inoculation interventions are designed to increase the client's sense of personal efficacy and control.

Specific Clinical Applications

Behavioral interventions have been applied to a diverse range of physical problems. Problems that have been most frequently treated using behavioral interventions include hypertension, coronary heart disease, headache, and chronic pain.

Essential Hypertension

Essential hypertension refers to chronically high blood pressure with no discernible organic etiology. Essential hypertension is a potent risk factor for diseases of the heart and blood vessels, which constitute major causes of death in the United States. The major treatment of hypertension is pharmacological. However, although drug treatments have been proven effective in lowering blood pressure on a short-term basis, their long-term effectiveness has been seriously questioned (Appel, Saab, & Holroyd, 1986). Hence, a variety of behavioral interventions have been used with hypertensive patients. Self-control techniques have been used to modify undesirable behavior patterns associated with hypertension. Desirable goals for change include weight reduction, restriction of sodium intake, reduction of alcohol intake and smoking, and increase in exercise (Johnston & Steptoe, 1989).

Furthermore, a large percentage of hypertensive patients do not comply with prescribed medication regimens (Sackett & Snow, 1979). Thus, behavioral techniques such as shaping and contingency contracting have been used to increase medication compliance (Johnston & Steptoe, 1992). Finally, behavioral interventions have been used to directly modify high blood pressure levels. For example, modifications in blood pressure achieved using relaxation training have been found to generalize to the work setting (Southam, Agras, Taylor, & Kraemer, 1982) and to persist in both settings at 15-month follow-up (Agras, Southam, & Taylor, 1983). However, changes in blood pressure resulting from biofeedback have been modest and do not appear to generalize to the home situation (Goldstein, Shapiro, Thanonapam, & Sambhi, 1982). Since biofeedback is more expensive and time consuming than relaxation training, the latter technique is preferred for use with hypertensives.

Unfortunately, behavioral techniques for lowering blood pressure have fared poorly in direct comparisons with pharmacological treatment. A variety of behavioral treatment techniques have been analyzed; none has been proven as effective as drugs in reducing high blood pressure (Andrews, MacMahon, Austin, & Byrne, 1982). Thus, behavioral interventions such as relaxation training are most appropriate for individuals who do not respond to drug treatments, or as adjuncts to pharmacological management (Agras, 1984).

Coronary-Prone Behavior Pattern

The Type A behavioral style has been identified as a risk factor for coronary heart disease (Rosenman, Brand, Jenkins, Friedman, Straus, & Wurm, 1975). For example, individuals with Type A behavioral styles are twice as likely as others to develop coronary heart disease (CHD); Type A individuals are also more likely than others to have multiple coronaries following the initial attack.

Type A behavioral style is typically assessed using a combination of interview and self-report measures. Individuals are placed on a continuum ranging from high Type A to high Type B, the converse of the A style. Type A individuals have been described as competitive and high achieving, with an exaggerated sense of time urgency and easily arousable hostility (Rosenman, 1978). More recently, it has been learned that the link between Type A behavior pattern and heart disease is accounted for by the presence of high levels of anger, hostility, and aggression: "Workaholic" Type A individuals who are low in hostility have a much lower risk of developing CHD than those with high levels of hostility (Matthews, 1988; Smith, 1992).

Frequently, relaxation training has been used to modify the characteristically tense style of Type A individuals. Appel and associates (1986) have emphasized that the rationale for relaxation training must be presented in a way that appeals to the Type A individual. For example, relaxation training could be framed as a technique for maximizing behavioral productivity. Relaxation training has proven more effective than no treatment with Type A individuals (Jenni & Wollersheim, 1979; Suinn & Bloom, 1978). However, the effects of relaxation training on Type A individuals appear to be very complex, influencing some areas of heightened vulnerability to stress but not others (Haaga, Davidson, et al., 1994). Furthermore, multicomponent cognitive-behavioral interventions are superior to relaxation training in the treatment of Type A individuals, perhaps because these interventions target a broad range of coping behaviors (Haaga, 1987). For example, self-defeating behaviors and cognitions, such as the tendency to personalize social interactions and overreact to stress, would be brought to the individual's awareness through cognitive exercises.

Headache

Two major types of headache have been identified: *migraine and tension.* It is important to differentiate them in assessment, due to differences in recommended behavioral treatment techniques. "Classic" *migraine* headaches consist of a severe, pulsing pain that is localized on one side of the head. Classic migraine sufferers commonly report prodromal symptoms prior to the headache, such as visual disturbances, tension, or loss of energy. Migraine headaches are excruciatingly painful and are often accompanied by nausea. They are episodic and may occur as frequently as several times per week. "Common" migraine headaches are very similar, except that the pain begins without warning signs. Also, common migraines may be bilateral or may even affect the entire head region. The immediate cause of migraine is presumed to be dilation of the blood vessels in the cranial region.

Two different biofeedback methods have been used to treat migraine headache. One method (hand warming) involves training migraine patients to increase finger temperature using biofeedback signals. The alternative method involves training the patient to constrict the cranial arteries themselves by lowering extracranial artery pulsations. Although both methods have been effective with migraine sufferers, the cranial pulse treatment has proven superior to hand warming in reducing migraine pain (Blanchard et al., 1980; Elmore & Tursky, 1981).

Tension, or "muscle contraction," headaches involve dull, continuous pain that is often described as feeling like a tight band has been clamped around the head. Electromyographic (EMG) feedback, in which facial muscle tension is reduced, is most effective for tension headache (Haynes, Griffin, Moody, & Parise, 1975; Phillips, 1977). However, relaxation training appears to be as effective as biofeedback in the treatment of both migraine and tension headache (Jessup, 1989). Interestingly, several investigators have suggested that biofeedback has no direct effect on autonomic or sympathetic nervous system activity, but rather, increases patients' perceptions of self-efficacy and control (Fydrich, Rudy, & Turk, 1988). If this is true, it would explain why RT and biofeedback have equivalent effects with headache sufferers, even though no specific muscle group is targeted in RT.

Cognitive-behavioral interventions have proven effective with headache sufferers (Turk, Meichenbaum, & Genest, 1983). Many different factors appear to account for the success of these interventions, including the individual's age, gender, pain beliefs, and coping strategies (Williams & Thorn, 1989; Keefe, Caldwell et al., 1990). In addition, the manner in which CBT interventions are prescribed appears to play a role in treatment effectiveness. For example, one group of chronic headache pain sufferers was told to practice coping strategies for a designated amount of time each day, whereas another group was given vague instructions such as "practice as much as possible" (James, Thorn, & Williams, 1993). Those who received explicit instructions reported less pain intensity and less use of narcotic medication than those who received vague instructions.

Chronic Pain

Millions of Americans suffer from chronic pain, or pain that persists after physical healing should have occurred. Chronic pain is a poorly understood phenomenon that can exist without prior bodily trauma. Unlike acute pain, it does not serve a useful "signaling function" with respect to physical damage (Gotestam & Linton, 1986). Chronic pain may have multiple causes: it is not just a sensory "event" but also a personal construction influenced by prior learning, motivation, the patient's interpretation of the situation, and beliefs about the effects of pain (Melzack & Wall, 1965). Therefore, individualized assessment and treatment is essential.

Behavior therapy techniques are not appropriate for all chronic pain patients. Furthermore, there are many obstacles to the successful use of behavioral techniques with pain patients. For example, pain patients often possess a cognitive set of hopelessness and attribute the pain experience solely to organic factors (Gotestam & Linton, 1986).

Operant techniques have been used successfully in the management of chronic pain. According to operant theorists, behaviors signaling pain may come under the control of reinforcement contingencies such as increased social attention or sympathy. For example, Flor, Breitenstein, Birbaumer, and Furst (1995) found that spouse solicitousness was associated with heightened pain perception in chronic pain patients. Operant treatment of chronic pain involves reinforcing physical activity, gradually reducing reliance on medication, and ensuring that pain behaviors are not rewarded. Assertiveness and social skills training are used to provide patients with constructive ways of meeting their needs for social attention. For example, Gotestam (1983) developed a tridimensional program for the operant treatment of chronic pain. Patients were reinforced for increasing their activity levels and for gradually decreasing their dependence on pain medication. Finally, subjective experience of pain was decreased through a combination of relaxation training and cognitive procedures (Linton & Melin, 1983).

Although positive short-term effects have been reported, there are few controlled outcome studies of the effectiveness of operant interventions with chronic pain patients. Furthermore, once the contingencies have been removed, there is little evidence that positive treatment gains are generalized to different situations or maintained across time (Turk et al., 1992).

The most promising interventions for chronic pain have been cognitive-behavioral in nature (Turk & Rudy, 1989). The central idea is that patients' interpretations of pain sensations can have direct and indirect effects on psychophysiological processes that maintain and exacerbate pain (Turk & Rudy, 1986). For example, in many reports, high levels of self-efficacy have been related to increased tolerance of painful sensations (Turk et al., 1992). CBT techniques involve training pain patients to generate imagery focused on pleasant experiences incompatible with pain. Typically, patients are instructed to relax while vivid descriptions of pleasant fantasies are narrated. The fantasies are carefully constructed so that all sensory modalities are represented. For example, Pearce and Erskine (1989) described the treatment of a 35-year-old woman who suffered from chronic pelvic pain. The patient developed an image of the pain as a serpent that was eating her internal organs. Then she relaxed and engaged in deep breathing while imagining that the oxygen in her lungs was strengthening her white cells. Her final image was that the white cells attacked and vanquished the serpent. The effectiveness of CBT procedures such as these has been demonstrated with a variety of acute and chronic pain conditions (Turk et al., 1992; Jessup, 1989).

Prevention

The most challenging application of behavioral medicine techniques involves prevention of health-related problems. Chronic, life-threatening conditions such as heart disease, cancer, liver disease, dibetes mellitus, pulmonary disease, and AIDS affect large segments of the world population. All of these conditions are at least partly preventable (Oyama & Andrasik, 1992). Typical preventive strategies involve targeting behavior patterns that place people at elevated risk for chronic diseases, rather than attempting to intervene in ways that ameliorate risk. For example, the Stanford Three Community Project (Farquhar, Maccoby, Wood, Alexander, Breium, Brown, Haskell, McAlister, Meyer, Nash, & Stem, 1977) has served as a model of effective community intervention. This program focused on the prevention of cardiovascular disease through modification of high-risk behavior patterns. An intensive educational mass media campaign was launched in one town. The media campaign emphasized the dangers of smoking, obesity, and poor eating habits as risk factors for heart disease; moderate exercise and a low-fat diet were presented as desirable life-style changes. Another town received the same media campaign, but in addition, individuals screened as high risk for heart disease were given intensive individual instruction in behavior modification. A matched "control" town received no intervention.

Mass media efforts were successful in promoting healthful lifestyle changes and increased health-consciousness, even in the absence of face-to-face intervention. As expected, these gains were increased when intensive behavior modification was added to the media campaign. Changes in knowledge, behavior, and physiological "endpoints" improved with a second year of education. Comparable reduction of risk factors was reported in a large Finnish project, the North Karelia Study (Puska et al., 1978). Presently, eight other community intervention projects are being carried out in the United States and worldwide. Community education is not sufficient to stop high-risk behavior patterns in some individuals, but appears to provide a cost-effective starting point.

Chapter Summary

The newest subfield of behavior therapy involves applying behavioral techniques to the management and prevention of physical illnesses. Behavioral techniques such as biofeedback and relaxation training have been used to directly reduce patterns of maladaptive physiological responding, such as excessive muscle tension in headache sufferers. Methods such as self-monitoring, shaping, contingency contracting, and cognitive restructuring have been used to help patients comply with medical recommendations and to reduce maladaptive behavior patterns (such as smoking, drinking to excess, overeating) that place individuals at elevated risk for chronic diseases. Finally, health-related behavior patterns in entire communities have also been targeted for behavioral intervention. Thus, behavioral medicine is a versatile subfield of behavior therapy with great promise for the future.

Epilogue
Conclusions and Prospects

Martin, the client whose panic disorder was described in Chapter 4, took part in a brief, structured program of behavior therapy that illustrates some of its important features and raises some significant questions. Martin was initially offered treatment via graduated real-life practice, clearly a behavioral technique grounded in conditioning theory, but he actually followed a regimen of stress inoculation training and rational emotive behavior therapy, procedures based on cognitive formulations. The outcome of treatment was carefully evaluated by means of a battery of measures in the context of a research study. Martin followed standard treatment protocols, but his therapist took account of some of his unique circumstances in implementing these procedures.

As a Native American adjusting to two cultures at once, Martin found it poignant that his first panic attack occurred when he was crossing the bridge from the reservation to the town. He and his therapist readily acknowledged the importance of the symbolic bridge between Martin's two cultures, and recognized the unease, distress, and discomfort provoked by its demands. If Meichenbaum had presented his *constructive narrative* approach before Martin entered treatment, it seems likely that we would have found it helpful as a treatment focus. Nonetheless, Martin did respond well to treatment, and he found it liberating in more than one sense. He was eventually able to pursue his studies far from home and to make significant contributions to his chosen profession.

Behavior Therapy After 40 Years

As we argued in Chapter 1, behavioral techniques have a long history, but behavior therapy as a professional mental health enterprise began in the late 1950s. In that sense of the term, the first case of behavior therapy presented in this book (H. G. Jones, 1956) was published 40 years ago (as of the time of this writing). We have shown that those 40 years have witnessed rapid development in the concepts, procedures, and applications of behavior therapy.

Initially, innovators such as Joseph Wolpe and Teodoro Ayllon used conditioning and learning principles to design treatments for specific problem behaviors and clinical disorders. Their work was marked not only by conditioning applications but also by scientific validation of their procedures. Behavior therapists soon demonstrated that there was no empirical basis for the concerns of psychoanalysts that clients or patients would develop new symptoms after successful behavior-focused treatment. Behavioral treatment was indeed successful, and in a wide range of applications—more demonstrably so than any prior approach to psychological treatment. As the results of more and more successful behavioral interventions poured in to the established and new professional journals, behavior therapists had to rethink some of their theories. Some new techniques, such as flooding, were effective when the prevailing theories predicted they would fail.

Theorists gradually began to question the adequacy of classical conditioning and two-factor theory in explaining unnecessary anxiety in specific situations, and it became clear that more diffuse disorders such as depression and generalized anxiety deserved greater attention. Studies of operant learning showed that people respond less to the objective contingencies than to the contingencies as perceived by the individual. Advances in assessment allowed clinicians to monitor clients' self-reports, behavioral performances, and physiological responding in structured, objective, psychometrically respectable ways. In the 1970s, procedures aimed at cognitive modification were greeted enthusiastically by clinicians, researchers, and students. Behavior therapy was extended to such problems as distress in intimate relationships, nightmares and obsessional thoughts, and severe medical disorders in children and adults. Theorists debated whether the cognitive dimension of therapeutic processes and procedures is essential to behavior therapy.

In this context, an important direction for future progress is in theory. Clinicians tend to be impressed by new techniques and procedures, but without coherent guiding principles, treatment can easily become a haphazard assortment of interventions, blurring the important theoretical mechanisms at work. Cognitive treatment procedures have been immensely popular, but Peter Lang's bioinformational theory (see Chapters 7 and 8)—a monumental attempt to integrate clinical research findings with validated concepts from cognitive psychology—has attracted relatively little attention. Some behavior therapists go as far as to state that cognitive interventions, while often empirically supported, lack a *theoretical* base, given that clinicians have often ignored the experimental psychology of cognition, *cognitive psychology* (Beidel & Turner, 1986/1995).

Behavioral or Cognitive-Behavioral?

We stated in Chapter 4 that the social learning theory view is that the effective treatment procedures are usually behavioral, while the essential change process is cognitive. Recent empirical findings have challenged this view, in that cognitive procedures have been shown effective in the treatment of depression and panic disorder (although the critic could point to significant behavioral components in Beck's cognitive therapy and in Barlow's panic control therapy). Can we still encompass the varied theories (e.g., two-factor theory, bioinformational theory, self-efficacy theory) and techniques (e.g., systematic desensitization, participant modeling, cognitive therapy, stress inoculation training) by the phrase *behavior therapy?* We think so.

In the last few years, professional interest groups in the United Kingdom and the United States debated whether to change the names of their associations and their journals to reflect the popularity of cognitive concepts and techniques. The results were mixed. In the United States, the *Association for Advancement of Behavior Therapy* and its journal *Behavior Therapy* both retained their original names after a vote of the membership. In the United Kingdom, the British Association for Behavioural Psychotherapy is now the *British Association for Behavioural and Cognitive Psychotherapy,* and its journal Behavioural Psychotherapy is now *Behavioural and Cognitive Psychotherapy.*

Leading clinical theorists who favor cognitive interventions have been divided on changing the names of their therapies to reflect the *behavioral* dimension. Arnold Lazarus originally called his treatment approach multimodal behavior therapy (Lazarus, 1976), but dropped the "behavior" to rename his approach *multimodal therapy* (Lazarus, 1995). By contrast, Albert Ellis's approach, long known as rational-emotive therapy (Ellis & Harper, 1975), is now called *rational emotive behavior therapy* (Ellis, 1995).

A study we cited in Chapter 1 showed that names are important, and that *behavior modification* was often perceived as a negative label (Woolfolk, Woolfolk, & Wilson, 1977). But it is clear that there is no universal consensus on the appropriate name for this field in the late 1990s. Possibly a better name for the field would have been *experimental psychotherapy*, or a similar title, indicating the central importance of its scientific basis. Yet, the phrase *behavior therapy* continues to reflect the historical and conceptual continuity in this major mental health approach, grounded in experimental psychology and committed to logical verification of its concepts, and scientific validation of its procedures.

Theory and Principles or Specific Techniques?

Early behavior therapists such as Monte Shapiro and Joseph Wolpe viewed the enterprise not as a fixed set of procedures but as a flexible clinical approach, focused on the individual client and based on a unique behavioral analysis. There is a recent trend toward validation of empirically supported interventions for particular disorders, somewhat parallel to the endorsement of specific pharmaceutical products for the treatment of given disorders by the Food and Drug Administration in the United States (Crits-Christoff, Frank, Chambless, Brody, & Karp, 1995). There is a potential conflict here between two defensible viewpoints. One is that it is inappropriate and unethical for professionals to offer clients treatments that have not been endorsed as safe and effective by the professions involved, according to appropriate standards of scientific verification. The other is that it is inappropriate and unethical to prescribe a course of treatment to a client purely on the basis of that client having a given disorder, and ignoring elements of his or her personal uniqueness that may have a valid bearing on treatment selection.

Fortunately, the potential conflict here may be addressed by (1) identifying treatments that have been shown effective for clients sharing certain characteristics (such as the disorder they have), (2) assessing the characteristics of each client so as to determine which of the research-validated interventions shows the greatest promise of success, and (3) carefully monitoring therapeutic progress, abandoning interventions that are not working and introducing others as necessary. The catch is that clinicians do not yet have all the data they need to make such decisions in every case. When a client presents a set of issues for which research has not yet identified suitable treatments, the clinician can choose either not to work with the client or to be inventive and use behavioral principles to design a suitable intervention. We prefer the second of these approaches. If behavior therapists such as Isaac Marks (exposure *in vivo*) and Edna Foa (trauma processing) had not experimented with new techniques when confronted by relatively unresearched problems, behavior therapy would not exist.

The Standing of Behavior Therapy

Consistent with its standing as a leading approach, behavior therapy is covered prominently in textbooks on contemporary psychotherapies (e.g. Bongar & Beutler, 1995; Corsini & Wedding, 1995; Gurman & Messer, 1995), in addition to having its own immense professional literature. Behavior therapy's strength partly derives from its scientific grounding and the empirical validation of its procedures, and partly from its humane application of psychological principles to a wide diversity of clients and patients. Among the psychotherapies, behavior therapy has been viewed as particularly congenial to women (Brodsky & Steinberg, 1995), racial/ethnic minority groups (Casas, 1995; Johnson & Thorpe, 1994; Ramirez, 1991), and older clients (Gallagher-Thompson & Thompson, 1995), partly because it avoids value-laden theories of personality and psychopathology. However, there are no grounds for complacency here, and behavior therapists continue to strive for further inclusiveness and diversity among their own ranks and among the clients they serve (Beidel, 1996; Iwamasa, Nangle, & VanLooy-Larrabee, 1995).

We hope to see behavior therapy continue to expand its theoretical, technical, and human horizons in the coming years, its advances helped by professional people from the various mental health disciplines. We also hope that some of you will be among them.

References

Abramson, L. Y., & Alloy, L. B. (1990). Search for the negative cognition subtype of depression. In C. D. McCann & N. Endler (Eds.), *Depression: New directions in theory, research, and practice*. Toronto: Wall & Emerson.

Abramson, L. Y., & Metalsky, G. I. (1995). Hopelessness depression. In G. M. Buchanan & M. E. P. Seligman (Eds.), *Explanatory style*. Hillsdale, NJ: Lawrence Erlbaum.

Abramson, L. Y., Metalsky, G. I., & Alloy, L. B. (1989). Hopelessness: A theory-based subtype of depression. *Psychological Review, 96*, 358–372.

Abramson, L. Y., Seligman, M. E. P., & Teasdale, J. D. (1978). Learned helplessness in humans: Critique and reformulation. *Journal of Abnormal Psychology, 87*, 102–109.

Abruzzese, M. D. (1995). Don't have contempt prior to investigation. *The Behavior Therapist, 18*, 126.

Abueg, F. R., & Fairbank, J. A. (1992). Behavioral treatment of posttraumatic stress disorder and co–occurring substance abuse. In P. A. Saigh (Ed.), *Posttraumatic stress disorder: A behavioral approach to assessment and treatment* (pp. 111–146). New York: Macmillan.

Achenbach, T. M. (1985). *Assessment and taxonomy of child and adolescent psychopathology*. Newbury Park, CA: Sage.

Achenbach, T. M. (1993). Implications of multiaxial empirically based assessment for behavior therapy with children. *Behavior Therapy, 24*, 91–116.

Achenbach, T. M., & Edelbrock, C. S. (1978). The classification of child psychopathology: A review and analysis of empirical efforts. *Psychological Bulletin, 85*, 1275–1031.

Achenbach, T. M., & Edelbrock, C. (1983). *Manual for the child behavior checklist and revised child behavior profile*. Burlington: University of Vermont.

Achenbach, T. M., Howell, C. T., Quay, H. C., & Conners, C. K. (1991). National survey of competencies and problems among 4- to 16-year olds: Parents' reports for normative and clinical samples. *Monographs of the Society for Research in Child Development, 56*, 225.

Adams, P. (1973). *Obsessive children*. New York: Brunner/Mazel.

Agras, W. S. (1984). The behavioral treatment of somatic disorders. In W. D. Gentry (Ed.), *Handbook of behavioral medicine*. New York: Guilford.

Agras, W. S., Leitenberg, H., Barlow, D. H., & Burlington, M. A. (1967). Social reinforcement in the modification of agoraphobia. *Archives of General Psychiatry, 19*, 423–427.

Agras, W. S., Schneider, J. A., Arnow, B., Raeburn, S. D., & Telch, C. F. (1989). Cognitive-behavioral and response-prevention treatments for bulimia-nervosa. *Journal of Consulting and Clinical Psychology, 57*, 215–221.

Agras, W. S., Southam, M. A., & Taylor, C. B. (1983). Long-term persistence of relaxation–induced blood pressure lowering during the working day. *Journal of Consulting and Clinical Psychology, 51,* 792–794.

Alden, L. (1989). Short-term structured treatment for avoidant personality disorder. *Journal of Consulting & Clinical Psychology, 57,* 756–764.

Alexander, J., & Barton, C. (1976). Behavioral systems therapy for families. In D. Olson (Ed.), *Treating relationships.* Lake Mills: Graphic.

Alford, B. A., & Correia, C. J. (1994). Cognitive therapy of schizophrenia: Theory and empirical status. *Behavior Therapy, 25,* 17–33.

Al–Kubaisy, T., Marks, I. M., Logsdail, S., Marks, M. P., Lovell, K., Sungur, M., & Araya, R. (1992). Role of exposure homework in phobia reduction: A controlled study. *Behavior Therapy, 23,* 599–621.

Allsop, S., & Saunders, B. (1989). Relapse: A critique. In M. Gossop (Ed.), *Relapse and addictive behaviors* (pp. 249–277). New York: Tavistock.

Ambrosini, P. J., Metz, C., Prabucki, K., & Lee, J. (1989). Videotape reliability of the third revised edition of the K-SADS. *Journal of the American Academy of Child and Adolescent Psychiatry, 28,* 723–728.

American Association on Mental Retardation. (1992). *Mental retardation: Definition, classification, and systems of supports* (9th ed.). Washington, DC: Author.

American Psychiatric Association. (1952). *Diagnostic and statistical manual of mental disorders.* Washington, DC: Author.

American Psychiatric Association. (1968). *Diagnostic and statistical manual of mental disorders* (2nd ed.). Washington, DC: Author.

American Psychiatric Association. (1980). *Diagnostic and statistical manual of mental disorders* (3rd ed.). Washington, DC: Author.

American Psychiatric Association. (1987). *Diagnostic and statistical manual of mental disorders* (3rd ed., Revised). Washington, DC: Author.

American Psychiatric Association. (1989). *Treatment of psychiatric disorders: A Task Force Report of the American Psychiatric Association.* Washington, D.C.: Author.

American Psychiatric Association. (1994). *Diagnostic and statistical manual of mental disorders* (4th ed.). Washington, DC: Author.

American Psychological Association. (1982). *Ethical principles in the conduct of research with human participants.* Washington, DC: Author.

American Psychological Association. (1992). Ethical principles of psychologists and code of conduct. *American Psychologist, 47,* 1597–1611.

American Psychological Association. (1994). *Publication manual of the American Psychological Association* (4th ed.). Washington, DC: Author.

Anderson, B. F. (1966). *The psychology experiment: An introduction to the scientific method.* Belmont, CA: Wadsworth.

Andrews, G., MacMahon, S. W., Austin, A., & Byrne, D. G. (1982). Hypertension: Comparison of drug and non-drug treatments. *British Medical Journal, 284,* 1523–1526.

Angermeier, W. F. (1994). Operant learning. In V. S. Ramachandran (Ed.), *Encyclopedia of human behavior* (Vol. 3) (pp. 351–366). San Diego, CA: Academic Press.

Annis, H. M., Graham, J. M., & Davis, C. S. (1987). *Inventory of Drinking Situations (IDS). User's guide.* Toronto: Addiction Research Foundation.

Appel, M. A., Saab, P. G., & Holroyd, K. (1986). Cardiovascular disorders. In M. Hersen & A. S. Bellack (Eds.), *Handbook of clinical behavior therapy with adults.* New York: Plenum.

Appleby, I. L., Klein, D. F., Sachar, E. J., & Levitt, M. (1981). Biochemical indices of lactate-induced panic: A preliminary report. In D. F. Klein & K. Rabkin (Eds.), *Anxiety: New research and changing concepts* (pp. 411–423). New York: Raven.

Arlow, J. (1995). Psychoanalysis. In R. J. & D. Wedding (Eds.), *Current psychotherapies* (5th. ed.) (pp. 15–30). Itasca, IL: F. E. Peacock.

Asarnow, J. R., & Carlson, G. A. (1988). Childhood depression: Five year outcome following following combined cognitive-behavior therapy and pharmacotherapy. *American Journal of Psychotherapy, 42,* 456–464.

Asher, S. R. & Renshaw, P. D. (1981). Children without friends: Social knowledge and social skill training. In S. R. Asher & J. M. Gottman (Eds.), *The development of children's friendships.* New York: Cambridge University Press.

Auld, F., & Hyman, M. (1991). *Resolution of inner conflict: An introduction to psychoanalytic therapy.* Washington, DC: American Psychological Association.

Axelrod, S. (1983). Introduction. In S. Axelrod & J. Apsche (Eds.), *The effects of punishment on human behavior* (pp. 1–11). New York: Academic Press

Ayllon, T. (1963). Intensive treatment of psychotic behavior by stimulus satiation and food reinforcement. *Behaviour Research and Therapy, 1,* 53–61.

Ayllon, T., & Azrin, N. H. (1965). The measurement and reinforcement of behavior of psychotics. *Journal of the Experimental Analysis of Behavior, 8,* 357–383.

Ayllon, T., & Azrin, N. H. (1968). *The token economy: A motivational system for therapy and rehabilitation.* New York: Appleton-Century-Crofts.

Ayllon, T., & Haughton, E. (1964). Modification of symptomatic verbal behavior of mental patients. *Behaviour Research and Therapy, 2,* 87–97.

Ayllon, T., Haughton, E., & Hughes, H. B. (1965). Interpretation of symptoms: Fact or fiction? *Behaviour Research and Therapy, 3,* 1–7.

Azrin, N. H., Besalel, V. A., Bechtel, R., Michalicek, A., Mancera, M., Carroll, D., Shuford, D., & Cox, J. (1989). Comparison of reciprocity and discussion-type counseling for marital problems. *American Journal of Family Therapy, 8* (#4), 21–28.

Azrin, N. H., Besalel, V. A., & Wisotzck, I. E. (1982). Treatment of self-injury by a reinforcement plus interruption procedure. *Analysis and Intervention in Developmental Disabilities, 2,* 105–113.

Azrin, N. H., & Foxx, R. M. (1971). A rapid method of toilet training the institutionalized retarded. *Journal of Applied Behavior Analysis, 4,* 89–99.

Azrin, N. H., Sisson, R. W., Meyers, R., & Godley, M. (1982). Alcoholism treatment by disulfiram and community reinforcement therapy. *Journal of Behavior Therapy and Experimental Psychiatry, 13,* 105–112.

Baer, L., Hurley, J. D., Minichiello, W. E., Ott, B. D., Penzel, F., & Ricciardi, J. (1992). EMDR workshop: Disturbing issues? *The Behavior Therapist, 15,* 110–111.

Baker, R., Hall, J. N., & Hutchinson, K. (1974). A token economy project with chronic schizophrenic patients. *British Journal of Psychiatry, 124,* 367–384.

Baker, R., Hall, J. N., Hutchinson, K., & Bridge, G. (1977). Symptom changes in chronic schizophrenic patients on a token economy: A controlled experiment. *British Journal of Psychiatry, 131,* 381–393.

Baker, R. C., & Kirschenbaum, D. S. (1993). Self-monitoring may be necessary for successful weight control. *Behavior Therapy, 24,* 377–394.

Balaguer, A., & Markman, H. (1994). Mate selection. In V. S. Ramachandran (Ed.), *Encyclopedia of human behavior* (Vol. 3, pp. 127–135). San Diego, CA: Academic Press.

Baltes, M. M., & Lascomb, S. L. (1975). Creating a healthy institutional environment for the elderly via behavior management: The nurse as a change agent. *International Journal of Nursing Studies, 12,* 5–12.

Baltes, P. B., & Lindenberger, U. (1988). On the range of cognitive plasticity in old age as a function of experience: 15 years of intervention research. *Behavior Therapy, 19,* 283–300.

Bandura, A. (1965). Influence of models' reinforcement contingencies on the acquisition of imitative responses. *Journal of Personality and Social Psychology, 1,* 589–595.

Bandura, A. (1969). *Principles of behavior modification.* New York: Holt, Rinehart and Winston.

Bandura, A. (1971). Psychotherapy based upon modeling principles. In A. E. Bergin & S. L. Garfield (Eds.), *Handbook of psychotherapy and behavior change* (pp. 653–708). New York: Wiley.

Bandura, A. (1977a). Self-efficacy: Toward a unifying theory of behavior change. *Psychological Review, 84,* 191–215.

Bandura, A. (1977b). *Social learning theory.* Englewood Cliffs, NJ: Prentice-Hall.

Bandura, A. (1986). *Social foundations of thought and action.* Englewood Cliffs, NJ: Prentice-Hall.

Bandura, A. (1994). Self-efficacy. In V. S. Ramachandran (Ed.), *Encyclopedia of human behavior* (Vol. 4, pp. 71–81). San Diego, CA: Academic Press.

Bandura, A. (1995). Exercise of personal and collective efficacy in changing societies. In A. Bandura (Ed.), *Self-efficacy in changing societies* (pp. 1–45). Cambridge: Cambridge University Press.

Bandura, A., & Adams, N. E. (1977). Analysis of self-efficacy theory of behavior change. *Cognitive Therapy and Research, 1,* 287–308.

Bandura, A., Adams, N. E., Hardy, A. B., & Howells, G. N. (1980). Tests of the generality of self-efficacy theory. *Cognitive Therapy and Research, 4,* 39–66.

Bandura, A., Blanchard, E. B., & Ritter, B. (1969). The relative efficacy of desensitization and modeling approaches for inducing behavioral, affective, and attitudinal changes. *Journal of Personality and Social Psychology, 13,* 173–199.

Bardon, J. I., Bennett, V. C., Bruchez, P. K., & Sanderson, R. A. (1976). Psychosituational classroom intervention: Rationale and description. *Journal of School Psychology, 14,* 97–104.

Barkley, R. A. (1981). Hyperactivity. In E. J. Mash & L. G. Terdal (Eds.), *Behavioral assessment of childhood disorders.* New York: Guilford.

Barkley, R. A. (1989). Attention-deficit hyperactivity disorder. In E. J. Mash & R. A. Barkley (Eds.), *Treatment of childhood disorders.* New York: Guilford.

Barkley, R. A. (1990). *Attention-deficit disorder: A handbook for diagnosis and treatment.* New York: Guilford Press.

Barlow, D. H. (1980). Behavior therapy: The next decade. *Behavior Therapy, 11,* 315–328.

Barlow, D. H. (1988). *Anxiety and its disorders: The nature and treatment of panic and anxiety.* New York: Guilford.

Barlow, D. H., Cohen, A. S., Waddell, M. T., Vermilyea, B. B., Klosko, J. S., Blanchard, E. B., & DiNardo, P. A. (1984). Panic and generalized anxiety disorders: Nature and treatment. *Behavior Therapy, 15,* 431–449.

Barlow, D. H., Craske, M. G., Cerny, J. A., & Klosko, J. S. (1989). Behavioral treatment of panic disorder. *Behavior Therapy, 20,* 261–282.

Barlow, D. H., Hayes, S. C., & Nelson, R. O. (1984). *The scientist-practitioner: Research and accountability in clinical and educational settings.* Elmsford, NY: Pergamon Press.

Barlow, D. H., & Hersen, M. (1984). Single-case experimental designs (2nd ed.). New York: Pergamon.

Barlow, D. H., Mavissakalian, M. R., & Schofield, L. D. (1980). Patterns of desynchrony in agoraphobia: A preliminary report. *Behaviour Research and Therapy, 18,* 441–448.

Barlow, D. H., Rapee, R. M., & Brown, T. A. (1992). Behavioral treatment of generalized anxiety disorder. *Behavior Therapy, 23,* 551–570.

Barrios, B. (1988). On the changing nature of behavioral assessment. In A. S. Bellack & M. Hersen (Eds.), *Behavioral assessment* (3rd ed.). New York: Pergamon Press.

Barrios, B. A., & O'Dell, S. L. (1989). Fears and anxieties. In E. J. Mash & R. A. Barkley (Eds.) Treatment of child disorders. (pp. 167–221). New York: Guilford.

Barrowclough, C., Johnston, M., & Tarrier, N. (1994). Attributions, expressed emotion, and patient relapse: An attributional model of relatives' response to schizophrenic illness. *Behavior Therapy, 25,* 67–88.

Basic Behavioral Science Task Force of the National Advisory Mental Health Council (1996). Basic behavioral science research for mental health: Perception, attention, learning, and memory. *American Psychologist, 51,* 133–142.

Baucom, D. H. (1982). A comparison of behavioral contracting and problem-solving/communications training in behavioral marital therapy. *Behavior Therapy, 13,* 162–174.

Baum, M. (1970). Extinction of avoidance responding through response prevention (flooding). *Psychological Bulletin, 74,* 276–284.

Beach, S. R. H., & O'Leary, K. D. (1992). Treating depression in the context of marital discord: Outcome and predictors of response of marital therapy versus cognitive therapy. *Behavior Therapy, 23,* 507–528.

Beach, S. R. H., Sandeen, E. E., & O'Leary, K. D. (1990). *Depression in marriage: A model for etiology and treatment.* New York: Guilford Press.

Beach, S. R. H., Whisman, M. A., & O'Leary, K. D. (1994). Marital therapy for depression: Theoretical foundation, current status, and future directions. *Behavior Therapy, 25,* 345–371.

Beck, A. T. (1967). *Depression: Clinical, experimental, and theoretical aspects.* New York: Harper & Row.

Beck, A. T. (1972). *Depression: Causes and treatment.* Philadelphia: University of Philadelphia Press.

Beck, A. T. (1976). *Cognitive therapy and the emotional disorders.* New York: International Universities Press.

Beck, A. T. (1985). Generalized anxiety disorder and panic disorder. In A. T. Beck, G. Emery, & R. L. Greenberg (Eds.), *Anxiety disorders and phobias: A cognitive perspective* (pp. 82–114). New York: Basic Books.

Beck, A. T. (1995). Cognitive therapy: A 30-year retrospective. In S. O. Lilienfeld (Ed.), *Seeing both sides: Classic controversies in abnormal psychology* (pp. 303–311). Pacific Grove, CA: Brooks/Cole. (Original work published in 1991.)

Beck, A. T., Emery, G., & Greenberg, R. L. (1985). *Anxiety disorders and phobias: A cognitive perspective.* New York: Basic Books.

Beck, A. T., & Freeman, A. (1990). *Cognitive therapy of personality disorders.* New York: Guilford.

Beck, A. T., Kovacs, M., & Weissmann, A. (1975). Hopelessness and judicial behavior: An overview. *Journal of the American Medical Association, 234,* 1146–1149.

Beck, A. T., Laude, R., & Bohnert, M. (1974). Ideational components of anxiety neuroses. *Archives of General Psychiatry, 31,* 319–325.

Beck, A. T., & Rush, A. J. (1977). Cognitive approaches to depression and suicide. In G. Servan (Ed.), *Cognitive defects in development of mental illness* (pp. 234–257). New York: Brunner/Mazel.

Beck, A. T., Rush, A. J., Shaw, B. F., & Emery, G. (1979). *Cognitive therapy of depression.* New York: Guilford.

Beck, A. T., Ward, S. H., Mendelson, M., Mock, J., & Erbaugh, J. (1961). An inventory for measuring depression. *Archives of General Psychiatry, 4,* 561–571.

Beck, A. T., & Weishaar, M. E. (1995). Cognitive therapy. In R. J. Corsini & D. Wedding (Eds.), *Current psychotherapies* (5th ed.) (pp. 229–261). Itasca, IL: F. E. Peacock.

Beck, A. T., Wright, F. D., Newman, C. F., & Liese, B. S. (1993). *Cognitive therapy of substance abuse.* New York: Guilford.

Beck, J. G. (1993). Vaginismus. In W. O'Donohue & J. H. Geer (Eds.), *Handbook of sexual dysfunctions: Assessment and treatment* (pp. 381–397). Boston: Allyn and Bacon.

Beck, J. G., & Zebb, B. J. (1994). Behavioral assessment and treatment of panic disorder: Current status, future directions. *Behavior Therapy, 25,* 581–611.

Beech, H. R., & Vaughan, M. (1978). *Behavioral treatment of obsessional states.* New York: Wiley.

Beere, D. B. (1992). More on EMDR. *The Behavior Therapist, 15,* 179–180.

Beidel, D. C. (1996). Anxiety's cross–cultural and culturally specific nature. *Contemporary Psychology, 41,* 62.

Beidel, D. C., & Turner, S. M. (1995). A critique of the theoretical bases of cognitive-behavioral theories and therapy. In S. O. Lilienfeld (Ed.), *Seeing both sides: Classic controversies in abnormal psychology* (pp. 311–327). Pacific Grove, CA: Brooks/Cole. (Original work published in 1986.)

Beliard, D., Kirschenbaum, D. S., & Fitzgibbon, M. L. (1992). Evaluation of an intensive weight control program using a priori criteria to determine outcome. *International Journal of Obesity, 16,* 505-517.

Bellack, A. S., Hersen, M., & Himmelhoch, J. (1981). Social skills training, pharmacotherapy, and psychotherapy for unipolar depression. *American Journal of Psychiatry, 138,* 1562–1567.

Bellack, A. S., & Morrison, R. L. (1982). Interpersonal dysfunction. In A. S. Bellack, M. Hersen, & A. E. Kazdin (Eds.), *International handbook of behavior modification and therapy* (pp. 717–747). New York: Plenum Press.

Bellack, A. S., & Mueser, K. T. (1994). Schizophrenia. In L. W. Craighead, W. E. Craighead, A. E. Kazdin, & M. J. Mahoney (Eds.), *Cognitive and behavioral interventions: An empirical approach to mental health problems* (pp. 105–122). Boston: Allyn and Bacon.

Bell–Dolan, D. (1995). Separation anxiety disorder. In R. T. Ammerman & M. Hersen (Eds.), *Handbook of child behavior therapy in the psychiatric setting* (pp. 217–238). New York: Wiley.

Bem, S. (1967). Verbal self-control: The establishment of effective self-instruction. *Journal of Experimental Psychology, 74,* 485–491.

Benjamin, S., Marks, I. M., & Huson, J. (1972). Active muscular relaxation in desensitization of phobic patients. *Psychological Medicine, 2,* 381–390.

Bennett, G. A. (1986). Behavior therapy for obesity: A quantitative review of the effects of selected treatment characteristics on outcome. *Behavior Therapy, 17,* 554–562.

Bennun, I. (1987). Behavioral marital therapy: A critique and appraisal of integrated models. *Behavioral Psychotherapy, 15,* 1–15.

Bentall, R. P., Haddock, G., & Slade, P. D. (1994). Cognitive behavior therapy for persistent auditory hallucinations: From theory to therapy. *Behavior Therapy, 25,* 51–66.

Berger, R. M., & Rose, S. D. (1977). Interpersonal skill training with institutionalized elderly patients. *Journal of Gerontology, 32,* 346–353.

Bergin, A. E. (1970). A note on dream changes following desensitization. *Behavior Therapy, 1,* 546–549.

Bernard, M. E., & DiGiuseppe, R. (Eds.). (1989). *Inside rational-emotive therapy: A critical appraisal of the theory and therapy of Albert Ellis.* San Diego, CA: Academic Press.

Bernstein, D. A., & Borkovec, T. (1973). *Progressive relaxation training: A manual for the helping professions.* Champaign, IL: Research Press.

Bernstein, D. A., & Nietzel, M. T. (1974). Behavioral avoidance tests: The effects of demand characteristics and repeated measures on two types of subjects. *Behavior Therapy, 5,* 183–192.

Bernstein, D. A., & Nietzel, M. T. (1977). Demand characteristics in behavior modification: The natural history of a "nuisance." In M. Hersen, R. Eisler, & P. M. Miller (Eds.). *Progress in behavior modification* (Vol. 4) (pp. 119–162). New York: Academic Press.

Bernstein, G. A. & Garfinckel, B. D. (1988). Pedigrees, functioning, and psychopathology in families of school phobic children. *American Journal of Psychiatry, 145,* 70–74.

Best, J. A., Owen, L. E., & Trentadue, L. (1978). Comparison of satiation and rapid smoking in self-managed smoking cessation. *Addictive Disorders, 3,* 71–78.

Bierdman, J., & Steingard, R. (1989). Attention-deficit hyperactivity disorder in adolescents. *Psychiatric Annuals, 19,* 587–596.

Bijou, S. W. (1963). Theory and research in mental (developmental) retardation. *Psychological Record, 13,* 95–110.

Bijou, S. W., & Baer, D. M. (1966). Operant methods in child behavior and development. In W. K. Honig (Ed.), *Operant behavior: Areas of research and application* (pp. 718–789). New York: Appleton-Century-Crofts.

Biran, M., & Wilson, G. T. (1981). Treatment of phobic disorders using cognitive and exposure methods: A self–efficacy analysis. *Journal of Consulting and Clinical Psychology, 49,* 886–899.

Blackburn, I. M., Eunson, K. M., & Bishop, S. (1986). A two-year naturalistic follow-up of depressed patients treated with cognitive therapy, pharmacotherapy and a combination of both. *Journal of Affective Disorders, 10,* 67-75.

Blanchard, E. B. (1981). Behavioral assessment of psychophysiologic disorders. In D. H. Barlow (Ed.), *Behavioral assessment of adult disorders.* New York: Guilford.

Blanchard, E. B., Andrasik, F., Ahles, T. A., Teders, S. J., & O'Keefe, D. (1980). Migraine and tension headache: A meta-analytic review. *Behavior Therapy, 11,* 613–631.

Blanchard, E. B., & Epstein, L. H. (1978). *A biofeedback primer.* Reading, MA: Addison-Wesley.

Blanchard, E. B., Hickling, E. J., Taylor, A. E., Loos, W. R., & Gerardi, R. J. (1994). The psychophysiology of motor vehicle accident related posttraumatic stress disorder. *Behavior Therapy, 25,* 453–467.

Blanchard, E. B., Kolb, L. C., Gerardi, R. J., Ryan, P., & Pallmeyer, T. P. (1986). Cardiac response to relevant stimuli as an adjunctive tool for diagnosing post-traumatic stress disorder in Vietnam veterans. *Behavior Therapy, 17,* 592–606.

Blanes, T., Burgess, M., Marks, I. M., & Gill, M. (1993). Dream anxiety disorders (nightmares): A review. *Behavioural Psychotherapy, 21,* 37–43.

Blechman, E. A. (1980). Family problem-solving training. *American Journal of Family Therapy, 8* (3), 3–21.

Bleuler, E. (1950). *Dementia praecox or the group of schizophrenias.* New York: International Universities Press. (J. Zinkin, Trans.) (Original work published in 1911.)

Block, J., Block, J. H., & Gjerde, P. F. (1988). Parental functioning and the home environment in families of divorce: Prospective and current analyses. *Journal of the American Academy of Child and Adolescent Psychiatry, 27,* 207–213.

Bongar, B. (1991). *The suicidal patient: Clinical and legal standards of care.* Washington, DC: American Psychological Association.

Bongar, B., & Beutler, L. E. (Eds.). (1995) *Comprehensive textbook of psychotherapy: Theory and practice.* New York: Oxford University Press.

Bonvillan, J. D., Nelson, K. E., & Rhyne, J. M. (1981). Sign language and autism. *Journal of Autism and Developmental Disorders, 11,* 125–137.

Borkovec, T. D. (1978). Self-efficacy: Cause or reflection of behavior change? *Advances in Behaviour Research and Therapy, 1,* 163–170.

Borkovec, T. D., & Bauer, R. M. (1982). Experimental design in group outcome research. In A. S.Bellack, M. Hersen, & A. E. Kazdin (Eds.), *International handbook of behavior modification and therapy* (pp. 139–165). New York: Plenum Press.

Borkovec, T., Wilkinson, L., Folensbee, R., & Lerman, C. (1983). Stimulus control applications to the treatment of worry. *Behaviour Research and Therapy, 21,* 247–251.

Boudewyns, P. A., & Shipley, R. H. (1983). *Flooding and implosive therapy: Direct therapeutic exposure in clinical practice.* New York: Plenum.

Boudewyns, P. A., Stwertka, S. A., Hyer, L. A., Albrecht, J. W., & Sperr, E. V. (1993). Eye movement desensitization for PTSD of combat: A treatment outcome pilot study. *The Behavior Therapist, 16,* 29–33.

Boulougouris, J. C., & Marks, I. M., & Marset, P. (1971). Superiority of flooding (implosion) to desensitization for reducing pathological fear. *Behaviour Research and Therapy, 9,* 7–16.

Bowers, W. A. (1990). Treatment of depressed in-patients: Cognitive therapy plus medication, relaxation plus medication, and medication alone. *British Journal of Psychiatry, 156,* 73–78.

Brady, J. P., & Lind, D. L. (1961). Experimental analysis of hysterical blindness. *Archives of General Psychiatry, 4,* 331–339.

Brandon, T. H., Piasecki, T. M., Quinn, E. P., & Baker, T. B. (1994). Cue exposure treatment in nicotine dependence. In D. C. Drummond, S. T. Tiffany, S. Glautier, & B. Remington (Eds.), *Addictive behavior: Cue exposure and practice.* New York: Wiley.

Brantley, J. P., & Bruce, B. K. (1986). Assessment in behavioral medicine. In A. R. Ciminero, K. S. Calhoun, & H. E. Adams (Eds.), *Handbook of behvioral assessment* (pp. 673–721). New York: Wiley.

Brantner, J. P., & Doherty, M. A. (1983). A review of time out: A conceptual and methodological analysis. In S. Axelrod & J. Apsche (Eds.), *The effects of punishment on human behavior* (pp. 87–132). New York: Academic Press.

Braswell, L., & Bloomquist, M. L. (1991). *Cognitive-behavioral therapy with ADHD children.* New York: Guilford Press.

Breuer, J. (1989). Anna O. In P. Gay (Ed.), *The Freud reader* (pp. 61–78). New York: W. W. Norton. (Original work published in 1895.)

Breuer, J., & Freud, S. (1974). Studies on hysteria. In J. & A. Strachey (Eds. and Trans.). *The Pelican Freud Library* (Vol. 3). Harmondsworth, UK: Penguin. (Original work published 1895.)

Brewin, C. R. (1988). *Cognitive foundations of clinical psychology.* London: Lawrence Erlbaum.

Brodsky, A. M., & Steinberg, S. L. (1995). Psychotherapy with women in theory and practice. In B. Bongar & L. E. Beutler (Eds.), *Comprehensive textbook of psychotherapy: Theory and practice* (pp. 295–310). New York: Oxford University Press.

Bromberg, W. (1975). *From shaman to psychotherapist: A history of the treatment of mental illness.* Chicago: Henry Regnery Co.

Brown, P. (1990). The name game: Toward a sociology of diagnosis. In D. Cohen (Ed.), Special issue: Challenging the therapeutic state: Critical perspectives on psychiatry and the mental health system. *The Journal of Mind and Behavior, 11,* (3 and 4), 385–406 (139–160).

Brownell, K. D. (1981). Assessment of eating disorders. In D. H. Barlow (Ed.), *Behavioral assessment of adult disorders.* New York: Guilford.

Brownell, K. D. (1982). The addictive disorders. In C. M. Franks, G. T. Wilson, P. C. Kendall, & K. D. Brownell (Eds.), *Annual review of behavior therapy: Theory and practice* (Vol. 8). New York: Guilford.

Brownell, K. D. (1984). Behavioral, psychological, and environmental predictors of obesity and success at weight reduction. *International Journal of Obesity, 8,* 543–550.

Brownell, K. D. (1991). Dieting and the search for the perfect body: Where physiology and culture collide. *Behavior Therapy, 22,* 1–12.

Brownell, K. D., Hayes, S. C., & Barlow, D. H. (1977). Patterns of appropriate and deviant sexual deviations. *Journal of Consulting and Clinical Psychology, 45,* 1144–1155.

Brownell, K. D., & Jeffery, R. W. (1987). Improving long-term weight loss: Pushing the limits of treatment. *Behavior Therapy, 18,* 353–374.

Brownell, K. D., Marlatt, G. A., Lichtenstein, E., & Wilson, G. T. (1986). Understanding and preventing relapse. *American Psychologist, 41,* 765–782.

Brownell, K. D., & Stunkard, A. J. (1980). Exercise in the development and control of obesity. In A. J. Stunkard (Ed.), *Obesity.* Philadelphia: Saunders.

Brownell, K. D., & Wadden, T. A. (1986). Behavior therapy for obesity: Modern approaches and better results. In K. D. Brownell & J. P. Foreyt (Eds.) *Handbook of eating disorders: Physiology, psychology, and treatment of obesity, anorexia, and bulimia* (pp. 180–197). New York: Basic Books.

Brownell, K. D., & Wadden, T. A. (1991). The heterogeneity of obesity: Fitting treatments to individuals. *Behavior Therapy, 22,* 153–177.

Bryson, S. E., Clark, B. S., & Smith, I. M. (1988). First report of a Canadian epidemiological study of autistic syndromes. *Journal of Child Psychology and Psychiatry, 29,* 433–445.

Burns, L. E. (1977). *An investigation into the additive effects of behavioural techniques in the treatment of agoraphobia.* Unpublished doctoral dissertation, University of Leeds, UK.

Burton, R. (1898). *Burton's Anatomy of melancholy.* London: Chatto & Windus. (Author's final edition but not the last printing. First edition 1621.) (Original work published 1651–1652.)

Cadoret, R. J., Cain, C. A., & Grove, W. M. (1980). Development of alcoholism in adoptees raised apart from alcoholic biologic relatives. *Archives of General Psychiatry, 37,* 561–563.

Campbell, S. B. (1986). Developmental issues. In R. Gittleman (Ed.), *Anxiety disorders in children* (pp. 24–57). New York: Guilford Press.

Campbell, S. B., & Ewing, L. (1990). Follow-up of hard-to-manage preschoolers: Adjustment at age 9 and predictors of continuing symptoms. *Journal of Child Psychology and Psychiatry, 31,* 871–889.

Camper, P. M., Jacobson, N. S., Holtzworth-Munroe, A., & Schmaling, K. B. (1988). Causal attributions for interactional behaviors in married couples. *Cognitive Therapy and Research, 12,* 195–209.

Cantwell, D. P. (1990). Depression across the early lifespan. In M. Lewis & S. M. Miller (Eds.), *Handbook of developmental psychopathology* (pp. 293–309). New York: Plenum.

Cantwell, D. P., Baker, L., & Rutter, M. (1978). Family factors. In M. Rutter & E. Schopler (Eds.), *Autism: A reappraisal of concepts and treatment.* New York: Plenum.

Cantwell, D. P., & Rutter, M. (1995). Classification: Conceptual issues and substantive findings. In M. Rutter, E. Taylor, & L. Hersov (Eds.), *Child and adolescent psychiatry* (pp. 3–21). Oxford: Blackwell.

Carr, E. G., & Lovaas, O. I. (1983). Contingent electric shock as a treatment for severe behavior problems. In S. Axelrod & J. Apsche (Eds.), *The effects of punishment on human behavior* (pp. 221–245). New York: Academic Press.

Carstensen, L. L. (1988). The emerging field of behavioral gerontology. *Behavior Therapy, 19,* 259–281.

Carstensen, L. L., & Fisher, J. E. (in press). Treatment application for psychological and behavioral problems of the elderly in nursing homes. In P. A. Wisocki (Ed.), *Clinical behavior therapy for the elderly client.* New York: Van Nostrand Reinhold.

Casas, J. M. (1995). Counseling and psychotherapy with racial/ethnic minority groups in theory and practice. In B. Bongar & L. E. Beutler (Eds.), *Comprehensive textbook of psychotherapy: Theory and practice* (pp. 311–335). New York: Oxford University Press.

Caspi, A., & Moffitt, T. E. (1995). The continuity of maladaptive behavior: From description to understanding in the study of antisocial behavior. In D. Cichetti et al. (Eds.), *Handbook of development and psychopathology* (pp. 472–511). New York: Wiley.

Cautela, J. R., & Kearney, A. J. (1986). *The covert conditioning handbook.* New York: Springer.

Cautela, J. R., & Mansfield, L. (1977). A behavioral approach to geriatrics. In W. D. Gentry (Ed.), *Geropsychology: A model of training and clinical service* (pp. 21–42). Cambridge, MA: Ballinger.

Cavallaro, L. A. (1987). *Cognitive-behavioral assertiveness training with agoraphobics.* Unpublished doctoral dissertation, University of Maine.

Centers for Disease Control. (1992). Cigarette smoking among adults: United States, 1990. *Morbidity and Mortality Weekly Report, 4(20),* 354–355.

Chadwick, P. D. J., Lowe, C. F., Horne, P. J., & Higson, P. J. (1994). Modifying delusions: The role of empirical testing. *Behavior Therapy, 25,* 35–49.

Chandler, M. (1973). Egocentrism and antisocial behavior: The assessment and training of social perspective–training skills. *Developmental Psychology, 9,* 326–332.

Charlop, M. H., Milstein, J. P., & Moore. (1989). Teaching autistic children conversational speech using video modeling. *Journal of Applied Behavior Analysis, 22,* 275–286.

Cheshire, N. M. (1975). *The nature of psychodynamic interpretation.* London: John Wiley & Sons.

Chiauzzi, E. J. (1991). *Preventing relapse in the addictions.* New York: Pergamon Press.

Christensen, L., & Mendoza, J. L. (1986). A method of assessing change in a single subject: An alteration of the RC index. *Behavior Therapy, 17,* 305–308.

Cicchetti, D. (1989). Developmental psychopathology: Some thoughts on its evolution. *Development and Psychopathology, 1,* 1–4.

Ciminero, A. R., & Drabman, R. S. (1977). Current advances in the behavioral assessment of children. In B. B. Lahey & A. E. Kazdin (Eds.), *Advances in child clinical psychology.* New York: Plenum.

Clark, D. M. (1986). A cognitive approach to panic. *Behaviour Research and Therapy, 24,* 461–470.

Clark, D. M., & Beck, A. T. (1988). Cognitive approaches. In C. Last & M. Hersen (Eds.), *Handbook of anxiety disorders.* New York: Pergamon.

Clark, D. M., Salkovskis, P. M., & Chalkley, A. J. (1985). Respiratory control as a treatment for panic attacks. *Journal of Behavior Therapy and Experimental Psychiatry, 16,* 23–30.

Clark, P., & Rutter, M. (1981). Autistic children's responses to structure and to interpersonal demands. *Journal of Autism and Developmental Disorders, 11,* 201–217.

Clarke, G., Hops, H., Lewinsohn, P. M., Andrews, J., Seeley, J. R., & Williams, J. (1992). Cognitive-behavioral group treatment of adolescent depression: Prediction of outcome. *Behavior Therapy, 23,* 341–354.

Cloninger, C. R., Bohman, M., & Sigvardsson, S. (1981). Inheritance of alcohol abuse: Cross-fostering analysis of adopted men. *Archives of General Psychiatry, 38,* 861–868.

Cobb, J., McDonald, R., Marks, I., & Stern, R. (1980). Marital versus exposure therapy: Psychological treatments of co-existing marital and phobic-obsessive problems. *Behavioral Analyses and Modification, 4,* 3–16.

Cohen, M. S., & Cohen, E. K. (1981). Behavioral family systems intervention in terminal care. In H. J. Sobel (Ed.), *Behavior therapy in terminal care: A humanistic approach.* Cambridge, MA: Ballinger.

Cohen, P., Velez, N., Kohn, M., Schwab-Stone, M., & Johnson, J. (1987). Child psychiatric diagnosis by computer algorithm: Theoretical issues and empirical tests. *Journal of the Amercan Academy of Child and Adolescent Psychiatry, 26,* 631–638.

Cohen, S., Tyrell, D. A., & Smith, A. P. (1991). Psychological stress and susceptibility to the common cold. *New England Journal of Medicine, 325,* 606-612.

Coie, J. D., Belding, M., & Underwood, M. (1987). Aggression and peer rejection in childhood. In B. B. Lahey & A. Kazdin (Eds.), *Advances in clinical child psychology* (Vol. 2, pp. 125-158). New York: Plenum.

Coleman, R. E., & Beck, A. T. (1981). Cognitive therapy for depression. In J. F. Clarkin & H. I. Glazer (Eds.), *Depression: Behavioral and directive intervention strategies.* New York: Garland SPM Press.

Conduct Problems Prevention Research Group. (1992). A developmental and clinical model for the prevention of conduct disorders: The FAST Track program. *Development and Psychopathology, 4,* 509–527.

Cone, J. D. (1979). Confounded comparisons in triple response mode assessment research. *Behavioral Assessment, 1,* 89–95.

Cone, J. D. (1986). Psychometric considerations and the multiple models of behavioral assessment. In A. S. Bellack & M. Hersen (Eds.), *Behavioral assessment: A practical handbook* (3rd ed.) (pp. 42–66). Elmsford, NY: Pergamon Press.

Conger, J. (1951). The effects of alcohol on conflict behavior in the albino rat. *Quarterly Journal of Studies on Alcohol, 12,* 1–29.

Conway, A. V. (1978). Little Hans: Misrepresentation of the evidence? *Bulletin of the British Psychological Society, 31,* 285–287.

Cooper, J. E., Gelder, M. G., & Marks, I. M. (1965). The results of behavior therapy in 77 psychiatric patients. *British Medical Journal, 1,* 1222–1225.

Corrigan, P. W., & Liberman, R. P. (1994). *Behavior therapy in psychiatric hospitals.* New York: Springer.

Corsini, R. J., & Wedding, D. (Eds.). (1995). *Current psychotherapies* (5th ed.) Itasca, IL: F. E. Peacock.

Costello, A. (1991). Structured interviewing in child and adult psychiatry. In M. Lewis (Ed.), *Child and adult psychiatry: A comprehensive textbook* (pp. 47–63). Baltimore: Williams and Wilkins.

Costello, C. G. (1982). Fears and phobias in women: A community study. *Journal of Abnormal Psychology, 91,* 280–286.

Costello, E. J., Edelbrock, C. S., & Costello, A. J. (1985). Validity of the NIMH diagnostic interview schedule for children: A comparison between psychiatric and pediatric referrals. *Journal of Abnormal Child Psychology, 3,* 579–595.

Cote, G., Gauthier, J. G., Laberge, B., Cormier, H. J., & Plamondon, J. (1994). Reduced therapist contact in the cognitive behavioral treatment of panic disorder. *Behavior Therapy, 25,* 123–145.

Craighead, L. W. (1985). A problem-solving approach to the treatment of obesity. In M. Hersen & A. Bellack (Eds.), *Handbook of clinical behavior therapy with adults.* New York: Plenum.

Craighead, L. W., & Agras, W. S. (1991). Mechanisms of action in cognitive-behavioral and pharmacological interventions for obesity and bulimia nervosa. *Journal of Consulting and Clinical Psychology, 59,* 115-125.

Craighead, L. W., Craighead, W. E., Kazdin, A. E., & Mahoney, M. J. (1994). *Cognitive and behavioral interventions: An empirical approach to mental health problems.* Boston: Allyn and Bacon.

Craighead, L. W., Stunkard, A. J., & O'Brien, R. (1981). Behavior therapy and pharmacotherapy of obesity. *Archives of General Psychiatry, 38,* 763–768.

Crits-Christoff, P., Frank, E., Chambless, D. L., Brody, C., & Karp, J. F. (1995). Training in empirically validated treatments: What are clinical psychology students learning? *Professional Psychology: Research and Practice, 26,* 514–522.

Crowe, M. J. (1978). Conjoint marital therapy: A controlled outcome study. *Psychological Medicine, 9,* 623–636.

Curran, J. P. (1981). Social-skills and assertion training. In W. E. Craighead, A. E. Kazdin, & M. J. Mahoney (Eds.), *Behavior modification: Principles, issues, and applications* (2nd ed.) (pp. 243–263). Boston: Houghton Mifflin.

Curran, J. P., Monti, P. M., & Corriveau, D. P. (1982). Treatment of schizophrenia. In A. S. Bellack, M. Hersen, & A. E. Kazdin (Eds.), *International handbook of behavior modification and therapy* (pp. 433–466). New York: Plenum.

Curry, S., Wagner, E. H., & Grothaus, L. C. (1990). Intrinsic and extrinsic motivation for smoking cessation. *Journal of Consulting and Clinical Psychology, 58,* 310–316.

D'Amato, M. R. (1970). *Experimental psychology.* New York: McGraw-Hill.

Dattilio, F. M., & Padesky, C. A. (1990). *Cognitive therapy with couples.* Sarasota, FL: Professional Resource Exchange.

Davidson, R. J. (1992). Emotion and affective style: Hemispheric substrates. *Psychological Science, 3,* 39–43.

Davis, D. D., & Peterson, L. (1994). Cognitive and behavioral practice. *Cognitive and Behavioral Practice, 1,* 1–4.

Davison, G. C. (1968a). Systematic desensitization as a counter-conditioning process. *Journal of Abnormal Psychology, 73,* 91–99.

Davison, G. C. (1968b). The elimination of a sadistic fantasy by a client-controlled counter-conditioning technique: A case study. *Journal of Abnormal Psychology, 73,* 84–90.

Davison, G. C. (1969). Appraisal of behavior modification techniques with adults in institutional settings. In C. M. Franks (Ed.), *Behavior therapy: Appraisal and status* (pp. 220–278). New York: McGraw-Hill.

Davison, G. C., & Neale, J. M. (1990). *Abnormal psychology* (5th ed.). New York: John Wiley & Sons.

DeAngelis, T. (1995). New threat associated with child abuse. *The APA Monitor, 26* (4), 1, 38.

Deffenbacher, J. L., & Suinn, R. M. (1987). Generalized anxiety syndrome. In L. Michelson & L. M. Ascher (Eds.), *Anxiety and stress disorders: Cognitive–behavioral assessment and treatment* (pp. 332–360). New York: Guilford.

DiClemente, C. C., Prochaska, J. O., Fairhurst, S. K., Velicer, W. F., Valesquez, M. M., & Rossi, J. S. (1991). The processes of smoking cessation: An analysis of precontemplation, contemplation, and prepartation stages of change. *Journal of Consulting and Clinical Psychology, 59,* 295-304.

Dimeff, L. A., & Marlatt, G. A. (1995). Relapse prevention. In R. K. Hester & W. R. Miller (Eds.) *Handbook of alcoholism treatment approaches* (2nd ed.) (pp. 176–194). Boston: Allyn and Bacon.

Di Nardo, P. A., & Barlow, D. H. (1988). *Anxiety disorders interview schedule—Revised.* Albany: State University of New York at Albany, Phobia and Anxiety Disorders Clinic.

Di Nardo, P. A., & Di Nardo, P. G. (1981). Self-control desensitization in the treatment of a childhood phobia. *The Behavior Therapist, 4,* 15–16.

Dishman, R. K. (1991). Increasing and maintaining exercise and physical activity. *Behavior Therapy, 22,* 345–378.

Dix, T. (1991). The affective organization of parenting: Adaptive and maladaptive processes. *Psychological Bulletin, 110,* 3-25.

Dobson, K. S. (1989). A meta-analysis of the efficacy of cognitive therapy for depression. *Journal of Consulting and Clinical Psychology, 57,* 414–419.

Dobson, K. S., & Shaw, B. F. (1986). Cognitive assessment with major depressive disorders. *Cognitive Therapy and Research 10,* 13–29.

Dobson, K. S., & Shaw, B. F. (1995). Cognitive therapies in practice. In B. Bongar & L. E. Beutler (Eds.), *Comprehensive textbook of psychotherapy: Theory and practice* (pp. 159–172). New York: Oxford University Press.

Dodge, K. A. (1993). Social-cognitive mechanisms in the development of conduct disorder and depression. *Annual Review of Psychology, 44,* 559–584.

Dodge, K. A. (1989). Problems in social relationships. In E. J. Mash & R. A. Barkley (Eds.), *Treatment of childhood disorders.* New York: Guilford.

Dodge, K. A. & Somberg, D. R. (1987). Hostile attributional biases among aggressive boys are exacerbated under conditions of threats to self. *Child Development, 58,* 213–224.

Donovan, D. M., & Cheney, E. F. (1985). Alcoholic relapse prevention: Models and methods. In G. A. Marlatt & J. R. Gordon (Eds.), *Relapse prevention* (pp. 351–416). New York: Guilford.

Dow, M. G. (1994). Social inadequacy and social skill. In L. W. Craighead, W. E. Craighead, A. E. Kazdin, & M. J. Mahoney (Eds.), *Cognitive and behavioral interventions: An empirical approach to mental health problems* (pp. 123–140). Boston: Allyn and Bacon.

Drummond, D. C., Tiffany, S. T., Glautier, S., & Remington, B. (1995). Cue exposure in understanding and treating addictive behaviors In D. C. Drummond, S. T. Tiffany, S. Glautier, & B. Remington (Eds.), *Addictive behavior: Cue exposure and practice.* (pp. 1–20). New York: Wiley.

Dunlap, K. (1932). *Habits: Their making and unmaking.* New York: Liveright.

Durlak, J. A., Furhman, T., & Lampman, C. (1991). Effectiveness of cognitive-behavioral therapy for maladapting children: A meta-analysis. *Psychological Bulletin, 110,* 204–214.

D'Zurilla, T. J., & Goldfried, M. R. (1971). Problem-solving and behavior modification. *Journal of Abnormal Psychology, 78,* 107–026.

Eccles, A., Wilde, A., & Marshall, W. L. (1988). *In vivo* desensitization in the treatment of recurrent nightmares. *Journal of Behavior Therapy and Experimental Psychiatry, 19,* 285–288.

Echeburua, E., Corral, P., Garcia Bajos, E., & Borda, M. (1993). Interactions between self-exposure and alprazolam in the treatment of agoraphobia without current panic: An exploratory study. *Behavioural and Cognitive Psychotherapy, 21,* 219–238.

Ecker, W., & Engelkamp, J. (1995). Memory for actions in obsessive-compulsive disorder. *Behavioural and Cognitive Psychotherapy, 23,* 349–371.

Edelbrock, C., & Costello, A. J. (1988). Structured psychiatric interviews for children. In M. Rutter, A. H. Tuma, & I. S. Lann (Eds.), *Assessment and diagnosis in child psychopathology* (pp. 87–112). New York: Guilford.

Edwards, G., Orford, J., Egert, S., Guthrie, S., Hawker, A., Hensman, C., Mitchelson, M., Oppenheimer, E., & Taylor, C. (1977). Alcoholism: A controlled trial of "treatment" and "advice." *Journal of Studies on Alcohol, 38,* 1004–1031.

Egan, G. (1982). *The skilled helper.* Monterey, CA: Brooks/Cole.

Elkin, I., Shea, M. T., Watkins, J. T., Imber, S. D., Sotsky, S. M., Collins, J. F., Glass, D., Pilkonis, P. A., Leber, W. R., Docherty, J. P., Fiester, S. J., & Parloff, M. B. (1989). National Institute of Mental Health treatment of depression collaborative research program: General effectiveness of treatment. *Archives of General Psychiatry, 46,* 971–982.

Ellis, A. (1962). *Reason and emotion in psychotherapy.* New York: Lyle Stuart.

Ellis, A. (1979). A note on the treatment of agoraphobics with cognitive modification versus prolonged exposure in vivo. *Behaviour Research and Therapy, 17,* 162–164.

Ellis, A. (1988). *How to stubbornly refuse to make yourself miserable about anything—Yes, anything!* Secaucus, NJ: Lyle Stuart.

Ellis, A. (1995). Rational emotive behavior therapy. In R. J. Corsini & D. Wedding (Eds.), *Current psychotherapies* (5th ed.) (pp. 162–196). Itasca, IL: F. E. Peacock.

Ellis, A., & Harper, R. A. (1975). *A new guide to rational living.* No. Hollywood, CA: Wilshire.

Elmore, A. M., & Tursky, B. C. (1981). A comparison of two psychophysiological approaches to the treatment of migraine. *Heachache, 21,* 93–101.

Emmelkamp, P. M. G. (1974). Self-observation versus flooding in the treatment of agoraphobia. *Behaviour Research and Therapy, 12,* 229–237.

Emmelkamp, P. M. G. (1979). The behavioral study of clinical phobias. In M. Hersen, R. Eisler, & P. M. Miller (Eds.), *Progress in behavior modification* (Vol. 8, pp. 55–125). New York: Academic Press.

Emmelkamp, P. M. G., & Bouman, T. K. (1991). Psychological approaches to the difficult patient. In J. R. Walker, G. R. Norton, & C. A. Ross (Eds.), *Panic disorder and agoraphobia: A comprehensive guide for the practitioner* (pp. 398–429). Pacific Grove, CA: Brooks/Cole.

Emmelkamp, P. M. G., & Gerlsma, C. (1994). Marital functioning and the anxiety disorders. *Behavior Therapy, 25,* 407–429.

Emmelkamp, P. M. G., & Giesselbach, P. (1981). Treatment of obsessions: Relevant versus irrelevant exposure. *Behavioural Psychotherapy, 9,* 322–329.

Emmelkamp, P. M. G., Kuipers, A. C., & Eggeraat, J. B. (1978). Cognitive modification versus prolonged exposure in vivo: A comparison with agoraphobics as subjects. *Behaviour Research and Therapy, 16,* 33–41.

Emmelkamp, P. M. G., Mersch, P. P., & Vissia, E. (1985). The external validity of analogue outcome research: Evaluation of cognitive and behavioral interventions. *Behaviour Research and Therapy, 23,* 83–86.

Emmelkamp, P. M. G., Mersch, P. P., Vissia, E., & van der Helm, M. (1985). Social phobia: A comparative evaluation of cognitive and behavioral interventions. *Behaviour Research and Therapy, 23,* 365–369.

Emmelkamp, P. M. G., & Ultee, K. A. (1974). A comparison of "successive approximation" and "self-observation" in the treatment of agoraphobia. *Behavior Therapy, 5,* 605–613.

Emmelkamp, P. M. G., van der Helm, M., VanZanten, B., & Plochg, I. (1980). Contributions of self-instructional training to the effectiveness of exposure, comparison with obsessive-compulsive patients. *Behaviour Research and Therapy, 18,* 61–66.

Emmelkamp, P. M. G., & Wessels, H. (1975). Flooding in imagination versus flooding in vivo: A comparison with agoraphobics. *Behaviour Research and Therapy, 13,* 7–15.

Endicott, J., & Spitzer, R. L. (1978). A diagnostic interview—The schedule for affective disorders and schizophrenia. *Archives of General Psychiatry, 35,* 837–844.

Epstein, N., Evans, L., & Evans, J. (1994). Marriage. In V. S. Ramachandran (Ed.), *Encyclopedia of human behavior* (Vol. 3, pp. 115–125). San Diego, CA: Academic Press.

Erwin, E. (1978). *Behavior therapy: Scientific, philosophical, and moral foundations.* Cambridge: Cambridge University Press.

Estes, W. K., & Skinner, B. F. (1941). Some quantitative properties of anxiety. *Journal of Experimental Psychology, 29,* 390–400. Reprinted in Catania, A. C. (Ed.). (1968). *Contemporary research in operant behavior* (pp. 244–250). Glenview, IL: Scott, Foresman.

Evans, I. M., & Nelson, R. O. (1977). Assessment of child behavior problems. In A. R. Ciminero, K. S. Eyberg, & H. E. Adams (Eds.). *Handbook of behavioral assessment.* New York: Wiley.

Evans, I. M., & Robinson, C. H. (1978). Behavior therapy observed: The diary of a client. *Cognitive Therapy and Research, 2,* 335–355.

Evans, P. D., & Kellam, A. M. P. (1973). Semi-automated desensitization: A controlled clinical trial. *Behaviour Research and Therapy, 11,* 641–646.

Everaerd, W. (1977). Comparative studies of short-term treatment methods for sexual inadequacies. In R. Emme & C. C. Wheeler (Eds.), *Progress in sexology.* New York: Plenum.

Everaerd, W. (1993). Male erectile disorder. In W. O'Donohue & J. H. Geer (Eds.), *Handbook of sexual dysfunctions: Assessment and treatment* (pp. 201–224). Boston: Allyn and Bacon.

Everaerd, W. T., Rijken, C. C., & Emmelkamp, P. M. G. (1973). A comparison of "flooding" and "successive approximation" in the treatment of agoraphobia. *Behaviour Research and Therapy, 11,* 105–117.

Eysenck, H. J. (1952). The effects of psychotherapy: An evaluation. *Journal of Consulting Psychology, 16,* 319–324.

Eysenck, H. J. (1961). The effect of psychotherapy. In H. J. Eysenck (Eds.), *Handbook of abnormal psychology: An experimental approach.* New York: Basic Books.

Eysenck, H. J. (Ed.). (1964). *Experiments in behavior therapy.* New York: Pergamon.

Eysenck, H. J. (1966). Personality and experimental psychology. *Bulletin of the British Psychological Society, 19* 62, (1–28).

Eysenck, H. J. (1978). Expectations as causal elements in behavioral change. *Advances in Behaviour Research and Therapy, 1,* 171–175.

Eysenck, H. J. (1984). Is behavior therapy on course? *Behavioural Psychotherapy, 12,* 2–6.

Eysenck, H. J., & Rachman, S. (1965). *The causes and cures of neurosis.* London: Routledge and Kegan Paul.

Fagerstrom, K. O., & Melin, B. (1985). Nicotine chewing gum in smoking cessation: Efficiency, nicotine dependence, therapy duration, and clinical recomendations. In J. Grabowski & S. M. Hall (Eds.), *Pharmacological adjuncts in smoking cessation.* Washington, DC: U.S. Government Printing Office.

Fairbank, J. A., & Brown, T. A. (1987). Current behavioral approaches to the treatment of posttraumatic stress disorder. *The Behavior Therapist, 10,* 57–64.

Fairbank, J. A., & Keane, T. M. (1982). Flooding for combat-related stress disorders: Assessment of anxiety-reduction across traumatic memories. *Behavior Therapy, 13,* 499–510.

Fairburn, C. G. (1983). The place of a cognitive behavioral approach in the management of bulimia. In P. L. Darby, P. E. Garfinkel, D. M. Garner, & D. V. Coscina (Eds.), *Anorexia nervosa: Recent developments in research.* New York: Alan R. Liss.

Fairburn, C. G. & Cooper, Z. (1993). The eating disorder examination (12th ed.). In C. G. Fairburn & G. T. Wilson (Eds.), *Binge eating: Nature, assessment, and treatment* (pp. 317–360). New York: Guilford.

Fairburn, C. G., Cooper, Z., & Cooper, P. J. (1986). The clinical features and maintenance of bulimia nervosa. In K. D. Brownell & J. P. Foreyt (Eds.), *Handbook of eating disorders.* New York: Basic Books.

Fairburn, C. G., & Wilson, G. T. (1993). *Binge eating: Nature, assessment, and treatment.* New York: Guilford Press.

Fairweather, G. W. (1964). *Social psychology in treating mental illness: Experimental approach.* New York: Wiley.

Fairweather, G. W., & Fergus, E. O. (1993). *Empowering the mentally ill.* Austin, TX: Fairweather.

Fairweather, G. W., Sanders, D. H., Cressler, D. L., & Maynard, H. (1969). *Community life for the mentally ill: An alternative to institutional care.* Chicago: Aldine.

Farberow, N. L. (1981). Assessment of suicide. In P. McReynolds (Ed.), *Advances in psychological assessment* (pp. 124–190). San Francisco: Jossey-Bass.

Farrell, A. D. (1993). Behavioral assessment with adults. In R. T. Ammerman & M. Hersen (Eds.), *Handbook of behavior therapy with children and adults.* Boston: Allyn and Bacon.

Farrell, B. A. (1981). *The standing of psychoanalysis.* Oxford: Oxford University Press.

Farrington, D. P., Loeber, R., & VanKammen, W. B. (1990). Long-term criminal outcomes of hyperactivity-impulsivity-attention-deficit and conduct problems in childhood. In L. Robins & M. Rutter (Eds.), *Straight and devious pathways from childhood to adulthood* (pp. 62–81). Cambridge, England: Cambridge University Press.

Favell, J. E. (Chairperson). (1982). Task Force Report: The treatment of self-injurious behavior. *Behavior Therapy, 13,* 529–554.

Feldman, M. P., & Peay, J. (1982). Ethical and legal issues. In A. S. Bellack, M. Hersen, & A. E. Kazdin (Eds.), *International handbook of behavior modification and therapy* (pp. 231–261). New York: Plenum Press.

Ferster, C. B., & Skinner, B. F. (1957). *Schedules of reinforcement.* New York: Appleton-Century-Crofts.

Feske, U., & Chambless, D. L. (1995). Cognitive behavioral versus exposure only treatment for social phobia: A meta-analysis. *Behavior Therapy, 26,* 695–720.

Finch, A. J., & Rogers, T. R. (1984). Self-report instruments. In T. H. Ollendick & M. Hersen (Eds.), *Child behavioral assessment.* (pp. 106–123). New York: Pergamon

Fiore, M. C., Novotny, T. E., Pierce, J. P., Giovino, G. A., Hatziandreu, E. J., Newcomb, P. A., Surawitz, T. S., & Davis, R. M. (1989). Trends in cigarette smoking in the United States: The changing influence of gender and race. *Journal of the American Medical Association, 261,* 49–55.

Firestar, M. (1993). Co-optation is beside the point. *Resources: Workforce issues in mental health systems, 5,* 15.

First, M. B., Frances, A., & Widiger, T. A. (1992). DSM-IV and behavioral assessment. *Behavioral Assessment, 14,* 297–306.

Fish, J. M. (1992). EMDR workshop and openness. *The Behavior Therapist, 15,* 180.

Fisher, K. J., Glasgow, R. E., & Terborg, J. R. (1990). Work site smoking cessation: A metaanalysis of long-term quit rates from controlled studies. *Journal of Occupational Medicine, 32* (5), 429–439.

Fitzgibbon, M. L., & Kirschenbaum, D. S. (1990). Heterogeneity of clinical presentation among obese individuals seeking treatment. *Addictive Behaviors, 15,* 291–295.

Flament, M. F., Koby, E., Rapoport, J. L., Berg, C. J., Zahn, T., Cox, C., Denckla, M., & Lenane, M. (1990). Childhood obsessive-compulsive disorder: A prospective follow-up study. *Journal of Child Psychology and Psychiatry, 31,* 363–380.

Flament, M. F., Whitaker, A., Rapoport, J. L., Davies, M., Berg, C. Z., Kilikow, K., Sceery, W., & Schaffer, D. (1988). Obsessive-compulsive disorder in adolescence: An epidemiological study. *Journal of the American Academy of child and Adolescent Psychiatry, 27,* 764–771.

Flor, H., Breitenstein, C., Birbaumer, N., & Furst, M. (1995). A psychophysiological analysis of spouse solicitousness towards pain behaviors, spouse interaction, and pain perception. *Behavior Therapy, 26,* 255–272.

Foa, E. B., & Kozak, M. J. (1986). Emotional processing of fear: Exposure to corrective information. *Psychological Bulletin, 99,* 20–35.

Foa, E. B., Riggs, D. S., Massie, E. D., & Yarczower, M. (1995). The impact of fear activation and anger on the efficacy of exposure treatment for posttraumatic stress disorder. *Behavior Therapy, 26,* 487–499.

Foa, E. B., Steketee, G., & Rothbaum, B. O. (1989). Behavioral/cognitive conceptualizations of post-traumatic stress disorder. *Behavior Therapy, 20,* 155–176.

Forehand, R., & Long, N. (1988). Outpatient treatment of the acting-out child: Procedures, long-term follow-up data, and clinical problems. *Journal of Consulting and Clinical Psychology, 49,* 342–351.

Forehand, R. L., & McMahon, R. J. (1981). *Helping the noncompliant child: A clinician's guide to parent training.* New York: Guilford Press.

Foster, S. L., Bell-Dolan, D. J., & Burge, D. A. (1988). Behavioral observation. In A. S. Bellack & M. Hersen (Eds.), *Behavioral assessment: A practical handbook* (pp. 119–160). Elmsford, NY: Pergamon Press.

Foxx, R. M., & Azrin, N. H. (1972). Restitution: A method of eliminating aggressive-disruptive behavior of retarded and brain-damaged patients. *Behaviour Research and Therapy, 10,* 15– 27.

Foxx, R. M., & Azrin, N. H. (1973). The elimination of autistic self–stimulatory behavior by overcorrection. *Journal of Applied Behavior Analysis, 6,* 1–14.

Foxx, R. M., & Bechtel, D. R. (1983). Overcorrection: A review and analysis. In S. Axelrod & J. Apsche (Eds.), *The effects of punishment on human behavior* (pp. 133–200). New York: Academic Press.

Foy, D. W., Donahoe, C. P., Carroll, E. M., Gallers, J., & Reno, R. (1987). Posttraumatic stress disorder. In L. Michelson & L. M. Ascher (Eds.), *Anxiety and stress disorders: Cognitive-behavioral assessment and treatment* (pp. 361–378). New York: Guilford.

Foy, D. W., Osato, S. S., Houskamp, B. M., & Neumann, D. A. (1992). Etiology of posttraumatic stress disorder. In P. A. Saigh (Ed.), *Posttraumatic stress disorder: A behavioral approach to assessment and treatment* (pp. 28–49). New York: MacMillan.

Foy, D. W., Resnick, H. S., Sipprelle, R. C., & Carroll, E. M. (1987). Premilitary, military, and postmilitary factors in the development of combat-related posttraumatic stress disorder. *The Behavior Therapist, 10* (1), 3–9.

Frame, C. L., Matson, J. L., Sonis, W. A., Fialkov, M. J., & Kazdin, A. E. (1982). Behavioral treatment of depression in a prepubertal child. *Journal of Behavior Therapy and Experimental Psychiatry, 13,* 239–243.

Frame, C. L., Robinson, S. L., & Cuddy, E. (1992). Behavioral treatment of childhood depression. In S. Turner, K. S. Calhoun, & H. E. Adams (Eds.), *Handbook of clinical behavioral therapy.* New York: Wiley.

Francis, G. (1995). Obsessive-compulsive disorder. In R. T. Ammerman & M. Hersen (Eds.), *Handbook of child behavior therapy in the psychiatric setting* (pp. 253–268). New York: Wiley.

Frank, E., Anderson, B., Stewart, B. D., Dancu, C., Hughes, C., & West, D. (1988). Efficacy of cognitive behavior therapy and systematic desensitization in the treatment of rape trauma. *Behavior Therapy, 19,* 403–420.

Frank, E., Kupfer, D. J., Wagner, E. F., McEachran, A. B., & Cornes, C. L. (1991). Efficacy of interpersonal psychotherapy as a maintenance treatment of recurrent depression: Contributing factors. *Archives of General Psychiatry, 48,* 1053–1059.

Franks, C. M. (1969). Introduction: Behavior therapy and its Pavlovian origins: Review and Perspectives. In C. M. Franks (Ed.), *Behavior therapy: Appraisal and status.* New York: McGraw–Hill.

Franks, C. M. (Ed.). (1969). *Behavior therapy: Appraisal and status.* New York: McGraw-Hill.

Franks, C. M. (Ed.). (1985). Foreword. In N. H. Hadley (Ed.), *Foundations of aversion therapy.* New York: Spectrum.

Franks, C. M. (1987). Behavior therapy with children and adolescents. In G. T. Wilson, C. M. Franks, P. C. Kendall, & J. P. Foreyt (Eds.), *Review of behavior therapy: Theory and practice* (Vol. 11, pp. 234–287). New York: Guilford.

Franks, C. M., & Wilson, G. T. (Eds.). (1975). *Annual review of behavior therapy: Theory and practice* (Vol. 3). New York: Brunner/Mazel.

Franks, C. M., & Wilson, G. T. (1978). Recent developments in behavioral assessment. In C. M. Franks & G. T. Wilson (Eds.), *Annual review of behavior therapy: Theory and practice* (Vol. 6). New York: Brunner/Mazel.

Freeman, A., Pretzer, J., Fleming, B., & Simon, K. (1990). *Clinical applications of cognitive therapy.* New York: Plenum Press.

Freeman, A., & Reineke, M. A. (1993). *Cognitive therapy of suicidal behavior.* New York: Springer.

Freeman, A., & Reinecke, M. A. (1995). Cognitive therapy. In A. S. Gurman & S. B. Messer (Eds.), *Essential psychotherapies: Theory and practice* (pp. 182–225). New York: Guilford.

Freud, S. (1955). Analysis of a phobia in a five-year-old boy. In J. Strachey (Ed. and Trans.), *The standard edition of the complete psychological works of Sigmund Freud* (Vol. 10, pp. 5–149). London: Hogarth Press. (Original work published 1909).

Freund, B., Steketee, G. S., & Foa, E. B. (1987). Compulsive activity checklist (CAC): Psychometric analysis with obsessive-compulsive disorder. *Behavioral Assessment, 9,* 67–79.

Friedman, J. M., & Chernen, L. (1987). Sexual dysfunction. In L. Michelson & L. M. Ascher (Eds.), *Anxiety and stress disorders: Cognitive-behavioral assessment and treatment* (pp. 442–464). New York: Guilford.

Friedman, J. M., Weiler, S. J., LoPiccolo, J., & Hogan, D. R. (1982). Sexual dysfunctions and their treatment. In A. S. Bellack, M. Hersen, & A. E. Kazdin (Eds.), *International handbook of behavior modification and therapy* (pp. 653–682). New York: Plenum.

Friedman, M. A. & Brownell, K. D. (1995). Psychological correlates of obesity: moving to the next generation. *Psychological Bulletin, 117,* 3–20.

Fuchs, C. Z., & Rehm, L. P. (1977). A self-control behavior therapy program for depression. *Journal of Consulting and Clinical Psychology, 45,* 206–215.

Fuller, R. K. (1995). Antidipsotropic medications. In R. K. Hester & W. R. Miller (Eds.), *Handbook of alcoholism treatment approaches* (2nd ed.) (pp. 123–133). Boston: Allyn and Bacon.

Fuller, R. K., Branchey, L., Brightwell, D. R., Dermon, R. M., Emrick, C. D., Iber, F. L., James, K. E., Lacoursieve, R. B., Lee, K. K., Lowenstam, I., Maany, I., Neiderheiser, D., Nocks, J. J., & Shaw, S. C. (1986). Disulfiram treatment of alcoholism: A Veterans Administration cooperative study. *Journal of Nervous and Mental Diseases, 256,* 1149–1455.

Gallagher-Thompson, D., & Thompson, L. W. (1995). Psychotherapy with older adults in theory and practice. In B. Bongar & L. E. Beutler (Eds.), *Comprehensive textbook of psychotherapy: Theory and practice* (pp. 359–379). New York: Oxford University Press.

Garfinkel, P. E., & Garner, D. M. (1982). *Anorexia nervosa: A multidimensional perspective.* New York: Brunner/Mazel.

Garfinkel, P. E., Kline, S. A., & Stancer, H. C. (1973). Treatment of anorexia nervosa using operant conditioning techniques. *Journal of Nervous & Mental Disease, 157,* 428–433.

Garner, D. M. (1991). *Eating Disorder Inventory-2: Professional manual.* Odessa, FL: Psychological Assessment Resources.

Garner, D. M. (1994). Bulimia nervosa. In C. G. Last & M. Hersen (Eds.), *Adult behavior therapy casebook.* New York: Plenum Press.

Garner, D. M., & Bemis, K. M. (1982). A cognitive-behavioral approach to anorexia nervosa. *Cognitive Therapy and Research, 6,* 123–150.

Garner, D. M., Rockert, W., Olmsted, M., Johnson, C., & Coscina, D. (1985). Psychoeducational principles in the treatment of anorexia and bulimia. In D. M. Garner & P. Garfinkel (Eds.), *Handbook of psychotherapy for anorexia and bulimia.* New York: Guilford Press.

Geer, J. H., & Silverman, I. (1967). Treatment of a recurrent nightmare by behavior modification procedures. *Journal of Abnormal Psychology, 72,* 188–190.

Gelder, M. G., Bancroft, J. H. J., Gath, D. H., Johnston, D. W., Mathews, A. M., & Shaw, P. M. (1973). Specific and nonspecific factors in behavior therapy. *British Journal of Psychiatry, 123,* 445–462.

Gelder, M. G., & Marks, I. M. (1966). Severe agoraphobia: A controlled prospective trial of behavior therapy. *British Journal of Psychiatry, 112,* 309–319.

Gelder, M. G., Marks, I. M., & Wolff, H. (1967). Desensitization and psychotherapy in the treatment of phobic states. *British Journal of Psychiatry, 113,* 53–73.

Gillan, P., & Rachman, S. (1974). An experimental investigation of desensitization in phobic patients. *British Journal of Psychiatry, 124,* 392–401.

Glasgow, R. E., & Bernstein, D. A. (1981). Behavioral treatment of smoking behavior. In C. K. Prokop & L. A. Bradley (Eds.), *Medical psychology: A new perspective.* New York: Academic Press.

Glassman, A. H. (1993). Cigarette smoking: Implications for psychiatric illness. *American Journal of Psychiatry, 50,* 546–553.

Gold, J. A. (1984). *Principles of psychological research.* Chicago: Dorsey.

Gold, S. R., & Gold, R. G. (1993). Sexual aversions: A hidden disorder. In W. O'Donohue, & J. H. Geer (Eds.), *Handbook of sexual dysfunctions: Assessment and treatment* (pp. 83–102). Boston: Allyn and Bacon.

Goldfried, M. R. (1980). Psychotherapy as coping skills training. In M. J. Mahoney (Ed.), *Psychotherapy process: Current issues and future directions.* New York: Plenum.

Goldfried, M. R. (Ed.). (1980). Special issue: Psychotherapy process. *Cognitive Therapy and Research, 4,* 271–306.

Goldfried, M. R., & D'Zurilla, T. J. (1969). A behavior-analytic model for assessing competence. In C. D. Spielberger (Ed.), *Current topics in clinical and community psychology* (Vol. 1). New York: Academic Press.

Goldfried, M. R., & Kent, R. N. (1972). Traditional versus behavioral assessment: A comparison of methodological and theoretical assumptions. *Psychological Bulletin, 77,* 409–420.

Goldfried, M. R., & Linehan, M. M. (1977). Basic issues in behavioral assessment. In A. R. Ciminero, K. S. Calhoun, & H. E. Adams (Eds.), *Handbook of behavioral assessment* (pp. 15–46). New York: Wiley.

Goldiamond, I. (1965). Self–control procedures in personal behavior problems. *Psychological Reports, 17,* 851–868.

Goldiamond, I. (1976). Self–reinforcement. *Journal of Applied Behavior Analysis, 9,* 509–514.

Goldsmith, J. B., & McFall, R. M. (1975). Development and evaluation of an interpersonal skill-training program for psychiatric inpatients. *Journal of Abnormal Psychology, 84,* 51–58.

Goldstein, A. J., & Chambless, D. L. (1978). A reanalysis of agoraphobia. *Behavior Therapy, 9,* 47–59.

Goldstein, A. P., Sprafkin, R. P., & Gershaw, N. J. (1976). Structured learning therapy: Training for community living. *Psychotherapy: Theory, Research, and Practice, 13,* 374–377.

Goldstein, J. B., Shapiro, D., Thanonaparn, C., & Sambhi, M. P. (1982). Comparison of drug and behavioral treatments of essential hypertension. *Health Psychology, 1,* 7–26.

Goldstein, M. J. (1996). Treating the person with schizophrenia as a person. *Contemporary Psychology, 41,* 256–258.

Goldstein, W. (1985). *An introduction to the borderline conditions.* Northvale, NJ: Jason Aronson.

Goodwin, D. W., Schulsinger, F., Hermansen, L., Guze, S., & Winokur, G. (1973). Alcohol problems in adoptees raised apart from alcoholic biological parents. *Archives of General Psychiatry, 28,* 238–243.

Goodyer, I. M. (1990). *Life experiences, development, and childhood psychopathology.* New York: Wiley.

Gotestam, K. G. (1983). A three-dimensional program for chronic pain. *Acta Psychiatrica Scandinavica, 67,* 209–217.

Gotestam, K. G., & Linton, S. J. (1986). Pain. In M. Hersen & A. S. Bellack (Eds.), *Handbook of clinical behavior therapy with adults.* New York: Plenum.

Gottesman, I. I. (1991). *Schizophrenia genesis: The origins of madness.* New York: W. H. Freeman.

Gottman, J. M. (1979). *Marital interacting: Experimental Investigations.* New York: Academic Press.

Graziano, A. M., & Mooney, K. C. (1980). Family self-control instruction for children's fears: A review. *Psychological Bulletin, 86,* 804–830.

Graziano, A. M., & Katz, J. N. (1982). Training paraprofessionals. In A. S. Bellack, M. Hersen, & A. E. Kazdin (Eds.), *International handbook of behavior modification and therapy* (pp. 207–229). New York: Plenum Press.

Graziano, A. M., Mooney, K. C., Huber, C., & Ignasiak, D. (1979). Self-control instruction for children's fear–reduction. *Journal of Behavior Therapy and Experimental Psychiatry, 10,* 221–227.

Greenwald, R. (1996). The information gap in the EMDR controversy. *Professional Psychology: Research and Practice, 27,* 67–72.

Greif, E., & Matarazzo, R. G. (1982). *Operant learning in physical rehabilitation.* New York: Springer.

Greist, J. H., Marks, I. M., Berlin, F., Gournay, K., & Noshirvani, H. (1980). Avoidance versus confrontation of fear. *Behavior Therapy, 11,* 1–14.

Grinker, R. R., Miller, J., Sabshin, M., Nunn, R., & Nunnally, J. (1961). *The phenomena of depression.* New York: Harper.

Grosscup, S. J., & Lewinsohn, P. M. (1980). Unpleasant and pleasant events, and mood. *Journal of Clinical Psychology, 36,* 252–259.

Gross, A. (1984). Behavioral interviewing. In T. H. Ollendick & M. Hersen (Eds.), *Child behavioral assessment.* New York: Pergamon.

Guevremont, D. C. & Spiegler, M. D. (1990, November). *What do behavior therapists really do? A survey of the clnical practice of AABT members.* Paper presented at the twenty-fourth annual convention of the Association for Advancement of Behavior Therapy, San Francisco.

Gunderson, J. G. (1984). *Borderline personality disorders.* Washington, DC: American Psychiatric Press.

Gurman, A. S. (1980a). Behavioral marriage therapy in the 1980s: The challenge of integration. *American Journal of Family Therapy, 8*(2), 86–96.

Gurman, A. S. (1980b). Foreword. In R. B. Stuart (Ed.), *Helping couples change: A social learning approach to marital therapy.* New York: Guilford.

Gurman, A. S., & Messer, S. B. (Eds.). (1995). *Essential psychotherapies: Theory and practice.* New York: Guilford.

Guthrie, E. R. (1935). *The psychology of learning.* New York: Harper.

Guttmacher, L. B., & Nelles, C. (1984). In vivo desensitization alteration of lactate-induced panic: A case study. *Behavior Therapy, 15,* 369–372.

Haaga, D. A. F. (1987). Treatment of the Type A behavior pattern. *Clinical Psychology Review, 7,* 557–574.

Haaga, D. A. F., & Davison, G. C. (1989). Outcome studies of rational-emotive therapy. In M. E. Bernard & R. DiGiuseppe (Eds.), *Inside rational-emotive therapy: A critical appraisal of the theory and therapy of Albert Ellis* (pp. 155–197). San Diego, CA: Academic Press.

Haaga, D. A. F., Davidson, G. C., Williams, M. E., Dolezal, S. L., Haleblian, J., Rosenbaum, J., Dwyer, J. H., Baker, S., Nezami, E., & DeQuattro, V. (1994). Mode-specific impact of relaxation training for hypertensive men with Type A behavior pattern. *Behavior Therapy, 25,* 209–223.

Haaga, D. A. F., Dyck, M. J., & Ernst, D. (1991). Empirical status of cognitive therapy of depression. *Psychological Bulletin, 110,* 215–236.

Haaga, D. A. F., & Stewart, B. L. (1992). Self-efficacy for recovery from a lapse after smoking cessation. *Journal of Consulting and Clinical Psychology, 60,* 24–28.

Haddock, G., Bentall, R. P., & Slade, P. (1993). Psychological treatment of chronic auditory hallucinations: Two case studies. *Behavioral and Cognitive Psychotherapy, 21,* 335–346.

Hafner, R. J. (1977). The husbands of agoraphobic women and their influence on treatment outcome. *British Journal of Psychiatry, 131,* 289–294.

Hafner, R. J. (1982). The marital context of the agoraphobic syndrome. In D. L. Chambless & A. J. Goldstein (Eds.), *Agoraphobia: Multiple perspectives on theory and treatment* (pp. 77–117). New York: Wiley.

Haggard, H. W. (1946). *Devils, drugs and doctors: The story of the science of healing from medicine-man to doctor.* New York: Pocket Books. (Original work published in 1929.)

Hagopian, L. P., & Ollendick, T. H. (1993). Simple phobia in children. In R. T. Ammerman & M. Hersen (Eds.), *Handbook of behavior therapy with children and adults* (pp. 123–136). Boston: Allyn and Bacon.

Hagopian, L. P., Weist, M. W., & Ollendick, T. H. (1990). Cognitive-behavior therapy with an 11-year old girl fearful of AIDS and illness: A case study. *Journal of Anxiety Disorders, 4,* 257–265.

Hahlweg, K., & Markman, H. J. (1988). Effectiveness of behavioral marital therapy: Empirical status of behavioral techniques in preventing and alleviating marital distress. *Journal of Consulting and Clinical Psychology, 56,* 440–447.

Hall, J. N., Baker, R. D., & Hutchinson, K. (1977). A controlled evaluation of token economy procedures with chronic schizophrenic patients. *Behaviour Research and Therapy, 15,* 261.

Hall, W., & Heather, N. (1991). Issue of statistical power in comparative evaluations of minimal and intensive controlled drinking interventions. *Addictive Behaviors, 16,* 83–87.

Hamilton, E. W., & Abramson, L. Y. (1983). Cognitive patterns and major depressive disorder: A longitudinal study in a hospital setting. *Journal of Abnormal Psychology, 92,* 173–184.

Hamilton, M. (1960). A rating scale for depression. *Journal of Neurology, Neurosurgery, and Psychiatry, 23,* 56–61.

Hammen, C. (1991). *Depression runs in families: The social context of risk and resilience in children of depressed mothers.* New York: Springer-Verlag.

Hammersley, (1992). Cue exposure and learning theory. *Addictive Behaviors, 17,* 297–300.

Hansen, D. J., St. Lawrence, J. S., & Christoff, K. A. (1985). Effects of interpersonal problem-solving training with chronic aftercare patients on problem-solving component skills and effectiveness of solutions. *Journal of Consulting and Clinical Psychology, 53,* 167–174.

Harrell, T. H., Chambless, D. L., & Calhoun, J. R. (1981). Correlational relationships between self-statements and affective states. *Cognitive Therapy and Research, 5,* 159–173.

Harrington, R., Fudge, H., Rutter, M., Pickles, A., & Hill, J. (1991). Adult outcomes of childhood and adolescent depression; II. Links with antisocial disorders. *Journal of the American Academy of child and Adolescent Psychiatry, 31,* 103–111.

Harris, B. (1979). Whatever happened to little Albert? *American Psychologist, 34,* 151–160.

Harris, F. C., & Phelps, C. F. (1985). Anorexia nervosa. In M. Hersen & A. Bellack (Eds.), *Handbook of clinical behavior therapy with adults.* New York: Plenum.

Harris, G. M., & Johnson, S. B. (1983). Coping imagery and relaxation instructions in a covert modeling treatment for test anxiety. *Behavior Therapy, 14,* 144–157.

Harris, K. (1985). Conceptual, methodological, and clinical issues in cognitive-behavioral assessment. *Journal of Abnormal Child Psychology, 13,* 373–390.

Harris, S. L. (1994). Treatment of family problems in autism. In In E. Schopler & G. B. Mesibov (Eds.), *Behavioral issues in autism* (pp. 161–177). New York: Plenum.

Harris, S. L., & Ferrari, M. (1988). Developmental factors and their relationship to the identification and treatment of behavior problems of children. In J. C. Witt, S. N. Elliot, & F. M. Gresham (Eds.), *Handbook of behavior therapy in education* (pp. 311–341). New York: Wiley.

Harris, S. L., Handleman, J. S., Kristoff, B., Bass, L., & Gordon, R. (1990). Changes in language development among autistic and peer childen in segregated and integrated preschool settings. *Journal of Autism and Developmental Disorders, 20,* 23–31.

Harris, S. L., & Powers, M. D. (1984). Diagnostic issues. In T. H. Ollendick & M. Hersen (Eds.), *Child behavioral assessment* (pp. 166–194). New York: Pergamon.

Harris, S. L., & Romanczyk, R. G. (1976). Treating self-injurious behavior of a retarded child by overcorrection. *Behavior Therapy, 7,* 235–239.

Harter, S. (1984). The perceived competence scale for children. *Child Development, 53,* 87–97.

Hartmann, D. P., & Barrios, B. (1980). Book review (Paul & Lentz, 1977). *Behavior Therapy, 11,* 607–610.

Hartmann, E. (1984). *The nightmare: The psychology and biology of terrifying dreams.* New York: Basic Books.

Harvard Mental Health Letter. (1995). Update on mood disorders—Part II. *The Harvard Mental Health Letter, 11* (7), 1–4.

Harvey, M. R., & Herman, J. L. (1992). The trauma of sexual victimization: Feminist contributions to theory, research, and practice. *PTSD Research Quarterly, 3* (3), 1–7.

Hassard, A. (1993). Eye movement desensitization of body image. *Behavioural Psychotherapy, 21,* 157–160.

Hassard, A. (1995). Investigation of eye movement desensitization in pain clinic patients. *Behavioural Psychotherapy, 23,* 177–185.

Hathaway, S. R., & McKinley, J. C. (1951). *MMPI manual* (rev.). New York: The Psychological Corporation.

Hawkins, R. P. (1979). The functions of assessment: Implications for selection and development of devices for assessing repertoires in clinical, educational, and other settings. *Journal of Applied Behavior Analysis, 12,* 501–516.

Hay, W. (1982). The behavioral assessment and treatment of an alcoholic marriage. In W. Hay & P. Nathan (Eds.), *Clinical case studies in the behavioral treatment of alcoholism.* New York: Plenum Press.

Hayes, R. L., Halford, W. K., & Varghese, F. T. (1995). Social skills training with chronic schizophrenic patients: Effects on negative symptoms and community functioning. *Behavior Therapy, 26,* 433–449.

Hayes, S. C. (1981). Single case experimental design and empirical clinical practice. *Journal of Consulting and Clinical Psychology, 49,* 193–211.

Hayes, S. C., Follette, W. C., & Follette, V. M. (1995). Behavior therapy: A contextual approach. In A. S. Gurman & S. B. Messer (Eds.), *Essential psychotherapies: Theory and practice* (pp. 128–181). New York: Guilford.

Haynes, S. N. (1991). *Models of causality in psychopathology: Toward dynamic, synthetic, and nonlinear models of behavior disorders.* New York: Pergamon Press.

Haynes, S. N., Griffin, P., Mooney, D., & Parise, M. (1975). Electromyographic biofeedback and relaxation instructions in the treatment of muscle contraction headaches. *Behavior Therapy, 6,* 672–678.

Haynes, S. N., & O'Brien, W. H. (1990). Functional analysis in behavior therapy. *Clinical Psychology Review, 10,* 649–668.

Heath, D. B. (1987). Anthropology and alcohol studies: Current issues. *Journal of Studies of Alcohol, 55,* 5–17.

Heather, N. (1989). Psychology and brief interventions. *British Journal of Addiction, 84,* 357–370.

Heather, N, Kissoon-Singh, J., & Fenton, G. W. (1990). Assisted natural recovery from alcohol problems: Effects of a self-help manual with and without supplementary telephone contact. *British Journal of Addiction, 85,* 1177–1185.

Hecker, J. E., & Thorpe, G. L. (1987). Fear reduction processes in imaginal and in vivo flooding: A comment on James' review. *Behavioural Psychotherapy, 15,* 215–223.

Hecker, J. E., & Thorpe, G. L. (1989, Nov.). *Cognitive-behavior therapy in the treatment of phobias: Long-term follow-up.* Paper presented at the 23rd Annual AABT Convention, Washington, D.C.

Hecker, J. E., & Thorpe, G. L. (1992). *Agoraphobia and panic: A guide to psychological treatment.* Boston: Allyn and Bacon.

Heimberg, R. G. (1985). What makes traumatic stress traumatic? *Behavior Therapy, 16,* 417–419.

Hergenhahn, B. R. (1992). *An introduction to the history of psychology* (2nd ed.). Pacific Grove, CA: Brooks/Cole.

Herman, J. L. (1992). *Trauma and recovery.* New York: Basic Books.

Herrnstein, R. J. (1969). Method and theory in the study of avoidance. *Psychological Review, 76,* 49–69.

Herrnstein, R. J., & Hineline, P. N. (1966). Negative reinforcement as shock-frequency reduction. *Journal of the Experimental Analysis of Behavior, 9,* 421–430.

Hersen, M. (1982). Single-case experimental designs. In A. S. Bellack, M. Hersen, & A. E. Kazdin (Eds.), *International handbook of behavior modification and therapy* (pp. 167–203). New York: Plenum.

Hester, R. K. (1995). Behavioral self-control training. In R. K. Hester & W. R. Miller (Eds.) *Handbook of alcoholism treatment approaches* (2nd ed.) (pp. 1148–159). Boston: Allyn and Bacon.

Hetherington, E. M. (1984). Stress and coping in children and families. In A. B. Doyle, D. Gold, & D. S. Moskowitz (Eds.), Children in families under stress. *New directions for child development, 24,* 7–34.

Hetherington, E. M., & Martin, B. (1979). Family interaction. In H. C. Quay & J. S. Werry (Eds.), *Psychopathological disorders of childhood* (2nd ed.). New York: Wiley.

Hineline, P. (1977). Negative reinforcement and avoidance. In W. K. Honig & J. E. R. Staddon (Eds.), *Handbook of operant behavior.* Englewood Cliffs, NJ: Prentice-Hall.

Hinshaw, S. P. (1987). On the distinction between attentional deficits/hyperactivity and conduct problems/aggression in child psychopathology. *Psychological Bulletin, 101,* 443–463.

Hinshaw, S. P., Lahey, B. B., & Hart, E. L. (1993). Issues of taxonomy and comorbidity in the development of conduct disorder. *Development and Psychopathology, 5,* 31–49.

Hodges, L. F., Kooper, R., Meyer, T. C., Rothbaum, B. O., Opdyke, D., de Graaff, J. J., Williford, J. S., & North, M. M. (1995, July). Virtual environments for treating the fear of heights. *Computer: Innovative Technology for Computer Professionals,* pp. 27–34.

Hoehn-Saric, E., Maissami, M., & Weigand, D. (1987). Measurement of anxiety in children and adolescents using structured interviews. *Journal of the American Academy of Child and Adolescent Psychiatry, 26,* 541–545.

Hofer, M. A., Wolff, E. T., Friedman, S. B., & Mason, J. W. (1972). A psychoendocrine study of bereavement. *Psychosomatic Medicine, 34,* 481–504.

Hollon, S. D., & Carter, M. M. (1994). Depression in adults. In L. W. Craighead, W. E. Craighead, A. E. Kazdin, & M. J. Mahoney (Eds.), *Cognitive and behavioral interventions: An empirical approach to mental health problems* (pp. 89–104). Boston: Allyn and Bacon.

Hollon, S. D., DeRubeis, R. J., Evans, M. D., Weimer, M., Garvey, M. J., Grove, W., & Tuason, V. B. (1992). Cognitive therapy and pharmacotherapy for depression: Singly and in combination. *Archives of General Psychiatry, 49,* 774–781.

Hollon, S. D., Shelton, R. C., & Loosen, P. T. (1991). Cognitive therapy and pharmacotherapy for depression. *Journal of Consulting and Clinical Psychology, 59,* 88–89.

Holroyd, K. A., & Lazarus, R. S. (1985). Stress, coping, and somatic adaptation. In L. Goldberger & S. Brenitz (Eds.), *Handbook of stress.* New York: The Free Press.

Homme, L. E. (1965). Control of coverants: The operants of the mind. *Psychological Record, 15,* 501–511.

Hops, H., Willis, T. A., Patterson, G. R., & Weiss, R. L. (1971). *The marital interaction coding system (MICS).* Unpublished manuscript, University of Oregon.

Hops, S., & Greenwood, C. R. (1981). Social skills deficits. In E. J. Mash & L. G. Terdal (Eds.), *Behavioral assessment of childhood disorders.* New York: Guilford.

Hoza, B., Vallano, G., & Pelham, W. E. (1995). Attention Deficit/Hyperactivity Disorder. In R. T. Ammerman & M. Hersen (Eds.), *Handbook of child behavior therapy in the psychiatric setting.* New York: Wiley.

Hughes, H., & Haynes, S. N. (1978). Structured laboratory observation in the behavioral assessment of parent-child interactions: A methodological critique. *Behavior Therapy, 9,* 428–447.

Hughes, J. R., Gust, S. W., Skoog, K., Keenan, R. M., & Fenwick, J. W. (1991). Symptoms of tobacco withdrawal. *Archives of General Psychiatry, 48,* 52–59.

Hull, C. L. (1952). *A behavior system: An introduction to behavior theory concerning the individual organism.* New Haven, CT: Yale University Press.

Hunter, R., & MacAlpine, I. (1963). *Three hundred years of psychiatry, 1535–1860.* London: Oxford University Press.

Hussian, R. A. (1981). *Geriatric psychology: A behavioral perspective.* New York: Van Nostrand Reinhold.

Hussian, R. A., & Lawrence, P. S. (1981). Social reinforcement of activity and problem-solving training in the treatment of depressed institutionalized elderly patients. *Cognitive Therapy and Research, 5,* 57–69.

Hymel, S., Rubin, K. H., Rowden, L., & LeMare, L. (1990). Children's peer relationships: Longitudinal prediction of internalizing and externalizing problems from middle to late childhood. *Child Development, 61,* 2004–2021.

Institute of Medicine. (1990). *Broadening the base for treatment of alcohol problems.* Washington, DC: National Academy Press.

Isaacs, W., Thomas, J., & Goldiamond, I. (1960). Application of operant conditioning to reinstate verbal behavior in psychotics. *Journal of Speech and Hearing Disorders, 24,* 8–12.

Ito, R. J., Donovan, D. M., & Hall, J. J. (1988). Relapse prevention in alcohol aftercare: Effects on drinking outcome, change process, and aftercare attendance. *British Journal of Addiction, 83,* 171–181.

Iwamasa, G. Y., Nangle, D. W., & VanLooy-Larrabee, A. (1995). AABT and ethnic diversity: A review of convention programs of the past decade. *The Behavior Therapist, 18,* 49–51.

Iwata, B. A. (1987). Negative reinforcement in applied behavior analysis: An emerging technology. *Journal of Applied Behavior Analysis, 20,* 361–378.

Iwata, B. A., Dorsey, M. F., Slifer, K. J., Bauman, K. E., & Richman, G. S. (1982). Toward a functional analysis of self-injury. *Analysis and Intervention in Developmental Disabilities, 2,* 3-20.

Iwata, B. A., Zarcone, J. R., Vollmer, T. R., & Smith, R. G. (1994). In E. Schopler & G. B. Mesibov (Eds.), *Behavioral issues in autism* (pp. 131–160). New York: Plenum.

Jacobson, E. (1938). *Progressive relaxation.* Chicago: University of Chicago Press.

Jacobson, N. S. (1977). Problem-solving and contingency contracting in the treatment of marital discord. *Journal of Consulting and Clinical Psychology, 45,* 92–100.

Jacobson, N. S. (1978). Specific and nonspecific factors in the effectiveness of a behavioral approach to the treatment of marital discord. *Journal of Consulting and Clinical Psychology, 46,* 442–452.

Jacobson, N. S. (1984). A component analysis of behavioral marital therapy: The relative effectiveness of behavior exchange and problem-solving training. *Journal of Consulting and Clinical Psychology, 52,* 295–305.

Jacobson, N. S. (1985). The role of observational measures in behavior therapy outcome research. *Behavioral Assessment, 7,* 297–308.

Jacobson, N. S. (1985). Uses versus abuses of observational measures. *Behavioral Assessment, 7,* 323–330.

Jacobson, N. S. (1992). Behavioral couple therapy: A new beginning. *Behavior Therapy, 23,* 493–506.

Jacobson, N. S., & Baucom, D. H. (1977). Design and assessment of nonspecific control groups in behavior modification research. *Behavior Therapy, 8,* 709–719.

Jacobson, N. S., & Follette, W. C. (1985). Clinical significance of improvement resulting from two behavioral marital therapy components. *Behavior Therapy, 16,* 249–262.

Jacobson, N. S., Follette, V. M., Follette, W. C., Holtzworth-Munroe, A., Katt, J. L., & Schmaling, K. B. (1985). A component analysis of behavioral marital therapy: One-year follow-up. *Behaviour Research and Therapy, 23,* 549–555.

Jacobson, N. S., Holtzworth-Munroe, A., & Schmaling, K. B. (1989). Marital therapy and spouse involvement in the treatment of depression, agoraphobia, and alcoholism. *Journal of Consulting and Clinical Psychology, 57,* 5–10.

Jacobson, N. S., & Margolin, G. (1979). *Marital therapy: Strategies based on social learning and behavior exchange principles.* New York: Brunner/Mazel.

Jacobson, N. S., Waldron, H., & Moore, D. (1980). Toward a behavioral profile of marital distress. *Journal of Consulting and Clinical Psychology, 48,* 696–703.

James, D., Thorn, B. E., & Williams, D. A. (1993). Goal specification in cognitive-behavioral therapy for chronic headache pain. *Behavior Therapy, 24,* 305-320.

Jannoun, L., Munby, M., Catalan, J., & Gelder, M. (1980). A home-based treatment program for agoraphobia: Replication and controlled evaluation. *Behavior Therapy, 11,* 294–305.

Jannoun, L., Oppenheimer, C., & Gelder, M. (1982). A self-help treatment program for anxiety state patients. *Behavior Therapy, 13,* 103–111.

Janoff-Bulman, R. (1992). *Shattered assumptions: Towards a new psychology of trauma.* New York: The Free Press.

Jarvis, M. (1989). Helping smokers give up. In S. Pearce & J. Wardle (Eds.), *The practice of behavioral medicine* (pp. 285–305). Oxford: BPS Books.

Jason, L. A., McMahon, S. D., Salina, D., Hedeker, D., Stockton, M., Dunson, K., & Kimball, P. (1995). Assessing a smoking cessation intervention involving groups, incentives, and self-help manuals. *Behavior Therapy, 26,* 393–408.

Jeffery, R. W., Bjornson–Benson, W. M., Rosenthal, B. S., Kurth, C. L., & Dunn, M. M. (1984a). Effectiveness of monetary contracts with two repayment schedules on weight reduction in men and women from self-referred and population samples. *Behavior Therapy, 15,* 272–279.

Jeffery, W. W., Forster, J. L., & Snell, M. K. (1984b) Promoting weight control at the worksite: A pilot program of self-motivation using payroll-based incentives. *Preventive Medicine, 14,* 187–194.

Jehu, D. (1984). Clinical practice in behavioral treatment for sexual dysfunction: Programs and procedures. In C. M. Franks (Ed.), *New developments in behavior therapy: From research to clinical application* (pp. 231–279). New York: Haworth.

Jenni, M. A., & Wollersheim, J. P. (1979). Cognitive therapy, stress management training, and the type A behavior pattern. *Cognitive Therapy and Research, 3,* 61–73.

Jensen, J. A. (1994). An investigation of eye movement desensitization and reprocessing (EMD/R) as a treatment for posttraumatic stress disorder (PTSD) symptoms of Vietnam combat veterans. *Behavior Therapy, 25,* 311–325.

Jessup, B. A. (1989). Relaxation and biofeedback. In P. D. Wall & R. Melzack (Eds.), *Textbook of pain* (2nd ed.) (pp. 989–1000). New York: Churchill Livingstone.

Johnson, L. E., & Thorpe, G. L. (1994). Review of Psychotherapy and counseling with minorities: A cognitive approach to individual differences. *Behavioural and Cognitive Psychotherapy, 22,* 185–187.

Johnston, C., Pelham, W. E., & Murphy, H. A. (1985). Peer relationships in ADDH and normal children: A developmental analysis of peer and teacher ratings. *Journal of Abnormal Child Psychology, 13,* 80–100.

Johnston, W. L., Baumeister, A. A., Penland, M. J., & Inwald, C. (1982). Experimental analysis of self–injurious, stereotypic, and collateral behavior of retarded persons: Effects of overcorrection and reinforcement of alternative responding. *Analysis and Intervention in Developmental Disabilities, 2,* 41–66.

Jones, B. M., & Jones, M. K. (1976). Women and alcohol: Intoxication, metabolism, and the menstrual cycle. In M. Greenblatt & M. A. Schuckit (Eds.), *Alcoholism problems in women and children.* New York: Grune & Stratton.

Jones, H. G. (1956). Application of conditioning and learning techniques to the treatment of a psychiatric patient. *Journal of Abnormal and Social Psychology, 52,* 414–419.

Jones, H. G. (1984). Behavior therapy—An autobiographic view. *Behavioural Psychotherapy, 12,* 7–16.

Jones, M. C. (1924). Elimination of children's fears. *Journal of Experimental Psychology, 7,* 382–390.

Jones, J. C., & Barlow, D. H. (1992). A new model of posttraumatic stress disorder: Implications for the future. In P. A. Saigh (Ed.), *Posttraumatic stress disorder: A behavioral approach to assessment and treatment* (pp. 147–165). New York: Macmillan.

Judd, L. J. (1965). Obsessive-compulsive neurosis in children. *Archives of General Psychiatry, 12,* 136–143.

Kagan, J., Reznick, J. S., & Gibbons, J. (1989). Inhibited and uninhibited types of children. *Child Development, 60,* 838–845.

Kagan, J., Rosman, B. L., Day, D., Albert, J., & Phillips, W. (1964). Information processing in the child: Significance of analytic and reflective attitudes. *Psychological Monographs, 78*(1), 578.

Kahana, E., & Kahana, B. (1970). Therapeutic potential of age integration: Effects of age integrated hospital environments on elderly psychiatric patients. *Archives of General Psychiatry, 23,* 20–29.

Kahn, R. L. (1977). Perspectives in the evaluation of psychological mental health programs for the aged. In W. G. Gentry (Ed.), *Geropsychology: A model of training and clinical service* (pp. 9–19). Cambridge, MA: Ballinger

Kallman, W. M., Hersen, M., & O'Toole, D. H. (1975). The use of social reinforcement in a case of conversion reaction. *Behavior Therapy, 6,* 411–413.

Kane, M. T. & Kendall, P. C. (1989). Anxiety disorders in children: A multiple baseline evaluation of a cognitive– behavioral treatment. *Behavior Therapy, 20,* 499–508.

Kanfer, F. H. (1970). Self-monitoring: Methodological limitations and clinical applications. *Journal of Consulting and Clinical Psychology, 35,* 148–152.

Kanfer, F. H. (1971). The maintenance of behavior by self-generated stimuli and reinforcement. In A. Jacobs & L. B. Sachs (Eds.), *The psychology of private events: Perspectives on covert response systems.* New York: Academic.

Kanfer, F. H., Karoly, P., & Newman, A. (1975). Reduction of children's fear of the dark by competence–related and situational threat-related verbal cues. *Journal of Consulting and Clinical Psychology, 43,* 251–258.

Kanfer, F. H., & Saslow, G. (1969). Behavioral diagnosis. In C. M. Franks (Ed.), *Behavior therapy: Appraisal and status.* New York: McGraw-Hill.

Kanfer, R., Eyberg, S. M., & Krahn, G. L. (1992). Interviewing strategies in child assessment. In C. E. Walker & M. C. Roberts (Eds.), *Handbook of clinical child psychology* (pp. 49–62). New York: Wiley.

Kanner, L. (1943). Autistic disturbances of affective contact. *Nervous Child, 2,* 181–197.

Kaplan, H. S. (1974). *The new sex therapy.* New York: Brunner/Mazel.

Kaplan, M. (1995). A woman's view of DSM–III. In S. O. Lilienfeld (Ed.), *Seeing both sides: Classic controversies in abnormal psychology* (pp. 65–71). Pacific Grove, CA: Brooks/Cole. (Original work published in 1983.)

Kashani, J. H., Carlson, G. A., Beck, N. C., Hoeper, E. W., Corcoran, C. M., Mcallister, J. A., Fallahi, C., Rosenberg, T. K., & Reid, J. C. (1987). Depression, depressive symptoms, and depressed mood among a community sample of adolescents. *American Journal of Psychiatry, 144,* 931–934.

Kaslow, N. J., & Racusin, G. R. (1990). Childhood depression: Current status and future directions. In A. S. Bellack, M. Hersen, & A. E. Kazdin (Eds.), *International handbook of behavior modification and therapy* (2nd ed.) (pp. 649–667). New York: Plenum.

Katahn, M., Pleas, J., Thackrey, M., & Wallston, K. A. (1982). Relationship of eating and activity self-reports to follow-up maintenance in the massively obese. *Behavior Therapy, 13,* 521–528.

Katz, R. (1994). Post-traumatic stress disorder. In V.S. Ramachandran (Ed.), *Encyclopedia of human behavior* (Vol. 3, pp. 555–562). San Diego, CA: Academic Press.

Kazdin, A. E. (1978). *History of behavior modification: Experimental foundation of contemporary research.* Baltimore: University Press.

Kazdin, A. E. (1982). History of behavior modification. In A. S. Bellack, M. Hersen, & A. E. Kazdin (Eds.), *International handbook of behavior modification and therapy* (pp. 3–32). New York: Plenum.

Kazdin, A. E. (1985). Selection of target behaviors: the relationship of treatment focus to clinical dysfunction. *Behavioral Assessment, 7,* 33–47.

Kazdin, A. E. (1989). Childhood depression. In E. J. Mash & R. A. Barkley (Eds.), *The treatment of childhood disorders* (pp. 135–166). New York: Guilford Press.

Kazdin, A. E. (1993). Treatment of conduct disorder: Progress and directions in psychotherapy research. *Development and Psychopathology, 5,* 277–310.

Kazdin, A. E. (1994). *Behavior modification in applied settings* (5th ed.). Pacific Grove, CA: Brooks/Cole.

Kazdin, A. E. (1995a). Informant variability in assessment of childhood depression. In W. M. Reynolds & H. F. Johnston (Eds.), *Handbook of depression in children and adults.* New York: Plenum.

Kazdin, A. E. (1995b). *Treatment of antisocial behavior in children and adolescents.* Homewood, IL: Dorsey.

Kazdin, A. E. & Bass, D. (1989). Power to detect differences between alternative treatments in comparative psychotherapy outcome research. *Journal of Consulting and Clinical Psychology, 57,* 138–147.

Kazdin, A. E., & Bootzin, R. R. (1972). The token economy: An evaluative review. *Journal of Applied Behavior Analysis, 5,* 343–372.

Kazdin, A. E., Esveldt-Dawson, K., French, N. H., & Unis, A. S. (1987). Effects of parent management training and problem-solving skills training combined in the treatment of antisocial child behavior. *Journal of the American Academy of Child and Adolescent Psychiatry, 26,* 416–424.

Kazdin, A. E., French, N. H., Unis, A. S., Esveldt-Dawson, K., & Sherick, R. E. (1983). Hopelessness, depression, and suicidal intent among psychiatrically disturbed inpatient children. *Journal of Consulting and clinical Psychology, 51,* 504–510.

Kazdin, A. E., Siegel, T. C., & Bass, D. (1990). Drawing upon clinical practice to inform research on child and adolescent psychopathology: A survey of practitioners. *Professional Psychology: Research and Practice, 21,* 189–198.

Kazdin, A. E., Siegel, T. C., & Bass, D. (1992). Cognitive problem-solving skills training and parent management training in the treatment of antisocial behavior in children. *Journal of Consulting and Clinical Psychology, 60,* 733–747.

Kazdin, A. E., & Wilcoxon, L. A. (1976). Systematic desensitization and nonspecific treatment effects: A methodological evaluation. *Psychological Bulletin, 83,* 729–758.

Kazdin, A. E., & Wilson, G. T. (1978). *Evaluation of behavior therapy: Issues, evidence, and research strategies.* Cambridge, MA: Ballinger.

Keane, T. M. (1985). Defining traumatic stress: Some comments on the current terminological confusion. *Behavior Therapy, 16,* 419–423.

Keane, T. M., Fairbank, J. A., Caddell, J. M., & Zimering, R. (1989). Implosive (flooding) therapy reduces symptoms of PTSD in Vietnam combat veterans. *Behavior Therapy, 20,* 245–260.

Keane, T. M., & Kaloupek, G. G. (1982). Imaginal flooding in the treatment of a posttraumatic stress disorder. *Journal of Consulting and Clinical Psychology, 50,* 138–140.

Keane, T. M., Zimering, R. T., & Caddell, J. M. (1985). A behavioral formulation of posttraumatic stress disorder in Vietnam veterans. *The Behavior Therapist, 8,* 9–12.

Keefe, F. L., Caldwell, D. S., Williams, D. A., Gil, K. A., Mitchell, D., Robertson, C., Martinez, S., Nunley, J., Beckham, J. C., Crisson, J. C., & Helms, M. (1990). Pain coping skills training in the management of osteoarthritic knee pain: A comparative study. *Behavior Therapy, 21,* 49-62.

Keith–Spiegel, P., & Koocher, G. P. (1985). *Ethics in psychology: Professional standards and cases.* New York: Random House.

Kelleher, R. T. (1966). Chaining and conditioned reinforcement. In W. K. Honig (Ed.), *Operant behavior: Areas of research and application.* New York: Appleton-Century-Crofts.

Kelley, H. H., & Thibaut, J. W. (1978). *Interpersonal relations: A theory of interdependence.* New York: Wiley.

Kelley, K., & Dawson, L. (1994). Sexual orientation. In V. S. Ramachandran (Ed.), *Encyclopedia of human behavior* (Vol. 4, pp. 183–192). San Diego, CA: Academic Press.

Kelly, A. B., & Halford, W. K. (1995). The generalisation of cognitive behavioural marital therapy in behavioural, cognitive and physiological domains. *Behavioural and Cognitive Psychotherapy, 23,* 381–398.

Kendall, P. C. (1987). Cognitive processes and procedures in behavior therapy. In G. T. Wilson, C. M. Franks, P. C. Kendall, & J. P. Foreyt, *Review of behavior therapy: Theory and practice.,* New York: Guilford.

Kendall, P. C., & Braswell, L. (1985). *Cognitive-behavioral therapy for impulsive children.* New York: Guilford Press.

Kendall, P. C., Lerner, R. M., & Craighead, W. E. (1984). Human development and intervention in child psychopathology. *Child Development, 55,* 71–82.

Kendall, P. C., Pellegrini, D., & Urbain, E. S. (1981). Approaches to assessment for cognitive-behavioral interventions with children. In P. C. Kendall & S. D. Hollon (Eds.), *Assessment strategies for cognitive-behavioral interventions.* New York: Academic Press.

Kernberg, O. F. (1984). *Severe personality disorders: Psychotherapeutic strategies.* New Haven, CT: Yale University Press.

Keys, A., Brozek, J., Henschel, A., Michelson, O., & Taylor, H. L. (1950). *The biology of human starvation.* Minneapolis: University of Minneapolis.

Kiesler, D. J. (1966). Some myths of psychotherapy research and the search for a paradigm. *Psychological Bulletin, 65,* 110–136.

Kilpatrick, D. G., & Best, C. L. (1984). Some cautionary remarks on treating sexual assault victims with implosion. *Behavior Therapy, 15,* 421–423.

King, N. J., Cranstoun, F., & Josephs, A. (1989). Emotive imagery and children's nightime fears: A multiple baseline design evaluation. *Journal of Behavior Therapy and Experimental Psychiatry, 20,* 125–135.

King, N. J., Hamilton, D. I., & Ollendick, T. M. (1988). *Children's phobias: A behavioral perspective.* New York: Wiley.

Kirkley, B. G., Schneider, J. A., Agras, W. S., & Bachman, J. A. (1985). A comparison of two group treatments for bulimia. *Journal of Consulting and Clinical Psychology, 53,* 43–48.

Klein, D. F. (1981). Anxiety reconceptualized. In D. F. Klein & J. Rabkin (Eds.), *Anxiety: New research and changing concepts.* New York: Raven.

Klein, D. N. & Riso, L. P. (1995). Psychiatric disorders: Problems of boundaries and comorbidity. In C. G. Costello (Ed.) *Basic issues in psychopathology.* New York: Guilford.

Klein, R. G., & Manuzza, S. (1991). Long-term outcome of hyperactive children: A review. *Journal of the American Academy for Child and Adolescent Psychiatry, 30,* 383–387.

Kleinman, A. (1986). *Social origins of distress and disease: Depression, neurasthenia, and pain in modern China.* New Haven, CT: Yale University Press.

Koegel, R. L., Frea, W. D., & Surratt, A. V. (1994). Self-management of problematic social behavior. In E. Schopler & G. B. Mesibov (Eds.), *Behavioral issues in autism* (pp. 81–98). New York: Plenum.

Koegel, R. L., & Koegel, L. K. (1990). Extended reductions in stereotypic behavior of students with autism through a self-management treatment package. *Journal of Applied Behavior Analysis, 23,* 119–127.

Koegel, R. K., O'Dell, M. C., & Koegel, L. K. (1987). A natural language teaching program for nonverbal autistic children. *Journal of Autism and Developmental Disorders, 17,* 187–200.

Koegel, R. L., Schreibman, L., Britten, K. R., Burke, J. C., & O'Neill, R. E. (1982). A comparison of parent training to direct child treatment. In R. L. Koegel, A. Rincover, & A. L. Egel (Eds.), *Education and understanding autistic children.* San Diego, CA: College Hill Press.

Kohler, F. W., & Strain, P. S. (1990). Peer assisted interventions: Early promises, notable achievements, and future aspirations. *Clinical Psychology Review, 10,* 441–452.

Kolb, L. C. (1988). A critical survey of hypotheses regarding post-traumatic stress disorders in light of recent findings. *Journal of Traumatic Stress, 1,* 291–304.

Kosten, T. R., Rounsaville, B., & Kleber, H. D. (1983). Concurrent validity of the Addiction severity Index. *Journal of Nervous and Mental Diseases, 171,* 606–610.

Kovacs, M. (1985). The Interview Schedule for children (ISC). *Psychopharmacology Bulletin, 21,* 991–994.

Kovacs, M. (1989). Affective disorders in children and adolescents. *American Psychologist, 44,* 209–215.

Kovacs, M., Feinberg, T. L., Crouse-Novak, M. A., Paulaskos, S. L., & Finkelstein, R. (1984). Depressive disorders in childhood: A longitudinal prospectus study of characteristics and recovery. *Archives of General Psychiatry, 41,* 229–237.

Kovacs, M., Paulaskas, S., Gastonis, C., & Richards, C. (1988). Depressive disorders in childhood: III. A longitudinal study of comorbidity with and risk for conduct disorders. *Journal of Affective Disorders, 15,* 205–217.

Krasner, L. (1992). The concepts of syndrome and functional analysis: Compatible or incompatible? *Behavioral Assessment, 14,* 307–321.

Kuczmarski, R. J. (1992). Prevalence of overweight and weight gain in the United States. *American Journal of Clinical Nutrition, 55,* 495S-502S.

Ladd, G. W. (1985). Documenting the effects of social skill training with children: Process and outcome assessment. In B. H. Schneider, K. H. Rubin, & J. E. Ledingham (Eds.) *Children's peer relations: Issues in assessment and intervention.* New York: Springer-Verlag.

LaGreca, A. M., & Stone, W. L. (1992). Assessing children through interviews and behavioral observsations. In C. E. Walker & M. C. Roberts (Eds.), *Handbook of clinical child psychology* (pp. 63–84). New York: Wiley.

Lahey, B. B. & Loeber, R. (1994). Framework for a developmental model of oppositional defiant disorder and conduct disorder. In D. F. Routh (Ed.), *Disruptive behavior disorders in childhood* (pp. 139–180). New York: Plenum.

Lam, W., Sze, P. C., Sacko, H. S., & Chalmers, T. C. (1987). Meta-analysis of randomized control trials of nicotine chewing gum. *Lancet, 2,* 27–30.

Lane, R. D., & Jennings, J. R. (1995). Hemispheric assymetry, autonomic asymmetry, and the problem of sudden cardiac death. In R. J. Davidson & K. Hugdahl (Eds.), *Brain assymetry._* Cambridge, MA: MIT Press.

Lang, P. J. (1965). Behavior therapy with a case of anorexia nervosa. In L. P. Ullman & L. Krasner (Eds.). *Case studies in behavior modification.* New York: Holt, Rinehart, and Winston.

Lang, P. J. (1968). Fear reduction and fear behavior: Problems in treating a construct. In J. M. Shlien (Ed.), *Research in psychotherapy* (Vol. III). (pp. 90–103). Washington, DC: American Psychological Association.

Lang, P. J. (1979). A bio-informational theory of emotional imagery. *Psychophysiology, 16,* 495–512.

Lang, P. J. (1985). The cognitive psychophysiology of emotion: Fear and anxiety. In A. H. Tuma & J. D. Maser (Eds.), *Anxiety and the anxiety disorders* (pp. 131–170). Hillsdale, NJ: Lawrence Erlbaum.

Lang, P. J., & Lazovik, A. D. (1963). Experimental desensitization of a phobia. *Journal of Abnormal and Social Psychology, 66,* 519–525.

Lang, P. J., Lazovik, A. D., & Reynolds, D. J. (1965). Desensitization, suggestibility, and pseudotherapy. *Journal of Abnormal Psychology, 70,* 395–402.

Lansing, M. D., & Schopler, E. (1978). Individualized education: A public school model. In M. Rutter & E. Schopler (Eds.), *Autism: A reappraisal of concepts and treatment.* New York: Plenum.

LaPointe, K. A., & Harrell, T. H. (1978). Thoughts and feelings: Correlational relationships and cross–situational consistency. *Cognitive Therapy and Research, 2,* 311–322.

Lapouse, R., & Monk, M. A. (1959). Fears and worries in a representative sample of children. *American Journal of Orthopsychiatry, 29,* 803–818.

Lapsley, D. K. (1994). Id, ego, and superego. In V. S. Ramachandran (Ed.), *Encyclopedia of human behavior* (Vol. 2, pp. 579–588). San Diego, CA: Academic.

Laski, K. E., Charlop, M. H., & Schreibmen, L. (1988). Training parents to use the natural language paradigm to increase their autistic children's speech. *Journal of Applied Behavior Analysis, 21,* 391–400.

Last, C. G., & Francis, G. (1988). School phobia. In B. Lahey & A. Kazdin (Eds.), *Advances in clnical child psychology* (Vol.11). New York: Plenum.

Last, C. G., Hersen, M., Kazdin, A. E., Finkelstein, R., & Strauss, C. C. (1987). Comparison of DSM–III separation anxiety and overanxious disorders: Demographic characteristics and patterns of comorbidity. *Journal of the American Academy of Child and Adolescent Psychiatry, 26,* 527–531.

Last, C. G., & Strauss, C. C. (1990). School refusal in anxiety-disordered children and adolescents. *Journal of the American Academy of Child and Adolescent Psychiatry, 29,* 31–35.

Layden, M. A. (1982). Attributional style therapy. In C. Antaki & C. Brewin (Eds.), *Attributions and psychological change.* New York: Academic.

Lazarus, A. A. (1971). *Behavior therapy and beyond.* New York: McGraw-Hill.

Lazarus, A. A. (1973). Multimodal behavior therapy: Treating the "Basic Id." *Journal of Nervous and Mental Disease, 156,* 404–411.

Lazarus, A. A. (1976). *Multimodal behavior therapy.* New York: Springer.

Lazarus, A. A. (1987). Some significant differences and more significant similarities. *American Psychologist, 42,* 101.

Lazarus, A. A. (1989). Multimodal therapy. In R. J. Corsini & D. Wedding (Eds.), *Current psychotherapies* (4th ed.). Itasca, IL: F. E. Peacock.

Lazarus, A. A. (1989). The practice of rational-emotive therapy. In M. E. Bernard & R. DiGiuseppe (Eds.), *Inside rational-emotive therapy: A critical appraisal of the theory and therapy of Albert Ellis* (pp. 95–112). San Diego, CA: Academic.

Lazarus, A. A. (1995). Multimodal therapy. In R. J. Corsini & D. Wedding (Eds.), *Current psychotherapies* (pp. 322–355). (5th ed.). Itasca, IL: F. E. Peacock.

Lazarus, R. S., & Folkman, S. (1982). Coping and adaptation. In W. D. Gentry (Ed.), *Handbook of behavioral medicine.* New York: Guilford.

Lease, C. A., & Strauss, C. C. (1993). Separation anxiety disoprder. In R. T. Ammerman & M. Hersen (Eds.), *Handbook of behavior therapy with children and adults* (pp. 93–107). Boston: Allyn and Bacon.

Lehrer, P. (1978). Psychophysiological effects of progressive relaxation in anxiety neurotic patients and of progressive relaxation and alpha feedback in nonpatients. *Journal of Consulting and Clinical Psychology, 46,* 389–404.

Lehrer, P. M. & Woolfolk, R. L. (1984). Are stress reduction techniques interchangeable, or do they have specific effects? A review of the comparative empirical literature. In R. L. Woolfolk & P. M. Lehrer (Eds.) *Principles and practices of stress management.* New York: Guilford.

Leiblum, S. R., & Pervin, L. A. (Eds.). (1980). *Principles and practice of sex therapy.* New York: Guilford.

Leitenberg, H., Agras, W. S., Allen, R., & Butz, R. A. (1975). Feedback and therapist praise during treatment of phobia. *Journal of Consulting and Clinical Psychology, 43,* 396–404.

Leitenberg, H., Agras, W. S., Edwardes, J. A., Thompson, L. E., & Wincze, J. P. (1970). Practice as a psychotherapeutic variable: An experimental analysis within single cases. *Journal of Psychiatric Research, 7,* 215–225.

Leitenberg, H., Agras, W. S., Thompson, L. E., & Wright, E. E. (1968). Feedback in behavior modification: An experimental analysis in two phobic cases. *Journal of Applied Behavior Analysis, 1,* 131–137.

Leitenberg, H., Gross, J., Peterson, J., & Rosen, J. C. (1984). Analysis of an anxiety model and the process of change during exposure plus response prevention treatment of bulimia nervosa. *Behavior Therapy, 15,* 3–20.

Leitenberg, H., Rosen, J. C., Gross, J., Nadelman, S., & Vara, L. S. (1988). Exposure plus response-prevention treatment of bulimia nervosa. *Journal of Consulting & Clinical Psychology, 56,* 535–541.

Lelliott, P., & Marks, I. (1987). Management of obsessive-compulsive rituals associated with delusions, hallucinations and depression: A case report. *Behavioral Psychotherapy, 15,* 77–87.

Lemere, F., & Voegtlin, W. L. (1950). An evaluation of the aversion treatment of alcoholism. *Quarterly Journal of Studies on Alcohol, 11,* 199–204.

Lenzenweger, M. F., & Gottesman, I. I. (1994). Schizophrenia. In V. S. Ramachandran (Ed.), *Encyclopedia of human behavior* (Vol. 4, pp. 41–59). San Diego, CA: Academic.

Leonard, H. L., Goldberger, E. L., Rapoport, J. L., Cheslow, D. L., & Swedo, S. E. (1990). Childhood rituals: Normal development or obsessive-compulsive symptoms? *Journal of the American Academy of Child and Adolescent Psychiatry, 29,* 17–23.

Leopold, R. L., & Dillon, H. (1963). Psycho-anatomy of a disaster: A long term study of post-traumatic neuroses in survivors of a marine explosion. *American Journal of Psychiatry,* 913–921.

Letourneau, E., & O'Donohue, W. (1993). Sexual desire disorders. In W. O'Donohue & J. H. Geer (Eds.), *Handbook of sexual dysfunctions: Assessment and treatment* (pp. 53–81). Boston: Allyn and Bacon.

Levis, D. J. (1982). Experimental and theoretical foundations of behavior modification. In A. S. Bellack, M. Hersen, & A. E. Kazdin (Eds.), *International handbook of behavior modification and therapy* (pp. 33–56). New York: Plenum.

Lewinsohn, P. M. (1975). The behavioral study and treatment of depression. In M. Hersen, R. M. Eisler, & P. M. Miller (Eds.), *Progress in behavior modification.* New York: Academic.

Lewinsohn, P. M., & Arconad, M. (1981). Behavioral treatment of depression: A social learning approach. In J. F. Clarkin & H. I. Glazer (Eds.), *Depression: Behavioral and directive intervention strategies.* New York: Garland STPM Press.

Lewinsohn, P. M., Hoberman, H. M., Teri, L., & Hautzinger, M. (1985). An integrative theory of depression. In S. Reiss & R. Bootzin (Eds.), *Theoretical issues in behavior therapy.* New York: Academic.

Lewinsohn, P. M., & Lee, W. M. L. (1980). Assessment of affective disorders. In D. H. Barlow (Ed.), *Behavioral assessment of adult disorders.* New York: Guilford.

Lewinsohn, P. M., & Libet, J. (1972). Pleasant events, activity schedules, and depression. *Journal of Abnormal Psychology, 79,* 291–295.

Lewinsohn, P. M., Youngren, M. A., & Grosscup, S. J. (1979). Reinforcement and depression. In R. A. Depues (Ed.), *The psychobiology of depressive disorders.* New York: Academic.

Ley, R. (1987). Panic disorder: A hyperventilation interpretation. In L. Michelson & L. M. Ascher (Eds.), *Anxiety and stress disorders: Cognitive-behavioral assessment and treatment* (pp. 191–212). New York: Guilford.

Lichtenstein, E., & Brown, R. A. (1982). Modification of cigarette dependence. In A. S. Bellack, M. Hersen, & A. E. Kazdin (Eds.), *International handbook of behavior modification and therapy.* New York: Plenum.

Lichtenstein, E., & Danaher, B. G. (1976). Modification of smoking behavior: A critical analysis of theory, research, and practice. In M. Hersen, R. Eisler, & P. M. Miller (Eds.). *Progress in behavior modification.* New York: Academic.

Liebowitz, M. R., Stone, M. H., & Turkat, I. (1986). Treatment of personality disorders. In A. J. Frances & R. E. Hales (Eds.), *American Psychiatric Association annual review* (pp. 356–393). Washington, DC: American Psychiatric Press.

Linehan, M. M. (1981). A social-behavioral analysis of suicide and parasuicide: Implications for assessment and treatment. In J. F. Clarkin & H. I. Glazer (Eds.), *Depression: Behavioral and directive intervention strategies.* New York: Garland STPM Press.

Linehan, M. (1993). *Cognitive-behavioral therapy of borderline personality disorder.* New York: Guilford.

Linehan, M. M., Goodstein, J. L., Neilson, S. L., & Chiles, J. A. (1983). Reasons for staying alive when you are thinking of killing yourself: The reasons for living inventory. *Journal of Consulting and Clinical Psychology, 51,* 276–286.

Linehan, M., Heard, H. E., & Armstrong, H. E. (1993). Naturalistic follow-up of a behavioral treatment for chronically suicidal borderline patients. *Archives of General Psychiatry.*

Linton, S. J., & Melin, L. (1983). Applied relaxation in the management of chronic pain. *Behavioural Psychotherapy, 11,* 337–350.

Lipke, H. J. (1992). Stance for Shapiro. *The Behavior Therapist, 15,* 215–216.

Lipsky, M. M., Kassinove, H., & Miller, N. J. (1980). Effects of rational-emotive therapy, rational role-reversal, and rational-emotive imagery on the emotional adjustment of Community Mental Health Center patients. *Journal of Consulting and Clinical Psychology, 48,* 366–374.

Litten, R. Z., & Allen, J. P. (Eds.). (1992). *Measuring alcohol consumption: Psychosocial and biochemical methods.* Totowa, NJ: Humona Press.

Lochman, J. E. (1992). Cognitive-behavioral intervention with aggressive boys: Three-year follow-up and preventive effects. *Journal of Consulting and Clinical Psychology, 60,* 426–432.

Lochman, J. E., Lampron, L. B., Gemmer, T. C., & Harris, S. R. (1987). Anger coping intervention with aggressive children: A guide to implementation in schoolsettings. In P. A. Keller & S. R. Heyman (Eds.), *Innovations in clinical practice: A source book.* (Vol. 6, pp. 339–357). Sarasota, FL: Professional Resource Exchange.

Locke, E. A. (1971). Is "behavior therapy" behavioristic? (An analysis of Wolpe's psychotherapeutic methods). *Psychological Bulletin, 70,* 318–327.

Locke, H. J., & Wallace, K. M. (1959). Short marital adjustment and prediction tests: Their reliability and validity. *Marriage and Family Living, 21,* 251–255.

Loeber, R. (1988). Natural histories of conduct problems, delinquency, and associated substance use: Evidence for developmental progressions. In B. B. Lahey & A. E. Kazdin (Eds.), *Advances in child clinical psychology* (Vol. 11, pp. 73–124). New York: Plenum.

Loeber, R., Wung, P., Keenan, K., Giroux, B., Stouthamer-Loeber, M., Van Kammen, W. B., & Maughan, B. (1993). Developmental pathways in disruptive child behavior. *Development and Psychopathology, 5,* 101–131.

Logue, A. W. (1995). *Self-control: Waiting until tomorrow for what you want today.* Englewood Cliffs, NJ: Prentice Hall.

LoPiccolo, J. (1994). Sexual dysfunction. In L. W. Craighead, W. E. Craighead, A. E. Kazdin, & M. J. Mahoney (Eds.), *Cognitive and behavioral interventions: An empirical approach to mental health problems* (pp. 183–196). Boston: Allyn and Bacon.

Lovaas, O. I., & Simmons, J. Q. (1969). Manipulation of self-destruction in three retarded children. *Journal of Applied Behavior Analysis, 2,* 143–157.

Lubin, B. (1967). *Manual for depression adjective checklists.* San Diego, CA: Educational and Industrial Testing Service.

Lucas, J. A. (1994). Panic disorder. In V. S. Ramachandran (Ed.), *Encyclopedia of human behavior* (Vol. 3, pp. 389–400). San Diego, CA: Academic.

Luce, S. C. (1986). Residential behavior therapy with autistic children and adolescents. In F. J. Fuoco & W. P. Christian (Eds.), *Behavior analysis and therapy in residential programs.* New York: Van Nostrand.

Luria, A. (1961). *The role of speech in the regulation of normal and abnormal behaviors.* New York: Liveright.

MacDonald, M. L., & Butler, A. K. (1974). Reversal of helplessness: Producing walking behavior in nursing home wheelchair residents using behavior modification procedures. *Journal of Gerontology, 29,* 97–101.

MacPhillamy, D. J., & Lewinsohn, P. M. (1982). The Pleasant Events Schedule: Studies on reliability, validity, and scale intercorrelations. *Journal of Consulting & Clinical Psychology, 50,* 363–380.

Maher, B. A. (1966). *Principles of psychopathology: An experimental approach.* New York: McGraw-Hill.

Mahoney, M. J. (1977). Publication prejudices: An experimental study of confirmatory bias in the peer review system. *Cognitive Therapy and Research, 1,* 161–175.

Mahoney, M. J. (1980). *Abnormal psychology: Perspectives on human variance.* San Francisco: Harper & Row.

Mahoney, M. J., & Arnkoff, D. B. (1978). Cognitive and self–control therapies. In S. L. Garfield & A. E. Bergin (Eds.), *Handbook of psychotherapy and behavior change* (2nd ed.). New York: Wiley.

Mahoney, M. J., & DeMonbreun, B. G. (1977). Psychology of the scientist: An analysis of problem–solving bias. *Cognitive Therapy and Research, 1,* 229–238.

Mahoney, M. J., & Mahoney, K. (1976). *Permanent weight loss.* New York: Norton.

Malcolm, J. (1982). *Psychoanalysis: The impossible profession.* New York: Vintage Books.

Mansdorf, I. J., & Lukens, E. (1987). Cognitive-behavioral psychotherapy for separation anxious children experiencing school phobia. *Journal of the American Academy for Child and Adolescent Psychiatry, 70,* 222–225.

Marcus, M. D., Wing, R. R., Ewing, L., Kern, E., Gooding, W., & McDerott, M. (1990). Psychiatric disorders among obese binge eaters. *International Journal of Eating Disorders, 9,* 69-77.

Margolin, G., & Weiss, R. (1978). Comparative evaluation of therapeutic components associated with behavioral marital treatment. *Journal of Consulting and Clinical Psychology, 46,* 1476–1486.

Marks, I. M. (1969). *Fears and phobias.* London: Heinemann Medical.

Marks, I. M. (1970). Agoraphobic syndrome (phobic anxiety state). *Archives of General Psychiatry, 23,* 538–553.

Marks, I. M. (1972). Perspective on flooding. *Seminars in Psychiatry, 4,* 129–138.

Marks, I. M. (1981a). Behavioural concepts and treatments of neuroses. *Behavioural Psychotherapy, 9,* 137–154.

Marks, I. M. (1981b). *Cure and care of neuroses: Theory and practice of behavioral psychotherapy.* New York: Wiley.

Marks, I. M. (1987). *Fears, phobias, and rituals: Panic, anxiety, and their disorders.* New York: Oxford University Press.

Marks, I. M., & Gelder, M. G. (1965). A controlled retrospective study of behavior therapy in phobic patients. *British Journal of Psychiatry, 111,* 571–573.

Marks, I. M., & Mathews, A. M. (1979). Brief standard self-rating for phobic patients. *Behaviour Research and Therapy, 17,* 263–267.

Marlatt, G. A. (1983). The controlled-drinking controversy: A commentary. *American Psychologist, 38,* 1097–1110.

Marlatt, G. A., & Donovan, D. M. (1981). Alcoholism and drug dependence: Cognitive social learning factors in addictive disorders. In W. E. Craighead, A. E. Kazdin, & M. J. Mahoney (Eds.), *Behavior modification: Principles, issues, and applications* (2nd. ed.) (pp. 264–285). New York: Houghton Mifflin.

Marlatt, G. A., & Gordon, J. R. (Eds.) (1985). *Relapse prevention: Maintenance strategies in the treatment of addictive behaviors.* New York: Guilford.

Marmor, J. Foreword. In R. B. Sloane, F. R. Staples, A. H. Cristol, N. J. Yorkston, & K. Whipple (1975), *Psychotherapy versus behavior therapy* (pp. xv–xviii). Cambridge, MA: Harvard University Press.

Martin, G., & Pear, J. (1978). *Behavior modification: What it is and how to do it.* Englewood Cliffs, NJ: Prentice-Hall.

Martindale, C. (1978). The therapist-as-fixed-effect fallacy in psychotherapy research. *Journal of Consulting and Clinical Psychology, 46,* 1526–1530.

Mash, E. J., & Hunsley, J. (1990). Behavioral assessment: A contemporary approach. In A. S. Bellack, M. Hersen, & A. E. Kazdin (Eds.), *International handbook of behavior modification and therapy* (2nd ed.) (pp. 87–106). New York: Plenum.

Mash, E. J., & Lee, C. M. (1993). Behavioral assessment with children. In R. T. Ammerman & M. Hersen (Eds.), *Handbook of behavior therapy with children and adults* (pp. 13–31). Boston: Allyn and Bacon.

Mash, E. J., & Terdal, L. G. (1988). Behavioral assessment of child and family disturbance. In E. J. Mash & L. G. Terdal (Eds.), *Behavioral assessment of childhood disorders.* (2nd. ed.). New York: Guilford.

Masserman, J. H. (1943). *Behavior and neurosis.* Chicago: University of Chicago Press.

Masters, W. H., & Johnson, V. E. (1966). *Human sexual response.* Boston: Little, Brown.

Masters, W. H., & Johnson, V. E. (1970). *Human sexual inadequacy.* Boston: Little, Brown.

Masterson, J. F. (1985). *Treatment of the borderline adolescent: A developmental approach.* New York: Brunner/Mazel.

Mathews, A. (1978). Fear-reduction research and clinical phobias. *Psychological Bulletin, 85,* 390–404.

Mathews, A., Bancroft, J., Whitehead, A., Hackman, A., Julier, D., Gath, D., & Shaw, P. (1976). The behavioural treatment of sexual inadequacy: A comparative study. *Behaviour Research and Therapy, 14,* 427–436.

Mathews, A. M., Gelder, M. G., & Johnson, D. W. (1981). *Agoraphobia: Nature and treatment.* New York: Guilford.

Mathews, A. M., Johnson, D. W., Lancashire, M., Munby, M., Shaw, P. M., & Gelder, M. G. (1976). Imaginal flooding and exposure to real phobic situations: Treatment outcome with agoraphobic patients. *British Journal of Psychiatry, 129,* 362–371.

Mathews, A. M., Johnston, D. W., Shaw, P. M., & Gelder, M. G. (1974). Process variables and the prediction of outcome in behavior therapy. *British Journal of Psychiatry, 125,* 256–264.

Mathews, A. M., & Rezin, V. (1977). Treatment of dental fears by imaginal flooding and rehearsal of coping behavior. *Behaviour Research and Therapy, 15,* 321–328.

Mathews, A. M., & Shaw, P. (1973). Emotional arousal and persuasion effects in flooding. *Behaviour Research and Therapy, 11,* 587–598.

Mathews, A. M., Teasdale, J., Munby, M., Johnston, D., & Shaw, P. (1977). A home-based treatment program for agoraphobia. *Behavior Therapy, 8,* 915–924.

Matthews, K. A. (1988). Coronary heart disease and type A behaviors: Update on and alternative to the Booth-Kewley and Friedman (1987) qualitative review. *Psychological Bulletin, 104,* 373-380.

McCaffrey, R. J., & Fairbank, J. A. (1985). Behavioral assessment and treatment of accident–related posttraumatic stress disorder: Two case studies. *Behavior Therapy, 16,* 406–416.

McClanahan, L. E., & Krantz, P. J. (1981). Accountability systems for protection of the rights of autistic children and youth. In G. T. Hannah, W. P. Christian, & H. B. Clark (Eds.), *Preservation of client rights: A handbook for practitioners providing therapeutic, educational, and rehabilitative services.* New York: Macmillan/Free Press.

McCrady, B., Stout, R., Noel, N., Abrams, D., & Nelson, H. (1991). Comparative effectiveness of three types of spouse involved alcohol treatment: Outcomes 18 months after treatment. *British Journal of Addiction, 86,* 1415–1424.

McGee, R., Freehan, M., Williams, S., & Anderson, J. (1992). DSM–III disorders from age 11 to age 15. *Journal of the American Academy of Child and Adolescent Psychiatry, 31,* 50–59.

McGee, R., Freehan, M., Williams, S., Partridge, F., Silva, P. A., & Kelly, J. (1990). DSM–III disorders in a large sample of adolescents. *Journal of the American Academy of child and Adolescent Psychiatry, 29,* 611–619.

McGee, R., & Share, D. L. (1988). Attention deficit hyperactivity disorder and academic failure: Which comes first and what should be treated? *Journal of the American Academy of child and Adolescent Psychiatry, 27,* 318–325.

McFall, R. M., & Lillesand, D. B. (1971). Behavior rehearsal with modeling and coaching in assertive training. *Journal of Abnormal Psychology, 77,* 313–323.

McFall, R. M., & Marston, A. R. (1970). An experimental investigation of behavior rehearsal in assertive training. *Journal of Abnormal Psychology, 76,* 295–303.

McFall, R. M., & Twentyman, C. T. (1973). Four experiments on the relative contributions of rehearsal, modeling, and coaching to assertive training. *Journal of Abnormal Psychology, 81,* 199–218.

McGlynn, F. D. (1973). Graded imagination and relaxation as components of experimental desensitization. *The Journal of Nervous and Mental Disease, 156,* 377–385.

McGlynn, F. D., Mealiea, W. L., & Landau, D. L. (1981). The current status of systematic desensitization. *Clinical Psychology Review, 1,* 149–179.

McLellan, A. T., Kushner, H., Metzger, D., Peters, R., Smith, I., Grissom, G., Pettinati, H., & Argeriou, M. (1992). The fifth edition of the Addiction Severity Index. *Journal of Substance Abuse Treatment, 9,* 199–213.

McMahon, R. J. (1984). In T. H. Ollendick & M. Hersen (Eds.), *Child behavioral assessment* (pp. 80–105). New York: Pergamon.

McMahon, R. J. (1994). Diagnosis, assessment, and treatment of externalizing problems in children: the role of longitudinal data. *Journal of Consulting and Clinical Psychology, 62,* 901–917.

McMahon, R. J. & Wells, K. C. (1989). Conduct disorders. In E. J. Mash & R. A. Barkley, (Eds.), *Treatment of childhood disorders* (pp. 73–134). New York: Guilford.

McNally, R. J. (1994). Introduction to the special series: Innovations in cognitive-behavioral approaches to schizophrenia. *Behavior Therapy, 25,* 1–4.

McNally, R. J. (1995). Cognitive processing of trauma-relevant information in PTSD. *PTSD Research Quarterly, 6* (2), 1–6.

McWhirter, D. P., & Mattison, A. M. (1980). Treatment of sexual dysfunction in homosexual male couples. In S. R. Leiblum & L. A. Pervin (Eds.), *Principles and practice of sex therapy* (pp. 321–345). New York: Guilford.

Meadows, E. A., & Barlow, D. H. (1994). Anxiety disorders. In V. S. Ramachandran (Ed.), *Encyclopedia of human behavior* (Vol. 1, pp. 165–173). San Diego, CA: Academic.

Meichenbaum, D. H. (1966). Sequential strategies in two cases of hysteria. *Behaviour Research and Therapy, 4,* 89–94.

Meichenbaum, D. (1971). Examination of model characteristics in reducing avoidance behavior. *Journal of Personality and Social Psychology, 17,* 298–307.

Meichenbaum, D. H. (1974). Self–instructional training: A cognitive prosthesis for the aged. *Human Development, 17,* 273–280.

Meichenbaum, D. H. (1977). *Cognitive-behavior modification: An integrative approach.* New York: Plenum.

Meichenbaum, D. H. (1995). Cognitive-behavioral therapy in historical perspective. In B. Bongar & L. E. Beutler (Eds.), *Comprehensive textbook of psychotherapy: Theory and practice* (pp. 140–158). New York: Oxford University Press.

Meichenbaum, D. H., & Butler, L. (1982). Cognitive ethology: Assessing the streams of cognition and emotion. In K. Blankstein, P. Pliner, & J. Polivy (Eds.), *Advances in the study of communication and affect.* New York: Plenum.

Meichenbaum, D. H., & Cameron, R. (1973). Training schizophrenics to talk to themselves: A means of developing attentional controls. *Behavior Therapy, 4,* 515–534.

Meichenbaum, D. H., & Cameron, R. (1983). Stress innoculation training: Toward a general paradigm for training coping skills. In D. H. Meichenbaum & M. Jaremko (Eds.), *Stress reduction and prevention.* New York: Plenum.

Meichenbaum, D. H., & Goodman, J. (1971). Training impulsive children to talk to themselves: A means of developing self-control. *Journal of Abnormal Psychology, 77,* 115–126.

Meichenbaum, D. H., Gilmore, J. B., & Fedoravicius, A. (1971). Group insight versus group desensitization in treating speech anxiety. *Journal of Consulting and Clinical Psychology, 36,* 410–421.

Meichenbaum, D. H., & Turk, D. (1982). Stress, coping, and disease: A cognitive-behavioral perspective. In R. Neufeld (Ed.), *Psychological stress and psychopathology.* New York: McGraw-Hill.

Meichenbaum, D., & Turk, D. (1987). *Facilitating treatment adherence.* New York: Plenum.

Menninger, K. (1958). *Theory of psychoanalytic technique.* New York: Basic Books.

Merckelbach, H., Hogervorst, E., Kampman, M., & de Jongh, A. (1994). Effects of "eye movement desensitization" on emotional processing in normal subjects. *Behavioural and Cognitive Psychotherapy, 22,* 331–335.

Metropolitan height and weight tables for men and women. (1983). *Statistical Bulletin, 1,* 2–9.

Meyer, V. (1957). The treatment of two phobic patients on the basis of learning principles. *Journal of Abnormal and Social Psychology, 55,* 261–266.

Meyer, V., & Gelder, M. G. (1963). Behavior therapy and phobic disorders. *British Journal of Psychiatry, 109,* 19–28.

Mikulincer, M., & Solomon, Z. (1988). Attributional style and combat-related posttraumatic stress disorder. *Journal of Abnormal Psychology, 97,* 308–313.

Miles, T. R. (1966). *Eliminating the unconscious: A behaviourist view of psycho-analysis.* Oxford: Pergamon Press.

Milgram, S. (1974). *Obedience to authority.* New York: Harper & Row.

Miller, G. E., & Prinz, R. J. (1990). Enhancement of social learning family interventions for child conduct disorder. *Psychological Bulletin, 108,* 291–307.

Miller, P. M., & Hersen, M. (1976). Modification of marital interactions between an alcoholic and his wife. In J. D. Krumboltz & L. E. Thorson (Eds.), *Counseling methods.* New York: Holt, Rinehart, and Winston.

Miller, P. M., Hersen, M., Eisler, R. M., & Elkin, T. E. A. (1974). A retrospective analysis of alcohol consumption on laboratory tasks as related to therapeutic outcome. *Behaviour Research and Therapy, 12,* 73–76.

Miller, P. M., Hersen, M., Eisler, R. M., & Watts, J. G. (1974). Contingent reinforcement of lowered blood/alcohol levels in an outpatient chronic alcoholic. *Behaviour Research and Therapy, 12,* 261–263.

Miller, W. R. (1982). Treating problem drinkers: What works? *The Behavior Therapist, 5,* 15–18.

Miller, W. R., Brown, J. M., Simpson, T., Handmaker, N. S., Bien, T. H., Luckie, L. F., Montgomery, H. A., Hester, R. K., & Tonigan, J. S. (1995). What works? A methodological analysis of the alcohol treatment outcome literature. In R. K. Hester & W. R. Miller (Eds.) *Handbook of alcoholism treatment approaches* (2nd. ed.) (pp. 12–44). Boston: Allyn and Bacon.

Miller, W. R., & Hester, R. K. (1980). Treating the problem drinker: Modern approaches. In W. R. Miller (Ed.), *The addictive behaviors: Treatment of alcoholism, drug abuse, smoking, and obesity.* New York: Pergamon.

Miller, W. R., & Hester, R. K. (1995). Treatment for alcohol problems: Toward an informed eclecticism. In R. K. Hester & W. R. Miller (Eds.), *Handbook of alcoholism treatment approaches* (2nd ed.) (pp. 1–11). Boston: Allyn and Bacon.

Miller, W. R. & Rollnick, S. (1991). *Motivational interviewing: Preparing people to change addictive behavior.* New York: Guilford.

Miller, W. R., Tonigan, J. S., & Longabaugh, R. (1994). *DrInC: An instrument for assessing adverse consequences of alcohol use.* Rockville, MD: National Institute of Alcohol Abuse and Alcoholism.

Millet, P. E., & Schwebel, A. I. (1994). Assessment of training received by psychology graduate students in the area of chronic mental illness. *Professional Psychology: Research and Practice, 25,* 76–79.

Millon, T. (1981). *Disorders of personality: DSM-III, Axis II.* New York: Wiley.

Millon, T. (1987). On the genesis and prevalence of the borderline personality disorder: A social learning analysis. *Journal of Personality Disorders, 1,* 354-372.

Milne, D. (1986). *Training behavior therapists: Methods, evaluation and implementation with parents, nurses and teachers.* London: Croom Helm.

Mineka, S. (1985). Animal models of anxiety-based disorders: Their usefulness and limitations. In A. H. Tuma & J. D. Maser (Eds.), *Anxiety and the anxiety disorders* (pp. 199–244). Hillsdale, NJ: Lawrence Erlbaum.

Mineka, S., & Kihlstrom, J. F. (1978). Unpredictable and uncontrollable events: A new perspective on experimental neurosis. *Journal of Abnormal Psychology, 87,* 256–271.

Minuchin, S., Rosman, B., & Baker, L. (1978). *Psychosomatic families.* Cambridge, MA: Harvard University Press.

Mischel, W. (1968). *Personality and assessment.* New York: Wiley.

Mitchell, J. E. (1990). *Bulimia nervosa.* Minneapolis, MN: University of Minnesota Press.

Mitchell, J., McCauley, E., Burke, P. M., & Moss, S. J. (1988). Phenomenology of depression in children and adolescents. *Journal of the American Academy of Child and Adolescent Psychiatry, 27,* 12–20.

Mize, J., & Ladd, G. (1990). Toward the development of successful social skills training for preschool children. In S. R. Asher & J. D. Coie (Eds.), *Peer rejection in childhood* (pp. 338-364). Cambridge: Cambridge University Press.

Moffitt, T. E. (1990). Juvenile delinquency and attention deficit disorder: Boys' developmental trajectories from age 3 to age 15. *Child Development, 61,* 893–910.

Monti, P. M., Binkoff, J. A., Abrams, D. B., Zwick, W. R., Nirenberg, T. D., & Liepman, M. R. (1987). Reactivity of alcoholics and nonalcoholics to drinking cues. *Journal of Abnormal Psychology, 96,* 122–126.

Monti, P. M., Rohsenow, D. J., Rubonis, A. V., Niaura, R. S., Sirota, A. D., Colby, S. M., Goddard, P., & Abrams, D. B. (1993). Cue exposure with coping skills treatment for male alcoholics: A preliminary investigation. *Journal of Consulting and Clinical Psychology, 61,* 1011–1019.

Moos, R. H., & Billings, A. G. (1982). Conceptualizing and measuring coping resources and processes. In L. Goldberger & S. Breznitz (Eds.), *Handbook of stress.* New York: The Free Press.

Morgan, G. D., Ashenberg, Z. S., & Fisher, E. B. (1988). Abstinence from smoking and the social environment. *Journal of Consulting and Clinical Psychology, 56,* 298–301.

Morokoff, P. J. (1993). Female sexual arousal disorder. In W. O'Donohue, & J. H. Geer (Eds.), *Handbook of sexual dysfunctions: Assessment and treatment* (pp. 157–199). Boston: Allyn and Bacon.

Morris, R. J., & Kratochwill, T. R. (1983). *Treating children's fears and phobias: A behavioral approach.* Elmsford, NY: Pergamon.

Morrison, A. P., Haddock, G., & Tarrier, N. (1995). Intrusive thoughts and auditory hallucinations: A cognitive approach. *Behavioural and Cognitive Psychotherapy, 23,* 265–280.

Morrison, R. L. (1988). Structured interviews and rating scales. In A. S. Bellack & M. Hersen (Eds.) *Behavioral assessment: A practical handbook* (3rd ed.) (pp. 252–277). New York: Pergamon.

Moskowitz, D. S., Schwartzman, A. E., & Ledinham, J. E. (1985). Stability and change in aggression and withdrawal in middle childhood and adolescence. *Journal of Abnormal Psychology, 94,* 30-41.

Mowrer, O. H. (1947). On the dual nature of learning as a reinterpretation of "conditioning" and "problem-solving." *Harvard Educational Review,* 102–148.

Mowrer, O. H. (1960). *Learning theory and behavior.* New York: Wiley.

Mowrer, O. H., & Mowrer W. M. (1938). Enuresis: A method for its study and treatment. *American Journal of Orthopsychiatry, 8,* 436–459.

Moye, J., & Brown, E. (1995). Postdoctoral training in geropsychology: Guidelines for formal programs and continuing education. *Professional Psychology: Research and Practice, 26,* 591–597.

Mumford, S. J., Patch, I. C. L., Andrew, N., & Wyner, L. (1975). A token economy ward programme with chronic schizophrenic patients. *British Journal of Psychiatry, 126,* 60–72.

National Institute of Mental Health. (1991). *Caring for people with severe mental disorders: A national plan of research to improve services.* DHHS Pub. No. (ADM)91–1762. Washington, DC: Government Printing Office.

National Institute on Alcohol Abuse and Alcoholism. (1983). *Special report to the U.S. Congress on alcohol and health.* Washington, DC: U.S. Government Printing Office.

National Institute on Alcohol Abuse and Alcoholism (1990). *Seventh special report to the U.S. Congress on alcohol and health* DHHS. Pub. No. ADM 90–1656. Washington, DC: Government Printing Office.

Nay, W. R. (1977). Analogue measures. In A. R. Ciminero, K. S. Calhoun, & H. E. Adams (Eds.), *Handbook of behavioral assessment.* New York: Wiley.

Neale, J. M., & Oltmanns, T. F. (1980). *Schizophrenia.* New York: Wiley.

Neisworth, J. T., & Madle, R. A. (1982). Retardation. In A. S. Bellack, M. Hersen, & A. E. Kazdin (Eds.), *International handbook of behavior modification and therapy* (pp. 853–889). New York: Plenum Press.

Nelson, G., & Walsh–Bowers, R. (1994). Psychology and psychiatric survivors. *American Psychologist, 49,* 895–896.

Nelson, R. E., & Craighead, W. E. (1977). Selective recall and negative feedback, self-control behaviors, and depression. *Journal of Abnormal Psychology, 86,* 379–388.

Nelson, R. O. (1977). Assessment and therapeutic functions of self–monitoring. In M. Hersen, R. Eisler, & P. M. Miller (Eds.), *Progress in behavior modification.* New York: Academic.

Nelson, R. O. (1983). Behavioral assessment: Past, present, and future, *Behavioral Assessment, 5,* 195–206.

Nelson, R. O., & Barlow, D. H. (1981). Behavioral assessment: Basic strategies and initial procedures. In D. H. Barlow (Ed.), *Behavioral assessment of adult disorders.* New York: Guilford.

Newman, C. F. (1994). Understanding client resistance: Methods for enhancing motivation to change. *Cognitive and Behavioral Practice, 1,* 47–69.

Neziroglu, F. A., & Yaryura-Tobias, J. A. (1993). Body dysmorphic disorder: Phenomenology and case descriptions. *Behavioural Psychotherapy, 21,* 27–36.

Niaura, R. S., Rohsenow, D. J., Binkoff, J. A., Monit, P. M., Pedraza, M., & Abrahams, D. B. (1988). Relevance of cue reactivity to understanding alcohol and smoking relapse. *Journal of Abnormal Psychology, 97,* 133–152.

Nishith, P., Hearst, D. E., Mueser, K. T., & Foa, E. B. (1995). PTSD and major depression: Methodological and treatment considerations in a single case design. *Behavior Therapy, 26,* 319–335.

Norman, W. H., Miller, I. W., & Dow, M. G. (1988). Characteristics of depressed patients with elevated levels of dysfunctional cognitions. *Cognitive Therapy and Research, 12,* 39–52.

Novaco, R. W. (1975). *Anger control: The development and evaluation of an experimental treatment.* Lexington, MA: D. C. Heath.

Nowicki, S., & Strickland, B. R. (1973). A locus of control scale for children. *Journal of Consulting and Clinical Psychology, 40,* 148–154.

O'Brien, J. S. (1979). A modified thought stopping procedure for the treatment of agoraphobia. *Journal of Behavior Therapy and Experimental Psychiatry, 10,* 121–124.

O'Brien, W. H., & Haynes, S. N. (1993). Behavioral assessment in the psychiatric setting. In A. S. Bellack & M. Hersen (Eds.), *Handbook of behavior therapy in the psychiatric setting* (pp. 39–71). New York: Plenum.

O'Donohue, W. T., Fisher, J. E., & Krasner, L. (1986). Behavior therapy and the elderly: A conceptual and ethical analysis. *International Journal of Aging and Human Development, 23,* 1–15.

O'Donohue, W., & Geer, J. H. (Eds.) (1993). *Handbook of sexual dysfunctions: Assessment and treatment.* Boston: Allyn and Bacon.

O'Farrell, T. J. (1995). Marital and family therapy. In R. K. Hester & W. R. Miller (Eds.) *Handbook of alcoholism treatment approaches* (2nd ed.) (pp. 195–220). Boston: Allyn and Bacon.

O'Farrell, T. J., Choquette, K. A., Cutter, H. S. G., Brown, E. D., & McCourt, W. F. (1993). Behavioral marital therapy with and without additional relapse prevention sessions for alcoholics and their wives. *Journal of Studies on Alcohol, 54,* 652–668.

O'Farrell, T. J., & Cowles, K. S. (1989). Marital and family therapy. In R. K. Hester & W. R. Miller (Eds.), *Handbook of alcohol treatment approaches: Effective alternatives* (pp. 183–205). New York: Pergamon.

O'Farrell, T. J., Cutter, H. S. G., Choquette, K. A., Floyd, F. J., & Bayog, R. D. (1992). Behavioral marital therapy for male alcoholics: Marital and drinking adjustment during the two years after treatment. *Behavior Therapy, 23,* 529–549.

O'Hara, P. (1994). Nicotine dependence. In C. G. Last & M. Hersen (Eds.), *Adult behavior therapy casebook* (pp. 79–94). New York: Plenum.

Ohman, A., Erixon, G., & Lofberg, I. (1975). Phobias and preparedness: Phobic versus neutral pictures as conditioned stimuli for human autonomic responses. *Journal of Abnormal Psychology, 84,* 41–45.

O'Leary, K. D. (1984). The image of behavior therapy: It is time to take a stand. *Behavior Therapy, 15,* 219–233.

O'Leary, K. D., & Johnson, S. B. (1979). Psychological assessment. In H. C. Quay & J. S. Werry (Eds.), *Psychopathological disorders of childhood* (2nd ed.). New York: Wiley.

Ollendick, T. H. (1979). Behavioral treatment of anorexia nervosa: A five-year study. *Behavior Modification, 3,* 124–135.

Ollendick, T. H. (1983). Reliability and validity of the Revised Fear Survey Schedule for children (FSSC-R). *Behaviour Research and Therapy, 21,* 685–692.

Ollendick, T. H., & Cerny, J. A. (1981). *Clinical behavior therapy with children.* New York: Plenum.

Ollendick, T. H., & Francis, G. (1988). Behavioral assessment and treatment of children's phobias. *Behavior Modification, 12,* 165–204.

Ollendick, T. M., Hagopian, L. P., & Huntzinger, R. M. (1994). Cognitive-behavior therapy with nightime fearful children. *Journal of Behavior Therapy and Experimental Psychiatry.*

Ollendick, T. H., & Hersen, M. (1984). An overview of child behavioral assessment. In T. H. Ollendick & M. Hersen (Eds.), *Child behavioral assessment* (pp. 3–19). New York: Pergamon

Ollendick, T. M., & Huntzinger, R. M. (1990). Separation anxiety disorder in childhood. In M. Hersen & C. G. Last (Eds.), *Handbook of child and adult psychopathology: A longitudinal perspective* (pp. 133–149). New York: Pergamon.

Ollendick, T. M. & King, N. J. (1994). Diagnosis, assessment, and treatment of internalizing problems in children: The role of longitudinal data. *Journal of Consulting and Clinical Psychology, 62,* 918–927.

Ollendick, T. M., Ollier, K., & Yule, W. (1991). Fears in British children and their relationship to manifest anxiety and depression. *Journal of Child Psychology and Psychiatry, 32,* 321–331.

Olmsted, M. P., Davis, R., Garner, D. M., Eagle, M., & Rockert, W. (1991). Efficacy of brief psychoeducational intervention for bulimia nervosa. *Behaviour Research and Therapy, 29,* 71–83.

Olson, S. L. (1992). Development of conduct problems and peer rejection in preschool children: A social systems analysis. *Journal of Abnormal Child Psychology, 20,* 327–350.

O'Neil, P. M., & Jarrell, M. P. (1992). Psychological aspects of obesity and dieting. In T. A. Wadden & T. B. VanItallie (Eds.), *Treatment of the seriously obese patient* (pp. 252–270). New York: Guilford.

Orlinsky, D. E., & Howard, K. I. (1995). Unity and diversity among psychotherapies: A comparative perspective. In B. Bongar & L. E. Beutler (Eds.), *Comprehensive textbook of psychotherapy: Theory and practice* (pp. 3–23). New York: Oxford University Press.

Osborne, J. G., & Adams, D. L. (1970, April). *Delays in token exchange and presentation in a token economy.* Paper presented at the Western Psychological Association Convention, Los Angeles.

Oyama, & Andrasik, F. (1992). Behavioral strategies in the prevention of disease. In S. M. Turner, K. S. Calhoun, & H. E. Adams (Eds.) *Handbook of clinical behavioral therapy.* New York: Wiley.

Palace, E. M., & Johnston, C. (1989). Treatment of recurrent nightmares by the dream reorganization approach. *Journal of Behavior Therapy and Experimental Psychiatry, 20,* 219–226.

Parks, C. W., & Hollon, S. D. (1988). Cognitive assessment. In A. S. Bellack & M. Hersen (Eds.), *Behavioral assessment: A practical handbook* (3rd ed.) (pp. 341–374). New York: Pergamon.

Patterson, G. R. (1969). Behavioral techniques based upon social learning: An additional base for developing behavior modification technologies. In C. M. Franks (Ed.), *Behavior therapy: Appraisal and status* (pp. 341–374). New York: McGraw-Hill.

Patterson, G. R. (1976). The aggressive child: Victim and architect of a coercive system. In L. A. Hammerlynck, L. C. Handy, & E. J. Mash (Eds.), *Behavior modification and families.* New York: Brunner/Mazel.

Patterson, G. R. (1982). *A social learning approach, Vol. 3: Coercive family process.* Eugene, OR: Castalia.

Patterson, G. R., Capaldi, D., & Bank, L. (1991). An early starter model for predicting delinquency. In D. J. Pepler & K. H. Rubin (Eds.), *The development and treatment of childhood aggression* (pp. 139–168). Hillsdale, NJ: Erlbaum.

Patterson, G. H., Hops, H., & Weiss, R. L. (1975). Interpersonal skills training for couples in early stages of conflict. *Journal of Marriage and the Family, 37,* 295–303.

Patterson, W. M., Dohn, H. H., Bird, J., & Patterson, G. A. (1983). Evaluation of suicidal patients: The SAD PERSONS scale. *Psychosomatics, 24,* 343–349.

Paul, G. L. (1966). *Insight versus desensitization in psychotherapy: An experiment in anxiety reduction.* Stanford: Stanford University Press.

Paul, G. L. (1967a). Insight versus desensitization in psychotherapy two years after termination. *Journal of Consulting Psychology, 31,* 333–348.

Paul, G. L. (1967b). Strategy of outcome research in psychotherapy. *Journal of Consulting Psychology, 31,* 109–118.

Paul, G. L. (1969). Behavior modification research: Design and tactics. In C. M. Franks (Ed.), *Behavior therapy: Appraisal and status.* New York: McGraw-Hill.

Paul, G. L. (1969). Chronic mental patient: Current status—Future directions. *Psychological Bulletin, 71,* 81–94.

Paul, G. L., & Lentz, R. J. (1977). *Psychosocial treatment of chronic mental patients: Milieu versus social learning programs.* Cambridge, MA: Harvard University Press.

Pavlov, I. P. (1927). *Conditioned reflexes: An investigation of the physiological activity of the cerebral cortex* (G. V. Anrep, Trans.). London: Oxford University Press.

Payne, P. V., & Halford, W. K. (1990). Social skills training with chronic schizophrenic patients living in community settings. *Behavioural Psychotherapy, 18,* 49–64.

Pazulinec, R., Meyerrose, M., & Sajwaj, T. (1983). Punishment via response cost. In S. Axelrod & J. Apsche (Eds.), *The effects of punishment on human behavior* (pp. 71–86). New York: Academic.

Pearce, S., & Erskine, A. (1989). Chronic pain. In S. Pearce & J. Wardle (Eds.), *The practice of behavioral medicine* (pp. 83–112). Oxford: BPS Books.

Peck, D. F. (1973). Operant assessment of hearing range in a nonverbal retardate. *Behavior Therapy, 4,* 319–320.

Peck, D. F., & Thorpe, G. L. (1971, Sept.). *Experimental foundations of token economies: A critique.* Paper presented at the Third Annual Conference of the Behavioural Engineering Association, Wexford, Ireland.

Pelham, W. E., & Hinshaw, S. (1992). Behavioral intervention for attention deficit disorder. In S. M. Turner, K. S. Calhoun, & H. E. Adams (Eds.), *Handbook of clinical behavior therapy* (pp. 259–283). New York: Wiley.

Pelham, W. E., & Milich, R. (1991). Individual differences in response to ritalin in classwork and social behavior. In L. Greenhill & B. P. Osman (Eds.), *Ritalin: theory and patient management* (pp. 203–221). New York: Mary Ann Liebert.

Pelham, W. E., Milich, R., Murphy, D. A., & Murphy, H. A. (1989). Normative data on the IOWA Conners teacher rating scale. *Journal of Clinical Child Psychology, 18,* 259–262.

Pendery, M., Maltzmann, I., & West, L. J. (1982). Controlled drinking by alcoholics? New findings and a reevaluation of a major affirmative study. *Science, 217,* 169–175.

Perri, M. G., Shapiro, R. M., Ludwig, W. W., Twentyman, C. T., & McAdoo, W. G. (1984). Maintenance strategies for the treatment of obesity: An evaluation of relapse prevention training and posttreatment contact by mail and telephone. *Journal of Consulting & Clinical Psychology, 52,* 404–413.

Persons, J. B. (1991). Psychotherapy outcome studies do not accurately represent current models of psychotherapy: A proposed remedy. *American Psychologist, 46,* 99–106.

Persons, J. B. (1994). Cognitive behavior therapy. In V. S. Ramachandran (Ed.), *Encyclopedia of human behavior* (Vol. 1, pp. 617–626). San Diego, CA: Academic.

Peterson, A. L., & Azrin, N. H. (1992). An evaluation of behavioral treatments for Tourette syndrome. *Behaviour Research and Therapy, 30,* 167–174.

Peterson, C. (1982). The learned helplessness and attributional interventions in depression. In C. Antak & C. Brewin (Eds.), *Attributions and psychological change* (pp. 97–118). New York: Academic.

Peterson, C. (1994). Learned helplessness. In V. S. Ramachandran (Ed.), *Encyclopedia of human behavior* (Vol. 3, pp. 57–66). San Diego, CA: Academic.

Peterson, C. (1995). Explanatory style and health. In G. M. Buchanan & M. E. P. Seligman (Eds.), *Explanatory style* (pp. 233–252). Hillsdale, NJ: Erlbaum.

Peterson, C. & Bossio, L. (1991). *Health and optimism.* New York: Free Press.

Peterson, C., & Seligman, M. E. P. (1984). Causal explanations as a risk factor for depression: Theory and evidence. *Psychological Review, 91,* 347–374.

Peterson, C., & Seligman, M. E. P. (1985). The learned helplessness model of depression: Current status of theory and research. In E. E. Beckman & W. R. Leber (Eds.), *Handbook of depression: Treatment, assessment, and research* (pp. 914–939). Homewood, IL: Dorsey.

Pfiffner, L. J., O'Leary, S. G. (1995). Psychological treatments: School-based. In J. L. Matson (Ed.), *Hyperactivity in children: A handbook.* Boston: Allyn and Bacon.

Phillips, C. (1977). The modification of tension headache using EMG biofeedback. *Behaviour Research and Therapy, 15,* 119–129.

Phillips, L., Draguns, J. G., & Bartlett, D. P. (1975). Classification of behavior disorders. In N. Hobbs (Ed.), *Issues in the classification of children.* San Francisco: Jossey-Bass.

Piaget, G. W., & Lazarus, A. A. (1969). The use of rehearsal-desensitization. *Psychotherapy: Theory, research, and practice, 6,* 264–266.

Pierce, W. D., & Epling, W. F. (1995). *Behavior analysis and learning.* Englewood Cliffs, NJ: Prentice Hall.

Pinkerton, S., Hughes, H., & Wenrich, W. W. (1982). *Behavioral medicine: Clinical applications.* New York: Wiley.

Pinkston, E. M., Linsk, N. L., & Young, R. N. (1988). Home-based behavioral family treatment of the impaired elderly. *Behavior Therapy, 19,* 331–344.

Pinto, A., & Francis, G. (1993). Obsessive-compulsive disorder in children. In R. T. Ammerman & M. Hersen (Eds.), *Handbook of behavior therapy with children and adults* (pp. 155–166). Boston: Allyn and Bacon.

Pittman, D. J., & Tate, R. L. (1969). A comparison of two treatment programs for alcoholics. *Quarterly Journal of Studies on Alcohol, 30,* 888–899.

Pokorny, A. D. (1968). Myths about suicide. In H. L. P. Resnick (Ed.). *Suicide behaviors.* Boston: Little, Brown.

Pomerleau, C. S., Pomerleau, O. F., Majchrzak, M. J., Kloska, D. D., & Malakuti, R. (1990). Relationship between nicotine tolerance questionnaire scores and plasma cotinine. *Addictive Behaviors, 15,* 73–80.

Pomerleau, O. (1981). Underlying mechanism in substance abuse: Examples from research on smoking. *Addictive Behaviors, 6,* 187–196.

Pomerleau, O. F., & Brady, J. P. (Eds.). (1979). *Behavioral medicine: Theory and practice.* Baltimore: Williams and Wilkins.

Porter, R. (Ed.). (1991). *The Faber book of madness.* London: Faber & Faber.

Porzelius, L. K., Houston, C., Smith, M., Arfken, C., & Fisher, E. (1995). Comparison of a standard behavioral weight loss treatment and a binge eating weight loss treatment. *Behavior Therapy, 26,* 119–134.

Premack, D. (1965). Reinforcement theory. In D. Levine (Ed.), *Nebraska symposium or motivation* (pp. 123–180). Lincoln: University of Nebraska Press.

Preskorn, S.H. (1995). Mental disorders are medical diseases. In W. Barbour (Ed.). *Mental illness: Opposing viewpoints* (pp. 29–36). San Diego, CA: Greenhaven Press.

Pretzer, J. & Fleming, B. (1989). Cognitive-behavioral treatment of personality disorders. *The Behavior Therapist, 12,* 105–109.

Prochaska, J. O., Diclemente, C. C., Velicer, W. F., & Rossi, J. S. (1993). Standardized, individualized, and personalized self–help programs for smpoking cessation. *Health Psychology, 12,* (5), 399–405.

Prochaska, J. O., Velicer, W. F., Guadagnoli, E., Rossi, J. S., & DiClemente, C. C. (1991). Patterns of change: Dynamic typology applied to smoking cessation. *Multivariate Behavioral Research, 26,* 83–107.

Puig–Antich, J. (1982). Major depression and conduct disorder in puberty. *Journal of the American Academy of Child and Adolescent Psychiatry, 21,* 118–128.

Puska, P., Virtamo, J., Tuomilehto, J., Maki, M., & Neitaanmaki, L. (1978). Cardiovascular risk factor changes in three year follow-up of a cohort in connection with a community program (the North Karelia project). *Acta Medica Scandinavica, 204,* 381–388.

Quay, H. C. (1986). Classification. In H. C. Quay & J. S. Werry (Eds.), *Psychopathological disorders of childhood* (3rd ed.) (pp. 1–34). New York: Wiley.

Rachlin, H. (1976). *Introduction to modern behaviorism* (2nd ed.). San Francisco: W. H. Freeman.

Rachman, S. (1971). Obsessional ruminations. *Behaviour Research and Therapy, 9,* 229–235.

Rachman, S. (1976). The modification of obsessions: A new formulation. *Behaviour Research and Therapy, 14,* 437–443.

Rachman, S. J. (1977). The conditioning theory of fear-acquisition: A critical examination. *Behaviour Research and Therapy, 15,* 375–387.

Rachman, S. J. (1978). An anatomy of obsessions. *Behavioural Analysis and Modification, 2,* 253–278.

Rachman, S. (1985). A note on the conditioning theory of fear acquisition. *Behavior Therapy, 16,* 426–428.

Rachman, S. J., & Hodgson, R. I. (1974). Synchrony and desynchrony in fear and avoidance. *Behaviour Research and Therapy, 12,* 311–318.

Rachman, S. J., & Hodgson, R. J. (1980). *Obsessions and compulsions.* Englewood Cliffs, NJ: Prentice-Hall.

Rachman, S. J., Marks, I. M., & Hodgson, R. (1973). The treatment of obsessive-compulsive neurotics by modelling and flooding in vivo. *Behaviour Research and Therapy, 11,* 463–471.

Rachman, S. J., & Teasdale, J. (1969). *Aversion therapy and behavior disorders.* Coral Gables, FL: University of Miami Press.

Rachman, S. J., & Wilson, G. T. (1980). *The effects of psychological therapy* (2nd ed.). Oxford: Pergamon.

Ramirez, M. (1991). *Psychotherapy and counseling with minorities: A cognitive approach to individual differences.* Boston: Allyn and Bacon.

Ramm, E., Marks, I. M., Yuksel, S., & Stern, R. S. (1981). Anxiety management training for anxiety states: Positive compared with negative self-statements. *British Journal of Psychiatry, 140,* 367–373.

Rankin, H., Hodgson, R., & Stockwell, T. (1983). Cue exposure and response prevention with alcoholics: A controlled trial. *Behaviour Research and Therapy, 21,* 435–446.

Rapee, R. M., & Barlow, D. H. (1991). The cognitive-behavioral treatment of panic attacks and agoraphobic avoidance. In J. R. Walker, G. R. Norton, & C. A. Ross (Eds.), *Panic disorder and agoraphobia: A comprehensive guide for the practitioner* (pp. 252–305). Pacific Grove, CA: Brooks/Cole.

Rapoport, J. L. (1986). Childhood obsessive compulsive disorder. *Journal of Child Psychology and Psychiatry, 27,* 289–295.

Raw, M. (1978). The treatment of cigarette dependence. In Y. Israel, F. B. Glaser, H. Kalant, R. E. Popham, W. Schmidt, & R. G. Smart (Eds.), *Research advances in alcohol and drug problems* (pp. 441–485). New York: Wiley.

Rees, V. W., & Heather, N. (1995). Individual differences and cue reactivity. In D. C. Drummond, S. T. Tiffany, S. Glautier, & B. Remington (Eds.), *Addictive behavior: Cue exposure and practice* (pp. 99–118). New York: Wiley.

Rehm, L. P. (1977). A self-control model of depression. *Behavior Therapy, 8,* 787–804.

Rehm, L. P. (1981). A self-control therapy program for treatment of depression. In J. F. Clarkin & H. I. Glazer (Eds.), *Depression: Behavioral and directive intervention strategies.* New York: Garland STPM Press.

Rehm, L. P. (1988). Self-management and cognitive processes in depression. In L. B. Alloy (Ed.), *Cognitive processes in depression.* New York: Guilford.

Rehm, L. P. (1989). Behavioral models of anxiety and depression. In P. C. Kendall & D. Watson (Eds.), *Anxiety and depression: Distinctive and overlapping features.* New York: Academic.

Rehm, L. P., Fuchs, C. Z., Roth, D. M., Kornblith, S. J., & Romano, J. M. (1979). A comparison of self–control and assertion training treatments of depression. *Behavior Therapy, 10,* 429–442.

Reiss, S. (1980). Pavlovian conditioning and human fear: An expectancy model. *Behavior Therapy, 11,* 380–396.

Reiss, S., Peterson, R. A., Gursky, D. M., & McNally, R. J. (1986). Anxiety sensitivity, anxiety frequency, and prediction of fearfulness. *Behaviour Research and Therapy, 24,* 1–8.

Rescorla, R. A. (1988). Pavlovian conditioning: It's not what you think it is. *American Psychologist, 43,* 151–160.

Rescorla, R. A., & Solomon, R. L. (1967). Two-process learning theory: Relationships between Pavlovian conditioning and instrumental learning. *Psychological Review, 74,* 151–182.

Resick, P. A., Jordan, C. G., Girelli, S. A., Hutter, C. K., & Marhoefer-Dvorak, S. (1988). A comparative outcome study of behavioral group therapy for sexual assault victims. *Behavior Therapy, 19,* 385–401.

Reynolds, W. M. (1989). *Reynolds Child Depression Scales.* Odessa, FL: Psychological Assessment Resources.

Reynolds, W. M. (1995). Assessment of depression in children and adolescents by self-report. In W. M. Reynolds & H. F. Johnston (Eds.), *Handbook of depression in children and adults* (pp. 205–234). New York: Plenum.

Richards, W. S., & Thorpe, G. L. (1978). Behavioral approaches to the problems of later life. In M. Storandt, I. C. Siegler, & M. F. Elias (Eds.), *The clinical psychology of aging* (pp. 253–276). New York: Plenum.

Riggs, D. S., Hiss, H., & Foa, E. B. (1992). Marital distress and the treatment of obsessive compulsive disorder. *Behavior Therapy, 23,* 585–597.

Riley, A. J., & Riley, E. J. (1978). A controlled study to evaluate directed masturbation in the management of primary orgasmic failure in women. *British Journal of Psychiatry, 133,* 404–409.

Rimmele, C. T., Howard, M. O., & Hilfrink, M. L. (1995). Aversion therapies. In R. K. Hester & W. R. Miller (Eds.), *Handbook of alcoholism treatment approaches* (2nd ed.) (pp. 134–147). Boston: Allyn and Bacon.

Risley, T. R. (1968). The effects and side effects of punishing the autistic behaviors of a deviant child. *Journal of Applied Behavior Analysis, 1,* 21–34.

Risley, T. R., & Edwards, K. A. (1978). *Behavioral techniques for nursing home care: Toward a system of nursing home organization and management.* Paper presented at the First Annual Nova Behavioral Conference on Aging, Port St. Lucie, FL.

Roberts, M. C., & La Greca, A. M. (1981). Behavioral assessment. In C. E. Walker (Ed.), *Clinical practice of psychology: A practical guide for mental health professionals.* New York: Pergamon.

Robins, C. J., & Hayes, A. M. (1995). The role of causal attributions in the prediction of depression. In G. M. Buchanan & M. E. P. Seligman (Eds.), *Explanatory style* (pp. 71–98). Hillsdale, NJ: Erlbaum.

Robins, L. N., Heltzer, J. E., Croughan, J., & Ratcliff, K. S. (1981). National Institute of Mental Health diagnostic interview schedule: Its history, characteristics, and validity. *Archives of General Psychiatry, 38,* 381–389.

Robinson, J. C., & Lewinsohn, P. M. (1973). Behavior modification of speech characteristics in a chronically depressed man. *Behavior Therapy.*

Robinson, L. A., Berman, J. S., & Neimayer, R. A. (1990). Psychotherapy for the treatment of depression: A comprehensive review of the controlled outcome research. *Psychological Bulletin, 108,* 30-49.

Rodin, J. (1980). The externality theory today. In A. J. Stunkard (Ed.), *Obesity.* Philadelphia: Saunders.

Rodin, J., & Salovey, P. (1989). Health psychology. *Annual Review of Psychology, 40,* 533–579.

Rohsenow, D. J., Monti, P. M., & Abrams, D. B. (1995). Cue exposure treatment in alcohol dependence. In D. C. Drummond, S. T. Tiffany, S. Glautier, & B. Remington (Eds.), *Addictive behavior: Cue exposure and practice* (pp. 169–196). New York: Wiley.

Rohsenow, D. J., Monti, P. M., Rubonis, A. V., Sirota, A. D., Niaura, R. S., Colby, S. M., Wunschel, S. M., & Abrams, D. B. (1994). Cue reactivity as a predictor of drinking among male alcoholics. *Journal of Consulting and clinical Psychology, 62,* 620–626.

Rohsenow, D. J., Niaura, R. S., Childress, A. R., Abrams, D. B., & Monti, P. M. (1990). Cue reactivity in addictive behaviors: theoretical and treatment implications. *International Journal of the Addictions, 25,* 957–993.

Romanczyk, R. G., Kent, R. N., Diament, C., & O'Leary, K. D. (1973). Measuring the reliability of observational data: A reactive process. *Journal of Applied Behavior Analysis, 6,* 175–184.

Rose, R. M., Jenkins, C. D., & Hurst, M. W. (1978). *Air traffic controller health change study.* Report to the Federal Aviation Administration.

Rosen, G. M. (1975). Is it really necessary to use mildly phobic analogue subjects? *Behavior Therapy, 6,* 68–71.

Rosen, G. M. (1992). A note to EMDR critics: What you didn't see is only part of what you don't get. *The Behavior Therapist, 15,* 216.

Rosen, J. C., Orosan, P., & Reiter, J. (1995). Cognitive behavior therapy for negative body image in obese women. *Behavior Therapy, 26,* 25–42.

Rosenfarb, I., & Hayes, S. C. (1984). Social standard setting: The Achilles heel of informational accounts of therapeutic change. *Behavior Therapy, 15,* 515–528.

Rosenman, R. H. (1978). The interview method of assessment of the coronary-prone behavior pattern. In T. M. Dembroski, S. M. Weiss, J. H. Shields, S. G. Hayes, & M. Feinleib (Eds.), *Coronary-prone behavior.* New York: Springer.

Rosenman, R. H., Brand, R. J., Jenkins, C. D., Friedman, M., Straus, R., & Wurm, M. (1975). Coronary heart disease in the Western Collaborative Group Study: Final follow-up experience of 8 1/2 years. *Journal of the American Medical Association, 233,* 872–877.

Rosenman, R. H., Friedman, M., Straus, R., Wurm, M., Kositichek, R., Hahn, W., & Werthessen, N. T. (1964). A predictive study of coronary heart disease. *Journal of the American Medical Association, 189,* 103–110.

Rosenthal, B. S., & Marx, R. D. (1981). A comparison of standard behavioral and relapse prevention programs. *Obesity Bariatric Medicine, 10,* 94–97.

Rosenthal, T., & Bandura, A. (1978). Psychological modeling: Theory and practice. In S. L. Garfield & A. E. Bergin (Eds.), *Handbook of psychotherapy and behavior change* (2nd ed.) New York: Wiley.

Rossiter, E., & Wilson, G. T. (1985). Cognitive restructuring and exposure in the treatment of bulimia nervosa. *Behaviour Research and Therapy, 23,* 349–360.

Roth, D., & Rehm, L. P. (1980). Relationships among self-monitoring processes, memory, and depression. *Cognitive Therapy and Research, 4,* 149–158.

Rothbaum, B. O. (1992). How does EMDR work? *The Behavior Therapist, 15,* 34.

Rothbaum, B. O., & Foa, E. B. (1992a). Cognitive-behavioral treatment of posttraumatic stress disorder. In P. A. Saigh (Ed.), *Posttraumatic stress disorder: A behavioral approach to assessment and treatment* (pp. 85–110). New York: MacMillan.

Rothbaum, B. O., & Foa, E. B. (1992b). Exposure therapy for rape victims with post-traumatic stress disorder. *The Behavior Therapist, 9,* 219–222.

Rothbaum, B. O., Hodges, L. F., Kooper, R., Opdyke, D., Williford, J. S., & North, M. (1995). Virtual reality graded exposure in the treatment of acrophobia: A case report. *Behavior Therapy, 26,* 547–554.

Rubin, K. H. (1985). Socially withdrawn children: An "at risk" population? In B. H. Schneider, K. H. Rubin, & J. E. Ledingham (Eds.), *Children's peer relations: Issues in assessment and intervention* (pp. 125–140). New York: Springer-Verlag.

Rude, S. S., & Rehm, L. P. (1991). Response to treatment for depression: The role of initial status on targeted cognitive and behavioral skills. *Clinical Psychology Review, 11,* 493–514.

Rush, A. J., Beck, A. T., Kovacs, M., & Hollon, S. (1977). Comparative efficacy of cognitive therapy and pharmacotherapy in the treatment of depressed outpatients. *Cognitive Therapy and Research, 1,* 17–37.

Russell, M. A. H., Armstrong, E., & Patel, U. A. (1976). The role of temporal contiguity in electric aversion therapy for cigarette smoking: Analysis of behavior changes. *Behaviour Research and Therapy, 14,* 103–123.

Rutter, M. (1966). Behavioral and cognitive characteristics of a series of autistic children. In J. Wing (Ed.), *Early childhood autism.* Oxford: Pergamon.

Rutter, M. (1983). Stress, coping, and development: Some issues and some questions. In N. Garmezy & M. Rutter (Eds.), *Stress, coping, and development.* New York: McGraw-Hill.

Rutter, M. (1986). The developmental psychopathology of depression: Issues and perspectives. In M. Rutter, C. E. Izard, & P. B. Read (Eds.), *Depression in young people* (pp. 3–30). New York: Guilford.

Rutter, M. (1989). Isle of Wight revisited: Twenty-five years of child psychiatric epidemiology. *Journal of the American Academy for Child and Adolescent Psychiatry, 28,* 633–653.

Rutter, M., Bailey, A., Bolton, P., & Le Couteur, A. (1993). Autism: Syndrome definition and possible genetic mechanisms. In R. Plomin & G. E. Mclearn (Eds.), *Nature, nurture, and psychology* (pp. 269–284). Washington, DC: APA Books.

Rutter, M., Mawhood, L., & Howlin, P. (1992). Language delay and social development. In P. Fletcher & D. Hale (Eds.), *Specific speech and language disorders in children* (pp. 63–72). London: Whurr Publishers.

Rychtarik, R. G., Silverman, W. K., Van Landingham, W. P., & Prue, D. M. (1984). Treatment of an incest victim with implosive therapy: A case study. *Behavior Therapy, 15,* 410–420.

Sacco, W. P., & Beck, A. T. (1985). Cognitive therapy of depression. In E. E. Beckham & W. R. Leber (Eds.), *Handbook of depression: Treatment, assessment, and research* (pp. 3–38). Homewood, IL: Dorsey.

Sackett, D. L., & Snow, J. C. (1979). The magnitude of compliance and noncompliance. In R. B. Hayes, D. W. Taylor, & D. L. Sackett (Eds.), *Compliance in health care.* Baltimore, MD: Johns Hopkins University Press.

Saigh, P. A. (1985). On the nature and etiology of traumatic stress. *Behavior Therapy, 16,* 423–426.

Saigh, P. A. (1992a). History, current nosology, and epidemiology. In P. A. Saigh (Ed.), *Posttraumatic stress disorder: A behavioral approach to assessment and treatment* (pp. 1–27). New York: Macmillan.

Saigh, P. A. (Ed.). (1992b). *Posttraumatic stress disorder: A behavioral approach to assessment and treatment.* New York: Macmillan.

Salkovskis, P. M. (1983). Treatment of an obsessional patient using habituation to audiotaped ruminations. *British Journal of Clinical Psychology, 22,* 311–313.

Salkovskis, P. M. (1985). Obsessional-compulsive problems: A cognitive-behavioural analysis. *Behaviour Research and Therapy, 23,* 571–583.

Salkovskis, P. M., Richards, H. C., & Forrester, E. (1995). The relationship between obsessional problems and intrusive thoughts. *Behavioural and Cognitive Psychotherapy, 23,* 281–299.

Salkovskis, P. M., & Warwick, H. M. C. (1986). Morbid preoccupations, health anxiety and reassurance: A cognitive-behavioural approach to hypochondriasis. *Behaviour Research and Therapy, 24,* 597–602.

Salter, A. (1949). *Conditioned reflex therapy.* New York: Creative Age Press.

Sanchez, V. C., Lewinsohn, P. M. & Larson, D. (1980). Assertion training: Effectiveness in the treatment of depression. *Journal of Clinical Psychology, 36,* 526–529.

Sancillo, M. F. M. (1987). Peer interaction as a method of therapeutic intervention with children. *Clinical Psychology Review, 7,* 474–500.

Sanders, M. R., & Dadds, M. R. (1993). *Behavioral family intervention.* Boston: Allyn and Bacon.

Sarason, I. G., & Sarason, B. R. (1981). Teaching cognitive and social skills to high school students. *Journal of Consulting and Clinical Psychology, 49,* 908–918.

Sato, R. A., & Heiby, E. M. (1991). Depression and post– traumatic stress disorder in battered women: Consequences of victimization. *The Behavior Therapist, 14,* 151–156.

Sattler, J. M. (1988). *Assessment of children* (3rd ed.). San Diego: Jermoe M. Sattler.

Schachter, S. (1978). Pharmacological and psychological determinants of smoking. *Annals of Internal Medicine, 88,* 104–114.

Schachter, S., & Singer, J. E. (1962). Cognitive, social, and physiological determinants of emotional state. *Psychological Review, 69,* 379–399.

Schaefer, H. H., & Martin, P. L. (1969). Behavioral therapy for "apathy" of hospitalized schizophrenics. *Psychological Reports, 19,* 1147–1158.

Schnurer, A. T., Rubin, R. R., & Roy (1973). Systematic desensitization of anorexia nervosa as a weight phobia. *Journal of Behavior Therapy and Experimental Psychiatry, 4,* 149–153.

Schopler, E., Reichler, R. J., Bashford, A., Lansing, M. D., & Marcus, L. M. (1990). *Psychoeducational profile—Revised.* Austin, TX: Pro-Ed.

Schreibman, L., Charlop, M., & Kurtz, P. F. (1992). Behavioral treatment for children with autism. In S. M. Turner, K. S. Calhoun, & H. E. Adams (Eds.), *Handbook of clinical behavioral therapy* (pp. 337–354). New York: Wiley.

Schukit, M. A. (1994). A clinical model for genetic influences in alcohol dependence. *Journal of Studies of Alcohol, 55,* 5–17.

Schwartz, G. E., & Weiss, S. M. (1978). *Proceedings of the Yale conference on behavioral medicine.* DHEW Publications (NIH) 78–1424.

Schwartz, R. M., & Gottman, J. M. (1976). Toward a task analysis of assertive behavior. *Journal of Consulting and Clinical Psychology, 44,* 910–920.

Scott, A. (1993). Consumers/survivors reform the system, bringing a "human face" to research. *Resources: Workforce Issues in Mental Health Systems, 5,* 3–6.

Scotti, J. R., Schulman, D. E., & Hojnacki, R. M. (1994). Functional analysis and unsuccessful treatment of Tourette's syndrome in a man with profound mental retardation. *Behavior Therapy, 25,* 721–738.

Seligman, M. E. P. (1971). Phobias and preparedness. *Behavior Therapy, 2,* 307–320.

Seligman, M. E. P. (1973). Fall into helplessness. *Psychology Today, 7,* 43–48.

Seligman, M. E. P. (1975). *Helplessness: On depression, development, and death.* San Francisco: W. H. Freeman.

Seligman, M. E. P. (1989). Explanatory style: Predicting depression, achievement, and health. In M. D. Yapko (Ed.), *Brief approaches to treating anxiety and depression.* New York: Brunner/Mazel.

Seligman, M. E. P., & Yellen, A. (1987). What is a dream? *Behaviour Research and Therapy, 25,* 1–24.

Selye, H. (1936). A syndrome produced by diverse nocuous agents. *Nature, 138,* 32.

Selzer, M. L. (1971). The Michigan Alcohol Screening Test: The quest for a new diagnostic instrument. *American Journal of Psychiatry, 127,* 1653–1658.

Serbin, L. A., Peters, P. L., McAfter, V. J., & Schwartzman, A. E. (1991). Childhood aggression and withdrawal as predictors of adolescentpregnancy, early parenthood, and environmental risk for the next generation. *Canadian Journal of Behavioral Science, 23,* 318–331.

Shapiro, E. S. (1984). Self-monitoring procedures. In T. H. Ollendick & M. Hersen (Eds.), *Child behavioral assessment* (pp. 148–165). New York: Pergamon.

Shapiro, F. (1989). Eye movement desensitization: A new treatment for post–traumatic stress disorder. *Journal of Behavior Therapy and Experimental Psychiatry, 20,* 211–217.

Shapiro, F. (1991a). Eye movement desensitization and reprocessing procedure: From EMD to EMD/R—A new treatment model for anxiety and related traumata. *The Behavior Therapist, 14,* 133–135.

Shapiro, F. (1991b). Eye movement desensitization and reprocessing: A cautionary note. *The Behavior Therapist, 14,* 188.

Shapiro, F. (1992). Dr. Francine Shapiro responds. *The Behavior Therapist, 15,* 111, 114.

Shapiro, F. (1995). *Eye movement desensitization and reprocessing: Basic principles, protocols, and procedures.* New York: Guilford.

Shapiro, M. B. (1966). The single case in clinical-psychological research. *Journal of General Psychology, 74,* 3–22.

Shaw, B. F., Vallis, T. M., & McCabe, S. B. (1985). The assessment of the severity and symptom patterns. In E. E. Beckham & W. R. Leber (Eds.), *Handbook of depression: Treatment, assessment, and research* (pp. 372–407). Homewood, IL: Dorsey.

Sheldon-Wildgen, J., & Risley, T. R. (1982). Balancing clients' rights: The establishment of human-rights and peer-review committees. In A. S. Bellack, M. Hersen, & A. E. Kazdin (Eds.), *International handbook of behavior modification and therapy* (pp. 263–289). New York: Plenum Press.

Sher, K., & Levenson, R. (1983). Alcohol and tension reduction: The importance of individual differences. In L. Pohorecky & J. Buick (Eds.), *Stress and alcohol use.* New York: Elsevier.

Sherman, W. M. (1990). *Behavior modification.* New York: Harper & Row.

Shiffman, S., Read, L., Maltese, J., Rapkin, D., & Jarvik, M. E. (1985). Preventing relapse in ex–smokers: A self-management program. In G. A. Marlatt & J. R. Gordon (Eds.), *Relapse prevention* (pp. 472–520). New York: Guilford.

Sieber, J. E. (1994). Will the new code help researchers to be more ethical? *Professional Psychology: Research and Practice, 25,* 369–375.

Siegel, J. M., & Spivack, G. (1976). Problem-solving therapy: The description of a new program for chronic psychiatric patients. *Psychotherapy: Theory, Research, and Practice, 13.*

Silva, P. de, Rachman, S., & Seligman, M. (1977). Prepared phobias and obsessions: Therapeutic outcome. *Behaviour Research and Therapy, 15,* 65–78.

Silverman, W., & Eisen, A. R. (1992). Age differences in the reliability of parent and child reports of child anxious symptomotology using a structured interview. *Journal of the American Academy of Child and Adolescent Psychiatry, 31,* 117–124.

Silverman, W. & Kearny, C. A. (1993). Behavioral treatment of childhood anxiety disorders. In V. B. VanHaselt & M. Hersen (Eds.), *Handbook of behavior therapy and pharmacotherapy for children: A comparative analysis.* New York: Grune & Stratton.

Silverman, W. K., & Nelles, W. B. (1988). The anxiety disorders interview schedule for children. *Journal of the American Academy of Child and Adolescent Psychiatry, 27,* 772–778.

Simons, A. D., Murphy, G. E., Levine, J. L., & Wetzel, R. D. (1986). Cognitive therapy and pharmacotherapy for depression: Sustained improvement over one year. *Archives of General Psychiatry, 43,* 43-48.

Sinnott, A., Jones, R. B., Scott-Fordham, A., & Woodward, R. (1981). Augmentation of in vivo exposure treatment for agoraphobia by the formation of neighborhood self-help groups. *Behaviour Research and Therapy, 19,* 339–347.

Skinner, B. F. (1953). *Science and human behavior* (pp. 227–241). New York: The Free Press.

Skinner, B. F. (1961). *Cumulative record* (enlarged edition). New York: Appleton-Century-Crofts.

Skinner, B. F. (1961). What is psychotic behavior? In B. F. Skinner, *Cumulative record* (enlarged edition). New York: Appleton-Century-Crofts.

Skinner, B. F. (1966). Operant behavior. In W. K. Honig (Ed.), *Operant behavior: Areas of research and application.* New York: Appleton-Century-Crofts.

Sloane, R. B., Staples, F. R., Cristol, A. H., Yorkston, N. J., & Whipple K. (1975). *Psychotherapy versus behavior therapy.* Cambridge, MA: Harvard University Press.

Smith, G. B., Schwebel, A. I., Dunn, R. L., & McIver, S. D. (1993). The role of psychologists in the treatment, management, and prevention of chronic mental illness. *American Psychologist, 48,* 966–971.

Smith, J. E., & Meyers, R. J. (1995). The community reinforcement approach. In R. K. Hester & W.

R. Miller (Eds.), *Handbook of alcoholism treatment approaches* (2nd ed.) (pp. 251– 266). Boston: Allyn and Bacon.

Smith, T. W. (1989). Assessment in rational-emotive therapy: Empirical access to the ABCD model. In M. E. Bernard & R. DiGiuseppe (Eds.), *Inside rational-emotive therapy: A critical appraisal of the theory and therapy of Albert Ellis* (pp. 135–153). San Diego, CA: Academic.

Smith, T. W. (1992). Hostility and health: Current status of a psychosomatic hypothesis. *Health Psychology, 11,* 139-150.

Sobell, L. C., & Sobell, M. B. (1992). Timeline followback: A technique for assessing self-reported ethanol consumption. In J. Allen & R. Z. Litten (Eds.), *Measuring alcohol consumption: Psychosocial and historical methods* (pp. 41–72). Totwota, NJ: Humana Press.

Sobell, L. C., Toneatto, T., Sobell, M. B. (1994). Behavioral assessment and treatment planning for alcohol, tobacco, and other drug problems: Current status with an emphasis on clinical applications. *Behavior Therapy, 25,* 533–580.

Sobell, M. B., & Sobell, L. C. (1973). Individualized behavior therapy for alcoholics. *Behavior Therapy, 4,* 49–72.

Sobell, M. B., & Sobell, L. C. (1978). *Behavioral treatment of alcohol problems: Individualized therapy and controlled drinking.* New York: Plenum.

Sobell, M. B., & Sobell, L. C. (1982). Controlled drinking: A concept coming of age. In K. R. Blankstein & J. Polivy (Eds.), *Advances in the study of communication and affect* (Vol. 7) *Self-control and self-modification of emotional behavior.* New York: Plenum.

Sobell, M. B., & Sobell, L. C. (1984). The aftermath of heresy: A response to Pendery et al.'s (1982) critique of "Individualized behavior therapy for alcoholics." *Behaviour Research and Therapy, 22,* 413–440.

Sobell, M. B., & Sobell, L. C. (1993). *Problem drinkers: Guided self-change treatment.* New York: Guilford.

Solberg, L. I., & Kottke, T. E. (1992). Smoking cessation strategies. In M. F. Fleming & K. L. Barry (Eds.), *Addictive disorders.* St. Louis: Mosby.

Solomon, R. L., Kamin, L. J., & Wynne, L. C. (1953). Traumatic avoidance learning: The outcomes of several extinction procedures with dogs. *Journal of Abnormal and Social Psychology, 48,* 291–302.

Solomon, R. L., & Wynne, L. C. (1954). Traumatic avoidance learning: The principles of anxiety conservation and partial irreversibility. *Psychological Review, 61,* 353–385.

Solomon, Z., Mikulincer, M., & Flum, H. (1988). Negative life events, coping responses, and combat–related psychopathology: A prospective study. *Journal of Abnormal Psychology, 97,* 302–307.

Solyom, L., McClure, D. J., Heseltine, G. F. D., Ledwidge, B., & Solyom, C. (1972). Variables in the aversion relief therapy of phobics. *Behavior Therapy, 3,* 21–28.

Southam, M. A., Agras, W. S., Taylor, C. B., & Kraemer, H. C. (1982). Relaxation training: Blood pressure lowering during the working day. *Archives of General Psychiatry, 39,* 715–717.

Spanier, G. B. (1976). Measuring dyadic adjustment: New scales for assessing the quality of marriage and similar dyads. *Journal of Marriage and the Family, 38,* 15–28.

Spiegel, T. A., Wadden, T. A., & Foster, G. D. (1991). Objective measurement of eating rate during behavioral treatment of obesity. *Behavior Therapy, 22,* 61-67.

Spitzer, R. L., Endicott, J., & Robins, E. (1978). Research diagnostic criteria. *Archives of General Psychiatry, 35,* 773–782.

Spitzer, R. L., & Williams, J. B. (1985). *Instruction manual for the structured clinical interview for DSM-III.* New York: Biometrics Research Department, New York State Psychiatric Institute.

Spivak, G., & Shure, M. B. (1974). *Social adjustment of young children: A cognitive approach to solving real-life problems.* San Francisco: Jossey-Bass.

Stampfl, T. G., & Levis, D. J. (1967). Essentials of implosive therapy: A learning-theory-based psychodynamic behavioral therapy. *Journal of Abnormal Psychology, 71,* 496–503.

Stanek, L. J. (1993). Manipulative language, discriminatory practices. *Resources: Workforce issues in mental health systems, 5,* 9–10.

Stanley, L. (1980). Treatment of ritualistic behavior in an eight-year-old girl by response prevention. *Journal of Child Psychology and Psychiatry, 21,* 85–90.

Stanley, M. A., & Wagner, A. L. (1994). Obsessive-compulsive behavior. In V. S. Ramachandran (Ed.), *Encyclopedia of human behavior* (Vol. 3, pp. 333–344). San Diego, CA: Academic.

Stark, K. D., & Bookman, C. (1992). Childhood depression: Theory and family-school intervention. In M. Fine & C. Carlson (Eds.), *Handbook of family-school intervention: A systems perspective* (pp. 247–271). Orlando, FL: Grune & Stratton.

Stark, K. D., Reynolds, W. M., & Kaslow, N. J. (1987). A comparison of the relative efficacy of self–control therapy and a behavioral problem-solving therapy for depression. *Journal of Abnormal Child Psychology, 15,* 91–113.

Stark, K. D., Swearer, S., Delaune, M., Knox, L., & Winter, J. (1995). Depressive disorders. In R. T. Ammerman & M. Hersen (Eds.), *Handbook of child behavior therapy in the psychiatric setting* (pp. 269–300). New York: Wiley.

Steinbruck, S. M., Maxwell, S. E., & Howard, G. S. (1983). A meta-analysis of psychotherapy and drug therapy in the treatment of unipolar depression with adults. *Journal of Counseling and Clinical Psychology, 51,* 856–863.

Steketee, G. (1993). Social support and treatment outcome of obsessive compulsive disorder at 9-month follow-up. *Behavioural Psychotherapy, 21,* 81–95.

Steketee, G. (1994). Behavioral assessment and treatment planning with obsessive compulsive disorder: A review emphasizing clinical application. *Behavior Therapy, 25,* 613–633.

Steketee, G., & Foa, E. B. (1987). Rape victims: Post-traumatic stress responses and their treatment: A review of the literature. *Journal of Anxiety Disorders, 1,* 69–86.

Steketee, G., & Frost, R. O. (1994). Measurement of risk-taking in obsessive-compulsive disorder. *Behavioural and Cognitive Psychotherapy, 22,* 287–298.

Stern, R., & Marks, I. M. (1973). Contract therapy in obsessive-compulsive neurosis with marital discord. *British Journal of Psychiatry, 123,* 681–684.

Stockwell, T. (1995). Anxiety and stress management. In R. K. Hester & W. R. Miller (Eds.) *Handbook of alcoholism treatment approaches* (2nd ed.) (pp. 242–250). Boston: Allyn and Bacon.

Stokes, T. (1995). A wrongly filled tabula rasa? [Review of R. Van Houten & S. Axelrod (Eds.), Behavior analysis and treatment.] *Contemporary Psychology, 40,* 428–430.

Stone, A. A., Bovbjerg, D. M., Neale, J. M., & Naploi, A. (1992). Development of cold symptoms following experimental rhinovirus infection is related to prior stressful events. *Behavioral Medicine, 18,* 115-120.

Stone, A. A., Valdimarsdottir, H. B., Katkin, E. S., Burns, J., & Cox, D. S. (1993). Effects of mental stressors on mitogen-induced lymphocyte esponses in the laboratory. *Psychology and Health, 8,* 269-284.

Strain, P. S. (1977). Effects of peer social initiations on withdrawn preschool children: Some training and generalization effects. *Journal of Abnormal Child Psychology, 5,* 445–455.

Strain, P. S., & Fox, J. J. (1981). Peers as behavior change agents for withdrawn classmates. In B. B. Lahey & A. E. Kazdin (Eds.), *Advances in child clinical psychology* (Vol. 4). New York: Plenum.

Straw, M. K., Straw, R. B., Mahoney, M. J., Rogers, T., Mahoney, B. K., Craighead, L. W., & Stunkard, A. J. (1984). The Master questionnaire: Preliminary reports on an obesity assessment device. *Addictive Behavior, 9,* 1–100.

Strauss, C. C. (1994). Overanxious disorder. In T. Ollendick, N. J. King, & W. Yule (Eds.), *Interna-*

tional handbook of phobias and anxiety disorders in children and adults (pp. 187-206). New York: Plenum.

Strauss, C. C., Lease, C. A., Last, C. G., & Francis, G. (1988). Overanxious disorder: An examination of developmental differences. *Journal of Abnormal Child Psychology, 16*, 433–443.

Street, L. L., & Barlow, D. H. (1994). Anxiety disorders. In L. W. Craighead, W. E. Craighead, A. E. Kazdin, & M. J. Mahoney (Eds.), *Cognitive and behavioral interventions: An empirical approach to mental health problems* (pp. 71–87). Boston: Allyn and Bacon.

Stromberg, C. D., Haggarty, D. J., Leibenluft, R. F., McMillian, M. H., Mishkin, B., Rubin, B. L., & Trilling, H. R. (1988). *The psychologist's legal handbook*. Washington DC: The Council for the National Register of Health Service Providers in Psychology.

Stromberg, C., Schneider, J., & Joondeph, B. (1993). Dealing with potentially dangerous patients. *The Psychologist's Legal Update, 2*. Washington, DC: National Register of Health Service Providers in Psychology.

Strupp, H. H. (1978). In S. Garfield & A. Bergin (Eds.), *Handbook of psychotherapy and behavior change*. New York: Wiley.

Stuart, R. B. (1980). *Helping couples change: A special learning approach to marital therapy*. New York: Guilford.

Stunkard, A. J., & Kaplan, D. (1977). Eating in public places: A review of reports of the direct observation of eating behavior. *International Journal of Obesity, 1*, 89–101.

Stunkard, A. J., & Messick, S. (1979). *A new scale to assess restrained eating*. Unpublished manuscript, University of Pennsylvania.

Stunkard, A. J., & Wadden, T. A. (1992). Psychological aspects of severe obesity. *American Journal of Clinical Nutrition, 55*, 524S–532S.

Sturgis, E. T., & Gramling, S. E. (1988). Psychophysiological assessment. In A. S. Bellack & M. Hersen (Eds.), *Behavioral assessment: A practical handbook* (3rd ed.) (pp. 213–251). Elmsford, NY: Pergamon.

Suinn, R. M. (1995). Schizophrenia and bipolar disorder: Origins and influences. *Behavior Therapy, 26*, 557–571.

Suinn, R. M., & Richardson, F. (1971). Anxiety management training: A nonspecific behavior therapy program for anxiety control. *Behavior Therapy, 2*, 498–510.

Suinn, R. M., & Bloom, L. J. (1978). Anxiety management training for pattern A behavior. *Journal of Behavioral Medicine, 1*, 25–35.

Sullivan, K. T., & Bradbury, T. N. (1996). Preventing marital dysfunction: The primacy of secondary strategies. *The Behavior Therapist, 19*, 33–36.

Swan, G. E., & MacDonald, M. L. (1978). Behavior therapy in practice: A national survey of behavior therapists. *Behavior Therapy, 9*, 799–807.

Swedo, S. E. & Rapoport, J. L. (1989). Phenomenology and differential diagnosis of obsessive-compulsive disorder in children and adolescents. In J. L. Rapoport (Ed.), *Obsessive-compulsive disorder in children and adolescents* (pp. 13–32). Washington, DC: American Psychiatric Press.

Swedo, S., Rapoport, J. L., Leonard, H., Lenane, M., & Cheslow, D. (1989). Obsessive–compulsive disorder in children and adolescents: Clinical phenomenology of 70 consecutive cases. *Archives of General Psychiatry, 46*, 335–341.

Szasz, T. (1990). Law and psychiatry: The problems that will not go away. In D. Cohen (Ed.), Special issue: Challenging the therapeutic state: Critical perspectives on psychiatry and the mental health system. *The Journal of Mind and Behavior, 11*, (3 and 4), 557–564 (311–318).

Szasz, T. (1995). Mental disorders are not medical diseases. In W. Barbour (Ed.), *Mental illness: Opposing viewpoints* (pp. 37–42). San Diego, CA: Greenhaven Press.

Taplin, P. S., & Reid, J. B. (1973). Effects of instructional set and experimenter influence on observer reliability. *Child Development, 44*, 547–554.

Tate, J. C., & Schmitz, J. M. (1993). A proposed revision of the Fagerstrom tolerance questionnaire. *Addictive Behaviors, 18,* 135–143.

Taylor, S. E. & Brown, J. D. (1988). Illusion and well-being: A social psychological perspective on mental health. *Psychological Bulletin, 103,* 193-210.

Thase, M. E., Simons, A. D., Cahalano, J., McGoory, J., & Harden, T. (1991). Severity of depression and response to cognitive behavior therapy. *American Journal of Psychiatry, 148,* 784–789.

Thibaut, J. W., & Kelley, H. H. (1959). *The social psychology of groups.* New York: Wiley.

Thompson, R. L. (1994). Classical conditioning. In V. S. Ramachandran (Ed.), *Encyclopedia of human behavior* (Vol. 1, pp. 591–601). San Diego, CA: Academic.

Thompson-Pope, S. K. & Turkat, I. D. (1989). Paranoia about paranoid personality research. *Journal of Clinical Psychology, 50,* 310.

Thorley, G. (1984). Review of follow-up and follow-back studies of childhood hyperactivity. *Psychological Bulletin, 96,* 116–132.

Thorndike, E. L. (1898). Animal intelligence: An experimental study of the associative processes in animals. *Psychological Review (Monograph Supplement 2, No. 8)* 1, 16.

Thorpe, G. L. (1971). Dream changes following desensitization. *Behavior Therapy, 2,* 627.

Thorpe, G. L. (1975). Desensitization, behavior rehearsal, self-instructional training and placebo effects on assertive-refusal behavior. *European Journal of Behavioral Analysis and Modification, 1,* 30–44.

Thorpe, G. L. (1977). Behavior therapy or behaviorism? (Correspondence). *AABT Newsletter, 4* (4) 7.

Thorpe, G. L. (1989). Confounding of assessment method with reaction assessed in the three systems model of fear and anxiety: A comment on Douglas, Lindsay, and Brooks. *Behavioural Psychotherapy, 17,* 191–192.

Thorpe, G. L. (1994). Agoraphobia. In V. S. Ramachandran (Ed.), *Encyclopedia of human behavior* (Vol. 1, pp. 57–69). San Diego, CA: Academic.

Thorpe, G. L., Barnes, G. S., Hunter, J. E., & Hines, D. (1983). Thoughts and feelings: Correlations in two clinical and two nonclinical samples. *Cognitive Therapy and Research, 7,* 565–574.

Thorpe, G. L., & Burns, L. E. (1983). *The agoraphobic syndrome: Behavioural approaches to evaluation and treatment.* Chichester, UK: Wiley.

Thorpe, G. L., Burns, L. E., Smith, P. J., & Blier, M. J. (1984). Agoraphobia: Research developments and clinical implications. In C. M. Franks (Ed.), *New developments in behavior therapy* (pp. 281–317). New York: Haworth.

Thorpe, G. L., Freedman, E. G., & Lazar, J. D. (1985). Assertiveness training and exposure in vivo for agoraphobics. *Behavioural Psychotherapy, 13,* 132–141.

Thorpe, G. L., Freedman, E. G., & McGalliard, D. W. (1984). Components of rational-emotive imagery: Two experiments with nonassertive students. *Journal of Rational Emotive Therapy, 2,* 11–19.

Thorpe, G. L., & Hecker, J. E. (1991). Psychosocial aspects of panic disorder. In J. R. Walker, G. R. Norton, & C. A. Ross (Eds.), *Panic disorder and agoraphobia: A comprehensive guide for the practitioner* (pp. 175–207). Pacific Grove, CA: Brooks/Cole.

Thorpe, G. L., Hecker, J. E., Cavallaro, L. A., & Kulberg, G. E. (1987). Insight versus rehearsal in cognitive-behavior therapy: A crossover study with sixteen phobics. *Behavioural Psychotherapy, 15,* 319–336.

Thorpe, G. L., Parker, J. D., & Barnes, G. S. (1992). The Common Beliefs Survey III and its subscales: Discriminant validity in clinical and nonclinical subjects. *Journal of Rational-Emotive and Cognitive-Behavior Therapy, 10,* 95–104.

Thorpe, J. G., Schmidt, E., Brown, P. T., & Castell, D. (1964). Aversion-relief therapy: A new method for general application. *Behavior Research and Therapy, 2,* 71–82.

Toseland, R., & Rose, S. D. (1978). A social skills training program for older adults: Evaluation of three group approaches. *Social Work Research Abstracts.*

Trexler, L. D., & Karst, T. O. (1972). Rational-Emotive Therapy, placebo, and no-treatment effects on public-speaking anxiety. *Journal of Abnormal Psychology, 79,* 60–67.

Trimble, M. R. (1981). *Post-traumatic neurosis: From railway spine to the whiplash.* Chichester, UK: Wiley.

Trower, P. (1995). Adult social skills: State of the art and future directions. In W. O'Donohue & L. Krasner (Eds.), *Handbook of psychological skills training: Clinical techniques and applications* (pp. 54–80). Boston: Allyn and Bacon.

Turk, D., Meichenbaum, D., & Genest, M. (1983). *Pain and behavioral medicine.* New York: Guilford.

Turk, D. C., & Rudy, T. E. (1986). Assessment of cognitive factors in chronic pain: A worthwhile enterprise? *Journal of Consulting and Clinical Psychology, 54,* 760-768.

Turk, D. C., & Rudy, T. E. (1989). An integrated approach to pain treatment: Beyond the scalpel and the syringe. In C. D. Tollison (Ed.), *Handbook of chronic pain management* (pp. 222-237). Baltimore, MD: Williams & Wilkins.

Turk, D. C., Rudy, T. E., & Sorkin, B. A. (1992). Chronic pain: Behavioral conceptualizations and intervention. In S. Turner, K. S. Calhoun, & H. E. Adams (Eds.), *Handbook of clinical behavioral therapy* (pp. 373-395). New York: Wiley.

Turkat, I. D. (1990). *The personality disorders: A psychological approach to clinical management.* New York: Pergamon.

Turkat, I. D., & Carlson, C. R. (1984). Symptomatic vs. data based formulation of treatment: The case of dependent personality. *Journal of Behavioral Therapy and Experimental Psychology, 15,* 153–160.

Turkat, I. D., & Maisto, S. A. (1985). Personality disorders: Application of the experimental model to the formulation and modification of personality disorders. In D. H. Barlow (Ed.), *Clinical handbook of personality disorders.* New York: Guilford.

Turner, S. M., Beidel, D. C., Dancu, C. V., & Keys, D. J. (1986). Psychopathology of social phobia and comparison. *Journal of Abnormal Psychology, 95*(4), 389–394.

Ullman, L., & Krasner, L. (1975). *A psychological approach to abnormal behavior* (2nd ed.). Englewood Cliffs, NJ: Prentice-Hall.

USDHHS. (1990). *The health benefits of smoking cessation: A report of the Surgeon General* (DHSS Publication # CDC 90-8416). Washington, DC: Government Printing Office.

Vaillant, G. E. (1983). *The natural history of alcoholism: Causes, patterns, and paths to recovery.* Cambridge, MA: Harvard University Press.

Vandereycken, W., Kog, E., & Vanderlinden, J. (1989). *The family approach to eating disorders.* New York: PMA Publishing.

Van der Kolk, B. A. (1987). *Psychological trauma.* Washington, DC: American Psychiatric Press.

Vygotsky, L. (1962). *Thought and language.* New York: Wiley.

Waddell, M. T., Barlow, D. H., & O'Brian, G. T. (1984). A preliminary investigation of cognitive and relaxation treatment of panic disorder: Effects of intense anxiety versus "background" anxiety. *Behavior Research and Therapy, 22,* 393–402.

Walen, S. R., DiGiuseppe, R., & Dryden, W. (1992). *A practitioner's guide to rational-emotive therapy* (2nd ed.). New York: Oxford University Press.

Waltz, J., & Jacobson, N. S. (1994). Behavioral couples therapy. In L. W. Craighead, W. E. Craighead, A. E. Kazdin, & M. J. Mahoney (Eds.), *Cognitive and behavioral interventions: An empirical approach to mental health problems* (pp. 169–181). Boston: Allyn and Bacon.

Wanberg, K. W., & Horn, J. L. (1983). Assessment of alcohol use with multi-dimensional concepts and measures. *American Psychologist, 38,* 1055–1069.

Watson, D. L., & Tharp, R. G. (1985). *Self-directed behavior: Self-modification for personal adjustment* (4th ed.). Monterey, CA: Brooks/Cole.

Watson, J. B., & Rayner, R. (1920). Conditioned emotional reactions. *Journal of Experimental Psychology, 3,* 1–14.

Watson, J. P., & Marks, I. M. (1971). Relevant and irrelevant fear in flooding: A cross-over study of phobic patients. *Behavior Therapy, 2,* 275–293.

Webster-Stratton, C., & Hammond, M. (1990). Predictors of treatment outcome in parent training for families with conduct problem children. *Behavior Therapy, 21,* 319–337.

Webster-Stratton, C., & Herbert, M. (1994). *Troubled families-problem children.* New York: Wiley.

Wechsler, D. (1974). *Manual for the Wechsler Intelligence Scale for Children-Revised (WISC–R).* New York: Psychological Corporation.

Weiner, H. (1994). The revolution in stress theory and research. In R. P. Liberman & J. Yager (Eds.), *Stress in psychiatric disorders* (pp. 1–36). New York: Springer.

Weinman, B., Gelbart, P., Wallace, M., & Post, M. (1972). Inducing assertive behavior in chronic schizophrenics: A comparison of socioenvironmental, desensitization and relaxation therapies. *Journal of Consulting and Clinical Psychology, 39,* 246–252.

Weintraub, W. (1981). Compulsive and paranoid personalities. In J. R. Lion (Ed.), *Personality disorders: Diagnosis and management.* Baltimore: Williams & Wilkins.

Weiss, G., & Hechtman, L. T. (1993). *Hyperactive children grown up* (2nd ed.). New York: Guilford.

Weiss, R. L., & Cerreto, M. C. (1980). The martial status inventory: Development of a measure of dissolution potential. *American Journal of Family Therapy, 8,* 80–85.

Weiss, R. L., Hops, H., & Patterson, G. R. (1973). A framework for conceptualizing marital conflict, a technology for altering it, some data for evaluating it. In F. W. Clark & L. A. Hamerlynck (Eds.), *Critical issues in research and practice: Proceedings of the Fourth Banff International Conference on Behavior Modification.* Champaign, IL: Research Press.

Weiss, R. L., & Perry, B. (1979). *Assessment and treatment of marital dysfunction.* Eugene, OR: Oregon Marital Studies Program.

Weiss, R. L., & Wieder, G. B. (1982). Marital distress. In A. S. Bellack, M. Hersen, & A. E. Kazdin (Eds.), *International handbook of behavior modification and therapy* (pp. 767–809). New York: Plenum.

Weissman, M. M. (1985). The epidemiology of anxiety disorders: Rates, risks, and familiar patterns. In A. H. Tuma & J. D. Maser (Eds.), *Anxiety and the anxiety disorders* (pp. 275–296). Hillsdale, NJ: Lawrence Erlbaum.

Wells, K. C. (1984). Review of "A social learning approach, Vol. 3: Coercive family process," by G. R. Patterson. *Behavior Therapy, 15,* 121–127.

Werry, J. S. (1994). Diagnostic and classification issues. In T. Ollendick, N. J. King, & W. Yule (Eds.), *International handbook of phobias and anxiety disorders in children and adults* (pp. 21-42). New York: Plenum.

Wesolowski, M. D., & Zawlocki, R. J. (1982). The differential effects of procedures to eliminate an injurious self-stimulatory behavior (digito-ocular sign) in blind retarded twins. *Behavior Therapy, 13,* 334–345.

Whalen, C. K. (1989). Attention deficit and hyperactivity disorders. In T. H. Ollendick & M. Hersen (Eds.), *Handbook of child psychopathology.* New York: Plenum.

Whalen, C. K., & Henker, B. (1976). Psychostimulants and children: A review and analysis. *Psychological Bulletin, 83,* 1113–1130.

Whalen, C. K., Henker, B., Buhmester, D., Hinshaw, S. P., Huber, A., & Laski, K. (1989). Does stimulant medication improve the peer status of hyperactive children? *Journal of Consulting and Clinical Psychology, 57,* 545–549.

Whalen, C. K., Henker, B., & Dotemoto, S. (1981). Teacher response to methylphenidate v. Placebo status of hyperactive boys in the classroom. *Child Development, 52,* 1005–1014.

Whalen, C. K., Henker, B., & Henshaw, S. P. (1985). Cognitive-behavioral therapies for hyperactive children: Premises, problems, and prospects. *Journal of Abnormal Child Psychology, 13,* 391–410.

Whisman, M. A. (1993). Mediators and moderators of change in cognitive therapy of depression. *Psychological Bulletin, 114,* 248–265.

Whitaker, A., Johnson, J., Shaffer, B. T., Rappoport, J. L., Kalikow, K., Walsh, B. T., Davies, M., Braiman, S., & Dolinsky, A. (1990). Uncommmon troubles in young people: Prevalence estimates of selected psychiatric disorders in a nonreferred adolescent population. *Archives of General Psychiatry, 47,* 487–496.

Wilkins, W. (1971). Desensitization: Social and cognitive factors underlying the effectiveness of Wolpe's procedure. *Psychological Bulletin, 76,* 311–317.

Wilkins, W. (1979). Expectancies in therapy research: Discriminating among heterogeneous nonspecifics. *Journal of Consulting and Clinical Psychology, 47,* 837–845.

Wilkins, W. (1983). Failure of placebo groups to control for nonspecific events in therapy outcome research. *Psychotherapy: Theory, Research, and Practice, 20,* 31–37.

Williams, D. A., & Thorn, B. E. (1989). An empirical assessment of pain beliefs. *Pain, 36,* 351–358.

Williams, J. B. W., & Spitzer, R. L. (1995). The issue of sex bias in DSM-III: A critique of "A woman's view of DSM-III" by Marcie Kaplan. In S. O. Lilienfeld (Ed.), *Seeing both sides: Classic controversies in abnormal psychology* (pp. 71–76). Pacific Grove, CA: Brooks/Cole. (Original work published in 1983.)

Williams, J. G., Barlow, D. H., & Agras, W. S. (1972). Behavioral measurement of severe depression. *Archives of General Psychiatry, 27,* 330–333.

Williams, S. L., & Rappoport, A. (1983). Cognitive treatment in the natural environment for agoraphobics. *Behavior Therapy, 14,* 299–313.

Williamson, D. A., Davis, C. J., Duchman, E. G., McKenzie, S. J., & Watkins, P. C. (1990). *Assessment of eating disorders: Obesity, anorexia, and bulimia nervosa.* New York: Pergamon.

Williamson, D. A., Cubic, B. A., & Fuller, R. D. (1992). Eating disorders. In S. Turner, K. S. Calhoun, & H. E. Adams (Eds.), *Handbook of clinical behavioral therapy* (pp. 355–371). New York: Wiley.

Willner, A. G., Braukman, C. J., Kirigin, K. A., & Wolf, M. M. (1978). Achievement place: A community model for youths in trouble. In D. Marholin (Ed.), *Child behavior therapy* (pp. 239–273). New York: Gardner.

Wilson, G. T. (1973). Counterconditioning versus forced exposure in extinction of avoidance responding and conditioned fear in rats. *Journal of Comparative and Physiological Psychology, 82,* 105–114.

Wilson, G. T. (1980). Toward specifying the "nonspecific" factors in behavior therapy. In M. J. Mahoney (Ed.), *Psychotherapy process: Current issues and future directions.* New York: Plenum. (Pp. 283–307).

Wilson, G. T. (1981a). Behavioural concepts and treatments of neuroses: Comments on Marks. *Behavioural Psychotherapy, 9,* 155–166.

Wilson, G. T. (1981b). Some thoughts about clinical research. *Behavioral Assessment, 3,* 217–225.

Wilson, G. T. (1982). Psychotherapy process and procedure. The behavioral mandate. *Behavior Therapy, 13,* 291–312.

Wilson, G. T. (1984). Clinical issues and strategies in the practice of behavior therapy. In C. M. Franks, G. T. Wilson, P. C. Kendall, & K. D. Brownell (Eds.), *Annual review of behavior therapy: Theory and practice* (pp. 291–320). (Vol. 10) New York: Guilford.

Wilson, G. T. (1993). Assessment of binge eating. In C. G. Fairburn & G. T. Wilson (Eds.), *Binge eating: Nature, assessment, and treatment* (pp. 227–249). New York: Guilford.

Wilson, G. T. (1995). Behavior therapy. In R. J. Corsini & D. Wedding (Eds.), *Current psychotherapies* (5th ed.) (pp. 197–228). Itasca, IL: F. E. Peacock.

Wilson, G. T., & Brownell, K. D. (1980). Behavior therapy for obesity: An evaluation of treatment outcome. *Advances in Behavior Research and Therapy, 3,* 49–86.

Wilson, G. T., & Davison, G. C. (1971). Fear reduction processes in systematic desensitization: Animal studies. *Psychological Bulletin, 76,* 1–14.

Wilson, G. T., Nathan, P. E., O'Leary, K. D., & Clark, L. A. (1996). *Abnormal psychology: Integrating perspectives.* Boston: Allyn and Bacon.

Wing, R. R., & Jeffery, R. W. (1979). Outpatient treatments of obesity: A comparison of methodology and clinical results. *International Journal of Obesity, 3,* 261–269.

Wolf, M. M., Risley, T. R., & Mees, H. L. (1964). Application of operant conditioning procedures to the behavior problems of an autistic child. *Behavior Research and Therapy, 1,* 305–312.

Wolpe, J. (1958). *Psychotherapy by reciprocal inhibition.* Stanford, CA: Stanford University Press.

Wolpe, J. (1973). *The practice of behavior therapy* (2nd ed.). New York: Pergamon.

Wolpe, J. (1975). Foreword. In R. B. Sloane, F. R. Staples, A. H. Cristol, N. J. Yorkston, & K. Whipple. *Psychotherapy versus behavior therapy* (pp. xixxx). Cambridge, MA: Harvard University Press.

Wolpe, J. (1976). Behavior therapy and its malcontents: II. Multimodal eclecticism, cognitive exclusivism and "exposure" empiricism. *Journal of Behavior Therapy and Experimental Psychiatry, 7,* 109–116.

Wolpe, J. (1981). *Our useless fears.* Boston: Houghton Mifflin.

Wolpe, J. (1982a). Behavioristic psychotherapy: Its character and origin. In J. Wolpe, *The practice of behavior therapy* (3rd ed.) (pp. 1–12). New York: Pergamon.

Wolpe, J. (1982b). Review of "Cure and care of neuroses," by I. M. Marks. *The Behavior Therapist, 5,* 37.

Wolpe, J. (1982c). *The practice of behavior therapy* (3rd ed.). New York: Pergamon.

Wolpe, J. (1990). *The practice of behavior therapy* (4th ed.). New York: Pergamon.

Wolpe, J., & Lang, P. J. (1969). *Fear survey schedule.* San Diego, CA: Educational and Industrial Testing Service.

Wolpe, J., & Lazarus, A. A. (1966). *Behavior therapy techniques.* New York: Pergamon.

Wolpe, J., & Rachman, S. (1960). Psychoanalytic "evidence": A critique based on Freud's case of little Hans. *Journal of Nervous and Mental Disease, 131,* 135–148.

Woodward, R., & Jones, R. (1980). Cognitive restructuring treatment: A controlled trial with anxious patients. *Behavior Research and Therapy, 18,* 401–407.

Wooley, S. C., & Kearney-Cooke (1986). Intensive treatment of bulimia and body image disturbance. In K. D. Brownell & J. P. Foreyt (Eds.), *Handbook of eating disorders.* New York: Basic Books.

Wooley, S. C., Wooley, O. W., & Dyrenforth, S. R. (1979). Theoretical, practical, and social issues in behavioral treatments of obesity. *Journal of Applied Behavior Analysis, 12,* 3–25.

Wooley, S. C., Wooley, O. W. (1984). Should obesity be treated at all? In A. J. Stunkard & E. Stellar (Eds.), *Eating and its disorders* (pp. 185–192). New York: Raven Press.

Woolfolk, A. E., Woolfolk, R. L., & Wilson, G. T. (1977). A rose by any other name . . . : Labeling bias and attitudes toward behavior modification. *Journal of Consulting and Clinical Psychology, 45,* 184–191.

Woolfolk, R. L., & Richardson, F. C. (1984). Behavior therapy and the ideology of modernity. *American Psychologist, 39,* 777–786.

Worsley, J. L. (1970). The causation and treatment of obsessionality. In L. E. Burns & J. L. Worsley (Eds.), *Behavior therapy in the 1970's.* Bristol: John Wright.

Wright, J. H., & Davis, D. (1994). The therapeutic relationship in cognitive-behavioral therapy: Patient perceptions and therapist responses. *Cognitive and Behavioral Practice, 1,* 25–45.

Yates, A. J. (1962). *Frustration and conflict.* London: Methuen.

Yates, A. J. (1970). *Behavior therapy.* New York: Wiley.

Yates, B. T. (1985). *Self-management: The science and art of helping yourself.* Belmont, CA: Wadsworth.

Yoman, J. (1996). The good news for behavior therapy's converted. [Review of P. W. Corrigan & R. P. Liberman, Behavior therapy in psychiatric hospitals.] *Contemporary Psychology, 41,* 64–65.

Young, J. & Swift, W. (1988). Schema-focused cognitive therapy for personality disorders: Part I. *International Cognitive Therapy Newsletter, 4,* 13-14.

Yufit, R. I. & Bongar, B. (1992). Structured clinical assessment of suicide risk in emergency room and hospital settings. In B. Bongar (Ed.), *Suicide: Guidelines for assessment, management, and treatment.* New York: Oxford University Press.

Zeiss, A. M., Lewinsohn, P. M., & Munoz, R. F. (1979). Nonspecific improvement effects in depression using interpersonal, cognitive, and pleasant events focused treatments. *Journal of Consulting and Clinical Psychology, 47,* 427–439.

Zelman, D. C., Brandon, T. H., Jorenby, D. E., & Baker, T. B. (1992). Measures of affect and nicotine dependence predict differential response to smoking cessation. *Journal of Consulting and Clinical Psychology, 60,* 943–952.

Zigler, E., & Phillips, L. (1960). Social effectiveness and symptomatic behaviors. *Journal of Abnormal and Social Psychology, 61,* 231–238.

Zimmerman, J., & Grosz, H. J. (1966). "Visual" performance in a functionally blind person. *Behaviour Research and Therapy, 4,* 119–134.

Zung, B. J. (1979). Psychometric properties of the MAST and two briefer versions. *Journal of Studies on Alcohol, 40,* 845–859.

Name Index

Subject Index